A. Asa Eger is Associate Professor in the Department of History at the University of North Carolina, Greensboro. He holds a PhD in Islamic Archaeology from the University of Chicago.

'This is a long-awaited and much-needed contribution to the study of the Byzantine–Islamic frontier that will force a step-change in approaches to the study of the region as well as to the study of medieval frontier societies and their archaeology. The author is to be congratulated on a clear, concise and well-argued analysis of complex textual and archaeological data.'

John Haldon, Shelby Cullom Davis '30 Professor of European History, and Professor of Byzantine History and Hellenic Studies, Princeton University

'Dr Eger's *The Islamic–Byzantine Frontier* is a well-constructed, original, and convincing book that challenges conventional opinions on the Islamic–Byzantine frontier, and in doing so raises important theoretical and methodological questions on understanding the dynamics of frontier zones in general. His study further weakens the conventional view of frontiers as sparsely populated, marginal, and disconnected peripheries. The "core and periphery" model for explaining the geopolitical patterning of settlements has never seemed so outdated, given the compelling argumentation presented in Dr Eger's ground-breaking study.'

Alan Walmsley, Professor of Islamic Archaeology and Art, University of Copenhagen

THE ISLAMIC–BYZANTINE FRONTIER

Interaction and Exchange Among Muslim and Christian Communities

A. Asa Eger

I.B. TAURIS
LONDON · NEW YORK

Paperback edition published in 2017 by
I.B.Tauris & Co. Ltd
London • New York
www.ibtauris.com

Hardback edition first published in 2015 by
I.B.Tauris & Co. Ltd

ISBN: 978 1 78453 919 1
eISBN: 978 0 85773 674 1
ePDF: 978 0 85772 685 8

A full CIP record for this book is available from the British Library
A full CIP record is available from the Library of Congress

Library of Congress Catalog Card Number: available

Typeset in Garamond Three by OKS Prepress Services, Chennai, India

To my parents

You should know that an area does not become illustrious by the number of its settlements, but rather by the importance of its rural districts

Muqaddasī, *Āḥsan al-taqāsīm fī ma'rifat al-iqlīm*, 1906, p. 228. Translation by Basil Collins, *The Best Divisions for the Knowledge of Regions*, 2001, p. 189.

CONTENTS

List of Figures and Tables ix
Acknowledgements xii
List of Abbreviations xv

Introduction Islamic Frontiers, Real and Imagined 1

Part 1 The Syro-Anatolian *Thughūr* **23**

1. The Central *Thughūr*: The Two Amuqs 33
2. The Central *Thughūr*: The Steppe and the River 69
3. The Eastern *Thughūr* 102
4. The Jazīra (Balikh and Khābūr River Valleys) 127
5. The Western *Thughūr*: Crossroads of Cilicia 158

Part 2 Hydraulic Villages and Fortified Castles: A Narrative of Settlement **183**

6. Prologue: Upland Settlements in the Late Roman Period (Fourth to Seventh Centuries) 187
7. Hydraulic Villages in the Early Islamic Period (Seventh to Tenth Centuries) 198
8. The Byzantine Frontier (Seventh to Tenth Centuries) 246

9. Epilogue: Fortified Castles of the Middle Islamic/Middle Byzantine Period (Tenth to Fourteenth Centuries) 264
10. Frontier or Frontiers? Interaction and Exchange in Frontier Societies 277
Conclusions Dismantling and Rebuilding the Frontier 310

Notes 315
Bibliography 371
Index 400

LIST OF FIGURES AND TABLES

Figures

Figure 1: The *thughūr* and *'awāṣim* 7

Figure 2: Tribes on the *thughūr* 24

Figure 3: The *thughūr* with natural features represented 35

Figure 4: The Central *thughūr* 36

Figure 5: The Amuq Plain 37

Figure 6: The Amuq Plain, Late Roman through Middle Islamic sites 42

Figure 7: The Kahramanmaraş Plain, Early Islamic through Middle Islamic sites 43

Figure 8: Domuztepe, the Late Roman and Early Islamic excavated building (photo courtesy of S. Campbell) 44

Figure 9: Nahr Sajūr Survey, Late Roman and Islamic sites 45

Figure 10: Jabbūl Survey, Late Roman through Middle Islamic sites (based on Yukich 2012) 46

Figure 11: Birecik-Carchemish Survey (Tigris-Euphrates Archaeological Reconaissance Project) and Jerablus Tahtani Survey (Land of Carchemish Project), Late Roman through

Middle Islamic sites (based on Wilkinson 2004, Figures 7.8, 7.9, 7.10, 9.1; Wilkinson 2007, Figure 1; Algaze et al. 1994, Figure 17) 80

Figure 12: Tell Rifa'at Survey, Late Roman through Middle Islamic sites (based on Matthers 1981) 86

Figure 13: Sweyhat Survey, Late Roman through Middle Islamic sites 90

Figure 14: The eastern *thughūr* 103

Figure 15: Adıyaman Survey, Late Roman and Islamic sites (based on Blaylock et al., 1980, Figure 30) 111

Figure 16: Group II, Karababa Basin Surveys, Late Roman through Middle Islamic sites (based on Wilkinson 1990: Figures 5.4 and 5.7; Redford 1998, Figure 7.2; Algaze et al. 1992, Figure 14; Gerber 1994, pp. 327 and 331) 113

Figure 17: Aşvan and Altınova Surveys, Byzantine and Islamic sites (based on Whallon 1979, Figure 3) 120

Figure 18: The Jazīra 132

Figure 19: Harran Survey, Late Roman and Islamic sites (based on Yardımcı 2004, 393 and 394) 133

Figure 20: Group I, Khābūr Survey sites, Late Roman and Islamic sites 137

Figure 21: Balikh Survey, Late Roman through Middle Islamic sites (based on 1996, pp. 345 and 348) 149

Figure 22: Group II, Khābūr Survey sites, Late Roman/Sāsānian through Middle Islamic sites 150

Figure 23: Middle Euphrates Survey, Late Roman through Middle Islamic sites (based on Berthier 2001, Map D) 151

Figure 24: The western *thughūr* 163

Figure 25: Cilicia Survey (based on Seton-Williams 1954) 164

Figure 26: Yumurtalık-Iskenderun Survey, Late Roman through Middle Islamic sites 166

Figure 27: Tüpraş Field/Ḥiṣn al-Tināt, eastern gate and internal rooms (courtesy of M.-H. Gates) 172

Figure 28: Comparative Early Islamic way stations. From top left, clockwise: Ḥiṣn Maslama sketch adapted from Haase 2006; Tell Brak; Kurban Höyük from Algaze 1990, Figure 124; Ḥiṣn al-Tīnāt by the author 227

Figure 29: Caliphal renovations, and bar graph 235

Figure 30: The Byzantine frontier 247

Tables

Table 1: Surveys on the *thughūr*, late period settlement 29

Table 2: Settlement patterns on the *thughūr* 185

ACKNOWLEDGEMENTS

If one looks hard enough, one can see just about anything. A patch of grass, when stared at for hours, is still an unremarkable patch of grass. Yet when one gets down on hands and knees, an entire microcosm unfolds, a multitude of creatures moving around and interacting with one another, and with the growing world around them. This book first began as an unnamed, unremarkable low-mounded patch of land, AS 257, that I surveyed along with other members of my team in 2001 in the Amuq Valley. The site soon turned out to be quite revealing. It was one of three, evenly spaced along a canal and newly founded in the seventh century. The canal was among several channels irrigating the Amuq Valley and in one of many lowland plains settled, irrigated and cultivated on the Islamic–Byzantine frontier. So my interest expanded and took shape, initially as a dissertation and finally into a study of the landscape of the entirety of the frontier and its neighbouring lands. Not a microcosm.

The entire process is the product of much wonderful collaboration and could not have been done without the inspiration, motivation, assistance and cooperation of a large and significant group of individuals. From the onset, I would like to thank my incredible University of Chicago dissertation committee: my advisor Donald Whitcomb, Fred Donner and Walter Kaegi, all three of whom have returned to the *thughūr* many times throughout their scholarship and together formed the perfect team. I would also like to thank Adam Smith, who, as an outside reader, provided an important anthropological perspective on the research. In the field, my list of colleagues to whom I owe great debts of gratitude is happily long, and to name but a select few: Tony Wilkinson, Jesse Casana, Aslıhan Yener, David Schloen, Fokke Gerritsen, Rana Özbal, Tasha Vorderstrasse, Timothy Harrison, Steve Batiuk and Amir Sumak'ai Fink for the Amuq survey; Liz Carter, Stuart Campbell, Liz Mullane, Mhairi Campbell, Claire Heywood, Ben Gearey, Will Fletcher and Kate Grossman for the Maraş Survey; and Marie-Henriette Gates, Fran Cole, Salima Ikram, Ben Claasz Coockson, Rado Kabatiarova, Tim Beach, Canan Çakırlar, Carolyn Swan and the tireless Turkish and American undergraduates for the Tupraş Field survey and excavations. Many people who have provided me along the way with useful insights and comments great and small must be thanked: Hugh Kennedy, McGuire Gibson, Gil Stein, Scott Branting, Seth Richardson, John Woods, Carrie Hritz, Linda Wheatley-Irving, Rana Mikati, and Derek Krueger; and my support group while at Chicago: Alyssa Gabbay, Pat Wing, Mayte Green, Adrian de Gifis, Vanessa de Gifis, Jonathan Brown, Yuval ben Bassat, Nukhet Varlık and Noha Forster.

This book was largely written during my stay as a Fellow at Dumbarton Oaks in the spring of 2012. My fellow Byzantine Fellows, lovingly strengthened by Margaret Mullett and the larger Dumbarton Oaks community, provided stimulating conversations. The library and gardens formed a perfect setting in which to write on landscapes. In particular, this book could not have been completed without the meticulous comments of John Haldon and the second anonymous reviewer throughout. Andrea de Giorgi, Lynn Swartz Dodd, Ian Straughn, Jason Ur, Gunder Varınlıoğlu, Michael Decker, Charles Gates, Stephen McPhillips, Bethany Walker and Alyssa Gabbay all provided comments, corrections, citations and clarity to individual chapters. Many thanks are also due to Ari Lukas, Luke Kaiser, Claire Ebert and Reed Goodwin for assistance with producing the geographic information system-based maps and to Kyle Brunner, Ian McDonald, Maria Marsh, and Allison Walker for all their help in editing. A last note of gratitude is for my family and friends, whose persistent support and encouragement was boundless and enabled me to traverse this frontier wilderness, this excellent country, these beautiful lands, with their parts untamed and parts organized, teeming with activity.

LIST OF ABBREVIATIONS

AST	*Araştırma Sonucları Toplantısı.*
Borders Barriers	*Borders, Barriers, and Ethnogenesis: Frontiers in Late Antiquity and the Middle Ages*, edited by F. Curta (Turnhout: Brepols, 2005).
Byzantine Trade	*Byzantine Trade, 4th–12th Centuries: The Archaeology of Local, Regional and International Exchange.* Papers of the thirty-eighth Spring Symposium of Byzantine Studies, St. John's College, University of Oxford, March 2004. Edited by Marlia Mundell Mango (Burlington, VT: Ashgate Variorum, 2009).
Castrum 3	*Guerre, fortification et habitat dans le monde méditerranéen au Moyen Âge*, edited by A. Bazzana (Madrid: Casa de Velázquez, 1988).
Castrum 7	*Zones côtières littorales dans le monde méditerranéen au Moyen Âge: défense, peuplement, mise en valeur*, edited by J.-M. Martin (Madrid: Casa de Velázquez, 2001).

Continuity and Change	*Continuity and Change in Northern Mesopotamia from the Hellenistic to the Early Islamic Period: Proceedings of a Colloquium Held at the Seminar für Vorderasiatische Altertumskunde, Freie Universität Berlin, 6th–9th April, 1994*, edited by K. Bartl and S. Hauser (Berlin: Dietrich Reimer Verlag, 1996).
Countryside	*Archaeology of the Countryside in Medieval Anatolia*, edited by T. Vorderstrasse and J. Roodenberg (Leiden: Nederlands Instituut voor het Nabije Oosten, 2009).
EI2	*Encyclopedia of Islam: New Edition*, edited by P. Bearman, Th. Bianquis, C. E. Bosworth, E. van Donzel, and W. P. Heinrichs (Leiden: Brill, 1960–).
Frontiers in Question	*Frontiers in Question: Eurasian Borderlands, 700–1700*, edited by D. Powers and N. Standen (New York: St. Martin's Press, 1999).
KST	*Kazı Sonucları Toplantısı.*
Medieval Frontiers	*Medieval Frontiers: Concepts and Practices*, edited by D. Abulafia and N. Berend (Burlington, VT: Ashgate, 2002).
Medieval Frontier Societies	*Medieval Frontier Societies*, edited by R. Bartlett and A. MacKay (New York: Oxford University Press, 1989).
Mu'jam (1955–7)	Yāqūt, *Mu'jam al-buldān* (Beirut: Dār Sādir, 1955–7).
Mu'jam (1990)	Yāqūt, *Mu'jam al-buldān* (Beirut: Dār al-Kutub al-'Ilmiya, 1990).

Residences, Castles, Settlements	*Residences, Castles, Settlements. Transformation Processes from Late Antiquity to Early Islam in Bilad al-Sham. Proceedings of the International Conference held at Damascus, 5–9 November 2006*, edited by K. Bartl and A.-R. Moaz (Rahden/Westfalen: Verlag Marie Leidorf GmbH).
Shifting Frontiers	*Shifting Frontiers in Late Antiquity: Papers from the First Interdisciplinary Conference on Late Antiquity, The University of Kansas, March 1995*, edited by R. W. Mathisen and H. S. Sivan (Brookfield, VT: Variorum, 1996).
TAÇDAM	*Ilısu ve Karkamış Baraj Gölleri Altında Kalacak Arkeolojik ve Kültür Varlıklarını Projesi* (Salvage Project of the Archaeological Heritage of the Ilısu and Carchemish Dam Reservoirs Activities), edited by T. Numan, J. Özturk, and J. Velibeyoğlu, 4 vols (Ankara: METU, 1999–2002).
Ta'rīkh (English)	Ṭabarī, *Ta'rīkh al-rusul wa-al-mulūk* (The History of al-Ṭabarī: an annotated translation), general editor: Ehsan Yar-Shater (Albany: State University of New York Press, 1985–2007).
Ta'rīkh (Arabic)	Ṭabarī, *Ta'rīkh al-rusul wa-al-mulūk* (Leiden: Brill, 1901).
Upper Syrian Euphrates	*Archaeology of the Upper Syrian Euphrates: The Tishrin Dam Area. Proceedings of the International Symposium Held at Barcelona, January 28th–30th 1998*, edited by G. del Olmo Lete and J.-L. Montero Fennollós (Barcelona: Sabadell, 1999).

INTRODUCTION

ISLAMIC FRONTIERS, REAL AND IMAGINED

Standing on a high point in the Cilician Gates north of Ṭarsūs, surveying his former lands stretched out before him, the Byzantine Emperor Heraklios allegedly uttered his most famous lament, a farewell: 'Peace unto thee, O Syria, and what an excellent country this is for the enemy [...]. What a benefit you will be to your enemy, because of all the pasturage, fertile soil, and other amenities you provide.'[1] The occasion, the retreat of the Byzantine army from Syria in around the late 630s in advance of the approaching Arab army, is one that was to resound emphatically in the works both of Islamic and of Christian writers, and to create an enduring topos: that of the Islamic–Byzantine frontier. For centuries, Byzantine and Islamic scholars have evocatively sketched a contested border: the annual raids that took place between *dār al-Islām* (House of Islam) and *dār al-ḥarb* (House of War), the line of fortified strongholds defending Islamic lands, the no man's land in between, and the birth of *jihād*. Others depicted the frontier as a wilderness settled by the Arabs. These accounts are not without politico-religious impact. In their early representations of a Muslim–Christian encounter, accounts of the Byzantine–Islamic frontier are charged with significance for a future 'clash of civilizations' that envisions a polarized world in which Muslims and Christians fight, rest, fight again, and maybe eventually destroy each other; a battle with high stakes over a fault line established from the very earliest period of Islam.[2]

Frontiers have long served as temptingly rich fodder for historians, ideologues and archaeologists, who transformed these shared spaces easily into whatever best serves the historical/ideological needs of the time. The Byzantine–Islamic frontier has not escaped such manipulations. The most prevalent depiction, that of the region as an empty space after the departure of Heraklios' armies which was then built up by the Arabs, is one that is not confirmed by archaeological evidence, but which nevertheless served the needs of those who put it forth. What is at stake is the continuous simplification of Muslim–Christian encounters throughout history and the appropriation of an assumed or envisioned past that has been grafted onto modern interactions. Yet, it is important to acknowledge that there are two visions of the frontier, an ideological one and a physical one, each supported by its own categories of evidence whether historical or archaeological. Both views are crucial to constructing (and deconstructing) Islamic frontiers and should be viewed as superimposed layers that impart different meanings, whether real or imagined. This volume contributes to a more complex vision of the frontier than traditional historical views by juxtaposing layers of a real ecological frontier of settlement and interaction with an imagined military/religious ideological frontier.

Unexplored Spaces

The aftermath of the departure of Heraklios, the Byzantine army, and his citizens recedes in our imaginations like water after a flood. Yet, it is worth remaining a bit longer and delving more deeply into this literary world. The establishment of a lasting frontier took about 80 years, until *c.*720. During this initial stage, the Arabs apparently found a ghost country, a wilderness whose forts had been apparently systematically destroyed and whose inhabitants had been deliberately removed in a scorched-earth policy in the wake of the Byzantine Emperor Heraklios' retreat. Balādhurī (d. *c.*892), the ninth-century Islamic historian, recorded: 'What is known to us is that Heraclius moved the men from these forts, which he *unsettled* [*sha'athaha*]. So when the Muslims made their raids, they found them vacant.'[3] Ṭabarī (838–923) similarly wrote that he took with him the people of the fortresses located between Iskandarūna and Ṭarsūs in the Cilician Plain.[4] Islamic texts state that when the Arab armies arrived at Ṭarsūs, they found it abandoned and in ruins. Similarly, although after the initial conquests, the Byzantines abandoned the fortresses of Germanikeia (or Mar'ash) at the end of the seventh century and Sīs (Sīsiya) at the beginning of the eighth or ninth century and fled to the mountains leaving these cities to fall into ruin (*kharāb*).[5] Accounts use the word *'imāra* (rebuild), whose root has a greater range of implications than simply restoring buildings. The word refers to cultivated land, crops, or food supplies unavailable to the Arab armies due to Heraklios' destruction of the land.[6] In a larger sense, the word connotes becoming prosperous, populous and civilized, implying a sense of organization that reverses *sha'atha*. It also has meaning in a religious and obligatory sense, used for the lesser year-round pilgrimage (*'umra*) to Makkah and Madīnah. The routine destruction of fields is hardly mentioned in textual sources; cultivation of lands appears slightly more frequently.[7] Nevertheless, these wider meanings add a level of necessity to rebuilding: the need to build from the ashes something that was better than its predecessor. As such, despite the remains of a pre-existing civilization, the perception by the Arab armies of their frontier environment was not only as a wilderness but as unexplored space.

A century later and on the other side of the Islamic world, the Umayyads were negotiating a similar frontier with the post-Visigothic Christian Asturians in Spain (al-Andalus). When the Umayyad armies arrived they established the northern frontier at the Duero Valley, which they noted was 'depopulated'.[8] Like Heraklios, the Asturian King Alfonso II (759–842) took the existing population and left the valley an empty land that was then settled or populated (*repoblación*) by Arab and Berber tribes. These lands were not empty. Scholars have reinterpreted the verb *poblar* not necessarily to mean 'to populate' but 'to organize an area administratively'. The *populator* was a ruler who not only gathered his people together but organized the cultivation of a previously uncultivated territory.[9] The association with the first Arab and Berber tribes and the need to not only populate, but to administrate and cultivate an emptied space is strikingly similar to the case of the Islamic–Byzantine frontier. Christian frontier ideology behaves much the same way. A similar event occurred in 965 when, after most of the Syro-Anatolian *thughūr* had been reconquered by the Byzantines, the Emperor Nikephoros Phokas (912–69) asked Syrian Jacobites to resettle the area, filling in the 'deserted' towns.[10] In a similar vein, the tenth-century Byzantine writers used the term *eremos*, or desert, to refer to lands beyond the *oikoumenē*, which carried with it implied meanings of the uncivilized and uninhabited.[11] Such spaces, while not physically bare of people and habitation, are perceived by contemporaries as relatively 'empty'.

The vision of the Islamic–Byzantine frontier as a no man's land is further augmented by the misconception that there existed a line composed of individual forts (using the singular form of *thughūr*, the *thaghr*) evenly spaced and strategically situated at key mountain passes and routes stretching from Ṭarsūs in the west to Malaṭiya in the east and even farther into Armenia. Although these have been demonstrated to be fortified towns and not isolated fortresses, and part of a deep zone of settlement rather than a 'line', their military character is still highlighted while their economic potential is seen only as a later ninth-century phenomenon.[12] Until the 720s there was a good deal of back-and-forth campaigining through both summer and winter seasons; the Arabs first tried to seize and settle Byzantine territory as part of Rashidūn and early Umayyad expansionist policies.[13] But, while they largely failed on the plateau and beyond the mountain chains, they succeeded in the area of the Taurus and Anti-Taurus Mountain line. From the death of Sulaymān and reign of 'Umar II, (*c.*717) and throughout the 'Abbāsid period (749–*c.*965 until the Byzantine reconquest, *c.*965–1050), following the first real Byzantine offensive by Constantine V (718–75) in 746 and 747, military strategy on both sides pursued a policy of defence, stabilization, and fortification while campaigining took on a symbolic, almost peculiar, form.[14] From these frontier settlements, religious warriors would undertake summer annual raids or *ṣawā'if* (singular *ṣā'ifa*) or *jihād* against non-Muslims north into Byzantine lands – a process recorded in the literature for virtually every year for the next two centuries, in a perpetual war between Islamic lands and Byzantine lands, the *dār al-Islām* and *dār al-ḥarb*, or, as it was sometimes known, *bilād al-kufr* – 'land of the infidel' – as it appears in juridical writings. The Byzantines would also retaliate, once a year. Strangely, in the wake of this ritualized conflict, the opposing armies never took any land and only held enemy forts for a token period of time. Indeed a quick look at the ninth-century Islamic historian al-Ṭabarī has the feel of reading the weekly police blotter: each year begins or ends with what raids were carried out into foreign lands and who led them.

The perspective of an imagined frontier in the pages of Early Islamic and Christian sources seems like an easy target that is already distorted, a straw man. Yet, modern scholarship made very few inroads in the region and continued to espouse uncritically the traditional text-based view virtually extolling the peculiarities of the back-and-forth raids.[15] Earlier scholarship on Byzantine and Islamic frontiers reflected the historiographical modes of its times. Indeed, the consideration of this period as a Dark Ages by scholars has further created an intellectual and chronological frontier.[16] Recently, in the past 30 years, several works directly or in passing have challenged this 'traditional' perception of the frontier and its Dark Ages, most notably the writings of J. Haldon, H. Kennedy, P. von Sivers, A. M. Abu Ezzah, I. Straughn, M. Bonner, M. A. Shaban, and K. Durak.[17] There are, however, few synthetic approaches that examine the physicality of the frontier from a military, economic, and transhumant perspective. Similarly, there are few works on the frontier that have examined it over a continuous stretch of time from the seventh to the tenth centuries, or even looking at patterns before and after, from the fourth to the fourteenth centuries, regardless of political periodizations. Unfortunately, in the absence of archaeology and the changing or evolving settlement patterns of the region, the militarized episodes are still taken at face value; the frontier remains frozen in an endless time loop. For some, the frontier is still a no man's land; for others, however, the frontier was not entirely depopulated: whoever lived there were passive actors in a larger epic drama, extras on a film set.[18] This notion echoes the famous Ottoman historian Paul Wittek's own Turnerian views on the frontier: 'a frontier culture will be, in most cases, necessarily primitive. It will be a cast-off from the high culture of the interior, mixed to such a degree with the waste products of the enemy's culture, that it will share nothing essential in common with that culture whose defender and champion it vaunted itself as being.'[19] Building an alternative model in reaction to this view, therefore, is not a straw-man argument for the simple reason that this view has become thoroughly entrenched in subsequent scholarship, which repeatedly projects the idea of a no man's land of Cilicia or the Duero Valley onto the entirety of the frontiers between Islamic and Christian lands.

At the onset, the Islamic–Byzantine frontier was not such a wilderness as has been previously emphasized. It was neither impassable nor empty. The first such frontier was established at the northern extent of the province of Shām (modern south-east Turkey and northern Syria). It extended from the Mediterranean Sea at Anṭākiya to the Euphrates. The Arabs met with little resistance when they took over its major cities and towns in 638. Many citizens, particularly of the upper classes, left if they had not already done so. Anṭākiya in the mid-seventh century lost its importance as a regional capital and became first a military post and then a small provincial town. The capital of the region on the Islamic frontier shifted further east to Ḥalab (Aleppo). The hinterland of Anṭākiya, the Amuq Plain (formerly a borderland in the early Umayyad period), was also subsumed within the frontier zone. In the Umayyad period, the Islamic–Byzantine frontier was pushed farther north and established along the southern edge of the Taurus Mountains, stretching from south-west to north-east, encompassing the Cilician Plain from the Lamas River to the west, incorporating the whole of the Amanus Mountain range, the Kahramanmaraş Plain (the northern extension of the Amuq Plain), the rolling hills, river valleys, and lowland steppes of the Euphrates region, and the Anti-Taurus and intermontane plains of the Upper Euphrates. This entire region was the province of *al-thughūr* (Figure 1).

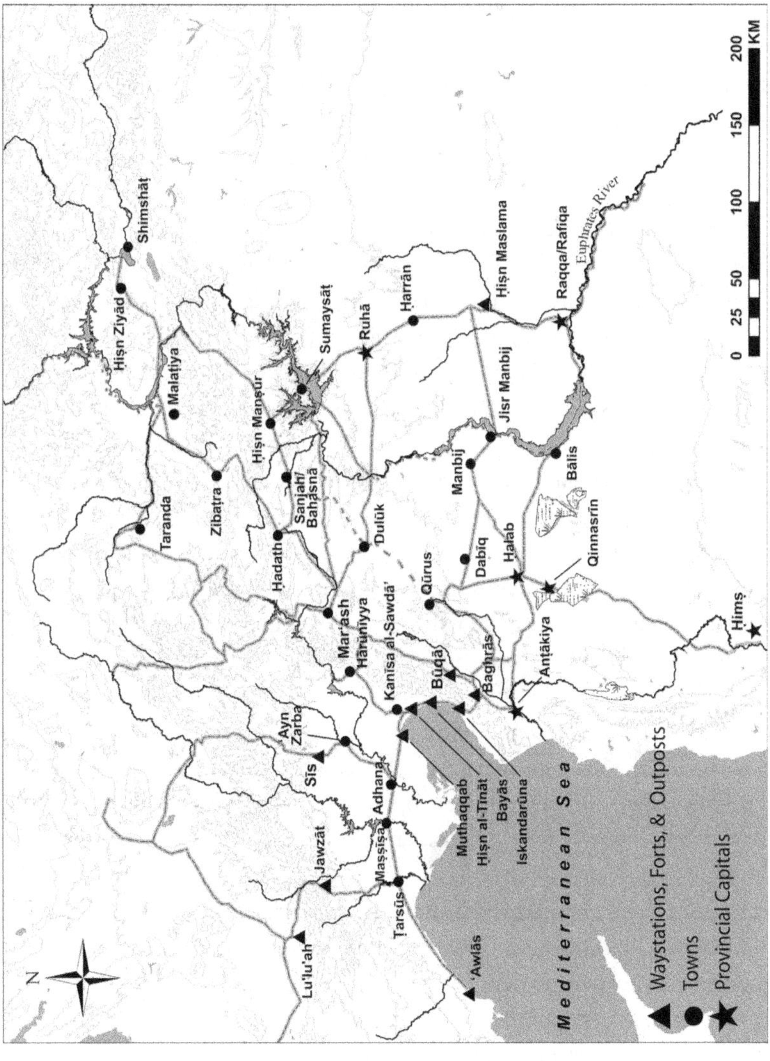

Figure 1 The *thughūr* and *ʿawāṣim*

The root of the term *thaghr* (plural *thughūr*) can mean frontier, mouth, or front teeth, likened to the towering Taurus Mountains dividing Byzantine and Islamic lands. *Thaghra* (plural *thaghar*) can mean a mountain pass, chink or crevice, and gap or breach in a wall (*thalma*).[20] A logical meaning of *thughūr* in the frontier sense, combining the ideas of gaps and teeth, would refer to the spaces between the teeth, the river gorges that passed through the mountains which linked Islamic and Byzantine lands and were crucial for the movement of armies, nomadic groups, traders, and religious pilgrims. Similarly, the Byzantines called these passes *stomata*, or mouths. The landscape of the *thughūr* was criss-crossed with roads connecting settlements: large cities that had functioned as important urban centers in the preceding centuries; towns and forts, way stations, small villages, farms, and monasteries, inhabited by Syriac-speaking Christians; and pastoral camps of Arab tribes, often invisible in texts, who roamed the area before the arrival of Islam.

The frontier as a wilderness is not yet confirmed by the archaeological evidence, supporting the fact that these events were stories and topoi rather than eyewitness testimony. Excavations at major frontier settlements such as Ṭarsūs, Anṭākiya, and Sumaysāṭ show no dramatic destruction, ruin, or burning of these cities in the seventh century. It must be remembered that much of the frontier, the northernmost lands of Islamic *bilād al-shām*, lies in a fertile agricultural zone that receives ample annual rainfall. Surveys reveal newly founded sites and irrigation systems. In Spain, the persistence of habitation of seventh- and eighth-century sites with Roman or Gothic and Arab and Berber toponyms belies any depopulation. The idea of an empty frontier falls in line with an academic view that has been strongly questioned and largely abandoned in the last 30 years, namely, the decline of settlement after the Islamic conquests in the seventh century.

Although archaeological investigation would normally not expect to perceive short-term depopulation followed by resettlement, the type of absolute depopulation described in the texts is doubtful. Deliberate destruction and the burning of forts would leave archaeological traces, besides involving an excessive amount of labour for a people in retreat. Furthermore, while many city-dwelling elites and garrisons may have fled with the Islamic conquests, many other people remained, particularly those peoples settled in rural areas, many of which were isolated and monastic communities of non-Chalcedonian Miaphysite and other Christian orders.[21] This is also suggested by Ṭabarī's mention of Heraklios depopulating only the 'people of the fortresses', suggesting that non-military and non-official inhabitants remained. Survey evidence shows that Islamic settlement was initially very limited and focused on administrative urban areas and irrigated agricultural estates in the plains. Settlement by Muslims would have been even more marginal on the edges of Islamic territory. Arab tribes who practiced nomadic or semi-nomadic pastoralism and were either Christian or Muslim were also part of the landscape, but often archaeologically invisible. While initially reduced, an empty landscape of smoke and ruin did not exist save in the perceptions of contemporaries.

Creating a concept of a mythic wilderness is a potent legitimizing tool for a new rising power, and important to the construction of a new ideological frontier. This concept functions as a process, according to I. Kopytoff, which begins with the creation of an institutional vacuum: 'The definition of the frontier as "empty" is political and made from the intruders' perspective.'[22] Abandoned buildings and burned lands can imply a time ripe for a new beginning and, metaphorically speaking, new growth. Indeed, the same themes of ruin and compulsion to rebuild using the civilizing concept of *'imāra* repeats in key moments of political maneouvering on the Early Islamic frontier. Both the settlements of Adhana and Maṣṣīṣa were described as ruined (and abandoned) until the 'Abbāsids arrived. Similarly, the Caliph al-Mahdī (r. 775–85) at the start of the 'Abbāsid caliphate sent his Khurāsānī horsemen to Ṭarsūs only to find it in ruins, which he then ordered rebuilt. Not long after, Hārūn al-Rashīd (r. 786–809) did the same for Ṭarsūs in 806–7.[23] These narratives serve to deny an even earlier Islamic historical claim to the settlements by the Umayyads.

Historians, archaeologists, and frontier scholars working on parallel cases now generally accept that medieval frontiers were never conceived as specific borders of demarcation between two entities in binary opposition, but rather were complex zones that were defined both by their inhabitants and by their character as peripheral lands in relation to their central ruling bodies, which fluctuated over time.[24] Further, frontiers are dynamic processes embodying the cultural interactions taking place within these diverse societies, including adaptation, acculturation, assimilation, and the cultural ambiguity of ethnic and religious groups. In some cases these interactions created new societies (ethnogenesis), uniquely born out of living within a peripheral sense of place. Some archaeologists have argued that contrary to the assumption that the central place typifies culture, it is precisely this interconnectedness of societies and visible process of social change on the frontier that should draw attention to its cultural importance. Taken even further, the processes of frontiers are not rooted to a fixed periphery but are moveable, and even manifest internally within settled societies.

Concepts of territory during the medieval period did not define space and frontier as we do today. Geographers described their world in terms of itineraries and traveling distances rather than geographical space; political maps were later institutions. Territories were demarcated physically, often by single points or boundary markers.[25] Natural features, such as the Taurus Mountains, were also used to delimit areas. This can be seen in the early maps of some of the Muslim geographers such as Muqaddasī (b. 945) and Idrīsī (d. 1165/6), which show abstracted lines for mountain ranges and coasts. Cartographers abstracted space in conceptualized ways, showing only the largest and most significant areas rather than depicting their worlds comprehensively and accurately.[26] The articulation of rule was over people rather than physical land. Similarly, forts were always described by who controlled them, rather than as physical markers of a frontier.[27] There were no political boundaries or unified agreements on the *thughūr* by geographers. Rather, 'frontier' was articulated as the distance away from the capital or urban center, that is, the core–periphery model.[28] This division of core and periphery, however, was not universally fixed. The capital was only given prominence and value through the ideologies and myths created by the ruler (or his propagandists) as specific situations and challenges arose.[29]

Furthermore, the capital (via the caliph) moved to the frontier several times throughout the Early Islamic period.

Several important studies on specific Roman, Byzantine, and medieval frontiers around the Mediterranean have advanced the conceptualization of territory significantly, and are useful as they illustrate the complexity of frontiers. Roman frontiers, whose infamous *limes* were once conceived of as strict boundaries, are now regarded as interactive zones of commercial and cultural contact.[30] J. F. Drinkwater, based on the research of the fourth/fifth-century Frankish border, states that the frontier was a 'stage show with created threats to mask internal instability'.[31] Byzantine rulers demonized the local 'barbarians' and actively employed aggressive policies towards them in part for self-aggrandizement and to justify keeping a military force on the frontier for internal security and tax collection, thereby adding a layer of political and religious ideology. Similarly, the landscape was appropriated symbolically in the reoccupation of cities and other features. From an analysis of Islamic frontiers, T. Rooke argues that part of the process of establishing political sovereignty involved 'imposing new boundaries on the past and/or old boundaries on the present [. . .] establish[ing] the stories of events [and] interpreting aggressive attempts at regional hegemony [. . .] as glorious defensive anti-colonial struggle'.[32] Part of this discourse involved establishing foreign invaders and occupants not only as enemies and the 'other' but as a destructive force, for the purposes of forging political unity. Taking this view further, D. Miller states:

> Anthropologists have shown us clearly that the first ethnographies of frontier native populations are always written by imperial intruders who consistently interpret the *pathological* militarized state of native society, which is the product of their own intrusion, as the *normal* state of native society, subsequently using the resultant stereotype of war-like 'barbarians' as a justification, often after the fact, for aggression.[33]

Shrouding the frontier and enemy in religious and apocalyptic rhetoric was one response to crisis, and it justified aggression. For the

Byzantines, the seventh through ninth centuries were angst ridden; lost borders were attributed to a difficulty in defining God's realm. The other side of the frontier became part of a dichotomous good/evil eschatological narrative of the post-apocalyptic rise of the heretical nomadic steppe lands of Gog and Magog.[34]

Subsequent aggressive policies and economic policing on the part of the central state backlashed, eventually leading to social competition and the rise of local charismatic leaders on the frontier who were detrimental to the central state.[35] As the idea of the central state disintegrated in the Middle and Late Islamic periods, so too did the idea of a physical frontier. Rather, everyone was located somewhere on the frontier and often those on the frontier had more in common with each other than with the central state. As such, the periphery was repositioned as the center and from it radiated spheres of influence encompassing human frontiers of religious plurality, ethnic diversity, and cultural production.[36] The frontier became a matter of perspective.

The Great Divide

This book contributes to the conversations by researchers of frontier studies, and reaches towards students and scholars in environmental history. It also addresses both archaeologists and historians in the fields of Byzantine and Islamic studies. This is no easy task. Despite attempts in modern scholarship to mediate the two forms of historical inquiry through an interdisciplinary approach, the fields of Byzantine–Islamic archaeology and history continue to operate in separate spheres, only occasionally utilizing, in uncritical and cursory ways, information the other field has produced. Two challenges in particular can be considered for this study: the physical landscape and environment as a holistic object of study and the centuries of transition as more precisely defined. In order to understand the formation, nature, and process of the Islamic–Byzantine frontier and test the textual model it is necessary to start from the ground up, we need to first examine the archaeological evidence before reintroducing the textual evidence and configuring the two data sets.

Byzantine and Islamic archaeology has, with a greater emphasis on the latter, traditionally focused on only the most urban and religious manifestations of the physical world. Amidst the urban network was a thriving rural landscape of villages and multi-ethnic communities, many of which were non-Muslim. Outside the villages and settled communities were many nomadic tribes whose transhumant ways of life often moved out of the range of the Empire. Beyond the Empire was frontier. To understand the *thughūr* is to examine first and foremost its rural settlements and land-use patterns, breaking the mould of an uncultivated landscape dominated by a few forts. The textual bias towards the urban elite and literate classes supplies mainly rich political and religious information but prevents us from hearing potential voices that are non-urban, and which live outside the framework of the Empire. Newer consideration of Syriac sources provides more details of towns, villages, and monasteries; the itineraries and routes taken; or the ways of life and occupations of local inhabitants, albeit sometimes coloured by religious convictions and hyperbole.[37]

Islamic archaeology in particular, as a form of historical archaeology, emerged as a text-driven field, rooted in narratives and using them as guides to search out the nature of this seemingly urban culture and religion. For example, the material culture from the early excavations of the ʻAbbāsid capital of Sāmarrā', thought to be a short-lived settlement according to texts (836–83 or 892), was consequently first dated to these years, which then served as a dating benchmark for many other sites until recently. Newer research has expanded the scope of urbanism, focusing on the urban landscape and the elements of empire: cities and towns, mosques and other urban institutions, primary centers of production, and intercity networks of trade and economy. Though these projects have been less reliant on historical documents, texts still serve as important supplemental and often legitimizing tools for excavation. As a result, the belief that Islam was an urbanizing civilization is constantly upheld by those who search for it in cities and towns. Gradually, and very recently, studies of rural settlement and material culture driven by social and economic inquiries, often in relation to urban networks, are being considered that can potentially examine new systems of locally organized culture.

Studies on the rural Byzantine and Islamic landscape have had differing results and agendas. Often these remain as singularly focused excavations arguing for an urban model of comparison by patterns of physical resemblance or material culture production. However, the rise of landscape archaeology and the study of the settled environment mainly, through regional surveys and remote sensing using aerial photography and satellite imagery, have, in the past 20 years, significantly expanded our knowledge of rural agrarian systems of settlement and land use, giving voice to the 'silent majority'. Even more importantly, landscape archaeology is a diachronic method. It allows us to glimpse the *longue durée* history of humans and nature symbiotically, affecting and reacting to one another in a constant yet inseparable relationship.

Consideration of post-seventh-century periods in this field is still quite nascent, but developing at a rapid pace. Irrigation and agricultural innovations historically tied to Early Islamic-period developments (the Green Revolution) are now largely disproved and have been contextualized in a much longer history of agrarian transmission. Ever more Near Eastern surveys, though not all, are considering medieval settlement processes and their profound effect on the environment, some of which will be examined closely in this volume.[38] Researchers in Spain have uncovered a rural network of Early Islamic and post-*reconquista* multi-ethnic villages centered on hydraulic features, using surveys, aerial photography, and linguistic continuities rather than excavation. Archaeology in the *thughūr* region is not entirely underdeveloped; it is possible to re-evaluate what has already occurred with an eye toward the Early Islamic period, configured by newer survey evidence.

A common yet distinctive pattern revealed in the periods of the Late Hellenistic through Islamic was a key shift in settlement, termed 'the Great Dispersal', from nucleated city states on tells of the third and second millennium BCE and earlier to scattered villages and farms throughout the landscape.[39] Settlement steadily increased, the peak in most areas occurring in the fifth and sixth centuries with an explosion of sites everywhere. Sites tended to be diffuse and very small (less than 1 ha) with no topographic relief, only distinguishable by scatters of pottery, roof tiles, and building stones. Surveys that prioritized the recording of tells produced skewed settlement patterns for the first millennium CE. Furthermore, not every landscape was equally preserved. Settlements in arid and montane landscapes, such as the infamous Syrian Jibāl (apparent by its better-known name of the Dead Cities), represented a rare landscape of survival based mainly on the durability of stone as a construction material and the fact that their upland location was unaffected by flooding and sedimentation. In the low plains of the *thughūr*, most of which were seasonal or permanent wetlands, settlements were built of local materials, such as mud brick and reeds. This distinction has created an archaeological bias towards finding sites whose remains are visible, large, or striking, while elusive settlements built of perishable materials in more biodegradable surroundings have been overlooked.[40]

A noticeable lacuna in both the Near East and Spain is the existence of the nomad or semi-pastoralist, particularly given the strong association with the initial spread of Islam through Arab tribes. This is no trivial omission; pastoral groups represent an unquantified but substantial segment of the population (Figure 2, p. 24).[41] On the *thughūr*, these populations would have occupied the seemingly inhospitable wilderness regions of marshes and mountains. Their interaction with settled societies and competition over land and resources was at the heart of virtually every conflict, imagined or otherwise. In certain periods, pastoral groups may have outnumbered settled groups. In the archaeological record, these moments show periods of decline. For example, once the fifth-century landscape was universally accepted by scholars as a high point for settlement and population, the point of change was marked by the middle of the seventh-century period with the spread of the mainly pastoralist Muslim tribes. The question of seventh-century decline after the conquests is linked to the visibility of these earliest settlements, and a finer focus on periodization is still necessary.

The issue of chronology, crucial to both historians and archaeologists, is a second challenge, particularly for the elusive transition from the Late Roman (fourth to mid-seventh centuries) to the Early Islamic period (mid-seventh to mid-tenth centuries;

640s to 960s for the frontier).[42] Typically, discrepancies in chronology are exacerbated by the disciplinary divide between archaeology and history; the first two centuries of Islamic rule, where texts are few, are best informed by archaeological evidence, albeit broadly dated, and the subsequent centuries by textual evidence, which is often retrospective, elitist, and government approved. Transformation in the seventh century occurred unevenly, with political changes manifesting as the quickest and most visible, followed by economic reorientation, and finally the cultural (and material cultural) milieu evincing the most gradual response. It follows that settlement patterns and environmental change would also not be readily or quickly apparent. The invisibility of the seventh century has been typically interpreted as a period of decline, the end of the Classical world. *Thughūr* text-based studies have tended to omit this century and the period that followed entirely, and to focus rather on the Roman to Late Roman *limes* or Middle Byzantine reconquest of the tenth century through the Crusades. From landscape surveys, Late Roman and/or Early Islamic decline is partly determined via interpretation of lack of identifying ceramic diagnostics, particularly since Roman *terra sigillata*, Late Roman finewares (mostly ending in the mid-seventh century), and Islamic glazed wares (mid-eighth century/early ninth century and beyond) are easily spotted on walking surveys, are easily dated, and dominate assemblages. Mid-seventh to mid-eighth-century/ninth-century ceramics are often harder to identify, and accordingly suggest a drop or gap in settlement in the first century of Islamic occupation. As a result, survey ceramic analyses, often done without a specialist on board, have swung toward the cautious, often identifying 'late period sites' as dating from the Roman to Early Islamic, or the first century BCE to tenth century CE.

Three decades of scholarship by Islamic archaeologists have resoundingly discarded the notion of seventh-century decline, recognizing the archaeological, and in some cases economic, continuity from the Late Roman to Early Islamic Near East.[43] For some archaeologists, the notion of decline was not dispensed with entirely but simply pushed further to the 'Abbāsid period, or back to the early sixth-century Persian conquests. This was based on an over-reliance on misdated coins and ceramics and the wish to align historical-political timelines with material culture. In the archaeological context, Late Roman to Early Islamic continuity has in recent times created a redefined transitional period encompassing the sixth to eighth centuries.

This macroscopic view of continuity, however, highlights two important factors of settlement patterns: 1) that there was never a period of total abandonment in the Early Islamic period; and 2) that sites with Late Hellenistic/Early Roman to Early Islamic occupation are often a part of a different system of settlement patterns than pre-Roman or post-Early Islamic occupied sites. While this transition correctly identifies the difficulty in assigning ceramic typologies to political changes, such a fluid categorization limits the study of the last centuries of Byzantium, the beginnings of Early Islam, and the identification of its initial settlement. At a very general level, absolute continuity between the Classical and Islamic periods is not tenable; change carried political, religious, and cultural implications and occurred on every level, from material culture to rural sites and urban cities to trade networks and land-use projects. With regard to the Islamic–Byzantine frontier, its formation and choices for settlement have become blurred in favour of a general continuity. In this way, the challenges of transition and landscape archaeology, with its reliance on surface ceramics, are intertwined.

Can a landscape–archaeology approach detect socio-political and religious differentiations, or is this perspective perhaps too coarsely grained to pick up such subtlety? This question becomes particularly salient in border zones or frontiers and time periods that have been determined to be transitional. The task of correlating political/cultural periods to archaeological and geomorphological time seems an oversimplification of two very different data sets. However, I would argue that the opposite is true. The process of transformation occurred over an important benchmark in the Near East – that is, the Islamic conquest. As such, it is essential to combine archaeological and historical methods to take advantage of this cultural shift and reveal the new populations, communities, settlements, and material cultures that were introduced or developed as a response to cultural mixing. When this cultural shift is overlaid on a profoundly transformed landscape, it allows for a greater distinction to be made between the Late Roman and Early Islamic periods. Such a combined study can inform whether settlement and land use was linked more with cultural and ethnic practices or evolved naturally as a response by any culture to the changing landscape.

Layering the **thughūr**

It is hoped that this volume will provide alternative routes, contributing toward a re-articulation of the Islamic landscape that synthesizes original survey and excavation work and other published and unpublished archaeological evidence. The focus is on the Early Islamic period, but patterns and changes in the landscape are traced over a millennium from the Late Roman through to the Middle Islamic/ Byzantine periods, the fourth to fourteenth centuries. Furthermore, this study will examine the points of congruity or incongruity between the archaeology of the frontier and its text-based narratives. This study does not begin with the assumption that parts of the frontier were more militarized than others, whether through the perception of a religious battleground, the presence of fortified garrison towns, or a strategic division of the region. The spiritual landscape or conceptual frontiers of the Islamic Empire will not be addressed here, but recent studies have admirably shown how these spaces can be seen as ways of imagining imperial control, articulating dominion, controlling the greater world, discrediting parts of it, and claiming others.[44]

As already discussed, either as a line or defence-in-depth zone, fortified garrison towns are implied from textual sources. Caliphs established camps, fortified them with walls, and garrisoned them, leading some to argue that they followed a similar pattern to the *amṣâr*, newly-founded garrison towns throughout Islamic territory established in the seventh century.[45] However, as nearly all of these *thughūr* towns were Byzantine cities and none have been excavated, there is no archaeological evidence to suggest how they were planned and whether they functioned primarily as garrison towns. Only two of these settlements have been excavated (Ṭarsūs and Ḥiṣn al-Tīnāt), and two have been intensively mapped and surveyed ('Ayn Zarba and possibly Hārūnīyya) in the past 20 years (and mainly in the past ten years). At present, the results do not give us an idea of these towns as fortified garrisons; however, future work may alter our understanding. Textual analysis of the usage of military or non-military terminology in relation to these towns, while not a part of this study, should be undertaken in the future as it may add a further dimension in tandem with the archaeology to how these towns were perceived. This study will examine frontier towns as one of a number of settlement types and discuss their geographic location, chronology, and economic viability as part of the larger frontier landscape.[46]

Although textual references at times suggest a division of the frontier into a more vulnerable front-line zone (*thughūr*) and rear-line (*'awāṣim*) province, reputedly for defence and supply, these divisions only occur from the end of the eighth century and the frontier did not remain static but developed over time. Shaban first commented that the creation of the *'awāṣim* was intended to produce a more tightly controlled and closer defence system, and primarily to curb investment in the upkeep and garrisoning of more exposed *thughūr* towns. Bonner argues that this division was an idealized and political administrative move to enable the 'Abbāsids to assert authority over former Umayyad lands and prevent the growth of local power.[47] Abu Ezzah argues that this division was arbitrary and flexible, and that the list of *'awāṣim* towns changed from author to author. In reality this designation did little to affect the everyday life or fate of frontier settlements.[48] The limit of the short-lived first frontier was at the provinces of Ḥimṣ (Emesa) and Qinnasrīn (Chalcis). These and other towns gradually became subsumed as the Islamic conquests expanded northwards to the Taurus Mountains and beyond. Eventually, the Taurus demarcated a rough upper limit of settlement for the *thughūr.* In an archaeological study of frontier landscapes, however, the frontier should be divided first by its natural topography, then by its settlements, and consideration given to *all* parts of the frontier and beyond. While seemingly similarly arbitrary, this division is grounded in historical perspectives and serves two purposes. In the medieval world, with regards to maps and boundaries, spaces were conceived in relation to natural features and chief cities that ruled districts. Further, by drawing attention to the environmental features of the frontier we can closely examine in a Braudelian fashion patterns of settlement and subsistence that cut across textually informed ideological constructions of the frontier.

This book will ultimately argue that the frontier, both real and imagined, is a framework where processes of interaction and exchange took place between communities. The argument will build slowly in two analytical sections. Part 1 (Chapters 1 to 5) provide chronologically grounded archaeological evidence for the environment from geomorphology, natural resources and products, and routes. Following this, survey and excavation data examine the several specific categories of settlement and land-use activities throughout the entire *thughūr*, including northern Syria and Mesopotamia. The model of analysis used for all the data, often statistical and technical in nature, is derived from surveys of the two large plains: the Amuq Plain of Anṭākiya in *al-ʿawāṣim* and the Kahramanmaraş Plain of Marʿash, the forward post of Anṭākiya in *al-thughūr*. Data for the elusive Late Roman to Early Islamic periods will be gleaned from recent high-resolution surveys and older low resolution surveys from both the *thughūr* and *ʿawāṣim* regions, reassessed to produce a clear image of settlement patterns during this time. The Jazīra river valleys of the Balikh and Khābūr, not formally part of the frontier, are analyzed as a comparative or counterpoint to the rest of the frontier. A central question will be to what extent these various regions, such as the Amuq (part of *al-ʿawāṣim*) and the Jazīra, displayed similarities in the settlement and land-use characteristic of a larger frontier province, showed differences supporting textual reference to administrative provincial jurisdictions, or diverged into a topographically-based set of contiguous river valleys and plains each with their own micro-regional patterns. Results will show that for most of the frontier, with the exception of the region around Ḥalab and most of the Jazīra, Early Islamic sites were reduced by half from the Late Roman period. More specifically, seventh- to eighth-century sites were fairly few, although they included new foundations, while eighth- to tenth-century sites were more numerous. This is not evidence of a 'no man's land' on the frontier nor of a continuously inhabited landscape, but rather of one that underwent a substantial reduction of population but became the focus of settlement and economic development.

Part 2 synthesizes settlement patterns, land use, and social interactions in their environmental and historical contexts. Historical evidence from primary texts including geographies written mainly in Arabic; Islamic histories; Byzantine military treatises; and, most importantly from a rural perspective, Greek and Syriac saints' lives all provide contextual frameworks and at times explanations for the patterns of settlement and land use. Chapters 6 to 9 present a narrative of settlement that incorporates wider Anatolian survey evidence and the Islamic–Christian *thughūr* of al-Andalus. While the primary locus of discussion is the Early Islamic period, the narrative can be extended to trace change from the Late Roman to the Early Islamic and the Early to Middle Islamic transitions and periods of occupation (or lack thereof).[49] The development of agricultural estates and irrigation, networks of way stations, adaptations to the spread of marshlands, and the eventual rise of villages and fortified castles are keyed into historical narrative. Chapter 10 closely examines the nature of different types of social interaction and exchange on the *thughūr*, besides those stemming from *jihād* and apocalyptic ideologies, such as trade and market economy, fluctuating tribal identities, and the rhythms and movements of pastoral populations. I argue that the frontier was layered and constituted three types of interactions: external (competition for resources between groups), internal (political relationships between the central state and peripheral groups), and ideological (military and religious conflict). Movement and communication across frontier spaces consisted primarily of upland and lowland interactions that were not limited to a singular monumental frontier. Instead, these are duplicated across time over localized environmental frontiers constituting ecological 'niches' of liminal space. This volume contributes to a more complex vision of the frontier than traditional historical views by juxtaposing layers of a real ecological frontier of settlement and interaction with an imagined military/religious ideological frontier.

PART 1

THE SYRO-ANATOLIAN *THUGHŪR*

Throughout the history of the *thughūr*, Islamic authors frequently refer to two geographical divisions on the frontier: the Syrian west (*thughūr al-shāmīya)* and the Jazīran east (*thughūr al-jazarīya*), with the Amanus Mountains and town of Mar'ash as the fulcrum. These divisions are not so much geographical (typically, all lands west of the Euphrates are part of Bilad al-Sham) as military, referring to the backgrounds of the soldiers on the fronter and a two-pronged double-flank style of summer raids from the left and right (*al-ṣā'ifa al-yusrā*, *al-ṣā'ifa al-yumnā*) to the Byzantine frontier. Further, they are mentioned by some geographers, such as Istakhrī and Ibn Ḥawqal, but not others, such as Muqqadasī.[1] Topographically, the frontier can be divided into three large areas, each with smaller micro-regions that are bounded by natural geographic features (Figure 3, p. 35). The western frontier, or Cilician Plain, stretches from Rough Cilicia to the Amanus Mountains. The central frontier (from the Amanus to the Euphrates River) can be subdivided into two areas: the western rift valley of the Amuq and Kahramanmaraş Plains and the eastern hilly steppe and plain of the Nahr Quwayq and Jabbūl Lake. The eastern frontier (east of the Euphrates, including the Upper Euphrates to the Tigris River) includes the Karababa, Malaṭiya, and Elazığ (Keban) Plains to the north. In presenting them, we can follow a central to east to west schematic, tracing roughly the path of interest taken by

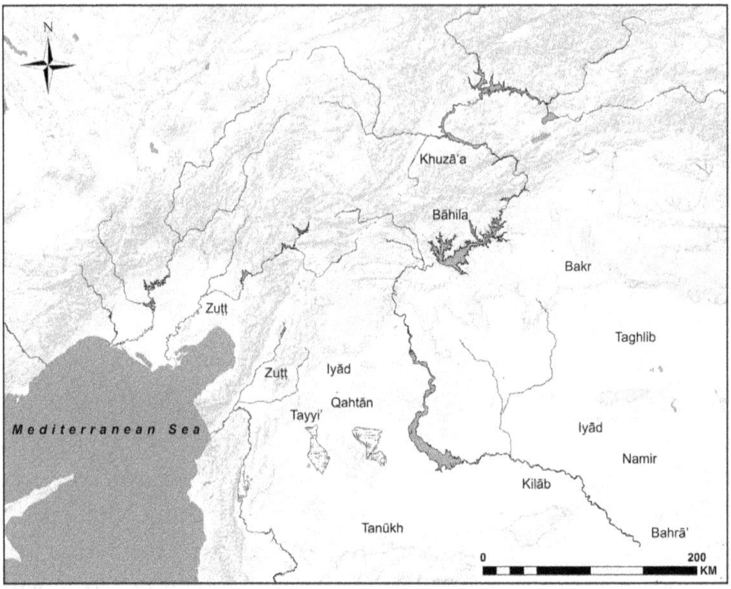

Figure 2 Tribes on the *thughūr*

Islamic rulers in establishing permanent settlements following the conquests. By comparison, the Balikh and Khābūr Plains are examined to see how they relate to the eastern *thughūr* or the Jazīra. In the interest of space and focus, the Tigris region and north-east including Mawṣil, Armenia, Ādharbāyjān, and Arrān will not be included. In the manner of the Islamic geographers such as Muqaddasī, the following five sections will analyse each of these areas in turn building up the landscape from its environmental features; resources; natural passes and routes; rural settlements; tell, upland settlements and monasteries; way stations; and chief towns. Unlike Muqaddasī, a hierarchy is implied but not imposed. Rather, the main aim is to uncover what archaeological evidence exists for the *thughūr* and how this evidence can be used to seek out not only the historically known *thughūr* settlements, but the lesser-known settlements that lay in between, invisible in the texts. These elusive communities, their interactions with one another, and their use of the land are integral elements in understanding the frontier landscape.

Methodology

Surveys along the *thughūr* have actually been fairly well represented in publications. However, the majority of surveys before 1980 have still treated late-period sites very cursorily, giving only a limited depiction of settlement. Although a few exceptions have provided substantial detail of the Roman and post-Roman landscape, there is presently no sufficient information overall to be comparable or consistent with recent data. This is a result of targeting earlier periods for specialized research and unfamiliarity with the late-period ceramics. Recent surveys and excavations with comprehensive strategies aimed at a holistic recording of the landscape in all periods, however, such as the Amuq and Kahramanmaraş regional surveys and several Euphrates salvage surveys and Jazīra surveys, counterbalance the weaker data sets.

The primary goal of most recent surveys in the Near East is to expand on earlier tell-based surveys by variations in site type and distribution. Non-mounded sites, flat scatters in the plains, sites in upland valleys, and high-elevation plateaus are considered alongside tells. Land-use features associated with sites such as canals, roads, field terraces, presses, and mills are also recorded as part of the landscape. The landscape itself is also the subject of investigation, and newer methods utilizing geomorphology, remote sensing, and geographical information systems (GIS) help greatly in tracking changes to the environment through climatic shifts and land use over time. Surveys rely on surface collection of sites, which are susceptible to variations in visibility due to ground cover and surveyor subjectivity. Second, the main chronological indicators are unstratified ceramics from largely rural sites, which are often dominated by coarsewares in their assemblages. The trend towards localized traditions of many coarsewares and some finewares makes dating often difficult and broader, to within one or two centuries. As a result, surveys have often been regarded as secondary after excavation data, where ceramics are stratified and dating is refined by numismatic, epigraphic, and scientifically-dated evidence. However, surveys remain the *only* method of investigating the landscape, its settlements, and land-use patterns over time and the relationship of these to the environment. This is particularly the case for the Islamic–Byzantine frontier, for which there have been around 35 surveys and only a handful of excavations of sixth- to tenth-century sites.

Not all of these surveys can be taken at face value or compared with one another as their methods differ radically, their results are inconsistent, and their treatment of the Islamic period is general at best. Meaningful comparison and reinterpretation is required, and it reveals pertinent general information that should not discarded outright as it supports the evidence from higher-resolution Islamic-focused surveys. As a result, surveys can be divided into four main groups: (1) extensive and coarse low-resolution large-area surveys; (2) intensive and high-resolution large-area surveys; (3) extensive and fine high-resolution large-area surveys; and (4) intensive high-resolution small-area surveys around sites and with reliable dating for the Islamic periods. Surveys ranged in methodologies, and, as a result, intensive or extensive classifications are on a scale: intensive surveys typically employed walking transects and off-site investigation while extensive surveys also used vehicles and were tell-focused.[2] Low-resolution and high-resolution refers specifically to the reliability of dated ceramics from the Islamic period that employ subdivisions. The coarse low-resolution surveys of the first group will be briefly described along with their general observations. The second and third groups will be analysed more comprehensively, taking into consideration the strong caveat that these high-resolution surveys had more finely tuned Islamic chronologies that allow subdivision. Recent excavations and a greater understanding of transitional and Early Islamic ceramics also permit more accurate dating of sites previously categorized by very general (at best) or incorrect chronologies. Even while this book is being written, new surveys and excavations are being conducted. Salvage excavations of rural and urban sites around the frontier carried out by Turkish museums add a significant level of information that unfortunately cannot be included in this study, as most of these are never published. Future work should add them to the larger data set. Using mainly survey data with some supplemental excavation evidence when available, these areas will be examined from an Early Islamic perspective that considers more broadly what came before and after. As labels and periods differ from survey to survey, it is necessary to configure the evidence into accepted chronologies while the original period designations will be parenthetically mentioned.

Certain trends can be detected that show general and specific Early Islamic frontier settlement patterns that are present throughout the frontier, and, at the same time, variations in micro-regions.[3] Some analysis tools that have been used for other surveys with good results, such as calculating sites per square kilometer, aggregate site area per period, and site catchment areas, will not be systematically used here. Many of these surveys are not comparable on these levels. For example, the Amuq was surveyed for more than 15 years. More than 300 sites were found in an area of almost 2,000 km^2, while the Nahr Quwayq was surveyed for two years in which 80 sites were found in an area of nearly 2,500 km^2. Many more sites are clearly visible with remote sensing techniques. Within these areas, one survey focused on uplands as well as lowlands while the other did not. Site area calculation also represents a challenge. Many older surveys did not note site areas; however, it is possible to calculate them with the help of satellite imagery or aerial photography. Such a huge undertaking is beyond the scope of this book, but is currently being conducted in the region.[4] Figuring out chronologies from such surveys still poses a problem. As such, comparing site signatures and numbers remain useful for this study. The main reason for this is that we are investigating relatively short-term changes in the landscape around settlements from the fourth to fourteenth centuries, how they are occupied, whether they continue, and, if not, when they are abandoned.

Yet, for the Islamic–Byzantine frontier, how can we refine the data futher and determine settlement patterns during the entangled, transitional sixth to eighth centuries? Or make claims as to which settlements were Islamic and which Christian? In approaching these questions, a model is applied to the Amuq and Kahramanmaraş surveys that views sites with certain criteria leaving room for nuance and degree, rather than labelling sites statically as transitional (Late Roman to Early Islamic), or one or the other (Late Roman or Early Islamic). There are discerning factors in settlement choices from the Late Roman to the Early Islamic periods resulting from human responses to environmental changes (such as marshification). These features can be linked to ethnic and cultural differences; new settlements of Muslims differed in many cases from Byzantine Christians who were already living in the plain. In order to tackle the issue of ethnic representation on the frontier, the argument initially needs to be framed in a different way. The primary element of the model differentiates the sites in terms of newly-founded *de novo* settlements and those that had preexisting occupations which continued. Sites with known Islamic or Late Roman pottery were 'definite', whereas sites with general coarsewares that were not diagnostic enough were 'indefinite'. These criteria include arbitrary and multiple categories and subcategories of: (1) newly-founded *versus* preexisting settlements; (2) chronology (seventh to eighth centuries, eighth to tenth centuries, tenth to eleventh centuries, twelfth to fourteenth centuries); (3) definite *versus* indefinite occupation (based upon known diagnostic ceramic evidence); (4) site size (small: 1 ha and below, medium: 1.01 to 8 ha, large: over 8 ha); and (5) assemblage size (light: 1–2 sherds, moderate: 3–7 sherds, heavy: 8 + sherds).[5] Survey pottery is notoriously difficult to pin down, particularly when there is no related local stratified excavation. Furthermore, pottery of the Late Roman to Early Islamic transition can also be difficult to differentiate. Definite occupation refers to the presence of at least one known diagnostic ceramic, while indefinite refers to possible ceramic presence that is ambiguously dated. The point is not to achieve total accuracy of which site was occupied where and for how long. General and even more specific trends will still arise, providing a long-term view of landscape history. For maps, a more conservative representation is given; only sites with definitive occupation are shown. Textual references to settlements – though very few for rural farms, estates, villages, and small towns – can provide useful evidence. Of course, no such archaeological model is foolproof and neither is textual evidence; settlements could and did often have mixed populations. Taken in total, these criteria can be used to develop hypothetical ethno-cultural inferences of population and demography in both a transitional period and a culturally-mixed frontier zone that are not limitations, but rather expose the rich complexity of interaction in the frontier zone (Table 1).

Table 1 Surveys on the *thughūr*, late period settlement[6]

Survey	Late Roman			Early Islamic			Middle Islamic			Islamic–General				Total Survey	
	Sites	Aggregate Area (ha)	Site/km^2	Sites	Aggregate Area (ha)	Site/km^2	Sites	Aggregate Area (ha)	Site/km^2	Sites	Aggregate Area (ha)	Site/km^2	Total Sites	Area (km^2)	Survey Date
Central															
Amuq	136	1735	0.07	67	1950	0.04	126	1260	0.07	—			330[a]	1875	1930s, 1995–2011
K.Maraş	115[f]		—	31	75	0.03	47	140	0.04	—			61	1100	1993–95, 97
Tabqa Reservoir	26	194	0.02	—	115	0.09	19	0		—			37	1350	1964
Tabqa Dam	3		0.47	2		0.31	4		0.63	8		1.25	34	6.4	1968
Sajur	41[b]	354	0.03	—		—	—		—	25	217	0.02	77	1323	1977, 79
Gaziantep	6			—		—	—		—	17			216	—	1971
Jabbul	53	319	0.05	52	295	0.05	—	284	—	—			140	1120	1939, 96
Jarablus Tahtani	12/13			5/6			1			—			23	—	2006
Carchemish-Birecik	42	279	0.23	3	20	0.02	15	58	0.08	—			68	186	1989
Tell Rifa'at	38	758	0.02	31	706	0.01	38	761	0.02	—			84	2400	1977–79
Sweyhat	7	59	0.12	4	12	0.07	1		0.02	—			32	60	1974, 91–92
Eastern															
Adıyaman	38	308	0.02	—	—	—	—	—	—	119	302	0.06	100	2156	1985–88
Keban	4	16	0.01	—	—	—	22	—	—	40	100	0.77	52	323	1967

Table 1 (*continued*)

Survey	Late Roman			Early Islamic			Middle Islamic			Islamic–General				Total Survey	
	Sites	Aggregate Area (ha)	Site/ km^2	Sites	Aggregate Area (ha)	Site/ km^2	Sites	Aggregate Area (ha)	Site/ km^2	Sites	Aggregate Area (ha)	Site/ km^2	Total Sites	Area (km^2)	Survey Date
Kurban Höyük	18	58	0.02	5	22	0.01	8	33	0.01	—			25	1000	1980–84
Gritille	17	42	0.40	2	7	0.05	7	21	0.16	—			19	43	1982–84
Titriş Höyük	33	97	0.19	0	0		4	22	0.02	—			30	177	1991
Lidar Höyük	28	89	0.19	11	50	0.07	—	—		—			29	150	1978–80
Bozova-Urfa	13[f]	83	0.02	10	42	0.01	—	—		—			21	800	1978–80
Western															
Cilicia (BIA)	46	390	0.01	20	298	0.00	39	177	0.01	—			145	7585	1951
Cilicia (Bilkent)	13	39		3	33		8	23		—			25	1268	1991
Kırıkköprü	4		0.62	1		0.15	1		0.15	—			6	6.5	2005
Jazira															
Harran	103[b]	797	0.05	—	—	—	—	—	—	175	1202	0.09	206	2000	1989
Khabūr (Van Liere and Lauffray)	34[c]	1758	0.00	—	—	—	—	—	—	—	—	—	38	16245	1954–55
E. Khabūr	53	894	0.02	—	—	—	—	—	—	94	1426	0.97	97	2300	1976–66,9
U. Khabūr	29	336	0.01	14	—	—	—	—	—	15	252	0.00	55	4770	1989
North Jazira	41	153	0.09	51[d]	785	0.11	28	398	0.06	—	—	—	96	475	1986–90
Tell Beydar	13	49	0.03	8	63	0.02	2	3	0.00	—	—	—	69	450	1997–98

Table 1 (*continued*)

Survey	Late Roman			Early Islamic			Middle Islamic			Islamic–General			Total Sites	Total Survey Area (km^2)	Survey Date
	Sites	Aggregate Area (ha)	Site/ km^2	Sites	Aggregate Area (ha)	Site/ km^2	Sites	Aggregate Area (ha)	Site/ km^2	Sites	Aggregate Area (ha)	Site/ km^2			
Tell Hamoukar	4	131	0.03	30[d]	292	0.18	9	189	0.07	—	—	—	26	125	1999
Tell Leilan	—	—		17	388	0.01	41	966	0.02	—	—	—	35	2040	1995
Tell Brak	22[c]			—		—	—		—				56	170	1978
Balikh	23	98	0.01	55	391	0.03	12	91	0.01	—			65	2074	1983
Middle Euphrates	18	173	0.01	73[d]	550	0.06	68[e]	408	0.05	146			111	1300	1987–90

These numbers cannot be taken as firm dates in every case, depending on the quality of each survey. Indefinite sites are not included, although sites with 'light' ceramic assemblages are. Please refer to the text for each of these surveys for comments on methodology. Aggregate areas are inexact as they reflect the total area of the site as delineated from CORONA satellite imagery and GIS. While most sites were traced, not all were found or are preserved. Further, this number should be taken as an estimate as it is impossible, without excavations, to know how much of the site was occupied in any given period.

[a]Includes only sites until 2004. Sites from 2005–11 have not yet been published.

[b]Roman and Late Roman are undifferentiated.

[c]Roman through Islamic are undifferentiated.

[d]Includes a total of transitional seventh-century, Umayyad, and 'Abbāsid periods.

[e]Includes several subdivided periods between the late tenth to fourteenth centuries.

CHAPTER 1

THE CENTRAL *THUGHŪR*: THE TWO AMUQS

You will depart and alight at a meadow with ruins (marj dhī ṭulūl).[1]

The above quote is taken from Early Islamic eschatological texts, describing the Amuq Plain, or Plain of Antioch, as a frontier battleground for one of the final apocalyptic wars. It was also a battleground for the early conquests where Arab armies camped on al-ʻAmq, the large fertile Plain of Antioch or Amuq, and chased the fleeing Byzantines. It also, however, succinctly frames how archaeologists have traditionally regarded the Amuq Plain and other similar geographic regions all over the Near East, which are dotted with tells (*tulūl*) mainly of the fourth to second millennia BCE. Indirectly, it alludes to the historical view of the frontier landscape during and following the Islamic conquests as uninhabited. Recently, close attention has been given to the non-tell landscape of the Classical, Late Antique, and medieval periods. Surveys in the Amuq and Kahramanmaraş Plains revealed a crucial series of dramatic changes that occurred in a relatively short period of time between the Late Hellenistic and Early Islamic periods. In the Late Hellenistic and Early Roman periods there was a rise in dispersed, low, mounded or flat settlements in both lowlands and uplands, and an increase in cultivation. By the Late Roman and Early Islamic periods, the seasonal wetlands had expanded into a permanent lake and marsh.

The results dispel the idea of the Amuq, a historically known frontier zone, as a no man's land, but do raise many questions as to what changes occurred in the landscape during the transitional Late Roman to Early Islamic periods. From the Late Roman to the Early Islamic period, a shift occurs that follows certain patterns of continuity, while at the same time presenting new forms of settlement and land use linked to complex factors combining landscape response and ethnic and cultural practice.

The Environment

The area of the central *thughūr* is bounded by the Amanus Mountains to the west, the Euphrates River to the east, Ḥalab to the south, and the Taurus Mountains to the north; a square area roughly 170 × 170 km (28,900 km^2) (Figure 3). It was in reality northern Syria, considered as such by authors of the day, and topographically more Syria than Anatolia. It includes two main geographical areas, the subjects of this and the next chapter. The first area, the lowland rift-valley river-plain area in the west, is a northern extension of the Great Rift Valley connecting East Africa and the Red Sea. This valley is broken up into two discrete plains, both referred to by the same name in Islamic periods: *al-'amq*, meaning the depression or lowland. The southern one is the large triangular-shaped Amuq Plain fed by four rivers, the Nahr 'Āsī (Orontes), Nahr 'Afrīn ('Afrīn), Nahr al-Aswad (Kara Su), and Nahr Yaghrā (Yaghrā, no longer extant), and was dominated since the Hellenistic period by a large lake, now drained (Figure 4). The Amuq measures about 670 km^2 and is indeed a low-lying depression, 90–100 meters above sea level (from here on, m.a.s.l.) receiving a relatively high amount of rainfall for the region (500–700 mm/annum). Modern Antakya receives even more, owing to its location in a narrow ravine (1,132 mm/annum) (Figure 5).

The long corridor of the Kara Su Valley connects the Amuq to the northern plain. The Kahramanmaraş Plain (al-'Amq al-Mar'ash) is actually two plains. The northern funnel-shaped plain immediately south of the modern city of Kahramanmaraş is watered by the Ak Su

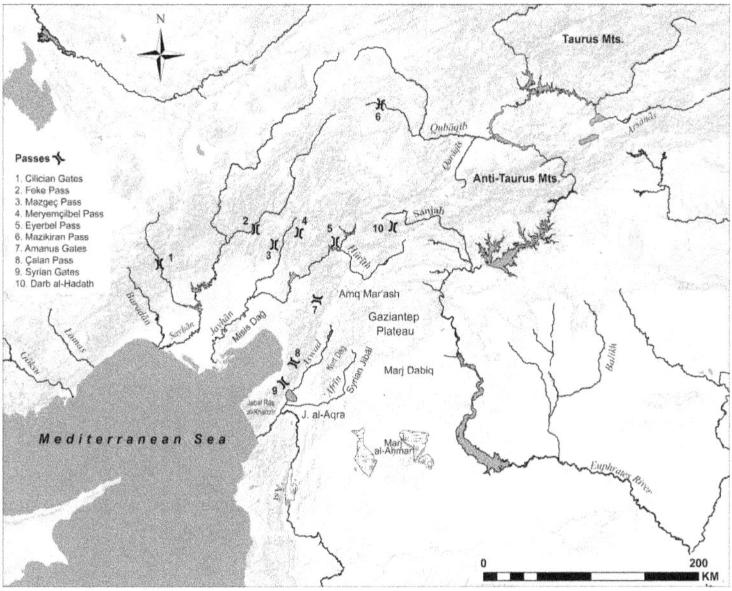

Figure 3 The *thughūr* with natural features represented

(Nahr Ḥūrīth) coming down from the north-east, originating at 'Ayn Zanīthā; the Erkenez Su from the east, and the smaller Organ Çay to the south-west. The southern plain was mainly a wetland traversed by the Ak Su (Nahr Ḥūrīth). It is considerably lower (500 m.a.s.l.) than the northern plain (1,800 m.a.s.l.). As a result, the southern plain was dominated until recently by two wetland areas: the Sağlık Lake, or Gavur Göl, and the Mizmilli Marsh. The smaller plains are connected by a narrow corridor and surrounded by the Taurus Mountains. The average rainfall is more than the Amuq, *c*.800–900 mm/annum. To the west of the two Amuqs are the imposing Amanus Mountains and to the east lies the hilly region of northern Syria, the Syrian Jibāl. Nearly the whole of the central frontier was within the Mediterranean vegetation zone, dominated by pine and oak in the uplands, that stretches from the coast over the Amanus Mountains and across much of the *thughūr*, lessening until it reaches the Euphrates River.

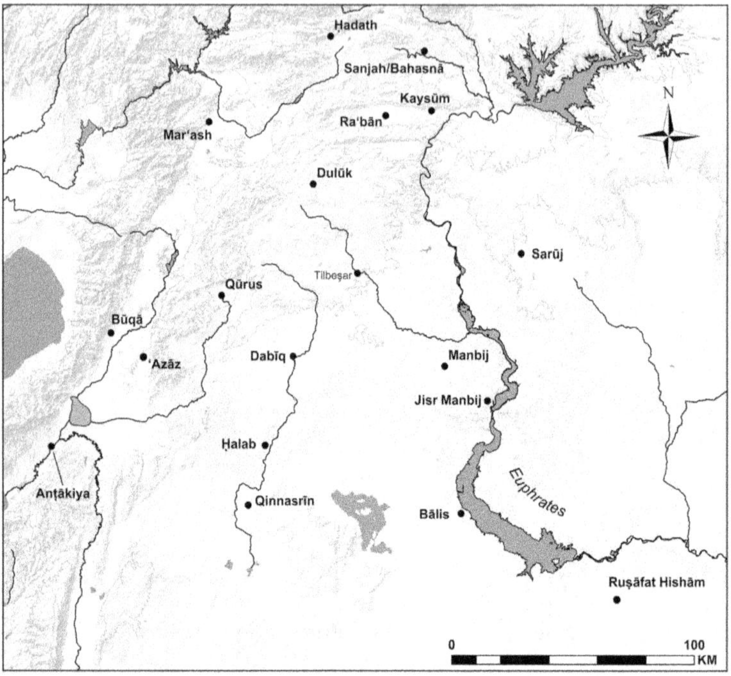

Figure 4 The Central *thughūr*

An important process induced mainly by human factors that took place in the sixth to eighth centuries was marshification, the growth and spread of marsh. The two Amuqs were always susceptible to water-logging, and marshes had occurred in earlier periods. However, the spread and then collapse of the intensive upland cultivation, mining, and deforestation seen in the growth and spread of Seleucid/Hellenistic to Late Roman sites on the slopes contributed to an erosion-prone landscape. Similarly on the plain, extensive irrigation and canal building during these same periods followed by abandonment of maintenance procedures contributed to the creation of a precarious and unbalanced ecological system. Abandonment of upland settlements and terraces also destabilized the topsoil. Natural processes such as more humid climatic conditions, greater precipitation, more frequent storms, and occasional seismic activity

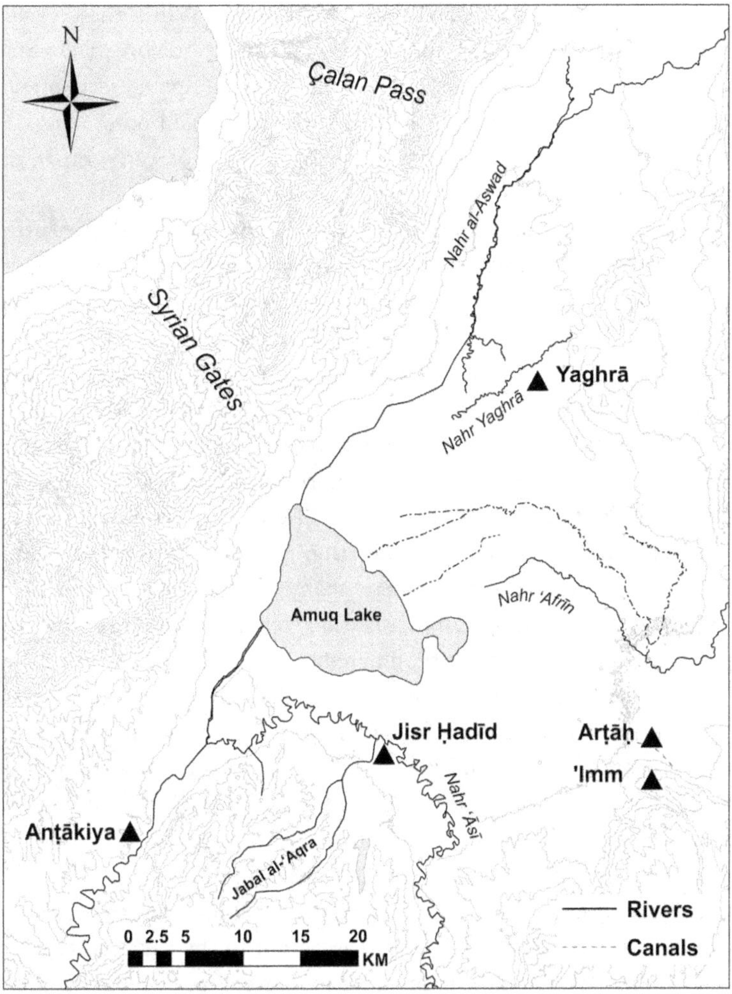

Figure 5 The Amuq Plain

in turn led to river flooding and avulsion, slope erosion, plain aggradation, and canal sedimentation. As a result the plains gradually filled, transforming seasonal lakes and marshland to permanent marsh. The early formation and expansion of the marsh, especially during seasonal inundations, would also have encouraged upland settlement, which in turn caused increased sedimentation in the form of erosion and avulsion on the plain. While these cycles based on human land use were in effect before the first millennium BCE, the combination of the spread of upland settlements and the intensification of agricultural, irrigation and other land-use activities was a crucial element in the process of early medieval marshification.[2]

Numerous authors from the fourth to tenth/eleventh centuries made repeated references to the cultivation of the lands around Anṭākiya, and certainly the Amuq and Kahramanmaraş Plains. The dominant crops included the typical Mediterranean triad of wheat, grapes and olives. Wheat and also barley grew in the lowland plains. Muhallabī, writing at the end of the tenth century, stated that olive oil from this region between Anṭākiya and Ḥalab, at places such as Artāḥ/'Imm in the Amuq, was an important and prolific industry and clearly desired, as it was exported to 'Iraq. This shows continuity with Late Roman olive oil production for the same region of the Syrian Jibāl upland sites, where many presses were found, and corroborates the heavy emphasis that scholars have traditionally placed on this local industry, but not to its exclusion. Water mills surveyed in the Amuq Plain indicate flour-processing activities, likely present throughout the region, while canals in all areas were instrumental in maximizing the output of certain crops as farmers would not have been able to depend on rainfall alone. Timber for construction and fuel was taken from the Amanus Mountains. The Amuq Survey documented steatite (soapstone) mines in the Amanus near Anṭākiya, and stone quarries in the Jabal al-'Aqra that loomed over Anṭākiya's eastern side. Fish was caught in the Lakes of Antioch and Yaghrā. We can also assume that reeds were harvested from these wetland areas for local construction. Glazed ceramic production in Anṭākiya and ceramic wasters and glass vitrified slag in small rural sites indicate a widespread craft specialization throughout the frontier countryside. Silk and cotton textiles were also similarly manufactured in Anṭākiya.

The major towns of Anṭākiya and Mar'ash were located in the lowland western rift valley, along with the fortified enclosure of Būqā and many other small rural settlements and towns such as

'Imm and Yaghrā. The main west–east route was along the Nahr al-'Āṣī to Jisr al-Ḥadīd then to 'Imm and Ḥalab, east out of the plain via the 'Afrīn Valley. The central frontier was in many ways a fulcrum balancing western and eastern frontiers. It connected to the western frontier towns via two key Amanus passes, the Belen and Bahçe; smaller secondary tracks from Ḥiṣn al-Tīnāt towards modern Hassa in the Kara Su Valley north of the Amuq Plain, and towards İslahiye (Nicopolis) in the same valley south of the Kahramanmaraş Plain; and a third route between Osmaniye and possible Hārūnīyya and İslahiye.[3] From Mar'ash, the road ascended the Bahçe Pass (also known as the Amanus Gates, Darb al-'Ayn, Darb al-Lukkām and Arslanlı Bel) to Hārūnīyya. From Anṭākiya, the road climbed through the Belen Pass (or Syrian Gates, Baylān, Darb Anṭākiya or Darb Baghrās) to Iskandarūna on the coast. The only definite north–south route was Anṭākiya–Baghrās–Būqā–Mar'ash through the rift valley corridor. North of Mar'ash was the Eyerbel Pass (also called the Ak Yol, or 'White Road') through the Taurus Mountains. One route followed the Nahr Ḥūrīth west of Mar'ash into the mountains to Göksun–Kemer–Sarız, then on to Kayseri in Byzantine Cappadocia (Figure 3).

Survey Methodology

Two large surveys in the Amuq and Kahramanmaraş Plains provide a spatial and temporal multilayered picture of Late Roman and Early Islamic settlement that can be used as a model for analysing settlement data from other surveys on the frontier. This model can try to overcome some of the challenges faced by 'late period' representation on archaeological surveys.

Group I: Extensive/Low-Resolution/Large-Area Surveys

R. Braidwood's groundbreaking survey in 1937 recorded only 17 sites of 'Late Roman' occupation. His total decrease in Phase S pottery (including brittle red wares dated to the 'Early Christian' era, 350–650) led to the incorrect hypothesis that few sites in the plain were occupied at this time despite the massive presence of nearby

Antioch.[4] Decades of improved ceramic dating demonstrates that brittlewares continue through until the tenth century. Braidwood acknowledged this discrepancy and concluded that: 'In all probability, the landowners lived in the great towns up on the hills or in Antioch, while the peasant population lived in reed huts in only semi-permanent villages much as the fellahin do today.'[5]

Early studies in the Kahramanmaraş plain were conducted by J. Garstang (1907) and J. Du Plat Taylor (1949). Similar to Braidwood, Du Plat Taylor in her 1949 survey in the Kahramanmaraş Plain wrote:

> A feature of the plain was the number of late Roman settlements; these were built on the flat ground and must have marked outlying farms, as similar structures were also visible on the tops of several of the *hüyüks.* These settlements were shown by a scatter of cut stones, building debris, roof tiles and later Roman coarse wares. In some cases they occupied an area up to an acre in extent.[6]

It is not necessary to go into detail about the results of both Braidwood's and Du Plat Taylor's surveys, as newer surveys have since expanded on them.

Group II: Intensive/High-Resolution/Large-Area Surveys

The University of Chicago's Amuq Valley Regional Project, building on Braidwood's 1930s' survey, directed by A. Yener, was conducted between 1995 and 2005 by various field directors including T. J. Wilkinson, J. Casana and F. Gerritsen and was renewed by A. Yener and A. Green in 2008 and L. Swartz Dodd in 2009–12.[7] The total number of sites surveyed increased dramatically from 178 sites, found by Braidwood, to 397. For the first ten years until 2005, ceramics were collected from 287 out of 355 sites; the remainder included Braidwood sites that are now in restricted military zones, those that are now in Syria, or sites where no collection was possible as they were cemeteries or salvage excavations conducted by the Hatay Museum. Study of the post-Roman ceramics for these 287 sites was carried out by A. U. de Giorgi (Roman/Late Roman),

T. Vorderstrasse (Middle Islamic/Late Islamic), and myself (Late Roman/Early Islamic/Middle Islamic).

The Kahramanmaraş Survey was carried out in 1993–4 by E. Carter (University of California, Los Angeles) and then in 1995 and 1997. N. Um initially examined the Islamic-period ceramics in the field, J. Vroom studied a small portion post-survey, and D. Whitcomb in 2001[8] and myself in 2003 and 2006 analysed all the collections comprehensively.[9]

There were some methodological differences between the two surveys. The Amuq Survey included urban surveys of the present-day towns of Demirkopru (Jisr al-Hadīd) and Yenişehir ('Imm), whereas a proper investigation of the major city of Kahramanmaraş is lacking, save for a collection from the citadel mound. The Kahramanmaraş Survey, however, found numerous encampment sites and temporary settlements, which were unfortunately few and far between for the Amuq.[10] An architectural survey of the city of Anṭakiyā by H. Pamir and G. Brands from 2004 to 2009 greatly increased our knowledge of the city plan, its walls and water-supply systems.[11]

One strong method of analysis is statistical as surveys have information on many sites and how many of these were settled in each period. Crunching numbers, so to speak, while technical and difficult to read, is a valuable way to compare the number of settlements between periods and how many of these were newly founded or continuously occupied and preexisting. In the Amuq, the peak in settlement was in the Roman (or Early Roman) period with 72 per cent of sites occupied (Figure 6).[12] This decreases in the Late Roman period to 47 per cent – a trend not seen in many other parts of the Near East, particularly the southern Levant, which chart an even greater peak in settlement (Figure 6). Only 3.5 per cent of the Late Roman sites were new settlements, meaning the majority were continuously occupied from the Roman period. Only sites with definite ceramic identifications are considered, omitting more ambiguous coarsewares, handles and bases. However, even including sites with indefinite Late Roman attribution brings the percentage to around that of the Roman period and not greater, countering a fairly

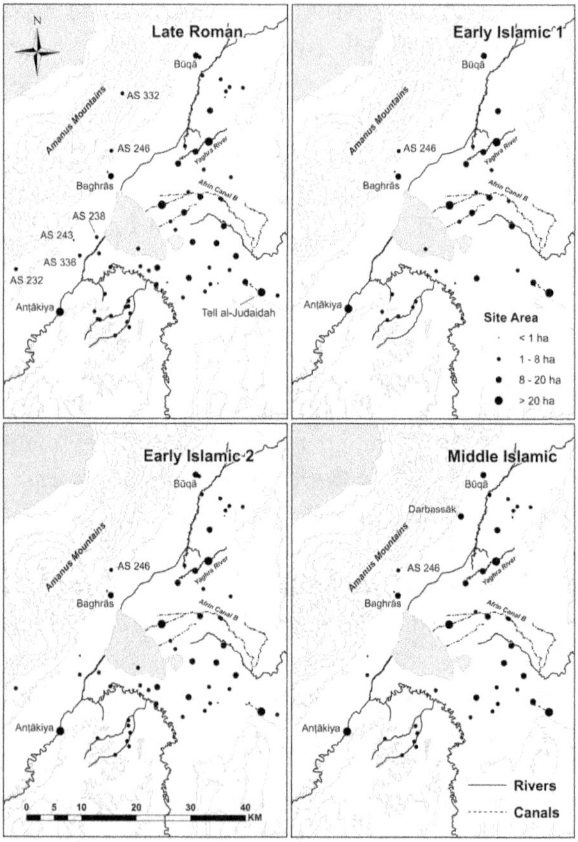

Figure 6 The Amuq Plain, Late Roman through Middle Islamic sites

common trend in Near Eastern settlement that shows a peak in settlement with the Late Roman period.

The Early Islamic period did not have a direct continuity from the Late Roman period, as is shown by the number of sites occupied overall and by the quantity of newly-established Early Islamic period sites (*de novo*) as compared with Late Roman sites that continued into the Early Islamic (preexisting). In the Early Islamic period there the number of sites was reduced by nearly half (Figure 6). 23 per cent of sites (67 of 287) in the Amuq were definitely occupied, as compared to 47 per cent (136 of 287) in the Late Roman period. The picture

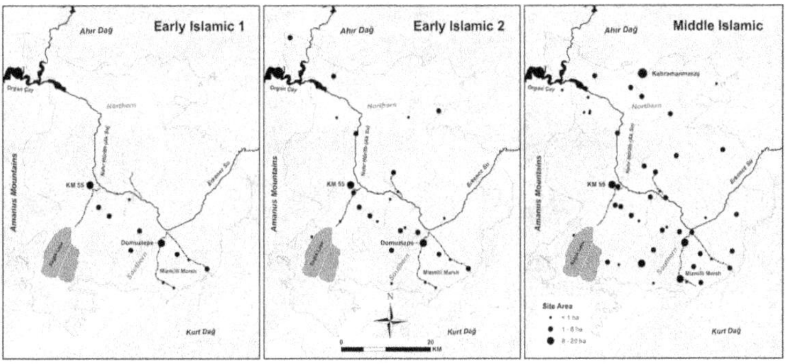

Figure 7 The Kahramanmaraş Plain, Early Islamic through Middle Islamic sites

changes little with the addition of indefinitely occupied sites (77 per cent Late Roman, 46 per cent Early Islamic). The lack of direct continuity between the Late Roman and Early Islamic periods is also reflected in the number of new *versus* preexisting sites. Although 9 per cent (six of 67) of the Early Islamic period sites occupied were newly founded and 72 per cent were preexisting, the latter only encompass 39 per cent of definite Late Roman sites. In other words, more than half of the Late Roman sites did *not* continue into the Early Islamic period. We can also examine with finer tuning when in the Early Islamic period sites were settled. 25 (37 per cent of the total number of Early Islamic sites) were settled already in the seventh to eighth centuries while 42 (63 per cent of the total number of Early Islamic sites) were first occupied in the eighth to tenth centuries. This clearly shows an increase in habitation from the Umayyad to 'Abbāsid periods.

By contrast, in the Middle Islamic period 44 per cent of sites (126 of 287) were inhabited, mainly between the early twelfth and early fourteenth centuries. Roughly half (47 per cent) of these were Early Islamic sites that continued, meaning that the other half of Early Islamic sites were abandoned by the mid-tenth century – generally viewed in the archaeological record as a poorly settled period, coinciding with the loss of 'Abbāsid hold on the frontier followed by a century or so of Byzantine reconquest and the rise of nomadic groups.

Figure 8 Domuztepe, the Late Roman and Early Islamic excavated building (photo courtesy of S. Campbell)

In the Kahramanmaraş Survey, 254 sites were identified in the plains, surrounding upland valleys, and central upland outcrops in the center of the plain. Of the located sites, 31 were identified as definitely Early Islamic (12 per cent) (Figure 7).[13] This compares with the Late Roman sites, which ranged from 88 to 143, averaging at around 115 (45 per cent) or about twice the number in a ratio of 2:1 Late Roman: Early Islamic sites.[14] Nine of the definite 31 Early Islamic sites were newly established, representing only 4 per cent of the total. Overall, the settlement pattern of the Kahramanmaraş Plain shows a 2:1 ratio of Late Roman sites to Early Islamic. Furthermore, only about 39 per cent of sites were initially occupied in the seventh to eighth centuries while 61 per cent were first occupied in the eighth to tenth centuries. A total of 47 sites (19 per cent) were inhabited in the Middle Islamic period, 27 (or 57 per cent) of which were new sites while 20 (43 per cent) were preexisting (Figure 8).

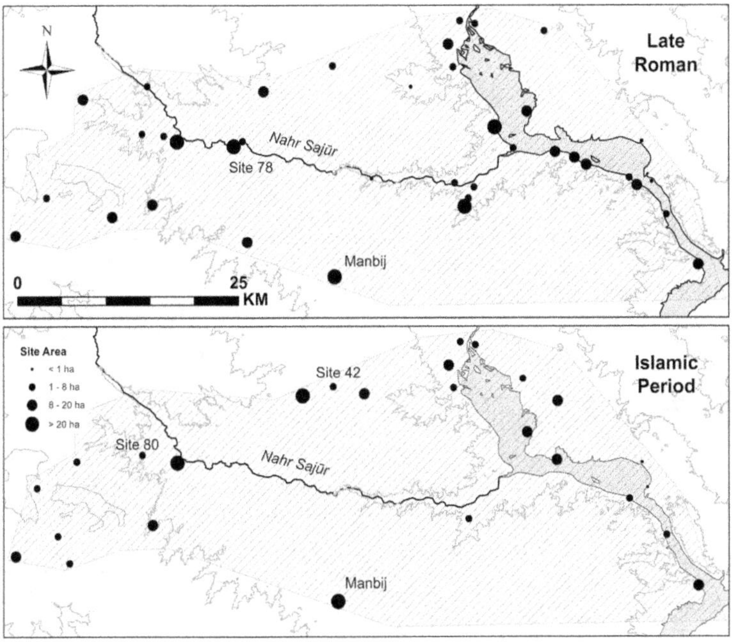

Figure 9 Nahr Sajūr Survey, Late Roman and Islamic sites

A comparison of the settlement patterns of the Kahramanmaraş and Amuq Plains is quite striking. Both show a similar 2:1 ratio of Late Roman to Early Islamic sites.[15] There are some differences, however. It is important to observe that newly-established Early Islamic settlement in the Kahramanmaraş region was only slightly less in magnitude than that in the Anṭākiya region. A comparison of relative chronologies (while tentative) also shows very slight differences, both within each region and comparatively (for Amuq sites: 37 per cent for the seventh to eighth century, 63 per cent for the eighth to tenth century *versus* Kahramanmaraş sites: 39 per cent for the seventh to eighth century, 61 per cent for the eighth to tenth century).

The percentage of Late Roman settlements is the same for the two survey areas (49 per cent definite for the Amuq *versus* an average of 45 per cent for Kahramanmaraş). What is known is that by the

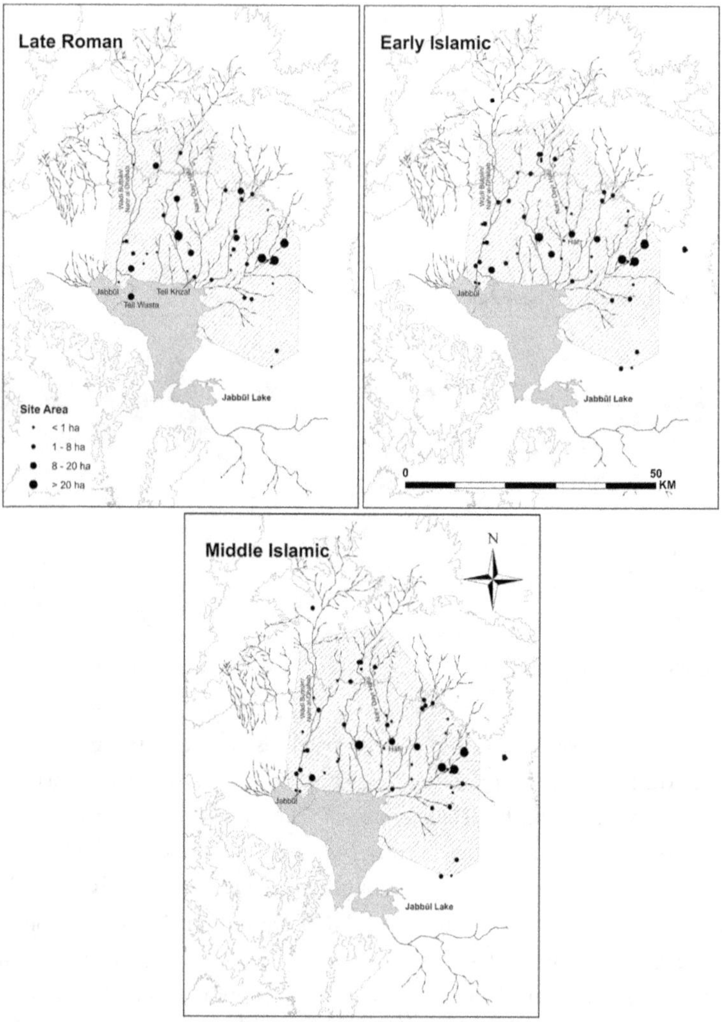

Figure 10 Jabbūl Survey, Late Roman through Middle Islamic sites (based on Yukich 2012)

seventh-century Early Islamic period there are twice as many sites in the Antioch region as there are in the Kahramanmaraş (23 per cent for the Amuq versus 12 per cent for Kahramanmaraş). Even if the indefinite Early Islamic sites were to be considered with the definite sites in total, the ratio is still maintained (49 per cent for the Amuq *versus* 24 per cent for Kahramanmaraş). The main difference lies in the number of preexisting Late Roman sites continuing into the Early Islamic period. Thus, while the levels of *de novo* Early Islamic sites are more or less consistent for both regions (7 per cent for the Amuq and 4 per cent for Kahramanmaraş), those for the preexisting Late Roman to Early Islamic sites are not (21 per cent for the Amuq and 9 per cent for Kahramanmaraş).

This neither illustrates fluid continuity into the Early Islamic period from the seventh century nor marked abandonment from the seventh to tenth century as a 'no man's land' frontier region. Methodological factors for those projects that have argued for seamless continuity come to mind, and they cannot be overruled – for example, ceramic redating[16] or indeterminate ceramic identification.[17] These interpretations compensated for earlier practices of supposing marked decline in settlement either at the end of the Late Roman period (with the arrival of the Muslims) or the end of the Roman period.

Canal, River and Marsh Sites

In the lowlands of the Amuq and Kahramanmaraş Plains, the largest and most important sites in terms of physical size and assemblage in the Early Islamic period were flat or low-mounded sites grouped as part of systems oriented along canal or river systems and in the expanding lake and marshlands. During the Late Roman to Early Islamic transition, canals continued to be used, as evidenced by the presence of Late Roman sites and large, newly-established Early Islamic sites on the same canals. In the Amuq, sites along the canalized 'Afrīn River in the center of the plain were evenly spaced, newly-founded between the second half of the seventh century and the early eighth century, comprised the largest Early Islamic sites found in the Amuq in terms of size (25–35 ha), and had moderate to heavy ceramic assemblages. All of these sites were double mounded, spread out to either side of the canal or divided into two low mounds on one side of it. Milling would have been a primary activity, as evidenced by the regular occurrence of large masonry blocks and millstones. Dams could have spanned the canals between the double-mounded sites. As the wetlands grew, occupation moved eastward away from the marsh in the Middle Islamic period. However, the expansion of wetlands did not cause these settlements to be suddenly abandoned. Rather, these shifts were gradual.

Sites were also concentrated similarly along rivers such as the Yaghrā, no longer extant, which flowed from the Gölbaşı Lake into the Lake of Antioch. These sites averaged 12 ha and were evenly spaced, but, unlike the canal sites, were mainly preexisting as they were built on a continuously flowing river. The Yaghrā River sites had larger assemblages, both by comparison with their previous Roman and Late Roman occupations and with the ʻAfrīn sites, even though the expansion of wetlands was more extensive for the Yaghrā River area than that of the ʻAfrīn canals. As in the ʻAfrīn region, occupation very gradually shifted from south to north from the Late Roman to Middle Islamic period, showing adaptation to the spreading marsh. Indeed, since the Middle Islamic period the Yaghrā River has became entirely subsumed within the wetlands. The sites were not totally abandoned; Middle Islamic period inhabitants built the sites higher and subsisted within a permanent wetlands environment. Although the process of marshification was more extensive for the Yaghrā River sites than for the ʻAfrīn Canal sites, the former were larger sites in terms of assemblages. Some exhibited glass slag vitrification, suggesting local industries. The sites also occupy midpoints on the east–west land route that crossed the northern part of the Amuq at the edge of the marsh, near the present-day Kırıkhan–Reyhanlı road. On the Orontes River, in the southern part of the plain, two newly-founded Early Islamic sites with light assemblages were situated between the towns of Jisr al-Ḥadīd and Anṭākiya; one of them extended into the Middle Islamic period. Sites also occurred along the Kara Su River and road leading to Marʻash. As such, canals and rivers became deliberate focal points for settlement for farmsteads or villages. In some cases, these were settled peripherally to Late Roman sites.

In the Kahramanmaraş Plain, it is possible to detect three canal systems – and possibly two more. A conspicuous pattern of newly-established Early Islamic sites, arranged linearly where several tributaries of the Ak Su River drained into the Mizmilli marsh, indicate the presence of canal systems. These sites have some of the largest assemblages for the Early Islamic period and only slight representation in the Middle Islamic. Despite their assemblage size, two of them were flat and rather small physically and founded in the seventh century, while the third, at the end of the canal line, was located at the edge of the uplands and included a tell settlement and preexisting Late Roman occupation. Another canal is suggested by a string of three sites just south of the aforementioned canal. Two of these sites were flat, while one was a high tell that encompassed a wider area than the others. The 'anchor' site at the end of the canal line was associated with small mounds perceived as individual buildings, a wine or olive press, an irrigation system, a quarry and graves. These sites exhibited continuity from Late Roman to the Early Islamic tenth century, with virtually no Middle Islamic representation. As such, this linear string suggests an earlier Late Roman canal that was still utilized in the subsequent centuries. The tell sites on each canal were very similar in size and appearance. Both had small villages around the mound: lower towns that likely were the focus of settlement, and which monitored water use to adjacent fields and maintained the canal.

On the western side of the plain, two small newly-founded eighth- to tenth-century sites that had no Middle Islamic period occupation were aligned, suggesting that canalization of the western Ak Su drainage continued in the Early Islamic period. The sites are also in line with the south–north road from Anṭākiya to Mar'ash. Three sites were linearly arranged and evenly spaced between this western canal and the central outcrop of the plain. While two of these sites continued from the Late Roman period, one of them was occupied only from the eighth century; all continued into the Middle Islamic period and beyond. Two of these sites were small low multiple-mounded sites and the surveyors described them as a group of farmhouses. These three sites indicate either a road or another canal system from the Late Roman period and earlier. A canal flows north and east of the south-eastern site today. The middle site, KM 5, was fairly large compared to others in this period (4 ha) and was a low double-mounded/flat site with a heavy Early Islamic assemblage but significantly lighter Middle Islamic and Late Islamic assemblages. The settlement is a possible candidate for Mar'ash. North of the central outcrop and Ak Su River, two sites (one currently along the Ak Su River itself), with occupation from the Late Roman to Middle Islamic represented in light assemblages, formed a small line. The northernmost site was a high tell with the possible outline of a fort on top, visible in the CORONA image. This grouping dated to between the eighth and tenth centuries. A few further sites were interspersed along the Ak Su River, including one consisting of a mound and lower town. Although it faced the northern canal site on the opposite bank, as seen in the CORONA imagery, it is unlikely that it was situated on the river itself, as it was fairly flat. This might suggest that the Ak Su's course traversed the plain more to the south at the time, and that even this river site was originally on its northern bank. A second site on or near the river, 10 km away, lay at the eastern end of the plain as one exits toward Ḥadath.

As the marshes spread, inhabitants adapted to life amidst the wetlands, while some founded marsh settlements from the start. Within the Amuq Lake, surveyors discovered a very low and flat mound dating from 650–750. The site was occupied in the Hellenistic period (and earlier), with uncertain continuity into the Roman and Late Roman periods. The site would have been an island, possibly built up with reed platforms. That it was located within the boundaries of the lake is evident not only by the paler soils visible in the CORONA images, but by a cover of freshwater gastropods on the site.

Yaghrā and 'Imm, Two Christian/Muslim Villages in the Amuq Plain

Smaller towns, often overlooked, filled in the spaces between the larger *thughūr* settlements and small unidentified rural farms. Consideration of these towns is important, as they gained prominence and operated with a degree of self-sufficiency not seen previously. Two river/canal towns in the Amuq Plain with both archaeological and textual evidence can give us a better idea of the nature of these settlements and which communities inhabited them.

The settlement of Yaghrā is known only in Middle Islamic texts as a village on a river of the same name and near a small lake known for its plentiful fish (Buḥayrah Yaghrā, 'Ayn as-Sallūr {Spring of the Catfish}, Casal Sellorie, and the fishery of Agrest in Crusader texts). It should be identified as Muratpaşa (AS 25), the largest of the three Yaghrā River sites and the one with the largest Middle Islamic assemblage.[18] The Late Roman occupation is presumed by its 'indefinite' attribution, given a large potential assemblage and a preexisting Roman component. Yet, Abū al-Fidā' in the fourteenth century described its population as Christian.[19] Interestingly, a Middle Islamic Qur'anic monumental inscription reportedly from the site mentions the Mamlūk Sultan al-Ashrāf Īnāl (d. 1461), and the settlement appears in an account describing a visit by the Sultan Qāitbāy in 1477.[20] One can posit that the settlement had a mixed community of Christians and Muslims.

In the south-eastern corner of the plain, on a raised flat plateau, a small canal was discovered measuring 3.4 km in length and visible in the CORONA imagery linking watermills and terrace walls at one end to a reservoir (lake) at its source near the village of Yenişehir and the large site of AS 345. Three major Late Roman sites were evenly spaced along this canal. In the Early Islamic period, this system continued and even expanded with the inclusion of a smaller Late Roman site, which grew in the Early Islamic period, and the addition of a major new Early Islamic site approximately 2 km away from the canal but still irrigated by it. In 1997, a survey recorded a full set of descending penstock water mills at Khirbet al-Tahun east of AS 347. Although the mills were of Roman construction based on architectural parallels, the mainly Late Roman pottery and few examples of Roman and Early Islamic pottery suggest they were in use throughout the Late Roman period and into the Early Islamic.

The site, designated AS 345, can be identified as 'Imm (Greek Imma), a third-century town placed on the important route that traversed the southern Amuq (parts of which are extant with wheel ruts) and connected Anṭākiya (20 Roman miles/29.6 km away) and Qinnasrīn (Greek Chalcis, 29 Roman miles/42.92 km distant), which appeared on the Peutinger Table map in the mid-fifth century and which also connected the communities scattered about the northern corridor of the Amuq Plain to Qūrus (Greek Cyrrhus, about 65 km away). In the mid-fifth century, Theodoret, the Bishop of Cyrrhus (393–457), mentioned 'Imm as 'a large and well-populated village' where the monk Palladius performed a judicial miracle during a crowded traders' fair.[21] An epigraphic identification appears in an early sixth-century Greek inscription, found in the modern town of 'Imm (Yenişehir), referring to a bishopric and the people of 'Imm (Imminoi).[22] Surveys in and around the town itself (AS 344 and AS 345) found many transitional seventh-, seventh- to eighth-, and eighth- to tenth-century ceramics and architecture, specifically in three areas: (1) a Late Roman building with an octagonal wall (possibly a church), converted into a Middle Islamic fortification (*kale*); (2) a stepped podium-type structure; and (3) city walls. Late Roman materials (fifth- to seventh-century African Red Slip and Phocean wares, predominantly) were collected in the first two of the surveyed sectors, and many architectural fragments were noted including columns, capitals, architraves, cornices, lintels and door frames. While little can be said about the structures and their relation to the urban layout, some more definite information about the town during Late Antiquity can be extrapolated from an inscription documented in 1999, now lost, mentioning an archbishop. A millhouse, possibly Middle or Late Islamic, was fed from a spring and the lake. Although textual evidence from the Early Islamic period is scant, later testimony can give some idea of the Early Islamic town. Ibn Buṭlān in 1051, travelling from Ḥalab to Anṭākiya, passed through a wealthy Christian town (*balda*) named 'Imm, where he spent the night. He remarked on its springs of water with fish, four churches, one mosque, and mills.[23] The letter is preserved in Yāqūt (1179–1229) who, in his gazetteer, adds that all the inhabitants are Christian and descended from ancient times (*wa qad nasaba ilayhā qadīman*). The Christian character of this town in the early eleventh century is highlighted by its raising of pigs (*mushārīr al-khanāzīr*) and the great number of permissible places for women, prostitutes and wine (*mubāh al-nisā' wa al-zanā wa al-khumūr āmrun 'aẓīmun*), not to mention that by this time the Muslim call to prayer had to be given secretly. By 1280, the settlement is referred to as a village (*qarya*) and, as suggested from its name, was fortified and appeared as Ḥiṣn 'Imm, but was also still predominately Christian.[24]

The settlement of nearby Artāḥ (Greek Artesia) is buried under the modern town of Reyhanlı. Numerous documents locate an important Roman settlement that preceded the sixth-century monastery at this settlement.[25] It is briefly mentioned both in Islamic and Middle Byzantine texts as early as 900, and may be one of 'Imm's satellite settlements that eventually became linked to it as a conglomerate town when a *strategos* of Artach or Artāḥ along with 'Imm is mentioned.[26] The survey discovered fragments of mills and other traces of architecture in the gardens of modern houses.

Such attention given to a village (a non-urban entity) in the historical accounts is encouraging and very useful, and it corroborates the archaeological evidence. While 'Imm was relatively larger than many other villages of the plain, it does not appear as an urban center, definitive bishopric, or sizable political entity. During much of the Early and Middle Islamic periods, at least until the thirteenth century, the village maintained its preexisting Syrian Christian community, seen from travellers' observations and the ratio of four churches to one mosque; however, it still was politically administered by Muslims. Its strategic location on the eastern access to the Amuq at the junction of plain and limestone massif was important both militarily and commercially, as seen in the above texts. At the same time, 'Imm's closed irrigated agricultural system of satellite sites, canals, mills and terraces show that the town was self-sufficient to a degree, not wholly reliant on the now-reduced former urban metropolis of Antioch. The settlement of Artāḥ demonstrates the continual process of conglomeration from farm to village to town in the Middle Islamic period.

Domuztepe: An Excavated Christian Village in the Kahramanmaraş Plain

In the Kahramanmaraş Plain, a Hellenistic through Middle Islamic/Middle Byzantine rural settlement occupation was excavated on a small scale in 2004–6 at the summit of Domuztepe (KM 97), a Late Neolithic site currently being excavated by the University of Manchester and previously together with the University of California, Los Angeles. The site is a rather large tell, but slightly mounded, averaging 8–10 m to a gradual rise of 14 m above the Kahramanmaraş Plain. It shared the extensive wetlands of the Ak Su eastern drainages with the *de novo* sites immediately to the west, and may have been part of this canal system. The stratigraphy in the small excavated area concerned (a single 10 × 15 m trench with an additional 5 × 5 m trench called Operation 7), in relation to the poorly preserved architecture, proved difficult to disentangle as the entire stratigraphic range from the Hellenistic period onwards was compressed into a little over a meter of deposition. Nevertheless, the site shows a certain level of continuity from the Late Roman period until the tenth century.[27]

At some time, probably during the Late Roman period (in the fourth century), a large square enclosure was built with thick exterior ashlar stone walls bonded with mortar (Figure 8). The enclosure had several rooms paved with terracotta tiles and white limestone tessera. In one room, the mosaic floor was badly damaged and excavation revealed a probably buried deposit of 287 Constantinian coins dated mainly from 313 to 347. Subsequent alterations were made, such as the addition of external square buttresses and long subdivided storage magazine-type spaces that probably date to the Late Roman and Early Islamic periods. Early Islamic ceramics were found in association with the remains of a large wall and several small subsidiary walls. Post-Chalcolithic architecture elsewhere on the site and the remains of a presumed Roman Period causeway over a small stream or canal show that more of the tell was occupied, although how extensively and in which period is unknown. On the whole, the ceramics were of local provenance and included virtually no imported wares, with the exception of one sherd. A local farmer discovered a large chancel screen fragment in the field just west of the summit. The decorated screen would have been part of a church, as yet undiscovered. To the south of the summit, a roughly rectangular cemetery was found while excavating the prehistoric phases of the tell (Operation 1). In 2005, a sounding 65 m west of Operation 1 revealed another burial, indicating that the area of the cemetery may have extended towards the summit, making it larger than previously assumed.[28] The cemetery contained approximately 48 bodies (both men and women) dating to the ninth/tenth centuries.[29] Based on the position of the bodies, they were identified as Christian burials. Finally, preliminary analysis of the animal bone assemblage from the sounding excavation at the summit revealed the presence of a higher amount (14 per cent) of pig bone compared to other identifiable species (cattle, sheep and goat) in the Early Islamic levels, with indications that pigs were raised at the site.[30]

The occupation at Domuztepe presents a special case where ethno-religious explanations for settlement can be tested with the combination of archaeological evidence showing diet, religious structures and burial practice, coupled with historical context. The results suggest that a small but long-standing Christian community was living atop a tell situated in the marshy lowland plain from the Late Roman to the early Middle Islamic/Middle Byzantine period. The lack of imported ceramics suggests weaker ties with larger urban towns and/or reliance on local manufacturing centers, possibly even at the settlement itself. Christians, mainly Jacobite Syriac Orthodox communities, are known from the Mar'ash area in the Early Islamic period. Several texts state that in 778 the Byzantines relocated many Jacobites from there to Thrace due to reasons of religious persecution. The text of a Syriac inscription from the Church of St Sergius at Ehnesh (Gümüşün), not far from Domuztepe on the Turkish lower Euphrates, corroborates the Byzantine displacement of its Syriac communities at this time.[31] The Muslims also displaced Jacobites to Ramla on account of Muslim scouts and spies being captured by the 'Rhomaye' (Byzantines).[32] The continuity of settlement indicated by the small excavations at Domuztepe does not illustrate any disruption, destruction or sudden abandonment of the settlement.

Routes and the Spaces in Between

Like canals and rivers, roads were focal points for site location. In the seventh and early eighth centuries, six large preexisting sites with heavy-assemblage sites interspersed along the west–east Anṭākiya–Ḥalab road continued and grew while some smaller Late Roman sites were abandoned or perhaps consolidated. Two sites located midway between Anṭākiya and Baghrās on the south–north route were founded in the Late Roman period, and replaced earlier sites near by. Indeed, one of these (AS 243) was the largest newly-established Late Roman site that had replaced earlier small settlements. In the eighth century, many smaller low sites of light to medium size and assemblage began filling in the spaces between these and the villages/small towns of Jisr al-Ḥadīd and 'Imm along the road. These sites no doubt highlight the importance of the road connecting Anṭākiya with the larger urban center of Ḥalab. There were also some small settlements, many newly founded, on the eastern perimeter road from 'Imm to Yaghrā, skirting the edge of the plain.

Only one of these sites is known by name. Jisr al-Ḥadīd ('Iron Bridge'; Greek Gephyra, or 'Bridge'), beneath the modern town bearing the same name in translation, Demirköprü, was known for its Roman bridge, the only remaining element from that period in the city, which spanned the Orontes River and which has been used continuously until the present day. This bridge would have been part of the main east–west route from Anṭākiya to Ḥalab. An additional east–west thoroughfare, indicated on the Peutinger Table, places Jisr al-Ḥadīd on the road into the 'Afrīn Valley. In the Early Islamic period, as in the Late Roman, Jisr al-Ḥadīd was surrounded by satellite sites radiating north of it towards the lake. These sites may have formed a similar complex of settlements around canal systems, as seen at 'Imm.

Off-road sites – that is, those whose location does not coincide with any known or obvious road, track or water channel – included eight that were mainly small with light assemblages. These began to fill in the irrigated and marshy plain between the Orontes and 'Afrīn

River basins, also in the eighth century. Indeed, Braidwood noted this area as having the densest concentration of 'Mediterranean-Arab Wares' in the Amuq, which he dated very generally from 630 until 1800.[33] Yet, on account of alluvial fans of the 'Afrīn, this area received very little sedimentation and was not a permanent wetland but probably flooded only seasonally. Ceramic wasters, glass slag, and terracotta piping indicate small local production centers not entirely dependent on the larger towns.

In the Kahramanmaraş Plain two preexisting Late Roman sites were located at either end of the roughly 10 km-wide narrow corridor separating the northern and southern plains. Both had late seventh/ early eighth to tenth-century ceramics, and both had bridges close by, allowing them to control river and road traffic between these plains. The southernmost of these sites was close to the presumed Late Roman site of Germanikeia, and is a second candidate for the location of Marʿash. An important pattern in the Middle Islamic period involved key sites along the land routes (which followed the river course) coming down the Kahramanmaraş Plain from north-west to south-east, many of which were newly established or enlarged. A cluster of three newly-established sites in the northern plain was detected on the western side of the plain. These sites were located near the Ak Su at the mouth of the Organ Çay Valley, at the point where a tributary fed into the river. This group shows that in the Middle Islamic period: (1) some settlement developed in the northern plain; (2) these sites consisted of nucleated conglomerate villages; (3) they were focused along the river and land route from the northwest; and (4) they included tell sites.

For off-road sites, a similar but less intensive process was noted in the southern Kahramanmaraş Plain on the edges of the marsh. By contrast, the northern plain had very few Early Islamic sites; only five out of more than 60 were occupied. They were located at the mouths of valleys, near streams and transhumance trails leading into the uplands. One site (KM 180) occupied an important strategic position as it stood in the Eyerbel Pass, which provided access from the plain to the Anatolian Plateau via Kokussos. None of these northern plain sites, however, were suggestive of any strategically placed or fortified sites that guarded the mountain passes on the edges of the Byzantine frontier. All of the sites in the northern plain were small, both in terms of assemblage and physical size; most were probably modest farmsteads that were only sparsely inhabited in the eighth to tenth centuries. Sites were often preexisting with no seventh-century component, indicating that they may have been abandoned for a century or so before a process of reoccupation occurred.

Alkım's survey has virtually no late information, yet the village of Ulucak/Kazan Ali in a valley at the entrance to the Bahçe Pass/Darb al-ʿAyn featured a 200-m wall 2–3 m thick, dated by him to the Late Roman period and used in the seventh century.

These smaller eighth-century sites did not have any secondary function as way stations and were mostly likely farms, indicating minor settlement growth in the second phase of the Early Islamic period following the transition and initial settlements of the first century after the Islamic conquest: a 'filling in' of the plain, or a process of sedentarization.

Upland Sites: Monasteries, Tells, Fortresses

While the majority of tell sites had no evidence of Early Islamic occupation, several did. Of the definite Early Islamic sites in the Amuq, eight (12 per cent) were tell sites. All of these had light to moderate Early Islamic assemblages. Yet, at three of them pottery came from the bases of tells in what was perceived as a lower town. In contrast to the Late Roman period, there were very few upland sites. Three small Late Roman upland fortifications were found in the Amanus, including Kale Tepe (AS 336) above Kırıkhan at 960 m.a.s.l., comprising a square enclosure measuring 20 m to a side built with large ashlar blocks and enclosed by a perimeter wall. AS 332 (Fenk Kale) yielded very little pottery overall but was similar in size and plan architecturally, and may have also been a Late Roman military site. AS 238 (Serinyol Kale) lay midway between Antioch and Baghrās, and was also square (9.3 m per side) with a vaulted roof and sitting on a larger rectangular platform (30 × 34 m). These sites showed no continuity as Early Islamic fortifications. Texts mention that various villages around the Amuq Plain were subdued during the seventh-century conquests, indicating their pre-Islamic existence. During his conquest of the region, Mu'āwiya found the forts along the eastern Amanus (Anṭākiya to Ṭarsūs) vacant (*khāliyatān*), and so he reoccupied them. It is unclear whether this was a literary trope or if these were actually uninhabited or abandoned at the time of the conquests.[34]

In the Kisecik Valley and uplands, west of Anṭākiya in the Amanus Mountains, five sites were identified and all were occupied in the Late Roman period. The furthest one up the valley (AS 232) was a Late Roman foundation. Of the five sites, only one – in the immediate vicinity of copper, gold and steatite mines – continued to be occupied. Intensive survey within the Jabal al-'Aqra east of Anṭākiya (not the Jabal al-'Aqra or Mount Cassius at the Orontes Delta), west of the Orontes River and south of the plain, shows a great dispersal of sites in the Late Roman period to the slopes, hilltops and valley floors, which was reduced by two-thirds in the Early Islamic period. Of these, most only bore slight continuity into the late seventh century and thus could be seen as continuing Late Roman sites. Those sites that showed eighth- to tenth-century Early Islamic occupation were the larger ones, located on valley floors in key areas (such as the valley mouth), were seen also in the Kahramanmaraş Plain, and all continued into the Middle Islamic period.[35]

Only one site in the Kahramanmaraş Valley (KM 66) was a definite upland site occupied in the Early Islamic period. However, surveyors noted that this hilltop site at the edge of the plain also had a lower town. Furthermore, mosaic floors were found at the upland site, suggesting that it too may have been a Late Roman settlement that continued.

Tell al-Judaidah was a *koinóbion* (community) monastery dated to the sixth century, with the remains of a small brick-and-stone church and attached room (a possible tomb), a residential building with rooms and a large central space with a mosaic, several outlying buildings, two pit burials, and a cistern surrounded by an enclosure wall.[36] Two complete reliquaries and part of another were found. It would have been associated with the nearby village of Imma. In the

ʿAfrīn Valley, Miaphysite intellectual centers flourished in the seventh century. Tell Jandārus (Gindaros, surveyed only by Braidwood as AS 58) was a coenobitic foundation (one of the earliest in northern Syria), founded in 330, appearing in the Peutinger Table as a stop on the road after Jisr al-Ḥadīd, and described by Malalas (491–578) in the sixth century as a walled town known as Gindaroupolis.[37] Michael the Syrian (1126–99) mentioned that after the Byzantine reconquest, four new Jacobite bishoprics were established in the villages around Marʿash. These included Arabissos (991–1002), Gihan near the convent of Barid (965–1038), Gudpai (40 km from Kahramanmaraş, 1027–30), and Karshena (1047–66).[38] It is likely that some of these were not so new or lay in proximity to known settlements, as evidenced by Arabissos. Further, the known placement of Arabissos (modern Elbistan)[39] and the convent of Barid on an upper course of the Jayhān,[40] both in the Taurus Mountains north of Kahramanmaraş, suggest that the new focus of bishoprics was not on the plain but in the Byzantine-controlled uplands. Taken together with the Amuq evidence, it can be concluded that those upland sites that were occupied may have been continued from the Late Roman period or, in certain cases, fulfilled special functions, either religious or industrial, as in the case of the Kisecik mining site.

In the Middle Islamic period, tells became more frequent choices for settlement. These were often surmounted by remains of square forts or churches, as noted in the Kahramanmaraş Survey. Many of these tells were either fortified or used as cemeteries in the Middle Islamic Period. One example was the settlement of Darbassāk (or Darbsāk, Greek Trapezon, Crusader Trapesac, modern Terbezek/Ala Beyli/Beyzil Bostan and the pilgrimage burial place of Beyazid-i Bestami, AS 346), farther north along the Amanus range from Baghrās. Darbassāk (from the same root as Dayr Bassāk, although possibly not referring to a monastery but a pass) was built on a flattened limestone plateau (hence the Greek name Trapezon, 'tabletop') that guarded a mountain pass (the Çalan Pass) – albeit a much smaller, narrower and more sinuous one than the Belen Pass – that began in the plain from the settlement of Celanlı.[41]

Abū al-Fidā' noted a Friday Mosque, and springs and gardens around it.[42] Darbassāk was built by Armenians and refortified in the Crusader Period, and consisted of a large castle on a high and natural rocky outcrop at the base of the Amanus Mountains. Middle and Late Islamic pottery was apparent on the surface. No Late Roman or Early Islamic site was found around the Middle Islamic period castle, although no intensive survey was conducted. Classical masonry and other architectural fragments reused in the castle suggest that a nearby site existed.

Way Stations

In the Early Islamic period, upland sites for fortifications were eschewed for fortified square enclosures built on important land routes on the plain. The Anṭākiya–Mar'ash road was a well-known and traversed route towards two Taurus passes. At the northernmost extent of the Amuq Plain in the Kara Su River Valley is Kırmıtlı (AS 190), thought to be identified as Būqā, initially built and fortified by the Caliph Hishām in the first half of the eighth century and continuing past the Byzantine reconquest, according to textual evidence. It comprised a square enclosure measuring 70 × 70 m, with stone walls and rooms around the perimeter and corner towers dated by ceramics to the eighth to tenth century and Middle Islamic periods.[43] There was also a low building mound to the east and north-east with large cobble walls, and a flat area to the south of the enclosure with numerous basalt columns, which may have been an open courtyard or perhaps a mosque. Just west of the enclosure was a well-built and partially preserved square tower structure, which seems later in date – likely Middle Islamic, as the settlement continued until the fourteenth century. The settlement was important both for its strategic location, as it offers a long view north up the Kara Su Valley and south to the Amuq Plain (to which it also guards the entrance), and for its location as a way station between Anṭākiya and Mar'ash, a distance of approximately 150 km as the crow flies. The settlement is about 50 km north of Anṭākiya, a little more than an average day's travel.

Baghrās would have also been a stopping point and divergence for those turning towards the Belen Pass, which connected the Anṭākiya–Iskandarūna route and the south–north Anṭākiya–Mar'ash road. The settlement of Baghrās, guarding this pass, has traditionally been identified with the fairly well-preserved upland castle that overlooks a small side valley in the Amuq Plain. However, this was the Middle Byzantine and Crusader settlement, dating from the second half of the tenth century onwards, as confirmed by the ceramic evidence from the Amuq Survey. The Peutinger Table lists the settlement as Pagaris, the Theodosian Tables as Pagras, and the Jerusalem Itinerary as Pangrios, suggesting that it was an important stop on the main road. The proposed identification for the Late Roman and Early Islamic settlement of Baghrās is AS 248, a roughly rectangular site situated at the foot of the Belen Pass through the Amanus, and roughly located between two identical large, round hills. Early Islamic material was found under the remains of an Ottoman *khān* at the northern end of the large Roman and Late Roman site. This suggests that the Early Islamic occupation may have been reduced from the 3 ha Classical and Late Antique settlement,[44] or that it may have been founded peripheral to the settlement. Local villagers attest to having excavated what appears to be a bathhouse and mosaic floors roughly in the center of the site. Accounts say that Nikephoros Phokas in the late tenth century took Baghrās and rebuilt it in three days during the Byzantine reconquest.[45] It is difficult to extricate the Middle Byzantine construction from the later Crusader and Armenian building in this fairly well-preserved and precariously situated structure. Traces of walls noted on the southern end of the site were identical in masonry style to those at Darbassāk.[46] Tenth- and eleventh-century moulded buffware and coloursplash/polychrome sgraffiato ceramics were found in the vicinity. The Late Roman and Early Islamic lowland settlement was not abandoned. Ibn Ḥawqal, writing in the tenth century, mentioned Ḥiṣn Baghrās and his account includes a Friday Mosque (*masjid al-jāmi'*) and large population.[47] In later centuries, there is evidence for other structures and settlement outside the walls of the castle. A bathhouse and gate associated with twelfth- to fourteenth-century Middle Islamic pottery were recorded on the slopes below the fortification. Water mills found in the vicinity on the Karamurt stream show that the area was still being used and was perhaps relatively self-sufficient into the Late Islamic period. Abū al-Fidā' in the fourteenth century described springs, gardens and fields all around Baghrās.[48]

A second candidate for the settlement is Çakallı Karakol (AS 246), which stood near by on a hill near the old Belen Pass road and just north of AS 246. Compared with AS 248, this site was larger (4.2 ha), with a heavy ceramic assemblage from the Hellenistic to Middle Islamic periods and a gap in the seventh century. Its Early Islamic ceramics belong almost entirely to the late eighth to tenth centuries, with ninth/tenth-century wares predominating.[49] From the Middle Islamic period, the site shows the largest assemblage of any other in the Amuq Survey. Texts mention that Baghrās was first refortified by Hishām as a *ḥiṣn*, and along with (Ḥiṣn) Būqā, Ḥiṣn Qatraghāsh and Ḥiṣn Mūra formed a system of settlements protecting either side of two Amanus passes, the Belen and Çalan/Sariseki. Other Islamic documents describe the settlement of Baghrās as a town (*madīna*) at the foot of the Amanus Mountains (*liḥf jabal al-lukām*).[50] The town had a minbar and guesthouse (*dār ḍiyāfa*) founded by Zubayda, Hārūn al-Rashīd's wife. The settlement of Baghrās protected a small side valley that led into the Belen Pass and may have been the route taken to cross the mountains, differing from the modern access.

The next stopping point would have been around İslahiye (Greek Nikopolis) and Fevzipaşa/ancient Zincirli, although no surveys have been conducted there yet. In the Kahramanmaraş Plain, one site in particular could qualify as a way station. KM 42 had one of the largest assemblages of Early Islamic ceramics on the plain from the mid- to late seventh/early eighth century. The Middle Islamic period assemblage was smaller. The site was located at the northern edge of the central outcrop in the southern plain, near a spring and not far from the Ak Su. A large wall was detected made of sandstone blocks in pebble cement and a square enclosure 50 m per side within an area of 2.3 ha, easily visible in a CORONA image. Just east of the site was a single-period eighth- to tenth-century site that was perhaps linked with KM 42, totaling 8.2 ha. Both sites were built over alluvial fans.

Although the surface ceramics suggest that KM 42 was not newly built in the early eighth century, as the aforementioned two way stations were, it may have been expanded or renewed and formed part of the same system.

Towns

The central *thughūr* was dotted with sizable towns, nearly all previously Early Byzantine (Late Roman), many first settled in the Umayyad or even Rashidūn period, and many part of the first limits of the frontier, which later became the zone of the *'awāṣim*. Alternating between the capitals (*qaṣabāt*) of this zone were the three towns of Anṭākiya, Bālis and Manbij, which, through various periods, also functioned as caliphal headquarters and mints. At the same time, none of these towns was the capital of the region, but rather they were satellites of the urban nodes of Qinnasrīn and, later, Ḥalab.

The scope of this volume necessitates that only a few comments should be made about Anṭākiya with regard to its changing status as a city in relation to its hinterland. By the Early Islamic period, Anṭākiya was greatly reduced from its Late Roman extent. However, the reduction of the city's settlement should not be viewed as an Early Islamic phenomenon. Although Libanius and Malalas described it as a city that constantly outgrew its borders, evidence for the shrinking of Anṭākiya's urban sprawl is found as early as the reign of Justinian (r. 527–65), who reduced the 'uselessly large wall'.[51] Transformations of social and civic institutions also contributed to the changes seen in the city. Traditionally, historians have argued that the reasons for its decline, whether Late Roman/Early Byzantine or Early Islamic, include a litany of natural and man-made disasters including earthquakes, invasions and plagues that befell the city in the sixth and seventh centuries.[52] There is some archaeological evidence for this. North of the city, an exposed section revealed a neighbourhood or series of rooms, walls and floors that had evidently suffered from earthquake damage. Collapsed roofs overlying human bones atop the floors were visible. The lack of Early Islamic-period ceramics led to the conclusion that this northern extent of the city was not reoccupied after the destruction.[53] Apart from this example, there is little real evidence for citywide destruction or a large exodus of its citizens, although a gradual depopulation of the city's Byzantine elite likely occurred during the Persian and Islamic conquests in the seventh century. Although smaller in scale (and, likely, population), the city transitioned with little disruption into the Early Islamic period and the following Middle Byzantine period after reconquest in the second half of the tenth century, increasing in growth and religious, economic, and building activity.

The changes affecting Anṭākiya need to be contextualized within larger environmental shifts caused mainly by anthropogenic land-use factors in its hinterland, the Amuq Plain. The beginning of the city's transformation by the mid-sixth century coincides with the spread and permanence of wetlands in the plain; the reduction in the quantity of settlements and aggregate land use, also in the plain; the peak in upland sites; and the rise of self-sufficient minor towns. Anṭākiya, located in a narrow valley with very little cultivatable land, was previously greatly dependent on the Amuq Plain for agricultural production, as was clearly described in Libanius' (314–94) fourth-century panegyric to the city. These environmental and settlement pattern shifts would have necessitated that Anṭākiya, too, develop more self-sufficient subsistence strategies, as described in numerous tenth-century Islamic and Christian accounts of the city. Indeed, the gaps between the standing sixth-century walls and the contracted Early Islamic period city were repurposed as green spaces for fields, pasturages, orchards, gardens and mills. The Amuq Survey noted two mills at the northern end of the city: one on the Orontes River and one along a mountain ravine that was canalized. Cemeteries were also brought inside the walls. Within the city, the main colonnaded street, originally thought to have been abandoned by the mid-sixth century, may have been built in the mid- to late seventh century.[54]

Evidence from the Princeton excavations of the 1930s for local coarseware and fineware ceramic production of Syrian yellow glaze, turquoise and Champlevé wares attests to a continuity in ceramic industries from at least the late eighth to twelfth/thirteenth centuries.[55] While Syrian yellow glaze and turquoise glazed wares were distributed throughout the frontier, Champlevé is entirely absent and must therefore have been an export-only ceramic found in Byzantine lands. Lavish baths and theaters, crumbling relics in the new medieval city, were repurposed as kiln sites, while the main *cardo* was altered but maintained and still functioned as a primary artery for mercantile and production activities. At the same time, many imported wares from eastern lands as far as China affirm Anṭākiya's role on the Silk Road. Al-Mināʿ, though no longer linked to Anṭākiya via the unnavigable Orontes River but connected by land, still served the city as its port. Al-Mināʿ (modern Liman Mahallesi) was the port of Anṭākiya in the Orontes Delta. Nearby Sabuniye, which was also occupied from the Late Roman through Middle Islamic/Middle Byzantine periods, was not the principal port but likely a small agricultural settlement.[56]

Texts show that underlying the city and its economy, populations were completely mixed, with various Christian communities (Syriac, Melkite, Georgian, Armenian) and Islamic groups (Persian, Zuṭṭ, Syrian Arab). The transformative process of Anṭākiya from metropolis to a frontier town raises the question as to whether all of the major *thughūr* towns underwent similar changes, becoming self-sufficient to a degree yet strongly connected by their economy and communities to the frontier districts, and linked to the greater Byzantine and Islamic worlds.

Marʿash was an integral town of the central *thughūr*, controlling key passes through the Taurus Mountains and is considered the divide between the western *thughūr al-shamīya* and eastern *thughūr al-jazarīya*. Its location is still unknown despite its constant conflation with modern Kahramanmaraş, which has a Middle Islamic/Middle Byzantine/Crusader/Armenian fortress; there is no evidence for this connection whatsoever. The three possibilities for this site, which likely continued from the Late Roman settlement of Marasion (and not Germanikeia, as is often assumed) are KM 5 (4 ha) in the southern plain along a road and/or canal, KM 54 at the entrance to the narrow Ak Su corridor leading into the northern plain, and the gradual slopes just south of the modern town of Kahramanmaraş in the northern plain. The clear focus of Early Islamic-period settlement in the southern irrigated and wetland plain compared with the relatively depopulated northern plain is suggestive that Mar'ash, too, was part of this pattern. Arguments can, however, also be made for the northern-plain location using Evliya Çelebi's (1611–82) seventeenth-century description of a ruined city just south of the modern town of Kahramanmaraş.[57] Although the city changed hands from Byzantine to Islamic several times, it was rebuilt three times in the Umayyad period by Mu'āwiya, al-'Abbās b. al-Walīd I, Marwān II and later by Hārūn al-Rashīd, and was known to have had strong double city walls, a ditch, congregational mosque, markets, a garrison and inner fortress through various times in its history. It was also the likely hometown of the Byzantine Emperor Leo III (b. 685). It is noteworthy that Abulustayn/Arabissos (modern Afşin), north of Mar'ash, was not truly part of the Islamic side of the *thughūr* until the Mamlūk period in the fourteenth century, despite the fact that it sat within the relatively expansive Elbistan Plain and not far from Ṭaranda. Tīzīn was an *'awāṣim* settlement whose location is indefinite but presumed to be at the village of Oğulpınar, 7.5 km west of 'Imm and Artaḥ. It appears to have been newly founded.

Conclusions

The two Amuqs comprised a micro-region within the frontier and central *thughūr*. In the Amuq Plain, there is both a random dispersal of sites for the Late Roman period and a discernible pattern of sites aligned along the major highways that ringed the plain and in upland valleys. By the Early Islamic period, Anṭākiya was transforming into a regional town, small sites in the plain were becoming larger towns. There was a focus on settling along canals, rivers and in marsh from the seventh century onwards in order to maximize irrigation-based land use in the plain, and small sites began to fill in the plain from the eighth century. Settlements in the Kahramanmaraş Plain were fewer, perhaps owing to its more northerly frontier status, but focused similarly on canals, rivers, marshlands, and key routes traversing the southern part of the plain. Hardly any abutted the foothills of the Taurus Mountains and the upper tributaries of the Ak Su River near the modern city of Kahramanmaraş. Settlement numbers in both plains were roughly half those of the Late Roman period.

CHAPTER 2

THE CENTRAL *THUGHŪR*: THE STEPPE AND THE RIVER

> *And we found all the country between Halab and Antakiya populous, nowhere ruined abodes of any description. On the contrary, the soil was everywhere sown with wheat and barley, which grew under the olive trees; the villages ran continuous, their gardens full of flowers, and the waters flowing on every hand, so that the traveler makes his journey here in contentment of mind, and peace and quietness.*[1]

Medieval Islamic historians tell us that some time in the early 'Abbāsid period, the Caliph Hārūn al-Rashīd apportioned most of the eastern half of the central frontier area to a second line of defence and winter garrisons called *al-'awāṣim* (the protectresses).[2] Were these lands around the provincial capital of Ḥalab (Aleppo) similarly settled, as in the western half? An archaeological examination of sites on the ground reveals similarities with the Amuq lowlands' settlements and key differences that underline the necessity to view the *thughūr* not as one singular entity, but as several linked micro-regions.

The Environment

Bordering the Amuq Plain to the east is the series of upland hills at 600–800 m.a.s.l., known collectively as the Syrian Jibāl, including roughly, from west to east, the Jabal Duwaylī, Jabal al-'Alā, Jabal Barisha, Jabal Halaqa, and Jabal Sim'ān (Figure 3). The Jabal al-Summāq was also part of this region, and together these hills were often called the Massif of Belus, limestone massif, or *massif calcaire*, home of the northern group of the well-known Dead Cities. The Jabal Zawiya, or Jabal Rīḥa, and Jabal Waṣṭanī lay farther south. These hills had hardly any perennial streams and received between 400 and 800 mm/annum of rain. The Kurt Dağ is a low basaltic range farther north of the 'Afrīn Valley. Further east and north is the second main geographical area of the central *thughūr*, also divided into two topographical regions: north and south. The north was dominated by the Gaziantep Plateau, a region of rugged limestone hills and steppe scored with east–west Euphrates tributaries forming discrete river valleys. Some of these include, from north to south, the Nahr Aswad (Kara Su), Nahr Marzabān (Greek Marsyas, Turkish Merzumen Dere), Nahr Karzīn (Nizip Çay), Nahr al-Amarna, and Nahr Sajūr. The southern part is roughly along the modern Syrian–Turkish border, between Carchemish and Dabīq south to Ḥalab and Bālis on the Euphrates. Here, the steppe flattens out slightly into a large limestone plain covered in *terra rossa* with some low hills, well watered and incised by several north–south flowing wadis that widen farther towards the south. Among them, the western one is the Nahr Quwayq, or Qoueiq (Greek Chalus), flowing into the marshy salt flats (Marj al-Aḥmar and Buḥayrah al-Matkh, 'the Lake of Mud') around Qinnasrīn. Between the Nahr Quwayq and the Euphrates River is the Wādī Buṭnān ('the Middle Wadi')/Nahr al-Dhahab ('the River of Gold', Greek Dardas)[3] and Nahr Dayr Hafir, which all drain into the second, and larger, shallow salt flat, the Jabbūl Lake (Sabkhat al-Jabbūl) and its wetlands. The annual rainfall for the eastern central *thughūr* is lower than for the western, at 200–250 mm for the Buḥayrah al-Matkh, Jabbūl Lake, and Nahr al-Dhahab until Ḥalab and the Euphrates from Bālis to the Nahr Sajūr, and 300–350 mm/annum for most of the Nahr Quwayq, thus placing much of it in the marginal dry-farming/irrigation zone and high area for pastoralism. The alluvial floodplain of the braided and meandering Euphrates River was a landscape of trees, backswamps, abandoned channels, and wetland vegetation, and it created rich zones for cultivation – particularly between Zeugma/Birecik and Raqqa. North of this area until the Karababa Basin, the Euphrates flowed through the narrow Karakaya Gorge. Settlement was generally a slight distance away from the floodplain on river terraces at 6 m.a.s.l.[4]

The cultivated and irrigated lands around Ḥalab were repeatedly noted by travellers, geographers, and historians. The Euphrates River in particular, and its tributary valleys and wadis created desirable fertile lands for agriculture. The opening quote to this chapter, written by Ibn Buṭlān, a physician travelling from Ḥalab to Anṭākiya in 1051, captures the landscape and its settlements and land use at their peak in the Islamic period. The cultivation of wheat, barley, and especially the region's famous olives dominated here, as it did in the Amuq Plain, although irrigation was more of a necessity. Fruit and nut trees (pistachio, fig, and pear) and shrubs such as sumac and others used in dyeing and tanning also grew in the central hills. Some of these agricultural products were also exported out of the *thughūr* to Iraq, Syria, Egypt, and the west. East of Ḥalab, cotton, onion, garlic, and coriander were grown in the Wādī Buṭnān, and in 'Azāz cotton was exported to the western Mediterranean at least by the fourteenth century. The Kara Su Valley of Ra'bān was also a cotton-producing region.[5] Small towns, such as al-Bāb/al-Buzā'ah in the Wādī Buṭnān also exported a thick cotton cloth known as a *kirbās* to Damascus and Egypt. Raisins were exported from Manbij. Salt was extracted from the Jabbūl Lake, and fish from this and the Ḥadath/Gölbaşı Lake fed by the Nahr Jūrīth or Ḥūrīth.

These areas along the wadis, rivers, and lake/wetlands were grassy steppes with permanent and seasonal wet pastures, excellent for grazing by nomadic and semi-pastoralist groups including the nomadic Ṭayyi', who inhabited the plains between Ḥalab and Qinnasrīn and the western banks of the Euphrates near Manbij, and the nomadic Qays farther south along the Euphrates near Bālis and Qāṣirīn (Figure 2). Christian groups who settled before the arrival of Islam and eventually converted remained in the area, including the Iyad, whose lands were around the Syrian Jibāl north of and close to Ḥalab, Kafar Tab, al-Ma'arra, Sarmīn, and Nasab, and the semi-nomadic Tanūkh south of Ḥalab to Qinnasrīn. Various names for the Christian Arabs in Syriac and Greek reflect the existence of tribal names and religious identity: for example, *tayyāyē* (Ṭayy'), *'arbāyē*, *tanūkāyē* (Tanūkh), *'aqūlāyē* ('Uqayl), and *ṭu'āyē*.[6] Also in this area were the nomadic Quḍā'a-descended Qaḥṭān tribes (consisting of the clans of Janab, 'Ulaym, Zubayr, and 'Adī of Kalb). In addition, there were lesser-known clans such as the Judhām, Balqayn, Balī, and 'Āmila, and the Bajila clan mentioned in eighth-century Syria. The presence of many nomadic and semi-nomadic tribes underscores the importance of pastoralism as a form of subsistence in this marginal rainfall zone, particularly east of the Nahr Quwayq.

Ḥalab was the southern anchor for the central *thughūr* and sites spread east, west, and north of this capital. The eastern steppe and hilly country contained most of the smaller towns, which appeared less often in texts, although many were identified as part of the *'awāṣim*: Dābiq, Tīzīn, Ra'bān, Manbij, Dulūk, Kaysūm, and Sanjah/Bahasnā. Ḥadath, sometimes called Ḥadath al-Ḥamrā' (the Red), guarded an important pass of the same name, Darb al-Ḥadath (Pass of News) or later the perhaps more fortuitously named Darb al-Salāma (Pass of Safety). From here, a route went via the Kanlı Yol ('Bloody Road') towards Plasta and Lykandos in the Byzantine Taurus. The central *thughūr* was not an abandoned no man's land but was dotted with major and minor towns, evenly spaced and criss-crossed with east–west roads, illustrating how well connected and well travelled this region actually was in the Early Islamic period. These included the routes of Anṭakīya–(Arṭāh/'Imm)–(possibly Tīzīn)–the Dana Plain–(Athārib)–Ḥalab–(Nā 'ūrah-Khusaf)–Bālis, and Anṭākiya–Qūrus (via the Nahr 'Afrīn valley), then 'Azāz. From there, the road could go north-east to Dūluk-Ra'bān or east to Dābiq-Manbij–Jisr Manbij, and Mar'ash-Ḥadath (via the Nahr Hūrīth valley) to Sanjah/Bahasnah. From the topography, additional connections can be inferred from Mar'ash to Dulūk, Mar'ash to Ra'bān, and Manbij to Ḥalab via the Wadī Butnān. There is no definite south–north route, aside from the one linking the two Amuqs; however, two additional routes can be suggested: one that linked Qūrus–Dulūk–Ra'bān-Kaysūm–Sanjah/Bahasnā in the center of the region, and one that linked Bālis–Jisr Manbij–Ra'bān–Ḥadath and travelled along the Euphrates by land, passing two way stations on the river until it became more deeply incised and then cut north-west away from the river. Routes connected with eastern frontier towns via land and Euphrates River crossings at Jisr Manbij and further north between Birecik and Zeugma, possibly at the way station site of Pınar Tarlası – a route only revealed in a survey. From Mar'ash, one route went to Kukusos via the Eyerbel Pass and a second to Lykandos via the Jayhān River gorge. Abulustayn (Greek Arabissos) in the Elbistan Plain sat astride and connected these two Byzantine towns.

Survey Methodology

This region has been fairly well surveyed, with projects covering large tracts of land between the Syrian Jibāl and the Euphrates. Only the central plateau north and south of Gaziantep, which was the focus of just one survey in 1971, comprises an underrepresented area in need of future work. A review of survey methodology, beginning with the older and less useful surveys, will reveal the basis of data collection and the limitations present, which might justify whether the conclusions merit a re-analysis or not.

Group I: Extensive/Low-Resolution/Large-Area Surveys

Moving from south to north, Euphrates surveys were conducted in the area between Raqqa and Bālis as salvage projects before flooding from impending dam constructions. The Tabqa Reservoir Survey was one such, conducted in 1964 by R. S. Solecki of Columbia University and M. van Loon of the Oriental Institute at the University of Chicago. Their small team identified 56 sites approximately 50 km north and south of Bālis. Owing to the pattern of preservation, these were concentrated on the low river terrace between the floodplain and the uplands. The chronologies used by the surveyors are slightly problematic, as they are based on some misdated ceramic types. There were 12 Roman sites (64 BCE–330 CE) characterized by 'bright-red slipped pottery', which appears to be *terra sigillata*; however, van Loon later writes that 'both surface and core are red' and that they have a slip ranging in colour 'from orange to red, with a mat surface', adding that 'Some sherds with a metallic black surface [...] appear to be variants of the same ware, due to firing accidents [...]. Other shapes include bowls with thickened rims resembling a *cyma reversa* molding.'[7] These are more suggestive of Late Roman finewares – Late Roman C (LRC)/Phocaean red slip specifically – primarily as the *terra sigillata* core is characteristically cream-colored. LRC is the most commonly distributed fineware in inner Syria and the Euphrates region in the fifth and sixth centuries. LRC often has a discoloured, black, or gray rim due to stacking in the kiln. Two of the most common forms – LRC Hayes Form 10, with its characteristic thickened rim and absence of rouletting, and Form 3, with its 'keel'-shaped rim – may conform to the 'cyma reversa molding' description. Settlement in this area peaked in the Late Roman (Byzantine) period (330–638), with 26 sites (46 per cent of sites surveyed). The surveyors' diagnostic ceramic was 'dark red and black corrugated pottery' with grit and thin-walled, wide, and flat handles, and sometimes 'ledge-like lugs in the shape of obtuse handles'.[8] These are the ubiqitious brittleware cooking pots that range from the Roman to Early Islamic periods and cannot be definitively dated as Late Roman. Certainly the ledge-like triangular handle belongs to the Early Islamic holemouth pot, dating from the eighth to the tenth centuries. This demonstrates the existence of Early Islamic sites – although none are mentioned, leaving a gap in settlement of nearly four centuries. The Middle Islamic period (eleventh to thirteenth centuries) had a secondary peak with 19 sites (34 per cent), 11 with blue or green glazed sherds and eight with 'contemporary or later unglazed wares'.[9] Some ware descriptions are provided, but since there are no published drawings or photographs it is difficult to know how to assign these chronologies. In the end, the settlement distributions indicate similar major and minor peaks in the Late Roman and Middle Islamic period, respectively, but these sites cannot be taken at face value as well dated.

The Tabqa Dam Euphrates Survey, a small area salvage survey carried out in 1968, identified 34 sites. The surveyors noted that many of the Classical sites had Islamic remains.[10] Yet, the chronologies of the sites are inconsistent. Some are designated by a specific century, while most are called 'Arab' with no further designation. Some sites are misdated, the map is incomplete, and only the major sites and tells were visited.[11]

The Jabbūl Survey, first conducted in 1939, included the area north of the Jabbūl Lake between Ḥalab and the Euphrates north to Manbij.[12] The surveyors recorded 109 sites, although focusing on pre-Roman-period tell sites. Roman and Late Roman periods were conflated at Phase X, and the latter period apparently was not well represented. Phase XI, the Islamic period, was similarly not well defined, with blue and white glazed pottery mentioned as the only hallmark diagnostic. The dearth of Late Roman pottery is a factor of poorly understood coarsewares, a problem the surveyors themselves mentioned and which was later amended when the region was resurveyed in 1996.

Surveys of the Nahr Sajūr and the Euphrates River between Jarablus and Qal'at Najm above the Tishrin Dam on both banks were conducted in 1977 and 1979 (Figure 9). A major aim was to obtain a geomorphological record of the region. Archaeology of the late periods is poorly represented. The 1977 survey located 30 sites, and the 1979 survey located 47 more sites and revisited many of the 1977 sites. Both surveys were, by the surveyors' own admission, rapidly undertaken using a Volkswagen bus to visit main tells rather than walking transects across the landscape. Unfortunately, the data for the Late Roman and Islamic periods are largely unusable. The 1977 survey noted a large number of small Late Roman settlements but hardly any Roman sites, yet a review of the site catalogue for the 1979 material shows only two Late Roman sites and many Roman sites. The problem again seems to be one of consistency and confusion between Roman and Late Roman wares. Further, the surveyors noted only whether sites were Islamic or not, thereby failing to distinguish between Early, Middle, or Late. The problems are confirmed by the 'Roman/Byzantine' and Islamic pottery plates, which have several incorrect identifications and incomplete ware descriptions but do include Early Islamic examples (some of them in the 'Roman/Byzantine' plate). This suggests that the Early Islamic ceramics were generally dated earlier, justifying at least in part H. de Contenson's contention that the Islamic pottery is thirteenth to fourteenth century or more recent (he includes Ottoman tobacco pipes).[13] Although glazed wares are mentioned, no information about them has been published. De Contenson states that the Roman and Late Roman periods had a high density of 41 tells occupied (53 per cent), while the Islamic had 26 (34 per cent). Reevaluation of the ceramic plates reveals Early Islamic sites at Taafliye (Site 80) and Soueida (Site 78) with transitional seventh- and eighth- to tenth-century brittleware forms, listed as Roman/Byzantine types in the literature. These sites are both on the Nahr Sajūr tributary. Youssef Bey (Site 42), located on the Nahr Amarna north of the Sajūr, seems to have an Early Islamic buffware jar. It does not appear in the Jarablus Tahtani Survey, which overlaps the area. Unfortunately, beyond these rough notes nothing further can be extrapolated from the published evidence. These three sites, all on Euphrates tributaries, lie within the districts of Baq'ā al-'Ays (between the Euphrates and Nahr Sajūr) and Baq'ā Rabī 'a (from the Nahr Sajūr towards Ḥalab), mentioned by Yāqūt.[14]

Unfortunately, there is little than can be extrapolated from the 1971 publication of the Gaziantep Survey as the site gazetteer, focusing on tell settlements, was not always complete with chronologies and not systematic. Of the 216 sites found, 17 were Hellenistic (8 per cent) and 76 were Roman (35 per cent), showing the general patterns of dispersal during this period.[15] For the Late Roman period, only six sites (2.7 per cent) were documented, and for the Islamic period there were 17 sites (8 per cent). It immediately seems strange that in the Late Roman period there was a drastic reduction in settlement, particularly when neighbouring regions and other surveys (the Amuq and the Kahramanmaraş Plains, the Syrian Jibāl) found evidence of continuity from the Roman to the Late Roman periods. In some cases, there was a slight increase or decrease in settlement between the periods, but in no case was there a drastic decline. The lack of Late Roman sites might stem from problems with the surface pottery. Most likely, it has to do with a conflation of Roman and Late Roman pottery similar to the conflation for the Islamic periods, where there is no differentiation between Early and Middle.

Group II: Intensive/High-Resolution/Large-Area Surveys

The new Jabbūl Survey was part of the Umm al-Marra regional project with clearer phasing, better distinguishing knowledge of Early Islamic and Middle Islamic ceramics, and consideration of environmental and land-use elements (Figure 10).[16] A total of 91 additional sites was recorded beyond 53 from the original survey that were revisited. From the Roman period, 60 sites (42 per cent) were recorded, followed by 53 (37 per cent) from the Late Roman (Byzantine) period, and 52 (36 per cent) from the Early Islamic period. The Middle Islamic period was not included in the publication. This new Jabbūl Survey overlapped slightly with the Rifaʿat Survey.

On the modern border between Syria and Turkey, the Tell Jerablus Tahtani Survey, known as the Land of Carchemish Project, was conducted in the vicinity of the site just south of Carchemish in 2006 (Figure 11).[17] In all, 23 sites were recorded, including non-tell settlements, with close attention paid to shifts in the patterns and land use for all periods. One of the goals of the survey was to expand beyond the Euphrates floodplain (8 km to the west), in order to avoid the inevitably skewed record of settlement that would result from limiting the investigation to that area. The Tell Jarablus Tahtani Survey revealed an even more pronounced Late Roman to Early Islamic pattern of more than half the sites abandoned, with 12 or 13 Late Roman sites (average 54 per cent) to five (or six) Early Islamic sites (average 30 per cent) and only one Middle Islamic site (4 per cent).

Equally encouraging, the Tigris–Euphrates Archaeological Reconnaissance Project directed by G. Algaze in 1989–90 yielded very interesting Early Islamic settlement patterns in the Birecik area further north on the Euphrates (Figure 11).[18] The area of the project included both sides of the Euphrates River up to an elevation of 400 m, from Halfeti in the north down to Carchemish in the south (60 km long and 186 km^2 in area), and avoided many high terraces. A total of 85 sites was recorded with varying types and sizes, and the geomorphological impact was discussed.[19] Chronology was broken down into Late Roman/Early Byzantine and Medieval, including

Early and Middle Islamic subphases. Settlement peaked in the Late Roman period, with 42 sites represented, followed by three in the Early Islamic period, and 15 in the Middle Islamic period.

Group III: Extensive/High-Resolution/Large-Area Surveys

West of this area, the Tell Rifaʿat Survey – encompassing the area from Ḥalab north to Azaz, east to Bāb and south to the Jabbūl Lake – was a regional survey around Tell Rifaʿat undertaken from 1977 to 1979 by the Institute of Archaeology of London University. The Tell Rifa'at Survey is problematic, however, and can only be considered Islamic-focused based on reinterpretation of its results (Figure 12). The 3,400 km^2 survey focused predominately on tell sites, and included a total of 88 sites (eight of which lay outside the survey boundaries). As such, it was not high-resolution. Several problems, which posed challenges to understanding the results, are worth mentioning as limitations to the data.

First, sites from the 1977 preliminary publication were completely renumbered in the 1979 version in order to keep them in alphabetical order. Equally confusingly, these names appear inconsistently with different spellings and variations throughout the 1977 and 1979 publications. Individual ceramic reports for the Hellenistic, Roman and Late Roman finewares by P. Kenrick, Late Roman and Islamic coarsewares by A. Northedge, and Islamic glazed wares by M. Bernus Taylor provide an attention to late periods that is not always present, specifically the useful contribution by Northedge on a category that is often completely ignored.[20] However, these ceramic reports are never integrated into a discussion on the settlement patterns of these periods, leaving the reader to do much of the analysis. Further, the reports are of varying consistency and style and sometimes include sites that others omit. The report on Islamic glazed wares is the most problematic as the black-and-white basic ink drawings are virtually unusable. Despite these limitations, when the reports are synthesized and reinterpreted using the three criteria of site morphology and size, assemblage size, and narrower dating (as used in the western central *thughūr*), the results are rather different than those for settlement patterns anywhere else on the frontier.

Second, it is possible to begin to differentiate among sites using ceramic assemblage size as a criterion – reconstructable for the Islamic glazed wares, but not completely as the coarsewares and Late Roman finewares do not provide this level of data.

Lastly, unlike what has appeared at the Amuq and Kahramanmaraş Surveys and elsewhere on the Euphrates, here there *is* a direct continuity from Late Roman to Early Islamic periods and even an increase in sites, as seen in the Balikh Valley. Combined with the other ceramic reports, Northedge's dating would result in 38 definite (43 per cent) and one indefinite Late Roman sites and 31 definite (35 per cent) and one indefinite Early Islamic sites, a slight decrease (by 18 per cent) but not by a half or even three-quarters.[21] The Middle Islamic period experienced resurgence, with 38 definite sites (43 per cent) and two indefinite sites occupied.

Group IV: Intensive/High-Resolution/Small-Area Surveys

Fortunately, the Tabqa Dam region was resurveyed in 1974 by D. Whitcomb and T. Holland, and again in 1991–2 by T. J. Wilkinson as the Sweyhat Survey, a regional survey around the site of Tell Sweyhat on the river terrace at the edge of the Euphrates River floodplain (Figure 13). In total, 30 sites were recorded, including non-tell settlements. Roman, Late Roman, Early and Middle Islamic periods were treated separately and Early Islamic sites were analysed with mapping and remote-sensing techniques. Key Islamic ceramic assemblages were also published separately by Donald Whitcomb.[22] The Sweyhat Survey found that in the Roman period (Phase XII) four sites were occupied, jumping to seven in the Late Roman period (Phase XIII, 23 per cent) and showing a peak in settlement. In the Early Islamic period (Phase XIV) there were four sites occupied (13 per cent), and there was one Middle Islamic period site.

Settlement along the Euphrates River

Despite the salvage nature of the Euphrates surveys and the lack of attention paid to Islamic settlement in the earlier steppe surveys, patterns indicate that Early Islamic settlement focused on canals and

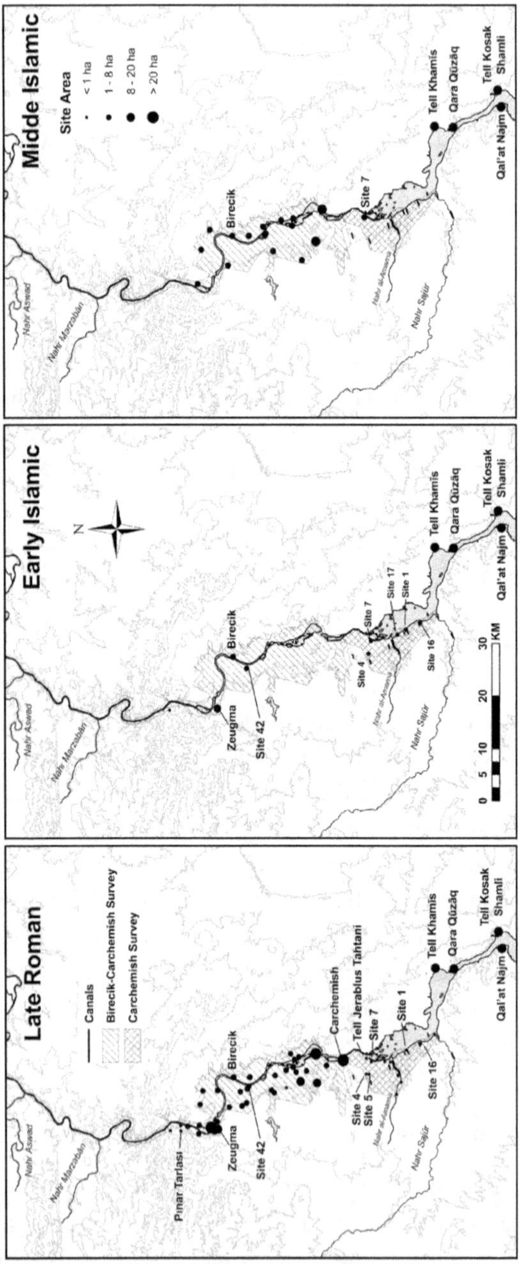

Figure 11 Birecik-Carchemish Survey (Tigris-Euphrates Archaeological Reconaissance Project) and Jerablus Tahtani Survey (Land of Carchemish Project), Late Roman through Middle Islamic sites (based on Wilkinson 2004, Figures 7.8, 7.9, 7.10, 9.1; Wilkinson 2007, Figure 1; Algaze et al. 1994, Figure 17)

rivers in the plains but tended to be less prolific along the Euphrates River itself and confined to a few key settlements (Figure 13). Of the Islamic settlements from the Tabqa Dam Euphrates Survey, the main ones were Bālis (Greek Barbalissus/Meskene), Qasirīn (Dibsi Faraj) (Greek Athis/Neocaesareia/Kaiserion), and Abū Hurayra (Greek Hararis) – the infamous location of Ṣiffīn (where Mu'āwiya and 'Alī fought). While some towns like Bālis thrived, others may have been abandoned (as Abū Hurayra was), while others still became smaller towns or rural settlements, as can be seen at Dibsi Faraj. Still others, assumed from texts, were never located, such as Dawsar, a Euphrates River crossing on the Ḥalab–Raqqa road and the Late Roman and Early Islamic precursor to Qal'at Ja'bar, mentioned from the ninth century onwards.[23]

Excavations at Dibsi Faraj, identified with Early Islamic Qaṣirīn, between 1971 and 1974 revealed occupation until the tenth century. The site, 17 km south-east of Bālis on a plateau overlooking the Euphrates, is at the southernmost edge of what can be regarded as North Syria and the *thughūr*/'*awāṣim* territory, yet it can be considered here on the basis of its close ties with other frontier sites through its ceramics. Excavators noted a grand L-shaped building, employing reused stone for its foundations and mud brick for a superstructure, constructed over part of the citadel basilica in Area 0.[24] The fourth-century church had already been razed by the time of the sixth century and a new one begun but never completed, leaving the area an opportune one on which to build a new structure in the Early Islamic period. Ceramics and a bronze-coin hoard in earth fill under the floor, whose latest-published dated coin is 728, provide a possible *terminus post quem*.[25] The new L-shaped structure incorporated the same basilica plan as the basilica, but the side aisles and nave became an open courtyard, the apse became an *iwan*, and the side pastophories became flanking rooms; it was a residence of some distinction and importance, which likely continued into at least the mid-eighth century with datable coins of the Umayyad (723, 734 with Wasiṭ, Mawṣil, Qinnasrīn, and Dimashq mints) and 'Abbāsid (one of 750) periods and with ceramics. Harper alludes to a local coarseware ceramic industry in the region, and elsewhere mentions that the extramural public baths (Area 3) were repurposed in the Early Islamic period, although for what remains unknown. Coins range from 708 to the Ayyubid Period. Settlement was recorded elsewhere on the tell, and outside the walls a lower city lay to the south and south-east along a wadi that flowed into the Euphrates.

Geomorphological surveying and remote sensing of the area by T. J. Wilkinson recorded the remains of a major canal preserved 2.3 km away with a plastered conduit running parallel to the Euphrates and estimated at 8.5–20 km in length, which could have had smaller, perpendicular offshoots.[26] This canal, dated by Early Islamic coins from the excavated fill, is identified as the Nahr Maslama that Maslama b. ʿAbd al-Malik (d. 738) had built in the first quarter of the eighth century, and which flowed from Bālis to Buwaylis ('Little Bālis', unidentified) to Qāṣirīn, ʿAbidīn, and to Ṣiffīn according to Balādhurī and the Syriac *Chronicle of Zuqnīn*.[27] The latter chronicler adds that he built forts and villages along the canal. The Early Islamic canal replaced a previous canal system, which was perhaps also associated with small agricultural Late Roman and Early Islamic sites near the settlement. A 4 km-long qanat brought water from the southern limestone steppe north towards the lower town of the settlement. The qanat, like those around the settlement of al-Andarīn (Greek Androna) south of Ḥalab, may date to the Late Roman occupation.[28] *Qadus* jars belonging to the pot-garland *saqiya* lifting device were found at the site.[29] The Tabqa Reservoir Survey also noted that Dibsi Faraj, as well as Abū Hurayra and Qal'at Ja'bar, was watered by gravity-fed channels of the Euphrates that are relict. They assigned a Late Roman date to the irrigation systems, linking them with the peak in sites, although the dating of this survey is problematic. Indeed, the importance of irrigation, as well as mention of a preexisting system, is implied not only by the site's location at the edge of the desert and marginal rainfall zone (*c.*250 mm/annum), but also by Theophanes' (758/760–817) account of the Battle of Ṣiffīn in 657. Here, Muʿāwiya's (602–80) troops 'captured the water [supply], while the Caliph ʿAlī's [r. 656–61] men were reduced to thirst and were deserting'.[30] The excavators of Dibsi Faraj noted extensive damage, which they attributed to an 859 earthquake. The settlement never recovered fully. Preexisting buildings were reused and reinhabited on a smaller scale for another century or so, evident also by some tenth/eleventh-century graves placed within the destroyed L-shaped seventh- to eighth- century building. The numismatic evidence points to continuity until the thirteenth century.

Tell Sweyhat showed some evidence, although slight, of domestic/rural occupation during the Late Roman period, which was a peak in settlement. By the Early Islamic period, all but one of these sites was abandoned. However, there were three important new Early Islamic foundations near Tell Sweyhat whose composition could be discerned from the topography and aerial photographs. These were treated separately by D. Whitcomb, who observed them as deliberately sited away from the tell on low, flat depression sites, the 'inversion of the tells or mounds'.[31] All three sites consisted of several blocks of residential buildings around a larger rectilinear walled enclosure. At Khirbet Dhiman (SS11) there were three blocks of structures, consisting of two to four rectangular courtyard buildings 20–25 m long per side with a walled enclosure (a) 70 × 70 m on the periphery. At Khirbet al-Hamra (SS7) there were two housing blocks consisting of three to four houses in linear units and a smaller rectilinear enclosure (f), also at the periphery of the site. At SS12, there were small buildings around one larger rectilinear enclosure 18 × 18 m. The first two were rather substantial villages (SS11: 9ha; SS7: 5 ha) calculated to have populations of 864–1,350 people at SS11 and 360–563 people at SS7. The last-named site (SS12: 0.8 ha) was posited as a sheikh's residence. They were only in use for a short period, from about 750 to 800. Furthermore, the Early Islamic foundations were built on land that was only marginally occupied in the Roman period. The settlements demonstrate an increased sedentarization in the early 'Abbāsid period, with multi-structure settlements suggestive of a conglomeration of buildings and a hierarchical component.

Early Islamic irrigation was also recorded farther up the Euphrates in the Jerablus Tahtani Survey (Figure 11). Late Roman sites were located along the Euphrates River and along the year-round-flowing Nahr al-Amarna tributary as dispersed, small, flat sites – the peak of a trend that began in the Hellenistic/Roman periods. Of the five Early Islamic sites, three were evenly spaced along the Euphrates (Site 1, on the lower town of the tell; Site 16 at the junction of the Sajur tributary; and Site 7 on a floodplain terrace) and two were clustered together on an upper terrace (350–400 m.a.s.l.) west of the river (Site 4, a flat site; and Site 5, a low tell). In this area, nearly all Early Islamic sites were founded on preexisting Late Roman ones. Sites 4 and 7 were the only Late Roman/Early Islamic sites. The sole single-period settlement was Site 17, a way station. Notably, this small area featured extensive canal systems – also preexisting, and continuing to be used in the Early Islamic period. A 9–14-m-wide canal on the west bank of the Euphrates ran parallel to the river and was flanked by evenly spaced Late Roman sites, one of which continued into the Early Islamic period, indicating that the canal may have been in use similarly. Flowing into this network, a wadi system was canalized with a rock-cut channel probably in the Roman period and remained in use into the Early Islamic, evident as flowing past Sites 4 and 5, and possibly connecting to a water mill near Site 7. Artificial stone canals channelled water from the Wādī Seraisat to flow into Site 1's lower town, and possibly also into a penstock water mill. Close by was evidence for baking lime and pottery manufacture. The overall system was of a main parallel feeder canal alongside the Euphrates with eight recorded smaller, perpendicular side channels along each tributary wadi, 20–100 cm wide, 30–100 cm deep, cut into bedrock or lined with ashlar blocks to augment water collected from annual rainfall.[32] Some of these may have functioned as qanats. Quarries and road tracks, more difficult to attribute to a specific period, were present in association with the same Late Roman/Early Islamic sites.

In the Tigris-Euphrates Archaeological Reconnaissance Project, the surveyors linked the growth of newly-founded 20 ha sites and satellite farmsteads to the use of the Euphrates both as bridge and border in Seleucid/Roman and Partho-Sāsānian imperial policies (Figure 11).[33] For the Early Islamic period (Period 13a), only three sites with small occupations were identified based on diagnostic Early Islamic pottery of color-splash and cut (excised) glazed wares: the important river crossing of Zeugma, a small rural settlement, and a way station.[34] Islamic Zeugma (Area D, Site 19) encompassed 2.5 ha of land on a hill overlooking the Euphrates. Geomorphologically, the settlement was located at 395–400 m.a.s.l. on a pediment, a spoon-shaped erosional surface with no perennial streams and shallow groundwater. A scatter of mid-eighth- to mid-ninth-century pottery stretched over an area 180 m in diameter. The occupation of Zeugma in the Early Islamic period was greatly reduced from the 87 ha settlement in the Late Roman period. Excavations at Zeugma revealed Islamic material only in Trench 1, in poorly stratified contexts. Ceramics confirm the Early Islamic date, as a lack of sgraffiato wares implies that the settlement did not continue much past the ninth century.[35] This does not correspond exactly with the textual evidence as Zeugma appears only in Michael the Syrian's chronicle, which provides a list of bishops of Zeugma between 818 and 1048.[36] Another possibility is that the settlement may have been reduced to a monastery or small Christian settlement, although it seems too minor and lacking in note to have functioned as a bishopric.[37] The other two Early Islamic sites avoided tell locations and were located on the low terraces just near, but not directly along, the riverbank. This was ideal, because the river followed an incised course in this section and rarely shifted. Well-developed paleosols made the soil suitable for irrigable agriculture. Karapınar Harabe (Site 42) was on a low ridge between two incised wadis on the Nizip Plateau near a spring. The excavators noted that the site was Islamic, but they did not specify a more exact periodization. The published ceramics are positive indicators that it was occupied in the Early Islamic period.[38]

A general pattern emerges from the Euphrates River sites. The known Euphrates crossings, including Jisr Manbij, all lie directly across from tributaries. The tributaries would not necessarily have all been navigable but it is reasonable to assume that transportation routes for migration and caravans, which followed land routes, would run along watercourses when possible. This tributary/river-crossing pattern may help guide researchers to detect more crossings at points of confluence. Way stations, discussed in Chapter 7, were sometimes associated with tributaries or functioned as crossings, but these created a south–north land route.

Settlement in the Nahr Quwayq Plain

The Nahr Quwayq was a hinterland for Ḥalab (Figure 12). Its most noticeable settlement patterns, one that diverged slightly from that in other frontier regions, occurred along the rich Nahr Quwayq

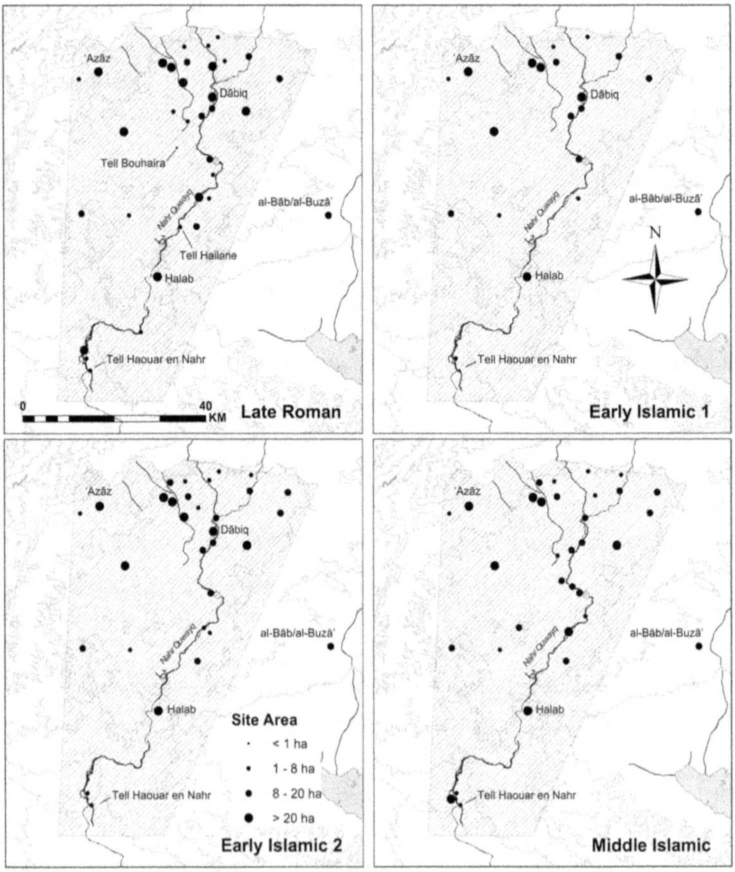

Figure 12 Tell Rifa'at Survey, Late Roman through Middle Islamic sites (based on Matthers 1981)

Valley that joined with two other branches just south of the Syrian–Turkish border and flowed south to Ḥalab. The pattern was of either river or canal sites, as the meandering action of the stream may have been canalized in parts. It is here that the number of sites occupied decreased only slightly from the Late Roman period, as opposed to dropping by half as it did elsewhere. Sites were oriented along the three main northern branches of the river and, after they converged, along the river itself. Slight differences are visible between Late Roman and Early Islamic settlement patterns in this area. Late Roman settlement was evenly dispersed from the northern limit of the survey (Turkish border) down to Tell Hailane, roughly 10 km north of Ḥalab. From the confluence of streams to Tell Hailane, there were eight sites, two of which were newly founded. Tell Hailane is most likely Ḥaylān, mentioned by Yāqūt as one of the villages of Ḥalab whose spring water filled the pools of Ḥalab's *masjid jami'* via a 12 km-long canal.[39] Interestingly, the latest ceramics from the survey were fifth-century. Early Islamic settlement was densest in the fertile northern area of the three branches but sparser south of their convergence at Tell Haouar en Nahr, with only four evenly spaced sites down to Ḥalab. This drop in numbers is emphasized by six new sites that appear in the Middle Islamic period. Most of the Early Islamic sites recorded throughout the Tell Rifa'at Survey had been inhabited since the seventh century (22 out of 29, or 76 per cent of the total), all preexisting the Late Roman period, and seven were newly established in the eighth century (24 per cent of Islamic sites).[40] This indicates that many sites survived past the seventh century conquests, the reverse of what was seen in the Amuq and Kahramanmaraş Surveys. Sites founded in the eighth century were part of the pattern of sedentarization. Three of the seven eighth-century new sites were at least of a medium assemblage, considering only the enumerated published glazed wares. Five of these seven were north of the survey area, in the well-watered zone where the Nahr Quwayq flowed alongside two other streams and settlement was densest. South of Ḥalab a string of Late Roman sites, including one newly established and one transitional, helps to date a possible canalized branch of the river before it entered the Buḥayrah al-Matkh wetland.[41] This process definitely continued into the eighth century and even grew in the tenth to fourteenth centuries. East of the Nahr Quwayq towards the town of Bāb and the Nahr al-Dhahab, only one of two Late Roman settlements continued into the Early Islamic period. West of the Nahr Quwayq, Late Roman settlement was denser than in the Early Islamic period as well, with the important settlement of ʿAzāz.

This site in the district of ʿAzāz was appropriately named, as the settlement of ʿAzāz (Greek Arsace, Mammisea, Ariseria; Crusader Artasia/Arthusa), and was recorded by the Rifa'at Survey as Tell Azaz. It was the heaviest site in terms of ceramic assemblage from the Early Islamic period, and continued in the Middle Islamic period.[42] Furthermore, it had Late Roman pottery into the middle of the seventh century. Texts before the Crusader period hardly mention the settlement, despite its archaeological importance. It may not be well known in Early Islamic texts in part because it might have been a monastery, Dayr Shaykh, mentioned by Yāqūt also as Dayr Tell ʿAzāz, presumably at what he described as the *madīnah laṭīfah* (fine town) of ʿAzāz. Yāqūt includes in his account verse by Isḥāq al-Mawṣilī (767–850), who stopped there, giving us clues to the date and relative importance of the town.[43] Several other villages (mentioned as *qurā* by Yāqūt) lay in the district of ʿĀzāz and possessed mosques and markets – for example, Kfar Lahthā, Mannagh/Mannaʿ, Yabrīn, Arfād, and Tubbal – while Īnnib was a *ḥiṣn*.

As the surveyors recorded mainly tells, these site types predominate. However, flat or low-mounded sites are also mentioned. Most of the new seventh-century sites were near tells, but half of the new eighth-century sites were flat sites. It is evident today from CORONA and other satellite imagery that most of these tell sites would have had lower towns, likely the focus of Late Roman and Early Islamic settlement. Toponyms such as Tell Bouhaira (Lake Mound) support the presence of wetland, as does the observation made by the surveyors that the area floods in the winter.[44] It is tempting to consider the use of tells and lower towns together as most sites in the Nahr Quwayq would have been surrounded by a seasonal marsh. Yet, all the new eighth-century flat sites were founded on the river and in the marsh. Thus, Early Islamic settlement focused on the river valley itself and any canalized portions. There were virtually no upper-slope sites recorded in the survey, which may be due to extensive erosion, mentioned by the surveyors themselves. This would have been a contributing factor to the marshification in the lowland valleys.

Marsh Settlement around the Jabbūl Lake

Other marsh and lake sites were also present in and around al-Matkh around and south of Qinnasrīn the Jabbūl Lake (Sabkhat al-Jabbūl) (Figure 13). The site of Tell Wasta (Site 145) was an island within the Jabbūl Lake west of Ḥalab and dated to the Late Roman period.[45] Ṭabarī mentioned a former companion of Marwān and one of his cavalry officers named Abū al-Ward (Majza'ah b. Kawthar b. Zufar b. al-Kilābī), who swore an oath of allegiance to the ʻAbbāsids. He lived with Maslama b. ʻAbd al-Malik's descendants at Bālis and a village called Nāʻūra ('Waterwheel'), located between Ḥalab and Bālis, in 749/50.[46] Although as yet unidentified, from the toponym we can surmise that this last site was built along a canal or tributary and involved in irrigation and perhaps milling. Al-Sarakhsī (d. 899), travelling between Ḥalab and Bālis, stopped at the settlement and noted that there was a small stone fort belonging to Maslama b. ʻAbd al-Malik. About 13 km east was the village of Muhammad b. al-ʻAbbās al-Kilābī, known as Qaryat al-Thalj. While travelling between Ḥalab and Bālis, al-Sarakhsī (833/7–99) observed that it was well-watered with canals from the Nahr Quwayq.[47] Ṭabarī also mentioned an agricultural settlement called Zarāʻat Banī Zufar or Khusāf, where an ʻAbbāsid officer had manhandled the sons of Maslama b. ʻAbd al-Malik and their wives while staying at Maslamah's fort (presumably in the same village, but perhaps the one at Nāʻūra). Abū al-Ward defended his neighbours, killed the officer, and joined the ʻAbbāsid opposition.[48] Al-Sarakhsī mentions the region around Khusāf as watered by canals, but during his travel across the plain water was scarce.[49] Khusāf should be the same as Tell Khzaf, surveyed in the Jabbūl Survey of 1939 and described as a large

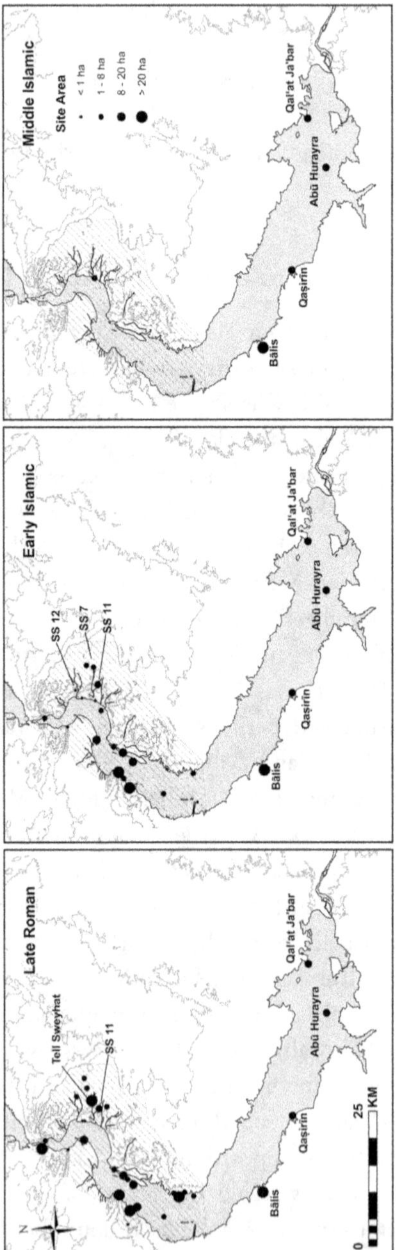

Figure 13 Sweyhat Survey, Late Roman through Middle Islamic sites

mound with a shrine on top and a cemetery to the north on the north-eastern shore of the Jabbūl Lake. A CORONA image clearly shows the mound and several other anomalies around it, including a canal that may be part of the Early Islamic site near the modern village of Khusāf. Interestingly, the newer survey of the Jabbūl Plain discovered Late Roman but no Early Islamic ceramics at the site. However, Yāqūt states that there are ruins for 50 km around the vicinity.[50] The historical anecdote provides insight into the links between Umayyad 'princely residences' and canal infrastructure with 'Abbāsid sedentarization practices. Even villages possessed 'forts' or residences set aside for important local rulers and officials in the Umayyad period, which pattern corresponds well with the Sweyhat 'sheikh's house' in the surveyed sites of the second half of the eighth century. These local centers, where Umayyad officials promoted agricultural and irrigation enterprises, became focal points for larger conglomerate villages with more buildings and higher population in the 'Abbāsid period. Both Nā'ūra and Khusāf appear on an itinerary followed in 900 by the Caliph al-Mu'taḍid, which connected the route Funduq al-Ḥusayn to al-Iskandāruna in the western *thughūr* to that of Baghrās–Anṭākiyah–Artāḥ–al-Athārib–Ḥalab–al-Nā'ūra–Khusāf–Ṣif-fīn–Bālis–Dawsar–Baṭn Dāmān–Raqqah.[51]

Upland Sites: Monasteries and Tells and the Syrian Jibāl

Tells were not primary areas of settlement. Along the Euphrates in the Tishrin Dam area, several tells were excavated as salvage projects by the Syrian Archaeological Mission of the University of Barcelona between 1988 and 1998, revealing cemeteries from the Islamic period such as Tell Kosak Shamli (Qusaq Shamalī), Tell Jarablus Tahtani (Jarāblūs Taḥtānī), Tell Khamīs, and Qara Qūzāq (Figure 11).[52] Tilbeşar (Arabic Tall Bashīr, Crusader Turbessel), 25 km south-east of Gaziantep in the Sajūr River valley, is a high mound excavated by a French team from 1994. Hellenistic and Roman finds were too sporadic to denote a real occupation, and Late Roman pottery was notably absent. Yet, a small assemblage of Early Islamic ceramics was found on the slopes of the tell, as well as to the north, north-east and south of the mound.[53] This may have been a Christian community, perhaps monastic, as suggested, albeit tentatively, by a Syriac inscription reused in a later wall on top of the tell but mentioning a building founded in the eighth century.[54] The occupation was limited, particularly in contrast to the eleventh to twelfth centuries, from which period pottery was observed throughout the site and on the tell summit, confirming Crusader and Mamlūk historical accounts that only mention the settlement from the eleventh century onward. Numerous cave dwellings on either side of the Euphrates in this area, posited as monasteries (eremitic or lavratic), were recorded and also associated at times with dovecotes.[55] One can imagine in one of these Saint Theodota of Amida (d. 698), who carved out such a cave in precisely this region where he lived for at least eight months.

One of the most important Miaphysite schools was located on the Euphrates across the river from the tell of Carchemish (Europa), the celebrated Syriac monastic center Qenneshrē/Qinnisrē ('Eagle's Nest'). On the rocks above the tell was a chapel dedicated to Thomas the Apostle. There was a mill and river crossing at this point.[56] Qenneshrē was occupied without pause from the fifth century to the 'Abbāsid period, as were many other places. It was torched and sacked in 811 by a Rabī'a follower of Naṣr al-'Uqayli.[57]

Jabbūl (Gabbula) was another Christian community on the edges of the Jabbūl Lake, and a conical tell with a lower city, likely involved in the salt-extraction industry. Hāfir was a village surrounding a tell between Bālis and Ḥalab associated with Dayr Hāfir, which one can assume followed the same tell/lower-town arrangement.[58] It was resurveyed by the new Jabbūl Survey as Site 34, occupied in the Early Islamic period.[59] Other monasteries in the vicinity of Ḥalab included 'Ammān, Ballāḍ, Hashyān, and Khunāṣira (Greek and modern Anasartha, 55 km south-east of Ḥalab).[60] Both Khunāṣira and Jabbūl featured Christian communities, and were new bishoprics with *kastra* in the fourth and fifth centuries before achieving town status.[61]

There was only one recorded Middle Islamic site in the Jerablus Tahtani survey: at the top of Tell Jerablus Tahtani, and dated 900–1250. Middle Islamic settlement in the Birecik–Carchemish Euphrates area contrasted significantly with that from the Early Islamic period, with 15 widely scattered sites settled. These were all smaller settlements occupying earlier multi-period tells. Middle Islamic period fortresses were constructed in the eleventh century, such as Ja'bar and Qal'at Najm.[62] From the Gaziantep Survey, a castle was found near Gaziantep by the mounds of Turlu, Battal, and Arıl. It was not situated in the lowland plains, but on a natural rise.

The most important group of upland sites in the central *thughūr* area are the well-known rural villages and monasteries of the Syrian Jibāl, frequently termed the 'Dead Cities': those remarkably preserved settlements on the limestone hills between Anṭākiya and Ḥalab, or the *massif calcaire.* The region has been documented extensively, which has engendered debates over the function of these settlements and their place in the surrounding Late Antique landscape.[63] The traditional view proposed by Tchalenko was that these communities were part of a unique settlement pattern of the fifth and sixth centuries involved in the monoculture of the olive. Indeed, the perseverance of the term 'Dead Cities' exacerbates the supposed peculiarity of these sites. This perception can and must be revised. First, the Syrian Jibāl sites are part of the same Late Roman dispersed landscape as the upland settlements of the Amuq, which happens to be rather well preserved. Second, they were largely self-sufficient communities that grew a range of produce and raised animals. Their economy may be seen more dynamically as encompassing both local production and the long-distance olive-oil trade until around the seventh century when the loss of distant markets necessitated a restructuring of olive-oil exports to the immediate region.[64] Third, many of these villages lasted well into the ninth and tenth centuries.

Unfortunately, space does not allow individual sites from previous surveys of the limestone hills to be systematically examined here – yet as both Late Roman and Early Islamic sites their consideration cannot be ignored, particularly as they offer a view into a well-preserved Christian community living on the Islamic *thughūr.* The roughly 700 villages concerned are self-contained and are built with an inward focus and no surrounding fortifications. There is also a lack of public buildings except for an abundance of churches, which are not always distinguishable from other (mostly farm) buildings. The most common structure by far was the two-story house built of limestone, wherein the upper floor was residential and the ground level was used for the raising of animals. Water was collected through the use of rooftop cisterns for rainwater and wells dug in the limestone; no aqueducts have been discovered. However, recent research has shown an elaborate locally-designed system of excavated or natural underground channels connecting these wells to subterranean cisterns for reserve water supply. These were simply utilized; when they overflowed, they were diverted off into fields.[65] Soundings excavated in the upland village of Déhès by R. Tate and J.-P. Sodini revealed a diverse agriculture including olives, grapes, beans, vegetables, and fruit, as well as the rearing of sheep and cattle, leading the excavators to postulate a relative degree of self-sufficiency which may have lasted until the tenth century.[66] Numerous presses capable of producing significant quantities of surplus oil are a noteworthy feature. Stone field boundaries appear to have been used to demarcate tracts of land between villages and to have functioned also as animal pens, another important element in the subsistence economy of the uplands. The villages were linked by tracks rather than by any main road, although routes down to the plains were essential in facilitating exchange with market towns.[67] Many also had inns for travellers (*pandocheion*). The implied landscape seems to consist of self-sufficient communities that augmented their mixed economy by participating in the external trade in olive oil, perhaps linked with LR1 amphorae production. About 61 sites were identified as monasteries, nearly always deliberately placed within 1 km or 2 km of other settlements.[68] Like tell monasteries and their lower towns, they were usually built on hilltops above villages, though still within view and close proximity. Despite this closeness, the presence of an enclosure wall has raised questions as to the relationship between village and monastery. As it enclosed a large open space, it may perhaps best be explained as a protected space for cultivation and a refuge for the nearby community. In some, a free-standing square tower (*ṣauma'ah*) has been identified as a hold-over from the pillar upon which Stylite saints sat. The *Life* of St. Simeon of the Olives (d. 734) mentions holy men ensconcing themselves in such towers *(pyrgoi)* in monasteries. Devotional communities may have developed out of such small sites. These towers could also act as lookout posts in times of uncertainty. The presence of a refuge and lookout tower immediately raises a question as to the date of these structures. D. Hull assigned a fifth- to sixth-century date, following stylistic grounds and previous scholars. The only excavations, at the village of Déhès (not a monastery), whose ceramics were reanalysed by Magness, revealed that all the houses examined were built in the second half of the sixth to seventh century, and that seventh-century pottery was present in all of the earliest floors, radically shifting the date for at least this settlement from the fourth century.[69] Furthermore, the site continued to be used until the ninth and tenth centuries. Not every one of the 700 villages would have continued into the Early Islamic period. Nevertheless, like Déhès, many of the sites including monasteries on the Syrian Jibāl did so, or were newly-established sites for Christian groups who migrated towards the relatively inaccessible uplands. Places of importance, like the pilgrimage center of Dayr Sim'an, were fortified in the tenth century. Muslims also lived in the uplands, although we can assume they did so in far smaller numbers, as evidenced by the small presence of some newly-built mosques and the repurposing of older structures into mosques, like the addition of a *mihrab* to the *andron* in Dayr (Deir) Seta.[70]

Way Stations

Two way stations marked newly-spaced stopping points on the south–north Bālis–Jisr Manbij–Ra'bān–Ḥadath (and beyond, through the Darb al-Ḥadath) route, which followed the Euphrates River on its western bank (Figure 11). From the Jarablus Tahtani Survey, Site 17 was 2 km north-east of Site 1 on a limestone rise above the Euphrates featuring a 25 × 25 m square building with corner towers of rubblestone. A bottle-shaped cistern was found in the center of the site, with a well nearby.[71] Directly across the river was a tributary wadi heading north-east to Sarūj, suggesting that this also may have been a river-crossing point (perhaps nearer to Site 1: Khirbet Seraisat from the Jarablus

Survey). The site lay *c.*47 km north of the presumed settlement of Jisr Manbij, around Qalʿat Najm.

Pınar Tarlası (Site 4 in G. Algaze's survey around Birecik) was a rectangular structure measuring 80 × 70 m (0.56 ha in area), well built and preserved to 1 m high with stone facing, and dated only to the mid-eighth to mid-tenth centuries.[72] It was located on an upper part of a narrow alluvial fan overlying a low river terrace at 375 m.a.s.l. The site is about 50 km north of Site 17 along the Euphrates and about 35 km south of Raʿbān, thereby occupying a stopping point on that north–south route. Pınar Tarlası marked a further important node; north of it the Euphrates is more incised and the land route north towards Ḥadath likely diverged from it towards Sumaysāṭ or Kurban Höyük on the eastern *thughūr*, a distance of about 60 km away. Pınar Tarlası would also have been situated on the two east–west routes from Dulūk (one long day's journey, or 45 km, to the west) to al-Ruhā (modern Urfa, nearly three days, or 85 km, to the east) or Sumaysāṭ. It may have replaced Late Roman Zeugma and preceded Middle Islamic Bira (modern Birecik) as a crossing point on the Euphrates River, where travellers could go along a tributary river valley directly across Site 4 (past modern Ayran) as far as Sumaysāṭ.[73]

Towns

The same settlement patterns are visible in the larger *thughūr* towns that frequently appear in accounts of the frontier. Most of these became part of Hārūn's *ʿawāṣim* province. In fact, from both Ibn Khurradādhbih's (w. 850 or 885/6) and Ibn al-Faqīh's (al-Hamdānī) (w. 903) lists, five out of seven (Manbij, Bālis, al-Jūma, Ruṣāfat Hishām, and Qūrus) are located in this area.[74] The exceptions are Anṭākiya and Tīzīn (and Ibn Khurradādhbih mentions also Būqā). Interestingly, he writes of Qūrus as a *kūra*, raising the possibility that the other entries also refer not only to towns but to districts.[75] Balādhurī in 869, and later Yāqūt, mentions Manbij, Tīzīn, Qūrus and Anṭākiya, adding Raʿbān and Dulūk and all the places between.[76] Writing in 967–88, Ibn Ḥawqal, a native of the region and the geographer most closely linked to it, lists only Bālis, Sanjah and Sumaysāṭ. Ibn Shaddād (1216/17–85) lists Baghrās, Darbassāk, Artāḥ (all in the Amuq Plain), Kaysūm, and Tell Qabbasin. All of these towns can be grouped together chronologically.

Bālis (Greek Barbalissus, modern Eski Meskene), on the west bank of the Euphrates River, was roughly equidistant between Ḥalab and Raqqa and was the first town one encountered when entering Syria from 'Iraq. Yāqūt mentioned that it was once a river crossing, but it now lies 8 km away from the shifted course of the Euphrates.[77] Excavations from 1927–30 uncovered an Umayyad mosque similar to the one in Damascus. Subsequent work from 1970 to 1973 by a team from the Institut Français d'Études Arabes de Damas and the Direction des Antiquités Nationales de Syrie uncovered parts of the Islamic city, including houses, streets, possible shops, a neighbourhood mosque, and a larger mosque.[78] The peak of settlement and architecture was an Ayyūbid period enclosure fortified by a wall with towers; however, 'Abbāsid foundations existed for the two mosques. Excavations by a team from Princeton University and the Syrian Directorate of Antiquities uncovered the Late Roman walled city, which had continued to be used, and the Umayyad *qaṣr* measuring 67 × 77 m, peripheral to the earlier city and looking down on it from a ridge, and perhaps that of Maslama b. 'Abd al-Malik or his brother Sa'id al-Khayr, both of whom built canals in the area. The *qaṣr* of Bālis was not just a residential palace or 'desert castle'; canals and work rooms for the preparation and cleaning of sheep wool were found within and around it. The settlement, like Dibsi Faraj, lies in the transitional rainfall zone, making irrigation necessary. T. Leisten argues that the Marwānid estate was a focal point and production center for surrounding villages and encampments, and was mainly settled by the Qays tribe.[79] The *qaṣr*, a Marwānid stronghold, was dismantled for building materials sometime in the first two decades of the early 'Abbāsid period, although early 'Abbāsid houses are recorded outside the enclosure.

A group of minor settlements taken during the Early Islamic conquests by Abū 'Ubayda during the reign of 'Umar I (r. 634–44) included Ra'bān, Dulūk, Qūrus and Manbij. Ra'bān (Greek Araban) is located in the center of a lowland river valley at the confluence of a Euphrates tributary, the Kara Su, and a smaller river that flows around the eastern side of the site. The valley is surrounded by two upland ranges to the north and south. Like a miniature Ḥalab, the site has a high flat-topped tell, known as Altıntaş Kalesi, with later Middle/Late Islamic remains and a lower city that completely encircles the tell with circuit walls – likely the focus of Early Islamic settlement, as suggested by Yāqūt, who mentions a fortress *under* a hill (*qal'a taḥt jabal*).[80] Dulūk (Greek Doliche), in the Gaziantep Steppe/Plateau incorporated a long natural rocky outcrop and lower town. Qūrus (Greek Cyrrhus), in the 'Afrīn Valley, also displaying a tell/lower town arrangement, had a fort named for one of Abū 'Ubayda's commanders who occupied it, although it is unclear when it was built. No caliphal or any other directed building or repair activities are known for these four settlements, which all had strong Syriac Orthodox Christian communities and a series of bishops into the tenth century. Qūrus also had a population of Slavs. Manbij (Greek Bambyke-Hierapolis) occupies the same site and is largely obscured by the modern town. It was described by Islamic geographers as well-watered and walled, with markets. The Jabbūl Survey noted robbed walls in the modern town. Jisr Manbij on the Euphrates is not definitively located and little is known about it. Ṭabarī mentioned that 'Alī crossed the river at Jisr Manbij on his way to Ṣiffīn in 656/7.[81] It might be associated not with the Middle Islamic fortress Qal'at Najm 25 km due east of Manbij, but with its lower town, described by the Jabbūl Survey as Hellenistic–Roman, and nearby Tall Najm, described by the Nahr Sajūr Survey as Byzantine/Islamic. As a river crossing, it may have been a double site spanning both banks. Directly opposite, on the east bank of the Euphrates, two settlements are visible in CORONA imagery on either side of a tributary which is today entirely flooded. The east bank settlements are at a bend in the Euphrates and sit just north of it, on a higher terrace above a large alluvial river plain.

Dābiq (Greek Dabekon), presumably identified with the modern town in Syria, was located in the central steppe/plain. It was briefly a headquarters for the Caliph Sulaymān (r. 715–17), and building activity is only recorded when a *ribāṭ* was built by Qāsim, Hārūn al-Rashīd's son, in 804. It is one of the few central *thughūr* settlements not associated with the *'awāṣim* or a Middle Islamic successor. The Rifa'at Survey found Late Roman pottery. The Early Islamic ceramic assemblage was, curiously, very light according to what can be extrapolated from the ceramics found. The town lies at the confluence of two of three major streams of the Nahr Quwayq and consists of two tells connected by a saddle on the west side of the river and a lower town extending east and south, as visible on the CORONA. Yāqūt called it a *qarya*. The settlement is perhaps most known for its surrounding plain, the Marj Dabīq, a seasonally inundated wetland/pasture where tribes and armies camped in the winter before summer expeditions into the Taurus Mountains.

Ruṣafa, or Ruṣafāt Hishām, is mentioned as an *'awāṣim* settlement, but it is far to the east of the central *thughūr* and closer to Raqqa. It lies south of the east–west course of the Euphrates and was a Byzantine and Ghassānid capital before Hishām turned his attention to it. Recent excavations have uncovered extensive small *quṣūr*-type residences with gardens, canals, and other irrigation features.[82] It is more similar to the "desert castles" than a *thughūr* town, but possesses signs of the same Umayyad canal-building entrepreneurship. It is on a tributary called al-Zaurā (the Crooked). Interestingly, Ibn Buṭlān mentioned that it was mainly a Christian community and a way station. The settlement was an important crossroads for routes from Dimashq (the well-known and ancient Strata Diocletiana) and routes from Ḥimṣ.

Ḥadath (Greek Adata), an important town outpost guarding a key Taurus Mountain pass, was a Late Roman settlement that was a 'new foundation' under al-Mahdī in the late eighth century – founded, like the settlements of Kanīsāt al-Sawdā', Hārūnīyya and 'Ayn Zarba in the western *thughūr*, either by him or his son, Hārūn. Indeed, during Hārūn's caliphate, more than half of the known central *thughūr* settlements – Anṭākiya, Baghrās, Bālis, Dābiq, Ḥadath, Manbij and Mar'ash – received considerable repairs and new constructions. Many of these were part of the *'awāṣim* administrative unit. It is mentioned that Ḥadath's sun-dried brick (*libin*) walls were repaired after having 'melted' from winter rains, and that a mosque was built. The site, in a fertile plain with rivers and lakes, has rather well-built limestone-ashlar mortared city walls with square buttresses, although the date for this enclosure is uncertain. The mention of unbaked brick for city walls stands out; however, this may refer to upper courses or internal walls only. Reference is made in 785/6 to market traders who fled during a Byzantine raid, indicating another level of population present besides a garrison.[83] The settlement also had a Christian community and bishopric in the ninth century.

The towns in the last group of these settlements – Kaysūm (Greek Kaisou) and Sanjah-Bahasnā (Greek Octacuscum, Syriac Bet Hesnā) – only briefly appear in ninth- and tenth-century histories of the region, respectively. It is assumed that Kaysūm and Sanjah-Bahasnā, which replaced Ḥadath, were former Late Roman towns but this is unverified, although they are places of Syriac communities.[84] Dionysius of Tell Maḥrē (818–45) studied at the Monastery of Mar Jacob in Kaysūm the early ninth century. None of these towns are associated with caliphal building activities. Al-Jūma, described by several authors as part of the *'awāṣim*, is hardly mentioned anywhere else and has not been located. Yet, it is referred to indirectly on numerous occasions when other villages are part of its district, which lies in the Afrīn Valley. As such, it may have been more importantly considered as a district rather than a town.[85]

Conclusions

In the area between Ḥalab and the Euphrate – the steppe and the river – as in the area of the two Amuqs, sites followed water channels, canals and rivers, and were also located around lakes and marshlands. Yet, the eastern central *thughūr* was more densely settled than the western *thughūr* in the Early Islamic period, with many sites exhibiting continuity through the seventh-century period of transition. More settlements were built near, around, or even on top of tells, although some of these combined Christian monasteries with lower towns. The Euphrates River region, by contrast, was only sparsely settled, with evenly spaced settlements. These served mainly as way stations and towns for routes running parallel to the river, and some functioned as river crossings at points of confluence with tributaries. The Euphrates

River was also canalized, with a main feeder channel and smaller conduits. The density of settlements in the Ḥalab steppe, where most of the *'awāṣim* towns are located begs the question of whether this administrative unit contributed to the increased population and sedentarism of the region. While this may certainly be an important factor, the survey evidence shows that most sites had been continuously inhabited since before Hārūn's reapportionment. It seems more practical to assign the relative prosperity to the importance of Ḥalab as the chief city, and that this area, as a micro-region, was part of the first frontier of settlement. A second major reason would be that increased settlement into the arid parts of the steppe was made possible through the heavy attention paid to the development of irrigation works by locals, the elite and caliphs.

CHAPTER 3

THE EASTERN *THUGHŪR*

Then Mar Theodota went out to go to the region of the fortresses {al-ḥuṣūn} and passed by Bīlū and Pīlīn and the rest of the districts that are there. So he said to his disciple, 'Joseph, my Son, let us go and visit those Syrian Orthodox who are in flight because of neediness and the great number of the Arabs. We will pray for them and encourage them in the hope of faith, for I know that the Romans are driving them out so they will change their faith.[1]

The eastern *thughūr* encompassed a very large area, including the Upper Euphrates and the lands east toward the Tigris River all the way into the Taurus Mountains to the north. Sites were concentrated in the geographically discrete mountain-ringed lowlands of the Karababa Basin, Malaṭiya Plain (Tohma Basin) and Elazığ Plain (Keban Basin). The largest of the well-known towns were Sumaysāṭ and Malaṭiya, with other settlements functioning more as fortified outposts or *maslaḥa* that changed hands and loyalties often. There have been many surveys in this region owing mainly to the salvage dam projects of the Güneydoğu Anadolu Projesi (GAP) along the Euphrates River. These northern upper reaches of the Euphrates in the eastern *thughūr* possessed similar patterns of settlement to those seen in the central frontier, but quite different densities, types and irrigation strategies. Early Islamic sites were fewer the farther north one progressed and were centred on natural springs.

The Environment

The first of these micro-regions, the Karababa Basin of the Euphrates, was not immediately adjacent to any passes, but it was a major transition point between the North Syrian steppe and the eastern Taurus Mountains (and Anatolian Plain beyond) (Figure 14). As such, most of its inhabitants were semi-pastoralists and transhumant to a degree. The basin, defined mainly by surrounding limestone plateaus, begins upstream of the Karakaya (Halfeti) Gorge (near the Atatürk Dam today) and widens eastward to Gerger as the Euphrates traverses across the plain east–west for about 100 km. Precipitation in the Karababa Basin averages between 400 and 600 mm/annum, higher than levels in northern Syria. Prior to the construction of dams, flooding usually occurred every spring (from March to June, peaking in April and May), while August and September had the

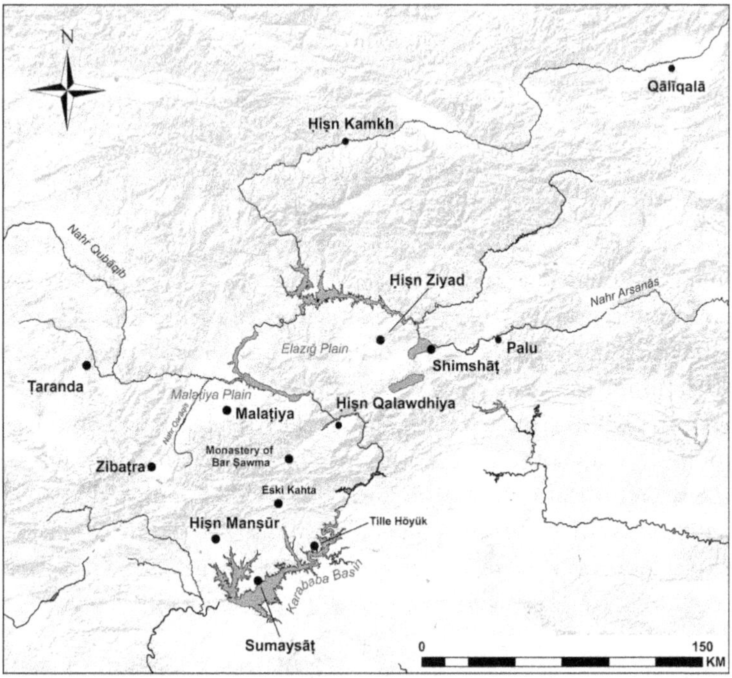

Figure 14 The eastern *thughūr*

lowest flow rates for the Euphrates. Besides the Euphrates as the main contributor of water, most of the streams and tributaries north and west of the region in the Adıyaman Plain limestone plateau and some to the east such as the Incesu (Nahr al-Azaz), empty into this lowland – as does snowmelt from the surrounding limestone hills and springs on the edges of the river terraces. The west bank of the Euphrates from the Adıyaman Plateau had many of these springs. These small spring-fed tributaries formed isolated fertile geomorphological strips, dictating settlement between the Euphrates and the Balikh Valley.

Three distinct vegetation zones intersect here. The aforementioned Mediterranean zone reaches its limits at the Euphrates River and Ruhā (Greek Edessa, modern Urfa). South and east of this zone is the Irano-Turanian Steppe, low rolling hills that range from the Urfa-Gaziantep Plateau down into the North Syrian Plain. The steppe vegetation was used by pastoralists as a grazing resource, predominately in the winter and early spring. By summer, the pastoralists moved their flocks north to the base and foothills of the eastern Taurus Mountains in the Kurdo-Zagrosian steppe–forest zone. The basin itself consists of separate Pleistocene river terraces with a calcium carbonate and cobble conglomerate, descending towards the Euphrates River. The lowest of these terraces is 400 m.a.s.l. and 20 m above the Euphrates. These are overlaid by reddish-brown calcareous soil eroded from the plateaus: important for cultivation, primarily of wheat and secondarily of barley, as well as viticulture on marginal soils and slopes. Fruit and nut trees (such as almond) on the slopes were the most well-suited and well-known product of the region. Other patches of irrigable and arable land comprise alluvial-silt areas laid down when the Euphrates shifted course and cut into the cliffs, creating wetlands around and in rivers (on islands) that served as good pasture areas. The dry-farming technique practiced in the early twentieth century was a winter activity: September sowing and July harvest. Although the area was within an adequate rainfall zone, lands for grazing were present and extensive.[2] As such, the basin was a nucleus of human activity and settlement, as well as transportation and trade, as it was the most northern part of the Euphrates that was navigable. The river was spanned by floating pontoon bridges in key locations. The region includes the *thughūr* settlements of Ḥiṣn Manṣūr (modern Adıyaman) and Sumaysāṭ (modern Samsat).

The northern- and easternmost part of the *thughūr* is also the most mountainous, leaving behind the steppe lowlands of northern Syria and crossing over into the rugged highlands of eastern Anatolia and Armenia. Despite this, settlement was concentrated in several large plains that push up against the Taurus Mountains and are fed by the Euphrates and its tributaries. The second micro-region, the Malaṭiya Plain – surrounded by the Anti-Taurus Mountain ranges to the west, south and east, and the Hekimhan Mountains to the north – is a semi-enclosed basin, 900 m.a.s.l. and watered by both the Euphrates and the Nahr Qarāqīs (Greek Melas, modern Tohma Çay), a tributary of the Qubāqib (modern Sultan Suyu) which crosses the basin west–east before emptying into the Euphrates.[3] The plain, known for the major town of Malaṭiya, is not completely level but is marked by some undulating ridges and tells. To the south-west is a small extension formed by the Nahr Qarāqīs. Here was also located the town of Zibaṭra. Iron was mined in the Taurus, probably in proximity to Zibaṭra, which was known for this activity. Ibn Serapion described the Nahr Qubāqib as originating in Byzantine lands and flowing into the Euphrates, where there was a great bridge named after this river.

To the east, the Elazığ Plain consists of broad river valleys that are ideal for both agriculture and pastoralism. This third micro-region is watered by the intersection of the Euphrates or Western Euphrates (local Karasu) and Nahr Arsanās or Arasnās (Greek Arsanias, modern Murad Su) Rivers, which continue into the Malaṭiya Plain. There are several other wide, fertile valleys in this area, such as the Aşvan Valley, which is north and east of the Keban Dam and the Altınova Valley (Uluova or Mollakendi Ovası), which is south-east of Elazığ. The plains are 700–845 m.a.s.l. There is also a lake, the Hazar Gölü, which may correspond with 'Hūrē, mentioned as a lake with islands and fish by Theodota of Amida.[4] Geomorphological work has demonstrated deforestation in the uplands by the first century BCE, leading to significant erosion on the plain.[5] This region experiences a combination of the long Middle Eastern hot summers and the short Anatolian cold winters, with significant precipitation in the uplands during the winter and early spring. The annual rainfall is 400–600 mm/annum, although the Altınova receives more rain on account of its location on the edge of the Taurus in the 600–800 mm/annum zone. The Elazığ Plain, was called *thughūr al-bakriya*, or the northern frontier of the tribe of Bakr (Diyār Bakr). The *thughūr al-bakriya* included the settlements of Ḥiṣn Qalawdhiya, Ḥiṣn Ziyād, Ḥiṣn Kamkh and Shimshāṭ, corresponding with the 'region of the fortresses' (*al-ḥuṣūn*) mentioned in the *Life* of Theodota of Amida.

These were the three major intermontane plains that lay between the Taurus and Anti-Taurus Mountain ranges. Although oak-juniper forests are attested in the Bronze Age for all three plains, much of the area would have been deforested and eroded, most likely during the Hellenistic to Early Islamic periods. The timber that was grown was not tall enough for use in shipbuilding. However, wild cypress is thought to have grown in the eastern Taurus, which had been already deforested by the third millennium BCE. The Euphrates would have facilitated timber transport. In addition, medlar, pear, gum mastic, sumac, walnut and almond trees grew in this region.[6] Near the plains were important copper, tin, lead-silver, iron and – to a lesser extent – gold deposits.

Various tribal groups claimed these lands. The Bāhila grazed in the Karababa Basin and the Khuzā'a of the Ṭayyi' tribe did the same in the Malaṭiya Plain (Figure 2). The northernmost of these settlements, including Ṭaranda and other towns north towards Sivas (Greek Sebasteia) and Tephrikē (modern Divrik), were controlled by the heterodox and persecuted Christian (mainly Armenian) Paulicians (Baylaqanī).

Land routes were preferred over Euphrates travel. The Mar'ash–Ra'bān–Sumaysāṭ route traversed the Karababa Basin, while another west–east route connected Ḥadath–Sanjah/Bahasnā–Ḥiṣn Manṣūr. The key south–north route came from Raqqa and travelled up the length of the Balikh Valley to Ḥarrān and Ruhā and then crossed the Euphrates at Sumaysāṭ and the Ḥiṣn Manṣūr. This stretch, about 180 km in length, probably traced the Balikh River and Nahr al-Azaz. Another route may have connected Raqqa with Sumaysāṭ via Sarūj. To skirt the Anti-Taurus Mountains and reach the northernmost settlements, three routes were possible: (1) from Ḥadath via the Gölbaşı Valley to Zibaṭra, thence to Malaṭiya via the Qarāqis River, a branch of the Qubāqib/Sultan Su (itself a tributary of the Tokhma Su); (2) from Sumaysāṭ or Ḥiṣn Manṣūr via the Euphrates past Ḥiṣn Qalawdhiya into the Malaṭiya Plain from the east (probably that shown on the Peutinger Table); or (3) from Sumaysāṭ to Ḥiṣn Manṣūr up the Kahta Su in the mountainous interior.[7] In this most elevated part of the *thughūr*, an east–west route would have linked Malaṭiya to Ḥisn Ziyād and Shimshāṭ and the north–south Euphrates route to Tephrikē and west via the Karasu to Ḥiṣn Kamkh and eventually Qālīqalā. Routes to Byzantine lands west of Malaṭiya traversed the Mazikiran Pass at Ṭaranda and modern Gürün in the foothills of the Ṭaurus, leading to Qaysarīya (Greek Caesarea Mazaca, modern Kayseri) in Cappadocia.

Survey Methodology

The eastern *thughūr* has been unevenly surveyed. Projects have focused mainly on the Euphrates River floodplains and their major tributaries as salvage ahead of impending dam construction. Despite the high variance in survey methodologies over time, it is possible to extract information about the Late Roman, Early and Middle Islamic period landscape.

Group I: Extensive/Low-Resolution/Large-Area Surveys

The earliest surveys of this region, beginning in 1975, focused only on main tells and castles and presented a chronology that was difficult to interpret on several levels, at least for the Late Roman and Islamic periods. A classic example is the one conducted in 1975 by the Middle East Technical University from the Keban Dam down to the Karababa Basin.[8] As many projects were of a salvage nature, reports were not always final and teams did not have late-period ceramic specialists. For example, reference to many 'Byzantine yellow-glazed wares' is unclear, but likely indicates the monochrome yellow (mustard and dark yellow) glazes or other glazes of the Middle Islamic period rather than the Early Islamic yellow glazes discovered around Raqqa, Anṭākiya and Ṭarsūs.

The British Institute's Adıyaman Survey between 1985 and 1991 focused on the Euphrates Valley, Kahta Çay tributary and the relatively lowland areas (below 550 m.a.s.l.) of the Çakal, Kalburcu and Ziyaret tributaries and the Turuş area below Sumaysāṭ (Figure 15).[9] The general pattern of settlement perceived was a clustering of sites around the confluence of the Çakal Çay and Kalburcu Dere tributaries. Out of 281 sites, there were 103 for the Roman period, 38 of which continued into the Late Roman period. These data should be taken cautiously, as the excavators did little to distinguish the Roman from the Late Roman period ceramics.[10] In the Islamic periods, there were 119 sites, but only 73. However, only 73 are listed on the phase map. Although the Islamic periods were divided into Early and Middle for the pottery plate, there was no such differentiation on the phase map.

The Keban Reservoir Area Survey, conducted in 1967, was also a salvage dam project. The goal was to search for early domestication and agriculture in the Elazığ Plain, including the Aşvan and Altınova River Valleys located to the north-west and south-east of Elazığ and Harput, respectively (Figure 17). The surveyors concentrated on tell sites and found 44 new sites in addition to eight that were already recorded. Islamic periodization was confusing, as it seemed to fall either within the Middle Islamic (termed 'Byzantine-Selcuk' and mainly 1200–1400, but presumably fourth to fourteenth century) or the Late Islamic (termed 'Medieval' and presumably Ottoman to present) periods. However, Islamic *pottery* was classified in general categories that were largely undifferentiated, such as 'Medieval Brick Ware' which encompassed virtually all redwares including all brittlewares from the Late Roman to Middle Islamic periods. Only those sites with sgraffiato or glazed ware (monochrome glazes) showed Middle Islamic occupation; however, one must bear in mind the possibility of early glazes. Early Islamic occupation was very difficult to identify, as it was grouped with 'Byzantine'.

A 1972–6 survey of Malaṭiya by J. Yakar and A. Gürsan-Salzmann focused exclusively on pre-Classical sites. Current survey around Arlsantepe in the Malaṭiya Plain has yielded few results for the Late Roman and Early Islamic periods. Focusing on the history of the region until the second millennium, publication of the survey results from 2003 showed that 33 sites were discovered, 16 of which were post-Classical. Unfortunately, no further distinguishing periodization was given. However, all of the sites were located on the plain.[11]

Group II: Intensive/High-Resolution/Large-Area Surveys

Finer chronological assessment was present in a survey surrounding Kurban Höyük on the southern bank of the Euphrates, conducted between 1980 and 1984 by the Chicago Euphrates Archaeological Survey (Figure 16).[12] This covered a 1,000 km^2 area, with a 5 km radius around the tell. Building up from the previous explorations of the major tells, emphasis was placed on single-period sites, flat sites and field scatters. There were 18 Late Roman sites, five Early Islamic and eight Middle Islamic sites out of a total of 47. Four other Euphrates River surveys were centered on key sites. The Gritille Regional Survey was conducted between 1982 and 1984, covering an area of 43 km^2 in a 5 km radius around the site, which included two terraces parallel to the Euphrates: an upper one at 450 m.a.s.l. and a lower at 400 m.a.s.l.[13] The main area of the survey comprised the west bank of the Euphrates and the perennial springs and seasonal watercourses that emptied into the river in an area including Gritille. Between the late Iron Age and Late Hellenistic/Roman period, settlement density here jumped from two or three to seven sites out of a total of 25. By the Late Roman period, there were 17 sites. The Middle Islamic period had a second peak in sites, totaling eight. A similar localized survey was conducted across the river by Wilkinson in 1991, covering 7.5 km^2 around the site of Titriş Höyük, 20 km east of Kurban Höyük. The site was situated in a 50 km^2 lowland plain and corridor, allowing natural passage via land routes between Gaziantep to the west and Āmid (modern Diyarbakr) Ruhā and Ḥarrān to the east. Of the 40 sites found in the Titriş Survey, 33 were Late Roman, as compared to 20 for the Roman period, showing a significant peak in settlement. Two surveys were conducted around Lidar Höyük (the regional Bozova-Urfa Survey and the immediate Lidar Höyük Survey). Despite the fact that the Bozova-Urfa Survey focused on 40 of the major tells of the area, the surveyors heavily emphasized that tell settlement ended in the Hellenistic period and did not pick up again until the Middle Islamic period.[14] As such, they cautioned against future tell-focused survey work that would fail to recognize primarily Roman to Early Islamic sites.

Settlement in the Karababa Basin

In the Adıyaman Survey, no major towns were established. Rather, many of these sites retained classic signatures of dispersed small farmsteads from this period, consisting of small ploughed-out field scatters of roof tiles and tesserae along terraces or bluffs overlooking tributary streams (Figure 15). Larger sites were located under or near modern villages. While the surveyors highlight only two Islamic sites, they point out the major settlement pattern that differentiates the Early from the Middle Islamic period: 'During the Medieval period there arose, at sites or places not previously outstanding, a number of centers (characterized by castles) which somewhat alter the pattern of earlier occupation when there were few major centers but numerous small agglomerations (villages, farmsteads and the like).'[15]

Only one plate of pottery is given with ceramics from four sites, thus making it difficult to reconstruct the dating for the sites. The ceramic identifications are for the most part correct. For the Early Islamic period pottery, numbers 4, 5, 6, 9 and 13 are grouped together, identifying Site 63 and Site 25 as Early Islamic. Both of these sites continued from the Late Roman period. It is possible that Site 25, which has multi-period occupation, was a tell, while Site 63, which only has Late Roman occupation, can be assumed to have been a flat site. For the Middle Islamic pottery, numbers 1, 2, 3 and 12 are grouped together. Number 7, the handle with snake application, should also be assigned to this group, identifying Sites 74, 63 and 14 as Middle Islamic. Of these three, Sites 74 and 14 have no Late Roman occupation. They do have occupation in the Early Bronze Age, suggesting that they were all tell sites abandoned in the Late

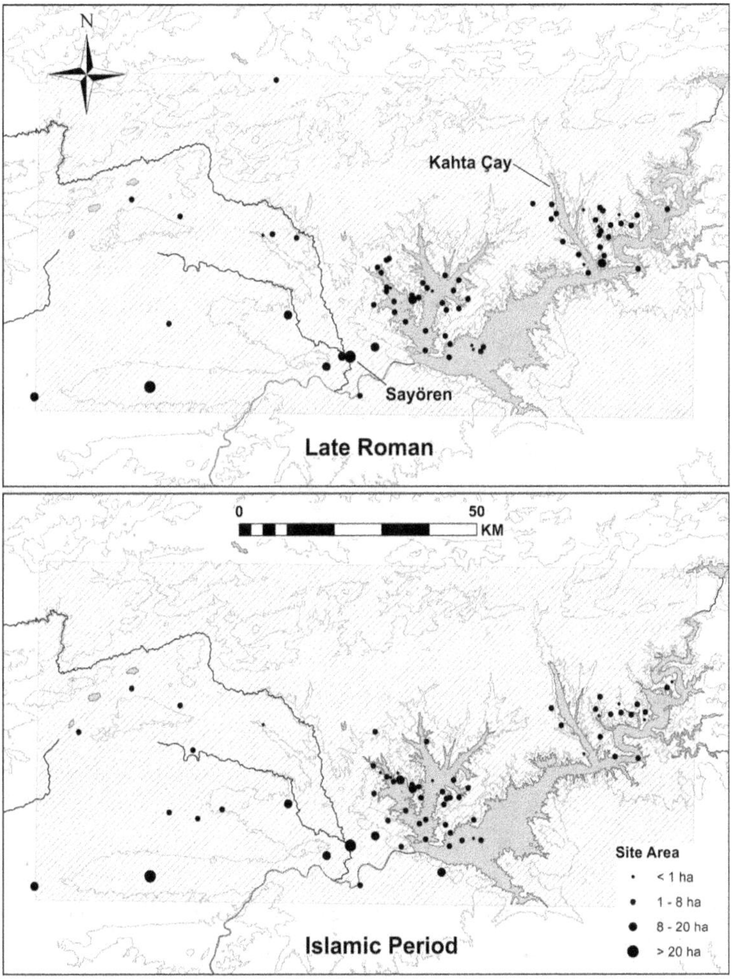

Figure 15 Adıyaman Survey, Late Roman and Islamic sites (based on Blaylock et al. 1980, Figure 30)

Roman (and presumably Early Islamic) period and reoccupied in the Middle Islamic. Numbers 8 and 10, called Early Islamic by the surveyors, cannot be further identified as no information is given about these decorated body sherds. From this single plate of pottery, two patterns arise: continuity of Late Roman–Early Islamic sites that avoided tells and a discontinuity with Middle Islamic sites that reoccupied earlier tells. Unfortunately, the survey maps show sites without their numbers so they cannot be re-mapped.

The first major trend discovered in the Kurban Höyük Survey was the dispersal of sites and population increase, beginning in the Late Hellenistic period and followed by a peak in settlement in terms of site quantity and aggregate settlement area between the fourth and sixth centuries (Figure 16). Similarly, slope erosion, gravel fans and valley aggradation resulting from deforestation was charted to have begun in the third millennium BCE. Settlement in the Late Hellenistic and Roman periods showed an increase in sites dated to the second century/early third century and then a slight gap in the third century. Many Late Roman period sites were continuations from the Seleucid/Roman period. The selection included: (1) medium-sized (3.0–6.5 ha in size) multi-period nodal sites dispersed along the Euphrates at 1.3–3.5 km intervals; (2) small settlements on the upland high terraces with springs, 0.9–1.5 ha in size; (3) sites in tributary river valleys, 0.6–1.0 ha in size; (4) very small sites and scatters and single buildings; (5) a small pastoral site (Site 26) in the limestone uplands with walls and a circular stone pen; and (6) two sites north of the Euphrates. During the Late Roman period, the same pattern of dispersal as seen in the Amuq Plain occurs, with settlement of small farmstead-type sites and movement towards the uplands. Also, the existence of pastoral sites in the uplands expands on the strictly agricultural system often modelled for the Late Roman period. Some of the multi-period nodal sites were also not tells, but larger, flat settlements evident from extensive field scatters, as for example at Sumaysāṭ where most of the population during this period were within the larger 50-ha lower town.

In the Early Islamic Period, there was a significant drop in seventh-century sites followed by a rise in the eighth century, which correlates to the patterns seen in the Amuq and Kahramanmaraş Plains. Yaslica (Site 18) to the south was a route site located on the Raqqa–Sarūj–Sumaysāṭ road. Site 6 was a river site on the İncesu Deresi and was initially a small Late Roman settlement that formed on the edge of Site 7. In the Early Islamic period, Site 6 grew in size

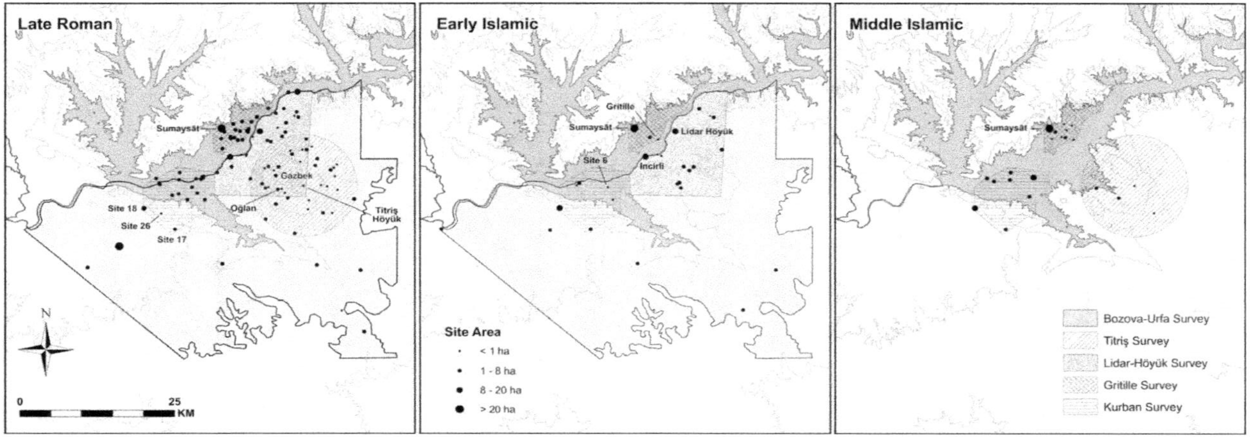

Figure 16 Group II, Karababa Basin Surveys, Late Roman through Middle Islamic sites (based on Wilkinson 1990: Figures 5.4 and 5.7; Redford 1998, Figure 7.2; Algaze et al. 1992, Figure 14; Gerber 1994, pp. 327 and 331)

into the tenth century and exhibited hydraulic features such as a water mill. This settlement was most likely continued as a point on the Ruhā–Sumaysāṭ road. The example of Site 6 shows that while all major Late Roman sites were abandoned during the late sixth or seventh centuries, some Early Islamic settlements continued, usually occupying border locations at the edge of a site's territory and associated with irrigation. The small number of Early Islamic sites led the surveyors to the conclusion that during this period the region had a low sedentary population, being chiefly occupied by pastoralists moving in and out of the frontier. The urban focus of the region would have been Sumaysāṭ, for which Kurban Höyük was a satellite settlement and way station (see Chapter 7). The Euphrates River would have been the main water source as the Roman aqueducts had fallen out of use; however, river sites were not resettled.

In the Middle Islamic period, the settlement of the landscape shifted and slightly intensified. Only Site 18 was preexisting from the Early Islamic period. Sites 17 and 18 – multi-period sites from the Late Roman period – were reoccupied; five other sites showed Middle Islamic period occupation. These tended to be ranged along both banks of the Euphrates River, 2 km to 4 km apart and 1 ha in size. The reintroduction of river sites on the Euphrates in the Middle Islamic period reinforces the pattern of discontinuity with Early Islamic river sites. There were also small Middle Islamic rural settlements and indications of pastoralism on the terraces.

The Gritille Survey sites tended to be small and occupied only for a single period or sporadically, as these were the satellite sites of the larger centers of Sumaysāṭ, Lidar and Gritille (Figure 16). Of the 25 sites surveyed, 21 were smaller than 0.5 ha and were classed accordingly as farmsteads. The Late Roman peak showed 'farmstead' sites evenly distributed around the tell of Gritille, which was not then occupied. On the lower terrace, sites were distributed along the Euphrates River course. Further, Late Roman pottery was found in field scatters all over the lower terrace, denoting the practice of manuring and intensive farming in fields alongside the river.

For the Early Islamic period, less well understood on this project, three sites (Sites 14, 17 and 27) were definitely occupied and three (Sites 11, 25 and 31) were possible Early Islamic sites.[16] From the published selected pottery, a sherd of moulded buffware from Site 11 is a strong indicator of Early Islamic period presence. While this feature is also seen from the Middle Islamic period on specific, local north-Syrian vessels such as pilgrim flasks, the low-relief design of circles and diamonds is strongly suggestive of ninth/tenth-century moulded buffware 'Mafjar' jugs and has parallels around the frontier in Anṭākiya, the Amuq Survey, Ḥiṣn al-Tīnāt and Ṭarsūs in the western and central *thughūr* and greater Bilād al-Shām. Three 'yellow and green glazed fine-to-medium grit-tempered red wares' are most likely Syrian yellow-glaze wares of the late eighth/early ninth century.[17] Of these Early Islamic sites, four (Sites 14, 17, 27 and 11) had preexisting Late Roman occupation. All of them were small, being less than 0.6 ha in size. All but one were located on the upper terrace: Site 27 was located midway up a tributary valley near a spring; Sites 14 and 17 were evenly distributed throughout a larger tributary valley; and Site 14 was sited near a spring. Only one of the Late Roman sites along the Euphrates was reoccupied (Site 11), showing the Early Islamic period avoidance of river sites.

Middle Islamic period occupation remained focused around springs, except for one river site. With the exception of fortified Gritille, the settlements remained smallish farmsteads but were larger than the Late Roman sites, averaging 1.19 ha in size. Thus, the total occupied area for both the Late Roman and Middle Islamic periods was the same, even though there were nearly half as many sites in the Middle Islamic. This pattern suggested a clustering of the population and cultivated fields (there was no evidence of manuring or field scatters), rather than the more dispersed Late Roman pattern. One explanation is that the unstable political landscape presented risks, resulting in nucleation and the abandonment of exposed Euphrates River sites.[18] Another explanation is that the clustering of sites around springs denoted small-scale agriculture and involvement with the nomadic/pastoral systems.[19] More specifically, the sites with springs would have accommodated groups of migrating herds in a cycle that also included post-harvest grazing among other activities. The sites were dependent on the regional centers of Gritille and Sumaysāṭ and were abandoned at the same time as these two towns were, during the late thirteenth/early fourteenth centuries. These were small settlements of mainly Christian agriculturalists and semi-pastoralists that could, in times of danger, seek safety within the larger fortified centers such as Sumaysāṭ, Tille and Lidar. By contrast, the dispersed Late Roman site patterns suggest a time of relative stability.

In the Titriş Survey sites also moved off the main mounds and occupied lower ones and there was an intensification of agriculture and movement towards a village/farmstead/villa economy (Figure 16).[20] The nature of the stony soil and the extensive manuring of sherds in the Late Roman period suggested a major viticulture economy. For the Early Islamic period, no sites were occupied in the ninth to tenth centuries and no mention was made of the seventh to ninth centuries. From his work at Kurban Höyük, Wilkinson suggested that the Late Roman settlement pattern and economical/agricultural system probably continued into the Early Islamic period. During the Middle Islamic period, four sites arranged along a watercourse were occupied – all formerly Late Roman settlements, including the mound of Titriş Höyük (Site 1).

Both Lidar Höyük Surveys yielded many of the same settlement patterns as the Titriş Survey, although with some variation (Figure 16). Roman to Early Islamic occupation on tells, when present (which was rarely), was often scanty and shifted to a lower town, as noted at Lidar Höyük. Roman to Early Islamic sites, although flat, developed into small mounds over time. The peak and densest trend in settlement in the Lidar Höyük Survey was reached in the fourth to sixth centuries, although in the Bozova-Urfa Survey, the Hellenistic period was the peak. In both, sites shifted from Hellenistic single farms under 1 ha in area to larger and more consolidated villages, evidenced by the grouping of Roman and Late Roman sites. These consolidated sites were also spaced approximately 2 km from one another in these valleys. In the Hellenistic period, sites chiefly dispersed along the Euphrates River shifted to terraces overlooking the river and to within side valleys in the Roman/Late Roman periods. This pattern indicates a variation in river-site avoidance that predates the Early Islamic period by several centuries.

Early Islamic settlement was sparse, with ten sites occupied in the Bozova-Urfa Survey (two main sites including Kurban Höyük, six with few finds and two with isolated sherds) and 11 sites in the Lidar Höyük Survey (five main sites; six smaller ones). Occupation in the Lidar region focused on two main areas: the previously densely settled Kantara Valley and the upland valleys of İncirli, Gazbek and Oğlan. Settlement mainly occurred in the seventh and eighth centuries.[21] Gerber posits that this may have been connected to an evacuation of the area by the Byzantines following the Islamic conquest; historical accounts mention the Byzantines resettling the Syrian population to Thrace. An interesting observation made by Gerber is that in the sixth century, settlement exploded on the hilly land between Ruhā and the Euphrates in part because the Byzantines were seeking refuge from the plains, whose resources were taken over by the demands of the Sāsānian armies and Bedouin tribes passing through.[22] This may explain why the hills and upland valleys east of Lidar were more densely settled in the Late Roman period than the Euphrates River region – a pattern seen elsewhere, such as in the Jabal al-ʿAqra and Syrian Jibāl. Environmental factors, such as a shift in the river or the spread of marsh, may have also contributed to the shift upland in the Late Roman period.

Rescue excavations at Tille Höyük revealed an Early Islamic occupation on the tell, which was located on the west bank of the Euphrates, east of Sumaysāṭ and Kahta (Figure 14). The tell was 26 m high although in the Euphrates valley it was located on a terrace just above the floodplain in the vicinity of springs. Early Islamic occupation was not located on the tell, save for two large pits that were found with ceramics and glass of the tenth century, according to the excavators and a coin dating to 741. The assemblage could be expanded somewhat earlier to the eighth century and possibly to the eleventh century.[23] What is immediately unusual is the complete lack of glazed wares for this Early Islamic assemblage and a seemingly discrete context for a collection of wares that span several centuries, which suggests two possibilities. At Tille and other rural sites during the Early Islamic period (or at least before the twelfth century), local ceramic traditions incorporating some typical frontier and North Syrian/Mesopotamian types – and, perhaps, even some more local wares – endured for longer periods and also dominated. The second possibility is that these pits were not discrete contexts at all, but large refuse pits (the excavators mention 'cess' pits), which were used to clear any rubbish from earlier centuries lying around (one cannot help but note the large amount of fragmentary glass). Also, no architectural phase is known from Tille during this period; as such, the pits may be related to something more ephemeral and a nearby settlement, such as the unexcavated lower town.

The site of Eski Kahta on the Kahta Çay River (Greek Nymphaios) lay at the edge of the Karababa Basin on the way north into the mountains (Figure 14). Surveys conducted by T. Goell between 1958 and 1961, in conjunction with excavations at the Seleucid settlement of Arsameia am Nymphaios across the river at Eski Kale, revealed Early Islamic splash glazes, polychrome sgraffiatos and even Chinese imports, as well as Middle Islamic twelfth- to fourteenth-century and Early Ottoman ceramics.[24] Goell and Otto-Dorn highlighted both local and imported wares and a more connected role for the settlement. The presence of a waster led the surveyor/excavators to suggest local rural production. While all of the finds were unstratified and mainly from fields around the village, the presence of an Early Islamic site here along the river may also be connected to a route into the mountains towards Malaṭiya, or at least to the Monastery of Bar Ṣawma.

Upland settlements were few and mainly monastic. After the Late Roman period, the surveyors of the Adıyaman Survey mention many Jacobite hermitages and monasteries that sprang up along the Euphrates in the Islamic periods. Another structure described is the church at Sayören, 200 m south of the village of the same name, but no date is given for it. In most cases these Christian structures begin appearing in the second half of the tenth century, after the Byzantine reconquest, through the twelfth century – for example, the fortified Church of Aharon near Malaṭiya, and the Monastery of Bar Ṣawma between Malaṭiya and Ḥiṣn Manṣūr in the district of Tepehan, village of Pereş (Figure 14).[25] There may have been mines in this region of the Anti-Taurus, as is suggested by mention of a blacksmith who made implements out of iron extracted from the uplands near Ḥiṣn Qalawdhiya (Greek Claudia/Claudioupolis).[26] In the Kurban Höyük area, Site 14, one of the Late Roman sites on the high terraces, only exhibited eighth-century brittlewares and nothing later. It is possible that this site possessed a church or monastery, which continued from the Late Roman period into the Early Islamic but was soon abandoned.

Settlement in the Malaṭtiya Plain (Tohma Basin) and Elazığ Plain (Keban Basin)

Survey around Malaṭiya has focused only on pre-Hellenistic periods, in tandem with excavations at Arslantepe. Stray finds from the eighth to eleventh centuries at the site suggest presence, but they are rather insignificant for the tell site. General settlement patterns from the Keban Dam project showed that only valleys with spring-fed streams had a reasonable number of settlements and associated agriculture (Figure 17). Most of the settlements were concentrated in the Altınova (38 sites) along the Haringet Çay stream and by the springs and in the Aşvan Valleys (eight sites) along two small and steep tributary stream valleys to the south of the Murat River Valley. Around the Aşvan area nine sites had 'Medieval' pottery and around Altınova 15 sites had 'Medieval' pottery. From the former, three sites in the Aşvan area and 13 in the Altınova area were all small occupations.[27]

Upon going through the individual site records and published information about the pottery, it is possible to detect a slight difference among site chronologies. For the Islamic period in general, ten sites were found in Aşvan and 30 in Altınova. Of these, three sites in the Aşvan area and 19 in the Altınova area qualified as Middle Islamic period. Early Islamic period sites that had no subsequent occupation would be the remaining seven sites of Aşvan and 11 sites of Altınova. Two sites (N52/7 and N52/8) in the Aşvan area that also

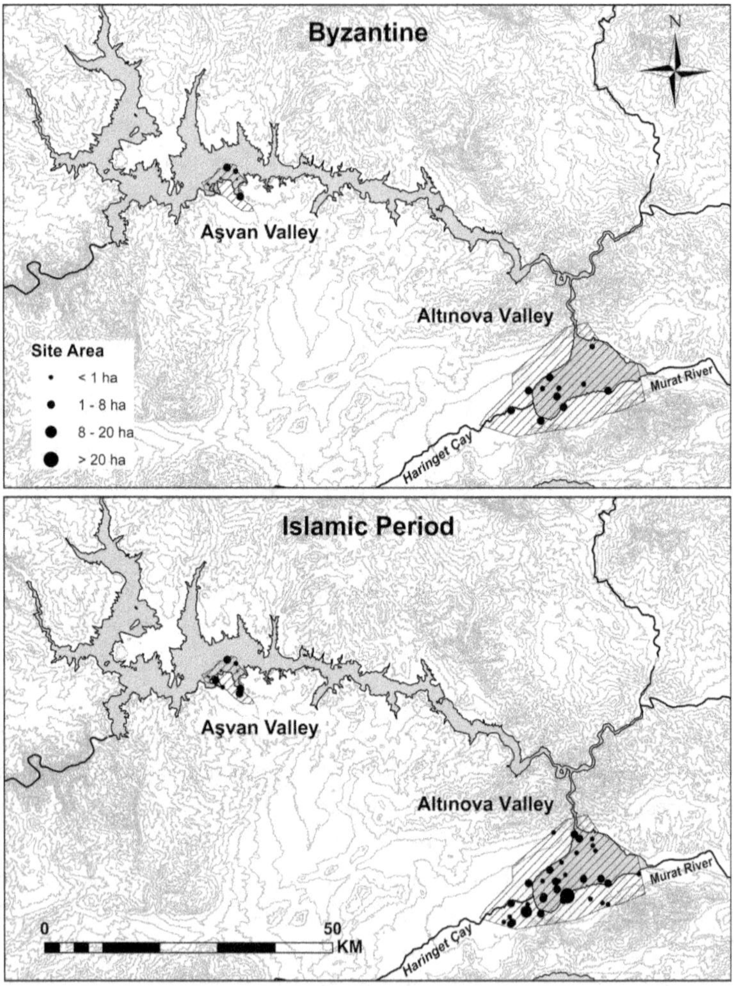

Figure 17 Aşvan and Altınova Surveys, Byzantine and Islamic sites (based on Whallon 1979, Figure 3)

had no preexisting occupation are likely candidates. Both of these had only 'Medieval Brick ware' assemblages and were river sites, not tells. but river sites. N52/7 was a surface scatter on a small natural rise near a stream north of the Murat River. N52/8 exhibited some ruined foundations on a small rise near a stream and spring. In the Altınova area, two sites (O54/17 and O54/18) were also surface scatters. O54/18's assemblage comprised only 'Medieval Brick ware'. From the surveyors, there was no clear pattern established in the Middle Islamic period. However, the fact that virtually all these sites were inhabited shows an extensive occupation. Furthermore, those sites yielding diagnostic Middle Islamic pottery (sgraffiato and monochrome glazed wares) constituted about half the total, or twice the number of sites without glazes. If one were to conjecture roughly about Early Islamic period settlement in the area without later occupation, then it would follow a pattern seen in other zones of the frontier: few Early Islamic period sites, followed by a more extensive occupation in the Middle Islamic period.

Way Stations

Two sites were located in close proximity east and west of Sumaysāṭ on the Euphrates. These were part of an east–west route that crossed the frontier. At Kurban Höyük on the Euphrates, a 57 × 57 m square building was excavated and dated to the ninth century as a single period of occupation with no reuse.[28] Only the building's foundations were preserved as it had no entrances. It also had no towers or buttresses, but rooms arranged around a courtyard. The ceramics included many splash-glazed varieties, yellow glaze and moulded buffwares. This was most likely a way station poised on the Raqqa–Sarūj–Sumaysāṭ road[29] linking northern Mesopotamia (al-Jazīra) with the *thughūr* and the Mar'ash–Ra'bān–Sumaysāṭ west–east road. Further upstream, a 20 × 18 m rectilinear building was excavated at Lidar Höyük. While originally thought to be Late Roman, it was later determined to be Early Islamic period and contemporaneous with the building at Kurban.[30] Another possible way station was Site 11 in the Gritille Survey. It was also a rectangular enclosure, measuring 57 × 51 m, whose main occupation was in the eighth to tenth centuries, as shown by the yellow-glaze and moulded buffwares. These three sites are too close together to be one day's travel apart (from Sumaysāṭ, Kurban Höyük is 11 km west; Lidar Höyük is 6 km east). Nevertheless, they speak to an intensification in way stations in this fertile and wide section of the Upper Euphrates known as the Karababa Basin. Ḥiṣn Manṣūr was also on this route connecting Sumaysāṭ (32 km to the south) and Malaṭiya (about 150 km to the north) and, I hypothesize, was part of this system, although it has not been excavated.

Towns

Sumaysāṭ, the largest settlement in the Karababa Basin (80 ha in area), was not near the frontier but was an important town and tell that functioned as the only major river crossing in the Karababa Basin until the traveller reached Malaṭiya and as a crossroads for routes from Raqqa to Malaṭiya and Ḥadath to Āmid (the *qaṣabah* of Diyar Bakr, Greek Amida, modern Diyarbakr). It was also the farthest point one could sail up the Euphrates River. The city was taken during the reign of ʿUmar I (r. 624–44) and, interestingly, its citizens were asked to make sure that travellers (i.e. Muslims) were guided properly and to maintain its bridges and roads.[31] The town was one of those most besieged of any *thughūr* settlement by both Byzantines and Islamic armies, likely on account of its well-connected location. Despite this, there are hardly any references to building activity except for rebuilding of the city walls in 813, most probably at the start of Ma'mūn's reign (his brother and predecessor Amīn paid little attention to the *thughūr*). Tenth-century descriptions do mention a congregational mosque and fortress on the mound, the *qal'āt al-ṭin* (Castle of Clay), which were perhaps constructed of mud brick. The town also had an important Christian community, surmised by a continuous line of bishops from the mid-eighth to twelfth centuries, interrupted only between 641 and 737. The town was a center for (indeed, the birthplace of) the Paulician movement. Excavations by Goell in 1967 on the tell exposed a palace or ruler's residence dated to the twelfth to thirteenth centuries, was associated with the local frontier dynasty, the Artūqids, and built of mud brick over reused stone foundations. The local construction style can be hypothesized for earlier periods. Stratified Early Islamic period deposits contained what appear to be mainly local ceramics forms and imported glass. Furthermore, there is direct continuity from the Late Roman to Early Islamic periods, with no period of abandonment. Sumaysāṭ is unusual in that it was an inhabited tell site. However, the Kurban Höyük Survey importantly noted a 50-ha lower town where most of the population during this period would have resided. The city wall, partly excavated, was a casemate (double wall), likely rebuilt many times, although the post-Roman construction was dated to the Artūqid period based on an inscription. The aqueduct from the Kahta River may have ceased working by the Early Islamic period. As such, the city would have depended on water-lifting devices. Islamic geographers mention that irrigation was necessary to supplement the region's rainfall.[32]

Another town, albeit a minor one, was Sarūj (Greek Battnae, modern Suruç), whose name in Arabic derived from the Syriac, Sarugh. CORONA imagery clearly shows, as late as the 1960s, a roughly square enclosure for the settlement measuring around 650 × 740 m (48 ha), which is now entirely invisible under the modern town. It had a notable Christian community, including the famous sixth-century bishop Jacob of Serugh (451–521), as well as a small Jewish community. Michael the Syrian mentions that Hārūn al-Rashīd brought water to it from the Euphrates via canals.[33]

In the Malaṭiya and Elazığ Plains, important towns were located mainly along the north–south and east–west routes that connected the frontier lands, rather than along the Euphrates River. Further, despite the mountainous terrain of the eastern *thughūr*, they were all situated in the lowlands. As such, the major settlements were used both as way stations and frontier posts.

Malaṭiya (Greek Melitene, modern Battalgazi) was the most important frontier city after Ṭarsūs, if one is to judge from its presence in written sources. As Ṭarsūs occupied the western end of the *thughūr*, Malaṭiya held the eastern position. Its site is walled and rectangular, measuring 500 × 300 m with a double wall, ditch and both square and polygonal prow-shaped towers and the river flows by its eastern side. Ibn Serapion (w. *c.*900) mentioned that watercourses were brought from Nahr Malaṭiya (modern Shakhma Su) into the city, thence flowing into the Qubāqib below the bridge on

Euphrates.[34] The city was first conquered during the reign of 'Umar I and then by Mu'āwiya and Hishām (r. 724–43) and rebuilt under al-Manṣūr (r. 754–75). Ibn Shaddād from Ya'qūbī (d. 897/8) states that the city was divided into seven quarters, one per tribe (i.e. Sulaym, Qays), which was also the basis for military organization. There was also a continuous line of bishops since at least the ninth century and possibly earlier. At times, Malaṭiya has been considered part of Byzantine land, according to Byzantine sources. While it was besieged several times, the city maintained its mainly Islamic status, which verged (like that of Ṭarsūs) on outright independence in several instances – particularly after a Byzantine siege in 926/7, when Baghdād was unable (or unwilling) to help.

South-west of Malaṭiya was Zibatra (Greek Sozopetra, modern Doğanşehir), a roughly square town enclosed by double city walls that are still visible, measuring 220 × 280 m. Ibn Serapion stated that the Qarāqīs passes near the city gate. It was a Late Roman period town taken in the late eighth century and rebuilt four times by al-Manṣūr, Hārūn al-Rashīd, al-Ma'mūn and al-Mu'taṣim (r. 833–42) – each time after a Byzantine attack. The last time, the caliph added four *ḥusun* around it. The town was also a bishopric, with bishops known from at least the second half of the eighth century to the Byzantine reconquest. Reaching westward towards Byzantine lands like a finger is the settlement of Ṭaranda (Greek Taranta). Its history is poorly known, but it had an Islamic garrison between 702 and 719 and was regarded as a Paulician fortress in the late ninth century (872). The settlement lay in the main valley as a *maslaḥa* (outpost) guarding the road connecting Malaṭiya and Cappadocia.

Ḥiṣn Ziyād and Shimshāṭ were located in the Elazığ Plain, farther upstream on the Euphrates. Ḥiṣn Ziyād (Greek Enzitene) in the eastern Altınova Plain appears only in the tenth century and was also the settlement of a Jacobite bishopric, although associated with a Slav who was appointed as ruler by Marwān II (r. 744–50). Shimshāṭ (Greek Arsamosata) on the Nahr Arsanās was rebuilt by the prolific Ṣāliḥ b. al-'Alī, who was associated with many activities during al-Manṣūr's reign. The site consists of an upland Hellenistic fort and a lower, walled Islamic town, although when in the Early Islamic period this was added is unknown. Ibn Serapion mentioned that there were six more forts, all unnamed, after Ḥiṣn Ziyād before the Nahr Arsanās joined the Euphrates.[35] Ḥiṣn Qalawdhiya was a *maslaḥa* of Malaṭiya, also rebuilt during al-Manṣūr's reign but presently unknown, although likely at the Late Roman settlement of Claudias (also unknown), which would have been corrupted to Qalawdhiya and located somewhere near the Euphrates (about 60 km southeast of Malaṭiya) in the vicinity of Koldere/Doğanyol – perhaps Kale, judging by the name, or Pütürge, where the remains of a Late Roman fortification were found.[36] In this situation, it would be *en route* from Sumaysāṭ/Ḥiṣn Manṣūr to Malaṭiya via the eastern Euphrates approach. Shimshāṭ and Ḥiṣn Ziyād would have lain on the route to Malaṭiya. In a sense, all three were outposts of Malaṭiya. We can also mention briefly the settlement of Pālūyah (modern Palu), which also corresponds with Bīlū and Pīlīn and is mentioned in the *Life* of Theodota of Amida as being in the 'region of the fortresses (Figure 14)'.[37]

Hisn Kamkh (Greek Kamacha) lay far to the north, adjacent to Armenian lands and was considered the town closest to the source of the Euphrates along with the unlocated Ḥisn al-Minshār. The settlement changed hands back and forth, but was taken during the caliphates of Mu'āwiya (r. 661–80) and Yazīd II (r. 720–4). The inhabitants of Ḥiṣn Kamkh helped defend it against Constantine V's attack. It was described as a castle with a lower town and fields along the riverbank and merchants (and, presumably, a market) were established there. Qālīqalā or Arḍ/Arzan al-Rūm (Greek Theodosiopolis, modern Erzurum) was first conquered by Ubaydalla b. 'Abd al-Malik under 'Abd al-Malik. It was retaken by Constantine V and rebuilt by al-Manṣūr. The site consisted of a castle with a lower town on the Nahr al-Furāt (Western Euphrates). Malaṭiya and Qālīqalā were among the locations settled by Jazīran soldiers, who were given lands to farm.[38]

Under al-Manṣūr, a policy of stabilization and refortification of the eastern *thughūr* is evident. He built in Zibaṭra, Malaṭiya, Shimshāṭ, Ḥiṣn Qalawdhiya, Ḥiṣn Kamkh and Qālīqalā at the far north-eastern end of the *thughūr* zone. Much of this work was carried out by his uncle, the governor Ṣāliḥ b. 'Alī. This work was an attempt to secure key road and river points within a frontier zone that remained as often in Byzantine hands or independently controlled as under caliphal control.[39]

Conclusions

The eastern *thughūr* was more sparsely settled with small rural settlements than the eastern central *thughūr* around Ḥalab and more similar to the Amuq and Kahramanmaraş Plains. Settlements were reduced by half from the Late Roman period. Route and river sites continued, although the Euphrates was only used as a crossing for land routes. Slight changes are noticeable from the Amuq and Ḥalab Plains, specifically the association of sites near springs and spring-fed streams, with far fewer notable canal-building projects. Practically, this can be explained by the fact that most of this region was within a rain-fed agricultural zone. Tells were still avoided for the most part, although some of the major towns like Sumaysāṭ and the farthest northern sites featured combinations of lower towns with tell or upland fortifications, perhaps alluding to a more unstable political landscape or local initiatives of self-preservation.

CHAPTER 4

THE JAZĪRA (BALIKH AND KHĀBŪR RIVER VALLEYS)

They came to own the lands – its rivers becoming their property –
Without commiting any injustice or seeking fame
You [the Caliph Hishām] *have been blessed with canals flowing from the hump of the Euphrates*
Among them the Hanī and another that flows in Qarqarā.[1]

The Jazīra, or northern Mesopotamia, is not considered part of the *thughūr* or *'awāṣim* provinces. Topographically, however, the region sits behind the eastern *thughūr* in the same way that the *'awāṣim* of North Syria sits behind the northernmost part of the central *thughūr*. Like the *'awāṣim*, it was an initial *thughūr* during the conquests. Al-Ṭabarī mentions that Qarqīsiyā and al-Mawṣil were *thughūr* cities of al-Kūfā in the early days of the conquest of 'Iraq in 638–9.[2] Archaeology provides a more nuanced view and a physical gauge. Evidence from survey does, in fact, show that these regions were not only distinctive but further broken down into micro-regions with differing patterns of settlement. While the western *'awāṣim* around Anṭākiya had nearly twice as many settlements as the frontier regions to the north (but half that of the Late Roman period), the number of settlements could not be considered dense and settlement patterns and processes over time were nearly identical. This is similar to, but also, in some respects different from the eastern *awāṣim* near Ḥalab, where patterns were similar but density was greater. The Jazīra, in contrast, exhibited Early Islamic period settlement patterns of densities that were twice as high or more as those of the Late Roman period and related to those in central lands rather than the frontiers. These patterns were visible in the main river valleys of the Balikh, Khābūr, and Middle Euphrates, but not on the eastern edges of the province. Increased settlement was a result of intensive agricultural and irrigation activities in major river valleys, increased personal attention and encouragement by the central state to settle in the late Umayyad and early ʻAbbāsid period, and numerous Christian communities already present.

The Environment

This region, administratively divided into three tribal districts, can be geographically divided into two main Euphrates tributary river valleys, whose watersheds were the nuclei of settlement: the Balikh in the Diyār Muḍar and the Khābūr in the Diyār Rabīʻa (Figure 18). Although separated by the modern Turkish–Syrian border, the Harran Plain and Balikh River Valley together form one topographic unit, a lowland incised by the Balikh River and other seasonal tributaries, such as the Jullab and Daysan (Kara Koyun) Rivers, which begin around Ruhā and flow south into Syria, emptying into the Euphrates – a distance of about 100 km. They comprise one region, but differing amounts of evidence from archaeological work and varying rainfall zones suggests two distinct areas. Like the Amuq Plain, the Harran Plain is a broad lowland about 400 m.a.s.l. It is bordered to the east by the Tektek Mountains and to the west by a series of low hills. The Harran Plain slopes north (470 m.a.s.l.) to south (345 m.a.s.l.), with a gradient of 0.2 per cent; it has no outcrops except for its many tells. This area receives 300–400 mm/annum of rain and the plain is very fertile and watered by the Jullab River, whose source comes from the mountains north of Ruhā. The river is the primary water source for the Harran Plain and empties into the Balikh. The Urfa-Harran Basin was very susceptible to flooding, as has been documented by Classical and medieval texts.[3] Wheat, lentils, chickpeas, fruit and vegetables were cultivated.

As one progresses south, the landscape becomes more sparsely vegetated into the steppes of northern Syria, and rainfall grows less frequent. The Balikh Valley Survey, while part of the same topographical region of semi-arid steppe, presents a slightly different scenario. Most of the valley is at or just below the 250 mm/annum rainfall isohyet zone, necessitating irrigation agriculture. Pastoralism would have been an important element on the largely unsettled upland pastures. Although part of the Jazīra, the region, as a fertile land south of the eastern frontier along the Taurus Mountains, is analogous to that between the *'awāṣim* region and the western frontier as a productive frontier hinterland. The floodplain of the Balikh basin is 70 km from east to west and about 100 km from north to south, and is bordered by limestone and gypsum plateaus. The river itself (Greek Bilecha) is narrow, 6 m wide, and originates in the subterranean springs in the Harran Plain at either 'Ayn al-'Arus or, according to Ibn Serapion, 'Ayn al-Dhabbāniyya or al-Dhahbāna. Several other streams flow into the Balikh, including the Wādī Ḥamar from the north-east, before it empties into the Euphrates at Raqqa.

To the east, the Khābūr was a similarly fertile area of several streams that were foci for settlement including, besides the Khābūr River (Greek Aboras or Khaboras), the Wādī al-Jaghjagh (Nahr al-Hirmas, Greek Mygdonius or Saocoras), Wādī Jarra, and Wādī Khanzīr flowing south from the Ṭūr 'Abdin uplands creating a well-watered north–south linear environment before gathering into the primary Khābūr River and flowing into the Euphrates. The Wādī Rudd crosses the southern portion of the plain, contributing to a wetland zone. The Khābūr originates near Ra's al-'Ayn at 'Ayn al-Zahiriyya, while the Hirmas' source is the Ṭūr 'Abdīn around Naṣībīn. Between these river valleys were pasturelands. Like the Balikh and Harran Plains, the northern half of the Khābūr and its far east, around Tell al-Hawa, were within the 350–450 mm rainfall zone, allowing dry farming, as in the Ḥarran Plain, while the southern half, in the 200–250 mm marginal zone when these two main rivers join, necessitated irrigation, similar to the Balikh region. Settlement and irrigation in the southern half of the Khābūr were focused mainly along the river itself on terraces as it cut through an upland plateau, the Jabal ʿAbd al-Azīz to the west, and Jabal Jembe and Jabal Sinjār to the east. Settlement patterns were also dictated by several geological sub-regions such as the arid Hemma basalt plateau near Tell Beydar, which was poor for agriculture but important for pastoralism.

The primary rain-fed crops grown between October and late May were wheat and barley, with legumes as a secondary crop. Cotton was a main summer crop grown in the Balikh, Harran, and Khābūr plains and exported to Syria, the Jazīra, and beyond. Michael the Syrian first mentions cotton grown in the Jazīra in 842.[4] Rice was also grown as a summer crop. Raqqa produced olive oil, soap and reed for pens – the last-named undoubtedly from its marsh grasses. The towns of the Jazīra were known for their nuts, including walnuts, nuts, pistachios and hazelnuts; fruit (raisins and figs); and dairy produce, including cooking butter and cheese. These were exported south to ʿIraq by land or river.

As implied by its famous dairy products, in addition to agricultural activity the Jazīra was most known for its pastures, ideal for animal husbandry, which supported otherwise relatively low crop yields (as compared to the much richer lands of southern ʿIraq).[5] The pasturelands between the Euphrates and the Tigris River (Nahr Dijla) were home to nomadic and semi-nomadic pastoralists from Northern Arabia well before the rise of Islam (Figure 2). The Bahrāʾ lived in the middle Euphrates area. The Taghlib were descended from the Northern Arabian Rabīʿa, and were largely Christian semi-settled groups who owned ploughable land and herds (*aṣḥāb ḥurūth wa-mawāsh*) in the Jazīra.[6] A clan of this tribe, the Hamdān, was already active in the seventh century, 300 years before their rise as an important independent dynasty. The Iyād and Namir were based south of the Taghlib. The Bakr, also descendant from the Rabīʿa, was a settled tribe with smaller subclans, such as the Thaʿlaba, ʿIjl, and Dhuhl. Several tribes were more nomadic than others, such as the Tamīm, Kilāb and Kalb, who were also partially Christian. They were active as major traders over the Taurus Mountains and also served as messengers, reputedly delivering, for example, the Prophet

Muḥammad's letter to Heraklios.[7] Indeed, the administrative subdivision of the province into three large tribal territories (Rabī'a, Bakr and Muḍar) as compared to the *ajnād* divisions of Syria reinforce the central state's acknowledgement of tribal influence and power.[8] Finally, it should be emphasized that the Jazīra, and in particular the area of Ṭūr 'Abdin, was home to many Christian communities, including those centered on monasteries and bishoprics.

Bisected by the major urban centers of Ruhā, Ḥarrān (Greek Karrhai) and Raqqa (Greek Kallinikos), the Harran Plain and Balikh River Valley formed a continuously utilized major transportation and trade route for south–north roads heading to the *thughūr* and its east–west routes. Indeed, 'Ḥarrān' comes from the Akkadian word for caravan route or way station. The name reverted to its Semitic origin in the Islamic period.[9] The Balikh route went: Raqqa–Ḥiṣn Maslama–Ḥarrān–Ruhā. The main towns of the Khābūr were located in its northern half: Ra's al-'Ayn to the west and Naṣībīn towards the center. A main east–west road connected these from Raqqa to Naṣībīn via the Balikh, then Ra's al-'Ayn, then Adhrama, Barqa'īd, Balad and Mawṣil. A south–north road followed the Khābūr on either side of the channel between Naṣībīn and Qarqīsiyā at the confluence of the Middle Euphrates River. A road connected Balad and Mawṣil with Qarqīsiyā via Sinjār across the arid eastern Khābūr. At the far west, a road connected Jisr Raqqa with Jisr Manbij via Dawsar. On a whole, the rural and pastoralist-dominated Jazīra was not evenly distributed with urban centers, necessitating way stations to act both as transportation foci and safe, well-watered stopping points for caravans passing through.

Survey Methodology

In general, transitional ceramics from the late Sāsānian to Early Islamic periods (sixth to eighth centuries) are more difficult to discern in the Jazīra than North Syria. This is mainly due to a lack of stratified contexts in excavated sites. In this region, rural/canal sites, and way stations are difficult to distinguish as separate sites, and even large sites had way stations attached. As such, they are considered together.

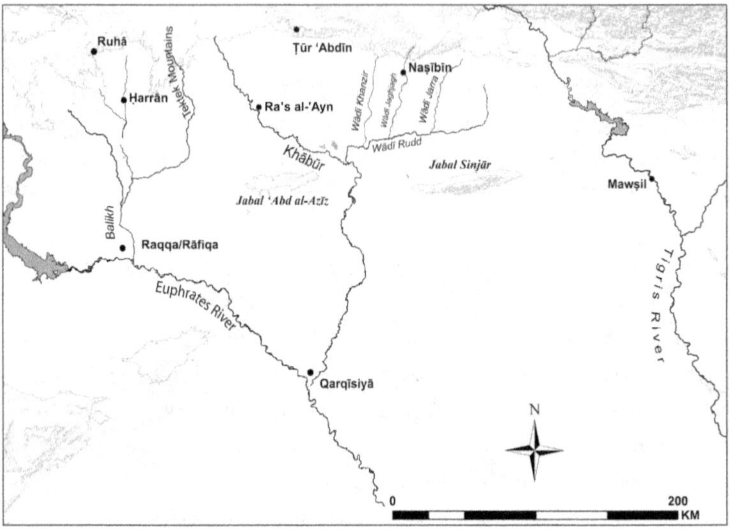

Figure 18 The Jazīra

Group I: Extensive/Low-Resolution/Large-Area Surveys

Several surveys in both the Balikh and Khābūr Valleys before 1990 did little to distinguish Late Roman/Sāsānian and Islamic period settlement, or else dated sites broadly as Islamic. The surveys show a continuity or increase in Islamic settlement.[10] However, these numbers cannot be taken in any meaningful way as the chronology employed was not subdivided between Early and Middle Islamic periods. As such, only general observations can be made.

The Harran Plain Survey, directed by Yardımcı, was part of the GAP salvage work (Figure 19). The team covered a large area of 2,000 km^2 and found a total of 208 sites (including Ḥarrān itself) in the lowland plain districts of Harran, Akçakale, and Mesudiye. The aim of the survey, besides the recording of the GAP project, was to complement the excavations on the mound of Ḥarrān. The surveyors concentrated on recording and measuring mainly tells and low mounds; however, they documented flat sites and the occasional ceramic scatter when found. While the publication is visually impressive, the dating for the Roman and Late Roman (or Parthian

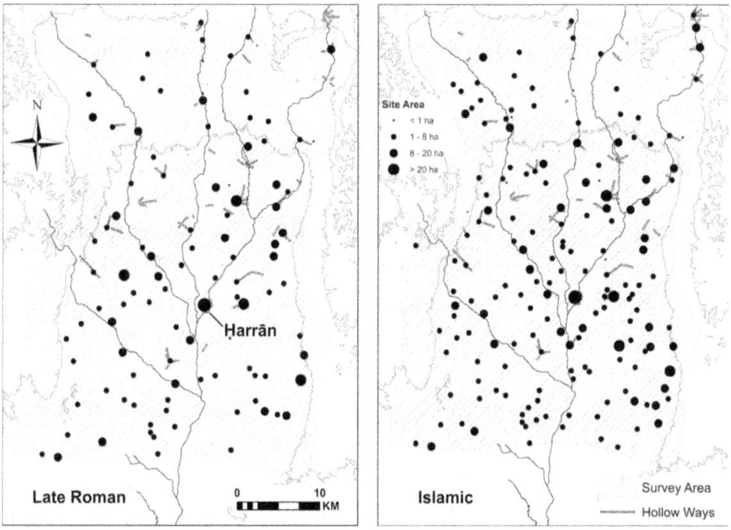

Figure 19 Harran Survey, Late Roman and Islamic sites (based on Yardımcı 2004, 393 and 394)

and Sāsānian) and Islamic periods is unspecified as compared, for example, to the three subdivisions that they employ within the Chalcolithic period. For the Classical periods, sites fall within the Hellenistic (18 sites) or Roman periods (103 sites) and there is absolutely no mention of Late Roman sites. For the Islamic periods, sites were dated only generally from the seventh to the twentieth centuries. From the settlement map, one can see that this is already problematic as 175 sites (out of 208) are Islamic, a number which is undifferentiated by sub-period and therefore meaningless. This large gap in the settlement record between the Roman and Islamic periods is unexplained. Presumably, Late Roman period sites are included within the Roman period. Very little systematic analysis can therefore be done; however, an extremely rough reinterpretation based on whatever ceramics were published reveals three main trends.[11] First, the Middle Islamic period had twice as many sites as the Early Islamic. In the latter period, 15 per cent of the total number of sites were occupied, while in the Middle Islamic period this number climbs to 30 per cent. This 2:1 ratio is also seen in other surveys throughout the frontier. Second, of the 15 sites with only definite Islamic occupation (single-period sites), 14 were flat or low-mounded. Of these, eight sites were definite Early Islamic period new foundations, five were possibly so, and one was not.[12] In the Middle Islamic period, about 40 sites were on tells while only 20 were on low mounds/flat sites. Third, the majority of the northern part of the plain was unoccupied in the Early Islamic period, the emphasis then being on the southern plain around the vicinity of Ḥarrān and the route between Ruhā and Ḥarrān. This pattern fits closely with that seen in the Kahramanmaraş Plain, with sites congregating in the wetlands of the lower part of the valley.

The Khābūr surveys include W. J. van Liere's and J. Lauffray's Khabur Survey (1954–5), D. Meijer's Eastern Khabur Survey (1976, 1977 and 1979) and B. Lyonnet's Upper Khabur Survey (1989) (Figure 20). Van Liere and Lauffray's survey was lacking in sufficient-quality ground control, quantifiable data, clear chronologies for the first millennium CE and phase maps – and, in many instances, resorted to guesswork based on site morphology and scale. However, even gross settlement patterns and general observations provide several insightful and clear trends in the Roman/Parthian, Late Roman/Sāsānian, and Islamic periods. From the large map, 15 towns, ten 'open towns', and 19 military camps were discernible, dating to the 'classique ou arabe' periods. Of this type, the authors correctly noted that many of these, assumed to be Roman military *limes* fortifications, are in fact Islamic sites.[13] Small hamlets, farms and other agricultural installations dotted the plains; there were more than 100 from the area west of Ra's al-'Ayn alone. Van Liere and Lauffray noted that, while Classical and Islamic period settlement was very dense in the Khābūr, the eastern edge was the least well inhabited.'[14]

Important observations can be obtained from van Liere and Lauffray's survey. All Late Roman/Sāsānian and Islamic period sites were founded near springs, rivers or wadis and were usually new foundations, away from tells although often quite near them as groups of low mounds several meters high, while the pre-Classical sites were more densely settled on the plateau. However, the surveyors noted that glazed green pottery was found on almost all tells, which may denote a Middle Islamic period occupation signifying a return to tells as a common pattern. At times, isolated farms or military posts were sited away from water sources. In addition to way stations and towns, surveyors recorded hundreds of hamlets and isolated farms on the borders of wadis and along the northern slopes of the Jabal ʿAbd al-Azīz. Several sites were also noted south of these mountains in the plateau area. The Khābūr River itself was more intensively occupied, with many preexisting Islamic sites along the river – sometimes as twin sites on either bank, sometimes as agglomerations of several sites. In the eastern portion of the Khābūr, the Diyār Rabīʿa, the number of towns, villages and farms decreased significantly in the Islamic period, although several large walled cities were recorded including a Roman/Late Roman 48-ha site identified with Thebeta. The surveyors argue that Islamic period occupation was confined primarily to the western and central portions of the Khābūr.

Meijer's survey of the eastern Khābūr from Tell Brak to the ʿIraq border recorded more than 300 sites, but listed only 290, of which 53 were Late Roman (Byzantine) and 94 were broadly Islamic period (Figure 20). The surveyors stated that Islamic period occupation was 'only indicated where a considerable presence was noted', and only illustrated two body sherds – moulded buff/creamware examples – in their type drawings. No phase maps were provided for any first millennium CE sites. From this information, it is difficult to gain a better understanding of their methods; however, on a rudimentary and largely meaningless level, there was denser settlement of Islamic as compared to the Late Roman period sites in the survey.

In 1989, B. Lyonnet conducted a survey in the upper Khābūr area between Hasseke to the south, Ra's al-ʿAyn to the north-west and Qāmishlī to the north-east. She surveyed 64 sites, focusing on tells. She recorded 29 definite and 14 indefinite Late Roman/Sāsānian period sites and 14 Early Islamic period sites. The decreased Islamic period presence led to some unfortunate conjectures about heavy taxation, endless war, disease and plague. Methodologically, the survey failed to consider satellite sites to tell and non-tell sites (although noting the former), which had been noted earlier by van

Liere and Lauffray as the key settlement characteristic of Roman/Parthian through Islamic period sites (Figure 20).

Group II: Intensive/High-Resolution/Small-Area Surveys

Intensive surveys from 1986 to the present mainly focused on large tells. They include the North Jazira Survey by T. J. Wilkinson, W. Ball, and D. Tucker (1986–90), Tell Beydar by Wilkinson and J. Ur (1997–8), Tell Hamoukar by Ur (1999) and Tell Brak by Ur, P. Karsgaard, and J. Oates (2003–6). These surveys have benefited from consistency of surveyors (namely Wilkinson and Ur) and, accordingly, identical methodologies and ceramic chronologies. The regional survey around Tell Leilan (1984, 1987, 1995 and 1997) can be placed in this category although it was larger in area (1,650 km^2) and benefited for one season (1995) from a closer study of its Islamic period ceramics (Figure 22).[15]

Between 1986 and 1990, the North Jazira Survey conducted fieldwork around the site of Tell al-Hawa, north-east of Jabal Sinjār on the eastern edge of the Khābūr area, with Wilkinson, W. Ball and D. Tucker. They recorded 184 sites within 475 km^2 and excavated four of them. The survey publication contains a wealth of information, considering closely the geomorphology, ethnographic studies and field scatters, hollow ways (radial routes from sites connecting to other sites), and non-tell settlements, in addition to the surrounding tells. Settlement levels dropped from 66 Parthian sites to 41 transitional Sāsānian-Early Islamic period sites to 37 Early Islamic period sites.[16]

More recently, surveys have been conducted around Tell Beydar, Tell Brak, Tell Hamoukar and Tell Leilan, some of the largest mounds in the Khābūr.[17] The Tell Beydar Survey, conducted in 1997 and 1998 by T. J. Wilkinson and J. A. Ur, discovered 82 sites within a 450 km^2 survey area.[18] Its focus was on recording non-tell sites: 13 of them were Sāsānian period, eight were definitely Early Islamic period (two were indefinite), and two sites were Middle Islamic period. The Tell Hamoukar Survey, an excellent example of survey publication, yielded interesting results. In it, the Sāsānian period (Period 15) experienced a drop in sites from 15 in the Parthian/

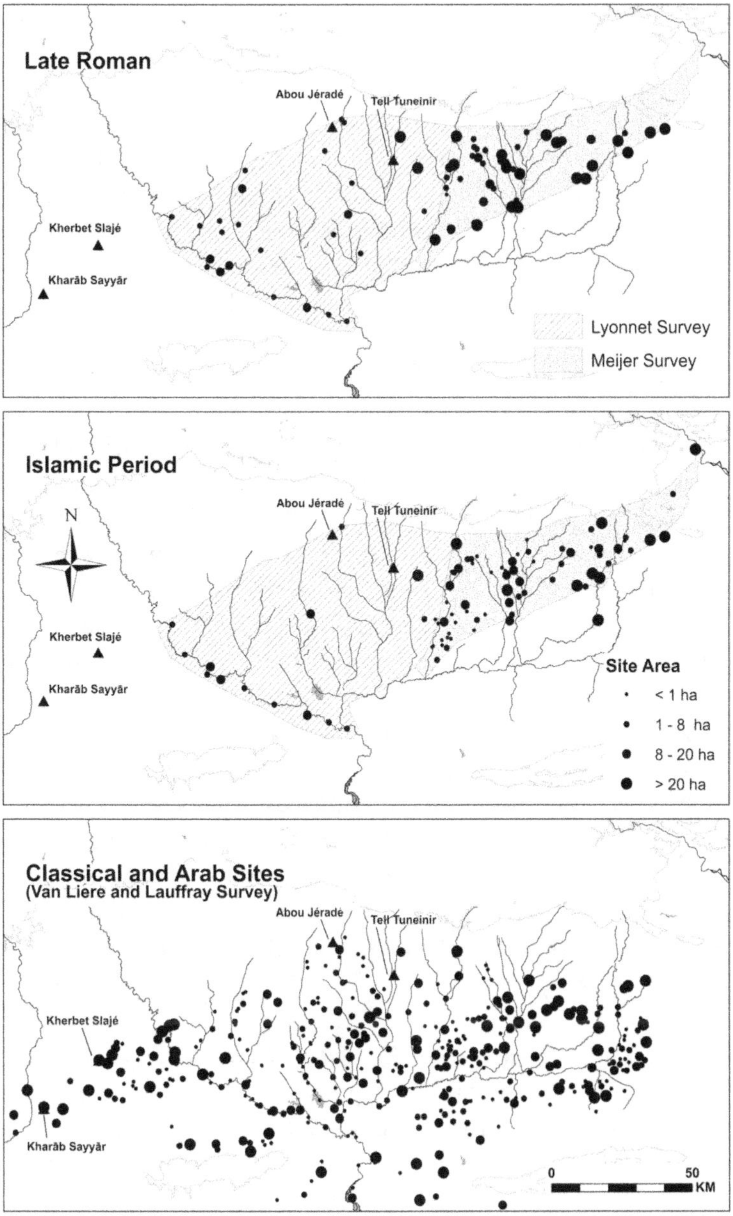

Figure 20 Group I, Khābūr Survey sites, Late Roman and Islamic sites

Roman to four, which then recovered to 15 in the Late Sāsānian/Early Islamic period (Period 16) and remained steady through the eighth to tenth centuries (Period 17, 13 sites).[19] In the Middle Islamic period, site occupation was greatly reduced to eight.

At Tell Leilan, the surveyors revisited several of Meijer and Lyonnet's sites. A total of 324 of them are recorded for the survey; however, only 104 were considered. Of these sites, 47 were Islamic period, with six subdivisions: (1) 'Early Islamic' (late eighth to ninth centuries): six sites; (2) 'Abbāsid (tenth to eleventh centuries): 13 sites; (3) Ayyūbid (twelfth to thirteenth centuries): 33 sites; (4) Mamlūk (late thirteenth to fourteenth centuries): 20 sites; (5) Late Islamic (fifteenth to sixteenth centuries): five sites; and (6) Ottoman (seventeenth to twentieth centuries): five sites. Like the Balikh Valley Survey, no seventh- to eighth-century Umayyad presence was detected, suggesting a combination of a low sedentary population and poor knowledge of the ceramics of this period. While the close study of the Islamic ceramics and settlement patterns reflects important advances in our knowledge of the Khābūr, the subdivisions employed by Vezzoli based on ceramic diagnostics are finely subdivided into narrow chronologies that are perhaps too optimistic, given our knowledge of ceramics of this period and region.[20] For example, the division between Early Islamic and 'Abbāsid is peculiar, and the two periods can be combined to roughly approximate an Early Islamic 2 period. This would make 17 sites rather than 19, as two were doubly counted. The Middle Islamic period showed a peak in settlement of more than double the previous total, or 41 sites (rather than 55) when the Ayyūbid and Mamlūk periods are combined.

Group III: Extensive/High-Resolution/Islamic-focused Surveys

The Balikh (1983) and Middle Euphrates (1987–90) Surveys are the most reliable for a nuanced discussion of Islamic period settlement of the Jazīra, the most comparable to the Amuq and Maraş Surveys, and perhaps the only ones that had an Islamic ceramic specialist, thus potentially readily identifying sites with Early Islamic period assemblages. The Balikh Survey was conducted by the University of

Amsterdam under M. N. van Loon and P. M. M. G. Akkermans (Figure 21). The project was intended to contextualize Tell Hammam et-Turkman in a regional survey. In total, 200 sites from all periods were found in a region that extended from Raqqa northwards to the Turkish border just south of Ḥarrān, following the Balikh River: an area of 2,074 km^2. K. Bartl was able to date the Islamic period ceramics more precisely, and accordingly to recognize sites and key settlement patterns between the sub-periods of the eighth to tenth, eleventh, and twelfth to thirteenth centuries. A total of 23 sites were definite Late Roman period, with an additional 14 indefinite. No less than 55 sites were definitely Early Islamic period (eighth to tenth centuries), with an additional 25 indefinite – an astonishingly high per centage of the total number of sites, which differs significantly from results from all other frontier regions. These sites were dated by stratified material at Raqqa and Madīnat al-Fār, and assemblages typically included common buffware basins with broad, slightly carinated rims, brittlewares and splash-glazed ceramics. By contrast, four were eleventh century and eight were twelfth to thirteenth centuries, although it is unclear whether the 25 indefinite Early Islamic period sites that the surveyors mention as being characterized by green or turquoise glazed monochrome sherds also date to these periods or are more transitional Sāsānian wares. The former seems more likely. Wilkinson conducted a hydrological and settlement survey, identifying important irrigation systems.[21]

At the farthest limits of our assessment, it is worth including the data and conclusions from the Middle Euphrates Survey, conducted between 1987 and 1990, as it is part of the same settlement phenomenon for the Balikh and Khābūr and is an example of remarkable, comprehensive, and well-presented research on Islamic settlement specifically, thereby confirming previously speculative patterns (Figure 23). The survey area was 1,300 km^2 along the Euphrates, up- and downstream from the confluence of the Khābūr in an area that was just below the level of rainfall required for dry-farming, at or less than 150 mm/annum. Out of the 209 sites identified, 171 were classified as settlements. Eighteen of these were Late Roman. However, in the Islamic period, 146 were occupied either permanently or seasonally. Of the permanent settlements, 31 were preexisting, while 72 were newly founded. The archaeologists excavated soundings and obtained carbon-14 dates, leading them to distinguish across at least six phases of Islamic settlement utilizing, for example, newly-founded 'Abbāsid single-period-occupation sites to establish localized internal chronologies in order to differentiate them from Umayyad sites. Site certainty, whether definite or indefinite, was also indicated.

Settlement in the Balikh Valley

In the Late Roman period, Edessa (Ruhā) and Karrhai (Ḥarrān) in the Harran Plain in the Osrhoene province were the focal points and urban centers in the Late Roman period, and were fortified by Justinian. The Balikh replaced them during the Early Islamic period (Figure 21). The first observation in the Balikh Valley noted by Bartl was the same dispersed pattern of settlement from the Roman/ Parthian period to the Islamic period thirteenth century. Late Roman period sites were typically small to medium, between 0.1 and 5.0 ha in area. Settlements were mainly evenly spread, with some clustering in the southern part of the valley. No less than 80 sites from the Islamic period were found. The earliest evidence came only from the mid-eighth century. As asserted by Bartl, the dearth of evidence for the Umayyad period is likely a manifestation of the difficulty in identifying the transitional pottery, specifically the coarsewares. The region is known textually from the Umayyad period, not least via the existence of Ḥiṣn Maslama (Madīnat al-Fār). The general size of all the sites on the survey (70 out of 80) from all periods was also small to medium, akin to the Late Roman period extent of 5 ha or less; however, most sites were small, being under 1 ha. These were posited as farmsteads. Three sites were medium-sized villages (5–10 ha) while four were large villages between 10 and 40 ha. Interestingly, 12 sites exhibited Roman to Islamic period continuity. Seven of these 12 were at the larger end of the small class (3–5 ha) of farmsteads, suggesting growth and consolidation of smaller sites.[22] This implies that the remaining 68 sites were founded *de novo*.

Work by Wilkinson as part of the the Western Jazira Archaeological Landscape Project showed that the Balikh landscape comprised a network of canals, marshes and dry riverbeds. Dominating this landscape in the sixth to eighth centuries was a major canal (Nahr al-Abbara/Nahr Turkmān), which was a straightened channel that ran parallel from the top of the Balikh Valley down its east side, irrigating large areas of land. It replaced an earlier, slightly smaller canal system (the Saḥlan–Ḥammām Canal), which was used from the Hellenistic period to the sixth century. It would have been a primary feeder, from which smaller secondary and tertiary canals would have branched off, as suggested by the presence of sluice stones found at intervals. After diverting water from the river, it emptied back into it just south of Tell Hammam et-Turkmān. Sites were conspicuously aligned along it in a linear fashion. The canal may be identified with one built by Hishām as caliph in 724, based on Syriac accounts such as that by Agapius of Manbij who said: 'He opened up many abundant water channels and it was he who drew water from the river above Kallinikos (Raqqa)' and, similarly, the anonymous author of the *Chronicle* of 819: 'and he [Hishām] diverted a river from the Euphrates to irrigate the plantations and the fields which he made near it.'[23] A canal, identified as the Nahr al-Nīl, brought water from the Euphrates to Raqqa passing through a circular enclosure surrounding an unfinished monument built by Hārūn al-Ra'shid and interpreted as a commemorative structure after his victory at Ḥiṣn Hiraqla (modern Ereğli) in 806.[24] A qanat was also discovered in the southern valley bringing water directly to Raqqa from the north, an area covered by around 20 early 'Abbāsid palaces, which thereby supply a date for the system.[25]

Two settlements in this area were attested historically as preexisting Roman period towns: the twin towns of Bāgharwān/Bājarwān (BS 108–10/Tall Damir al-Sharqī and al-Gharbī) on either side of the river and Tell Maḥrē (BS 142/Tell Sheikh Hassan, possibly Greek Therimachon). From the Umayyad period, survey evidence is slight. Only two sites were larger than 50 ha, and newly founded and historically attested: Bāghaddā/Bājaddā (BS 172, Khirbat al-Anbār, just south of Ḥiṣn Maslama), attributed as a Maslama foundation, and Madīnat al-Fār (over 100 ha), identified with Ḥiṣn Maslama (BS 187) and also named after its founder, the son of ʻAbd al-Malik. The sites of BS 108, 109 and 110 on both sides of the Balikh River formed one settlement, primarily dating to the ninth century. As a double site, it was similar to AS 29 on the Yaghrā River in the Amuq. This site was identified as Bāgharwān or Bājarwān, one of five named sites in the valley and a medium-sized center.[26] The city wall of Tell Maḥrē (Tell Sheikh Hasan) measured 450 × 450 m (20 ha) and enclosed a central mound, church and small mosque. The Late Roman period site was smaller, enclosing 7 ha. The main occupation was evident from the extensive eighth- to tenth-century ceramics littered over the site.[27] Ibn Khurradādhbih lists it on the Raqqa–Ḥarrān road as a stop, and Yāqūt calls it a fortified town.[28] At Bājaddā, the surveyors did not find Umayyad pottery. It was a flat-topped low mound encompassing a roughly square 800 × 700 m site. Sarakhsī describes it, in the late ninth century, as a walled city with gardens and a central well that irrigated the fields. Yāqūt states that Maslama b. ʻAbd al-Malik gave the land (*āqṭʻa* as *qaṭiʻa*) to one of his captains, Āsīd of the Sulaym, who walled the village and built it up.[29]

Ḥiṣn Maslama was a large walled compound (over 100 ha in size) with three elements, including a central elevated rectangular enclosure (80 × 40 m) consisting of two adjacent houses surrounded by a wall, and a large northern enclosure (330 × 330 m). It had corner towers and eight intermittent tower buttresses with gates along each wall, and an outer ditch and street grid. A southern compound consisted of loosely planned residences. The site of Ḥiṣn Maslama belonged to two phases: the first was scarcely represented and dated to the early eighth century, while the second dated to the late eighth/early ninth centuries. There is little evidence for continued occupation after 860. Most of the visible remains and large-scale buildings of the central enclosure, northern enclosure, and southern compound extension are attributed to the second ʻAbbāsid phase, but the dates of the city walls and gates are not known with any certainty.[30] Like Ḥiṣn Manṣūr, Ḥiṣn Maslama was associated with the Late Umayyad/Early 'Abbāsid period up until the caliphate of al-Mahdī (r. 775–87). Maslama b. 'Abd al-Malik controlled the territory of the frontier from Iskandarūna (modern Iskenderun) and Anṭākiya to the Balikh, and was governor of the Jazīra (708–9). The early 'Abbāsid caliphs allowed the territory to remain in his family's possession.[31] Whether Maslama and his family were supported by the caliphate, local tribal leaders or urban elites following the Umayyad demise is uncertain. In 779–80, al-Mahdī stayed at the site, where a descendant of Maslama, Muhammad b. Yazīd al-Umawī (known also as al-Ḥiṣnī), was still living as a poet. The 'Abbāsids, sympathetic to him as they were to Maslama, spared his life. Ḥiṣn Maslama was surrounded by canals bringing water from the Balikh 3 km away to irrigate fields, and may have been part of a settlement policy of granting incentives with agricultural lands. This suggests that the *ḥuṣūn* were not strictly fortified 'castles' *per se* but in some way developed from the *quṣūr* desert castles with their agricultural holdings. S. Heidemann argued that the lack of coins of Maslama as compared with the many coins of the local governor al-'Abbās b. Muhammad (759–72) indicated that the Umayyad site was possibly a self-sufficient agricultural estate (*ḍiyā'*), which transformed in the early 'Abbāsid period into an administrative center and/or market[32] or way station/garrison.[33] As a way station, it connected Raqqa and Ḥarrān on the south–north route and likely Jisr Manbij and Ra's al-'Ayn on the west–east route. The other main Balikh Valley sites mentioned from historical accounts besides Raqqa were Leontopolis (from the mid-fifth century onward), the Kadar or Amud Monastery, and Dabana/Davana Castle. A site (BS 273) with square enclosure walls of 250 m per side and visible entry, in the north-east part of the valley, which was also inhabited in the Early Islamic period, may have been the site of Dabana.

Settlement in the Khābūr Valley

We can only conjecture, based on general low-resolution survey observations and textual information, that the Khābūr region was as densely settled during the Islamic period as the Balikh. The Tell Beydar Survey in the western Khābūr noted a drop in sites from the

Sāsānian period, which the surveyors attributed to a low sedentary population (Figure 22). Alluviation on the valley floors would have obscured some sites. The main site type for the Early Islamic period was the small low mound (or mounds) less than 5 m high (typically 1–1.5 m high) and less than 3 ha (typically 1 ha) in area, of which there were seven. Less frequently, there were lower towns around tells, of which there was one site, and tells which were typically not occupied in the Sāsānian and Islamic periods; only three were occupied, but this is unclear from the publication. Of the tell sites, TBS 32, 55 and 59 are mentioned on the phase map but no Islamic phase is mentioned in the catalogue. Of the Early Islamic period sites (eight in number), three were new foundations: TBS 6, 17 and 57. TBS 6 and 17 were single-period sites (although TBS 6 had two small Iron Age mounds), and TBS 57 continued into the Middle Islamic period. Seven out of eight Early Islamic period sites were equally dispersed along the Wādī 'Awaidj on the floodplain's upper terrace and avoided the basalt terrace to the west. Only TBS 43 lay at the base of the basalt plateau, and also comprised an extensive lower town around a tell.

By contrast, settlement grew in the Early Islamic period, as is shown by the Tell Hamoukar Survey, starting in the Late Sāsānian–Early Islamic (Period 16). Settlements were typically structures dispersed within the boundaries of the site. They were also consolidated sites, many larger than 1 ha in area and unfortified.[34] While some were newly founded in the eighth to tenth centuries (Period 17), other Late Sāsānian/Early Islamic period sites were abandoned; similarly, some grew and some were reduced. However, in Period 16 only three sites were large, over 8 ha, and in Period 17 only one. Nearly all sites were on or very near wadis. Hollow ways were noted in this landscape – as were irrigation canals, mainly in the north and west, and likely dated to the Early Islamic period expansion. Two canal systems were identified: one in the north-east part of the survey and one near the largest sites of THS 54 and THS 50 in the west (Figure 22).

All but one of the sites in the Tell Leilan Survey were small- or medium-sized, at under 4 ha. They mainly centered on the wadi tributaries of the center and north-west of the survey area; the eastern and south-eastern areas were sparsely settled in the Early and Middle Islamic periods. Similarly, the number of Sāsānian–Early Islamic period sites in the North Jazira Survey dropped, further defining the eastern contour of the intensively settled Khābūr–Balikh area. This may have been due to site conglomeration from dispersed farms in the Parthian period to larger villages in the Sāsānian–Early Islamic period. As in the preceding Sāsānian period, these were low mounds where individual buildings were often discernible and depressions were dug throughout the site, to either hold water or for mud-brick extraction. Large enclosures date from this transitional period and were often sited near tells, such as was the case at Site 54, a 5.9-ha pentagonal enclosure that likely belonged to the Sāsānian period. A square enclosure, the more commonly seen model, on the edge of Site 110 had a 100 × 100 m embankment, formed either from dumped earth or from collapsed mud-brick construction.

New Early Islamic period sites were square enclosures that resembled way stations, and were eighth- to tenth-century in date. Site 4, just south-west of Tell al-Hawa, one of the small enclosures, was a single-period site dated to the second half of the eighth century, as it lacked Samarran ceramics according to the excavators, and measured 80 × 80 m. Site 47 measured 50 × 40 m. The excavators suggested that the largest of these (Site 54) was more military in character, possibly aimed at controlling local nomadic populations or the frontier itself, while smaller enclosures (*c.*2.4 ha) were way stations on routes (Figure 22).[35] Basic routes using those sites with the highest assemblage counts (in this case, Sites 23, 4, 1 and 29) were discernible from the south-east to the north-west (from Mawṣil to Nisibin). The settlement at Tell al-Hawa was off the tell in a series of low mounds, and comprised a lower town to the south-west (Sāsānian–Early Islamic period) and south-east (Middle/Late Islamic period).[36] In the Middle and Late Islamic periods, even fewer sites (28) were occupied. Surface collection at nearby Tell Hamoukar identified Early Islamic period ceramics only at the uppermost level of its Area A, which indicates a small settlement.[37] The surveyors of the North Jazīra project attributed decline in the eastern Khābūr to a non-settled population with falling grain yields (as evidenced by *kharāj* returns from the years *c.*800 to 1335).[38] The lack of major watercourses, springs or surface water that would have enabled irrigation cultivation of surrounding lands is an important factor, although the area is just within the limits for dry-farming cultivation. No major canal works were detected coming from the nearest stretch of the Tigris, more than 20 km away. More work is needed to elucidate these patterns, however, as the eighth to tenth centuries, a period of growth in settled populations as compared to nomadic groups, is represented by a decline in sites.

A notable exception was the Early Islamic site at Tell Brak, a way station originally identified as a Roman or Late Roman period *castellum* (Figure 22).[39] The fortified enclosure is 91 m per side and 0.73 ha in area, with 2.6 m-thick walls, 4.5 m-wide towers at every 7.5 m, and a 2 m-wide gateway. Survey around the entire area revealed only eighth- to tenth-century ceramics scattered around an area of 14 ha. In addition, J. Ur, P. Karsgaard, and J. Oates noted a canal drawing water from the Nahr Jaghjagh with three perpendicular offshoots observed between the river and the way station, indicating a focus of cultivated fields.[40] The canal curved around the site. Other features formed part of this Late Roman/Sāsānian and Islamic period landscape, including curvilinear walls above and along the Khābūr, which the surveyors posited were animal pens; hollow ways inscribed on the landscape as finer lines than their pre-Classical versions; and, finally, canals. Two types were identified: small canals connecting with *nāʿūra* or *sāqiya* water-lifting devices in lower ground around isolated farms, and grand canals running parallel to the Khābūr – all south of Ḥasaka and the confluence of the various wadis into one stream. These fed sites all along the river, driving the agricultural (and textile) economy of the region. Research in the lower Khābūr – based on geomorphological investigation, limited excavation and settlement proximal survey – has determined that the nearly 170 km of canals along the river were likely all dug at one time, during the Neo-Assyrian period (*c.*900–600 BCE); however, the network of distributed sites became denser from the Parthian–Islamic period until the Mongol conquest.[41] Decker estimates that the canals were large enough to irrigate 30,000 ha and provide for 62,000 inhabitants.[42]

Yāqūt mentions that the Khābūr from Ra's al-'Ayn to Qarqīsiyā on the Euphrates was in its past entirely navigable by small boats whereby people could visit each others' gardens and orchards, implying a dense network of canals.[43] The maintenance of such extensive canal systems would have been immense, and was unlikely to have been an immense effort that was unlikely to have continued unchanged for over a millennium. Although specifically indeterminate, parts of this system would have been maintained or re-excavated in the Early Islamic period.

Several important sites, particularly from the 'Abbāsid period, were developed along the main caravan road traversing the upper Khābūr and connecting Raqqa to Mawṣil, and mentioned by numerous geographers from the ninth to the eleventh centuries. From the western Khābūr, the main town was Ra's al-'Ayn, whose Islamic settlement lay north of the Late Roman period site (Figure 18). Kharāb Sayyār in the Wādī Ḥamar or Beni Siar, possibly identified with the settlement of Jārūd, measured 650 × 650 m (42 ha) and was only occupied from the second half of the eighth to the middle of the tenth century, with much of the building dating to the middle of the ninth (Figure 20). The site was walled with ditches, and also had gates enclosing a tell. Excavation and geophysical survey inside revealed a grid pattern of streets and a main, circular or octagonal building, and possibly a mosque in the north-west. There was also evidence for a residential structure, bathrooms and a bathhouse (with painted walls), which later became a workshop area. The tell possessed a multi-roomed building with stucco decoration. A *khān* was noted outside the walls. The water-supply system included canals and cisterns.[44] Kherbet Slajé, 4 km west of Tell Khanzir, was 1 km^2 and walled, with one quarter separately enclosed by another wall. Abou Jéradé was a 42-ha site around a tell. The site of Qantari, a Christian community as suggested by Syriac inscriptions on chancel screens, may have been a monastery. After Naṣībīn, the road first passed Adhrama, which may be identified as either Tell Sha'ir/Site 74 or Gir Sikha/Site 116 from the Tell Leilan Survey. Both sites are relatively close to one another and were the largest in the survey, with heavy assemblages beginning in the eighth century and continuing until the Late Islamic period.

Islamic-period-focused excavations were conducted at Tell Tuneinir between 1987 and 2004 by Michael and Neathery Fuller (Figure 20).[45] From short preliminary reports, the excavations show a fairly typical and unknown settlement in the Khābūr with both Syriac-speaking Christian and Muslim communities, which continued into the Middle Islamic period. It was laid out as an occupied high tell surrounded by a lower town dating mainly to the twelfth to thirteenth centuries. On the tell were houses, suggested as elite residences, based on material culture. The lower town featured two *khānāt*, a bathhouse and a market. Slightly farther away was a church and monastery. Early Islamic period presence was detected only in the last-named complex, which was occupied intensely until around the tenth century, and in a pit under the market.

Settlement on the Euphrates at the Confluence with Khābūr

An explosion of Early Islamic period settlement noted in the Middle Euphrates Survey mirrored and reinforced the Balikh and western/central Khābūr settlement patterns (Figure 23). Late Roman period sites at the limits of the Byzantine frontier were very few and mainly grouped around Buṣayra (Greek Kirkesion) and the Khābūr delta, with Dura-Europas notable in the southern part of the surveyed area. The sites were irrigated by the Nahr Semiramis on the east bank. Several sites, notably tells, in the immediate vicinity of Buṣayra continued into the seventh to eighth centuries. Early Islamic settlement exploded, but was confined to a 60-km length of the river encompassing two major canal systems, one on either side of the Euphrates. As main feeder channels, both followed the parallel course seen in all Euphrates, Balikh and Khābūr canals attested on surveys but were unlike the ʻAfrīn in the Amuq, whose channels were bifurcated and straightened, or the Ak Su in Maraş, where dendritic perpendicular canals began at the source. Beginning in the second half of the seventh century, settlement flourished on the east bank of the Euphrates. The sites here were mainly organized along a newly

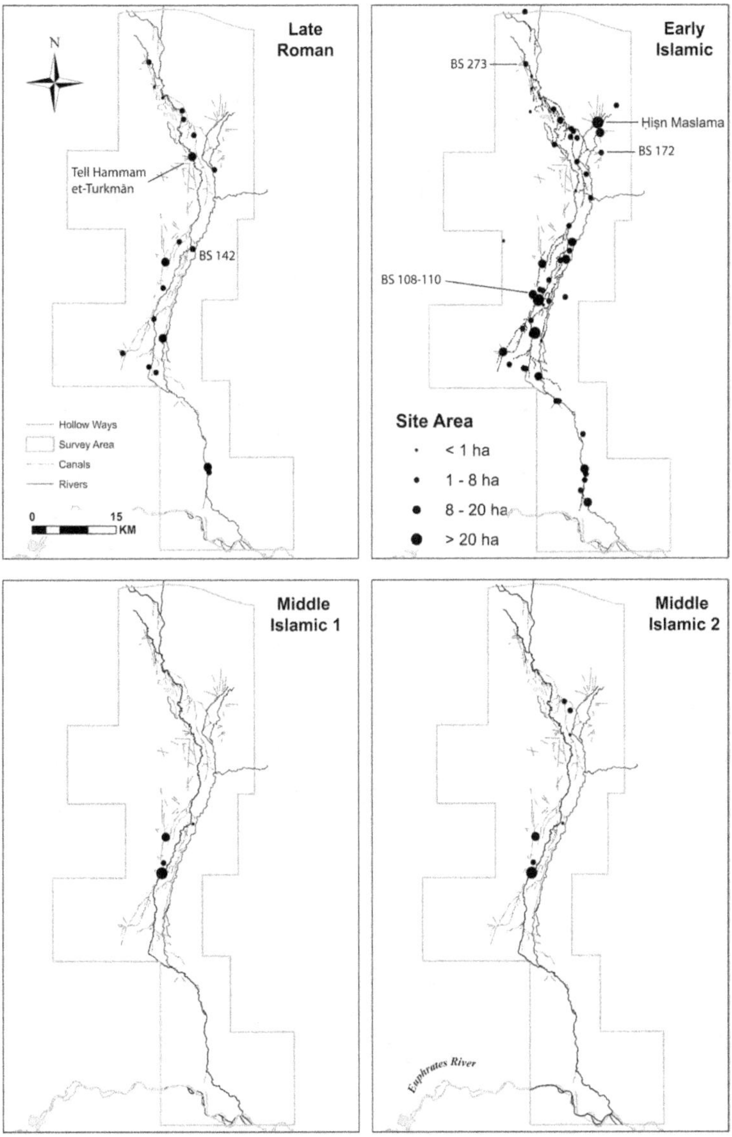

Figure 21 Balikh Survey, Late Roman through Middle Islamic sites (based on 1996, pp. 345 and 348)

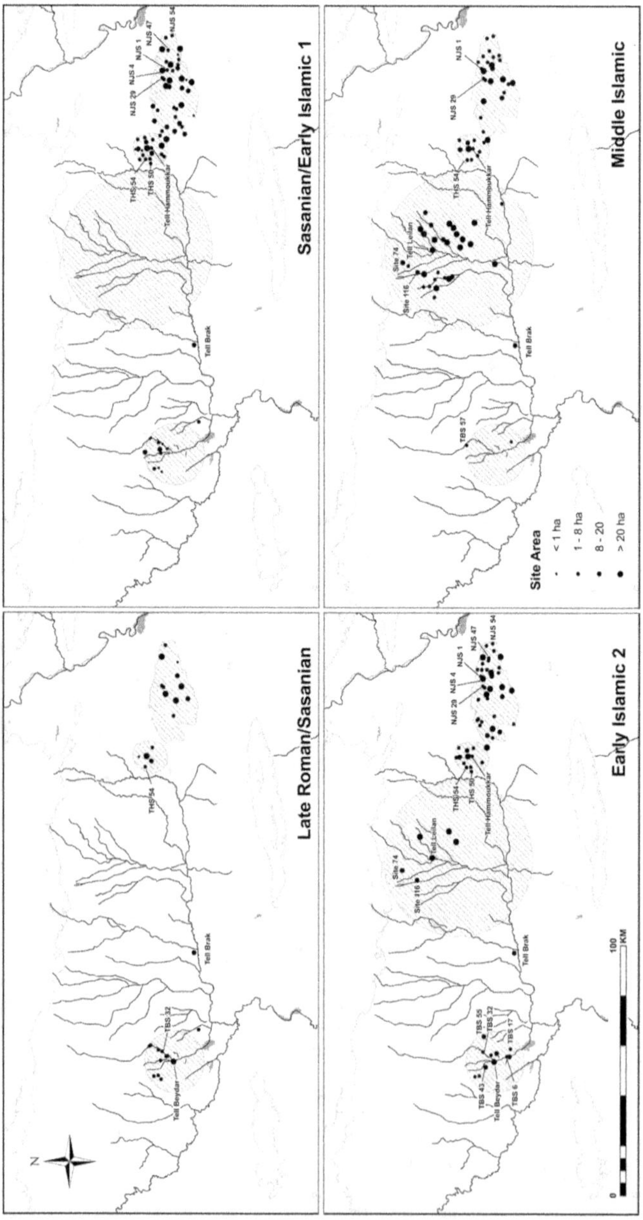

Figure 22 Group II, Khābūr Survey sites, Late Roman/Sāsānian through Middle Islamic sites

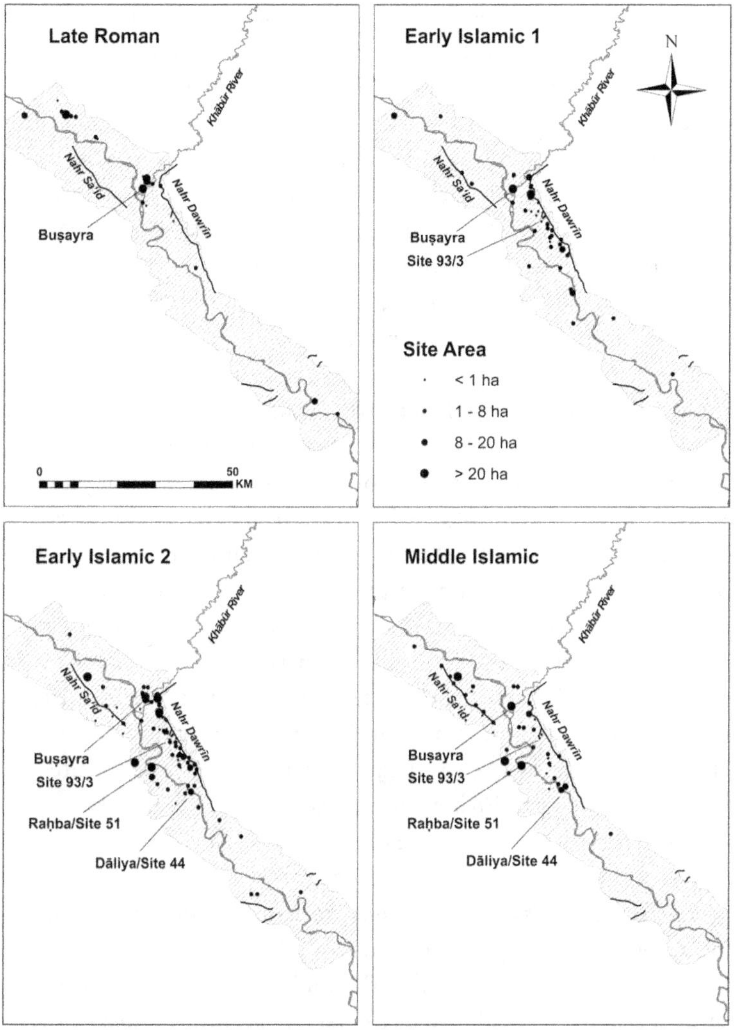

Figure 23 Middle Euphrates Survey, Late Roman through Middle Islamic sites (based on Berthier 2001, Map D)

built canal, the Nahr Dawrīn, which was visible intermittently for 50 km. Some 36 sites were situated along this canal, 26 of which were from the seventh to eighth centuries. Most continued past the eighth century and more were founded and occupied until the end of the ninth century, from which period sedimentation was noted. The canal took water from the Khābūr and irrigated all of the Euphrates terrace land for a stretch of about 30 km downstream. The Nahr Dawrīn is not attested in historical accounts. Al-Ṭabarī mentions the donation of a piece of desolate land called Dawrīn, along with its villages, to Hishām, where the latter then turned into an estate from which he received revenue.[46] Most sites were flat and small, however. Excavations of Site 93/3 revealed a square enclosure, 15.5 × 15.5 m with 60 cm-wide walls. The walls enclosed six rooms and an entry chamber around an internal courtyard.

The Nahr Sa'īd flowed parallel to the Euphrates on its western bank for an intermittent length of 33 km. Settlement along it was less dense than on the Nahr Dawrīn, with only 14 associated sites – several of them tell sites. The use of tell sites is an interesting pattern, as many were not terribly high (maximum 6 m) and were newly-founded Islamic period sites, i.e. not pre-Islamic. They would have been in an advantageous position to avoid erosion caused by river avulsion, seen also with the Yaghrā River sites in the Amuq. Soundings across the canal and the dating of proximal sites by ceramics and radiocarbon, however, uniformly attest to a later date for this canal, beginning from the ninth century. Intact vessels of a *qadūs* or *sāqiya* type, but more spherical, were discovered at seven sites and were related to water-lifting devices mainly from the end of the tenth to the thirteenth centuries. These would have brought water to higher terraces and secondary canals, whose perpendicular traces were noted. The entire system continued to be used until the end of the fourteenth century. Two periods of abandonment are notable, however: the tenth century and the mid-late thirteenth century. As such, the archaeological evidence diverges from the textual evidence, which mentions that the canal was dug by Sa'īd al-Khayr b. 'Abd al-Malik. It may have been dug by the Umayyads but developed later as part of the 'Abbāsid ascendancy in the region.

Animal and plant remains allow an appreciation of the natural population of the survey region, and a better understanding of subsistence strategies. This information can in turn be hypothesized for our other survey regions where such studies were not conducted.

The crops that dominated this fertile oasis were the winter crops of wheat, barley, lentil, pea, chickpea and broad bean. The summer crops were millet, cotton, rice and sesame. The last three named require a hot climate and plenty of water – a challenge in the late spring to early fall months of this low rainfall zone. Rice, ideally grown in humid lowlands, consumed four times as much irrigation as cotton, and had to be immersed in 15 cm of water that was flowing, as salinization could affect its fertility.[47] The cultivation of these crops, probably for export, would have been an irrigation priority. Paleobotanists also identified some fruit, nuts and remains of grape through all periods; peach and date from the mid-eighth century; pomegranate, fig and plum from the tenth century onwards; and melon, cucumber, almond, caper and coriander occurred rarely.

Sheep and goats were the dominant species found in all periods, attesting to a mixed system of farming and pastoralism. Such evidence is useful in considering the role, amidst these irrigated and fertile reclaimed lands, of pastoralists who otherwise would be 'invisible' or marginalized to the uplands or areas beyond the green river valley. In addition, pig bone was virtually absent, but remains of water buffalo (*jamūs* or *Bubalis bubalis*) were found in canal soundings both at the site of Tell Guftān and at Tell Qaryat Medād.[48] These remains are rare, as water buffalo bones are difficult to distinguish from those of other cattle. Nevertheless, they suggest a possible mixed and symbiotic system of irrigated lands and water-buffalo rearing within and around them, the latter also being used as work animals that can in turn be projected on the Amuq and Cilician Plains where these animals were said to have been introduced in the Early Islamic period.

The main known towns of the Khābūr/Middle Euphrates confluence region that also functioned as stations on the Euphrates land route connecting 'Iraq and the Jazīra were Qarqīsiyā (Buṣayra), Raḥba and Dāliya. Raḥba, or Raḥba Malik b. Ṭawq, is identified with the site of Meyādīn/Site 51: early ninth to the middle of the eleventh century. The dates corroborate the textual evidence, which states that the town was founded by a leader of the Banū Taghlib during the reign of al-Ma'mūn (813–33) and had a river port (*furda*).

He developed the town as an economic center for merchants and traders to generate revenue.[49] Dāliya ('water-wheel') is identified with the site of al-Graiye 1/Site 44 (mid-eighth to the tweflth century), where remains were discovered of the foundation of a *na'ūra* within the river, following the town's namesake.

Towns

The only large settlements for the Diyār Muḍar were the twin *thughūr* towns of Raqqa and Rāfiqa, founded in 772, and Ḥarrān. Their sites are located just west of where the Balikh flows into the Euphrates on an elevated spur that would have protected it from the marsh and flood-prone rivers. Raqqa was the *qaṣaba* (provincial capital) of the Diyār Muḍar and one of the capitals of the *'awāṣim*. Rāfiqa, garrisoned by Khurāsānī troops, was erected by al-Manṣūr in order not only to create a headquarters for Byzantine raids but also to establish an 'Abbāsid presence on the frontier and ensure stability and loyalty from its populations. It may be the only frontier settlement in the region to have been newly founded deliberately as a garrison town (*wa lam yakun al-Rāfiqa āthar qadīm*).[50] The twin towns became a growing focus during the early 'Abbāsid period, much larger than in the previous Late Roman period settlement, with palatial residences and racetracks built to the north (under Hārūn al-Rashīd in 796–7) and an important industrial ceramic- and glass-manufacturing zone (al-Raqqa al-Muḥtariqa, 'Burnt Raqqa' and Tell Aswad), which grew between the two towns in 1815/16 and produced types found throughout the *thughūr*, Northern Syria and the Jazīra, including the yellow glaze wares of the late eighth to mid-ninth centuries. Al-Raqqa al-Muḥtariqa was enclosed by a wall dated to 815, and contained a market (Sūq al-Hishām) and caravansarai-type building (al-Funduq al-Qadīm). Additionally, the settlement includes a tell (Tell Bi'a) which was the location of Dayr Zakka (Mar Zakkā or the Monastery of Zacchaeus), in use from the sixth to the ninth century if not later. Two canals (one of them being the Nahr al-Nīl) watered the city and surrounding lands.[51] The town, thus, was an economic hub for the frontier and the Jazīra, acting as a protected port for goods and grain bound for Baghdād.[52] The area continued to be occupied until the eleventh century, after which settlement focus shifted to al-Rāfiqa in the twelfth and early thirteenth centuries.[53] Excavations at Ḥarrān have focused mostly on the tell and its Ayyubid structures, but recently also on the *masjid al-jāmi'a*. We know that irrigation works occurred near the town as references mention an Ismā'īl b. Ṣubayḥ, secretary under Mahdī and Hārūn, who commissioned a 16 km-long canal there called al-Jullāb.[54]

Conclusions

The Balikh and Middle Euphrates/Khābūr confluences, and possibly the western/central Khābūr areas, were unusual for the entire region because they exhibited nearly twice, if not more, the typical proportion of Early Islamic period sites to Late Roman period sites. The majority of the former were early 'Abbāsid, but they began at the end of the Umayyad period. All of these sites grew in the early 'Abbāsid period, and many were new foundations. Furthermore, many of them were associated with canal systems. A mixed cultivated/pastoralist system was adopted with a rotation of winter wheat and barley and summer rice and cotton, and the rearing of sheep, goats and possibly water buffalo. Rice and cotton demanded intensive irrigation strategies. Ibn Serapion described the Balikh as rich in estates (*ḍayā'ān)*, rural districts (*rasātīq*) and gardens (*basātīn*), suggesting a densely populated area.[55] Many of these early 'Abbāsid sites were square (in a few cases rectangular) fortified enclosures sited on main routes. Of these, some were of a larger size than the majority of *thughūr* sites and were small towns, while others were 70–90 m per side and acted as way stations. The archaeology complicates and challenges C. Robinson's recent view of Early Islamic settlement in the Jazīra, particularly along the Euphrates, Balikh and Khābūr Rivers, which according to Robinson 'failed to conduct the same forces of settlement and urbanization as did the Tigris; and such Muslim settlement there as there was in the Jazīra on the whole seems to have been conditioned by opportunism and desperation, rather than by the Qurashī élite's enthusiasm'.[56] The evidence from archaeological surveys, far better represented in these river valleys than anywhere else on the frontier, is not 'underdeveloped' but rather shows scanty occupation in the century immediately after the Islamic conquests, followed by rapid development of settlement, population and economy in the Middle Euphrates, Balikh and western and central Khābūr but not the eastern side.[57]

The presence of rural sites, irrigation systems and way stations link the Jazīra and the frontier. Like the Amuq Plain (and *'awāṣim*), the Balikh and Khābūr were important conduits to the *thughūr*, specifically to the eastern frontier. The chronologies of low sedentary Umayyad settlement followed by a steady growth in new settlement in the early 'Abbāsid period are also similar to those of the Amuq Plain. However, archaeological evidence shows that the Jazīra differed from the frontier substantially in density and demography. Several factors account for this. First, in the Late Roman/Sāsānian period, the Balikh and the Khābūr were less densely settled than the Near East as a whole in the fifth and sixth centuries. Second, between 796 and 808, Hārūn al-Rashīd moved from Baghdād to Raqqa/Rāfiqa, making it his temporary capital; it was already the provincial capital of the Diyār Muḍar. The city flourished, with markets, racetracks, palaces and workshops, and featured a high population density, urbanization and caliphal investment. Third, the region owed its efflorescence to close connections with the Euphrates, which linked two separate yet related spheres of economic activity: the central (southern) lands of 'Iraq and the Jazīra. This might explain why seventh- to eighth-century settlement in this region is more difficult to locate. Populations migrated or were relocated to this area, particularly during the Umayyad period; however, permanent settlement would have been light apart from some *quṣūr* and estates such as Hishām's residence at Ruṣāfa, the Umayyad palaces at Raqqa, and Marwān's II's residence at Ḥarrān. 'Abbāsid attempts to overcome this last Umayyad bastion during the revolution of 749–50 ultimately proved successful, and sparked an interest in garnering support from locals and repopulating it with sympathetic groups, providing incentives of land grants to soldiers and developing the region generally. Al-Manṣūr, al-Mahdī and Hārūn al-Rashīd all played significant roles in developing this area, giving it their personal attention – either with visits or temporary residence, evident of course in Raqqa/Rāfiqa, built up by al-Manṣūr and made a headquarters by Hārūn. Indeed, the proliferation of settlement is suggestive of intensive sedentarization, as seen to a lesser degree in the Amuq and Kahramanmaraş Plains. Agricultural production and way stations, promoting safer and more stable trade routes, engendered economic success. In the Balikh, an enormous increase in copper coinage, particularly during the reign of al-Mahdī, supports evidence of this infusion of economic activity.[58] Fourth, the corridor between Raqqa–Ḥarrān–Ruhā (Edessa) and Sumaysāṭ gave rise to an active and thriving Syriac Christian community, attested by a large number of scholars, bishops, patriarchs and saints who lived, worked, preached and wrote in this area between the seventh and ninth centuries, individuals who would have worked with numerous settlements – villages and monasteries alike. A famous local resident, Dionysius of Tell Maḥrē, mentions Jacobite monasteries throughout the Balikh Valley in the early 'Abbāsid period. The region was also full of Old and New Testament holy places: tombs of prophets whose shrines were cared for and venerated by both Christians and Muslims. Fifth, we can view this region of agricultural prosperity and entrepreneurship only relative to the frontier to the north and west. Sixth, the very thinly settled landscape following the tenth century can also be linked to the abandonment of irrigation systems and various political shifts leading to the presence of a largely nomadic population in the landscape. Unlike the frontier zone, where high-cost investment in irrigation agriculture may have been too risky to undertake, the Jazīra was relatively protected. This is an important contrast, showing that the Balikh, Middle Euphrates/Khābūr confluence, and the western/central Khābūr areas in the Jazīra were micro-regions. Although comparable with the spatial relationship of the Amuq hinterland plains to the Taurus, these valleys were not at all like the *thughūr* frontier zone or even the *'awāṣim* plains (the Amuq) situated well behind the Taurus Mountains.

CHAPTER 5

THE WESTERN *THUGHŪR*: CROSSROADS OF CILICIA

> *Returning from Baghdad, we went from al-Massîsah to Adhanah, passing through a prairie and villages which followed each other very closely, and many settlements.*[1]

Travellers and scholars throughout history have described the fertile and rich plain of Cilicia as the key crossroads between Anatolia and Syria. The few but well-travelled mountain passes leading in and out of the plain had already been memorialized in the Classical periods with names such as the Cilician Gates, Syrian Gates and Amanus Gates. As a major part of the Islamic–Byzantine *thughūr*, comprising roughly one-third of the frontier and the portion closest to Byzantine lands, these descriptions appear at odds with a notion of an impassable border or abandoned wilderness. Yet, more than any other frontier region, scholars frequently describe Cilicia in these extreme and conflicting terms: as a no man's land, deliberately vacated after the Byzantine emperor's dramatic departure, as a staging point for raids into Byzantine lands, and as a dangerous battleground at risk from raiding Byzantine armies. For Cilicia, these views mainly stem from ninth- and tenth-century geographical and historical texts, which detail significant caliphal-sponsored building activity focusing on constant refortification of the major cities and their walls. Accompanying these perceptions is the frequently cited and rich, preserved text of al-Ṭarsūsī (d. 1011), which gives us the most detailed view we have of life in the frontier city of Ṭarsūs, although one whose perspective was dictated heavily by the annual military raids. As such, Cilicia is often a stand-in for the entirety of the Islamic–Byzantine *thughūr*. In the face of unbalanced textual evidence focusing mainly on key cities, what can be said to test this contradiction of a settled yet empty landscape unchanged over 300 years, from the mid-seventh to the mid-tenth century? A nuanced analysis of the region that evaluates the archaeological data of settlement and material culture will better consider change in the region from the seventh to the tenth centuries, through a closer examination of site types beyond the major cities, networks of settlement, and the economy of the region itself as seen through its local production, land-use and trade. Returning to the final farewell of the Byzantine Emperor Heraklios at the Cilician Gates as he leaves these lands permanently, we understand his goodbye initially as a lament for losing such a rich province. Looking beyond and to the future, Heraklios imparts a motive for Byzantine and Islamic conflict across the frontier; abandoning the land and bestowing it upon the Muslims leads to the desire to re-establish the rich trade and productivity of Cilicia.

The Environment

The western part of the *thughūr* is referred to briefly in Yāqūt as Khadhqadūna since the time of Yazīd I b. Muʿāwiya (r. 680–3).[2] It consists of a clearly defined, large, lowland alluvial plain, the Cilician Plain or Cilicia Pedias (Smooth Cilicia), with an eastern extension: the coastal Plain of Issus (or Black Cilicia) that narrowly sweeps around the Gulf of Iskenderun (Figure 3). The plains are bordered on all sides by either highlands or sea: the Mediterranean to the south, the Amanus Mountains (Mauron Oros/Melantion Oros, Jabal al-Lukkām, or Black Mountain on account that it being thickly forested) to the east, the Taurus Mountains to the north, and mountainous Rough Cilicia to the west. The Lamas River (Greek Lamus) coursed through these highlands and was typically considered the westernmost boundary with Byzantium. Three rivers flow through the plain from the northern mountains and empty into the Mediterranean. They are, from west to east: the Baradān (Greek Cydnus), which flows through Ṭarsūs; the Sayḥān (Greek Sarus); and the Jayḥān (Greek Pyramus), named after the Sīr Daryā (Sayḥūn) and Amū Daryā (Jayḥūn) of the eastern Turkish frontier – the last-named being two of the four heavenly rivers of Paradise derived from the biblical Giḥon and Pishon.[3] These were major rivers of Islamic lands, appearing on geographical maps such as that of the province of Shām in Ibn Ḥawqal. Average rainfall in the Plain of Issus is high (*c*.950–1,050 mm/annum), as it is a narrow plain backed by the sharply rising Amanus Mountains, which trap weather systems moving eastward from the Mediterranean.

These rivers contribute to an extremely fertile and arable landscape, and at times in history a marshy wetland due in part to their meandering deltas. In antiquity, farmers here produced wheat, barley, lentils, beans and other legumes, sesame, millet, rice, olives, cotton and, in the eastern part and the Plain of Issus, date palms. Olive-oil production was particularly prolific and considered of high quality in Cilicia. More exotic resources included a large number of plants and tree extracts that were used as cooking herbs, medical remedies, incense and scents in perfume, such as crocus (for saffron) from the floor of the massive sinkhole of the Corycian Cave (modern Cennet or 'Heaven'), hyssop and thyme.[4] The Armenian geographer Ananias of Širak, who possibly wrote between 610 and 685, gave a lengthier account of these resources of Isauria, emphasizing them in contrast to those of other regions where he only described settlements. He added gum (*lini* and *xungs*), storax (*stirak*, resin of the sweetgum tree), colophane (*kučum*, or rosin, resin of the pine tree), obergomphis (*bŕgumbit'*), and calamite (*kalamita*, reed, ginger grass, or a fossilized extinct tree-like horsetail) from trees produced by the boring of a yellow-coloured worm with black markings.[5] From the storax, a perfume known as *may'a* from Salūqiyya (Greek Seleucia, modern Silifke) and Ajya (or Āyas, Greek Aigai, modern Yumurtalık) was a prized product exported to Islamic lands. Timber was harvested and sent downstream to coastal sites, particularly where the mountains were near, such as in the Plain of Issus where pine was floated down from the Amanus to Ḥiṣn al-Tīnāt and Iskandarūna, and in Rough Cilicia where cedar and cypress were harvested from the Taurus. These timbers, as well as pine, were greatly coveted for shipbuilding. Other woods, such as juniper, boxwood, oak and fir, were cut to make small boat parts; fuel for metal processing, pottery and glass kilns, and bathhouses; and building-construction components. Resin was tapped and also used in construction. Pastoralists sold their sheep and goat products in the cities, such as the coats of sheep wool famous in the markets of Maṣṣīṣa and known in both Islamic and Classical periods (as *cilicium*). Silver, copper, lead, tin and iron deposits were present in the Taurus.

The widespread growth of marsh, particularly by the early modern period, and the presence of malaria led many travellers and archaeologists to comment on the inhabitability of the plain. While marshes and lakes began to take shape and expand across these plains more permanently in the Late Roman/Early Islamic periods, such as the former Rhegma lagoon south of Ṭarsūs, the extent and danger of malaria were likely not seen as such serious hindrances to settlement as they would be in the modern era. The presence of Roman and Late Roman period towns such as Mallos, Sebaste, Korykos and Megarsos on the coast and at the mouths of the major rivers, and of smaller sites also suggests that the marsh, known in the early modern period, was not as widespread in Late Antiquity. Ancient accounts hardly mention the marshes of Cilicia, suggesting that these were later environmental changes.[6] Heavy deforestation and cultivation of the Taurus slopes may have led to widespread erosion, contributing to significant progradation of the Cilician coastline, a process seen also in the Plain of Issus.[7] Likewise, the same phenomenon of marshification, the process of land forming larger and permanent wetlands, seen in the Late Roman and Early Islamic periods in the nearby Amuq and Ghab Valleys of the Orontes and Southern 'Iraq, may also have occurred in Cilicia, although very little geomorphology has been conducted.[8] An exception is seen on the slopes of the western Amanus, where extensive erosion occurred at the end of and following the Late Roman period; a factor also contributing to the process of marshification. In the Early Islamic period, marsh dwellers or Zuṭṭ from south-eastern Islamic lands were also relocated and settled in wetland communities along with their water buffalo (Figure 2). The insurgent Jarājima/Mardaites dwelled in the Amanus Mountains and the Isaurians were a local independent group living in pockets of the highlands of Rough Cilicia.

The main roads from Islamic lands came over the Belen and Bahçe Passes across the Amanus into the plain (Figure 24). From Mar'ash, the road descended the Bahçe Pass to Hārūnīyya, south to Kanīsa al-Sawdā', then ran west to Maṣṣīṣa. From Anṭākiya, the road descended the Belen Pass to Iskandarūna, north along the coast to Bayyās, Ḥiṣn al-Tīnāt, around to al-Muthaqqab, and then met the former road at Maṣṣīṣa. The road from Muthaqqab west, although avoiding the coast, followed a straight route across the plain. From there, the road would have been a major one, connecting the large cities of Maṣṣīṣa, Adhana and Ṭarsūs before splitting into two routes: one towards Rough Cilicia and the coast at 'Awlās and Lamas, and the other north, traversing the Taurus Mountains and the Cilician Gates. A second, though less travelled northern route, went from Adhana north via the Sayḥān to Rodandos. A third northern route likely went from Maṣṣīṣa to 'Ayn Zarba, meeting the Kanīsa al-Sawdā'–Hārūnīyya–'Ayn Zarba route, then on to Sīs and via a pass to Feke and Saimbeyli. Two other passes crossed, one north of Kadirli to Kukusos via the Mazgaçbel/Mazgeç (also called the Çiçeklidere Yolu or 'Flowered Stream Road') Pass and another from Andrassos/Andırın to Kukusos via the Meryemçilbel Pass (Figure 3). In Rough Cilicia, the Göksu River also formed a pass from Saluqiyya, capital of the *kleisoura* of Seleukia, towards Claudiopolis (modern Mut) and on to Iconium (modern Konya).

Survey Methodology

Unfortunately, this region has only been the focus of archaeological work since 2004, and most of this work is still largely unpublished. Evidence from survey work is too insufficient to permit a full assessment of historical geography and settlement types, or to allow a

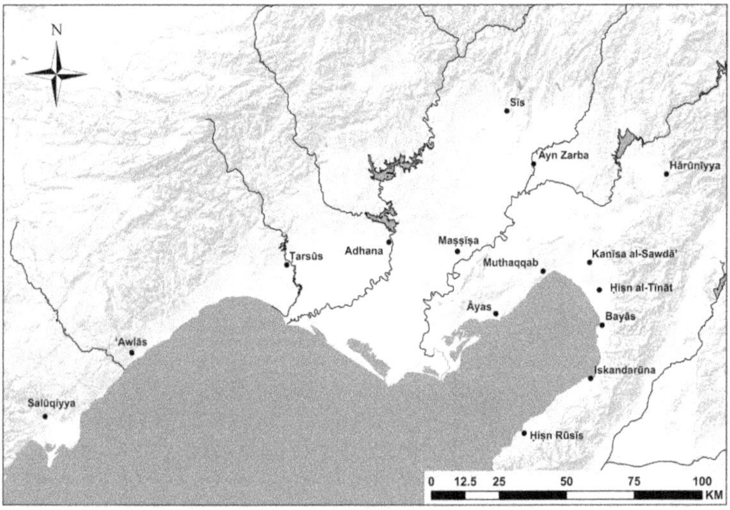

Figure 24 The western *thughūr*

finer dating of rural settlements in the seventh century. While archaeologists conducted many surveys within the very definable landscape, it is surprising that so little is understood of the seventh to eleventh centuries.[9]

Group I: Extensive/Low-Resolution/Large-Area Surveys

The British Institute of Archaeology in Ankara led the first survey in 1951, directed by M. V. Seton-Williams. As its intentions were to record and examine pre-Classical mounded sites in the Cilician Plain and around the Gulf of Iskenderun, the survey does not include many of the important Classical and post-Classical sites.[10] Seton-Williams conflated chronologies for the later periods, but conjectural guesses can be made based on finewares from tables that show sites by ware types (Figure 25). Hellenistic, Roman and Late Roman period wares are grouped together, but 46 have Late Roman period finewares ('Red'). 'Cooking Pots' and 'Wine Jars' are undifferentiated by period. The 'Coarse Red' category is also unclear. Islamic sites are more difficult to discern, as they are only presented in a single table with no phase map or text to describe the nature of settlement. Some

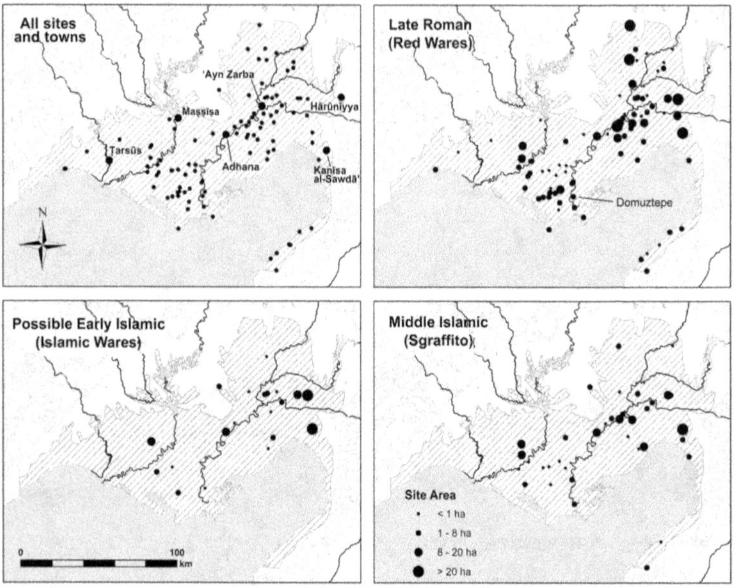

Figure 25 Cilicia Survey (based on Seton-Williams 1954)

20 sites have 'Islamic Wares', but 39 have 'Sgraffiato wares', a different category. Only very tenuous conjectures can be suggested. Perhaps these categories reflect Early Islamic (20 sites) and Middle Islamic/Middle Byzantine (39 sites) period groupings, thereby showing a 2:1 Late Roman and Middle Islamic to Early Islamic period ratio, and a major Late Roman period peak and minor Middle Islamic/Middle Byzantine period peak.

Group II: Intensive/High-Resolution/Large-Area Surveys

More recent surveys have been conducted in the eastern Cilician Plain, supplementing the missing information for settlement and adding to our knowledge of rural Cilicia. The Mopsos Survey covered the entire Plain of Issus itself and the Amanus foothills (A. Killebrew and G. Lehmann, 2004–9). It has found 195 sites, most of which have been dated from the Hellenistic to the Late Roman periods.[11] Preliminary results indicate that in the eastern Cilician Plain, settlement flourished and population expanded during the Roman/

Late Roman periods. The survey benefited from adequate field identifications. It is still unpublished, but will be comparable to the Amuq and Maraş Surveys – and I have begun to study the Islamic ceramics.

Group III: Intensive/High-Resolution/Small Area Surveys

Recently, small-area surveys have filled in regions of eastern Cilicia such as the coastal strip between Yumurtalık and Iskenderun (I. Özgen and M.-H. Gates in 1991); the small area north and south of Kinet Höyük along the coast (A. Eger and A. U. de Giorgi in 2005); a 15 km-radius area, including mainly the Amanus foothills, for geomorphological purposes (T. Beach in 1998–2010); and the area around Osmaniye and the Amanus foothills (F. Tülek in 2005–11). These surveys have not all been published. The Yumurtalık-Iskenderun Survey took place over two weeks in August of 1991 and focused on tells (and pre-Hellenistic sites) (Figure 26).[12] A total of 25 sites was recorded. I analyzed the ceramics in 2013. Of these sites, 13 were Late Roman period, three were definite Early Islamic while three were indefinite, and eight were Middle Islamic/Middle Byzantine period. The largest percentage of sites was Late Roman period (52 per cent), while in the Early Islamic period there was a drop to 12 per cent. Many Late Roman period sites were single-period non-tell settlements. Early Islamic period sites had light assemblages characterized by buff coarseware jars and brittleware cooking pots. The Kırıkköprü Survey was an intensive pedestrian investigation of the area immediately around Kinet Höyük in the Plain of Issus.[13] The area of the survey was a coastal strip roughly 3.5 km north to south by 2 km east to west. A total of six sites was found, four of them Late Roman and one an Early Islamic period site that continued until the early twelfth century. The results do not necessarily indicate a decline in Early Islamic period settlements; the four Late Roman period sites are discrete areas of bridge/road, houses, bath and cemetery that were likely all part of the same settlement – that of the Late Roman period coastal villa, or *mansion*, of Issus. The Early Islamic and Middle Islamic/Middle Byzantine period site can be identified with Ḥiṣn al-Tīnāt, while the successor site in the mid- to

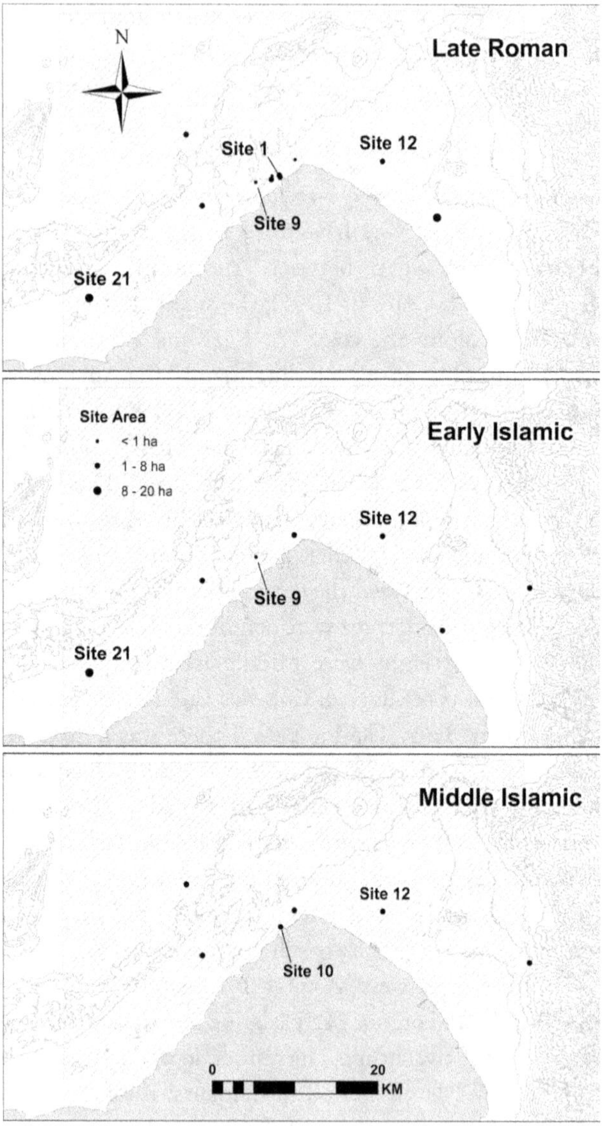

Figure 26 Yumurtalık-Iskenderun Survey, Late Roman through Middle Islamic sites

late twelfth to early fourteenth century is Kinet Höyük itself. A 15 km-radius geomorphology survey around Kinet Höyük conducted nearly every year between 1998 and 2010 by T. Beach identified many Late Roman sites on the western slopes of the Amanus. While unsystematic (and not intensive), in that archaeological site survey was not the primary goal, this investigation is worth mentioning here as part of the Kırıkköprü Survey. The Osmaniye Survey recorded a main Early Islamic period site; however, its preliminary reports do not provide a site gazetteer or maps with which to interpret any of the data.[14]

Settlement in Smooth Cilicia

So far, archaeological evidence affirms that Late Roman period settlement peaked with many sites in the uplands and on the slopes of the Amanus (as shown in the Mopsos and Kinet Höyük geomporphological surveys). Oil presses of the Roman and Late Roman periods have been found throughout Cilicia, attesting to the importance of the olive-oil industry. Excavations at Cilician Domuztepe between 1988 and 1999 revealed a fifth/sixth-century farm-estate that invested in the production of olive oil, as evidenced by a large-capacity olive-oil press and storage *pithoi*. That site did not continue into the Early Islamic period, but it remains useful as it is one of the only rural sites excavated in the plain and provides a hypothetical example of those that may have continued functioning.[15] Sites 9 and 10 from the Yumartalık-Iskenderun Survey were on an extinct volcano's caldera near Erzin. Site 10 had huge coarse-cut basalt stones set upright as an entrance to one of several buildings of indeterminate plan. The pottery was Late Roman period, fifth to seventh century, with one Early Islamic period seventh- to early-eighth-century mortar basin rim. Evidence also indicates that in the Early Islamic period the limit of the frontier was the plain itself, and there was no permanent Islamic settlement in the rugged, mountainous Rough Cilicia (Cilicia Trachea), ancient Isauria. Surveyors noted that Early Islamic period settlements were located on the broad river terraces and at the base of ancient tell sites, rather than on top of them. Many of the sites nearest the estuaries of the main rivers would have been surrounded by wetlands by at least the Early Islamic period.

Textual information unfortunately adds only several rural settlements in the Cilician Plain that have not been located. Yāqūt mentions Adhrama, a village between the Sayḥān and Jayḥān Rivers, and al-ʿAjlānīya in the Marj al-Dībāj pasture about 20 km from al-Maṣṣīṣa towards ʿAyn Zarba, likely in the vicinity of the modern village of Mercimek.[16]

Upland Sites: Monasteries, Tells, Fortresses

Upland sites were frequent in the Roman and Late Roman periods. The geomorphological survey around Kinet Höyük identified several sites on the western foothills of the Amanus between around 150 and 215 m.a.s.l. My examination of these collections showed at least six Roman and Late Roman sites dating until the seventh century, with evidence also for mosaics and tombs. A more intensive survey in 2010 of the Deli Çay and Tum Çay watersheds along these rivers were recorded by the Mopsus Survey and confirmed the presence of Late Roman farms. Inhabitants would have populated the coastal hills, cultivating olives and grapes. Around these sites, the slopes were extensively eroded to bedrock with large gullies and rills. The process of erosion began to occur in the Late Roman period and became more dramatic subsequently, when these sites (and their terraces) were abandoned.[17] One site (Site 6) along the Tum Çay itself had Roman through Early and Middle Islamic period occupation, and could be linked to a local system including Tupras Field/Ḥiṣn al-Tīnāt, watered by the same river. These sites were involved in collecting timber cut from the Amanus above and floated downstream.

Most Islamic sites in the western *thughūr* were situated in the plain, carefully avoiding any artificial or natural rise. There are very few monasteries mentioned in the region of the Cilician Plain. A Syrian Jacobite monastery, Ḥesnā Ḥamūṣā, likely in the foothills of the Amanus east of Osmaniye, has never been definitely located, although Ḥamūs, known more from the second half of the tenth century onwards, is associated with Gavur Kalesi in the Humus Suyu Valley. Bishops from Irenopolis (possibly Hārūnīyya) came from here, according to Michael the Syrian.[18] There was also a monastery on the Jabal Ra's al-Khanzīr (modern Hınzır Burnu) just south of Iskandarūna and Ḥiṣn Rūsīs or Rusūs (Greek Rhosus, modern Arsuz) called 'In Scopulo'. The area between modern Arsuz and the Orontes Delta, where the Amanus Mountains fall directly into the sea, is unsurveyed, and only a dirt road skirts the edge of the shore. Besides the monastery, it was also a place for timber felling.

Tell sites are unusual choices for Early Islamic period settlement, and very few have been definitively identified with the exception of Gözlü Kule in Ṭarsūs and, possibly, Muthaqqab. A small amount of evidence from the tenth and eleventh centuries has been found in layers under the more significant twelfth- to fourteenth-century occupation of the tell of Yumuktepe within Mersin.[19] From the Yumurtalık-Iskenderun Survey, Site 12 (Kara Höyük) is also Seton-Williams' Site 147, and Site 2 on the Mopsus Survey. The last-named did not record any Early Islamic period occupation. The site was a small, high (15 m) mound in a lagoonal area and very fertile. A moderate assemblage of ceramics was found both on the mound slopes and in the east field. The Yumurtalık-Iskenderun Survey Site 21 was a steep, conical mound (13 m) with a large terrace but not very high, and was also Seton-Williams' Yeniköy II. One brittleware holemouth cooking pot (light assemblage) was identified. Other tell settlements can be surmised from texts that mention three as being in the *thughūr*: Tell Jubayr, around 20 km from Ṭarsūs towards the Cilician Gates; and Tells Ḥūm and Ḥāmid, near Maṣṣīṣa – the latter, possibly beneath the town of modern Ceyhan.

Similarly rare are upland fort sites before the tenth century on the Islamic frontier. Ḥiṣn Qatraghāsh was known to have been the first fort built by Hishām with an architect (*muhandis*) from Anṭākiya. Although 'near Maṣṣīṣa', its presumed identification by Hellenkemper and Hild as Sarıseki Kalesi, a Crusader and Ottoman fortification on a flat rise within the coastal Plain of Issus cannot be verified as it falls within a military compound. Ḥiṣn Mūra, built at the same time, protected an Amanus pass ('Aqaba al-Baydā), and may be situated similarly in the still-accessible foothills. From this, we can infer that Ḥiṣn Qatraghāsh also protected a pass, the Çalan Pass. Baghrās and Būqā in the Amuq Plain of the central *thughūr* protected the Belen and the other end of the Çalan/Sarıseki Pass, respectively. These four settlements were all developed by Hishām in the first half of the eighth century as a small system of forts protecting major and minor passes across the Amanus Mountains. One may ask why such a system was necessary, given that the mountains were enclosed within Islamic lands. The investment shows a concern with upland mountain groups such as the Jarājima, who were notoriously difficult to control and who frequently raided towns and caravans.

Settlement in Rough Cilicia

In Rough Cilicia, surveys on the coast since 1962 and inland did not reveal any significant post-seventh-century occupation. Major towns such as Anemourion, Korykos, Korasion and Elaiussa-Sebaste, according to their excavators and surveyors, were largely abandoned by the end of the seventh century or moved in and upland. This seems to be corroborated by Ibn Khurradādhbih, who states:

> beyond Ṭarsūs on the seashore there are ruined Roman towns [*mudun*] like Qalamya, sixteen miles from Ṭarsūs, then Qurqus, ten miles from Qalamya, then Qarāsya, four miles from Qurqus, then Iskandarīyya twelve miles from Qarāsya, then Sabasṭya, four miles from Iskandarīyya, then Salūqiyya, four miles from the sea in a plain, then Nabīk, a fort [*ḥiṣn*] on a mountain.[20]

The inclusion of Nabīk, neither coastal nor a town but an upland *ḥiṣn* and, therefore, possibly inhabited and not ruined, is suggestive of the Byzantine population having abandoned the coasts for the more secure upland fortifications. One should not, however, rule out total abandonment. We can deduce coastal settlements, albeit perhaps ephemeral, based on Early Islamic period activity (or raids) for the procurement for shipbuilding of timber that was felled and sent down mountain streams to the coast in areas around Anamur (Anemorium), Salūqiyya (Seleukia/Silifke) and Lāmīs/ Elaiussa-Sebaste. R. Blanton's and N. Rauh's surveys around the western coast of Rough Cilicia concluded that there was an overall decrease in settlement and population in the periods 700–969 ('Early Byzantine') and 970–1071 ('Late Byzantine'), which had actually already begun in late sixth and early seventh centuries. The presence of sherds at Iotape, Selinus and Antiochia ad Cragum, and standing architecture such as a fortress-tower on the promontory of Selinus at the mouth of a river, may indicate other isolated Islamic period coastal settlements beyond the traditional frontier zone.[21] Middle Byzantine period building with the reconquest of Cilicia at Seleukia and Korykos indicates the importance of controlling this area, its resources and ports. Upland sites in Rough Cilicia were isolated, locally producing their own pottery. Excavations at Kilise Tepe in the Göksu River (Greek Calycadnus) valley floor, between 1994 and 2011, have revealed important evidence for local ceramic industries in the Late Roman period.[22] A dearth of excavations and knowledge of local ceramic traditions may play a role in the degree to which decline is emphasized, and is often attributed to Arab raiding.

Way Stations

The term *ḥuṣūn* in relation to the Early Islamic period in this region commonly referred to a series of way stations. Between Bayās and al-Muthaqqab, tenth-century Islamic geographers mention the fort of Ḥiṣn al-Tināt (Figure 27). The site can be identified with an area of land just south, and along the southern perimeter fence of, the large Botaş compound in a series of cultivated fields belonging to the Tüpraş oil company. The site is also about 900 m north of Kinet Höyük, a tall substantial multi-period harbour site, and the town of Issus, of Alexander and Darius fame. Indeed, the name Kinet most likely comes as a corruption of al-Tīnāt or 'the Figs', the abbreviated form of the fortified settlement mentioned in Muqaddasī.[23] The survey of the Tüpraş site, which I directed in association with Bilkent

Figure 27 Tüpraş Field/Ḥiṣn al-Tīnāt, eastern gate and internal rooms (courtesy of M.-H. Gates)

University and the University of North Carolina at Greensboro, consisted of four to five phases of construction ranging from the eighth to the early twelfth centuries, affirming its foundation in the early ʻAbbāsid period. Its earliest phase(s) (IV and V) revealed a series of well-built fortification walls with ashlars, although the orientation was difficult to ascertain. By the tenth century, some of these walls were incorporated into a square fortified enclosure with added corner towers and midpoint buttresses. Rooms were arranged around the interior perimeter of the walls, and there was likely a central courtyard. The eastern gate, the only entrance discovered, whose stones were partially robbed, was quite broad, estimated at *c.*4 m wide. Furthermore, the location of the site, abutting the coast with a presumed harbour and along the coastal road, disproves any military-strategic siting implied by the use of the term *ḥiṣn*, generally translated as 'fort'. Rather, the settlement was mentioned as a gathering and distribution point for cut timber from the nearby Amanus Mountains. Its enclosure would therefore have protected a coveted natural resource and functioned as a fortified way station on the main route between Syria and Anatolia. The southern Botaş company fence cut the site, which extended northwards and has been completely destroyed by a man-made waterway. Site 7, identified by the Yumurtalik-Iskenderun Survey, was near by, with a light Early Islamic and Middle Islamic period assemblage.

Other settlements that have not been identified may have also been part of this way station system, such as Ḥiṣn al-Mulawwān, located south of Maṣṣīṣa near the Jayḥān and coast (likely between Yumurtalık and Karataş, and possibly associated with Greek Mallus) and Ḥiṣn al-Mūra, located between Maṣṣīṣa and the Amanus Mountains. While this system of way stations occurred on routes throughout the *thughūr*, hostel or inn settlements, more explicitly named *funduq*, were mentioned mainly in Cilicia; they included al-Funduq near Maṣṣīṣa; Funduq al-Ḥusayn, either near Ṭarsūs or between Maṣṣīṣa and Iskandarūna, where the Caliph Mu'taḍid passed through in 900; and Funduq Bughā and Funduq al-Jadīd, between Adhana and Ṭarsūs. Funduq Bughā was constructed on the orders of Bughā al-Saghrīr (d. 862). That these settlements are referred to as *funduq* and not *ḥiṣn* may suggest that they were not fortified but rather for pilgrims and merchants, and were part of a similar system of way stations occupying intervals along the main route that connected all of the cities of Cilicia.

Towns

According to texts, the majority of Cilicia – with the exception of al-Maṣṣīṣa and al-Muthaqqab – was the last part of the *thughūr* to be built up.[24] 'Abd al-Malik (r. 683–705) rebuilt the first *thughūr* town, al-Maṣṣīṣa, constructing a mosque there. This account is probably not entirely accurate, as it is known that Mu'āwiya established a settlement at Ṭarsūs in 651/2, yet this may not have been anything more than military/nomadic encampments. The caliph's choice of Maṣṣīṣa as the initial focus of urban development on the frontier was a sensible one: it was an important central point and crossroads for Cilician traffic. For this reason, it is perhaps unsurprising (and unhelpful) that so many small settlements around the plain are described in geographies only as being 'near al-Maṣṣīṣa'. Between these routes were smaller way stations, known by name but not all identified.

Recent excavation, and site-survey ceramic analysis in the past decade, permits a greater understanding of the urban, built *thughūr*.

Many of the towns were not seriously renovated until the early 'Abbāsid period, yet we know that during the Umayyad expansion in the mid-seventh to mid-eighth century, the landscape was dotted with preexisting rural Christian sites, which were continuing cities as demonstrated by named bishoprics, the presence of seasonal pastoralists and military Arab camps, and at least one restored Islamic period town. In the Early Islamic period, the area included the main frontier towns of Ṭarsūs, Adhana and Maṣṣīṣa. Many Islamic geographers and historians wrote that three additional settlements, 'Ayn Zarba, Kanīsa al-Sawdā' and Hārūnīyya, were established in the 'Abbāsid period. The *thaghr* system encompassed other smaller settlements, such as the coastal forts of al-Muthaqqab, Iskandarūna, Bayās and the 'Abbāsid way station of Ḥiṣn al-Tīnāt. All of these comprised systems of nested networks that functioned in connection with one another.

What is immediately noticeable about the arrangement of Cilicia's three major cities in both the Late Roman and Early Islamic periods is that they are evenly spaced from one another, located on the three main rivers that water the plain, and are not on the coast but are roughly equidistant between the mountain passes and the sea. The advantages of a north–south and east–west centrality are apparent and probably cannot be overstated; they reflect the fact that Cilicia was indeed first and foremost a crossroads linking Anatolia to Syria and that it relied on transportation and trade through these land corridors. Secondarily, these settlements were linked to the sea. In the Late Roman period, accounts describe the Cilician Plain towns of Mopsuestia/al-Maṣṣīṣa on the Pyramus River/Nahr Jayḥān, Ṭarsūs on the Cydnus River/Nahr al-Baradān, and Antioch/Anṭākiya on the Orontes River/Nahr al-'Aṣī as navigable riverine ports. At some point, the rivers could no longer support shipping traffic due to silting of their beds. This may already have been a concern in the fourth and fifth centuries, when a law appeared in the Theodosian Code mandating that a fleet be responsible for clearing the Orontes River of 'obstructions' – whether natural silt accumulation or pirates is uncertain. Evidence that these cities continued to function as ports in the Early Islamic period is supported by the geographers' perceptions of them as coastal or sea-accessible settlements. However, on his tenth-century map, Ibn Ḥawqal indicates quite clearly that the settlements are on rivers and not on the coast. The estuaries of these rivers created increasingly permanent marshland that would also have deterred major urban settlement.

Excavations around the city at Ṭarsūs have revealed a mainly mid- to late-eighth-century settlement. On the prominent tell of Gözlü Kule south of the city, excavations since 2001 by a team from Boğaziçi University led by A. Özyar uncovered eighth- to eleventh-century domestic residences. The structures, at the summit of the hill overlooking the city, are plainly built but equipped with sophisticated septic drainage systems and pits that cut directly into Roman period and Iron Age levels. One building, with a poorly preserved possible niche, may have been a neighbourhood or private mosque, although this is still tenuous. The material finds, however, both from these excavations and from the original ones by H. Goldmann in the 1930s and 40s, include the richest and most diverse range of ceramics seen on the frontier, from locally-produced wares to imported high-quality ceramics such as luster- and cobalt-painted wares from 'Iraq and further east. Most evident was the range of shapes and glazes, using every possible glazing style on every possible form of vessel. Luster glass and a range of glass bottles for medicinal use are among the other high-quality and unusual objects found in this area.[25] At least in this part of the tell, very few remains of Late Roman period structures were found. In the lower city, an area of approximately 40 ha based on the Roman city wall, excavations at the Cumhuriyet Meydanı (Republic Square) from 1993 uncovered a main colonnaded east–west street (possibly the *dekoumanos*) with porticoed market buildings to either side. In the final periods there were many rebuildings alongside the street, and also pits – although it appears that the street itself was little changed. Holemouth brittleware cooking pots, dating between the eighth and tenth centuries, and associated coins constituted 30 per cent of the ceramic assemblage, indicating Early Islamic period presence in the lower town on the main streets as well. A small number of seventh/eighth-century brittleware forms were also uncovered, giving the only evidence for continuity in the city. A vertical-walled black holemouth cooking vessel may have been produced at Ṭarsūs. Kilns producing large numbers of LR 1, 5 and 6 amphorae types from the Cumhuriyet Meydanı excavations suggest not only ceramic production but local wine and/or olive-oil production that may have continued into the ninth century. While only limited excavation was done to either side of the colonnaded street, the space may be compared to Anṭākiya, where the Early Islamic period city to either side of the main *cardo* thrived and transformed into shops, residences, private potters' quarters and burial space. Also in the lower city, a Roman bath (known as Eski Hamam) was reused as a ceramic and glass kiln in the Early and Middle Islamic periods, indicating the existence of manufacturing and production. In both the lower and upper cities, the archaeological evidence from excavations reveals a strong eighth to tenth-century presence, with a slight seventh/eighth-century presence in the lower town. This may correspond with the textual evidence, which states that the settlement was initially a camp under Mu'āwiya in 651/2 and only developed permanently in 779 under al-Mahdī.

In Maṣṣīṣa, G. Salmeri and A. L. d'Agata recently surveyed the city wall (enclosing about 40 ha) and found it to have been built in successive phases from the fifth century until the thirteenth.[26] While the city may have been first settled under Mu'āwiya, accounts mention that 'Abd al-Malik refortified it, repairing the wall, installing a garrison, and building a mosque in 703–5. These texts also maintain that it was the focus of much activity under successive Umayyad caliphs, including Walīd, 'Umar II, possibly Hishām, and Marwān II. Under 'Umar II, the town of Kafarbayyā on the opposite bank of the river was built and quickly became a significant focus of settlement which is still visible today. At Adhana, the modern city prevents excavation but early digging in the Tepebağ quarter on the west bank of the river revealed Islamic remains, and travellers in the early twentieth century attributed the bridge as Islamic period and a fortification on the east bank as Byzantine. Textual records indicate that it was an encampment established by al-Walīd in 743 and not initialy built up until either 758/9 or 761/2 under al-Manṣūr.

The towns of Kanīsa al-Sawdā', 'Ayn Zarba and Hārūnīyya are mentioned by accounts as 'Abbāsid foundations and attributed most frequently to Hārūn al-Rashīd. The first two were former Late Roman towns, which appear on the fifth-century Peutinger Table as stops between Alexandretta and Mopsuestia. However, they may not have experienced substantial seventh- to eighth-century occupation, as is demonstrated by survey surface collections. Archaeological survey work has been done to varying degrees in all three sites. Kanīsa al-Sawdā' (The Black Church), the former Epiphaneia, is situated directly at the point where the narrow coastal corridor and easternmost extension of the Cilician Plain, known as the Plain of Issus, opens up into the plain. The site also sits on the eastern edge of an extinct volcano and a large basalt field, the source of its building materials, which gave rise to the Arabic name of the settlement. It is about 150 enclosing a natural outcropping, main colonnaded street, open colonnaded court or agora, and surrounding buildings such as a theatre and bath. The town was fed by an aqueduct that brought water down either from the Amanus Mountains or a local spring, and emptied into a *castellum divisorum* or nymphaeum. Observations by Jennifer Tobin between 1993 and 2000, and the Mopsus Survey in 2004, recorded the city plan, surviving architecture and collected ceramics. The ceramics demonstrated continuous strong Late Roman period occupation until the early seventh century, but very light seventh/eighth-century and slightly more of an eighth- to tenth-century presence. More recently, salvage excavations by the Hatay Museum under the direction of Ömer Çelik have revealed a bath with a later phase of Early Islamic period (eighth- to tenth-century) shops, a street, water system and a warehouse.[27] Historical accounts state that it was fortified by Hārūn al-Rashīd during his reign, in either 799 or 806. The Middle Islamic period occupation was heavily represented, with many ceramics dating from the twelfth to the fourteenth centuries. It is likely that one of the baths was transformed into a ceramic workshop producing specifically Port St. Symeon ware, ubiquitous throughout Cilicia.

'Ayn Zarba is located farther north up the Jayḥān from Maṣṣīṣa, on the way to the region's mountain passes. It is well sited just north of the Jayḥān, where the river is met by several small streams (such as the Sombaz Çayı, which fed one aqueduct to the site) before turning to the south and becoming more narrowly incised. A team directed by R. Posamentir conducted intensive geophysical prospection, surface collection, and architectural recording including the perimeter city walls.[28] It is evident that, like Ṭarsūs (and Anṭākiya), the main colonnaded *cardo* remained an important artery throughout the settlement's post-Classical history. Late Roman period ceramics continued until the early seventh century. My preliminary analysis shows that the site has only a slight ceramic presence in the seventh/eighth century, in contrast to a marked and major ceramic presence in the mid-eighth to tenth centuries. This latter was characterized by an overwhelming amount of brittleware holemouth rims and some moulded buffwares, but very few seventh-century diagnostics and a small number of Syrian yellow glaze wares. This suggests a stronger ninth-century occupation for the site as compared with the preceding centuries.[29] The findings partially corroborate the textual evidence, which mentions that the settlement was first built up by Hārūn al-Rashīd in either 796 or 804. The site continues until the fourteenth century; however, at some stage it contracts and a new wall using spolia and a moat/ditch is built. The contraction seems to have occurred by the sixth century, as argued by Posamentir. However, the upper courses, or second phase, are dated at least from the tenth century, as evidenced by tenth/eleventh-century turquoise glazed ceramics in the mortar of the wall.[30] The wall was likely partially or wholly repaired, and is attributable perhaps to the period of Byzantine reoccupation of the settlement in the last half of the tenth century.

Hārūnīyya was strategically sited on the plain guarding the easternmost south–north route into the Taurus and also the Darb al-'Ayn (or Bahçe Pass), one of the two main Amanus Mountain east–west passes leading to Mar'ash. Hārūnīyya, according to texts, was first fortified and garrisoned with a mosque by Hārūn al-Rashīd during the reign of his father, al-Mahdī. Its actual location is undetermined at present, and may be in one of two areas. The first is near Düziçi on the lowest slopes just above the smaller Düziçi Ovası, an enclosed plain in eastern Cilicia watered by the Deliçay River. This is also the settlement of Irenopolis, and Late Roman period ceramic and mosaic remains attest to this identification. However, apart from local claims and attributed Early Islamic finds, no definitive material culture of this period is noted from the town itself. The second possibility is Örenşehir, much nearer to the Jayḥān River, just north-west of Osmaniye on the road that forks off the Plain of Issus route and crosses the same mountain pass, the Darb al-'Ayn. The site is a square enclosure, 250 m per side, with round towers, and has been surveyed by F. Tulek and her team from Kocaeli University.[31] The ceramic assemblage contains nothing before the eighth century, indicating this site as a new 'Abbāsid foundation.[32] Its size, location and range of material culture suggests a stronger identification with Hārūnīyya than Düziçi, yet is much larger than the system of newly-founded way stations such as Ḥiṣn al-Tīnāt. However, at the same time we have no evidence for pre-Islamic period settlement unlike at 'Ayn Zarba and Kanīsa al-Sawdā'. Nevertheless, viewed in the context of these two sites, it forms part of a larger network of settlements developed at the same time.

These three towns together fill the eastern part of the Cilician Plain, are all equidistant from one another as points on a triangle, and are all placed in the plain in strategic locations. They were also part of the same route. The easiest route would have followed a narrow north–south valley between Kanīsa al-Sawdā' and Ḥārūnīyya (at Örenşehir) outlined by outcrops to the west and the Amanus Mountains to the east. It then followed the Jayḥān at its widest point, where it cuts east–west across the plain towards 'Ayn Zarba. The emphasis in developing these towns leading north indicates a desire to not only settle the eastern plain but also to improve networks of trade and security with the Jayḥān-Taurus Mountain pass leading to Feke and Kayseri in Cappadocia. Sīs, situated at the entrance to this pass, was heavily developed only later in the mid-ninth century, as is indicated by textual evidence.

Muthaqqab, Bayās and Iskandarūna comprise a third group of *thughūr* settlements that were located on the coast around the Plain of Issus, but were much smaller in size. Their Islamic period areas of occupation are less definitively identified, mainly because the coast has succumbed to heavy industrial development. At the northernmost point of the Bay of Iskenderun was the harbour site of Mutallip Höyük, which showed Roman and Islamic period remains (standing walls) on a tell and on a south-east terrace just to the east. The site can be likely identified with the *thaghr* al-Muthaqqab, and was surveyed briefly by M-H. Gates and İ. Özgen in 1991.[33] The ceramics from ten bags, however, included Late Roman until the early seventh century and Middle Islamic period, but no definitive Early Islamic period pieces. It is difficult to determine whether Early Islamic period settlement focused on the terrace at the base of the mound, as was characteristic, because the site is entirely subsumed by the Toros Gübre fertilizer plant. Muthaqqab was built, according to textual evidence, in the Umayyad period under either 'Umar II or Hishām. Bayās is even more obscure, and may have been located near the Payas Çayı under the site of a Crusader fort, which in turn may have been built over by a sixteenth-century Ottoman pentagonal fort still standing. Iskandarūna, a growing coastal town today, is difficult to pinpoint but may have been in the Esentepe and/or Çankaya neighbourhoods of the city. The town and region were known to be under the control of Maslama b. 'Abd al-Malik, but texts only mention that it was fortified by Hārūn al-Rashīd.

It is interesting to note the absence of coastal ports between Muthaqqab and the western boundary of the Cilician Plain, a coastline roughly 150 km long, particularly given the closer spacing of coastal ports along the Plain of Issus and the entire Levantine shore. This empty coastline, the 'belly' of the Cilician Plain comprising the three river deltas, was settled in the Classical periods, yet at present there is no textual evidence and no archaeological information to support the idea that any of these sites continued. On the western edge of the plain, where it lies adjacent to the region of Rough Cilicia, Ḥiṣn Āwlās possibly served Ṭarsūs as a port and/or replaced Qalamya (possibly Greek Kalanthia), which was destroyed. It may have been located at Karaduvar, a coastal suburb east of Mersin, as is indicated by Byzantine accounts and by Idrīsī, who states that it was two days from there to Salūqiyya. It is also possible that it was at Elaiussa-Sebaste near the mouth of the Lamīs River, although excavators emphasize that they have not found any significant post-seventh-century material there. The settlement of Lamīs, where Byzantine and Islamic prisoner exchanges took place, has also not been definitively located, although a medieval village and later-period castle by that name are present. From this point west, we can assume that former ports in Rough Cilicia became coastal stopping points and very small settlements for timber acquisition.

Conclusions

The picture of settlement for the western *thughūr* is still coming into focus. However, we can note several similar trends in patterns seen elsewhere on the frontier. Settlement peaked in the Late Roman period with sites on the plain and slopes of the Amanus and Taurus Mountains. The number of inhabited sites dropped significantly after the seventh century though not completely. Early Islamic period sites were situated on the plain and avoided the slopes with very few exceptions that were attributed to strategic locations near mountain passes. Early Islamic period sites also were very limited in Rough Cilicia with perhaps some small isolated Islamic sites near the coast, while Byzantine sites remained in the uplands. Major way stations and larger towns linked by a clear network of routes testify to the importance of Cilicia as a crossroads linking Byzantine and Islamic lands. The archaeological chronology seems to confirm the textual evidence at present: the majority of settlement was only from the eighth century on. Seventh/eighth century sites were few, though not completely absent. Publications from the many ongoing or recently completed projects in the next several years should provide a much fuller understanding of this key frontier region.

PART 2

HYDRAULIC VILLAGES AND FORTIFIED CASTLES: A NARRATIVE OF SETTLEMENT

In the days of old, cities were numerous in Rūm, but now they have become few. Most of the districts are prosperous and pleasant, and have (each) an extremely strong fortress, on account of the frequency of the raids which the fighters of the faith direct upon them. To each village appertains a castle, where in time of flight (they may take shelter).[1]

The above observation on Byzantine Anatolia, made by an anonymous geographer writing in Persian in 982–3 CE, succinctly describes two very different settlement patterns: one characterized by numerous cities before the tenth century, which changed to one characterized by defensible fortifications with villages attached. The process of settlement transformation encapsulated in this anecdote is precisely that observed in the western Mediterranean: *incastellamento*, or the villa-to-village model of transition from open, dispersed and largely unfortified lowland farms and towns to more nucleated but still dispersed, defensible fortified villages and castles in the uplands.[2]

From the archaeological evidence, this basic process has been shown in the Amuq Plain, Kahramanmaraş Plain, Plain of Issus, and other areas surveyed throughout not only the Near Eastern but also the Andalusian, or Spanish, *thughūrs* as a key settlement change that took place gradually from the Late Hellenistic to the end of the Early Islamic period and then rapidly during the Middle Islamic period. The nucleation of settlement in the landscape prior to the first millennium BCE is related to the presence of city states, while the subsequent dispersed settlement pattern is a result of the formation and expansion of larger territorial empires.[3] In the Middle Islamic period, sites, still located in all parts of the plains, grouped as larger villages around fortified high tells in a pattern that can be termed 'nucleated dispersal'. This is morphologically and chronologically similar to the process of *incastellamento* noted by archaeologists working in Spain and Italy, and draws from the political fragmentation and instability in the wake of declining empires. Here, independent rulers held, though did not necessarily live on, *iqṭā'* lands distributed around towns and districts. Such a pattern echoes the ancient city states with one major exception: these communities were not entirely independent, but were based still on a loose system of patronage and even cooperative rule, with tax collection, over a preexisting dispersed settled landscape. Unlike in the Early Islamic period, where in times of insecurity villagers withdrew into fortified cities, by the Middle Islamic period they retreated to protected elevated fortifications, some built by local rulers and some realized as community-based initiatives, showing that villagers also took matters of protection into their own hands.

Yet the motivations for and consequences of these transformations remain unclear. As such, the historical evidence for the Islamic–Byzantine frontier should not be avoided but rather configured with the archaeological picture. These archaeological and historical pieces can be assembled to form a diachronic narrative of the Islamic–Byzantine frontier, which addresses several key issues. Landscape archaeologists and medieval historians working on the other side of the Mediterranean Sea in the *thughūr* of al-Andalus, Italy and Sicily have demonstrated remarkably similar patterns that will be examined side by side. Although the importance of micro-regions is emphasized, comparing surveys across different geographies is important as it helps show broader patterns and avoids compartmentalization.

Although the Early Islamic period comprises the main body of the study, along with the Middle Byzantine period, the Late Roman and Middle Islamic periods will be similarly interrogated on a lesser scale, as a prologue and epilogue, using the same set of questions: (1) What are the main *types* of settlement from Anatolian and Andalusian surveys and what are their *distributions* and *patterns*? (Table 2). What other parallels are there for the settlement, settlement pattern, and environmental context from other areas of Anatolia and the Near

Table 2 Settlement patterns on the *thughūr*

Late Hellenistic, Roman, Late Roman and Early Islamic Period Patterns
- Settlement on low, flat sites, which over time could become small mounds.
- Avoidance of, or very scanty occupation on, tells (partially excludes Late Hellenistic).
- Occupation of lower towns beside tells.
- Small sites, often under 1 ha in size, and dispersed.
- Sites located near canal networks (partially includes Middle Islamic).

Early Islamic Period Patterns
- Sites located near springs, sites with hydraulic devices (water mills) [includes Middle Islamic].
- Sites in marshland or marsh-susceptible lowlands.
- Avoidance of upland sites.
- Sites established on periphery of larger earlier sites.
- Avoidance of major river-port sites.
- Half the number of sites occupied, as in the Roman or Late Roman (the highest peak) in certain micro-regions (not the Aleppo area, or parts of the Jazīra).
- Low sedentary population shared with pastoralists.

Middle Islamic Period Patterns
- Occupation on large, low, flat Early Islamic sites continued.
- Sites are clustered together and agglomerative.
- Settlement on tells, some following Hellenistic occupation.
- Tells often included as part of a low, flat site.
- Construction and occupation of upland castles.
- Revival (second highest peak) in settlement.

East? (3) What are the historical trajectories behind these settlements, including the movement and interaction of frontier populations? These questions will show that the frontier was more complicated than the concept 'no man's land' would indicate, and was characterized by peaks and reductions in settlement and population.

The narrative offers several means of analysis through problems associated with Islamic archaeology and the frontier, such as how to represent seventh-century continuity, the rural and environmental landscape, and archaeology and history. It allows for a differentiation to be made between the transitional periods of Late Roman and Early Islamic settlement. At the same time, it builds upon a symbiotic relationship between settlement and the changing environmental landscape of the frontier. In incorporating historical evidence, it provides political, economic and social contexts for shifts in settlement with changing trajectories of settled and nomadic peoples over time. Finally, in Chapter 10, the inhabitants of the frontier emerge, their interactions and exchanges are examined, and the notion of 'frontier' itself is challenged.

CHAPTER 6

PROLOGUE: UPLAND SETTLEMENTS IN THE LATE ROMAN PERIOD (FOURTH TO SEVENTH CENTURIES)

> *We have hills, either in our own territory or around it; some bisect the plain, others, with a broad sweep enclose the entrance or bar it in at the outer limits. Some of them differ in appearance from the level plains, for they are raised aloft, yet they vie in fertility with the lands at their feet. Farmers work there, in land no less desirable, driving their ploughs to the summits.*[1]

Evidence from regional surveys has shown that by the Late Roman period, settlement in the plains and surrounding foothills and uplands of the Islamic–Byzantine frontier reached its height, with sites dotting every part of the landscape and epitomized by the spectacular villages on the North Syrian Jibāl. This was a continuation and peak of the pattern of settlement that began in the first millennium BCE, *c.*900, termed the Great Dispersal by Wilkinson.[2] This sharply contrasts with patterns of nucleation in settlement seen mainly before the Hellenistic period or even the Iron Age. The nucleation of settlement prior to the first millennium has generally been attributed to local and central urban-based systems in the Bronze Age with more restrictive market economies.

Agriculturally dependent rural settlements linking to regional urban centers within larger and external-based economic and transportation networks exhibit settlement patterns of dispersal. These dispersed landscapes are indicative of expansive and diverse territories, unified under a protectorate empire. In the Late Roman period, the dispersal process was no less remarkable as it occurred in many lands that were only marginally productive – such as those that lay in northern Syria and Mesopotamia, whose annual rainfall was between 200 and 600 mm/annum. This was supported by a phenomenon of widespread urbanization spanning the fourth and fifth centuries.[3] The region between the Euphrates and Balikh Rivers experienced the largest settlement peaks from the fourth to the sixth centuries, including the areas of Birecik-Carchemish, Kurban Höyük, Gritille, Titriş, Lidar, Tell Rifaʿat, the Tabqa Reservoir, Sweyhat, eastern Cilicia/Plain of Issus, and likely the Nahr Sajūr and western Amanus slopes (Mopsos Survey), with sites indiscriminately occupying all parts of the landscape. All regions affected by this dispersal displayed a consistent, specific site type – the rural settlement in the plain – and a pattern of expansion into upland sites. However, the expansion of sites in the Late Roman period was not consistently seen in all parts of the Near East at precisely the same time.[4] Uneven settlement patterns were linked to several phenomena, and occurred in specific micro-regions within the larger landscape.

Rural Sites in the Plain

The apparent reduction of sites in the Late Roman period in the Amuq is not a rupture of settlement but shows a continuum from the Early Roman phase without apparent breaks. It was observed early on that Late Roman period sites differed significantly from pre-Roman and Middle Islamic/Medieval period ones. The former were dispersed and predominately small, flat scatters or low mounds, sometimes designated as farms or farmsteads and unwalled, some single-period, and averaging 1 ha in area. Tells in the eastern *thughūr*, such as those documented in the Bozova-Urfa and Lidar Höyük Surveys, also generally had no, or very scanty, remains. Their ceramics came from lower towns such as the village to the north of Lidar Höyük at the foot of the tell. As types, these sites bore signs of direct continuity from the Roman and, usually, Hellenistic periods. These patterns were common throughout the Near East and noted in many older surveys that were tell-focused, such as: the Khabur Survey by Liere and Lauffray; the Tell Rifa'at/Nahr Qoueiq, Adıyaman, Gritille, Titriş and Lidar Surveys; and in newer surveys that considered flat sites, such as the Jerablus Tahtani, Sweyhat, Balikh, Middle Euphrates, North Jazira and Beydar Surveys; and the eastern Cilicia/Plain of Issus Survey by Gates and Özgen. The Amuq, Tell Rifa'at, Kurban Höyük and Adıyaman Surveys also show evidence that the dispersed nature of sites was not completely haphazard but linearly organized along canals, rivers, tributary streams and routes through and around the plain. Indeed, sites can become useful proxies for canals, which are harder to detect but can be inferred. Small, newly-founded settlements were part of a continuing need to develop canal systems on the plain. Canal and river sites were not just intended for managing irrigation but also acted as natural field boundaries and transportation conduits, as explained by Libanius himself in his fourth-century panegyric to Antioch: 'The countryside is divided up between them [the rivers]; the river flows through the areas which derive no assistance from the lake; similarly, the lake extends over those areas where there is no aid from the river.'[5] A long, significant canal was observed running parallel to the Balikh River, and extensive qanat systems were mapped around al-Andarīn.[6] The Nahr Semiramis irrigated the lands along the Middle Euphrates. Along the Upper Euphrates River, the Kurban Höyük Survey noted sites at relatively short intervals, averaging 2.4 km apart. At the same time, the Lower Euphrates and Tigris of the Sāsānian Empire fed an interlocking dense network of canals of all scales, including the 230 km sixth-century Nahrawan Canal, which irrigated 8,000 m^2 of land. New sites were also founded at evenly spaced intervals along major routes. As agricultural settlements, these were involved in wheat, vine and olive production, as is demonstrated by the olive press found at the fifth/sixth-century site of Domuztepe in Cilicia, at AS 341, and a possible one at 204/Harranköy in the Amuq.

Tell sites were mainly avoided; however, there were some exceptions – usually taking one of five forms. The first type had small occupations, limited to isolated buildings or small villages that were not walled. The excavation of these in the Amuq is revealing; they show a greatly diminished settlement pattern as compared to the earlier Bronze and Iron Age occupational levels. At Çatal Höyük (AS 167), excavations uncovered a small fifth- and sixth-century village built over only part of the top surface. An example of the same type of settlement is the modern village of Atchana, clustered around the southern end of its tell (AS 136) while the rest, now a protected site, was never settled. The Middle and Late Bronze Age capital of the Amuq featured only a slight Late Roman period presence, from ceramics and rooftiles.[7] A second tell type was the monastery. At Tell al-Judaidah (AS 176) in the Amuq, a small monastery with chapel, residential building and cistern was noted.[8] The presence of monasteries on tells or hilltops demonstrates these communities' attempts to actively isolate themselves (to a degree) from the rest of society, in a process that begins in this period and continues through the Early and Middle Islamic periods. A third type was the cemetery. Some tells were also used for burial, such as Çatal Höyük in the Amuq whose cemetery was walled, and Zeytinlibahçe Höyük and Fıstıklı Höyük on the Euphrates where excavation uncovered Late Roman and Roman cemeteries, respectively.[9] Two other types are more transient and difficult to prove with concrete evidence. These were the use of tells as temporary military posts, better known in the Ottoman period, and pastoralist camps. Based on tenuous numismatic evidence, this light occupation is possible for Tell Kurdu (AS 94).[10] Such small inhabitation types, including tiny villages and lone farmhouses, monasteries, cemeteries, military posts and pastoralist camps, demonstrate the elusiveness and near invisibility of Late Roman (and Early Islamic) period occupation on tells. As such, tell occupation in the Late Roman period can be misleading in terms of data. While the sites may have been physically large or tall in relation to others, their settlements may have been very small, distorting analyses of area coverage by period as a comparative marker of settlement.[11]

Expansion of Upland Sites

One of the hallmarks of Late Roman period settlements is their wide dispersal in order to populate not only the plains but the uplands on foothills, in highland valleys and on plateaus and ridges. Some of these sites were tied to montane industries, such as stone quarrying and the steatite, copper and gold mines in the Amanus west of Antioch, whose attendant sites were all dated to the Late Roman period. Steatite was used both for everyday production in forming utensils and also decoratively, in making plaques with religious iconography. Other upland sites included fortifications. The three discovered in the Amanus overlooked the Amuq Plain and were high above olive-and vine-producing elevations. The site of Burç from the Adıyaman Survey was similar.[12] These Late Roman period military forts in the uplands resembled small, well-defended watchtowers. These were probably connected as part of a signalling system to warn against incursions. Forts or villages with towers gave a provided a defensive function to the many Late Roman period upland sites that were rural and agrarian in nature. The valleys east of Antioch and south of the Amuq and Orontes were teeming with sites on valley floors, slopes and hilltops of all types. Most were larger sites with finewares and mosaic floors suggesting villas, estates, churches and monasteries rather than single farms. Late Roman period settlements with fineware ceramic assemblages and associated agricultural activity, including terracing, were similarly seen on the other side of the Amanus on the upland slopes over the Plain of Issus. These settlements on the Syrian Jibāl, Amuq and the Orontes were incentives for military veterans to reclaim new agricultural areas, as attested by inscriptions.[13] Monastic communities and pilgrimage centers were also often characteristically sited in the uplands, and had a relationship with lowland or nearby upland villages. Monastic settlements, particularly as they continued during the Early Islamic period, will be discussed more fully in Chapter 7. For the present, it is important to note that their shift upland was gradual, beginning in the early fourth century and peaking in the mid-fifth to mid-sixth century. Similar settlement patterns show the highest peaks in the sixth century for the Jibāl in northern Syria. These upland settlements were self-sufficient to a degree, yet centered upon the export economy of olive oil – albeit not exclusively, but as a dominant element in trade with Constantinople and points in between.[14] Theodoret, Bishop of Cyrrhus in the 440s, wrote of this area: 'In the plain (*choria*) have been built villages both small and great, adjoining the hills on either side.'[15] Gindaros, in the uplands of the 'Afrīn Valley, was one such example of a monastery/large village or *kōmē*.[16] Upland sites were also detected as small farmhouses or villages in the Orontes Delta;[17] and on the western slopes of the Amanus, in both geomorphological and archaeological surveys; not to mention the monasteries on Mount Cassius. Caves were used by hermits near the Euphrates River. Similarly in Lycia, at the western end of the Taurus range, churches, monasteries and villages were found with associated wine and olive presses, terraced fields and animal pens.[18] The Kurban Höyük Survey discovered a Late Roman period pastoral upland site (Site 26) with an animal pen and sites on the high upland terraces around springs. New survey evidence has discovered fortified, isolated farmsteads with associated olive-oil and ceramic production in the Taurus Mountain highlands near Pisidia.[19] Local ceramic industries (including, we can presume, timber felling) also occurred in the Taurus Mountains of Rough Cilicia. In the case of the Amuq, the shift upland continued, so while the Jabal al-'Aqra provided a new economic focus away from Antioch in the fourth and fifth centuries, the Syrian Jibāl sites continued this phenomenon well into sixth and seventh until the ninth or even eleventh century, as is attested by Déhès.[20]

Changing geopolitical circumstances also provided motivations for populations who wished to seek refuge or remain apart. From the Amuq and Antioch region, several groups went up into the Byzantine-controlled upland territories in the Taurus or formed breakaway communities in the uplands, such as the Mardaites (Jarājima) of the Amanus. Gerber argues that around Lidar Höyük near Sumaysāṭ on the Euphrates, a concentration of Late Roman period upland settlement was keyed into displacement due to the sixth-century incursions of Persian armies and pre-Islamic Arab tribes on the plain competing for resources. Shifts to the isolated uplands away from the more vulnerable coastal plains also occurred in Rough Cilicia, starting in the late sixth/early seventh centuries – even before the Islamic conquests. At this time, Christian villages and monasteries were also established on the Ṭūr 'Abdin Hills, in the Jazīra (the future district of Diyār Bakr). In the *Life* of Simeon the Mountaineer (d. *c*.541), Simeon travels around the Anti-Taurus Mountains between Samosata (Sumaysāṭ) and Melitene (Malaṭiya) in the region of Claudia (Ḥiṣn Qalawdhiya, near the Upper Euphrates). There he encounters shepherds living in the uplands who are Christian but have no knowledge of any of Christianity's practices and are living amidst the remains of a long-abandoned church. He converts them and restores the church, thus re-Christianizing the uplands and pastoral communities.[21]

Settlement patterns in Late Roman (fourth century) and Visigothic (fifth to eighth centuries) period al-Andalus and Lombard Italy bear some similarity to those in the Near East, although the chronology needs to be reconfigured before it can be applied to Late Roman and Early Islamic period Anatolia and Syria – particularly as the Islamic conquest occurred approximately one century earlier in the Near East. Villas that outgrew their original functions as rural farm-estates and came to resemble cities, as well as cities themselves, were in a state of transition by the sixth/seventh centuries. These villas began to spread towards small hills or hillsides near larger cities. Hispano-Roman populations led by a Visigothic aristocracy fled from the lowlands to the mountains and began to create hilltop settlements (*oppida* or *ummahāt al-ḥuṣūn*). An example of this was in the aforementioned Duero Valley where, a century before the Muslim conquest, the country was 'depopulated' by Alfonso II and his people who left 'an empty buffer zone' between Islamic and Visigothic lands. Many of the upland settlements were dated from the sixth/seventh centuries and are identified as Hispano-Roman based on the survival of Latin toponyms.[22] Several other groups that left the cities and villas to which they were attached did not join the oppressive feudal Visigothic aristocracy,[23] but resettled in other areas. In Italy, this same process occurs as part of the first and second stage of transformation of the villa to village model: the desertion of the countryside by the aristocracy and abandonment of Roman villas followed by a shift to hilltop nucleated settlements in the sixth and early seventh centuries CE by the remaining peasantry.

Uneven Settlement Patterns and Ecological Transformations

While site types were consistent from region to region, settlement distribution was not. In the Bozova-Urfa Survey, the peak in settlement came in the Hellenistic period with a subsequent drop linked to the consolidation of sites. In the Amuq, the peak in settlement was reached in the Early Roman period and there was a significant decrease by the fourth century CE and virtually no new foundations. Three main patterns contributing to this reduction began to be set in motion: the rise of minor towns, the consolidation of rural sites, and the expansion of upland sites.

For the north-eastern Mediterranean, the role of Roman Antioch as a world city is well known. At the same time, its role as a parasitic settlement dependent on the bounty of its hinterland is suggested – not least by Antioch's own citizen Libanius, who wrote in the fourth century: 'By lake and river craft they empty the countryside of its produce and transport it to town.'[24] Interestingly, he elsewhere states that the population of the hinterland of Antioch had 'little need for the town, thanks to exchange among themselves'.[25] Libanius' descriptions of his town are rhetorical, part of his panegyric to Antioch, and cannot be taken at face value. Despite this, they provide some basic textual evidence that Antioch, which had no immediate agricultural capacity of its own, was part of a larger system of agricultural production, which included the Amuq Plain as a hinterland composed of small rural farms and villas linked to one another with networks such as barter and inter-village festivals and in less need than one might expect of urban assistance.[26] The inter-village fairs would also have replaced village shops as a milieu for trade and exchange.[27]

At the same time, small Roman period farms or minor route stations began to disappear; they were replaced in the fifth century by fewer consolidated villages or towns with markets, forming islands of self-sufficiency by incorporating surrounding satellite sites and elaborate connected systems of canals, water mills and agricultural lands. The largest newly-established Late Roman period settlement in the Amuq (AS 243), located on the Antioch–Germanikeia road, supplanted smaller Hellenistic and Roman period settlements in the immediate area – by then abandoned – showing a process of consolidation of rural sites. These sites, as yet unidentified, constituted consolidated large villages, or *kōmai megalai* or *metrokōmai*, which rose in importance, with their own annual fairs, agricultural production and artisans, as populated independent settlements.[28] As their *raison d'être* increased, based on location and services provided to surrounding settlements and independent links to the upland settlements in the Syrian Jibāl, Antioch began to contract, no longer being the preferred economic outlet. According to de Giorgi, the reduction in the number of farms in the Amuq Plain reflects the expansion of larger estates, owned by Antioch's wealthy families and officials, which incorporated smaller holdings and often entire villages and monopolized the city's markets.[29] By the end of the seventh century, a depopulation of the wealthier Byzantine citizens of Antioch seems to have occurred, but a mass exodus of the region is certainly unlikely. Such a shift would also have affected surrounding Late Roman period rural settlements dependent on the urban center and its markets, causing smaller farmsteads to be abandoned for more agglomerate villages with larger populations and more secure resources. By swinging toward the Jibāl, Antioch's economic pendulum broke with the tradition of town *and* country that was a hallmark of the Hellenistic and Early Roman periods.[30] In the Kahramanmaraş Plain similar trajectories can be deduced, although the precise chronology of when these occurred is unknown for the Late Roman period. Working backwards from the Early Islamic period, evidence of new or preexisting sites demonstrates that in the Late Roman period, more settlements were abandoned in Kahramanmaraş than in the Antioch region, where there is more continuity into the Early Islamic period. Germanikeia, identified as KM 55/Danışman Höyük and situated in the center of the plain between the northern and southern basins, was the local urban center for the region in the Hellenistic and Early Roman periods. In the Late Roman period, however, the site, if occupied at all, did not approach the size and extent of an urban settlement such as Antioch – nor did it continue to be an urban site, but may have shifted. Domuztepe in the plain, as revealed by excavations, was an important site. This is suggested by the Constantinian coin deposit excavated there in 2005. The deposit of 287 'billion' coins (bronze with silver coating) ranged mainly from 313 to 347 CE. It is unlikely that they represented a hoard of hidden savings as they were in circulation and were of low value, while several were debased. Sixty-five per cent were minted at Antioch, the closest mint.[31] The presence of the deposit gives evidence for the development of rural sites as local centers as early as the fourth century.

Although plain sites in the Amuq decreased; upland sites expanded. What accounted for this deliberate shift away from the plain? One incentive, and perhaps agricultural/environmental necessity, was the need to bring previously uncultivated and peripheral lands under the plow.[32] But this does not explain away the fact that there was no further explosion or peak of sites in the Late Roman period on the plain. The process of settlement shifting upland was a dynamic response to changing environmental and economic conditions, namely the steady growth of the lake and surrounding marshes. In the erosion-prone limestone/sandstone/shale uplands, a vicious cycle was engendered whereby the avoidance of marsh and the economic pressures of the mainly olive-oil export market led to dispersed upland settlement, deforestation and cultivation, which in turn loosened topsoils over a wide physical area that eroded on the plain during severe storms. This sediment filled in the canals and rivers, causing the channels to break their banks and flood the plain – a process of marshification that by the end of the Late Roman period had caused the spread of permanent wetlands, which in turn prompted inhabitants to continue shifting to the uplands where they intensified olive-oil and wine production.[33] Environmental disasters in the sixth and seventh centuries would have also played a role. In Antioch, a series of calamities – such as agricultural crisis, population reduction and nucleation, loss of a labour force in the seventh century, drought, insect plague and invasions that damaged the countryside – is often given as part of a range of explanations for Late Roman period decline. The same is true in al-Andalus.[34] Such litanies should always be taken with caution, and tempered with evidence from the material culture and from other contemporary sources, such as Arab accounts, which, interestingly, dwell far less on these natural disasters. Setting the literary tropes of disaster aside, it seems that there is some truth in the human response to changing environmental conditions. The process of environmental change, often linked to similar human activities, affected each ecosystem or micro-region differently and led to contraction and nucleation of settlements and populations. As C. Wickham has shown for the entirety of the Mediterranean region, it is crucial to understand these macro- and micro-regional patterns as they form the 'prologue' to Early Islamic period settlement patterns and constitute the basis of the trajectories of *incastellamento* that crystallized in the Middle Islamic period.[35] It is also during the Early Islamic period that we can investigate the survivial of Christian communities and their relationships with new Islamic settlements.

CHAPTER 7

HYDRAULIC VILLAGES IN THE EARLY ISLAMIC PERIOD (SEVENTH TO TENTH CENTURIES)

You [Hishām] *hewed out from the Euphrates flowing canals, blessed, and they have been constructed just as you wished.*
The mountains bowed to your wish; they were mute, while cut up by iron.
You arrived at the Hanî [canal] *and there gave thanks, for the solid mountain was leveled.*
Olives give a rich yield there and clusters of black grapes weigh down [the boughs of the vine].
The Hanî has become an earthy paradise, even the envious acknowledging that it is the everlasting [garden].
They bite their fingertips [with frustration and envy] *when they see these orchards ready for harvesting* [and they see] *pairs of fruit trees and date palms bearing a ripe yield.*[1]

In the Early Islamic *thughūr*, the number of sites occurring in nearly all surveys on the frontier was half the number from the preceding Late Roman period, a figure that illustrates neither fluid continuity nor a complete 'no man's land'. However, the numbers of seventh- to eighth-century sites were rather low as compared to sites of the eighth to tenth centuries, which increased. This pattern can be attributed to three early causative factors, including the voluntary emigration – and, in some cases, depopulation – of major Late Roman period settled areas to the uplands; the proportional rise (and advent) of pastoralist groups, whose sites are virtually invisible in the archaeological record; and the effects of war and conquest on local populations, also invisible on the ground. As the dust settled following these political and military upheavals, four interlocking processes of settlement and interaction developed from the seventh to the tenth centuries. Many preexisting communities remained, following the same patterns of settlement as in the Late Roman period. A small number of new seventh-century rural estates were founded along canals and rivers and tied to agricultural, caliphal and local entrepeneurship and land use. Environmental change and the growth of marshlands led to new adaptations in settlement. Finally, by the eighth century, the frontier showed signs of increased activity, settlement focus and sedentarization; more sites began to appear around the plains and along roads, including not only rural communities but a new system of way stations. Analysis of these four processes within the archaeological landscape, combined with textual information and parallel occurences, can allow us to detect Christian and Muslim communities and progress towards differentiating between these settlements. Furthermore, these processes offer other scenarios to the standard Muslim–Christian conflict narratives; they reveal gradual accommodation and adaptation among frontier groups.

Persisting Patterns of Settlement

The first process was one of continuity in settlement patterns. Many characteristics of Late Roman period settlements remained unchanged, such as the choice to occupy low mounds or flat sites rather than tells, the appearance of a small number of dispersed new sites, the consolidation of preexisting sites, and the reduction of major urban cities coupled with the prominence of minor towns as self-sufficient polities. Upland sites, settled densely in the Late Roman period, in some cases declined and in some cases stabilized owing to the severing of Late Roman urban–rural agricultural connections.

Plain Sites

The preference for non-tell sites on the plain was noted in nearly every survey, including the Amuq and Kahramanmaraş Surveys, van Liere and Laffray's Khābūr Survey, and the Harran, Sweyhat, Tille, Brak, Beydar, Adıyaman and Jerablus Tahtani Surveys. The two last-named specifically noted Late Roman to Early Islamic period continuity. In the North Jazira, Brak and Sweyhat Surveys, low-mounded sites were observed as small sites of one or several individual buildings. Many of these sites were along wadis, canals or around springs, as in the Amuq, Kahramanmaraş, Balikh, Rifa'at, Jerablus Tahtani, Tabqa Dam, Keban, Brak, Hamoukar, Beydar, Gritille, Middle Euphrates and various Khabur Surveys. Unlike the long-lived tell habitations, many of these sites were occupied for short periods, depending on environmental variability and irrigation enterprises.[2]

The Late Roman period transformation of major urban centers into contracted and smaller towns, and the rise to prominence of minor towns, advanced further in the Early Islamic period.[3] By the Early Islamic period, Anṭākiya was further reduced from its Late Roman period extent and became secondary in importance to the provincial capital city of Ḥalab, which was for a time the capital (*qaṣaba*) of the *'awāṣim* province. It was an example of *rus in urbe*, or countryside within the city, with green spaces for agricultural and pastoral activity and water milling within its walls. While Anṭākiya contracted, 'Imm and Baghrās grew, with water mills or canals and satellite sites. Such mills, for the grinding of grain, can be used as indicators of self-sufficiency, as they provided flour for their immediate settlements while surplus could have been exported via a canal or road system.

Decker raises the possibility that dispersed lowland settlement patterns and canal building in the Roman and Late Roman periods suggested a stable and secure landscape. He does, however, mention that during the Early Islamic period a decline in the number of settlements was seen in almost every survey on the frontier. His observations, with the added support of the Amuq and Kahramanmaraş data sets (unavailable at his time of writing), are correct in terms of settlement number for the most part. It is important to underscore the fact that flat sites are underrepresented. Older surveys that only recorded tells have skewed data for Roman to Early Islamic period settlement patterns. Moreover, the percentage of flat or low-mounded sites in newer surveys, while more accurate, is still lower than the actual number of settlements that existed. This is owing to the simple fact that these sites are less conspicuous, often buried under heavy sediment, and would have incorporated many biodegradable materials in their construction. Small flat scatters with scanty assemblages that are mainly undiagnostic also pose a problem of attribution. Regardless, these same patterns apply to Late Roman period sites. As the Amuq and Kahramanmaraş Surveys have shown, even if indefinite sites are included the potential number of sites occupied is increased for both Late Roman and Early Islamic periods, and Early Islamic occupation is still significantly reduced.

There were some exceptions to this regional phenomenon in several plains. In the eastern half of the central *thughūr*, Late Roman and Early Islamic period sites were about equal in number. Many of the settlements along the Nahr al-Quwayq and Nahr al-Dhib watercourses showed direct continuity across the seventh century. Behind the eastern *thughūr* in the Jazīra, the Balikh Valley, parts of the Khābūr Valley and the Middle Euphrates showed increased settlement. These exceptions can be initially explained by the fact that these settlements were located within the immediate influence of two large urban areas: Ḥalab and Raqqa/Rāfiqa, connected to southern 'Iraqi influence via the Euphrates, and were home to a large population of preexisting Christian communities.[4] Cultivated lands were not destroyed but were carefully enumerated and divided up among the new rulers, undoubtedly for taxation purposes and to determine which were abandoned and available for new settlers. An anonymous seventh-century chronicle in Syriac stated that Maslama b. 'Abd al-Malik, upon his appointment as governor of Mesopotamia, 'sent officers throughout Northern Mesopotamia to measure lands, make a census of vineyards, plantations, livestock, and people'.[5] The archaeology suggests micro-regions of differential growth that support the administrative divisions, at least from the eighth to the tenth centuries: the Jazīra was not the frontier. The *'awāṣim* (although only the area around Ḥalab) was also more densely settled than the rest of the frontier.

Decker considers the decline of the frontier as a potential shift of the sociopolitical climate.[6] However, Early Islamic period settlement types (low and flat) and distribution (dispersed) were, for the most part, the same as Late Roman. This would suggest, if one were to follow the same hypothesis, that a frontier of dispersed farms and villages near routes, and unwalled as opposed to walled tell settlements, suggests a measure of political and economic stability that endured following Persian and Islamic conquests. The frontier was less intensively settled, although it also comprised mixed religious and ethnic communities. Despite this 'mottled' landscape, plain settlements, mostly involved in agricultural pursuits, indicate a socioeconomic system of cooperative interaction and exchange for land resources.

Tell and Upland Sites

All surveys show that only a handful of tell sites were occupied, similar to the Late Roman period, but some tells – such as Çatal Höyük, Tell al-Judaidah and Tell Atchana in the Amuq Plain – had light evidence of occupation, and some of these had a lower town. These settlements did not continue into the Early Islamic period. In the Kahramanmaraş Plain, the number of tell sites was higher than elsewhere in the *thughūr* – nearly one-third the total number of sites. As in the Amuq, nearly all of these sites fell into the range 0–6 ha in area, and had small ceramic assemblages. An exception was KM 97/ Domuztepe, which covered 16 ha. In the case of the majority of tells that were not occupied, land on top was utilized for cemeteries. Recent work by J. Bradbury recorded burials atop tells as cairns or tumuli. Many lay within 500 m of Islamic sites, and were presumably linked to them. As unsettled areas, tell cemeteries were out of the way, and they show a pragmatic reuse of space. They were prominences in the landscape, recognized by settled or nomadic tribes and maintained over time owing to historical attachment and social memory. They also served to claim ancient sites.[7] Some tells were given over to farming or pasturing with small attendant settlements, much like they can be today. Others may have been for refuse, as suggested by Tille Höyük, which featured tenth-century pits of broken ceramic and glass with no associated architecture.

Surface survey and excavation at Domuztepe indicated the presence of a Late Roman period church, and possibly other buildings and a Christian cemetery. A short distance from Tell Tuneinir, a Syriac monastery with mainly Early Islamic period material culture was found to have been fitted with a large wine press. Following the example of Domuztepe, Tuneinir and the Amuq sites of Tell al-Judaidah and AS 275 in the Jabal al-ʿAqra (not to mention Qenneshre, the sites of the Syrian Jibāl and Ṭūr ʿAbdin), buildings atop tells and hills were frequently found to be churches, sometimes associated with small rural settled communities. These Christian settlements continued from the Late Roman into the Early Islamic period. Indeed, if one were to view a map of the *thughūr*, North Syria and northern Mesopotamia showing only monasteries, one would see a landscape dotted with hundreds of sites, many attested in texts. One would also discern that while many of these monasteries were in upland zones, a significant number were not – and instead were located on tells rising above lower towns with Muslim populations, the two communities living in close proximity. An interesting pattern arises of monastic communities on tells near lower villages and towns, such as Tell al-Judaidah, Qenneshrē, Gabbula/Jabbūl, Dayr Shaykh/Tell ʿAzāz, Dayr Hāfir and Tell Biʿa (Dayr Zakka), which may partially explain the habitation of tells in this region. Undoubtedly a considerable amount of interaction would have occurred between Islamic and Christian communities.[8] The specifics of their interactions are myriad, ranging from the hedonistic pleasures of daily life to long-term measures of stability. Muslims at times frequented monasteries for escapist pursuits, to drink wine, write poetry and dally with attractive youths. Monastic communities close to *thughūr* towns relied on them economically and for protection as stable-walled and guarded locations.[9] One can also detect clusters of monastic groupings: around the Black Mountain and Ra's al-Khanzir in the Orontes Delta; on the Syrian Jibāl; in the Plain of Ḥalab; around Qenneshrē; around the Anti-Taurus between Malaṭiya and Sumaysāṭ; and, most densely, between Sumaysāṭ and Raqqa in the Balikh and in the hills of the Ṭūr 'Abdin north of the Khābūr. These communities were not isolated – rather, they probably interacted in their own networks on several levels, exchanging people, ideas, financial support and even goods between monasteries. The last-named enterprise would have been critical, as these monasteries otherwise survived on endowments and gifts from wealthy community members. Monks and holy men, as understood through their recorded *Lives*, frequently journeyed back and forth between monasteries: St Simeon of the Olives, for instance, travelled between Ḥarrān and the Ṭūr 'Abdin at least four times, a distance of just under 230 km or about six days travel by animal. In this way, their frontier zone is a whole different layer interdigitated between the Islamic geographers' landscape of cities and towns, and enduring through periods of political and cultural transition. These monks would have rested in other monasteries along the way. As way stations, these could also have accommodated other travellers on the more remote routes.[10] Monasteries also supported local pastoralist and peasant populations, doubling as landholders, schools, hospitals and places of worship. Monks could perform funeral rites or exorcisms and arbitrate between populations.[11]

In the Early Islamic period, very few upland sites noted on surveys such as those of the Amuq, Kahramanmara and Kurban included slopes and foothills. None were newly founded. Those that were recorded were associated with mines, guarded important passes, or were vestigial sites from the Late Roman period that only bore slight continuity into the late seventh century. It would be wrong to attribute this simply to the reverberating effects of Islamic conquest. Many of the ties that linked upland agricultural enterprises with Antioch in the Late Roman period were severed due to the major transformations of that city and the reorganization of the economy into more immediate self-sufficient localities. Some upland sites, such as those in the side valleys of the Amuq and Site 14 in the Kurban Höyük Survey, only showed evidence of continuity until the eighth century. The upland sites that did continue were for the most part located on the valley floors or on nearby, low slopes.

Terracing was noted, although difficult to date. Yet, surveys in the side valleys of the Amanus revealed many Roman and Late Roman period sites and associated terraces, indicating cultivation, that were not used in the Early Islamic period. This settlement type, on tributaries and in side valleys, was fairly common and was seen in the Adıyaman, Gritille, Titriş and Bozova-Urfa Surveys. The lack of upland sites from the Early Islamic period is not an indication, however, that settlement patterns during this time reverted to those of the lowland, nucleated settlement centers seen in the Bronze and Iron Ages. Early Islamic period settlement avoided the uplands as a whole in favour of centralized canal, river and marsh locations. This is an important contrast, particularly due to the fact that much of the plain was given over to permanent and seasonal wetlands. Abandonment of upland sites and sites on slopes, as well as on unmaintained terraces, also contributed to erosion-prone surfaces, sedimentation on the plain and marshification.

The settlements of the Jabal al-ʿAqra show continuity in occupation until the tenth century – albeit restructured, less monumental and more isolated than before. Similarly, the Syrian Jibāl settlements represent a partially isolated pocket of Christians in villages and monasteries, who maintained active communities that were largely self-sufficient until the tenth century. Some of these communities may have been augmented by an influx of people from elsewhere in the seventh century, associated with the Persian and Islamic conquests or earlier sixth-century emigrations out of the cities. This was also noted in the Bozova-Urfa and Lidar Survey regions. While there is little evidence for lavish church-building following the seventh century (and no inscriptions after 610 as evidence of donors), perhaps tied into geopolitical and economic shifts for olive-oil export, these communities persisted and prospered, transforming spaces into more pragmatic arrangements and redirecting interactions and exchanges with closer towns, travellers (merchants, monks and pilgrims) and pastoralist groups. The *Life* of St Timothy of Khākhustā, who lived probably between 750 and 830, presents the landscape of the Syrian Jibāl as being full of Christian villages, whose inhabitants were described as relatively rich. These villagers interacted, traded and visited with one another frequently.[12] It is important to point out that isolated valleys in the uplands would also have been foci of settlement, such as the valley of Danā amidst the Syrian Jibāl. Preexisting Christian communities that had already shifted to the uplands by the Late Roman period would have continued certain long-standing traditional activities, such as olive-oil production, basketry, animal husbandry, weaving and carpentry, which would have afforded a degree of self-sufficiency if necessary.[13] They could have traded in travelling fairs at villages and towns in the plains, and procured manufactured items. Ibn Buṭlān said that the Monastery of Qal'at Sim'ān and its grounds were equal to half the city of Baghdād, providing the settlement with a yearly income of 400,000 dinars.[14] While undoubtedly an exaggeration, this suggests that monasteries were significant players in the local economy, and that the Jazīra and *'awāsim* were part of larger economies supplying Baghdād.

Irrigation, Social Organization and Subsistence Strategies

Archaeological and textual evidence supports the early introduction of new settlements and economic infrastructures on the Islamic frontier – the latter including hydraulic systems for transport, irrigation, and milling. In addition to irrigation activities, marshes, often overlooked as uninhabitable and undesirable environments, were loci of settlement and are important markers of landscape adaptation. These two processes are linked, and can be dated to as early as *c.*700 CE.

Canal and River Agricultural Estates

The second process of settlement and interaction was the development of new sites early in the seventh century that were linked to agriculture, state and local entrepreneurship; land ownership; and local economic development. While river and canal sites, along with canal building, had continued since the Late Roman period, new canals and their attendant communities became the first foci for seventh- and eighth-century settlement. These utilized systems of water sharing and canal management that were either cooperative or managed by one large estate.

In the Amuq, Kahramanmaraş and Balikh Valley Surveys, the biggest sites and those with the largest assemblage occurred as low mounds or flat scatters along canal systems, rivers and within or on the edges of expanding lakes and wetlands. These sites also reflect the gradual expansion and permanence of the marsh. Canal and river settlements were linearly arranged, evenly spaced, and sometimes constituted double sites, set on either bank, as seen in the Amuq Plain ('Afrīn Canal and Yaghrā River sites) and the possibly identified settlement of Bāgharwān in the Balikh. These sites were often newly established. In the Amuq, four out of eight newly-established sites were located on canals and were also among the largest in size and assemblage, with similar parallels in the Kahramanmaraş Plain showing that great importance was placed on irrigating the plain and controlling water resources from the onset of the Early Islamic period. Two of the remaining newly-founded sites were along the Kara Su River.

The Jabbūl Plain Survey noted more sites in the Late Roman and Early Islamic periods in the dryer eastern-steppe plain towards the Euphrates, linked with evidence of qanat and canal systems dated by their proximal sites. Several of these sites were rather large, measuring between 10 and 30 ha in size, with no defensive walls. They were similar to the 'Afrīn canal sites and were interpreted as estates or regional centers, while small 1 ha sites were interspersed among them – a pattern also noted in the Tabqa Dam Survey. Canals around Jerablus/Carchemish, drawing from the Euphrates, were observed by the surveyors who recorded four types: earthen, dug canals; rock-cut channels; built stone channels; and qanats. Most were Late Roman period installations that continued into the Early Islamic period. These can perhaps be identified though a mention, in the *Life* of Theodota of Amida, of irrigation ditches feeding fields of grain, fruit and produce around Qenneshrē.[15] A qanat was also identified running parallel to the Nahr Quwayq from Tell Hailane to Ḥalab. Canals and a qanat were also found to be associated with Dibsi Faraj. Canal features identified around Tell Brak in the Khābūr can be dated, at least partially, to the eighth to tenth century by the associated fortified, square enclosure/way station near the mound.[16] Many of these locations lay within the marginal rainfall zone, which averaged 250 mm/annum. Although yields were not as robust as those in southern 'Iraq, these canal systems were less vulnerable to the constant effects of sedimentation and salinization experienced in the Sawād lands south of Baghdād. Yet it is remarkable to note canal-building efforts in the Amuq Plain, which although having very low precipitation in the summer received enough rainfall per year, sustained permanent wetlands, so as to make irrigation less of a necessity but more of an economic investment that offered a secure cushion during drier years.

In addition, archaeologists working in al-Andalus, Sicily and the Balearic Islands noted many localized canal/settlement systems during this period. The Early Islamic period (mid-eighth to end of ninth century, 'Paleoandalusi') in al-Andalus was marked by a transformation in culture and settlement, with the advent of Arab and Berber tribal populations in 711.[17] Similar to the case in the Amuq and Kahramanmaraş Plains, water supply, canalization, irrigation and marshlands were elements that dictated new settlement in the Early Islamic period. Lowland hydraulic villages (*aldea* or *alquería*, from *al-qarya*: 'village' – typically a village and its territory) clustered around a shared water supply without attendant castles.[18] Sites were chosen for settlement not necessarily for their strategic location, but primarily for their proximity to water sources. The presence of many fragments of *na'ūra* jars (*qādūs*) links irrigation technology with material culture. In the Islamic period, patterns of evenly spaced *alquerías* dictated by canals and rivers were deemed to be the characteristic settlement type.[19]

Canal systems and sites are well attested in the Early Islamic period on the Syro-Anatolian frontier. Yet how these hydraulic estates or villages were settled, canals built and water distribution organized are more complicated. So, too, are issues of land tenure and taxation in relation to these systems. Ideas of irrigation and social organization have developed significantly since K. Wittfogel's theory of Oriental Despotism, which stated that totalitarianist empire-regimes became what they were because they were able to carry out and capitalize on large-scale irrigation projects using forced labour and to control water access through a hierarchical system. It is, rather, the reverse which holds true: large-scale empires enabled the development and spread of irrigation and water management in the Near East.[20] Scholars, in recognizing that local and chronological variations are paramount in any such claim, have typically argued for one of two revisionist models: either that irrigation was completely locally or tribally organized, or that canal- or qanat-building projects were initiated and encouraged as a state enterprise but maintained on a local level, thus partially embracing Wittfogel's scheme.[21] Archaeology alone cannot resolve this issue, not least because many examples of irrigation works, such as canals or water mills, are not easily dated. Without ceramic or inscription evidence, such features are best dated via their associated sites as an overall system, a technique which has already been demonstrated.

The Umayyad state was not an absolutist empire. Rather, it represented a dominant family within a minority group of Muslims in the largely Christian Levant. In this sense, the Umayyads early on utilized the fragmented nature of Muslim and Arab groups in the Near East to their advantage by typically employing policies of indirect administration, with incentives of wealth and prestige by conquest, to cohere tribes gradually. These policies may have been part of sedentarization strategies given to nomadic groups or soldiers on the frontier. Lands still occupied by non-Muslims were preserved but taxed with the *kharāj* land levy. Monasteries were included within this system, as is shown in the case of a young officer by the name of Sargīs (possibly a Christian) who was sent by Ilūsṭrayya, the *qā'id* (leader) of Sumaysāṭ, to collect the *kharaj* and *jizya* taxes on the Dayr Mār Sarjiyūs al-'Arīḍ (Monastery of Mar Sergios the Broad) located near Ḥiṣn Qalawdhiya.[22] Another example is shown when Iyād b. Ghanm conquered Raqqa and its region, leaving the majority of its land with already-established farmers (*al-fallāhīn* or *al-arīsīyīn*).[23] In other cases, Christian tenants paid their rents to

Muslim landlords or agents.[24] From the sources, land tenure and tax as they related to the survival and relative autonomy of Christian communities are difficult issues to quantify chronologically or geographically, as are individual cases of conversion, although general remarks can be made (see the section below on ethno-religious identity).[25] State or caliphal lands (*ṣawāfī*) were legally defined as lands appropriated during the time of conquests that had been abandoned because their occupants had fled or been killed, that belonged to former Byzantine or Sāsānian elites, or that comprised wetlands, posthouses or mills.[26] Until the time of Muʿāwiya, these lands were for Muslim fighters but were then transferred to the central state. They were granted to Muslims groups in several ways. *Qaṭīʿa* (plural *qaṭāʾiʿ*) were long-term or permanent, alienable and inheritable lands given to private ownership, often as estates, but whose produce was shared (*fayʾ*) or owners paid the *ʿushr*, or tithe, rather than the steeper *kharāj* land tax. The *qaṭāʾiʿ* lands could also be small, agricultural (*mazāriʿ*) or building (*masākin*) plots with housing, given to soldiers who paid little or no tax or paid directly to the ruler (*īghār*), and could be passed down as inheritance. After Muʿāwiya, instances of land grants increase, for example ʿAbd al-Malik gifts lands to frontier fighters in Maṣṣīṣa, the *thughūr* and the Jazīra.[27] This system in the tenth century became the *iqtaʿ* system of fixed-term concessions of land granted to officers or bureaucrats in exchange for service. Entrepreneurs who developed abandoned or previously non-agricultural lands with irrigation systems for cultivation were rewarded for their revitalization efforts on otherwise 'dead' lands (*mawāt*) by becoming landowners with tax exemptions on account of their prior investments. Furthermore, their tenure was secure; they could sell the lands or pass them down to kin.[28] A similar process had been used in the Roman and Late Roman periods as an impetus for veterans to settle in the uplands. Thus, whether directly, by owning lands, or indirectly, by granting them, the ruling Umayyad family took a personal interest in the frontier.

Canal digging was a costly enterprise, and one that subsequently required considerable upkeep to maintain the accompanying dams and outflows; remove sediment and overgrowth; and, particularly in southern 'Iraq, to deal with saline (*sabkha*) accumulations. Mention by Michael the Syrian of an unfinished canal project under Yazid b. Mu'awiya attests to this fact.[29] Frequent references in Balādhurī and Ṭabarī, as well as in Syriac accounts, speak of numerous canal-building activities by Umayyad and 'Abbāsid caliphs, princes, local rulers and governors, and members of the elite (most notably, the sons of 'Abd al-Malik).[30] They all built 'estates' (*ḍiyā'*) to support the intensive greening of both naturally fertile and previously uncultivated parts of the landscape. In the Balikh Valley, Maslama b. 'Abd al-Malik built a canal (Nahr Maslama) diverting the Balikh River to supply water to a large cistern measuring about 5.8 m square and 22 m deep, and both canal and cistern irrigated (*yusaqī*) lands around Ḥiṣn Maslama (BS 187/Madīnat al-Fār) at the local inhabitants' request.[31] He also established the settlement of Ḥiṣn Maslama itself, for Muslims who had recently received or occupied land possessions.[32] It is also possible that the Nahr Maslama is the same as the Nahr al-Abbara, dated to the sixth to eighth centuries, as both flowed along the east side of the Balikh where all of the major Early Islamic period sites (including Bāghaddā/probably BS 172, Mahrē/BS 142, and Bāgharwān/probably BS 108–10) were found. A secondary canal, flowing from the main Nahr al-Abbara to the settlement of Ḥiṣn Maslama, was recorded.[33] Many Early Islamic period field scatters alongside canals show archaeological evidence for the manuring and cultivation of irrigated land. Maslama also paid for and built a canal at Bālis, to irrigate its villages from the Euphrates. As the former inhabitants of this land had fled, it was initally granted to fighters and Syrian Arabs who converted and settled. It was eventually given as a *qaṭī'a* to his son, al-Ma'mūn.[34] In Raqqa, the Nahr al-Nīl Canal attributed to Hārūn al-Rashīd flowed into the western side of the city, past Hārūn's palaces, and functioned as a moat/ditch, or *khandaq*. Visible from aerial photography, it was a primary feeder canal about 12 m wide that emptied east of Raqqa into the marshy Balikh and Euphrates confluence.[35] A qanat fed the city's northern palaces and a canal passed through Hārūn al-Rashīd's victory monument west of the city, bringing water from the Euphrates. Irrigation canals were also noted with CORONA imagery in relation to a building complex north of the city.[36] Opposite the river was a canal 15 km long, beginning near Qal'at Namrud and ending at the confluence of the Balikh with the Euphrates. It can be identified as the Hanī Canal, attributed to Hishām in the *Chronicle of Zuqnin.* Agapius (d. 941/2) and the *Chronicle* of 1234 mention the destruction of the estates of Hishām along the Euphrates by Marwān II, indirectly alluding to the presence of caliphal lands. Ṭabarī refers to Hishām's money-generating estate at Dawrīn (comprising also its villages), which can be associated with the Nahr Dawrīn at the Khābūr and Euphrates confluence.[37] The Nahr Sa'īd was a large canal, built in Umayyad times, that diverted waters from the Euphrates in a loop to irrigate the district capital of Raḥba, and which flowed from Qarqīsiyā to Dāliya. The land was given as a *qaṭī'a* by Walīd to his brother Sa'id al-Khayr b. 'Abd al-Malik, who built the canal. Mahdī and Hārūn al-Rashīd's secretary built a canal feeding Ḥarrān called al-Jullāb.[38] On the Tigris, canals are known from Jazīra ibn 'Umar, a district capital north of Mawṣil (Mosul) situated on an island formed partly by the Tigris and partly by a diverted canal. Ra's al-'Ayn was irrigated by canals, as was a town of Maslama b. 'Abd al-Malik, given as a land grant to one his men, Usayd as-Sulamī, and possibly identified as Bājaddā.[39] Some of the *quṣūr* or 'desert castles', many which have elaborate irrigation systems, functioned as agricultural estates.[40]

Euphrates canals, due to the deeply incised nature of the northern portion of the river and high banks, would have required lifting devices such as waterwheels (*na'ūra* and *sāqiya*) to bring the water to the canals. Fragments of *qadus* jars found at Dibsi Faraj support the presence of such installations. Other waterwheels are inferred by villages named after water-lifting-device terms, such as Nā'ūra, between Ḥalab and Bālis near the Jabbūl Lake, and al-Dāliya (waterwheel) near al-Raḥba and the Nahr Sa'īd on the Euphrates. Hārūn al-Rashīd, while travelling down the Euphrates, observed *na'ūra* waterwheels at al-Raḥba. Similarly to the major 'Afrīn canal sites, many of these settlements were Early Islamic period foundations or else flourished in the Early Islamic period under the Umayyads, and were largely abandoned by the tenth century.

From textual references, we see that Maslama's canal-building projects are entrepreneurial and likely represent an investment in bringing provincial funds to the state capital. Syriac accounts all mention the activities of Caliph Hishām, who built canals and diverted water in the Balikh and 'established plantations and enclosed gardens and spent much money on creating these things'. We can return to the verse composed by Jarīr b. 'Aṭiya (*c.*650–*c.*728), which opens this chapter and which implies that Hishām's construction of the Hanī was a costly and enormous effort. Agapius states that he was the 'first of the Arabs to take on estates for himself' and received revenue from all of this. The Hanī Canal's revenue, according to Michael the Syrian, surpassed the amount collected from taxes in the entire empire.[41] Michael the Syrian and the author of the *Chronicle* of 1234 also allude to high taxation and tribute. This latter, anonymous, author also mentioned that Hishām used 'free and forced labour' in the undertaking of these canals.[42] In most cases, caliphs would have had a caretaker (*wakil*) to manage the estate, usually worked on by *mawālī*.[43] Apart from the standard paraphrasing that exists in the Syriac texts, these anecdotes illustrate caliphal irrigation activity in the Jazīra. Yet, and this cannot be overstated, caliphal or central-state initiatives as such must not be assumed to have been general practice. Even the Syriac authors allude to the fact that no other caliph before Hishām did any of these things. References to managing estates under the *diwān al-ḍiyā'* (office of estates) and *diwān al-mawārith* (office of estate inheritances) in the growing administrative framework of the 'Abbāsid state suggest that by the ninth century other landowners were running estates. The intensity of caliphal initiatives for irrigation projects and agricultural estates, however, greatly diminished after the caliphates of Manṣūr and Mahdī at the end of the eighth century.[44]

Evidence also exists for local initiatives on both the level of monastery and of village/town. Again, Syriac texts provide some insight, but rarely, as most are devoted to religious achievements in the *Lives* of saints. Simeon of the Olives built, in Naṣībīn (Greek Nisibis) and all around the Ṭūr 'Abdin, numerous monasteries equipped or associated with shops, inns, animal enclosures, olive groves, irrigation channels and mills. He even built a 'large and beautiful mosque' next to the church in Naṣībīn, a *madrasa* and a *pandocheion*, or way station. He paid for this work using gold and silver that his nephew found hidden as a hoard, a likely exception to the norm of funding monasteries by private donation and alms from wealthy urban elites or holy men who had died and willed their possessions. Proceeds from agricultural production and rent went to the monasteries themselves. Indeed monasteries, particularly large ones like Qartmīn (Mor Gabriel on the Ṭūr 'Abdin), could own other monasteries.[45]

Qudāma b. Ja'far alludes to local canal-digging in his discussion of sharing water rights, providing examples both hypothetical and anecdotal of individual and village irrigation efforts.[46] Such excavation was a shared activity, but cleaning out, damming and supervising the canals was directed by the Imām 'from the moneys of the Muslims'. However, during al-Mahdī's time, he cites another scholar who states that along the great rivers, digging, construction of bridges, canal clearing and dam maintenance were paid for by the state treasury.[47] The villagers around Bālis, who were Muslim, asked Maslama to build them a canal (the second Nahr Maslama) and gave him one-third of its produce (*ghullātihim*) as tithe for the government (*'ushr al-sulṭān*).[48] Normal *'ushr* – the tribute paid by Muslims, as opposed to the higher-rate, *kharāj*, tax paid by non-Muslims – of lands watered by artificial means was one-twentieth, or 5 per cent, as opposed to one-tenth or 10 per cent, as the name implies. This demonstrates the tax-incentive quality to irrigated lands common on the frontier. In Bālis, the lands were subject both to Muslim tithe to the state and yields to the landowner or patron.[49] Furthermore, this shows that local groups required state authority to assist them in land development and reclamation, at least concerning irrigation from the Euphrates, Tigris, and other major rivers of the region. Maslama, in his role as governor of the frontier from Cilicia to Mesopotamia, helped develop land with large-scale irrigation efforts, but the maintenance, organization and control was most likely left to the local communities. In this fashion, canal-building projects were 'agents in the settlement and colonization of areas that formerly had been sparsely settled', although, to be sure, they were not new innovations and in many cases replaced older hydraulic systems.[50]

Water milling was directly tied to irrigation practices, and was similarly a caliphal/state or private investment. In the Khābūr and Ṭūr 'Abdin and Tigris regions, mills had been known since at least the fourth century.[51] Caliphal mills (*'urūb*) were built at a high cost around Mawṣil, beginning in the Marwānid period, and were a major source of revenue.[52] Mills were similarly constructed at great expense by Hishām. They were also described at Naṣībīn and Qenneshrē along the Euphrates.[53] They could also become 'privatized'. What did the state gain from these irrigation and milling enterprises? Beyond a portion of the yields and a major source of revenue, these public works were incentives for frontier inhabitants to settle down and channel a degree of loyalty to the central state, thereby affording the latter a level of control. Further research, which correlates areas of irrigation temporally and geographically with taxation records, can consider whether such intensive irrigation projects were also designed to meet or mitigate the burdens of an increasingly demanding taxation system.[54] What can be considered here is how settlements and irrigation systems were organized spatially and socially.

A salient observation is that these canal systems, as seen from both archaeological and textual evidence, were rather conservative and localized *in scale*. None of them resembled the 230 km-long Nahrawan Canal built in the sixth century Sāsānian Empire, which was capable of irrigating 8,000 km^2 (800,000 ha) of land.[55] Even the potentially largest of the *thughūr* and Jazīra systems, such as the Nahr Dawrin or the Khābūr River zone, was estimated to irrigate only 30,000 ha. Based on this size, although the central administration continued to have a political and economic hand in irrigation works, canal construction, maintenance and organization was on the scale of a town – or the collective authority of multiple hydraulic villages.

The textual evidence for local-authority, state, or even caliphal-sponsored waterworks is significant and at the same time biased towards lauding the efforts of rulers in making even the most marginal areas fertile and economically viable. Community-initiated canal systems would, perforce, be invisible in the historical record, and inscriptions are scarce. For the region of al-Andalus, K. Butzer divided irrigation practice into a quasi-chronological tripartite system based on scale. The large scale of irrigation was a Roman period development, encompassing 50–100 km^2 on the major floodplains and coastal plains. These floodplains had large canals, which then broke off into secondary irrigation channels. By the fifth century, these irrigation systems began to collapse – a process that continued until the period of Early Islam, when these macro-systems were revitalized. Butzer wrote that the Islamic period regulation of water rights in al-Andalus was adapted from the Roman system, and was similar to certain practices in the Near East (the 'Syrian System'). These regulations attached proportional water allocations to property holdings. Representatives from major communities could bring their claims to the city. The meso- and micro-scales were more distinctly Islamic systems of organization. Meso-scale irrigation involved a small group of villages (typically seven) that shared water from springs and small rivers in an area 15–125 ha in size. Water may have been lifted by *cenias* (*saqiya* or pot-garland), stored in tanks, and then distributed to smaller canals. Irrigation was seasonal, usually between late June and mid-October; it was regulated by an irrigation officer, who allocated water rights to villages in groups of hours or days. The last degree of irrigation, micro-scale, involved small lots of land, around 1 ha in area, irrigated by springs, whose water was held in tanks or cisterns and was shared by small groups of landholders, rather than villages.

In Early Islamic period al-Andalūs, rather than centralized or municipal control and bureaucratic organization of irrigation, tribal organization took place on the scale of individual river valleys and plains. Furthermore, smaller meso- and micro-scales of irrigation correlated well with tribal organization, due to the necessary cooperation between groups and the rigid social ordering of 'hydraulic microspace': 'Not surprisingly, cooperation works better in small groups with similarity of needs and clear boundaries, and shared norms and patterns of reciprocity. In such communities monitoring is easier.' Although irrigated portions of land and villages may not always have been equal, the even distribution of water rights ensured that resources were not overused. Individual parcels of lands and equal water rights under smaller systems of irrigation ensured a level of self-regulation and enforcement. Evidence of cooperation and sharing was shown by the prioritizing of irrigation canals over mills, which were always placed at the end of the system so as not to disrupt the allocation of equal water rights and lead to conflict.[56]

Based on the persistence of Berber tribal names in modern toponyms, archaeologists in Spain and the Balearic Islands observed multiple tribal communities settled along the same canal with individual parcels of land of varying sizes. They argued that this showed cooperative organization and land use by tribal, segmentary groups, rather than a Visigothic pre-Islamic period feudal model.[57] Settlement and demographic expansion were negotiated by overlapping spaces that were shared, and included seasonal pastoralism.

Many similarities can be posited betwen the eastern and western Islamic frontiers. Qudāma b. Jaʿfar details the sharing and equalization of water rights between landowners upstream and downstream along rivers and canals, even the issue of giving more rights to the downstream farmer. The key difference with the local Andalusian system of organization is that for the Syro-Anatolian *thughūr* we have textual evidence for caliphal and princely canal-building programmes, which cannot be ignored. We can adapt Butzer's three-tiered structure to the *thughūr* evidence, bearing in mind these differences. The macro scale involved state building projects on major rivers, such as those for the long Euphrates, Balikh, and Khābūr Canals. It also included caliphal/state lands (*ṣawāfī*) and estates, such as those of Hishām on the Euphrates. At the meso scale, although the central administration continued to have a political and economic hand in irrigation works, canal construction, maintenance, and organization was carried out by a collective authority of multiple villages or estates – as in the Amuq Plain for the ʿAfrīn and ʿImm Canals, and in the Marʿash Plain, as well as for Bālis or Dibsi Faraj off the Euphrates. The influence of the caliph could offer a measure of support and protection, particularly in frontier lands. Those projects orchestrated with elite funds tended to appear in documents – as in the case of the *ṣawāfī* lands around Bālis, given as *qaṭī ʻa* – while the Amuq and Marʻash Canals may have been more in the way of community initiatives, and thus not mentioned in texts. Lastly, the micro scale would involve a system in which only communities beyond the influence of the central state, such as the mainly Christian groups in the Syrian Jibāl, were digging out their own irrigation systems, 'invisible' to the textual record.[58]

In all examples, however, local maintenance and organization would have been needed. Since irrigation strategies reduced water flow both in the main rivers and in subsidiary canals, settlement arrangements would have demanded cooperative and local systems of resource sharing, suggested by the relatively even distribution of sites along the channels. The exceptional work done in al-Andalus on irrigation and social organization is useful for suggesting models of community interaction and exchange on the Syro-Anatolian frontier. These hydraulic villages, occupying equidistant plots of land along canals and rivers, may have been organized by tribal, clan or religious affiliation (and exhibited differing tax status). Muslim and Christian communities may have shared the same water system, as perhaps they did at the Yaghrā River sites and at ʻImm and its satellite sites. Ethnographic first-person accounts by a villager and canal worker in southern ʻIraq show that community leaders and village or tribal *shaykhs* made decisions cooperatively in periodic meetings and determined how to divide up responsibility for maintaining the irrigation system, including assigning families rotational guard duties.[59] In many cases, knowledge of how to build and maintain canals was locally transmitted from preexisting farmers who were managing these systems before the Islamic conquest.

Archaeology can offer some spatial interpretation. In the Amuq, the sites on ʻAfrīn Canal B are 4.48, 6.1 and 35 ha in size from east to west, in the direction of its flow; the largest site sits at the end of the canal. For the ʻImma Canal system, the sites are 2.25, 1 and 4.5 ha; the largest is also at the end point, where a system of water mills was found. In the eastern Marʻash Plain, of the two canals recorded, the eastern one's sites were 1.13, 0.79 and 6 ha in area, while the western canal sites were 6, 2 and 4 ha. With all of these canals, the estimated site sizes were not equal and the middle site(s) were the smallest. In three examples, the last site on the system was the largest. Water rights would have been allocated in proportion to the amount of land and site size. The first and last positions on the canal would have been the most important: the former to manage the head dam and divert water, and the latter as this was the most likely location for milling industries (as seen at 'Imm), which were placed at the end of the system so as not to unfairly reduce water supply downstream. By contrast with an artificial system, the Yaghrā River sites were all the same size (around 12 ha each).

The use of tells in the Mar'ash canal systems may be similar to patterns in al-Andalus. In the west, defence was secondary to water supply. Forts that protected water systems and major canals, or were militarily strategic, and villages that administered water systems and canals were not mutually exclusive to any area. They were all part of the landscape, and often their roles cannot be clearly discerned. For example, tell sites with forts may be perceived as control points on higher ground. In the area around Torrent and Picanya, south of Valencia, six out of a group of ten villages had an associated tower-refuge.[60] In some cases, the fort was built on a tell and located at one end of the canal. It also stands to reason that a tell site in the center of a canal group could similarly have protected the supply. Both examples occur in the Mar'ash canals, and they underscore an association of defence with water supply – particularly necessary in areas so close to the Taurus frontier, as in the Mar 'ash Plain.

Marsh Settlements

The spread of wetlands was not a complete deterrent to settlement. In the Amuq, both the physical size and ceramic assemblages of the 'Afrīn Canal and Yaghrā River sites grew from the Late Roman period to the tenth centuries and showed a gradual chronological shift away from the marshes. Yet, while these shifts were made to accommodate the expanding lake and the encroaching wetlands, the sites were not immediately abandoned in the Early Islamic period. Rather they had a fairly notable overlap with each other, indicating that the sites lay in, or in close proximity to, wetlands throughout much of their occupation. Further, the Yaghrā River sites had larger assemblages than the 'Afrīn Canal sites, yet were more inundated by spreading wetlands.[61] As such, by the ninth and tenth centuries several of the former sites, namely those closest to the lake, had already become completely surrounded by wetlands. The same is true for the Nahr Ḥūrith/Ak Su Canal sites, centered on the wettest part of the Kahramanmaraş Plain. Although the low, flat site predominates, and there is a concentration of heavy assemblage settlements, what marks these sites out from the Amuq pattern is that they are physically much smaller. Furthermore, two of the three Nahr Ḥūrith/Ak Su Canal systems incorporate a tell and presumed lower town as part of the irrigation network. The near absence of Early Islamic period sites, whether *de novo* or preexisting, in the northern plain shows a restructuring of settlement towards the southern, more wetland areas.

In the midst of the swamps, a new site appeared in the seventh/eighth centuries, as an island within the Lake of Antioch that was of considerable size (3.3 ha) in its category. Tell Wasta (0.9 ha), in the salt marshes of the Jabbūl Lake, was a similar site, although of Roman/Late Roman period in date and situated on a natural rocky outcrop. These new sites were partially a response to the growth of marsh, caused by advanced erosion sedimentation on the plain and subsequent flooding of the rivers and canals of the previous periods. Each canal system also possessed an outlet, which was important for maintaining a regular water flow and level, which would have discharged water either back into rivers or, in smaller systems, into fields, thereby further contributing to the creation and expansion of wetlands.

In al-Andalus and Sicily, archaeologists have shown that many Early Islamic period hydraulic settlements were in marshlands.[62] Some were already settled by the sixth and seventh centuries by displaced populations moving towards the fertile coastal swamps on the Mediterranean and relying on a subsistence diet and economy of resources from the sea and marsh.[63] In the marshes (*marjal*) along the eastern littoral of al-Andalus (such as Olivia, Valencia, and Murcia/Orihuela), Late Roman period upland settlements were replaced by settlements along irrigation canals and river meanders that were part of the marsh landscape.[64] In Catalonia from the ninth to the eleventh centuries, irrigated lots of land producing fruit trees, legumes and vines were found in the intermittent beds of rivers as islands watered by surface canals or seasonal flooding. When they were not cultivated, they were used as pasturage. These areas were appropriately given the toponym al-Jazīra, or similar corruptions such as Algeciras or Alcira.[65] Primary texts support this type of new Islamic period settlement in marshes. By the start of the eleventh century, al-'Udhrī states that the Segura River ended in a marsh 'in a district of Muwalladūn in the direction of the alquería called al-Juzaira'.[66] In addition to the evidence of settlement patterns and toponyms, many of the ceramics found at these sites were not Late Roman period forms. In the marshland south of the Segura River, some sites were permanent villages built above the surrounding marsh on mounds (*cabezos*) and using the inundated landscape alternately for gardens and pasturage. These had associated irrigation using *nawā'īr* (singular *na'ūra*), and had land apportioned in fan-shaped patterns.[67] During this period, the Júcar River was a marsh floodplain irrigated with *nawā'īr*, and it possessed alquerias with present-day Latinized Arabic names, such as Alásquer (*al-'askar*, or the army) and Resalany (*ra's al-'ayn*). Both names are linked not only with the presence of eighth-century Islamic sites but the former suggests a possible military encampment, and the latter, localized around springs.[68]

Although today most wetlands in the *thughūr* region have been drained completely,[69] marshes have been documented in most other areas of Islamic–Byzantine frontier settlement, including the coasts and inland plains and valleys, until recently. Most of the coastline consisted of wetlands by the Early Islamic period. The Cilician Plain was dominated by marsh near the outlets of the Sayḥān and Jayḥān Rivers and the land along the coast between them. Travellers in the nineteenth and early twentieth century remarked on the extensive marshes of the southern Cilician Plain, which by recent history had few settlements, but they were used mainly as pasture for the fields of clover that covered the areas in spring when the winter floodwaters receded.[70] The area south of Ṭarsūs to the coast, watered by the Nahr al-Baradān, was also a marshland, as was the coastal Plain of Issus around Arsuz and Alexandretta (and Ḥiṣn al-Tīnāt and Kinet Höyük).[71] *Salina* basins were dug in many of these coastal wetlands for salt gathering.[72] Besides the Kahramanmaraş and Amuq Plains and the Jabbūl Lake east of Ḥalab, wetlands also existed in many other inland plains and valleys along the *thughūr* and *'awāṣim* frontiers. The Quwayq River, after flowing south through Ḥalab and Qinnasrīn, traverses the Marj al-Aḥmar (Red Meadow) for 19 km, emptying into the Buḥayra al-Matkh (Lake of Mud) marshes.[73] Perhaps most telling is the major Early Islamic period twin town grouping of Raqqa/Rāfiqa (sometimes referred to as Raqqa al-Sawdā') in the Jazīra of Northern Syria. The city was surrounded by marshland, particularly to the north and east near to the Balikh where a back-water swamp formed in a low-lying depression.[74] Indeed, the word *raqqa* in Arabic refers to marsh areas that form along rivers during seasonal flooding (further emphasized by the use of the term *raqqa al-sawdā'*, the black swamp). That Hārūn al-Rashīd chose to make the city his headquarters when he was attempting to endorse his campaign of Byzantine raiding ties together the importance of marsh and pasture for frontier settlement, whether nomadic or sedentary. Marshes can be assumed to have existed around the settlement of al-Raḥba at the point where the Khābūr empties into the Euphrates. *Al-raḥba* can be defined either as a town square or as another descriptive term for a low-lying wetland which is also fertile.[75]

The selection of Early Islamic period frontier sites near marsh and pasture is an important adaptive phenomenon that cannot be overlooked. Marshlands were vital ecological niches for certain types of inhabitant, supporting a way of life characterized by mixed cultivation, reed gathering (for house and boat construction), and fishing and hunting waterfowl that would have added new elements to the local economy.[76] Reeds were also used to make mats, some quite decorative, as in an example found near Ṭabarīyya (Greek Tiberias).[77] Marsh clay was also a valuable construction material that could be used in place of mortar. In the Amuq Plain, Cilicia and other parts of the frontier, marsh dwellers from the wetlands of southern 'Iraq were settled and adapted to a familiar way of life. In replicating similar settlements, they may have lived on islands or mounded settlements built up with reeds. Such marsh settlements of reed and mud brick are notoriously hard to discern in the archaeological record, and so it is certainly possible that the gap between the number of Late Roman and Early Islamic period sites is smaller than it appears. Furthermore, marshes were prime areas for pasture. This is important for large groups with herding animals or horses, such as pastoralists or armies. During the Early Islamic period, the Amuq Plain was a central staging area and pasturage for summer transhumance (and raids) over the Taurus Mountains into Byzantine land. The summer months would have been when the non-cultivated parts of the plain were driest. While animals could graze on whatever land lay fallow, the majority of irrigated and cultivated fields would have been off limits. Consequently, there would have been a shortage of pasture in the summer. In the winter, when the plain was fully inundated, pastoralists and armies remained and made use of it as a wet pasturage, particularly as the waters receded by early spring. Summer crops, such as rice and vegetables, could be grown within the marsh waters. Ethnographic evidence for the Ghab and southern 'Iraq points to such crops growing in standing water.[78] The fluctuating margins of marsh would also support dry-crop cultivation. Both cultivation and pasture were noted together around marshes in the Balearic Islands.[79] Marsh settlement constituted a new form of adaptation to an increasing wetlands environment previously regarded as marginal. The seasonal expansion and reduction of the marsh waters, and the constantly renewed pastureland, would have created a joint subsistence system. This dimorphic system would have reduced stress on water supply, thereby also limiting competition for water resources.[80]

Symbiotic Subsistence Strategies

Observing the close relationship between Early Islamic period settlement and irrigation strategies, and the appearance of non-native cultivars to the Middle Euphrates region, S. Berthier argues that there indeed was an Islamic agricultural revolution.[81] Yet other scholars like D. Samuel and M. Decker have demonstrated that nearly all the species concerned were cultivated prior to the Islamic conquest, and that water technologies and agrarian calendars with summer growing seasons were also present. Such a 'revolution' would have been gradual and diffused over time.[82] It was not an innovation in methods or materials but, more reasonably, an intensification of the land-reclamation, settlement and irrigation strategies that were already in place.

In the absence of a 'smoking gun' – the faunal and botanical material for the *thughūr* – we can suggest a mixed system of irrigated agriculture and cultivation, marsh subsistence and pastoralism in the Amuq, Mar'ash, Cilician and Malatiya Plains. Geomorphology confirms the presence of wetlands in all of these areas that became permanent by the Early Islamic period. Archaeology shows evidence for new irrigation works such as qanats, canals and mills in the Early Islamic period. The Jerusalem Talmud (redacted *c.*400–500) refers to rice production centers in the Hulath Antioch Valley, meaning the Hulah of Antioch – either the Amuq or Orontes Delta.[83] An inscription listing tariffs on products entering the Cilician city of Anazarbus in the sixth century includes rice among the items, and ninth-century tax lists state that rice was grown in the Great Swamp of Southern 'Iraq and in Cilicia around Ṭarsūs.[84] Ninth-century histories mention the presence of Zuṭṭ and their water buffalo in these frontier plain areas. During the Mamlūk period, yürük Türkmen nomads of the Dulghadıroğlu grew rice along the river valleys of the Cilician and Mar'ash Plains. These practices were resurrected in the Ottoman period, when rice is mentioned in *defters* as a frequent crop grown on reclaimed irrigated lands (*mavât*) furnished with canals in the Amuq, Cilicia and Malaṭiya (where it was quite extensive) Plains and elsewhere in Anatolia.[85] Small-scale settlements in these areas subsequently grew up along canals. Ethnographic evidence of rice cultivation was noted in the Mar'ash Plain in the early twentieth century, and from survey data in 1994.[86] Assembling all of these pieces, it is not an exaggerated claim to posit a single-season crop rotation of rice. Yet it is certainly possible in those dry-farming hot, relatively humid (more so for Cilicia and the Plain of Issus) and wet irrigated zones for a biannual growth cycle of each main crop to be achieved. On elevated parts of the plain and upper terraces, such as the margins of the Amuq on the 'Imm Plateau, wheat was grown, irrigated by canals, and ground into flour by mills during the winter months. In the wetlands and lower river terraces of the *thughūr*, crops such as rice, which required intensive water and labour management in their early stages, were grown in the partially receding waters during late spring/early summer. They may have been farmed by the Zuṭṭ along with their water buffalo, and by other groups during the late spring, summer and early autumn months – the months, also, of Islamic and Byzantine raiding.

Sedentarization and the Frontier Economy

In the late eighth/early ninth century, the frontier began to fill in with sites – many of them small and dispersed along routes, and involved in the local production of ceramics or glass. A specialized route site was the way station, also founded as part of a system or network of settlement in the early 'Abbāsid period. As the settlement patterns show, rural sites in the seventh/early eighth century were far fewer in number than sites in the eighth to tenth centuries. In the Amuq Plain, sites along the Kara Su River and urban nodes such as 'Imm and its surrounding sites had seventh- to tenth-century ceramics. However, the majority of preexisting Late Roman period sites in all other areas on the plain (the Orontes and 'Afrīn basins, Amanus Mountains and Jabal al-'Aqra) spanned the eighth to tenth centuries, indicating that they may have been reoccupied after a period of abandonment. The sites tended to be small, with light to medium assemblages.[87] New late-eighth-century settlements were also seen at the three sites from the Sweyhat Survey and in Early Islamic period sites on the Kurban Höyük Survey, where some were route sites. Many of these sites, as seen in the Amuq, were involved in local economies on the frontier, specifically ceramic and glass production and the baking of lime. The ceramics – namely, the yellow glazes and brittlewares, and likely the polychrome/

colour-splashed wares shown by the site assemblages – were overwhelmingly of local, North Syrian production with very few examples of finewares and imports. Kilns and wasters show that these finewares were produced at the nearest regional centers of Anṭākiya and Raqqa, and there is a strong likelihood that they were also manufactured at Ṭarsūs and Afamīyya. Evidence for local ceramic production is also suggested at Eski Kahta and Khirbet Seraisat (Site 1) from the Jerablus Tahtani Survey.

Fortified Square Enclosures (Way Stations)

Unlike in the Late Roman period, when small fortifications were built in the uplands, Early Islamic period fortifications took on a decidedly different shape and role. Sites such as Ḥiṣn al-Tīnāt in the Plain of Issus; Būqā in the Amuq; Kurban Höyük in the Karababa Basin; Site 17 from the Jerablus/Carchemish Survey; Site 4/Pınar Tarlası, also from the Birecik/Carchemish survey; Ḥiṣn Maslama in the Balikh; and Tell Brak in the Khābūr were all located on important south–north routes (Figure 28). They are also mainly single-period sites, founded in the eighth century and abandoned by the twelfth century. At sites, very few sporadic Roman or Late Roman period sherds have been found, giving too tenuous a pattern to qualify for a preexisting occupation. As frontier settlements, they were small by comparison to the *thughūr* towns. Rather, this new type of settlement – the fortified square enclosure – can be attributed to the Early Islamic period, as a mid-range settlement type between the larger and well-known urban centers and the rural villages and farms. These poorly known settlements, usually not identified or known by name in texts, can best be categorized as way stations. They have been found in other surveys and excavations throughout the Islamic–Byzantine frontier. The presence of more of these is possible, as many may have been misidentified Roman forts, such as Tell Brak. As such, these 'Abbāsid period way stations should revise preconceived notions of the Roman *limes* and encourage a closer look on the ground and ceramic dating at some of these 'Roman' *kastra*. They retained the classic Early Islamic period *qaṣr* architectural layout, but were smaller in general, showed variation in size, and were typically

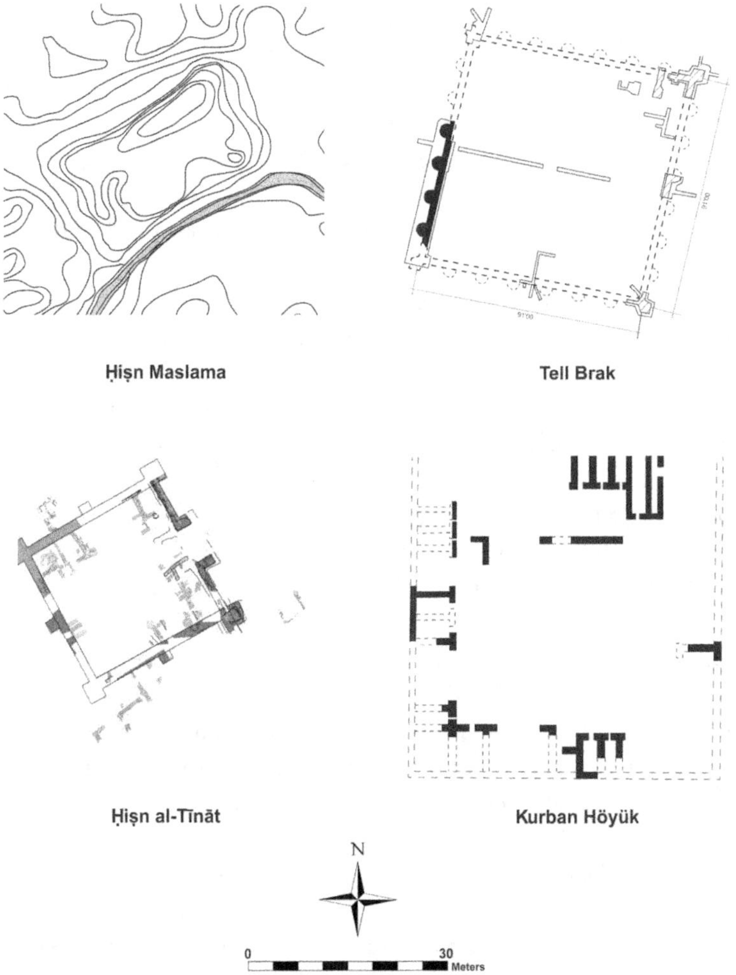

Figure 28 Comparative Early Islamic way stations. From top left, clockwise: Ḥiṣn Maslama sketch adapted from Haase 2006; Tell Brak; Kurban Höyük from Algaze 1990, Figure 124; Ḥiṣn al-Tīnāt by the author

undecorated as compared to their lavish predecessors. Although fortified with buttresses and towers, their walls would not have been able to withstand sieges by the Byzantine army, but as way stations they would have offered security from raiding parties of transhumant, nomadic or upland groups (such as the nearby Jarājima/Mardaites on the Amanus) or other bandits. In type, they are more similar to the modest enclosures attending the larger *quṣūr* seen in the caravan stops on the Darb Zubayda, the extramural residences at Ruṣafa, or the farms around al-Andarīn and Madaba. Neither are they *ribāṭ*, which were known to have been built mainly on the eastern Turkish and western coastal Byzantine frontiers and over time assumed a range of functions and associations including garrison, caravan rest stop, prisoner exchange, local refuge and military/religious stronghold for those wishing to serve on the frontier out of a responsibility to perform *jihād*. Excavated *ribāṭ* on the southern Levantine coast have been demonstrated to be mainly seventh-/early-eighth-century constructions, built over Late Roman period remains. Textual mention of *ribāṭāt* on the northern *thughūr* occurs in relation to buildings within towns, such as Ṭarsūs and Qūrus, rather than lone settlements. The fortified enclosures were probably referred to as *ḥuṣūn*, an inexact term that refers to all manner of fortifications.[88]

Ḥiṣn al-Tīnāt can serve to elaborate on the way station type as a textually known and excavated example. It was not only located on the land route from Iskandarūna into Cilicia but also on the coast as a port. Its third phase, which included the addition and thickening of external walls of the enclosure and domestic structures, including floors, hearths, and cooking and finewares outside and abutting the exterior walls, dated to the tenth century. Excavation on the coastline uncovered the edge of a wall, amphorae, and long pieces of timber – all suggestive of a dock for the port. Geophysical work indicated structures between these two areas, from the enclosure to the coast. Locally-made frontier ceramics and glass were present alongside imported ceramics, perfume and medicine bottles, bronze surgical tools, and glass bracelets from ʻIraq, Egypt and Byzantine lands. Material culture attested primarily to food production and trade; very few military artifacts were found at the site. As a result, the site, whose full size is still undetermined, was by the tenth century (and maybe earlier) not an isolated garrison structure but a coastal frontier settlement involved in trade and exchange.

These fortified way stations were all located in open and well-connected places and accessible by land and sea. This is a reflection of the larger Hellenistic to Early Islamic period settlement patterns already discussed, with some key differences. Interestingly, although sites were associated with smaller rivers and canals or coastal rivers, they eschewed the major rivers such as the Euphrates for settlement. Surveys such as Gritille, Birecik and Bozova-Urfa showed far fewer sites in the Early Islamic period and even Late Roman period on the Euphrates River as compared to Hellenistic and Roman period sites, which were more dispersed and placed at intervals along the west bank of the river. The few Euphrates River sites found on the various surveys were mainly on the upper terraces away from the river itself. The Northern Jazīra and Saddam Dam (Eski Mosul) Salvage Project Surveys similarly showed an avoidance of major river settlements in the Early Islamic period and a preference for sites associated with land routes, such as the lower-town Early Islamic period settlement at Tell al-Hawa adjacent to the 'Abbāsid Road' hollow way. However, S. Redford points out that while the Islamic geographers mention this type of transportation, emphasis seems to be placed far more on land routes where multiple routes of specific stops, and distances and times, are frequently given.[89] He therefore concludes that settlements such as Sumaysāṭ on the Euphrates were given importance to ensure safe river crossing rather than as a riverine port. This can be seen archaeologically from the settlement evidence. There is only a handful of spaced Euphrates River crossings including, besides Sumaysāṭ, Zeugma (Site 19) from the Birecik-Carchemish Survey (between which two was a gap of about 80 km), Qenneshrē and/or Khirbet Seraisat (Site 1) from the Jerablus Survey (a gap of about 60 km), Bālis (a gap of about 40 km), Jisr Manbij (a gap of about 65 km), and Raqqa (a gap of about 80 km). Shifts in the river in the Karababa Basin, where it was less deeply inscribed, might have deterred settlement; however, smaller undiscovered river crossings should not be entirely discounted.[90] Nevertheless, the distances between crossings were on average about 70 km. We know that long-distance travel on the Euphrates and Tigris did occur, from historical texts mentioning Caliph Hārūn travelling from Raqqa to

Baghdād and geographers stating that towns like Bālis and Jazīra Ibn 'Umar were ports (*furḍa*) for the frontier whose goods were shipped down to 'Iraq.[91] River transport may have been used for bringing regionally-specific goods to the markets, or even the elite households of the sprawling Baghdād metropolis.

The Hellenistic–Roman–Late Roman pattern of river settlements is suggestive of a border, using the river as the dividing line between the Parthians and Sāsānians. However, some sites do not seem to have been fortified in any way and were located on the either side of the river. Forts and watchtowers were placed near villages and other rural sites. The eastern *limes*, a subject of great discussion, was not a border but a military/economic settled zone. Similarly for the Early Islamic frontier (and the Middle Islamic), reoriented towards the north, this settlement pattern does not suggest any type of border, although it incorporates elements of a wide linear natural boundary, the Taurus Mountains. These mountains may have been *perceived* as a frontier, as they were pierced with established points at which traders or soldiers 'crossed' to the 'other side' – similar in some ways to the Byzantine–Sāsāanian frontier of the Euphrates River in the fifth and sixth centuries and the Byzantine–Bulgar frontier of the Danube from the eighth to the tenth centuries, which featured a built dike and line of settlements.[92] At the same time, the frontier suggests a network of stopping points across a border that would have facilitated trade and exchange. The early Islamic transhumant tribes avoided Euphrates River transportation for land-based caravan trade, which undoubtedly blended more easily into traditional pastoral routes. Further, long-distance trade was a necessary component for the revitalization of the northern Syrian and Mesopotamian economy.[93] In this marginal-rainfall 'zone of uncertainty,' agricultural production and animal husbandry were greatly ameliorated by far-reaching systems of trade and exchange that brought produce and animal-based products to 'Iraq and distributed manufactured goods around the frontier. P. Wheatley considered transportation foci as an important functional criterion in defining certain types of settlements and establishing links in criss-crossing networks: longitudinal routes connecting coastal towns with their interior; and 'inland ports' traversing the marginal regions from south to north.[94] Like canal building and other types of irrigation that began under the Umayyads, fortified way stations were part of an 'Abbāsid network of frontier development.

These sites were also situated within their own micro-environments. They were not only well connected by land and river routes but also took advantage of their immediate resources as marsh, river, or coastal sites. It is this localization in low areas that are cultivated and well irrigated, and which offered important subsistence strategies, that belies the impression of a random scattering of sites along the frontier – or, for that matter, any one explanation for site settlement, such as strategic or transportation locations. If ecological elements are a determining factor, then the settlements are not reliant solely on their position within systems of trade but also within rural networks involved in some form of land use that is self-sufficient to a degree. Ḥiṣn al-Tīnāt shows further how such a way station guarded and managed local resources. The small system of Early Islamic sites dispersed along the Tum Çay was part of an even smaller network facilitating the seaborne transport of timber. Their enclosures may not have been isolated, as geophysical evidence at Ḥiṣn al-Tīnāt suggests.

The fortified enclosures, when contextualized with earlier settlement patterns on the *thughūr*, stand in stark contrast to settlement in the seventh and early eighth centuries, which was sparse, consisting of a handful of key, newly-founded hydraulic farms and estates, a few reoccupied Late Roman towns, and a scattering of remaining Late Roman period villages. Evidence from some settlements may be ambiguous – pointing to use as either way stations or residences of local rulers, or both – such as the newly-founded enclosure in Site 11 from the Sweyhat Survey, whose size and early 'Abbāsid date is suggestive but also set apart from, though related to, a village. A fort/residence at Tell Khusāf was mentioned in the vicinity of that village. These settlements were part of an overall expansion, beginning in the late eighth/early ninth centuries, in which there was a significant increase in settlement in the landscape, with newly-founded or occupied major towns and villages. Inns for travellers (*funduq*, *khān*) that were not necessarily fortified also appear to increase during the ninth and tenth centuries through *waqf*, particularly in the area of the *thughūr*.[95] Together, both unfortified inns and fortified way stations were part of a new system designed to promote settlement and sedentarization, and also to build and protect the economic infrastructure of movement across the frontier. By the tenth century this must have been a significant feature of the *thughūr*, leading al-Muhallabī (d. 990) to call the frontier *bilād al-fanādiq* (land of the way stations).[96] At the same time, this example of state-sponsored intentionality, as argued by F. Donner, added a level of control on the frontier that reduced the risk to long-distance trade from raiding groups and prevented the rise of local autonomies.[97] As the landscape of the frontier is assumed to have been tumultuous in some fashion, these walled representations dominate their setting, disseminating power and providing refuge for the surrounding community, whether nomadic or sedentary. As such, they inherited a Classical legacy of settlements that were consolidated as fortified farms, religious buildings, and forts. At the same time, the imprint of a distinct and familiar Islamic Near Eastern architectural type, based on Umayyad and ʻAbbāsid forms and duplicated along the marginal frontier region, became a visual symbol for ʻAbbāsid authority.

Frontier Towns

Nearly all the cities of the *thughūr* were taken by treaty, not by force. Frontier towns, while not newly founded, experienced a surge of settlement and construction activity from the late eighth century/early ʻAbbāsid period. Cilicia, the western *thughūr*, provides a good example of this. New evidence at the frontier town of ʻAyn Zarba has shown that the site has only a slight ceramic presence in the seventh/early eighth century, in contrast to its major ceramic presence in the mid-eighth to tenth centuries. Preliminary examinations of ceramic assemblages, both from Gözlü Küle in Ṭarsūs and Örenşehir (a candidate for Hārūniyya) show parallel evidence. Texts refer to camps in Ṭarsūs in 651/2 and Adhana in 743 until the early ʻAbbāsid period, when the towns were developed and new refortification of

'Ayn Zarba, Hārūnīyya, and Kanīsa al-Sawdā' under Hārūn. Manṣūr in 756 gave Maṣṣīṣa the second name al-Ma'mura (from *'imara*), the 'colonized' or 'restored'. While these towns were certainly not newly founded, and very likely not completely abandoned (as evidenced by mention of bishoprics and the presence of camps), there may be some physical truth and archaeological correlation to their development in the early 'Abbāsid period. A hypothesis for urban development in Islamic period Cilicia might begin with encampment that grew separately from the continuously inhabited town. The *ḥīra* found at many sites is often the earliest Islamic period presence in the form of a camp outside a preexisting city that eventually becomes a permanent camp (*ḥāḍir*) and then an urban quarter.[98] Archaeological studies have been carried out in the Near East of the sedentarization of nomads, seen through the permanence of tent sites.[99] At Qinnasrīn, Whitcomb excavated an isolated two-room structure of two phases – the first of mud brick, and the second of stone – which he argued was an example of a tent that became a permanent foundation (*sibāt*) 'just before or during the early 'Abbāsid period'.[100] This is supported by a reference to the wealthy Banū Tanukh in the *Chronique* of Michael the Syrian, who observed that their camp outside Ḥalab had, by 813, become a sprawling town that was unwalled, lavish, and attracted merchants.[101] From the Tigris-Euphrates Carchemish-Birecik Survey, the continuation of Zeugma as an Early Islamic period site on a smaller scale was possibly a *ḥāḍir*, and Site 6 from the Kurban Höyük Survey also showed continuity from the Late Roman period, but only on the periphery of the site. In any case, for rural settlement, way stations and towns, the slight physical presence of the initial Early Islamic period settlement in contrast with the later Early Islamic period settlement is seen at other sites in more deliberate ways, connected to ideas of sedentarization. Settlements of the late eighth century (early 'Abbāsid period), by contrast, comprised large, square towns such as Doğanşehir/Zibaṭra (220 × 280 m in extent), Orensehir/possibly Hārūnīyya (250 × 250 m), Madīnat al-Fār/Ḥiṣn Maslama (330 × 330 m), Tell Sheikh Hasan/Tall Maḥrā (450 × 450 m), Kharāb Sayyar (650 × 650 m), and Khirbet Anbār/possibly Bājaddā (800 × 700 m), resembling Umayyad 'Anjar (310 × 370 m) in Lebanon.[102]

These towns were centers that developed from previously Umayyad agricultural estates.[103]

Examples of state- and/or military-sponsored sedentarization exist in the written record. Balādhurī describes an intentional sedentarization process during the seventh-century conquests, in the form of a report from Raqqa where the Caliph 'Uthmān (r. 644–56) orders Mu'āwiya, the governor of Syria, to settle both nomadic and settled tribes in non-urban areas all over the Jazīra:

> When Mu'āwiyah ruled over Syria and Mesopotamia [Jazīra] in the name of 'Uthmān ibn-'Affān, he was instructed by him to settle [*yanzila*] the Arabs in places far from the cities and villages, and allow them to utilize [*aytimāl*] the lands unpossessed by anyone. Accordingly, he caused the banu-Tamīm to settle at ar-Rābiyah; and a promiscuous multitude of Ḳais and Asad and others, in al-Māziḥīn and al-Mudaibir. The same thing he did in Diyār Muḍar. In like manner, he stationed the Rabi'ah in their Diyār.[104]

Other examples occur, with cultivated lands and irrigation as the incentive. Tribes from southern 'Iraq who demonstrated pro-Umayyad sentiments were encouraged to settle around places such as Qinnasrīn and were given lands in exchange for wages (*iqṭā'*) – for example, the Kinda (from Kūfa) and the Tanūkh. These tribes were administered by local governors and members of the Umayyad family in the seventh and early eighth centuries. A former Bedouin chief, Mālik b. Ṭawq al-Taghlibī, requested lands and waterwheels from Hārūn al-Rashīd at the future settlement of Raḥba near the outlet of the Khābūr River, on which to settle down and develop a town.[105] In the 'Abbāsid period, the areas of the eastern frontier as far as Malaṭiya were administered by governors who belonged to the tribes themselves, rather than members of the Umayyad family. Al-Manṣūr settled 4,000 soldiers in Malaṭiya, giving them plots of farmland (*iqṭā'*).[106] These were 'Abbāsid supporters, and this was undoubtedly partly a political move to unseat the pro-Umayyad tribal allies of Marwān II and weaken his power base in the central and eastern *thughūr* and Balikh. Mu'āwiya also transported Persians to Anṭākiya from Ba'alabakk, Ḥimṣ, Baṣra and Kūfā in 669/70.[107] It is likely that a small community of Persians were already in the city from the time of the first (540) and second (613) Persian conquests. The ethnic composition changed even more by the mid-eighth century, when professional troops from Khurāsān (*abnā'*) were settled alongside Syrian and Jazīran Arabs. Khurāsānī troops were also sent to Adhana, Ṭarsūs and 'Ayn Zarba. A remark on the rebuilding of Ṭarsūs during the caliphate of Mahdī describes the presence of troops from Samarqand, Khwārizm, Farghāna and other parts of Central Asia.[108] This mixing of armies with local Arab tribes and imported Persian soldiers was designed to unbalance the independent tribal chiefs and, using loyal 'Abbāsid troops, prevent them from controlling their own armies.

Tighter dating and correlation with texts may reveal that many of these examples of sedentarization can be attributed to the last half of the eighth century – and, increasingly and more specifically, to the caliphate of al-Mahdī and his son Hārūn al-Rashīd, who sponsored many renovations of frontier fortifications before he became caliph (Figure 29).[109] Under Manṣūr's reign there was a rebuilding programme of four towns between 756 and 760 carried out by Ṣāliḥ

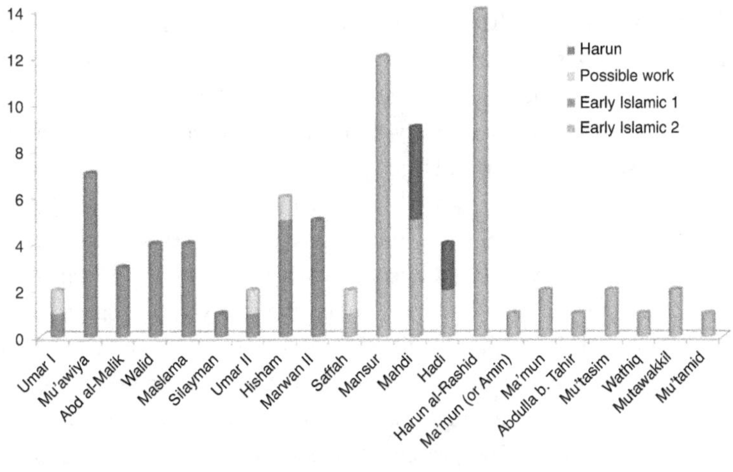

Figure 29 Caliphal renovations, and bar graph

b. ʿAlī. Indeed, Ṣāliḥ and his family inherited most of the northern Syrian and Mesopotamian Umayyad lands and were a very influential family in the *thughūr*.[110] Al-Mahdī (largely through Hārūn al-Rashīd and al-Ḥasān b. Qaḥṭaba, a Khurāsānī commander) carried out a large number of renovations and repairs to eight towns in all regions of the *thughūr*. During his own reign, Hārūn repaired six more sites and focused on three frontier posts in 799–800: ʿAyn Zarba, Kanīsa al-Sawdā' and Hārūnīyya; all three were located in a small area of the eastern Cilician Plain. Both caliphs also settled groups of Khurāsānīs, Yāmānīs, Jazīrans from Mawṣil, Syrians, and volunteers from ʿIraq and the Ḥijāz.[111] Indeed, al-Mahdī himself moved the capital from Baghdād to Ḥalab in 778, and Hārūn did similarly by establishing Manbij as a headquarters in 791 and moving the capital to Raqqa from 797 to 808.[112] Al-Mahdī and Hārūn personally went on expeditions into Byzantine lands, oversaw renovations of preexisting towns and the founding of new ones, resettled large populations of soldiers to the frontier, and, overall, implemented a new policy on the *thughūr* of direct participation.[113] This policy continued for the next 20 years. Ma'mūn (r. 813–17/19) died at the Cilician Gates, the pass between Muslim and Byzantine territory on the Taurus, and was buried at Ṭarsūs.[114] Muʿtaṣim headquartered at Dābiq and received his caliphate at Ṭarsūs. The involvement of these caliphs on the *thughūr* and in caliph-led 'show expeditions' was important as it indicated a physical and symbolic need to consolidate loyalties and sympathies to the central state and to galvanize the frontier communities, through military and political prestige and religious ideologies, in the face of a larger enemy.

Certainly, the anxiety caused by an uncontrolled nomadic population on the frontier is visible as a subtext for such a settling process.[115] Further, the report from Raqqa and other instances taps into the familiar trope of the need to settle the unexplored spaces and wildernesses of the empire. As C. Robinson argues, the report is full of generic motifs peppered with specific places and names so as to condense or 'telescope long processes of social change into specific historical events'.[116] The process of resettlement mimics very similar policies enacted by the Neo-Assyrian Empire in these same marginal lands, showing the need for a regime to build up and invest in an agriculture-based economy.[117] Indeed it has been argued that sedentarization occurred most frequently under strong administrations.

Gradual sedentarization also occurred on the frontier. Shifting economic realities; environmental conditions, such as numerous plagues, famine and earthquakes, as mentioned in texts; and marriage, social pressures and trend-setting behaviors were the main motivators. Although difficult to gauge accurately, most of the early Islamic tribes that were semi-nomadic eventually adopted sedentary practices, becoming farmers (*fallāḥūn*), husbandmen (*arīsīyūn*) or landowners. The practices of farming and irrigation would not have been that foreign, as many would have worked seasonally alongside and with farmers in settled communities, harvesting fields or digging canals and diversionary dams.

Historically, movement across the Islamic–Byzantine frontier in the conquest period was expansive, taking land and settlements, while by the ʻAbbāsid period annual raiding took no land and was seen as symbolic. The mainly Arab tribes often wintered during the first long-ranging conquests. This would have demanded a different sort of transhumance that was much more nomadic in nature. One mention of a raid on Euchaita after 640 recounts that the army, consisting of 5,000 Arabs, wintered around the city with mounts, pack animals and herds of cattle for subsistence, and 'a large captive band in men and animals from various provinces'.[118] However, annual raiding in the summer was recorded as early as 640, although certain years had winter raids (*shawātī* or *shatiya*) and certain raids ventured as far as Constantinople. In the ʻAbbāsid period, the regularization of annual raids increased while the longer winter forays decreased. Different types of land grants available to soldiers contributed to sedentarization, such as those of *qaṭīʻa* and *mawāt* lands that have already been discussed. Some soldiers gradually lost their *iqṭāʻ* lands and were forced to settle down and work their own plots or other people's lands themselves.[119] Individual or village-initiated agricultural entrepreneurship could be linked to these choices. The raiding strategies, from expansionist to symbolic, correspond to a process of sedentarization and are part of an evolutionary trajectory of nomadic to settled peoples.

The intensification of agriculture and irrigation, and the rise of way stations, feed into the economic model outlined by P. von Sivers.[120] This scenario diagrammed three approximate periods of development during the 'Abbāsid era on the *thughūr*, based on evidence from known historical events and actions and a prosopography of individuals known to have resided there. The first period (750–842) was characterized by the settlement of mainly Arab tribes and soldiers through fiscal incentives, coupled with the revenue from the larger local Christian population. Agriculture was the predominant enterprise. In the second period (842–78) – a short, transitional time – agricultural income declined and commercial activity began, athough it remained unprofitable as the central authority took up a defensive policy. Commercial routes were protected, however. Finally, in the third period (878–962), agricultural enterprise was slowly eclipsed by commercial expansion. This is supported by evidence of the conquest and post-conquest economy of the Jazīra.[121] Once the region was settled it gradually became linked within the commercial networks of the late ninth and tenth centuries. A prosopographical analysis further shows that over time the notable personages shifted from 'Abbāsid members and Khurāsānī military leaders on temporary assignments to Central Asians and assorted professional troops of the caliph who came permanently to reside in the frontier. These, and the class of scholars and ascetics, invested in commerce and became wealthy.[122] The blurring of ethnic groups on the frontier was facilitated by the importance of trade and economy. Interestingly, instances of defection and desertion were tied to commercial enterprises.[123] Markets as both measures and outputs of economic development can be strongly linked with the growth in settlement and sedentarization. The military had greater liberty to invest their spoils to make more money in trade and in the primarily tax-free land where they settled down, while non-military personnel and merchants (*ahl al-aswāq*) provisioned armies.[124]

These arguments are supported by the mention of markets and merchants in seven if not more frontier towns, including Adhana, Anṭākiya, Maṣṣīṣa, Ḥadath, Ḥiṣn Kamkh, Kanīsa al-Sawdā' and Sumaysāṭ, not to mention the inn at Baghrās, two unnamed *khānāt* in

Cilicia and the network of fortified enclosures throughout the frontier. The market economy served the frontier and Jazīra as well as channelling the movement of grain and goods to Baghdād. Of course, the other great market for frontier goods was Byzantium.[125] K. Durak's exhaustive study of Islamic–Byzantine trade between the ninth and eleventh centuries strongly shows the development of international trade between the two empires using a wide range of sources. He demonstrates that these sources' mentioning of international trade of Byzantine commodities in Islamic lands and *vice versa*, and Muslim merchants moving back and forth, does not appear substantially before the late ninth/early tenth century.[126] Durak describes four major periods: (1) mid-seventh- to mid-eighth-century land expansion and long-distance trade; (2) mid-eighth-century to *c*.900 expansion in the volume of trade; (3) *c*.912–69 diversification in Byzantine exports to Islamic lands, increased activity of merchants travelling between lands, and fewer restrictions on exports; and (4) 960s–70s, when these trends continued even more markedly as a result of Byzantine reconquest of the frontier.

Such shifts not only testify to the development of the economy of the *thughūr*, its interconnectivities and multi-ethnic populations, but also offer very pragmatic perspectives for settlement that trump purely religious motivations and even the simple acquisition of booty from raids. Ninth- and tenth-century military involvement entailed not only collecting booty for personal survival and trade but was also subsumed under larger ecologically-tied methods of subsistence, such as farming, herding, extracting agricultural revenue, trading, protecting the movement of goods, and commercial private enterprise. Depending on the season and specific intent of the raid, military endeavours across the frontier at times could certainly threaten both the local and the long-distance economy in the short term. At the same time, these expeditions did not disrupt trade and exchange, rather stimulating networks over time and increasing cost and communication.[127]

The frontier was not wholly dependent on its central lands, however, but was largely self-sufficient to a degree, using agricultural revenue to support military endeavours. Operating quietly in alternative yet intersecting topographies, Christian spaces, such as monasteries, also functioned not only as 'independent, self-perpetuating spaces of cultural production [. . .] no longer inextricably tied to the fortune of cities', but as an autonomous network of production, trade and exchange, route rest stations and refuges.[128] The degree of self-sufficiency does not refer to a closed and isolated system for the frontier in its entirety, as the latter was well connected with Byzantine and Islamic lands. Rather, the term here refers to more immediate micro-systems of land use between urban and rural settlements located within the frontier. For example, there is mention of *awqāf* from the *'awāṣim* area of Anṭākiya and Ḥalab from agricultural production supporting both military and religious institutions.[129] As the frontier was less strongly integrated into central economies, the military in their seasonal movements were tied to a system of farming and pastoralism, moving across the frontier and interacting with frontier societies on both the Byzantine and Islamic sides.

The archaeological evidence shows a similar basic transformation, with an earlier dating. Thus, agricultural enterprises had begun by *c.*700, and their irrigation systems were further intensified with newer ones built in the early 'Abbāsid period that *continued* until around the tenth century. Similarly, the protection of commercial routes and the development of a vibrant trade and commercial economy alongside irrigation systems can be seen with the rise of way stations *c.*750–800, also earlier than Sivers' model proposes. Such configurations of the physical and textual evidence should not be surprising. First of all, the dating of both data sets is fairly rough, despite the specificity of historical events. Second, the economic viability and revenue from the frontier would not have been instantaneous but would have taken several generations to develop. A basic sketch of four periods of frontier history may be conceived as: (1) 632–*c.*700, a period of wide-reaching conquests, and non-participation by caliphs as mainly Sufyanid policy, with continuous or expanded settlement in the Jazīra and areas around Ḥalab, but decreased settlement in the rest of the frontier; (2) *c.*700–*c.*750, a period of irrigation networks and estate building, mainly Marwānid policy, chiefly in the Jazīra and North Syria (later *'awāṣim*); (3) *c.*750–809, a period of development for frontier settlement on every level (building, agriculture/irrigation, commerce/trade, and manufacture) and the direct involvement of caliphs, mainly early 'Abbāsid policy throughout the entire frontier and Jazīra; and (4) 809–*c*.900, a period following civil war, when frontier settlements were largely left on their own, settlement and economy was well developed, and caliphal presence was minimal.[130] This last period may extend well into the tenth century, as it is difficult to assess Ḥamdānid local rule in the first half of the century and Byzantine reconquest in the second half as having any significant impact on settlement and economy.

Ethno-religious Identity in Frontier Communities

Who lived in these settlements, abandoned them, and resettled them? These questions are complicated, particularly from an archaeological perspective. The inhabitants of the frontier comprised rural and urban or settled, semi-nomadic or nomadic populations throughout the Early Islamic period. Archaeology has revealed key distinguishing factors in ceramics and settlement patterns. From textual evidence, we know that the frontier was composed of many different ethnic, religious, and political communities. As such, it is worth speculating whether the archaeological classifications of site categories can be further distinguished with ethnic associations. Ethnic groups, for the most part, also had certain identifiable religious affiliations, although the processes of conversion, cultural blending and political defection diluted clear representations of religious identity over time.

It should be emphasized that practicing Muslims on the frontier constituted a minority throughout the Umayyad and, partly, the 'Abbāsid periods. A well-known model for the process of conversion is that of R. Bulliet, who describes at the onset a slow shift to Islam that rapidly gathered influence. According to him, by 861, the stage of early adoption to Islam would have been reached by 16 per cent of the population and by 961, the period of early majority, 50 per cent of the population would have converted to Islam. Specifically for Syria, the Muslim majority was reached by the end of the ninth century, and certainly by start of the tenth century with the rise of the

Fāṭimids. Although Bulliet's dates seem too specific and somewhat arbitrary, a general pattern of a Muslim majority (50 per cent of the population converting to Islam) by the end of the Early Islamic period echoes the pattern of 50 per cent of Late Roman sites being occupied in the Early Islamic period. On the one hand, Bulliet argues that Islam was slow to penetrate rural areas, 'partly because [. . .] the remoteness of the countryside slowed the pace of conversion'.[131] On the other hand, non-Muslims would have had experienced more social and economic pressure to convert to the religion of the ruling class in urban areas than in the contryside. Christian elites who converted affected a cachet influential on other members of the community.[132] Once converted, as *mawālī* they were able to attain power and prestige as soldiers or civil servants – even to rule, as in the case of Maymūn b. Mihrān, secretary and administrator of the Jazīra under 'Umar II. There were also exceptions. Muslims and Christians intermarried, as seen in the case of Arab soldiers after the Battle of al-Qādisiyya (636) who married non-Muslim women as there were few alternatives. Christians also converted to Islam and back again as was politically, economically or even socially expedient.[133] Setting aside these exceptions, which of themselves fascinatingly complicate an otherwise difficult process, is it possible to pin down conversion processes utilizing archaeological evidence?

There are, of course, apparent problems in attempting to assign ethnic or religious markers to archaeological evidence: pots do not equal people. These problems can be exacerbated in the archaeology of any transitional period or culturally mixed frontier zone, itself an ambiguous space. Discerning difference and change in a heterogeneous cultural landscape could be seen as a forced exercise. Preexisting Syriac-speaking communities, Arab tribes, and resettled populations and soldiers – Khurāsānī, Christian or Muslim – coexisted on the frontier. How is one able to differentiate between these communities or account for settlements with mixed populations? Haldon and Kennedy established criteria for distinguishing Byzantine from Early Islamic period frontier forts based on differences between upland, defensible locations and lowland, open, urban layouts, respectively. Despite this, it is too simplistic to say that all upland communities on the Byzantine frontier were Christian and all lowland settlements on the Islamic frontier were Muslim. There is very little evidence for highland Muslims communities, with only a handful of exceptions such as Bara and Dayr Sim'ān with newly-built mosques and Dayr Seta, which featured a repurposed mosque.[134] Many preexisting Semitic eastern (Nestorian) and western (Miaphysite) Syriac- and Aramaic-speaking Christians who lived in northern Syria and the Jazīra remained settled as farmers and traders. They were referred to in Arabic as *Nabaṭ*, or Nabataean. Many ethnic Greeks (*rūmī*), mainly consisting of the urban ruling elite, left the cities, but a generally urban group of Greek speakers (Melkites) remained. Groups such as the Syriac Orthodox appear to have thrived in the *thughūr*, where virtually every major *thaghr* also had a bishop's seat for some or all of the Early Islamic period. Lesser towns like 'Imm, villages like Domuztepe, and towns with monasteries hovering on tells above them like 'Azāz, also had Christian communities. Similarly, certain Arab tribes, such as the Taghlib, were largely non-nomadic settled Christians. Ideally, markers such as tax status (*kharāj* and *jizya* vs. *'ushr*) would be useful in differentiating ethnic/rural identity within non-Muslim and Muslim rural communities, as we know that caliphs, like Manṣūr, initiated these land-tax cadastral surveys (*ta'dil*). Aside from the odd, isolated case, the textual record, at present, is not robust enough to attempt such an undertaking; the surveys are not all preserved. Some texts name villages and districts, but these lists do not exist for every province, including the *thughūr*. Elsewhere, information can be conflicting. At Bālis, there is evidence that an elite family of Greek brothers owned the settlement and surrounding villages at the time of the Islamic conquest.[135] Some of these lands were also granted to fighters, Syrian Arab converts who paid the *'ushr* in the time of Maslama.[136] Tracing an Early Islamic period signature in a pre-established Late Roman period landscape from ceramic surface collections becomes less clear. Islamic pottery is not indicative of Muslim settlement, and pre-Islamic period pottery traditions would have persisted. Indeed, there is an almost tautological danger of seeing difference because difference is implied.

In order to tackle the issue of ethno-religious representation on the frontier, the argument initially needs to be framed in a different way. Proceeding from the historical contexts, an examination of the sites using criteria gained from archaeological evidence – such as physical size and assemblage size, chronology, definite or indefinite occupation, and preexisting or newly-established settlement based on known ceramic types – has added levels of variance and degree to Late Roman and Early Islamic period settlements. The criterion of a site that was preexisting or newly founded is a key distinguishing marker between Late Roman and Early Islamic period sites and, hypothetically, Christian and Muslim communities. This conclusion is built on the textually-informed premise that many Christian groups, largely of the urban-dwellling elite classes, left the frontier regions for Byzantine lands and no new groups settled down in the countryside, whereas new Muslim groups settled or were settled in their place. Preexisting Christian villagers or nomads gradually converted. The model is, of course, flawed and leaves out individual variation: Muslims who defected to Byzantine lands or converted to Christianity, Byzantine prisoners taken from expeditions, or Christians who gave up their land to Muslims in cities and themselves resettled in newly-founded Muslim towns or became *mawālī* (see Chapter 10, section on Tribal Identity).[137] It also avoids the undoubtedly present yet complicated issue of hybridity and the syncretism of frontier societies. These distinctive examples, endemic in such societies, complicate binary narratives of Christian–Muslim interaction. However, archaeological evidence for long-term settlement patterns is itself rather coarsely grained. Following a Braudelian *longue durée* scheme, individuals, events and specific dates are omitted in the broader picture of communities and groups.

There is also precedent for such analysis. Some studies have been done to distinguish Christian and Berber settlements in al-Andalus. M. Acién Almansa demonstrated that areas of Berber settlement and Berber sites (often known from toponyms) had no Late Roman period pottery types and were mainly *de novo*.[138] S. Gutiérrez Lloret shows that marsh sites in the eighth and ninth centuries also did not contain any Late Roman period pottery, and therefore were established *de novo* with newer pottery forms.[139]

What can be suggested is that newly-founded settlements associated with new canal construction being the largest and most important sites on the plains, these were probably occupied or deliberately settled by Arab tribes and their clients (*mawālī*) and were largely non-Christian Muslim communities, perhaps organized by the local officials and members of the Umayyad ruling family. Late Roman settlements that increased significantly in the Early Islamic period (urban centers and river sites, such as the 'Imm and Yaghrā in the Amuq) may suggest mixed ethnic and religious Muslim and Christian communities resulting from incoming Muslims adding to a community of already-present Christians. That all of these sites expanded in the Early Islamic period from the seventh century onwards suggests that they may have become large, hydraulic villages or perhaps towns sited to control water rights and utilize the broad wetlands' resources. Marsh settlements, also part of the Early Islamic period settlement signature, were more specialized, and perhaps settled by relocated populations from other parts of the Islamic empire, such as the Zuṭṭ from the wetlands of southern 'Iraq. Fortified enclosures, similarly, were way stations that controlled frontier movement. By contrast, scattered Late Roman period sites that were reduced in physical size and/or assemblage size by the Early Islamic period on the plain, or that showed some continuity in the uplands, may represent persisting Christian communities that did not leave the region, such as those of the Syrian Jibāl.

The ethno-religious hypothesis shows processes of accommodation and adaptation among groups, although it does not take into account acculturation and assimilation processes (such as conversion), which would have occurred gradually over time. Nevertheless, all of these processes suggest that interaction on the frontier was not simply a matter of Muslim fighting against Christian in a holy war.

CHAPTER 8

THE BYZANTINE FRONTIER (SEVENTH TO TENTH CENTURIES)

I have headed for this kingdom, of whose like I have never heard for abundance of sweet odors, wilderness of living space, richness in resources of power and extensiveness of hills.[1]

A poet traveled through the Taurus Mountains on his way to join the campaign at Qurra (Greek Koron, headquarters of Cappadocia, near modern Çömlekçi/Ulukışla) in the summer of 830 or 832 and to recite a poem to Caliph al-Ma'mūn. On the way, he met an elderly man of the same tribe who was also journeying to Byzantine lands. When asked why, the old man's response, quoted above, like the poet's own motivation is complicated by a range of desires for the beauty of these unknown lands, the *dār al-ḥarb*. Much has been said about the Islamic side of the frontier, but the Byzantine frontier, wreathed in mountains, remains misty and obscure. One impediment has been traditional assumptions about a 'Dark Age' and decline; a viewpoint that has been challenged and reframed by several scholars.[2]

In the eighth century and later, Byzantine frontier sites were mainly rural, protected, and located in the mountains, often on marginal land where population was sparse and arable production limited (Figure 30). The environment of Cappadocia and the

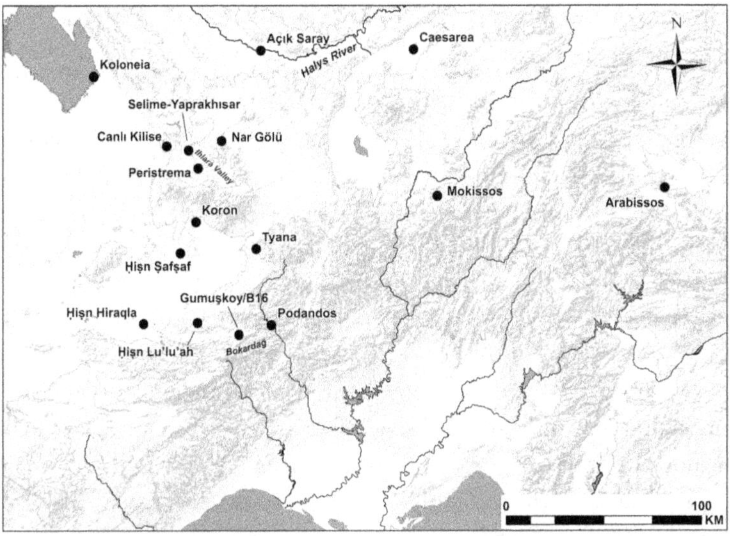

Figure 30 The Byzantine frontier

surrounding provinces on the high Anatolian plateau (at more than 1,000 m.a.s.l.) on the Byzantine frontier is a relatively dry continental and sub-desertic climate, receiving around 350 mm of rainfall per annum, and experiences extreme temperature differences between day and night. Geomorphological work shows alternating wet and dry periods between 500 and 1400, suggesting variance in the amount of rainfall.[3] Its mountainous rugged terrain, sandwiched between the Halys River to the north and the Taurus Mountains to the south, is pierced with dramatic, volcanic peaks 2,000–4,000 m high. Amidst these peaks are several relatively semi-arid treeless basins, conducive to the small-scale cultivation of crops (such as grapes), which can contend with the mineral-rich and water-retaining volcanic soil. How did the Byzantine communities subsist? To answer this question, we will examine what is known of Byzantine society in Cappadocia from the seventh to the tenth centuries, what its settlements looked like, and lastly what can be said about subsistence strategies for the Byzantine inhabitants of the frontier.

Frontier Society in the Middle Byzantine Period

What is known of these communities comes largely from texts that are military in nature. These imply that life on the plateau was unstable – any day could bring a Muslim raid. A host of economic changes affected the Byzantine Empire in the seventh and eighth centuries, including the diminishing of large-scale commerce, the termination of the *annona* grain supply to Constantinople, the privatization of certain sectors of the economy, and the loss of lands in the eastern and western provinces – all of which cumulatively led to a fiscal crisis.[4] *Curiales* (town councilmen), who were responsible for increased deficits, fled from their positions.[5] Towns lost their fiscal autonomy and were administered by the local elite and/or a local bishop and the church, while the central state cut back on its expenditures. In the second half of the seventh century and the early eighth century, Syrian cities lost their economic and political importance as self-governing centers of administration for the region and generators of imperial revenue. Many among the Byzantine population, particularly the wealthier urban officials, elite, merchants and aristocracy, left the cities to the local populace and withdrew to the Taurus Mountains, heading to Constantinople.[6] Heraklios, in al-Ṭabarī, says to his people: 'By God, that you give them [the Arabs] half of what Syria produces and take half, [provided that] the mountains of Rome [*jibāl al-rūm*, the Taurus Mountains] remain with you, is better for you than that they overpower you in Syria and share with you the mountains of Rome.'[7] Another instance records the departure of Byzantines from Sīs in Cilicia for the 'Greek Mountains'.[8] Many Byzantines migrated to the Byzantine provinces of Asia Minor, the districts that from the 640s onwards had become the command posts (*strategides*) for the armies of Anatolikon and Armeniakon, military units whose troops were under the authority of a *strategos* or general.[9]

Until the middle of the tenth century, there was no grand strategy on the part of the Byzantines to conquer Islamic lands, although imperial ideology consistently represented the emperor's remit as one in which the recovery of lost Roman territory was a prime duty (and even then the so-called reconquests of the period were more the result of military-magnate pressure than imperial government policy). By the time of the seventh through early ninth centuries, the cities and countryside on the Byzantine frontier were mostly left to their own devices to subsist and defend themselves; however, the central government at Constantinople still had influence. It raised taxes, maintained local armed forces, and funded fortifications at a local level. The church, which also owned lands, often worked together with the central state, maintaining imperial order. Local, individual, and community-based systems of power predominated in the provinces.[10] Out of this situation, several landowning elite families, which later formed the core of a military aristocracy in Anatolia, emerged from Cappadocia during this period. Relatively independent in their home region, they were nevertheless closely tied into court and imperial systems through their positions, titles, ranks and offices. This was in part because much of their wealth derived from imperial largesse and annual payments of gold coin as recompense for their service to the state.[11] Part of their wealth was also supplemented and expanded, we can assume without much evidence, from raiding operations in Islamic lands, along with agro-pastoral activities and horse breeding (for which the region was famous, not unlike the Jazīra, and which is attested from pre-seventh-century accounts). Horses were sold and mainly used for cavalry.[12] The rise and origins of this military aristocracy is rooted in both their involvement with the state and their provincial geographical situation. The economy and politics of the frontier-zone environment undoubtedly aided them in developing local power and building up networks of patronage and authority, through which they could also control local commerce.[13] Some of these Cappadocian families were of Armenian origin, and by the early tenth century many were powerful and independent – such as the famous Phokades, to which the Emperor Nikephoros Phokas (r. 963–9) belonged, as did his nephew Bardas Phokas (the Younger, d. 989), who rebelled against Basil II.[14] Other emperors, such as John Tzimiskes (r. 969–76) rose to power as military men on the frontier where, with the support of the provincial armies and the family loyalties that had developed across the generations, they were in a position to challenge the reigning emperor for power. Bardas Skleros is a further example, acclaimed emperor by his Cappadocian troops in defiance of Basil II in 976–9. The Scleros and Phocas families were rivals; relatives through marriage; and at times, in the eyes of the government at Constantinople, rebels. As such, they were not unlike the powerful tribal or local 'warlords' known from Islamic frontier regions, primarily after the weakening of the 'Abbāsid caliphate in the tenth century (see Chapter 9).[15] They portrayed themselves as beturbaned with decorated *aqbiya* (singular *qabā'*, kaftans) containing *ṭirāz* bands in the manner of Muslim elites, and dined and entertained guests in similar fashion – on cushions and rugs. In this fashion, the local elites exhibited acculturation with Muslim society, presenting themselves in the manner of a familiar authority figure that would be recognizable in Islamic eyes.[16]

Anxiety over the central state's ability to control the frontier populations is suggested by Emperor Constantine V, who split the military command of Opsikion – probably as a result of civil war in the early 740s. This is strikingly similar to Hārūn al-Rashīd's creation of the *'awāṣim*, which also had the function of a deployment and buffer zone whose instigation had likely been a destabilizing maneouver. It is very likely that it was the self-interested investment, particularly in land and livestock, undertaken by members of the provincial magnate elites in the course of the tenth century (when we have a little evidence), that drove some of the economic recovery of the Byzantine state at this time.[17]

Military organization in these frontier areas, as in other parts of the empire, depended largely on a core of small (probably very small) regular garrisons of full-time troops, largely cavalry, supported by a larger number of part-time militia, such as soldiers called up on a seasonal basis. Their duties, of course, entailed more specific roles in maintaining a watch on the passes into and out of imperial territory. In the tenth and eleventh centuries, when the Byzantine military gained territory on the Islamic frontier, the local troops were conscripted in the course of more aggressive offensive campaigns as scouts and skirmishers (*prokourstores*, *trapezitai*, *tasinakia*), employed alongside the professional forces of the *tagmata*, full-time paid units of both Byzantine and foreign origin. Perhaps an exceptional account, the *Chronographia* of Theophanes, recounts that Islamic forces defeated an army led by two generals and 'a throng of peasant militia' after initial defeat followed by a nine-month siege at Ṭuwāna (Greek Tyana) in Cappadocia in 707.[18] Since regular pay was often either unreliable or minimal, booty (*skula*) was an essential aspect of all warfare, whether in the form of livestock, grain or prisoners.[19] From the 680s into the middle of the eighth century, Byzantine forces generally avoided direct confrontation with the enemy, preferring to operate a hit-and-run, guerilla strategy where possible. A treatise on skirmishing warfare in the tenth century clearly stipulates that the response against enemy raids should be defensive, protecting people, animals and wealth above all, and only retaliating while the raiders were returning home, tired and laden with their booty. Byzantine strategy also included a measure of surveillance by mobile units in key positions and passes. The main goal of this was to function as part of an early-warning and evacuation system assisted by the military (*expelatores*), which affected settlement patterns.[20] How early this evolved is unclear; however, changing Byzantine policy towards an offensive strategy as early as the middle of the eighth century suggests a transforming imperial agenda.

Settlement on the Anatolian Plateau

There has hitherto been little evidence about frontier settlements from a Byzantine perspective. This is changing, with a growing interest in Cappadocia sparked initially by the attraction of the vibrantly painted cave churches, attesting to a persisting Christian community in the Middle Byzantine period. We have seen the shift to upland settlement already in the Late Roman period in the Amuq. This resembled the Visigoths' exodus from the Andalusian plains to upland fortified sites around the same time. This process continued into the tenth century and was noted not only by Byzantine military treatises but by Islamic geographers such as Ya'qūbī, who distinguishes Malaṭiya rising from the plain but surrounded by the mountains of the Byzantines (*Jibāl al-rūm*) and, in his oft-quoted observation (written *c.*891), 'The Byzantine border districts are a land of fortresses and villages, not of cities ...'[21] Ibn Ḥawqal notes (written *c.*977, revised 988): 'Rich cities are few in their [Byzantines'] kingdom and country, despite its situation, size and the length of their rule. This is because most of it consists of mountains, castles [*qilā'*], fortresses [*ḥuṣūn*], cave dwellings and villages dug out of the rock or buried under the earth.'[22] Ibn Khurradādhbih enumerated the fortresses (*ḥuṣūn*) of each Byzantine province. Their numbers far outweighed any mention of cities, towns, or villages.[23] The anonymous Persian author of the *Ḥudūd al-'Alām* (*c.*982) provides even more specific information about a previously urban settlement system replaced by a village/fortress-refuge dual arrangement, already discussed and quoted at the introduction to this current section (Part 2). The Arabic geographers used these terms deliberately and with greater specificity, differentiating between cities and fortified places.[24] Interestingly, Leo the Deacon (b. *c.*950), in his *History*, wrote of Nikephoros Phokas between 963 and 965 heading to the frontier in the land of Cappadocia 'whose people *were formerly* (*to prosthen*) called troglodytes (*Troglodytai*), because they dwelt (*to...hypodesthai)* in caves (*troglais)*, hollows (*xeramois*) and labryinths, as if in dens (*pholeois*) and holes (*hypiogais*)'.[25] Leo in all likelihood witnessed these dwellings himself. The comparison also implies not only a level of distinction from Leo's own urban world but a detached condescension, likening its subjects to burrowing animals.

Very limited survey or excavation has been done on the Taurus north of the *thughūr*, but several studies show interesting patterns. Excavation in Tyana revealed little of the seventh- to tenth-century settlement. The brief description of the post-seventh-century town mentioned a Middle Byzantine church from the tenth century.[26] A prehistoric survey in the Anti-Taurus north of Mar'ash noted that Classical sites were in the area of the Jayḥān River and Arabissos/ Elbistan Plain in the Anti-Taurus Mountains north of Mar'ash.[27] Although it is unknown whether Late Roman and Islamic period settlements shifted, it is important to consider that while some sites are considered as 'upland', many were sited in upland valleys and plains, albeit still inaccessible as they were nestled within or behind mountain ranges. Survey in the Peristrema Valley in Cappadocia showed that eighth- and ninth-century churches were more hidden within the gorge near Ihlara. The site of Selime, part of a cluster of tenth- to eleventh-century sites farther north on the Melendiz Suyu, was attenuated by a 200 m-long, 4 m-thick fortification wall with buttresses and a 3 m-deep dry moat to the exterior protecting the site from approach via the plateau above. Further gardens and dovecotes were often, though not always, also situated in courtyards of house complexes and fields between the rock-cut buildings and the river.[28]

Several settlement types are recorded in texts that point to very different patterns of settlement from those on the Islamic *thughūr*. Under threat of attack, villagers were to evacuate with their livestock to a designated, defensible mountain fortification called either *kataphygia* (fortified village for refuge) or *ochyrōmata* (refuge in the mountains). The *kataphygia* were not part of a formal network but an *ad hoc* system of out-of-the-way settlements used by the rural population in times of danger. The evacuations were seasonal, in keeping with the timing of Islamic raids. In Cappadocia, the objects of these raids were places known as *al-matāmīr* (singular *al-matmūra*), which refers to underground granaries or any subterranean or rock-cut settlements that were hidden from raiding Islamic tribes and armies. These terms were even used as town names. Abū Isḥāq took al-Matmūra on a raid in Cappadocia in 831. The granaries were used to protect the wealth of the community, and may have functioned as storehouses to stockpile provisions for troops moving across the *theme*. They are indicative of a rural population in unstable times.

The fact that Ibn Khurradādhbih took note of this process suggests that such places were known and an 'open secret', and may have been targets for Islamic raids. A valuable description of such a cave settlement is given anecdotally in his accounts, relayed in a story by Muhammad b. Mūsā, an astronomer who was sent by Caliph al-Wāthiq (r. 842–7) on a mission into Byzantine territory to find the place of the *aṣḥāb al-raqīm* or *ahl al-kahf* (the Cave of the Seven Sleepers) known from Sūra 18 of the Qur'ān. He was taken by a local frontier inhabitant to see the settlement of Qurra in the rural district (*rustāq*) of Kharama, whose entrance, among other features, the emissary observed rather closely:

> Then we continued our journey and arrived in four days, before a mountain whose diameter at its base was less than one thousand cubits. An underground tunnel, whose entrance opened at the entrance to ground level, gives access to the site of the people of the cave. We began by climbing on top of the mountain (*al-jabal*), where we saw a well of large size, cut in stone, at the bottom of which we could discern the water. We went down then up to the door of the underground tunnel, and, after having not even walked three hundred steps, we arrived at the same spot that we had looked down on before. One finds a portal whose ceiling is supported by columns carved in the rock, and from which are some of rooms. One of them, where the threshold rises to above ground to the height of [a] man, is closed by a door of stone cut by a pickaxe and it is there that the bodies are preserved. The gatekeeper, who is attending eunuchs of remarkable beauty, wanted to prevent us from seeing and touching them. To intimidate us, he said that anyone who would try to do so would bring about a terrible misfortune.[29]

The astronomer determines in the end that this is not the Cave of the Seven Sleepers, but what is relevant for us is the close detail given to the description of a Cappadocian dwelling.

Stables, such as those recorded at Açık Saray, Çanlı Kilise (identified as a *kōmē* or agricultural town) and Selime-Yaprakhısar (Wādī Salamūn), were also rock-cut and also effectively hidden from outsiders.[30] The last two examples were on hillsides overlooking plains. These were not monasteries but self-sufficient residences for landowning aristocrats who raised and bred horses, providing (or selling) them for military use. Çanlı Kilise, in addition to a church and around 30 residential units and seven stables (capable of holding at least 100 horses in total), had two areas identified as refuges for the population.[31] The priority to protect villagers and livestock (sheep and goats, but especially horses) from rustling, and settlements and granaries from looting, is an indication of the type of mobile booty collected by nomads. In the *Life* of Philaretus the Merciful (702–92), written by his grandson, we learn that he was a landowner from humble origins who owned 48 separate estates (*proástia*) in the regions of Paphlagonia, Pontus and Galatia, and who raised livestock: 600 head of cattle, 100 yoked pairs of oxen, 800 horses in pasturage, 80 saddle horses and mules, and 12,000 head of sheep. His estates were dispersed in locations with available and irrigated water, implying pragmatism with regard to existing infrastructural conditions.[32] He eventually loses his livestock-based wealth by giving away too much to those in need and succumbing to 'the cattle-lifting of the Ismaelites' (*dia te aixmalosias ton 'Ismaeliton*), the Islamic raiders.[33]

Two other types of such Byzantine settlement existed: *phrouria* (garrison stations for defence) and *aplekta* (fortified camps for the lodging of troops, military staging posts). They had a similar basic arrangement to previously mentioned examples: a perimeter wall, cisterns, enclosed buildings and empty space. In some cases, a tower or main structure may have served an additional function as the seat of a local military commander, or *tourmarchai*. Many of these settlements guarded routes and resources but, unlike the network of fortified-enclosure way stations on the Islamic side of the frontier, the *phrouria* were not readily accessible or open, while the *aplekta* were situated on roads. They may have been part of another system entirely. Surveys in Cappadocia recorded two sites on the Tyana–Mokissos route, as well as the site of Selime-Yaprakhısar on the Koloneia–Tyana route that could also have functioned as signalling stations.[34] The latter site may also have functioned as an *aplekton*. A system of fortifications is known to have been established between the Taurus Mountains and Constantinople, with warning fortifications placed every 50–100 km.[35] It is unlikely that such a planned construction of new forts across Anatolia took place before the tenth century – rather, existing forts and some new constructions were connected opportunistically, although strategically.[36]

Many similar shifts from *poleis* to upland *kastra* settlements that also functioned as signalling stations were recorded in other areas of Anatolia, such as Rough Cilicia/Isauria, Paphlagonia (north-central Anatolia),[37] Pontus (north-eastern Anatolia),[38] and Lycia (south-west Anatolia) and Pamphylia (south-central Anatolia) on the coast at the western end of the Taurus range. We can recall Ibn Khurradādhbih's reference to Nabīk in the mountains of Rough Cilicia. In Paphlagonia, surveys have discovered that Roman period sites were dispersed near river lowlands and mountain passes, but 20 fortified sites from the Middle Byzantine period were documented on natural prominences. These isolated, upland fortresses were more prevalent in times of instability, when the local population sought refuge in them temporarily. Such settlements were densely packed buildings arranged around a church on a hilltop. The fort of Dereğzi is an example of a newly-founded seventh-century hilltop fort built to protect the surrounding plain. In some cases individually defended upland settlements linked together to create a fortified area, such as Alexander's Hill at Sagalassos.[39] In Lykia and Isauria, fortified seventh-century Byzantine hilltop or upland settlements also reoccupied places last inhabited by Lykians and other groups.[40] Some similarity and some difference can be seen in a comparison with the villa-to-village model of *incastellamento* described above for the western Mediterranean, which defines this period as the third stage of social and settlement transformation with the reintroduction of a local aristocracy and agrarian specialization in *curtes*, or farm-manors, in the eighth to early ninth centuries. For the Cappadocian frontier at this time, however, the non-elite and military component of the frontier was still crucial.

While the synchronicity of lowland-to-upland *incastellamento* during this period all around Anatolia, al-Andalus and Italy is striking, the chronology and justification given by some scholars with regard to keying shifts in settlement patterns to specific historical events should be lengthened and unbound. It is unlikely that these shifts occurred contemporaneously with the Islamic conquests of the mid-seventh century. Rather, a gradual removal from coastal plains to the uplands in the Early Islamic period, and perhaps earlier, is more likely.[41]

Resource Protection and Pastoralism

It is worth considering what resources were peculiar to the montane Byzantines, which were important for subsistence or were worth defending. A major mountain resource was wood, particularly tall timbers of pine, cedar and oak, which was greatly valued for its use in building ships for naval and mercantile fleets. The intersection of the Taurus Mountains and the Mediterranean coast in Rough Cilicia, and the Feke Peninsula between Antalya and Fethiye, were known to be prime areas for forestry.[42] The shift of Late Roman period settlements after the seventh century from the contested coastal plain to the uplands is suggestive of a move to protect not only the communities themselves but also their timber sources. The Byzantine state also recognized this resource with the creation of the maritime *theme* of Kibyrrhaiotōn, encompassing the provinces of Lykia, Pamphylia and Cilicia Trachaeia or Rough Cilicia (Isauria). This was a move designed to protect timber resources and exact state control, further evidenced by decrees by ninth- and tenth-century emperors forbidding the sale of timber to Muslims who were raiding the coastline.[43] The Rough Cilicia Survey Project identified two relic cedar forests at 1,700 m.a.s.l. One had the remains of a Roman logging camp while the other, in the Biçkici Canyon, had a Late Roman through Middle Byzantine period (fourth to thirteenth centuries) defensive structure and evidence of continuous occupation.[44] That harvesting of timber for Islamic lands also occurred is referred to by al-Bīrūnī, who describes loggers from Ṭarsūs who were sufis (*abdâl*) before the Byzantine reconquest.[45] Timber was not the only resource of value from the forested slopes. Arboreal and plant extracts, such as saffron, known to grow in hidden and protected sinkholes, were sought-after items used for medicine, perfume, incense, and also for dyeing. These products were hard to obtain (one had to be sourced using snakes!) and sold at high prices.

Equally, we can assume that mines were an important resource. Currency from the seventh to tenth centuries (particularly petty coinage) dwindled in minting and circulation as a result of deliberate imperial policy from the 660s, leading to the continuous recycling of existing coinage, regionalized local economies, and a rise in non-monetary exchange (as in the barter of agricultural produce, livestock, or prisoners from raids) – particularly on the frontier, and for the payment of soldiers.[46] Maintaining currency and obtaining new supply was still an important activity and required control over metal sources, which were mined in the Taurus Mountains, Pontic Mountains and the Caucasus. Surveys in the Bolkardağ region of the Taurus Mountains, just west of the Cilician Gates, between 1983 and 1985, revealed evidence of a series of predominately silver but also iron, copper, lead, tin and gold mines (about 800 in all), smelting areas and 27 settlements that comprised regional centers during the eighth to tenth centuries. Most mine sites were on the steep slopes or cliffs of the southern part of the valley (where the survey focused). One such site, Gümüşköy/B16 ('Silver Village'), was on a mountaintop with the largest pottery spread of any site on the survey encompassing Early and Middle Byzantine periods and a coin of Romanos III (1028–35). It also had evidence of smelting and ores rich in cobalt, important for glass and pottery coloration. Chronology of these sites was determined by ceramics (the presence of glazed pottery), and the carbon-dating of a shovel handle found in a mine (700–850) and a wooden ladder (744 +/– 55 years). Fifty per cent of sites were dated to the seventh/eighth centuries.[47] Large iron deposits, as well as copper and zinc, were mined near Tephrikē and Malaṭiya, likely during this period.[48]

These mines and mining communities were located exactly between the Islamic and Byzantine frontiers and proximal to the expedition routes across the Taurus, and therefore must have been a protected, valuable resource. The settlements of Ḥiṣn Hiraqla, Ḥiṣn Lu'lu'a and Ḥiṣn Ṣafṣaf all border the Bolkardağ Valley to the north, but lie west of the main route from the Cilician Gates to Ṭuwāna (Tyana) and Qayṣariya (Kayseri) and *en route* to Qūniya (Konya).[49] Their frequent occurrence in historical sources as the object of raids (along with other similar settlements that have not been identified) has two linked explanations, neither of which is explicit in the written accounts: they were there to control the route to Konya and they protected the mining industry, a resource which the Islamic armies also sought to gain access to. There were several sources of lead throughout the Islamic world, and most silver was obtained from Central Asian sources. However, lead from the Taurus may have been important for the production of glazes for ceramics in frontier centers and elsewhere. Isotope analysis of Fusṭāt glazed wares show the use of lead from the Aladağ area of the Taurus Mountains, just north of Adhana, mainly on luster wares and manganese-glazed wares between 1125 and 1175.[50] The mines themselves could also be used as refuges (*ochyrōmata*), as is known from a famous expedition by Mu'taṣim in 838, during which inhabitants took refuge in the salt mines (*mallāḥa*) around Ankara.[51]

As has already been mentioned, horses were a specialty of the region. At times they were traded or sold in Islamic markets.[52] The relatively high investment in horse breeding and stabling demonstrates the need to protect this resource from raiding expeditions. Did the Byzantines practice pastoralism? Horse, cattle or sheep raising would have been more viable in the upland terrain, requiring less manpower and being a portable resource. In some cases, we are aware that Syriac-speaking Christians on the frontier also practiced pastoralism, as known from the fourth-century *Life* of John the Arab. Saint Michael Maleinos of Charsanion (894–961), uncle of Nikephoros Phokas, gave away all of his moveable possessions, including slaves and, most importantly, his immense flocks of grazing animals (*agelas bosxematon kai pantaon eidon apeiron plethos...*) of all kinds, to the poor when he renounced his worldly possessions.[53]

There is no reason to assume that Greek- or Syriac-speaking Christian groups did not move across the frontier seasonally or even permanently after the Islamic conquests. Christian pastoralism is further supported by textual evidence, such as the *Life* of Simeon the Mountaineer in the sixth century and the *Life* of Philaretus the Merciful of the early ninth century, as well as archaeological evidence for stables. The landscape, as noted already, was conducive to limited agriculture. In the correspondence from Hārūn al-Rashīd to Constantine VI on the cessation of their truce, the Caliph notes, 'whereas today, they [the Byzantines on the frontier] are prevented from cultivating their lands [...] they have abandoned the wheat fields, the fertile lands, and the water canals for the arid mountains'. Geomorphological evidence from cores taken in Nar Gölü near the settlement of Nazianzos in the Melendiz Ovası (the Peristrema or Ihlara Valley and Marj al-Usquf or 'Bishop's Meadow') in Cappadocia, and also in the highlands of Rough Cilicia, confirm this picture. Pollen evidence shows a long-term retrenchment of agricultural activity between 670 and 950 and a secondary woodland and shrub growth more suited to extremely limited pastoral activities (suitable for goats and pigs).[54] This is just the sort of minimalist livestock raising that farmers required for a balanced, mixed regime, rather than true, extensive stock raising, which appears in the second half of the tenth century. Set within this longer-term change was the short-term withdrawal of farming populations, until 780–90 due to the disruption caused by larger-scale and long-distance raiding. As Hārūn's correspondence indicates, by the second half of the eighth century the frontier was reasonably stable, recovered, and the same types of farming activities as before continued, although being limited and mixed with pastoralism.

Byzantine pastoralist populations practiced a form of transhumance by moving either from the valleys to the plateaus in the summer or from the same village to fortified upland sites and back based on the seasonal raiding calendar (semi-nomadic); or by moving from site to site continuously and treating each as a temporary camp (nomadic).[55] In a transhumance symbiotic model, herders graze sheep, goat and horses within range of villages and estates where animals were returned to rock-cut mangers, pens and stables. The best pastures were on the mountain slopes, such as those on Mount Erciyes. These could easily become depleted, however, necessitating longer-range grazing. Farmers cultivated on a limited scale, enhanced by manuring gathered from thousands of dovecotes found all over Cappadocia, and perhaps limited seasonally-based irrigation. They hid their harvests in fortified granaries. In al-Andalus and the Maghrib, ethnographic evidence shows how granaries in caves were protected and their locations hidden so as to be used by transhumant pastoralists when they returned to the site.[56] In mountainous Isauria, a variation is presented on this model whereby local groups would inhabit lower-elevation settlements in the autumn and winter, the time of olive harvesting, and move to the uplands, grazing flocks or harvesting grapes in intra-montane valleys in the spring and summer during the raiding season.[57] These patterns are often described in the textual sources and secondary literature as a defensive and reactive response to Islamic seasonal transhumance, which often ignores the fact that such patterns had long existed and were a part of the usual seasonal and regional economy. Yet, such responses evoke an almost tribal cohesion in Byzantine movements, and one that is echoed in Wickham's articulation of the transformations of early medieval society.[58] Indeed, local Byzantines responded and adapted to the dry mountain/plateau environment and precarious political/military atmosphere by implementing a transhumant economic subsistence strategy and inhabiting defensive settlements – codependent activities that were linked together as a form of easily mobile 'defensive agriculture', which occurs before the eleventh century.[59]

Byzantines practiced forms of raiding through an *ad hoc* army of local peasants who used guerilla and surveillance tactics and acquired booty whether as prisoners, livestock or other supplies.[60] This would have been crucial for subsistence, particularly in the fortified refuges where there was no food. In organized military expeditions, one-fifth or one-sixth of the booty went to the governor or emperor and the rest to the troops, mirroring exactly the *khums* (fifths) system of booty redistribution in Islamic raiding of Byzantine lands.[61] Not every raid was an organized military expedition. We can deduce that there were numerous small campaigns, as is alluded to by, for example, Emperor John Tzimiskes' (r. 969–76) decree on the tax of Muslim prisoners not obtained through official expeditions.[62] The Byzantines not only attacked Islamic raiders but raided Islamic frontier towns on the plain. Alternatively, they could sell their goods, such as the highly-valued sheep wool or skin and goat-hair clothes prized in Cilicia, at markets in the winter. This is intimated in the *Taktika* of Nikephoros Ouranos (w. *c.*1000), who wrote from his own experience as a soldier on the Byzantine–Islamic frontier, although by this time the military situation of the Byzantines had already changed: they had become a powerful military power with professional soldiers; the 300-year 'ideology' of raiding had shifted to a more formalized offensive of invasion and reconquest, and a good portion of the Islamic *thughūr* had already been taken. Nevertheless, the text is useful as Ouranos advises on stopping the flow of commercial traffic, which he describes thusly:

> In like fashion, they [the 'Saracens'] send word to bring them both cheese and flocks in return for a high price for these goods. The Saracens who are hard pressed in their fortress say these things to our people dwelling along the frontiers, and our people of low station and high, in their love of grain, furnish them not only with great quantities of grain and flocks but also with all number and manner of foodstuff in their possession.[63]

Most notable is the valuable exchange of pastoralist products (dairy and animals) from the Byzantines for highly desired grain from the Islamic frontiers, which is implicitly 'business as usual' *even during periods of wartime* on the frontier. Several Islamic authors such as Pseudo-Jāhiẓ, Ibn al-Faqīh and Ibn al-'Adīm, writing in the late ninth to tenth centuries, corroborate the pastoralist activities of the Byzantines and the trade in livestock and animal products, including carpets and textiles.[64] Similarly, on the Andalusian frontiers, Christian groups that had fled to the uplands conducted small-scale raids on large fortified villages as the primary method employed in the *reconquista*.[65] These movements are typical forms of transhumance behaviour. Although the Byzantines may not have identified themselves as nomadic or semi-nomadic, circumstances and adaptation to environmental realities necessitated that many individuals (though not, perhaps, the wealthy elite families) assume a gradually pastoralist, though still mixed, subsistence regime that evolved from more farming and fewer livestock to more livestock and less farming.[66] This does not represent a Byzantine Dark Age, despite the rural and pastoral focus on society, but rather an adaptive transformation. Farmers, particularly in times of instability, could employ mixed subsistence strategies or give up being tethered to their fields and become full- or part-time pastoralists.[67] The example of the Byzantine socioeconomic agenda teaches us a valuable lesson about the Islamic frontier which, from a subsistence perspective, was less about military strategy and religious war and more about environmental and economic resilience.

CHAPTER 9

EPILOGUE: FORTIFIED CASTLES OF THE MIDDLE ISLAMIC/ MIDDLE BYZANTINE PERIOD (TENTH TO FOURTEENTH CENTURIES)

During the Middle Islamic/Middle Byzantine period, there was a secondary peak in settlement, seen in all surveys in which chronological separation within the Islamic periods is possible. This 'minor' peak, while not as high as the 'major' one for the Late Roman period, is noticeable, particularly relative to the preceding Early Islamic period and also in relation to other previous chronological periods. These minor peaks were noted in the Nahr Sajūr, Tabqa Reservoir, Kurban Höyük and eastern Cilicia/Plain of Issus Survey by Özgen and Gates. Tell Rifa'at had about the same number of Middle Islamic/Middle Byzantine as Late Roman period sites. Tell Leilan also exhibited a peak; however, until the Late Roman/Sāsānian-period material is published, it is difficult to determine its relative number. More finely-tuned ceramic dating permits us to see that in the Amuq, Balikh, Northern Jazīra and Quwayq only about half the number of Early Islamic period sites continued to be occupied into the Middle Islamic/Middle Byzantine period and the majority of Middle Islamic/Middle Byzantine settlements were first occupied only from the late eleventh to early fourteenth centuries – one century later. As such, settlement patterns in the Middle Islamic/Middle Byzantine period demonstrate three characteristics. First, settlement can be separated into two phases, the poorly settled mid-tenth to mid-eleventh centuries (or Middle Byzantine period) followed by the late eleventh to early fourteenth centuries (Middle Islamic/Frankish periods). The second phase exhibits an important phenomenon of 'nucleated dispersal'. Second, while settlements were numerous and dispersed around the plains, they became even more consolidated over time, forming large villages arranged around the base of a tell, echoing Bronze Age patterns of nucleation. Corollary to this process, the third characteristic shows an inclusion of tells and uplands as sites for fortified towns and castles.

A Century of Discontinuity: Renomadization in the Tenth to Eleventh Centuries

Settlement patterns throughout the entire frontier show a marked abandonment of sites between the mid-tenth and mid-eleventh centuries, which was also represented with variations on a sub-regional level. In the Amuq, although settlement continued at the largest villages and towns, by the tenth century, two-thirds of the small and dispersed upland sites in the Jabal al-'Aqra in the Amuq, and many of the sites on the Syrian Jibāl, were abandoned, indicating a general trend. Many sites, including 'Imm and Tell Sultan (AS 32) on the Yaghrā River, continued only until the tenth century. In the Kahramanmaraş Plain, the abandonment of most canal sites by the Middle Islamic period suggests a different system of settlement, one that avoided flat canal sites in the inundated, expanded, marshy plains. Dibsi Faraj on the Euphrates declined in the tenth/eleventh centuries, although numismatic evidence continues until the thirteenth. In the Nahr Quwayq, virtually every Early Islamic period site continued into the Middle Byzantine period with the exception of six, five of which ended in the tenth century. Of the 12 new Middle Islamic/Middle Byzantine period sites, nine were founded in the eleventh, twelfth, or thirteenth centuries and three were founded in the tenth century (of which, the Ḥalab citadel was one). Bartl identified only four Middle Islamic sites out of a total of 80. Bartl and Berthier, from separate evidence in the Balikh Valley and Middle Euphrates Surveys, linked the drop in settlement with the political and economic fragmentation of the northern regions and the shift toward nomadism in the first phase of the Middle Islamic/Middle Byzantine period, followed by a brief secondary resurgence during the Zangid/Ayyūbid/Mamlūk period until the Mongol era.[1] Heidemann might bring this date even earlier, based on numismatic evidence, to the last third of the ninth century. He ties this in with the 'Abbāsid–Ṭūlūnid wars in the 880s, the Shi'ī Qarāmiṭa rebellions from 899 onwards, and the Ḥamdānī takeover of Raqqa in 942.[2] Rather than decline, this region seems to reflect a fragmentized and politically unstable rule by shifting from farmsteads to fortresses, from villa to village. Economic links with Baghdād and the towns of southern 'Iraq gradually weakened, affecting the economy of both the 'Abbāsid central state and the frontier and Jazīra. An increase in nomadism with the influx of Turkic and Arabian tribes may also have been influential on the disparity between agricultural settlements in the Early Islamic period and fortress settlements in the Middle Islamic, leading to a rise in extramural camps that would be difficult to detect in the archaeological record. From the Zangid/Ayyūbid periods until the end of the Mongol invasion, encompassing the Mamlūk period, the region experienced a brief, secondary prosperity.

The intervening century immediately following the Byzantine reconquests can be seen as simply another phase of decline, pushing the notion of decline from one transition of Islamic history (seventh century) to another. Part of the story of this 'lost century' may, in fact, stem from an ambiguity in the transitional nature of pottery, as the tenth century represents both a break (as in the dwindling use of unglazed brittlewares for cooking, in favour of glazed brittlewares or coarser and grittier cooking pots) and a development (as in the appearance of sgraffiato on splash-ware glazed vessels and the proliferation of turquoise glazes) in ceramic styles. Higher visibility of twelfth- to fourteenth-century glazed forms on surveys may also contribute to relative differences in this period and the subsequent one. Clear chronologies and ranges for tenth-century ceramics are poorly known. In the absence of archaeological evidence, historical processes can fill in the picture of frontier settlement. A different picture for tenth century continuity is also suggested textually by the observations of the Christian doctor Ibn Buṭlān, travelling through the Amuq Plain in 1051, who remarked on its prosperity, despite the ceramic evidence:

> and we found all the country between Halab and Antakiya populous, nowhere ruined abodes of any description. On the contrary, the soil was everywhere sown with wheat and barley, which grew under the olive trees; the villages ran continuous, their gardens full of flowers, and the waters flowing on every hand, so that the traveler makes his journey here in contentment of mind, and peace and quietness.[3]

However, the century or so of discontinuity is well attested, independently, in many historical accounts as a period of general decentralization in most of, but not the entire, frontier region. The Byzantine reconquest of the frontier after the first sieges in 956 was partly successful, as it took advantage of the growing internal crisis within the ʿAbbāsid caliphate that had already emerged by the early ninth century. This crisis was due to the rising influence of Kurdish and Daylamī (i.e. Būyid) groups and Arab Bedouin tribes, as well as a Turkish military class that was responsible for the elevation and reign of weak and easily manipulated rulers (such as Caliph Muṭīʿ [r. 946–74]). For the northern regions, the role of Arab tribes in relation to these other groups specifically set the stage for an increasingly unstable political landscape. These interactions were coupled with economic instability (tax crises, growing debt and bankruptcy) and the environmental degradation (fragility of unmaintained canal systems and salinization) of the southern ʿIraqī lowlands. This is reflected in surveys of southern ʿIraq, in which R. McC. Adams noted a period of economic and demographic decline.[4] The sedentarization of former troops; lack of land grants to new soldiers (Khurāsānīs and

Turks), who were paid in cash; and diminishing ties to the frontier with the movement of the capital to Samārrā', which was not linked to the Euphrates, were further factors that would have prevented investment in the frontier regions and, consequently, ensured less return. The agricultural boom of the Jazīra was short-lived, yet the region remained a viable source of grain despite being cut off from southern 'Iraq and held by local powers such as the Ḥamdānids.[5] Between 890 and 985, the Qarāmiṭa, Isma'īlī Shi'i followers, revolted against the 'Abbāsids in the Jazīra, 'Iraq and Arabia, stimulating, in part, movement of other Bedouin Arab tribes out of Arabia. The 'Abbāsid–Ṭūlūnid wars in the 880s also played a role.[6] The waning influence of the central government and large urban polities created a period of instability, both politically and economically.

In the mid-tenth century, Mas'ūdī observed that the villages of the Orontes Valley had become heavily depopulated due to 'official negligence', and were peopled by Bedouin.[7] Between the Byzantine reconquests and the Saljūq invasions (tenth to eleventh centuries), the largest Bedouin migration out of Arabia since the Islamic conquests changed the balance of tribes that had largely become sedentary on the *thughūr*. Some tribes were nomads (*ahl wabar lā madar*) and sedentarized (*ahl madar lā wabar*), and some were a mixture of both. As such, Syria and the Jazīra became renomadized as these tribes claimed pasture lands around major towns, which became their *de facto* permanent bases. By the tenth century, several important independent frontier dynasties, led by strong local rulers or 'warlords', formed from these tribes at the twilight of 'Abbāsid centralized power in the Jazīra (the western and central *thughūr* being in Byzantine hands). In this sense, they were not unlike the elite and increasingly militarized powerful Byzantine families of Cappadocia, their contemporaries across the frontier. Scholars, from Ibn Khaldūn to the present day, frequently observed cycles in history in which periods of political instability have traditionally favoured pastoralist power.[8] The most powerful of these Bedouin tribes were the aforementioned Ḥamdānids of the Banū Taghlib, who transformed into sedentary dynastic rulers around Ḥalab and Mawṣil. In the wake of the Ḥamdānids, came the former Qays tribes of the 'Uqayl, Kilāb

(Mirdāsids), and Numayrids and lesser tribes like the Qushayr and 'Aylān. The Mirdāsids took power around the lands between Ḥalab and Raḥba on the Euphrates in 1024, while the 'Uqayl were based around Mawṣil and Naṣībīn but eventually took Ḥalab in 1079. The Numayr were located along the east bank of the Euphrates south of Raqqa, and in the Balikh Valley towards Ḥarrān and Ruhā. Philaretos Brachamios, a former Byzantine general, was a rebel and warlord who held power around Mar'ash and Malaṭiya between 1071 and 1078. Political alliance was a crucial factor for the survival of local power. Several of these tribal dynasties paid allegiance either to the 'Abbāsids, the Fāṭimids, or the Byzantines. At the same time, they were difficult to control – as in shown by the case of the Numayrids. These were initially 'Abbāsid Jazīran troops that supported the Ḥamdānids and were given more power. They declared themselves independent, taking Raqqa and Ruhā and fighting the Byzantines. The role of the Bedouin tribes was made more complicated by the presence of the Daylamī Būyids, who were in effect controlling 'Abbāsid lands, vying with the Turkish military over control of Baghdād, and trying to take the Jazīra and parts of the *thughūr* for its agricultural and tax potential. The Būyid Mu'izz al-Dawla, after taking Baghdād in 945, attempted several times unsuccessfully to unseat Ḥamdānid power in the Jazīra. His son, Bakhtiyār ('Izz al-Dawla) tried again, this time forging an uneasy alliance with the head of the Turkish military faction, the general Sabuktakīn. They timed the expedition to coincide with the Byzantine reconquest against the Ḥamdānids, but failed again. 'Aḍud al-Dawla succeeded in taking Ḥamdānid mountain fortresses and dispersing their occupants between 977 and 980, but the Būyids' power waned and the northern regions were ceded to the 'Uqaylī and other tribes as *iqṭā'*.[9] The Kurdish Humaydī tribe, led by Bādh in their summer pastures in the Anti-Taurus Mountains, clashed with the 'Aḍud al-Dawla when trying to migrate towards their winter pastures in the Jazīra. Bādh similarly clashed with the Ḥamdānids, and the 'Uqaylī and Numayrī who supported them, over access to pasturelands.[10] The predominance of nomadic pastoralists on the frontier would have shifted the balance of agrarian lands towards pasture. The success of many of these dynasties arose not because they directly supported the urban populations and merchants, but because they facilitated an open commercial economy and controlled trade routes that were safe from other nomadic incursions, drawing to various degrees from the revenue of towns.[11] Pasture, and power over it, were prime motivational factors. Tribes formed alliances and participated in conflicts. The rise in power of certain tribal groups meant the decline of other tribes and their influence.

The transformation of the settled landscape of villages into a more transient landscape of camps has been difficult to detect from surveys in the heavily aggraded plains of the frontier, unlike those of the better-preserved upland sites. It is precisely this accrued level of aggradation from abandoned irrigation systems that may have contributed to this settlement transformation, as demonstrated by evidence of increased marshification.[12] Such ripples in the settled landscape adversely affected agricultural communities, spurring previously sedentarized tribes to return to nomadic lifestyles, and populations to shift and be shifted into new territories.

Parts of the frontier that were reconquered by the Byzantines fared differently, including the western *thughūr* and urban centers. Excavations at Ḥiṣn al-Tīnāt show continuity from the eighth to early twelfth centuries, with substantial refortification of the main enclosure some time in the tenth century, through reinforcement of its outer walls and the addition of towers. Anṭākiya grew in importance under Middle Byzantine rule. Kilns producing splash-glazed sgraffiato ware and turquoise-glazed creamware are noted from the Princeton excavations and would have been produced for the local region – as is evident from close parallels at Ḥiṣn al-Tīnāt and al-Minā', and inland sites towards Ḥalab in the Nahr Quwayq.[13] Textual accounts are also rich at this time, for both Anṭākiya and its surroundings.[14] A large number of coins from this period, specifically from the Çatal Höyük excavations in the Amuq, raise a further incongruity that may be explained by a high level of monetization even in rural areas or the presence of a military garrison at the site.[15]

Conglomerate Villages and Tell Occupation in the Late Eleventh to Early Fourteenth Centuries

In the second Middle Islamic phase, many large settlements were occupied and very few new ones were founded. This is seen in the large number of Early Islamic period sites that continued to be occupied, or were reoccupied a century later, and of pre-Early Islamic period sites reoccupied in the Middle Islamic period. These comprised scattered farms that had merged into sizable conglomerate villages and small towns, continuing the process of Late Roman and Early Islamic consolidation of villages and the equalization of cities and towns. The Kurban Höyük surveyors noted that Middle Islamic sites were clustered together, forming larger sites. Interestingly, Muqaddasī writes of the Amuq that, 'in this region villages (*qurā*) are more splendid and larger than most of the cities (*mudun*)'.[16] The town of Artāḥ (Greek Artesia) in the Amuq is a good example of a conglomerate village. The town is only known as a Middle Islamic/ Middle Byzantine period settlement, rather than an Early Islamic period one. Islamic authors, such as Ibn Shaddād, describe a small town (*madīnatūn saghiratūn*) that possessed gardens (*basāṭīn*), springs, (*'uyūn*), mills (*ārḥā'*) and villages (*qurā*). The four villages attached to the town are named, and include nearby Tell al-Judaidah. These various, rather insubstantial, sites likely depended on (and even comprised) Artāḥ – an example of nucleated dispersal, which was a Middle Islamic period phenomenon.[17] In the Amuq, Tell Maltah (AS 28) near the Yaghrā River is an example of this pattern. The site had Late Hellenistic and Middle Islamic but no Roman through Early Islamic period occupation. It could have been abandoned for nearby Tell Sultan (AS 32), perhaps due to a shift in the river. The days of canal building and intensive irrigation had passed; many of these waterways had dried up, collapsed or become marsh. As seen at Gritille and at Kurban Höyük, settlement was around springs and agriculture, and was probably practiced in extremely localized fields around sites with a heavy emphasis on nomadic pastoralism. However, both Gritille and Titris noted a return to settlement on river courses, such as the Euphrates, which featured sites from this period approximately every

3 km. Despite these settlement shifts, local industries of ceramic and glass did not disappear.

The example of the Andalusian *thughūr* offers a richer understanding of social organization and resource management. That landscape evolved from settlements around communal springs or canals that were tribe- or clan-based into periurban agglomerated villages (*huertas*) of the twelfth century. In these mixed-clan settlements, water-supply administration and access was privatized rather than communal. Expansion led to more social interaction and complexity between villages and varying tribal groups, which eventually led to a form of privatization.[18]

The tell, as a village's defensible high point, offered walled refuge for villagers and their livestock. The investigation of the post Early Islamic settlement is hampered by the fact that many villages today are built over the Middle and Late Islamic period sites, yet the fact that these modern-day continuities exist is evidence in and of itself. The tell sites were often small, similar to the few Late Roman and scanty Early Islamic period occupations of tells. Examples of this are numerous over the entire frontier, at such important sites as Çatal Höyük, Kinet Höyük, Coba Höyük in the Sakcegözü/Kahramanmaraş Plain and Tell Jerablus Tahtani (Site 22), as well as Mezraa Höyük, Akarçay Höyük, Şaraga Höyük and Gre Virike – all excavated, but initially recorded from the Birecik-Carchemish Survey.[19] Tells were occupied all over the Nahr Quwayq Plain, many continuing today with villages surrounding them in what would have been lower towns. These date mainly from the twelfth to the fourteenth centuries, which show a growth in sites in the Ayyūbid and Mamlūk periods around Ḥalab. At Tell Tuneinir in the Khābūr, a twelfth- to thirteenth-century site (Zangid and Ayyūbid) of 46 ha, the tell became a residential quarter while the large lower town was devoted mainly to commercial activities, as evidenced by the presence of two *khānāt*; a market with workshops for iron, glass, ceramic and textile working; and a bath. A mosque attached to the *khān* and a church suggest either Muslim and Christian communities living there, or a Christian community catering for Muslim caravans. During the political upheavals of the thirteenth century, the *khānāt* and market were burnt and destroyed violently, with evidence of weapons in the destruction levels. At Zeytinlibahçe Höyük on the Upper Euphrates, a Middle Islamic fortified building was discovered occupying much of the tell, with a 1.5 m-thick wall built along the tell's contour line interspersed with buttresses and watchtowers.[20] In a second phase of this fortified building, subdivided rooms and animal skeletons suggest that the fortified settlement also contained space for livestock. This is strongly reminiscent of *incastellamento* practices seen at earlier Byzantine upland sites, which incorporated open courtyards for villagers to bring their livestock to in times of trouble.

Fortified Upland Towns and Castles

In this unstable landscape, Bedouin tribes and other groups often used defensible fortifications or mountain strongholds as refuges. This is supported by extensive survey evidence, which shows that newly-founded sites on the frontier tended to be fortified upland castles first constructed in the Middle Byzantine period and throughout the Middle Byzantine/Cilician Armenian, Crusader, Saljūq, Ayyūbid and Mamlūk periods. Among the earliest would have been the castles of Baghrās, Anṭākya and ʿAyn Zarba, built in the tenth century by the Byzantines, and Qalʿat Ja'bar and Qalʿat Najm on the Euphrates River in the eleventh century by Bedouin Arab tribes such as the Banu Numayr. In the Adıyaman Survey, Kale Boğaz, 15 km south-west of Gölbaşı on the main road to Pazarcık, was a thirteenth- to fourteenth-century double-walled castle.[21] Monasteries like that of Qalʿat Simʿān, dedicated to St Simeon the Elder, and the Monastery of St Simeon the Younger overlooking the Orontes Delta were refurbished with outer fortified enclosure walls in the tenth century and later. Evidence from archaeological survey and textual sources in the Amuq suggests that these settlements were more than just isolated castles. In Baghrās, the construction of the castle was not at the expense of the lower town but rather part of an overall complex with mill irrigation that added a level of defence and refuge for the lower-town dwellers. Darbassāk in the northern Amuq plain on the eastern slopes of the Amanus had a similar complex of lower town and castle; however, unlike Baghrās, Darbassāk may not have been an Early Islamic settlement. As in fourteenth-century descriptions for these two settlements, the hilltop fortress of al-Rāwandān, across the Amuq in the 'Afrīn Valley in modern Syria, also had gardens, fruit trees and springs.[22] These mountain fortifications, some with lower towns, were of a single type, self-sufficient to a point, and part of a process of *incastellamento*. Their prominence within the literature of the Islamic geographers as *ḥuṣūn* is interesting. Many of these authors lived at the end of the 'Abbāsid period, when the frontier changed hands frequently and defensible castles were built. By the Middle Islamic period, many settlements, such as Baghrās, Darbassāk and even 'Imm, were named *ḥuṣūn* due to their strategic location as transportation nodes along military or trade routes. The term is not specific; rather, it refers to a fortified settlement in the most general sense.

Excavations at Çadır Höyük in northern Anatolia, a fortified tell occupied in the ninth and tenth centuries, revealed that the fortification wall surrounding the summit had been intended to protect a storage area and stable of livestock for the population that lived on a lower terrace.[23] Again, the Andalusian and Italian research offers useful models for comparison with and interpretation of the post-*thughūr* landscape. In the fourth stage of villa-to-village transformation for Italy and the west, hilltop villages (*castelli*) were fortified and rural markets and local governments emerged by the tenth century. *Incastellamento* began to occur by the end of the Early Islamic period, *c.*1000. The first phase was the transition from dispersed tribally-based *alquería* hydraulic sites to more nucleated groupings of village settlements around a fortification (the *ḥiṣn/qarya* model) at the end of the tenth century. Those castle names that were Arabized (e.g. Alcalá, from *qal'a*) were located in lowlands or at the margins of upland and lowland areas. Some of these forts reoccupied Classical sites. The earliest *ḥuṣūn* consisted of three elements: (1) a central residence; (2) a *sāluqiya*, or celoquia, where the *qā'id* (ruler) resided; and (3) a cistern and walled-in enclosure. This enclosure (*baqār* or albacar, 'the cattle') was most likely for the sheltering of livestock along with the rural population of the area. That the *ḥuṣūn* were used for refuge rather than for serving a military function is evident from two elements. First, the greatest density of these fortifications was in the southern large plains and river valleys of Castelló, Mijares and Palancia, where most of the population lived, rather than the northernmost frontier (*al-thughūr al-'alā'*) on the Christian border. This could indicate a general sense of instability and threat that was felt throughout al-Andalus. Second, the arrangement of fortifications on the *thughur al-'alā'* was not necessarily suggestive of a border line; rather, the *ḥuṣūn* protected the main cities, forming a defensive perimeter around them. This is seen in the city of Huesca, which had 12 *ḥuṣūn* around it. Textual information corroborates the use of upland fortifications for refuge, as in the Mudéjar Revolt of 1276–7 when Muslims 'emptied out their villages in the plains and went up with the beasts and clothing to the feet of the castle walls'.[24]

The *ḥuṣūn* were also responsible for protecting local resources. Besides looking after water sources, there were *ḥuṣūn* consisting of fortified granaries. One such, in the Valle de Ricota (middle Segura Valley, Murcia) called Cabezo de la Cobertera, was located on a steep mound 100 m above the river and is dated to the late twelfth to early thirteenth century. Individual cells contained both family quarters and storage areas, either for grain or animals. Although this granary was not explicitly a *ḥiṣn*, several *ḥuṣūn* also possessed collective storage spaces often associated with the *albacar*, such as those at Uxó, Monte Marinet, Silla, Montroy and la Magdalena. As pointed out by J. de Meulemeester, this is not unlike the role of churches during the same period, which also possessed storage spaces for a community's wealth, sometimes in separate cells.[25] A brief mention of Ismā'īl the ruler of Sebastea in Cappadocia, provides a counterexample. During a famine in the winter of 1173–4, he hoarded the wheat for himself and was subsequently killed, along with his entire household, by the villagers.[26] In this unstable landscape, trade continued: we can suppose that way stations continued to exist, and perhaps their guarantee of safety for travellers and goods was even more necessary. Ibn Jubayr (1145–1216) wrote:

> one of the astonishing things that is talked of, is that though the fires of discord burn between the two parties, Muslim and Christian, two armies of them may meet and dispose themselves in battle array, and yet Muslim and Christian travellers (*rifāq*) will come and go between them without interference.[27]

The system of *ḥuṣūn* from the tenth to the thirteenth centuries presented an inversion of the feudal model. These settlements are not following a clearly military borderline arrangement, nor do they function feudally as centers of urban power, tax collection or control over a rural population. Rather, these settlements were non-linear and defensive, comprised complexes, sheltered local populations, were used for grain storage, and functioned as holding areas for livestock.[28] The multiple functionality and high importance of refuge/defence for such fortifications puts these settlements in an entirely different class than castles in the Western European (and Christian Medieval) model.

A general yet clear picture emerges when the archaeological record is synthesized with the historical evidence of a transformation from far-ranging migration to restrained transhumance and increased economic entrepreneurship. Tribal identities also became more heterogeneous, including those for members of other tribes, non-Muslims and settled peoples from other parts of the Islamic world (Khurāsānī, Zuṭṭ, etc.). These multicultural groups formed their own frontier societies with their own economic interests – involving cultivation, pastoralism and trade. Middle Islamic/Middle Byzantine period settlement and population levels reached a secondary peak, wherein mixed communities agglomerated into towns with upland fortifications, a process of *incastellamento* that underscored basic upland and lowland interactions on the frontier.

CHAPTER 10

FRONTIER OR FRONTIERS? INTERACTION AND EXCHANGE IN FRONTIER SOCIETIES

Although each group likes to think of itself apart and contrasts its way of life with that of the other group, all are organized in a single economic system geared to the utilization of all the resources, agricultural and pastoral, of the total environment.[1]

In the seventh century, a popular apocalyptic story from the frontier town of Ḥimṣ in North Syria described the events that would lead up to the final conquest of Constantinople by the Arabs. This battle, coincidentally, takes place in the Amuq Plain. Strangely, a truce is drawn between the Byzantines and Arabs, and an alliance of the two is forged against the defecting North Arabian Muslims of Kūfā: 'The fighting of al-A'maq has been put among the tribulations (*fitan*) because a third of the Arabs, whole tribes with their banners, will join the infidels (*al-kufr*), and a group of the Hamra' will break away and join them also.'[2] Although the prophecy depicts a rivalry with the northern Arabs, the main hostility is directed at the Quḍā'a: the non-urban nomadic South Arabians of the Kalb Confederacy, who established themselves in northern Syria and the *thughūr* before the Islamic conquests: 'surely, the people will not stop until they will take (flocks of) sheep and milk them, competing with each other for them, until, when they have become numerous, they will leave the towns, communities, and mosques and lead a Bedouin life with them'.[3] The Quḍā'a's status as a free-ranging nomadic group who were already inhabitants of the frontier was the cause of much anxiety, and the South Arabians viewed them as defectors from Islam, moving to Byzantine land with their *mawālī*. This anxiety masks two conflicts. The first is a general tribal rivalry over land and resources; the second is between a peripheral group and a central authority. Both are two sides of the same coin and present ambiguity towards clear-cut ideas of *jihād* and a militarized Islamic–Byzantine frontier.

On the frontier, settlements were dictated by gradual responses and adaptations to changing landscapes, and by interactions between local peripheral groups with the central authority. Like the apocalyptic prophecies, these constitute three layers of frontier interactions: (1) ideological – military and religious conflict; (2) external – the competition over resources; and (3) internal – the political relationships between local peripheral groups and the central authority. In the first type of interaction, the space is a single physical boundary; in the last two types of interaction, the frontier becomes a set of peripheral environmental boundaries or localized zones composed of interactions between upland and lowland groups. These last two types are crucial in showing how the interactions between humans and their environment are part of complex adaptive systems that respond and contribute to larger historical cycles and, ultimately, to a deeper understanding of history. This chapter will examine these external and internal interactions in the light of ideological conflict on both frontier and frontiers.

External Interactions: Holy War or Competition for Resources?

From the archaeological evidence, certain ethno-religious characteristics were inferred from the various types of site that raise more questions than answers. Were these characteristics tied into shifting trajectories of lowland and upland settlements? For example, is it possible to say that the Byzantine frontier consisted of mountainous uplands while the Islamic frontier comprised lowland plains and marshes – and, by extension, that all upland settlements were occupied by Byzantine (and Christian) settlers and lowland settlements by Islamic nomads? Yaghrā and 'Imm in the Amuq Plain and Domuztepe in the Kahramanmaraş Plain have already been discussed as examples of preexisting Christian communities living on the plain. How would Christian settlements in Islamic lands be treated? Were these communities exempt or part of a protracted political/religious holy war between Christian and Muslim – or were they participants in an environmental/economic symbiotic relationship of land and water rights between the settled and the nomadic? This penultimate chapter cannot hope to answer all of these questions. Rather, it will present a range of frontier interpretations and construct a basic theoretical framework for understanding them.

C. Robinson outlines several models of interaction, all between nomads and settlers. In a mutualism model, there is symbiosis between both groups. In a conflict model, nomads are perceived as dangerous and uncontrolled entities who raid, taking prisoners and booty. A conflict model would also support a 'large scale investment in fortifications'.[4] Superficially, these models reflect the historical and archaeological perceptions that come from viewing the frontier in terms of layers in an environmental/economic symbiosis (archaeological mutualism) or a political/religious aggression (historical conflict). While potentially useful as theoretical frameworks, these two views are not mutually exclusive but represent different orders of layered views of the frontier. Further, these models are not completely adequate and leave out the role of environmental change and human adaptation to the landscape. Robinson states that a mutualism model would assume a political and environmental stability. This is not necessarily the case, as has been demonstrated from the archaeological data. The same is true for historical interactions across the frontier when placed in their environmental contexts. It is possible to show the gradual transformations and relationships between humans and their environment in both historical and archaeological layers on the frontier.

It would be the crudest simplification to see the frontier as inhabited by Muslim communities on one side and Christian ones on the other. Crucial to understanding the frontier as a complex landscape is the notion of tribal interaction. At the periphery of empire, the *thughūr* and its well-watered plains were home to many tribes, some preexisting and some settled since the Islamic conquests, some settled and some nomadic, and most somewhere in between. The interaction of these tribes with each other, with other settled communities, and with the central state illustrates many vectors taking place over time, rather than a unilinear interaction from one side of the frontier to the other. So, too, do the complexities of settlement. It should be emphasized that tribe and clan size, affiliation and grazing areas varied throughout the Early Islamic period of the seventh to tenth centuries. This was partially the case because while some tribes were nomadic, others (often the Christian ones) were sedentary – and some were both. However, the majority practiced a seasonal, annual transhumance, moving upland in summer for better pasture and returning to the lowland plains for winter pasture, which was not as far ranging as that practiced by the purely nomadic, migratory tribes of Central Asia, and perhaps one that employed a mixed strategy of sedentarism and pastoralism. This practice is also referred to as enclosed nomadism – that is, the nomads' range of mobility included a settled area of seasonal agriculture and adjacent uplands for pasture.[5] Semi-nomads had lowland camps and practiced limited agriculture, and semi-sedentarized nomads lived in permanent villages but became mobile part of the year. As most tribes practiced transhumance to a degree, I use the generic (though imperfect) terms 'pastoralist' or 'transhumant' to refer to both nomadic and semi-nomadic, or semi-sedentarized, groups.

The 'Abbāsid administrator and writer Qudāma b. Ja'far (d. 948) described the timing of the annual expeditions according to the most commonly-held views of those frontier folk participating:

> We shall now describe one of the raids (*al-ghazuwāt*) in order to get a surer understanding of this. We say that the most

> challenging raid for the skilled frontier-raiders is the so-called 'springtime' raid, which begins around 10 May (Ayyār), after the people have pastured their animals and when their horses are in good condition, and which lasts 30 days, through the remainder of May and ten days into June (Ḥazīrān). In the land of the Romans (*Bilād al-Rūm*), they find pastures for their livestock like a second spring. Then they return home and settle for 25 days, being the remainder of June and five days into July (Tammūz), until [their beasts are] rested and fattened. Then the people join in the summer raid, starting from 10 July and lasting 60 days. As for winter raids, everyone I know says that if these are necessary, they should not penetrate too far [into enemy territory], but only to the extent of about 20 days round-trip, just long enough that the raider can load sufficient provisions on horseback. They should be done by the end of February (Sabāṭ), and they should head out in the early days of March (Ādhār), for at that time they will find the enemy – themselves and their animals – weaker, and their livestock (*mawāshīhim*) greater. Then they return and vie with one another to put their animals to green pasture.[6]

The degree to which certain tribes were more settled or more pastoral than others differed among clans. Additionally, most pastoral tribes were probably associated with sedentary communities at the very least through economic ties and probably through a gradual process of nomadization to increased sedentarization that occurred over many generations. The gradual but continuous process of sedentarization led to most settlements being inhabited by tribesmen, many of whom had been nomadic, illustrating a more complicated interrelationship between settled and nomadic groups. Seasonal nomads belonging to permanent communities would be able to help year-round farmers in the intensive cultivating and harvesting of grains, grown during the winter months. A small but important point must be kept in mind, however. Not all Muslims were pastoralists, nor Christians sedentarists. Many of the Syriac-speaking Christians of the Jazīra and northern Syria – notably the holy men whose lives we know of, like John the Arab, Alexander the Sleepless, and even Symeon Stylites and other ascetics who called themselves *ṭūraiē* (men of the mountains) and *ra'iē* (shepherds) – also practiced a type of pastoralism in the days before the conquest, and it cannot be stated that when or if they settled down, they gave up the shephard's crook for the plow.[7] Indeed, the association of holy man and shepherd is a natural one, becoming a powerful metaphor and spiritual example: they were all 'shepherds' of God's flock. Prior to Islam, and perhaps even after, these holy men linked pastoralists to sedentarists, Arab tribes to settled communities, and often helped to settle disputes between them over land and water. The annual movements of crossing the Islamic–Byzantine frontier for summer raiding in uplands and winter retrenchment in lowlands describes in perfect terms, without political or religious ideologies, pastoralist transhumance movement. Competition for resources (i.e. grazing lands, water rights, the acquisition of livestock during raids, and even access to Taurus Mountain mines or tree stands) comprised certain interactions between Islam and Byzantium, pastoralists and settlers, or pastoralists and other pastoralists.[8]

Pastoralist presence and competition does not preclude the existence of a military agenda. The difference is a matter of perception, particularly with regard to frontier interaction. Pastoralists were not just herders moving their animals passively across the general background of the Middle East. Text-based historians often work in a rarified world of exceptional events and narratives. On the ground, the inhabitants of the frontier first and foremost had to survive, raise food, and feed, clothe and house family groups. Becoming part of the army was but one facet of frontiersmens' lives, but it did not define their existence or preclude other modes of subsistence or making a living. The inhabitants of the frontier could be '*auxilia* in imperial armies, *foederati*, phylarchs, traders, smugglers, messengers, agriculturalists, spies, scouts, boatsmen, guides, and pilgrims'.[9] It is known that the armies that crossed the frontier annually included nomadic and semi-nomadic groups. Even in the diverse tenth-century Islamic armies of the Ḥamdanids there were Daylamī, Turks, Kurds and Arabs (Bedouin).

Many of these groups were brought into the military to prevent potential rebellions. Kurdish and Arab soldiers, in particular, were known to have a propensity for plundering goods and animals while campaigning, from any and either side, as noted by Ibn Qalanisī (1070–1160).[10] Thus, the words of Caliph ʻUmar, resonate strongly: ʻI prefer to die between the two upright pieces of my wooden saddle as I travel through the land seeking God's bounty (*faḍl*), rather than be killed as a fighter in the *jihad* for the sake of God.'[11] As a personal anecdote and individual opinion, it bears little on the frontier tribesmen. Yet, ʻUmar was expressing a deep desire – as a pastoralist, or nomad, or soldier – to participate in his duty because it allowed him to see the world and earn some profit at the same time. ʻUmar is speaking for every man on the frontier.

The political and ethnic tribal conflicts that underpin historical accounts and apocalyptic literature reveal certain economic advantages of *jihād* policy. Conversion, a requirement of *jihād*, is seldom mentioned – if at all – in relation to the frontier conflict and raiding. Rather, what is mentioned is the amassing of tax or booty. Collection of the *jizya* tax and acquisition of booty were further requirements that could often prevent *jihād* violence. Ghevond's account of eighth-century ʻAbbāsid Armenia states that violence was used as a punishment if no tax was collected.[12] Groups who were encouraged by the central state to settle on the frontier (often through a rhetoric of *jihād*) were granted certain tax incentives.[13] Al-Mawardī (d. 1058) said that *jizya* should be paid immediately and treated like booty. The term booty must be clarified somewhat, as it has acquired a modern meaning of treasure or gold. Booty taken on tribal raids consisted of mobile products and resources such as livestock (sheep, goats, camels, and horses), silk and other textiles, grain and other produce, objects such as vases and furniture, and prisoners. The collection of enemy prisoners was important economically, as they were periodically traded for one's own men or goods. Prisoners were sometimes incorporated into their captor's tribal groups. These accounts imply that tribal raids or Islamic conquests and the collection of booty or tax, whether formal activities or not, were difficult to separate; and also that the practice of *jihād* against unbelievers had little to do with the religious spread of Islam and conversion, but was an economic war, depending on the acquisition of resources and payments as tribute to ensure security. Thus, although the Islamic invasions were recorded as a religious enterprise, the impulse and temptation to acquire economic resources was great. On the northern frontiers with Byzantium and Armenia, the ambiguity of state-sanctioned tax collection and conquests or independent raiding for booty was even greater. The elements of collecting booty to increase a resource base or for subsequent trade, and the method of raiding, typically characterize nomadic pastoralist subsistence strategies for sustaining an otherwise difficult way of life.

Muslim Classical authors write that the division of the *thughūr* into *thughūr al-shāmīya* and *thughūr al-jazarīya* was established in order to distinguish the regional, tribal makeup of the armies that crossed the frontier from either side. For example, Balādhurī wrote, 'Al-Manṣūr settled in Malaṭyah 4,000 fighters from Mesopotamia [*āhl al-Jazīra*], Malaṭyah being one of the Mesopotamian frontier towns [*thughūrihim*]'.[14] Ties between the state and the frontier frequently involved setting up local tribal leaders as governing administrators. Historians document many instances of local chiefs being appointed on the frontier. Moreover, accounts from the major cities of the frontier that had strong settled communities scarcely mention the role of administrators, implying perhaps that these chiefs were less firmly based or involved in urban life than we might expect.

The nomad/pastoralist as an auxiliary, soldier, spy, etc. certainly existed, but this fact also undermines a level of agency. The line is quite tenuous between nomad as soldier in an imperial army or transhumant tribe as the army unit, and the tribal leader as controlling the army. On the frontier, these lines were crossed all the time and the increasing introduction of non-Arab soldiers, such as Khurāsānīs and Turks, shows attempts by the central state to quash tribal autonomy; implying that such concerns were valid. Transhumant or nomadic tribes could have exacted a certain amount of self-directed motivation on the frontier by virtue of their power in local administration, the location of their homes on the margins of central lands, and their need for self-preservation. Steps could have been taken to ensure the safety of migration routes by occupying way stations or even building new ones and, at the same time, controlling trade routes. The controlling of trade routes, keeping them safe from bandits (i.e. other tribes), constituted a transhumant tribe's attempts to secure more regional power amidst a milieu of tribal diffusion. In this way, it was always possible that they, at times, brought a mob rule of sorts to the settled populations. Similar arguments of tribal autonomy have been used to explain the rise of the later Turkic nomadic groups in the same region. Most notable is a study of the Aqquyunlu tribal chiefs, who secured strategically-located strongholds on key migration routes along the Taurus farther east – thereby also controlling the eastern Anatolian trade, and collecting protection and toll money from merchants and traders, which functioned as an important source of revenue.[15]

Three examples of institutions and processes existed that demonstrated variations in frontier interaction and exchange the *ḥimā* system, the presence of markets and fair circuits, and tribal identity.

The Ḥimā *System*

While many tribal pasturelands were shared due to overlapping migrating routes, some systems protected pastures and routes via restricted access. The *ḥimā* (plural *aḥmā'*) was a protected tribal pasture that had a military aspect and had been known since pre-Islamic Arabia.[16] It was a secular parcel of land that was owned by and under the protection of a specific tribe, and provided access to grazing and water rights. Enforcement of this access or restriction was carried out by the clan or clans that temporarily settled there, and is an example of tribal solidarity. Restricted seasonal access allowed the vegetation to return the following year. Certain *aḥmā'* allowed only cattle and equids, barring sheep and goats which typically overgraze a piece of land. They were designed specifically for stock breeding. Some *aḥmā'* also had a permenant water supply. As such, the system had a component of sustainability and prevented lands from becoming desertified, overgrazed or deforested. In the Early

Islamic period, the *ḥimā* took on the function of a protected pasture for the mounts of the military, as well as the herds of the tribes. At the settlement of al-Rabaḍa the *ḥimā* was developed by 'Umar in 637 as a vast breeding ground for camels and horses, which numbered 40,000.[17] The *ḥimā* is also mentioned in relation to land around the frontier *ribāṭ* of North Africa as a protected pasture (called *qidāl*) and refuge from raids, not unlike the Byzantine fortified refuges with protected lands around them.[18] Evidence of the *ḥimā* in archaeological contexts is elusive. Clues might come from water installations such as reservoirs, wells and cisterns. One distinct possibility for a *ḥimā* is the large protected open spaces (*ḥayr*) of the *quṣūr* of Syro-Palestine, often thought to be hunting grounds. Throughout the frontier, the lowland marshes are frequently called *murūj* (singular, *marj*), meaning meadow pasturelands, and they appear often in conjunction with the operation of mustering troops for annual expeditions. Straughn hypothesizes that the settlement of new Early Islamic period communities in marsh/pasture lands throughout the frontier shows an intentional 'cultural logic' in creating a *ḥimā* space 'which has a particular designation in Islamic law as a public good that can serve the whole community as a pasture'.[19] These spaces would also reduce conflict and preserve grazing land, particularly in dry years when available pastures were limited.

The frontier of al-Andalus provides important parallels, showing that military pastures and transhumance were not just a product of the Near East but an environmental and economic strategy. Following the *reconquista*, specialized routes for moving sheep were created, or rather, became more separated from traditional routes which are documented since the sixth to seventh century if not earlier.[20] Often these routes deliberately moved between fallow fields, showing a symbiotic adjustment between settled and pastoralist groups. The routes were protected militarily, as were lowland pastures, and tolls were exacted on these sheep roads. Written accounts describe lowland shepherds in the uplands encountering competition from upland pastoralists. Finally, the collection of booty in the form of livestock also served to redistribute wealth across people, tribes and communities.[21]

Markets and Fairs

Soldiers or pastoralists who acquired various items of booty on excursions into Byzantine lands would need to sell or trade them. Such trade, a portion of which had to go to the state, also required pastoralists to interact with settled people in markets and fairs. Traditionally, pastoralist and settled groups have forged an important symbiosis wherein pastoralists require markets to sell or trade their dairy, wool (important for textiles) and meat to buy food (other meat, grain, produce) and manufactured goods, and settled groups required the reverse. Beyond the local economy, nomadic pastoralists on the frontier were necessary in conveying goods for international import/export between Byzantium and the Islamic lands – whether for legitimate trade, smuggling, tribute or gift exchange. The Prophet Muḥammad's envoy delivered goods for trade, along with a letter to Heraklios.[22] This economy, using nomadic or transhumant tribes as middlemen or brokers for items consisting mainly of crafts and luxury goods, was part of a larger frontier economy tapping into the Silk Route.[23] Texts mention a range of luxury goods imported from Byzantine lands, including arboreal extracts, herbs and horses (which we have already discussed), gold/silver utensils, lyres, brocades, female slaves and eunuchs. Excavations at Ṭarsūs uncovered a diverse assemblage of glassware interpreted as medical vessels and equipment.[24] It is possible that spices and extracts were bought and sold and prepared for medical use in the Ṭarsūs markets by pharmacists, continuing the local tradition of Dioskorides, the famous first-century CE medical author of *De Materia Medica*, who came from nearby Anazarba. Other Byzantine imports included birds of prey; hunting dogs; brocades, wool and linen; iron chairs decorated with gold; kitchen utensils of gold, silver and brass; and locks. Certain goods coming from Islamic lands and farther east, such as textiles from Syria, were bought and taken to Byzantium and even goods from Northern Europe arrived to the frontier.[25] The Church of Tokalı in Cappadocia used lapis, imported from Afghanistan, in its ninth to mid-tenth-century wall paintings.[26] Islamic sources mention the presence of *fanādiq* (singular, *funduq*) on routes not only in the Cilician plain but through the Taurus Mountain passes, including one north of Badhandūn (Greek Podandos, modern Pozantı), one near Qayṣariyya, and one between Mar'ash and Tzamandos.[27] According to Lewond, an Armenian historian who wrote in the eighth century, al-Mahdī established a free-trade system for Muslim merchants (trading in nearby Armenia) by abolishing duties.[28] The presence of local and international economies implies that markets were important in frontier towns, and that the frontier was open to trade.

The settlement pattern of major *thughūr* cities and villages in lowland areas on main routes rather than in defensible strongholds strongly suggests an open involvement with frontier trade and exchange. The network of fortified way stations on north–south routes across the frontier further supports economic development. Markets and merchants are mentioned for Adhana, Anṭakīya, Maṣṣīṣa, Ḥiṣn Kamkh, al-Kanīsa al-Sawdā', Ṭarsūs, Mar'ash (with extramural markets), Ḥadath (where there are the *ahl al-aswāq*), Shimshāṭ, Sumaysāṭ and smaller towns such as 'Imm in the Amuq. During the time of al-Ma'mūn, a new community called Kafarbayyā was built on the opposite bank of the Jayḥān from al-Maṣṣīṣa, and became its commercial center, with many *khāns*.[29] Ibn al-'Adīm observed that fine sheep-wool coats sold at al-Maṣṣīṣa for 30 dīnārs a piece. Indeed, it is logical to suppose that markets and merchants existed in every town. In the eastern Jazīra in Diyār Rabī'a, Ibn Ḥawqal mentioned the Sūq al-Aḥad (Sunday Market) near a river that flowed into the Greater or Upper Zāb River, a Tigris tributary at the foothills of the Zagros Mountains. Here lowland farmers, Kurdish highland dwellers (Hadhbaniya), Arabian Bedouin (Shaybān) and Christians (Sahārija) living in the town of Kafr 'Azzā interacted and exchanged goods in a seasonal fair.[30] Fairs corresponded with Christian feasts commemorating martyrs and were on fixed days of the year called *panegyris* or *tagūrtā*, the Syriac word for trade or commerce. Evidence from Arabic almanacs, calendars, and astronomical and chronological treatises from the ninth to thirteenth centuries shows that markets continued to occur after the Islamic conquest of the city. Of the fairs mentioned in these texts, four are in the *thughūr* and Jazīra: Ḥalab, Raqqa, Manbij and Raḥba following the post road (Ṭariq al-Barīd). Unlike many other fairs of Bilād al-Shām, all of these occurred in the autumn months, between September and November.[31] The timing was to take advantage of the fall harvest. Yet, it is interesting to note that soldiers and pastoralists would have been able to sell or trade booty acquired from raids soon after returning home from summer campaigns. Ibn Ḥawqal mentions this indirectly, drawing attention to an interregional trading network, when he describes Ḥalab up until the Byzantine reconquest as a populated city with beautiful markets where wealth and commerce benefited from its location 'on the high road between 'Iraq and the *al-thughūr*, and the rest of Syria'.[32] Furthermore, these fairs, often connected to shrines of Christian saints, were frequently outside or on the outskirts of the town, where settlers, pastoralists and foreigners could conduct business on neutral ground without needing to enter the town. The calendrical convergence of saints' days, agricultural activities, seasonal raiding and travelling fairs cannot be overlooked. Travelling markets and fairs passed through towns, creating an interdependent self-sufficient economic system between the transhumant tribes and various rural communities and contributing to the economic development of the *thughūr*.

Textual evidence also exists for the conjunction of fair circuits and the military in Byzantine lands during the Early Islamic period. Annual travelling fairs (*panegyreis*) occurred in major cities such as Trebizond, Ephesos, Sinope, Euchaita, Chonai, Myria, Thessaloniki and Nikomedia.[33] Localized trade and exchange took place, as well as the distribution of military pay. Economic exchange between Christians and Muslims also occurred in these regions. Under Leo III in 716, markets were established at 'Ammurīyya (Amorion) for the Islamic armies. Similarly, the Empress Irene was requested to establish a chain of markets for the returning Islamic armies in Bithynia.[34] As soldiers acquired booty or earned money through increased stipends (*'atā'*), they contributed to the frontier economy. Merchants and markets played a vital role in Byzantine and Islamic campaigining, linking settled and pastoralist groups, and strengthening local economies.

Tribal Identity

Transhumant tribal groups facilitated access rights to grazing lands, water sources and trade routes; protection under chiefs; and greater resistance in difficult times due to shared resources (i.e. maximizing grazing areas and minimizing herd loss) and market interaction. As such, tribes operated as political units and were not strictly genealogical or kinship based. The family comprised the most basic and smallest unit, and was generally blood linked. While many members shared kinship linkages, tribes could incorporate defectors from other tribes or from settled communities, prisoners taken during raiding, and any other type of recruits.[35] Captives from Byzantine lands, numbering in the thousands each year, are mentioned frequently as an important prize of raids. As this was a topos in the literature, the numbers are undoubtedly exaggerated. Nevertheless, even reducing this number to a more realistic figure and assuming that many could also have been sent back in exchange for Muslim prisoners of war during the well-known prisoner exchange rituals across the neutral zone of the Lāmus River west of Ṭarsūs, this would still have created a population of dislocated Byzantine captives on the frontier that had to be accounted for somehow.[36] As runaways, they could join bands or tribes, or become slaves. An important category in the Early Islamic period is that of the *mawālī* (converted Muslim, or client). Instances of *mawālī* joining groups and being treated as pure-blooded members can be seen in historical accounts, as in the example of Zurayq, a *mawlā* of the Khuzā'a Arab tribe, and Karbeas (Qarbiyās), the Paulician leader and a *mawla* of Ṭāhir b. al-Ḥusayn.[37] The Zuṭṭ and Sayābija, marsh dwellers in the *thughūr*, were originally from India and Indonesia, and came to the Islamic lands as *mawālī* of the Tamīm tribe. Ṭabarī describes a prisoner exchange that occurred in Constantinople where some Muslims chose not to return but convert and remain.[38]

Similarly, there are numerous instances of discontented individuals or groups that crossed the frontier to identify with the other side. Among Christians who sided with the Muslims against the Byzantines, the most famous group was the Paulicians, eastern dualist Christians accused of Manichean heresies. They inhabited the mountainous terrain north of Malaṭiya, towards Tephrikē under the control of Karbeas, and were eventually defeated by the Byzantines in 872 after ongoing attempts to subdue them. Armenians sought refuge from the Byzantines in Islamic-controlled Malaṭiya and Sumaysāṭ.[39] The Magaritai were Christians who converted to Islam.[40] Slavs came to Islamic lands during the rule of Mu'āwiya in 664/5 and under Justinian II and 'Abd al-Malik in 693 were settled on the frontier around Anṭākiya, Afāmiya (Apamaea) and Ḥiṣn Salmān in Qūrus, and took Arabic names.[41] There are also instances of frontier dwellers that sided with the Byzantines during raids and were swayed instead to serve in Islamic ranks alongside Arab soldiers, earning a salary, housing and status as a special youth corps (*al-fityān*).[42]

Movement across the frontier was not a one-way affair; Muslims helped Byzantine Christians as well, and were called *musta'riba*. Ṭabarī records that the Banū Taghlib, in the early days of the conquests (639–40), 'whether or not they had become Muslims' joined al-Walīd, except for the members of the Iyād b. Nizār tribe who left with all of their possessions for Byzantine territory. Caliph 'Umar wrote to the Byzantine emperor asking him to turn them back, lest 'we will surely dissolve our covenants with the Christians living under Arab sovereignty, and expel them'. A total of 4,000 returned, while the rest 'lagged behind scattering all over the border regions between Syria, al-Jazīra and Byzantine territory'.[43] Ṭabarī also tells us that in the year 837, Theophilus (829–942) attacked Zibaṭra and Malaṭiya and was joined by a group of Kurdish and Persian defectors known as the Muḥammira, whose commander was called variously Narsī or Narseh/Naṣīr/Nuṣayr or the Greek name Theophobus.[44] They were enlisted as regularly paid troops and given wives. Theophilus had an 'Ethiopian Unit', possibly comprising refugees from the East African Zanj canal workers from Southern 'Iraq. Theophilus also was known to have had, like his 'Abbāsid caliph contemporary al-Mu'taṣim, a personal bodyguard (*hetaireia*) of Khazars or Turks from the Farghana Valley.[45] The Ḥabīb clan of the Banū Taghlib in 935 allied themselves with the Byzantines and defected to Byzantine lands from the area of Ḥamdānid-controlled

Naṣībīn. The idea that they converted to Christianity may only partially be true, as many may still retained their Christian past identities. They numbered 12,000 horsemen with families and also took some neighbouring tribes with them; when they converted they were given lands, animals, clothes, and even valuable objects. A major motivation on the part of the Byzantine state was to gather manpower with a degree of control and semblance of loyalty on the frontier. This is an interesting example of the social pressures of tribal affiliations and decision making. The Ḥabīb, in turn, raided Islamic lands habitually every year during the harvest. They mainly raided in the Diyār Muḍar, taking several of the frontier forts, such as Ḥiṣn Ziyād and Ḥiṣn Manṣūr.[46] A short text from the *De cerimoniis* of Constantine VII Porphyrygenitos (r. 905–59) states that Muslims who are baptized can receive a start-up of some money, oxen, seed grain, and three years' tax exemption. Furthermore, households that take in converted captives (as 'sons-in-law', or *gambroí*) can also receive three years' tax exemption. Two points are salient here: a Byzantine version of tribal incorporation (in the unit of the family) and an attempt by the central state to encourage sedentarization and agrarian productivity.[47] Landless labourers and semi-pastoralists also comprised individuals or small groups who travelled looking for seasonal short-term work such as harvesting or construction.

The notion of an ancestral genealogy was often a binding mechanism for tribal solidarity (*'aṣabiya*) that was kept deliberately vague or mythic but was important nevertheless. The Muslim social historian Ibn Khaldūn comments that *'aṣabiya* was best obtained for alliances and for conquest when framed within religious ideology (such as *jihād*). Lindner's work on the early Ottomans as nomads provides valuable comparison. He argues against the prevailing *ghazī* thesis of Wittek, which states that the formation of the early Ottoman state in the late thirteenth century was an outcome of Ottoman religious warriors fighting a Muslim holy war. The absolutist political and religious agenda envisioned by Wittek was not the case in the formative periods; the Turkish tribe was not purely Muslim (rather syncretic), and their initial goals were not to convert Christians. Rather, the educated, orthodox, and sedentary, classes that became part of the administrative structure used the character of the *ghazī* as a way for them to retroactively understand the formation of the early Ottoman state, converting the 'nomadic pragmatist to a clever Holy Warrior' such as had been used to justify earlier Islamic expansion: 'As the Holy War, the jihad, was invoked for the initial Bedouin operations in early Islam, so too was the early Ottoman predation justified by the ghaza [raids].'[48] As such, the tribal unit was inclusive and functioned more or less as a politically-ordered group, not unlike an army garrison. Both were composed of tribal members who were mainly, but not necessarily, blood-linked (including prisoners, defectors and *mawālī*) and both were bound by ideological concepts: for tribal identity, the eponymous ancestor; for an army garrison, political/religious motivations. By extension, frontier conflict was a competition over resources for grazing and water rights, which combined ideological or military identity and solidarity with economic and environmental necessity.

Internal Interactions: Frontier Societies and the Central State

Having the frontier broken down into smaller micro-regions adds complexity to the notion of a singular entity. What can be said about the actual existence of several physical and geographical spaces? The physical frontier of the transhumant and sedentary societies comprised lowland plains that had become increasingly marshy in the winter, and mountain uplands that were only accessible via a handful of important passes in the summer months. Both mountains and marshes have traditionally been on the edges of settlement. This may in part be associated with modern perceptions that tend to dismiss such terrains as peripheral and uninhabited zones within the landscape – uncultivated landscapes 'gone wild'. On mountains, agriculture is seen as a difficult enterprise; in marshes, irrigation systems no longer function properly and insects and disease are rampant. This much is implied in a letter from Hārūn al-Rashīd to Constantine VI, sent from Raqqa in 796, in which Hārūn reminds Constantine how good life was during their peace treaty for the

Byzantine people, who 'abandoned the summits of the mountains and the beds of marshes and went, in the midst of their dwellings [...] digging canals, planting trees, and causing springs to burst forth, in such a way that they prospered'.[49] In addition, these spaces are conceived as obstacles to travel and transportation, particularly for the large commercial and trade-based economies that dominated the Near East following the first millennium BCE. These wildernesses were regarded as the realms of wild beasts, rebels and bandits, and social and political outlaws.

There is no shortage of instances in which local chiefs, warlords, rebels or self-proclaimed prophets positioned against the central Islamic state, ensconced themselves on the *thughūr* – most notably Marwān II, the last Umayyad caliph, during the 'Abbāsid Revolution in Ḥarrān.[50] Of course, these perceptions reflect a central state/settled point of view. It is also no coincidence that these regions figured prominently in the lives of pastoralist tribes. Pastoralists tend to be locally autonomous and governed by their own tribal group, and practice herding to various degrees. More clearly, mountain pastures provided summer grazing areas while marshes provided winter ones. Pastoralists did not regard movement between these as an impediment but rather a way of life. As they lived on the periphery of settled society and their movements were difficult to control, they were regarded as thieves and dissidents. Much as military expeditions and competition for resources were two sides of the same coin, the peripheral pastoralist was seen equally as a rebel or soldier, depending on the level of perceived control by the central state. Muqaddasī, referring to the nomads of the deserts (another type of environmental frontier), stated that they are both dangerous bandits and hospitable guides.[51] Regardless of political frontiers, each of these smaller ecological regions were themselves localized frontiers.

Mountains

Perhaps unsurprisingly, one of the last areas of Syria to be conquered was the mountains to the north, unlike the lowland communities that capitulated quickly.[52] The thickly forested mountains uplands were difficult to access and remained on the peripheries of settlement, often serving as refuges for native populations. In the *thughūr*, the mountains – specifically the Amanus range, including the Lebanon and Anti-Lebanon Mountains – were the abodes of the Jarājima (Mardaites), who had set up local autonomy.[53] It is mentioned that they were intentionally left by Heraklios to guard the frontier outposts, although this is surely a misrepresentation of a local populace that had no wish to evacuate or be resettled. The Jarājima were treated extensively by Balādhurī, who describes them as Christians who lived in the Amanus (al-Lukkam) in a town called al-Jurjuma between Bayās and Būqā near the Ma'din al-Zāj (Vitriol or Copperas [iron or ferrous sulphate] Mine).[54] Both Arabic and Syriac texts call them brigands (*luṣūs* in Arabic, *Garegūmāyē* or *Marīdayē* in Syriac) showing how they were regarded by either group.[55] They were neither Arab nor Byzantine. Some scholars have argued that they were were cavalry from Persia that had remained in Syria, cultivating tax-free plots of land on the 'frontier' in exchange for service.[56] Others have contended that they were of Armenian/Caucausus descent, from the highlands near Qālīqalā (Greek Theodosiopolis, modern Erzerum),[57] while some suggest that they were from the region of Late Hittite/Assyrian Gurgum, ancient Mar'ash.[58] They were nominally governed by Anṭākiya, and some barricaded themselves in the city during its conquest in 636. Following the fall of Anṭākiya, they retreated as a group to the mountains. The accounts are unclear as to whether they were mountain folk before the conquest with certain members living in the city, or if they retreated to a new upland residence upon the conquest. Nevertheless, the Jarājima were still problematic and deemed insurgents by the new Islamic rulers. During the conquests, Ḥabīb ibn Maslama al-Fihrī, the acting governor of Anṭākiya, attempted to forge a peace treaty in an effort to control them. Terms were established whereby the Jarājima would become spies, participating in raids, and were absolved from paying tax and allowed to keep any booty.[59] This arrangement extended to the citizens of al-Jurjuma, its merchants and employees, and to dependants and locals of surrounding villages – called *al-rawādif*, meaning 'those who follow'. Balādhurī also suggests that *al-rawādif* could refer to followers who joined their cause, such as former slaves of the Muslims, rather than just those who resided in the villages. Theophanes Confessor confirms this point, 'so that in a short time they grew to many thousands'.[60] However, the mountain people's allegiance only went as far as was convenient, and they continued to be a threat. Balādhurī mentions that in 'Abd al-Malik's time the Jarājima would raid the villages of Anṭākiya and the Amuq and strike at lagging Islamic troops during the annual summer expeditions. During the second *fitna* in 678/9–88, they allied with the Byzantines under Justinian II. They forayed as far south as Mount Lebanon and Mount Galilee, keeping only to the mountains and avoiding the plains. As such, they remained out of reach by any major army and their resistance was as much independently carried out as it was nominally a Byzantine incursion. On the one hand, the use of the Jarājima as buffers and allies of the Byzantines is typical of Byzantine warfare on the frontier. In this case, the Jarājima were seen as a potentially dangerous group and the Byzantines used them so they would remain *within* the Islamic frontier rather than raiding their own lands.[61] On the other hand, the inability of either the Byzantine or Islamic side to control them suggests that these mountain folk were self-governing and had little interest in alliances.

Eventually, several other peace treaties were made in efforts to control the Jarājima. Greek and Syriac authors such as Theophilus of Edessa, Theophanes Confessor, Agapius and Michael the Syrian – and the anonymous author of the *Chronicle* of 1234 – all mention that 'Abd al-Malik offered Justinian II money to remove 12,000 Jarājima, 'not including runaway levies and slaves'.[62] This attempt was not entirely successful, and most of the Jarājima settled in their Amanus Mountain homes while some joined the Islamic summer expeditions. In some cases, they were given money, wheat and oil, strikingly similar to the incentives offered to Arabs and other groups to settle on the *thughūr*, and showing an attempt to sedentarize rebellious mountain people on the plains. During a raiding campaign, Maslama b. 'Abd al-Malik under al-Walīd in 705/6 fought alongside one Maymūn al-Jurjumānī in the Taurus Mountains.[63] However, in

708, Maslama tried to settle them elsewhere in further efforts to control them or get them out of the way in places such as the lowlands – 'Amq Tīzīn, Mount Huwwār in the eastern Cilician plain near Hārūnīyya, Ḥimṣ, or Dimashq – or the Byzantine uplands: Sunh al-Lūlūn near Lu'lu'a. In one instance in the early 'Abbāsid period, a leader of the Jarājima – Bundār or Theodore – rallied other disenfranchised peasants and runaway slaves to revolt against taxation in Lebanon. They raided and plundered Ba'labakk and villages of the Biqā' Plain. Sāliḥ b. 'Alī, governor of Syria under al-Manṣūr, sent a force to root them out of their mountain stronghold and forcibly resettled them around the province. Cobb's analysis of this revolt argues that they were a nativist and messianic movement like other millenarian bandit cults in history, such as those participating in the Judaic revolt – also an upland/lowland conflict.[64]

What of the settlement of al-Jurjuma – was it a small urban area, or a large village in the mountains that would have merchants and dependent villages? The mention of dependent villages suggests a different pattern, given that settlement during both the Late Roman and Early Islamic periods focused on small, dispersed sites in the uplands. The settlements on the Syrian Jibāl, while larger entities with churches and other buildings, still did not possess communities of merchants and surrounding dependent villages. The *Tabula Imperii Byzantinii* mentions the modern toponym of Çomçom – between Kırıkhan and Sarıseki, but closer to the Amuq – although this identification seems to be based on the name alone, and was not verified.[65] Unfortunately, no survey in the heart of the Amanus range has been conducted other than on its eastern or western slopes and valleys. A common misconception is that the Amanus, like the Taurus, were a range of towering peaks. Yet, nestled amidst the peaks were many hidden and protected valleys. The presence of Crusader and Armenian castles in these valleys is proof of settlement, perhaps in connection with smaller paths between the Amuq and the coast that are less well known but which functioned in antiquity.

As Christians living within the Islamic frontier, the Jarājima were exceptions as targets of holy war, being given economic incentives and even recruited into seasonal raids/expeditions. Further, these Christians were semi-nomadic mountain dwellers whose practices (including raiding, collecting booty, and acquiring followers or defectors) were fairly overt and characterized them as a political tribe. As mountain dwellers they become bandits and political dissidents, and much anxiety is seen over the inability of either Islamic or Byzantine sides to control them and resettle them in the lowland plains. Taking into account their aforementioned attributes, they were not unlike the local frontier Byzantines whose transformation in lifestyle and settlement in mountain refuges was an environmental response to their political situation.

There are numerous other examples of frontier rebel groups ensconced in the mountains. Most similar to the Jarājima were the Armenian Ṭonrakians, including the Banū Bazrik (or Gharzik) and Banū Boghousag of Sevaverak (or Siberek), two different dissident groups of highland dwellers who lived in the Anti-Taurus Mountains south of Malaṭiya. They were nominally Christian, but considered bandits as they raided surrounding Muslim and Christian villages and monasteries alike, including the Monastery of Mar Bar Ṣawma, taking money and livestock. To prevent this, the rulers of Malaṭiya gave them lands around Ḥiṣn Qalawdhiya not far from the Euphrates.[66] The *abdāl* Sufis lived around Antakiya, Maṣṣīṣa and Ṭarsus, presumably in the uplands as they were foresters.[67] In al-Andalus, Roman Visigothic communities that occupied mountain sites following the Early Islamic conquests similarly practiced raiding and banditry on the lowland Islamic communities. Examples of Islamic groups living in the mountains exist as well. During the Umayyad–ʻAbbāsid transition in the mid-eighth century, certain groups took advantage of the political vacuum to establish themselves in the mountains and practice armed resistance. In some cases, they were settled there, as in the case of the *ashrāf ahl al-ʻIraq*, who were placed by ʻUthmān in the mountain passes north of Cilicia to get rid of them.[68] Qurra b. Thābit was one such local governor and tribal chief who raided the lowland towns, causing the local Arab and Christian communities of Mayyafāriqīn to form an alliance against the mountain folk.[69] In the very early eleventh century, key mountain areas such as the Jabal al-Summāq, Jabal al-Rawādīf (part of the Syrian Jibāl) and Jabal al-Lukkām (Amanus) 'were primarily inhabited by a tribally organized peasantry [*'ashā'ir*] who were fiercely antagonistic toward any type of outside authority'.[70] The Jabal al-Rawādīf, south of Anṭākiya, was populated by the al-Aḥmar and the Ghannāj under the local chieftain Naṣr b. Musarraf – the Mousaraph mentioned by the Byzantine historian John Skylitzes. In 1027, Musarraf started an insurrection against Byzantine-controlled Anṭākiya that lasted for five years. Similar rebellions were started by the Druze, who lived in 'virtually inaccessible strongholds' on the Jabal al-Summāq, and the Munqidh, who lived in the uplands near Shayzar farther south along the Orontes. The Byzantines attempted to control them by enlisting them in their armies to guard the mountain passes between Ḥalab and Anṭākiya. It is interesting to note that the Byzantine armies were divided into two groups of soldiers – the white (*ābyaḍ*) and the brown (*āsmar*) – reflecting the mix of people and use of tribesmen. The *āsmar*, perhaps composed of some of these groups, were given mountain passes to control, as this was in many ways their own territory.[71]

The similarity between the attempt by the Islamic rulers to control the Christian Jarājīma in the seventh and eighth centuries and the Byzantines to control the Bedouin tribes in the early eleventh centuries in the exact same region is striking. Both cases occur in the mountains of Anṭākiya, not on the Taurus Mountains of the Islamic–Byzantine frontier. The rebel mountain groups, who probably practiced a semi-nomadic/semi-settled strategy previously, were forced to adopt upland lifestyles to maintain local autonomy. As such, the interactions between Islam and Byzantium, or Muslims and Christians, regardless of who was in power, occur across a localized frontier of mountains and plain.

Marsh

Like the mountains, the marshes were also thought to be uninhabited wastelands. However, the wetlands were also localized frontiers where settlement and interaction was equally significant but qualitatively undetermined, particularly in the *thughūr*. As has been shown, by the Early Islamic period much of the lowland plains were seasonal-to-permanent marshes. Unlike the mountain areas, there are no good accounts of marshes on the frontier and how they supported settlement or group interaction, although there is limited work on marshes in the Classical periods.[72] Written accounts briefly and indirectly state that the mountain Jarājima also lived in the marshes of the Amuq Plain and farther north, but nothing further is mentioned.[73] There are, however, several specific references to marsh dwellers who were resettled from southern ʻIraq. An examination of their origins and settlements in the well-known marshes of southern ʻIraq (*al-Baṭā'iḥ*), an important parallel to the marsh settlements of the frontier, reveals the extent to which these spaces were localized frontiers.

Although infrequent, textual references to known structures, mainly in the marshlands of southern ʻIraq, appear throughout the Islamic periods and imply settlement on islands and reed platforms. More often, marshes and swamps are regarded as the hideouts of bandits and rebels. The presence of outlaw communities in the marshes would probably go unnoticed in any official or semi-official geographical or historical text, unless they proved especially rebellious. Furthermore, their absence from the geographical sources as properly named communities may be more a function of their size and loose tribal organization.

Muqaddasī mentions the settlement of al-Salīq, a preexisting Sāsānian city and a typical swamp settlement described as a *madīna* on the edge of a lagoon in the swamps of southern Iraq:

> The fields [of Salīq] extend right up to the outskirts of al-Kūfah, but the heat is very great, and the air foul and oppressive. The mosquitoes are a perfect pest, making life miserable. The food [of the inhabitants] is fish, their drink is warm water, and nights are a torture. [The populace] is boorish and its speech corrupt. There is a shortage of salt and great misery. However, [the district] is a source of abundant flour,

> has a benign government, abundant water and considerable quantities of fish. The city [of Sāliq] has a great name, and the inhabitants are without exception good fighters, and knowledgeable about the river. One of the localities is reminiscent in its pleasantness of the canal of al-Ubullah.[74]

Muqaddasī's skeptical views of marsh settlement should be taken with a grain of salt. Apart from his trademark descriptions of towns, which frequently alternate good qualities with bad, he was an urbanite from the high elevations of Jerusalem. That he viewed the government as benign and considered it a *madīna* based to some degree on its politics is interesting. Around the time of his writing, al-Salīq was in its second period of independent rule (*c.*983). During the first period (949–79), 'Imrān b. Shāhīn had established himself as an independent ruler and al-Salīq as his headquarters in the swamps, away from the eyes of the 'Abbāsid government. The 'Abbāsid armies made several attempts to depose him, all of which failed on account of their unfamiliarity with the wetlands terrain.[75] That an independent ruler could maintain power for at least 30 years in relatively close proximity to the seat of the government/capital lends great significance to the power of the marshlands as marginally viewed territory from a central-lands perspective.

The marsh dwellers and supporters of the independent insurgents consisted of several ethnic groups that became clients of Arab tribes and could, on political terms, be termed a sub-tribe or clan. Generally, literature describes the major insurgent rebellion of the marsh dwellers as the Zanj Revolt, a major episode appearing in several historical accounts but most notably in al-Ṭabarī who devotes significant attention. Although the Zanj were East African slaves brought to work the canals of southern 'Iraq, the term collectively refers to all non-Arab slaves including the Zuṭṭ from India and the Sayābija from Indonesia. The Zuṭṭ or Sindī were made up of two groups based on the different routes they took in migrating or being resettled from their Indus Valley homelands to the wetlands of southern 'Iraq. One group came to the Persian Gulf coasts in the early fifth century, although written accounts are divided as to why. Some say that the Zuṭṭ were musicians and entertainers also called Lūrī or Lūlī, 12,000 of which settled down at the behest of Bahram Gur. They were from the environs of Lūristān and the city of Mihrān, the area stretching from the northern shore of the Persian Gulf to Multān on the west side of the Nahr Mihrān. They were also former tribesmen, who were not farmers but pastoralists who lived in marshes and ate fish.[76] Others claim that they were brought by the last Sāsānid king as mercenaries against the Arabs. Balādhurī says that the Zuṭṭ, as well as the Sayābija and Andaghār, were Indians (Sindī) in the Persian army. Al-Ṭabarī first mentions them after the death of the Prophet, when they were made to rebel against the Arabs in the region of al-Khaṭṭ between Baḥrayn and al-ʻUmān. Al-Khwārazmī in the tenth century said that their original name was *jiṭ* (plural *juṭṭān* and ancient Getae), which was arabicized to Zuṭṭ and that they were also employed to protect roads (*badhraqa*).[77] Still other accounts suggest that they migrated naturally westward searching for pasture via a canal called the Nahr al-Zuṭṭ, which was dug for, or by, them in the marshlands of southern ʻIraq. A district in Khūzistān called Zuṭṭ may also indicate their migratory trajectory.[78] Whether or not they were deliberately settled, the Zuṭṭ were a nomadic people, migrating over distances with their families and livestock for better resources. Indeed, they are sometimes considered the forerunners of the Gypsies who migrated to Armenia, Anatolia and Europe. During the Islamic conquests, they converted and became *mawālī*, and were based around Baṣra. The second group came in the Umayyad period and was brought by Muhammad b. al-Qāsim al-Thaqafī, who was prefect (*ʻāmil*) of al-Ḥajjāj after his campaigns in the Indus Valley. They were settled in the area of Kaskar, east of Kūfa, in the lowlands of the Tigris around Wāsit with their families and livestock.[79] The Zuṭṭ also included deserters from the Persian cavalry (Asāwira), who were of Indian origin, much like the Jarājima of the Amanus. The Zuṭṭ revolted 813–33 and 834, and were subdued by being resettled by Muʻtaṣim's commander Ujayf, who sent 27,000 of them first to Khāniqīn north of Baghdād, then to ʻAyn Zarba on the *thughūr*.[80] The government armies had great difficulty quelling the revolt as they could only access the Zuṭṭ settlements by boat. This clearly reflects the perspective of the governmental central lands, which were unfamiliar with the territory and saw the swamps as the edges of civilization.

The Sayābija were another non-Arab marsh-dwelling group with debated origins. They were most likely from Sumatran Indonesia, and were also originally employed by the Sāsānians as treasury guards. They also lived in the region of Baṣra and were used to fight pirates, indicating that they were perhaps seafaring and used, like the Jarājima, as buffers against other maritime rebels.[81] Etymologically, the *sayābija* derives from the Tamil root word of 'sapa' or 'saba' (Arabic *zabag* via *sabag*), referring to a river estuary. The inhabitants of these environments were the Savaka, or people of the Saba, which was then Arabicized to *sayābija*.[82] Zakeri states that they were also possibly Persian cavalry, similar to the Jarājima, Zuṭṭ and Asāwira.[83]

The Zuṭṭ, Sayābija and Zanj show a clear ecological relationship with their surrounding wetland environment and are predecessors of the marsh dwellers of southern 'Iraq today. They subsisted on cattle and fish, as well as fruit and vegetables from surrounding orchards and gardens, date palms and, of course, they harvested reeds. In addition, they participated in various local industries such as weapons manufacture, boat building and clothing. The proliferation of markets and minting attest to a wide economic base that was in part facilitated by exchange and the trade of agricultural goods with Bedouin merchants. Furthermore, they practiced raiding (particularly on Baṣra);[84] however, no land of settlements were ever taken. Only what was mobile and useful was acquired, such as booty (money, horses, weapons), troops and boats (often with cattle and grain). This type of subsistence can be closely compared to the 'trade-and-raid' lifestyle of transhumant tribes who rely on both sedentary markets, to trade animal products for cultivated goods, and on the raiding of settlements. These raids – perceived as robbery and banditry by the central state, which could not readily control the marshes (it took them nine months to quell the 834 rebellion) – were probably designated as revolts when crescendoes of multiple insurgencies were reached. The central state had to resort to marsh warfare, with which their Turkic troops would have been most unfamiliar. Ṭabarī mentions that the Zuṭṭ, who were referred to on other occasions as 'frogs', attacked and travelled by skiffs, forcing the 'Abbāsid troops to do the same and to block canals.[85] In the fourteenth century, Ibn Baṭūṭa described the region as being full of Shi'i bandits who raided caravans.[86] Most importantly, the settlements and interactions of the marsh dwellers demonstrate an enduring, internal, localized frontier within Islamic lands. Further, they provide evidence for interpreting the sites and the interactions of the marsh dwellers on the Islamic–Byzantine frontier, who were the very same Zanj and Zuṭṭ relocated from southern 'Iraq.

Several previous settlements of Zuṭṭ to the *thughūr* had already taken place by Mu'āwiya in 669/70, who settled Zuṭṭ and Sayābija families from Baṣra in Anṭākiya and Būqā in the Amuq. No less than 4,000 water buffalo (*al-jamūs*), both male and female, were brought to the frontier under Caliph al-Walīd I. They were among thousands brought from India. An additional 4,000 female water buffalo and their Zuṭṭ masters were sent to Maṣṣīṣa by Yazīd b. 'Abd al-Malik, who took them from Muhallab, making the total at Maṣṣīṣa upwards of 8,000 water buffalo.[87] Beasts and masters were also living in the area of 'Ayn Zarba when, in 855, a Byzantine raid took a number of their women, children and livestock.[88] These three instances suggest either deliberately episodic resettlement policies or migratory routes of the pastoralist and nomadic marsh dwellers to the *thughūr* – or a combination of the two. Furthermore, they show how the central state was preoccupied with how to control the marsh dwellers of these localized frontiers.

Like the mountain frontiers, there was no specifically ethnic or religious attachment in these peripheral, localized spaces. Rather, the groups that inhabited them were often politically or economically marginalized. Abū al-Fidā' described the way of life of the marsh inhabitants in the Ghab Valley along the Middle Orontes in the fourteenth century, when the region was under

Mamlūk rule and relatively far from the Taurus Mountain border. These settlements were highly adaptive to the ecosystem and bear a very close resemblance to those of the marsh dwellers in southern 'Iraq. Abū al-Fidā' writes, 'there are Christian fishermen who live here in huts built on posts (*buyūt 'ala al-khawāzīq* [sing. *khāzūq*]), in the northern part of the lagoon. This lake is four times larger than the Afāmiya Lake. In the middle of the Lake of the Christians (*buḥairat al-naṣārā*) the dry land appears.'[89] When integrated within the larger economic framework of the Levant, the marsh dwellers may have maintained the Orontes waterways linking trade traffic between Ḥims, Ḥamā and Anṭākiya. What is interesting from the comments of Abū al-Fidā on the marsh dwellers is that they are Christian communities, rather than Muslim. From archaeological and literary evidence, virtually nothing is known about marsh dwellers in the Roman and Late Roman periods. This suggests that either the adaptive strategies of marsh settlement and subsistence were learned from the 'Iraqi (and Sindī) marsh dwellers that settled in the Early Islamic period, or developed independently and simultaneously as a response to the environment and political circumstances.

Environmental Frontiers: Upland and Lowland Interactions

Environmentally-determined localized frontiers show several types of interactions taking place, such as the competition for resources between pastoralist and settled groups, and pastoralist and other pastoralist groups, and security and counter-insurgency measures between the central state and its peripheral communities. These were not unique to specific ethnic groups and did not occur solely in the *thughūr*, but were adaptive, resilient responses to historical occurrences, thereby deconstructing the notion of a single, physical frontier. Further these interactions are similar to parallels in other periods of history which featured upland and lowland interactions between groups in the very same regions.

Pre-Islamic interactions occurred on the *thughūr* between the areas of the uplands of Isauria (or Rough Cilicia) and the marshy lowlands of the Cilician Plain (or Smooth Cilicia) in the Iron Age, Hellenistic/Persian, Roman and Late Roman periods. In pre-Classical periods, the large empires controlled the plains and coast but had limited power, often maintained by treaty, over the neighbouring highlands of Isauria. This was true of the Hittites, who created the Cilician Gates, the Assyrians whose center was Ṭarsūs, and the Achaemenids.[90] A story of the Persian King Datames (r. 385–62 BCE) shows a different type of interaction, besides just diplomacy and treaty writing. In efforts to control the mountains of Rough Cilicia, Datames both raided them intermittently and created alliances with other mountain chiefs, eventually prevailing. As a result, the central court from which he came deemed him a rebel governing an autonomous region and attacked him. B. Shaw shows how the 'mountains made the man' – that is, whether or not Datames intended to establish an autonomous base, his presence in such a region made him a political outlaw.[91] The mountains were examples of localized frontiers, and to properly deal with them one had to become a part of them. This created some anxiety on the part of the central state in managing the peripheries of empire. Datames' successful methods of raiding, forming tribal alliances and negotiating only loose control are strongly evocative of nomadic and settled interactions. Furthermore, they are similar to interactions that once occurred on the Islamic–Byzantine frontier – albeit nearly 1,000 years earlier, in a landscape governed by different political borders. What is consistent is the physical landscape itself and the perceptions of it.

The Romans and Byzantines had similar trouble with the mountain areas. Their goals, however, were not to bring them into the folds of the empire so much as to secure overland routes for communication, trade and transport. Attempts to root out mountain settlements on the Amanus were unsuccessful. Similarly, the Romans had to forge alliances, and in some cases gave areas of the mountains to local dynastic leaders as gifts, a practice seen often in the Early and Middle Islamic periods.[92] An important point is that the inhabitants of these regions, called by Cicero 'wild savages beyond the pale of civilization' were not just mountain dwellers (Amanienses) but ethnic Cilicians (linguistically Luwian) from the plains, who had moved upland to seek refuge, avoid oppression, maintain independence, and preserve ethnic and cultural ways of life.[93]

These interactions are also seen in the thirteenth century in Rough Cilicia with the Kahramanid Turkmen dynasty, who were described as pastoralists, lumberjacks and bandits, and more recently in the mid-nineteenth century, when the Ṭarsūs Ottomans attacked the Isaurian mountain dwellers, the Derebeys, who were considered outlaws (*sakı*) who raided the plains. The Ottomans dealt with the threat by giving them local power. The Derebeys became employed as middlemen to collect tribute and recruit soldiers, and then were given offices of power. However, the practice of using the local inhabitants as clients or buffers, as was seen with the Jarājima, could easily backfire. As much as a protection against an external threat, the military on the frontier were seen as insurance that they themselves would not defect – or worse, set up local power structures.

Cilicia was known in the Roman period for its mountain resources: timber and the products of sheep and goat herding, which would have been sold or traded on the plains.[94] As in the early Islamic period, interaction was also marked by a competition for resources. Further, these interactions between nomad and settler, nomad and nomad, and central state and periphery were enshrouded in a religious ideology that justified conflict, much as an ethic of *jihād* and apocalyptic literature did in the early Islamic period. Cilicia was the home of St Thekla, a fifth-century saint who was worshipped particularly in the areas between Rough Cilicia and the Cilician Plain, the localized frontier of settlement. Another personality was Konon of Bidana, who converted bandits 'not [only] in a spiritual sense, but also in an economic one, by turning them from wandering and free pastoralists to cultivators of the land who became his slaves'.[95] Through the religious lens of a local saint, the enemy was seen as sacrilegious and the saint and her worshippers as the bringers of a religious truth.

Upland and lowland frontiers are both physically and mentally constructed spaces:

> A prevalent ideology shared by most landowners tended to reflect, from their perspective, the political and military frontier between mountain and plain as a dividing line between the 'barbarian' and the 'civilized'. But there was an element of illusion in this idea, since montane societies, even if they rejected political and military forces directed against them, seem to have been open to, and permeable by, various cultural and economic forces stemming from the lowlands.[96]

The same processes of interaction were not unique to the Islamic–Byzantine frontier, either as a singular physical border or zone, or a special period of history. Examples are known from contemporary periods in west China and South East Asia, and between Vietnam and India, with similar attempts by a central state or settled population to control mountain groups with a concept of civilizing.[97] Furthermore, examples have shown that the inhabitants of localized frontiers who participated in upland and lowland interactions were not fixed but changed depending on historical events. The local Byzantine populace became mountain pastoralists during the seventh/eighth centuries, as did the local Hispano–Romano population, led by the Visigothic aristocracy of al-Andalus, at the end of the Late Roman period, and the Cilicians during the Roman period. The Jarājima in their mountain refuges similarly retreated to the Amanus with the arrival of the Islamic conquests. These movements are not bound to chronological, geographical or ethno-religious restraints but evince interactions between uplands and lowlands and have modern implications. We need not look too far into the past to find these in the very same spaces: the Kurds in the uplands of south-east Turkey, for example, PKK (Parti Karkerani Kurdistani, or Kurdistan Worker's Party) insurgents ensconced in the Amanus Mountains; or the Basque separatists of ETA (Euskadi Ta Askatasuna, or Euskadi {Basque country} and Liberty) in the

Pyrenees. Furthermore, they show the importance of localized frontiers, how they are created by historical occurrences and maintained by a level of environmental and economic resilience. These processes are part of a longer, cyclical history, in which patterns are repeated in an ebb and flow of complex, adaptive relationships between humans and the landscape.

CONCLUSIONS

DISMANTLING AND REBUILDING THE FRONTIER

The frontier in history, cultural consciousness, and current scholarship has always lingered just beyond the grasp of understanding. Indeed, its traditional definition, as a wilderness on the edge of civilization or as a boundary separating two entities, speaks of an otherness, a negative entity rather than a positive one. The archaeologist may feel this lack of specificity most keenly. How can he or she perceive frontiers? In the medieval periods, there were no linear boundaries. The concept of borders, so much a part of contemporary nationalism, may not have been felt as acutely.

Can a frontier be simply defined as a thinly settled area? The answer is no. Evidence has shown a more nuanced response. While some surveys on the *thughūr* show decreased settlement initially, the frontier fills in over time. The material culture of assumed Byzantine or Christian communities in proximity to Arab or Muslim communities (or *vice versa*) delineates a zone where two groups interacted over a 300-year period of time. While certain identity models can be put forth, ethnic or religious groups such as Arabs or Christians may not be readily identifiable within sites. Further, the prevailing material culture is not necessarily paradigmatic of a frontier society. Frontier settlements and societies, like those in the central Islamic landscapes of Early Islamic Palestine and Egypt, reflect the dominance of local traditions and industries, dictated in part by closer connections to and subsistence upon an immediate environment rather than more distant connections to centralized cities and societies. Frontier settlements may also differ from other similar examples that were situated in different elevations and terrain, or even from other more central Islamic lands that exhibit wider connections, the importation of material culture and animals, and the proximity to larger and denser settlements and urban areas. The core–periphery model, positioning the relationship between a central state and the frontier, can be dispensed with. As archaeological evidence is so site-specific, the idea of territoriality, when cast in an archaeological light, distinctly avoids political subjectivity. Reacting to political, subjectivist claims on the concept of territoriality, A. Smith states, 'Ecological change or alterations in the nutrient requirements of populations are the *only clear determinants* that might explain changes in attachments between people and place'.[1] Taken further, although categories of evidence may suggest ethno-religious frontier societies, to the archaeologist the frontier as an identifiable regional space is imperceptible. The *thughūr* becomes an imagined frontier composed of religious/political ideologies. Stripped of its ideology, archaeology is a substrate showing a region of continuity, ecological subsistence and local economy.

Of course, it is possible to debate whether one can escape ideology at all. Archaeology and its motivations for discerning truth or historical narrative in pseudo-scientific terms are also part of embedded ideologies, whether consciously constructed or not. The discourses of settlement and material continuity, environmental history and destabilizing Christian–Muslim interaction can also be perceived as the product of a liberal and reactive Western ideology. This ideology emerged in the early twenty-first century as a response to more than a decade of physical and propagandistic war between the US, Europe and the Middle East.

Thus, frontiers cannot be totally deconstructed or decoupled from ideologies, which, whether real or imagined, all have historical relevance. An ideology of frontier and articulated sense of place gives the Islamic–Byzantine *thughūr* poignancy. In this case, Islamic and Byzantine authors articulated a third layer: the imagined, uninhabited, uncivilized and shattered (*sha'atha*) 'no man's land', or *emeros*, waiting to be rebuilt (*'imāra*) and repopulated (*repoblación*). Woven through this process of reclamation was the political-religious ideology of a just or holy war (*jihād*). Holy war substantiated and divided the frontier into the metaphysical landscapes of *dār al-Islām* and *dār al-ḥarb*. Like the notion of a frontier, *jihād* was an elastic, idiosyncratic concept rather than a static and monumental one. The development of *jihād* must be seen as not only constantly changing, but changing to fit the political and social realities of relations with non-Muslim individuals, communities or empires. Apocalyptic narratives were important motivation for *jihād* conquests, and emerged from and of the *thughūr.* These two narratives were similar in that their mythology could also be altered to consider any actual event of 'war', whether a victory, defeat or political crisis. Both served as important elements in the religious frontier landscape, and were embraced by rulers and frontier inhabitants alike. The religious frontier of *jihād* and apocalypse appears on the pages of eschatological tales,[2] military campaigning books (Kitāb al-Siyar),[3] epic poems,[4] speeches,[5] and fantastical geographies.[6] The articulation of these conflicts constituted propaganda from central lands on how to effectively administrate the periphery, attract settlers to these cities, and build up the regional economy. These texts were also literary interactions in their own right. Religious ideology justified raiding between Muslims and Christians, and internally controlled the mixed frontier societies by galvanizing them towards an external threat and creating an antagonistic 'other'.

What, then, is left of the frontier or its inhabitants? Was there an Islamic, Byzantine, Muslim or Christian frontier to speak of – or was there just a set of groups living near each other, who were defined as a frontier population? Or was the frontier just a landscape composed of communities living side by side and competing with one another? Perhaps it is most accurate to conclude that the *thughūr* was none of these. It cannot be defined simply as a single physical space inhabited by people. Rather, it is the simultaneous accumulation of several layers of perception. One layer is a clearly-defined historical frontier actively imbued with a definitive purpose by its inhabitants. Another layer is an archaeological landscape, across which the transformations of settlements are passively dictated by changing environmental conditions. The *thughūr* is redefined as a framework where *processes of interaction* take place diachronically across these layers: the interaction, exchange and competition between groups, and between groups and their environment, that influence shifts in settlement and changes in landscape.

Studies of the political, social and cultural interactions on Islamic–Byzantine frontier from other disciplines have already begun to be explored in a process of studying the relationships of frontier groups with one another, with the central state, and with foreign lands. Art-historical studies can examine the process of acculturation of local cultures to new ruling groups, or the reverse: ruling groups adopting local styles using imported goods, local imitations and hybridizations based on style and technique.[7] They can also investigate the transmission of artists, architects and building supplies as a form of interaction.[8] There was no conflict of interest here; receptiveness to the 'enemy's' culture implies that it was perceived as somehow 'neutral', and not infected by the ideology of its foreign source.

Historical text-based studies have begun to examine the role of individuals who frequently crossed the porous frontier: scholars, geographers, physicians, merchants, diplomats, religious leaders, pilgrims and spies, whose roles were blurred.[9] Objects also travelled, whether as diplomatic gifts, relics, or books that were subsequently translated.[10] Within the frontier, important Syriac scholars lived in almost every town, including Anṭakiya, Malaṭiya, Sumaysāṭ, Ḥarrān, Raqqa, Sarūj, Manbij and Ruhā, as well as in monasteries. These monasteries were often visited by elite Muslims who wished to escape from the cities and indulge in wine, and at times in the attractiveness of its young male and female initiates.[11] These individual points of intersection between Islamic and Christian lands, or among Muslims in Christian spaces within Islamic lands, occurred everywhere, and their study can fine-tune the archaeologists' focus on groups. All these studies share in the idea that the frontier, whether regional or conceptual, is valuable as a discursive framework within which to study the process of interaction.

Much like Heraklios' destruction of the frontier, we have moved toward a final deconstruction. The frontier, no longer a means to an end, is a tool with which to address problems across disciplines. As such, the frontiers in history have become defined by the research and range of disciplines involved in their understanding. Perceptions of frontiers are a product of the disciplines that created them. It is no wonder that the frontier has been reified both by historians and by archaeologists as encompassing multivalent, pluralistic layers, as these perceptions have been motivated by the diverse disciplines and ambitious attentions brought to bear on the subject. The study of frontiers thus far has expanded into an interdisciplinary discussion that at the same time has raised certain borders. Examining the *thughūr* has shown how our own disciplines (whether archaeology, history, art history or literature) determine where we place our own frontiers and whether they are, in fact, real or imagined. In studying these sets of liminal processes and change, our own interdisciplinary interactions become imbedded participants in the creation of frontiers. At present, the state of the frontier seems not to reside in its function, which has been dismantled in its monumental form and rebuilt over and over again across diverse socio-physical geographies. A total deconstruction of the concept of the frontier would have made for a very short book. Rather, this deconstruction becomes a point of departure with which to rebuild or repopulate the frontier, bridging the disciplinary divide and creating something new in the process: an epistemological *'imāra*.

NOTES

Introduction Islamic Frontiers, Real and Imagined

1. The quote in two parts comes from two sources. The first: Balādhurī, *Futūḥ al-buldān* (Beirut: Dār al-Nashr lil-Jāmi'īyīn, 1957–8), p. 186. Translation following Hitti, *Origins of the Islamic State* (Piscataway, NJ: Gorgias Press, 2002), p. 210. The second of al-Azdī, *Ta'rīkh futūḥ al-Shām* (Cairo: Mū'assasat sijil al-'arab, 1970), 236-17-20. Translation following L. I. Conrad, 'Heraclius in Early Islamic Kerygma', in G. J. Renink and B. H. Stolte (eds), *The Reign of Heraclius (610–641): Crisis and Confrontation* (Dudley, MA: Peeters, 2002), p. 145. It is interesting to note the tradition of a letter supposedly sent by the Prophet Muḥammad to the Emperor Heraklios. In the letter, written several centuries later, the Prophet invokes the sin of the *arīsīyīn* (husbandmen or tillers of other's soil) on the Byzantines. Conrad has analysed this to read a reference to the Parable of the Husbandmen in Matthew 21: 33–41 but redirected whereby Heraklios and his Byzantine Christians should convert or else be 'driven out of the vineyard', and replaced by the Arabs who would better respect and rule in the name of God, the ultimate landowner. Idem, pp. 128–30.
2. S. P. Huntington, 'The Clash of Civilizations?', *Foreign Affairs* 72/3 (Summer 1993), p. 31.
3. Balādhurī, *Futūḥ al-buldān* (1957–8), p. 224. Translation mostly following P. K. Hitti, trans., *Origins of the Islamic State*, p. 253. The emphasis is mine. Hitti translated the verb *sha'atha* as to shatter, however the word implies a less aggressive act of disuniting, scattering, dissolving or disorganizing. This suggests that Heraklios did not destroy the forts but allowed them to fall into disrepair. Interestingly, of the Syriac authors only Dionysius of Maḥrē includes this account of North Syrian devastation, leading some to suggest a Miaphysite polemic against Heraklios; see R. Hoyland, trans. *Theophilus of Edessa's Chronicle*

and the Circulation of Historical Knowledge in Late Antiquity and Early Islam (Liverpool: Liverpool University Press, 2011), p. 107: fn. 231.

4. Ṭabarī, *Ta'rīkh*, 2.2396 (Arabic text) and vol. 12, p. 182 (English text).
5. This occurred in either 711–12/712–13 according to Ibn Shaddād, *al-'Alāq al-Khaṭīra fī Dhikr Umarā' al-Shām wa'l-Jazīra*, Vol. 2 (Damascus: Manshūrāt Wizārat al-Thaqāfah, 1956–91), p. 127 and others, or pp. 808–9/809–10, Balādhurī [after al-Wāqidī], *Futūḥ al-buldān* (Beirut: Mu'assasa al-Ma'arif, 1987), p. 233. Ibn Shaddād, *al-'Alāq al-Khaṭīra*, p. 153 (for Ṭarsūs), p. 128 (for Mar'ash), p. 127 (for Sīs).
6. Conrad, 'Heraclius in Early Islamic Kerygma', p. 146.
7. R.-J. Lilie, *Die Byzantinische Reaktion auf die Ausbreitung der Araber* (Munich: Institut für Byzantinistik und Neugriechische Philologie der Universität, 1976), cultivation: pp. 76–7, 114–15, destruction: p. 146.
8. T. F. Glick, *From Muslim Fortress to Christian Castle: Social and Cultural Change in Medieval Spain* (Manchester: Manchester University Press, 1995), p. 113.
9. E. Manzano Moreno, 'The Creation of a Medieval Frontier: Islam and Christianity in the Iberian Peninsula, Eighth to Eleventh Centuries', in *Frontiers in Question*, pp. 32–54; Glick, *From Muslim Fortress to Christian Castle*, p. 114.
10. J.-M. Fiey, 'The Syriac population of the Thughūr al-Shāmiya and the 'Awāṣim, and its relation with the Byzantines and Muslims', in M. A. al-Bakhit and R. Schick (eds), *Bilād al-Shām during the 'Abbāsid Period (132 A.H./750 A.D.–451 A.H./1059 A.D.)*, proceedings of the 5th International Conference on Bilad al-Sham (Amman: Lajnat Tārīkh Bilād al-Shām, 1991), p. 43.
11. A. Kazhdan and G. Constable, *People and Power in Byzantium* (Washington, DC: Dumbarton Oaks, 1982), p. 41; A. Rambaud, *L'Empire Grec au Dixième Siècle: Constantin Porphyrogénète* (New York, NY: Burt Franklin, 1963), p. 302, n. 6; Constantius VII Porphyrogenitus, *De Ceremoniis aulae Byzantinae* (lib. 1.84–2.56), J. J. Reisk, ed. (Bonn: Weber, 1829), p. 472.15, 486.12, 488.2.
12. W. A. Farag, 'Byzantium and its Muslim Neighbours During the Reign of Basil II (976–1025)', PhD dissertation, University of Birmingham, 1979, p. 12; J. F. Haldon and H. Kennedy, 'The Arab-Byzantine Frontier in the Eighth and Ninth Centuries: Military Organization and Society in the Borderlands', *Zbornik Radova Vizantoloski Institut (Recueil des Travaux de l'Institut d'Études Byzantines)* (Belgrade) 19 (1980), p. 109; H. Kennedy, *The Prophet and the Age of the Caliphates* (Essex: Longman, 1986), pp. 277–8; P. Wheatley, *The Places Where Men Pray Together: Cities in Islamic Lands, Seventh through the Tenth Centuries* (Chicago, IL: University of Chicago Press, 2001), pp. 120, 187, 262.
13. For an excellent, if now somewhat dated catalog and analysis of Byzantine and Arab sources for the early Islamic conquests at this period, see Lilie, *Die Byzantinische Reaktion*, pp. 133–42.
14. Ibid., pp. 162–9, which ascribes successful Byzantine defense after 720 to the themes and tegmata, pp. 287–338, esp. 338. A. M. Abu Ezzah, 'The Syrian Thughūr', PhD dissertation, University of Exeter, 1980, p. 69 attributes this to 'Umar II who ceased the expansionist aims of the earlier Umayyads and opened

diplomatic dialogues of religion with the Byzantine emperor, Leo III. However, several raids ventured far into Anatolian territory such as the Sea of Marmara (781 CE), Ephesus (798 CE), Ankara (806 CE), Cappadocia (830 and 831 CE), Amorion and Ankara (838 CE). These were not expansionist as they did not conquer Anatolian lands. Rather, these deep penetrations were usually led by the caliphs themselves, such as Hārūn al-Rashīd, Ma'mūn, and Mu'taṣim.

15. For instance, A. A. Vasiliev, *Byzance et les Arabes* (Bruxelles: Institut de philologie et d'histoire orientales, 1935); M. A. Cheïra, *La Lutte entre arabes et byzantins: La conquête et l'organisation des frontières aus XIIe et VIIIe siècles* (Alexandria: Société de publications Égyptiennes, 1947).
16. Mathisen and Sivan, Introduction, *Shifting Frontiers*.
17. J. Haldon, *Byzantium in the Seventh Century: the Transformation of a Culture,* Revised Edition (New York, NY: Cambridge University Press, 1997), pp. 1–2; Haldon and Kennedy, 'The Arab-Byzantine Frontier'; W. E. Kaegi, 'The Frontier, Barrier or Bridge?', *The 17th International Byzantine Congress: Major Papers* (New Rochelle, NY: A.D. Caratzas, 1986), pp. 279–303. See also Abu Ezzah, 'The Syrian Thughūr'; P. von Sivers, 'Taxes and Trade in the Abbasid Thughūr, pp. 750–962/133–351', *Journal of the Economic and Social History of the Orient* 25 (1982), p. 71; I. Straughn, 'Materializing Islam: An Archaeology of Landscape in Early Islamic Syria (c. 600–1000 CE)', PhD dissertation, University of Chicago, 2006; M. Bonner, *Aristocratic Violence and Holy War: Studies in the Jihād and the Arab-Byzantine Frontier* (New Haven , CT: American Oriental Society, 1996); M. Bonner, Introduction to M. Bonner (ed.) *Arab-Byzantine Relations in Early Islamic Times* (Burlington, VT: Ashgate, 2004), pp. xiii–lv; M. A. Shaban, *Islamic History: A New Interpretation,* Volume 2, *A.D. 750–1055 (A.H. 132–448)* (Cambridge: Cambridge University Press, 1976); K. Durak, 'Local, Regional, and International Trade in Medieval Cilicia: A case study of Byzantine-Islamic Trade in the 10th century', in *The Center and Periphery in the Age of Constantine VII Porphyrogennetos* (12–14 November 2009), Oxford Studies in Byzantium (2013, in publication); idem, 'Traffic across the Cilician Frontier: Movement of People between Byzantium and the Islamic Near East in the Early Middle Ages', in *Byzantium and the Arab World, Encounter of Civilizations*, Thessalonica (16–18 December 2011) (2013, in publication).
18. For example, R.-J. Lilie, 'The Byzantino-Arab Borderland from the Seventh to the Ninth Century', in *Borders Barriers*, pp. 13–21.
19. P. Wittek, 'Deux Chapitres de l'histoire des Turcs de Roum', *Byzantion* 11 (1936), pp. 285–319.
20. Ibn Manẓūr, *Lisān al-'Arab* (Egypt: Dar El-Hadith, 2003), Volume 1, pp. 676–8; J.G. Hava, *al-Faraid Arabic-English Dictionary,* Fifth Edition (Beirut: Dār el-Mashreq, 1982), p. 69.
21. H. Kennedy, 'Syrian Elites from Byzantium to Islam: Survival or Extinction?', in J. Haldon (ed), *Money, Power, and Politics in Early Islamic Syria: A Review of Current Debates* (Burlington, VT: Ashgate, 2010), pp. 181–200. Kennedy also

questions the existence of a no man's land, raising the likelihood that 'many may have sunk into poverty and obscurity'.

22. I. Kopytoff, 'The internal African frontier: the making of African political culture', in I. Kopytoff (ed.), *The African Frontier: The Reproduction of Traditional African Societies* (Bloomington: Indiana University Press, 1987), p. 25.
23. Ibn Shaddād, *al-'Alāq al-Khaṭīra*, p. 150.
24. See F. Curta, Introduction to *Borders Barriers*, pp. 1–9; see also the following edited volumes: *Medieval Frontier Societies*; *Shifting Frontiers*; *Frontiers in Question; Medieval Frontiers.*
25. P. Squatriti, 'Moving Earth and Making Difference: Dikes and Frontiers in Early Medieval Bulgaria', in *Borders Barriers*, pp. 59–60; W. Pohl, 'Frontiers and Ethnic Identities: Some Final Considerations', in *Borders Barriers*, pp. 255–65.
26. P. G. Dalché, 'De la Liste a la Carte: Limite et Frontière dans la Géographie et la Cartographie de l'Occident Médieval', in *Castrum* 7, pp. 19–31.
27. M. Kulikowski, 'Ethnicity, Rulership, and Early Medieval Frontiers', in *Borders Barriers*, pp. 247–54; Pohl, 'Frontiers and Ethnic Identities'.
28. R. W. Brauer, *Boundaries and Frontiers in Medieval Muslim Geography* (Philadelphia, PA: American Philosophical Society, 1995).
29. As such, J. Z. Smith argues against any universalizing mythology in Islam but an opportunistic value assigned to space: 'Map is not Territory', in Smith, J. Z., *Map is Not Territory: Studies in the History of Religions* (Chicago, IL: University of Chicago Press, 1993), pp. 289–310.
30. Traditional views in S. T. Parker, *Romans and Saracens: A History of the Arabian Frontier* (Winona Lake, IN: Eisenbrauns, 1986). To this we may add recent papers by A. M. Smith II, 'Reconsidering the *Territorium* of Roman Aila' and G. Davies, 'The Roman Fort at Yotvata in its Regional Context' (papers presented at the annual meeting of the American Schools of Oriental Research [ASOR], San Diego, CA, 2007). Administrative view in P. Mayerson, 'Towards a Comparative Study of a Frontier', *Israel Exploration Journal* 40/4 (1990), p. 267; B. Isaac, *The Limits of Empire: The Roman Army in the East* (New York, NY: Oxford University Press, 1992). Economic view in J. Eadie, 'Transformation of the Eastern Frontier', in *Shifting Frontiers*, pp. 72–82; J. Magness, *The Archaeology of Early Islamic Settlement in Palestine* (Winona Lake, IN: Eisenbrauns, 2003). Interactive zone in H. Elton, 'Defining Romans, Barbarians, and the Roman Frontier', in *Shifting Frontiers*, pp. 126–35; C. R. Whittaker, *Frontiers of the Roman Empire: A Social and Economic Study* (Baltimore, MD: Johns Hopkins University Press, 1994).
31. J. F. Drinkwater, '"The Germanic Threat on the Rhine Frontier": A Romano-Gallic Artefact?', in *Shifting Frontiers*, pp. 20–30.
32. T. Rooke, 'Writing the boundary, *Khitat al-Shām* by Muhammad Kurd 'Ali', in Y. Hiroyuki (ed.), *The Concept of Territory in Islamic Law and Thought*, (London: Kegan Paul International, 2000), p. 180.
33. D. H. Miller, 'Frontier Societies and the Transition Between Late Antiquity and the Early Middle Ages', in *Shifting Frontiers*, p. 169.

34. D. Olster, 'From Periphery to Center: The Transformation of Late Roman Self-Definition in the Seventh Century', in *Shifting Frontiers*, pp. 93–104; Pohl, 'Frontiers and Ethnic Identities'. See J. E. L. de Coca Castañer, 'Institutions on the Castilian-Granadan Frontier, pp. 1369–1482', in *Medieval Frontier Societies*, pp. 127–50; R. Amitai-Press, 'Northern Syria Between the Mongols and Mamluks: Political Boundary, Military Frontier, and Ethnic Affinities', in *Frontiers in Question*, pp. 128–52; A. Williams, 'Crusaders as Frontiersmen: The Case of the Order of St. John in the Mediterranean', in *Frontiers in Question*, pp. 209–27.
35. As seen on the Byzantine–Slavic Danube frontier: F. Curta, 'Frontier Ethnogenesis in Late Antiquity: The Danube, the Tervingi, and the Slavs', in *Borders Barriers*, pp. 173–204.
36. An example of this occurred with the large influx of Turks and Mongols to the Near East in the twelfth and thirteenth centuries, which turned the central lands of the Levant and Iraq into a frontier. For the Crusaders: R. Ellenblum, 'Were there Borders and Borderlines in the Middle Ages? The Example of the Latin Kingdom of Jerusalem', in *Frontiers in Question*, pp. 105–19; and J. Riley-Smith, 'Government and the Indigenous in the Latin Kingdom of Jerusalem', in *Medieval Frontiers*, pp. 121–31. For the Ottomans, see C. Heywood, 'The Frontier in Ottoman History: Old Ideas and New Myths', in *Frontiers in Question*, pp. 228–50. Most recent are A. Gabbay, *Islamic Tolerance: Amīr Khusraw and Pluralism* (New York, NY: Routledge, 2010); R. Haug, 'The Gate of Iron: The Making of the Eastern Frontier', PhD dissertation, University of Michigan, 2010; and M. Luce, 'Frontier as Process: Umayyad Khurasan', PhD dissertation, University of Chicago, 2009.
37. For example in the *Life* of St Simeon of the Olives, he writes of the Islamic conquest: 'After a little bit, the Arabs came and laid waste to all of the cities of the East'. *Life* of St Simeon of the Olives, text and translation by Jack Tannous, unpublished, number p. 10.
38. See also, for example, the recent Materiality in Islam Reserach Initiative, 'Materiality of the Islamic Rural Economy', held at the University of Copenhagen, pp. 24–25 August 2012, organized by S. McPhillips and P. Wordworth.
39. T. J. Wilkinson, *Archaeological Landscapes of the Near East* (Tucson: University of Arizona Press, 2003), particularly pp. 128–50.
40. Ward-Perkins, 'Land, Labour, and Settlement', *Cambridge Ancient History* 14 (2001), p. 324.
41. Most recent exceptions around the frontier region have been by surveys that have found campsites using intensive survey, see J. A. Ur and E. Hammer, 'Pastoral Nomads of the Second and Third Millenia AD on the Upper Tigris River, Turkey: Archaeological Evidence from the Hirbemerdon Tepe Survey', *Journal of Field Archaeology* 34 (2009), pp. 37–56; K. Alizadeh and J. A. Ur, 'Formation and Destruction of Pastoral and Irrigation Landscapes on the Mughan Steppe, North-Western Iran', *Antiquity* 81/311 (2007), pp. 148–60.
42. Throughout this book, the term Late Roman is used instead of Byzantine as a cultural designation rather than a political period. This is because there is direct continuity both in terms of settlement patterns and material culture with the

Roman period that is not easy to separate. Late Roman here refers to the conventional range of the Byzantine period (or early Byzantine; fourth through mid-seventh centuries), not to the chronological range sometimes attributed to the Late Roman period as an interstice between Roman and Byzantine (second–third centuries). In describing the central state and certain communities, particularly after the mid-seventh century, I retain the term Byzantine (i.e. Byzantine army, Byzantine reconquest). Middle Byzantine refers to those areas under Byzantine rule between the ninth and thirteenth centuries.

43. A. Walmsley, *Early Islamic Syria* (London: Gerald Duckworth & Co. Ltd., 2007), pp. 15–47.
44. I. Straughn, 'Materializing Islam'; T. Zadeh, Mapping Frontiers Across Medieval Islam: Geography, Translation, and the 'Abbasid Empire (London: I. B. Tauris, 2011); Z. Antrim, *Routes and Realm: The Power of Place in the Early Islamic World* (New York, NY: Oxford University Press, 2012, Second Edition, 2014, forthcoming).
45. For example, A. Northedge, 'Archaeology and New Urban Settlement in Early Islamic Syria and Iraq', in G. R. D. King and A. Cameron, *The Byzantine and Early Islamic Near East*, Vol. II, *Land Use and Settlement Patterns* (Princeton, NJ: The Darwin Press, Inc., 1989), pp. 232 and 265.
46. As a companion to this volume, and for more discussion on the frontier towns themselves, see A. A. Eger, *The Spaces Between the Teeth: A Gazetteer of Towns on the Islamic-Byzantine Frontier* (Istanbul: Ege Yayınları, 2012, Second Edition, 2014, forthcoming).
47. Bonner (*Aristocratic Violence and Holy War*, p. 66; 'The Naming of the Frontier: 'Awāṣim, Thughūr, and the Arab Geographers', *Bulletin of the School of Oriental and African Studies* 57 (1994), pp. 17–24) asserts that the creation of the *'awāṣim* in the first year of Hārūn al-Rashīd's reign was a political move designed to break up the province known as the Umayyad North (including Armenia, Azerbaijan, and the *thughūr*) and consolidate the frontier into a separate but unified administrative province that he could personally supervise and in which he would be able to eliminate local accumulations of power under stray commanders. Straughn states that territorial ambiguities may have been an indication that the articulation of the frontier was *not* a political enterprise, as then it would have been more clearly defined, 'Materializing Islam', p. 164.
48. Abu Ezzah states that the term *al-'awāṣim* was used interchangeably and inconsistently with *al-thughūr*; perhaps *al-'awāṣim* was a term given locally to a region as a matter of pride, 'The Syrian Thughūr', p. 94.
49. I use the term Middle Islamic to denote the tenth through fourteenth centuries. This term is slightly inaccurate and debated, given that during part of this period the frontier region was under Byzantine and Crusader/Frankish rule. This period has been called Middle Byzantine or, more commonly, Medieval. I use Middle Islamic as a generalizing term, and one that perhaps addresses the continuity of local traditions and cultural influence rather than political periodization – much like the use of Late Roman instead of Byzantine.

Part I The Syro-Anatolian *Thughūr*

1. Bonner, *Aristocratic Violence and Holy War*, pp. 57, 85, 140; Bonner, 'The Naming of the Frontier', p. 18.
2. Ur and Hammer, 'Pastoral Nomads', p. 38.
3. M. Decker has produced an overview of many of the surveys in the frontier region, with keen observations on settlement patterns in the Byzantine and Early Islamic periods and an important discussion on land-use strategies on the Byzantine (Cappadocian) frontier. He also draws attention to the importance of regional variation. See 'Frontier Settlement and Economy in the Byzantine East', *Dumbarton Oaks Papers* 61 (2007), p. 222; and idem, 'Settlement and agriculture in the Levant, 6th–8th centuries', in A. Borrut, M. Debié, A. Papaconstantinou, D. Pieri, and J.-P. Sodini (eds), *Le Proche-Orient de Justinien aux Abbasides: Peuplement et Dynamiques Spatiales* (Turnhout, Belgium: Brepols, 2011), pp. 1–6. Hugh Kennedy also refers to micro-regions in this area, Introduction, 'Syrian Elites from Byzantium to Islam: Survival or Extinction?', pp. xii–xiii.
4. In independent projects by T. J. Wilkinson (Fragile Crescent Project, Durham, UK), J. Casana and J. Cothren (Department of Anthropology and Center for Advanced Spatial Technologies, University of Arkansas), and myself. N. Galiatsatos, T. J. Wilkinson, D. N. M. Donoghue, and G. Philip, 'The Fragile Crescent Project (FCP): analysis of settlement landscapes using satellite imagery', *CAA 2009: Making History Interactive*, Williamsburg, VA, pp. 22–26 March 2009; J. Casana, J. Cothren, and T. Kalaycı, 'Swords into Ploughshares: Archaeological Applications of CORONA Satellite Imagery in the Near East', *Internet Archaeology* 32 (2012). Available at http://dx.doi.org/10.11141/ia.32.2 (accessed 3 May 2013).
5. For comparison with other survey methodologies: in the North Jazira Survey, assemblage size was divided between significant (more than six sherds) and minor (less than six) with the inference that minor sites may be nomadic temporary camps that morphologically have less ceramic refuse. Elsewhere, sites with one or two sherds are considered nomadic sites or sites with eight or fewer diagnostics. T. J. Wilkinson and D. J. Tucker, *Settlement Development in theNorth Jazira, Iraq: A Study of the Archaeological Landscape* (Baghdad: British School of Archaeology in Iraq, 1995), Table 12, pp. 69 and p. 71.
6. Current surveys are excluded from this table as they are largely unpublished save for preliminary reports and papers.

Chapter 1 The Central *Thughūr*: The Two Amuqs

1. Nu'aym b. Ḥammad, *Kitāb al-Fitan*, MS Brit. Mus. *Or*, 9449, folios 119b–20a, translated by W. Madelung, 'Apocalpytic Prophecies in Hims in the Umayyad Age', *Journal of Semitic Studies*, p. 174.

2. A. A. Eger, 'The Swamps of Home: Marsh Formation and Settlement in the Early Medieval Near East', *Journal of Near Eastern Studies* 70/1 (April 2011), pp. 55–79.
3. U. Bahadır Alkım, 'The Amanus Region in Turkey: New Light on the Historical Geography and Archaeology', *Archaeology* 22/4 (1969), pp. 280–9.
4. R. Braidwood, *Mounds in the Plain of Antioch* (Chicago, IL: University of Chicago, 1937), p. 46.
5. Ibid. See Wilkinson, *Archaeological Landscapes of the Near East*, pp. 128ff.; J. Casana, 'From Alalakh to Antioch: Settlement, Land Use, and Environmental Change in the Amuq Plain of Southern Turkey', PhD dissertation, University of Chicago, 2003, 254ff.
6. Du Plat Taylor, M. V. Seton-Williams, and J. Waechter, 'Excavations at Sakçe Gözü', *Iraq* 12 (1950), p. 61.
7. The Islamic material from the post 2005 surveys will be published in the forthcoming AVRP Vol. 2. F. Gerritsen, A. U. de Giorgi, A. Eger, R. Özbal, and T. Vorderstrasse, 'Settlement and Landscape Transformations in the Amuq Valley, Hatay: A Long-Term Perspective', *Anatolica* 34 (2008), pp. 241–314. For recent preliminary reports, see K. A. Yener, 'Amik Vadisi Bölgesel Projesi 2006 Yılı Yüzey Araştırmaları', *AST* 25/1 (2007), pp. 341–8; L. Dodd, A. Green, and A. Yener, 'The Amuq Valley Regional Survey Project 2009', *AST* 28.1 (2010), pp. 435–52; L. Dodd, A. Green, N. Highcock, L. Cadwell, and A. Yener, 'The 2010 Amuq Valley Regional Projects Survey', *AST* 29/2 (2011), pp. 205–24; J. Casana and T. J. Wilkinson, 'Settlement and landscapes in the Amuq region', in K. Aslhan Yener, (ed.), *The Amuq Valley Regional Reports, Vol. 1. Surveys in the Plain of Antioch and Orontes Delta Survey, 1995–2002* (Chicago, IL: Oriental Institute Publications, 2005), pp. 25–66; J. Casana, 'Mediterranean Valleys Revisited: Linking Soil Erosion, Land Use, and Climate Variability in the Northern Levant', *Geomorphology* 101/3 (2008), pp. 429–42; idem, 'Structural Transformations in Settlement Systems of the Northern Levant'. *AJA* 111/2 (2007), pp. 195–222; idem, 'The archaeological landscape of Late Roman Antioch', in I. Sandwell and J. Huskinson (eds), *Culture and Society in Late Roman Antioch: Papers from a Colloquium, London, 15th December 2001* (Oakville, CT: David Brown Book Company, 2002) pp. pp. 102–25.
8. D. Whitcomb, 'Letters from the Field: In Search of Lost Mar'ash', *The Oriental Institute News and Notes* 171 (Fall 2001).
9. A more recent Turkish survey in the Kahramanmaraş Plain and north of the city around the Elbistan and Afşin Plains has been ongoing since 2006, but preliminary reports focus only on the Iron Age and give no evidence on Late Roman or Islamic settlements. E. Konyar, 'Kahramanmaraş Yüzey Araştırması 2007', *AST* 26/2 (2008), pp. 175–86; idem, 'Kahramanmaraş 2009 Yılı Yüzey Araştırması', *AST* 28/2 (2010), pp. 263–71; E.Konyar, 'Surveys in Kahramanmaraş in 2010', *ANMED* 9 (2011), pp. 174–9; E. Konyar, M. Doğan-Alparslan, and M. Alparslan, 'Kahramanmaraş Yüzey Araştırması 2010', *AST* 29/2 (2011), pp. 35–50.

10. The corridor of the Kara Su Valley bridging the two plains has not been completely surveyed. The 2010–11 AVRP survey included the territory up to just north of Hassa, leaving the Gaziantep province mainly unsurveyed. An informal survey was carried out by U. Bahadır Alkım around 1955. See U. Bahadır Alkim, 'The Road from Samal to Asitawandawa', *Anadolu Araştırmaları* 2 (1965), pp. 1–45 and idem, 'The Amanus Region in Turkey', *Archaeology* 22 (1969) pp. 280–9. As the survey concentrated on Bronze and Iron Age transportation routes and their sites. There are hardly any Byzantine or Islamic sites mentioned. Future survey around the University of Chicago excavations at Zincirli may fill in this gap.
11. H. Pamir and G. Brands, 'The Asi Delta and Valley Archaeological Project in 2004: Samandağ and Antakya Surveys', *Anadolu Akdenizi Arkeoloji Haberleri* 3 (2005), pp. 103–9; idem, 'Asi Deltası ve Asi Vadisi Arkeoloji Projesi Antiocheia, Seleuceia Pieria ve Sabuniye Yüzey Araştırmaları 2004 Yılı Çalışmaları', *AST* 23/2 (2006), pp. 89–102; G. Brands and C. Meyer, 'Antioch-on-the-Orontes and Seleucia Pieria 2004: Preliminary Results of the Geophysical Survey', *Arkeometri Sonuçları Toplantısı* 21 (2005), pp. 149–54; H. Pamir and G. Brands, 'Asi Deltası ve Asi Vadisi Arkeolojisi Projesi Antakya ve Samandağ Yüzey Araştırmaları 2005', *AST* 24/2 (2007), pp. 397–418; H. Pamir, G. Brands, and F. Çevirici, 'Hatay Ili, Antakya, Samandağ ve Yayladağı Yüzey Araştırması 2006', *AST* 25/3 (2008), pp. 393–412; H. Pamir, G. Brands, and S. Nishiyama, 'Hatay Ili, Antakya ve Samandağ Yüzey Araştırması 2007', *AST* 26/3 (2009), pp. 1–12; H. Pamir, 'Hatay Ili Antakya, Samandağı, Altınözü ve Yayladağı Yüzey Araştırmaları 2009', *AST* 28/3 (2010), pp. 371–98; H. Pamir and İ. Yamaç, 'Hatay Yüzey Araştırmaları 2010 Antakya, Samandağ, Yayladağı ve Altınözü', *AST* 29/2 (2011), pp. 361–78.
12. This does not include the pp. 2008–12 material, not yet completed at the time of writing and part of the Late Roman material.
13. It should also be mentioned that not every site of the total number (254) could be dated, due to the lack (or near lack) of diagnostic ceramics. These sites were marked by architectural or industrial/installation traces and included tombs, quarries, and temporary encampments.
14. The wide number range reflects the fact that the Late Roman analysis, started by E. Laflı, was not finished at the time of writing and I am using my own approximations. E. Mullane carried out quantitative modelling of the results for the broad 'Early Historic' period (550 BCE–650 CE) and projected an average statistic of additional sites from the two intensive surveys onto the entire plain, coming up with a total of 264 sites and covering an area of 535 ha and estimated population of 62,000. The 'Medieval' period (pp. 650–1500) total number was slightly less (249 sites), but significantly less in total area (390 ha) and population (47,000), showing nucleated rather than dispersed settlement. E. Mullane, 'Patterns in the Past: Model Building and the Identification of Settlement Change in the Kahramanmarash Archaeological Survey Project, Turkey', MA thesis, UCLA, p. 2005.

15. Mullane (Ibid., 27) also demonstrated a halving of sites from the 'Early Historic' to 'Medieval' periods.
16. Magness, *The Archaeology of Early Islamic Settlement in Palestine*, p. 21.
17. G. Avni, *Nomads, Farmers, and Town-Dwellers: Pastoralist-Sedentist Interaction in the Negev Highlands, Sixth-Eighth Centuries CE* (Jerusalem: Israel Antiquities Authority, 1996), p. 8.
18. Yaghrā has also been incorrectly associated with the classical site of Meleagrum, mainly based on the corruption of the name. For a discussion, see A. U. de Giorgi, 'The Formation of a Roman Landscape: The Case of Antioch', *Journal of Roman Archaeology* 20 (2007), p. 293.
19. Abū al-Fidā', *Kitāb taqwīm al-buldān*, in M. Reinaud and M. le Baron MacGuckin de Slane, *Géographie d'Aboulféda. Texte Arabe publié d'après les manuscrits de Paris et de Leyde aux frais de la Société Asiatique* (Paris: Imprimerie Royale, 1840) pp. 41–2.
20. R. L. Devonshire, 'Relation d'un voyage du sultain Qâitbây en Palestine et en Syrie', *Bulletin de l'Institut Français d'Archéologie Orientale* 20 (1922), pp. 1–43. See A. Eger, 'Patronage and Commerce at the Twilight of Mamluk Rule: Two new Fifteenth Century Inscriptions from the Amuq Plain, Turkey,' *Journal of Islamic Archaeology* 1.1 (2014), pp. 53–72.
21. Theodoret, *A History of the Monks of Syria* (Kalamazoo, MI: Cistercian Publications, 1985) Vol. II, pp. 1–2, 69.
22. L. Jalabert and R. Mouterde, 'Gabal al-A'la', *Inscriptions Grecques et Latines de la Syrie*, Volume 2 (Paris: Libraire Orientaliste Paul Geuthner, 1939), 338 (#624); V. Chapot, *La frontière de l'Euphrate de Pompée à la conquiste Arabe* (Paris, A. Fontemoing, 1907), p. 343.
23. Ibn Buṭlān in Yāqūt, *Mu'jam al-buldān* (Beirut: Dār Sādr, 1955–7), 4.157.
24. Ibn Shaddād, *al-'Alāq al-Khaṭīra*, p. 138; P. Jacquot, *Antioche centre de tourisme* (Paris: Comité de tourisme d'Antioche, 1931), p. 442.
25. G. Tchalenko, *Villages antiques de la Syrie du Nord: Le massif du Bélus a l'époque romaine, I–III* (Paris: Paul Geuthner, 1953–8), p. 153.
26. Ibn Shaddad, 2. pp. 323–7.
27. E. Carter and S. Campbell, 'Report on the 2004 Excavation Season at Domuztepe', *KST* 27.1 (2005), p. 316; S. Campbell, 'Domuztepe 2005', *Anatolian Archaeology* 11 (2005), p. 15; idem, 'Domuztepe 2004 Excavation Season', *Anatolian Archaeology* 10 (2004), p. 5; idem, 'Domuztepe 2003', *Anatolian Archaeology* 9 (2003), p. 6. Limited information has been published thus far on the late periods at Domuztepe; see J. Snead, 'The Local Survey around Domuztepe', UCLA Archaeological Projects in Turkey. Available at www.humnet.ucla.edu/humnet/nelc/stelasite/james.html (accessed 3 May 2013).
28. Campbell, 'Domuztepe 2005', p. 15.
29. J. Pearson is currently working on the skeletal remains, which are as yet unpublished. Excavations of the cemetery are not complete, and more graves (five to ten) are expected to be found.
30. I am grateful to K. Grossman for making available her preliminary analysis on the faunal assemblage from Operation 7.

31. A. Palmer, *The Seventh Century in the West-Syrian Chronicles* (Liverpool: Liverpool University Press, 1993), p. 71.
32. For the Muslim-instigated displacements, see Michael the Syrian, *Chronique de Michel le Syrien*, Volume 2, edited and translated by J.-B. Chabot (Paris: Ernest Leroux, 1901), p. 526.
33. Braidwood, *Mounds in the Plain of Antioch*, p. 45.
34. Balādhurī, *Futūh al-buldān* (1957–8), p. 225.
35. Gerritsen et al., 'Settlement and Landscape Transformations', pp. 262–3, 272.
36. T. Vorderstrasse, 'The Romanization and Christianization of the Antiochene region: the material evidence from three sites', in I. Sandwell and J. Huskinson (eds), *Culture and Society in Later Roman Antioch* (Oakville, CT: David Brown Book Company, 2002), pp. 91–4.
37. Theodoret, *A History of the Monks of Syria*, II.9, n. pp. 8–9; J. S. Trimingham, *Christianity among the Arabs in Pre-Islamic Times* (Beirut: Librairie du Liban, 1990), p. 104; John Malalas, *The Chronicle of John Malalas*, E. Jeffreys, M. Jeffreys, and R. Scott, trans. (Melbourne: Australian Association for Byzantine Studies, 1986): 13.347, p. 452.
38. See G. Dagron, 'Minorités ethniques et religieuses dans l'Orient Byzantin à la fin du Xe et au Xie siècles: L'immigration Syrienne', *Travaux et Memoires* 6 (1976), pp. 177–216.
39. Known as a Classical site and surveyed by G. H. Brown, 'Prehistoric Pottery from the Antitaurus', *Anatolian Studies* 17 (1967), p. 162.
40. E. Honigmann, *Le Couvent de Barsaumā et le Patriarcat Jacobite d'Antioch et de Syrie* (Louvain: L. Durbecq, 1954), p. 47 and n. 2, pp. 52–54, 116.
41. al-Dimashqī, *Manuel de la Cosmographie du Moyen Age*, A. F. Mehren, trans. (Copenhagen: C. A. Reitzel, 1875), p. 280; Behā ed-Dīn, *Life of Saladin,* L.-C. Condor, trans., Palestine Pilgrims' Text Society 13 (New York, NY: AMS Press, 1971), p. 135; Marino Sanuto, *Secrets for True Crusaders, to Help Them Recover the Holy Land.* Part 14 of book 3, Aubrey Stewart, trans., Palestine Pilgrims' Text Society 12 (New York, NY: AMS Press, 1971), p. 4 (as Trapasa); Ibn Shaddād, *al-'Alāq al-Khaṭīra*, p. 419. Indeed, one possible translation of Darbassāk, or *darb assāk*, may refer to a narrow path.
42. Abū al-Fidā', *Kitāb taqwīm al-buldān*, p. 261.
43. Balādhurī, *Futūḥ al-buldān* (1957–8), p. 229; Yāqūt, *Mu'jam al-buldān* (1955–7), 1.510; Ibn Shaddād, *al-'Alāq al-Khaṭīra*, pp. ii. 422. The site revealed one third-century ceramic sherd and three other sherds of indeterminate Byzantine or Early Islamic date. These may be associated with a nearby bath and tell. A. Eger, 'The Early Islamic Period (mid 7th to mid 10th centuries)' in Gerritsen et al., 'Settlement and Landscape Transformations', pp. 270–1.
44. Casana, 'From Alalakh to Antioch', p. 308.
45. See A. Eger, *The Spaces Between the Teeth: A Gazetteer*, p. 50 and R.W. Edwards, *Fortifications of Armenian Cilicia* (Washington, DC: Dumbarton Oaks Research Library and Collection, 1987), p. 416.
46. See also Edwards, *Fortifications of Armenian Cilicia*, p. 253, plates 246a, 247a, b.

47. Ibn Ḥawqal, *Kitāb ṣūrat al-arḍ* (Beirut: Manshurāt Dār Maktabat al-Ḥayā, 1964), p. 169.
48. Abū al-Fidā', *Kitāb taqwīm al-buldān*, p. 259.
49. Balādhurī, *Futūḥ al-buldān* (1957–8), p. 225.
50. Yāqūt, *Marāṣid al-ittilā' 'ala asma' al-amkina wa al-biqā'* (Beirut: Dār al-Jīl, 1992), p. i.209.
51. Procopius, *Of the Buildings of Justinian*, A. Stewart, trans., Palestine Pilgrims' Text Society 2 (New York, NY: AMS Press, 1971), p. 68.
52. For example, H. Kennedy, 'The Last Century of Byzantine Syria: A Reinterpretation', *Byzantinische Forschungen* 10 (1985), pp. 141–83.
53. Casana, 'From Alalakh to Antioch', 295; T. J. Wilkinson, 'Archaeological Survey in the Amuq Valley', *The Oriental Institute 2001–2002 Annual Report* (2002), p. 23.
54. Magness, *The Archaeology of Early Islamic Settlement in Palestine*, p. 344.
55. A. A. Eger, '(Re)Mapping Medieval Antioch: Urban Transformations from the Early Islamic to Crusader Periods', *Dumbarton Oaks Papers* 67 (2013).
56. T. Vorderstrasse, *Al-Mina: A Port of Antioch from Late Antiquity to the End of the Ottomans* (Leiden, the Netherlands: Nederlands Instituut Voor Het Nabije Oosten, 2005).
57. Evliya Çelebi, *Seyahatnâmesi*, S. A. Kahraman and Y. Dağlı, translit. (Istanbul: Yapı Kredi Kültür Sanat Yayıncılık, 1999), vol. 3, p. 102.

Chapter 2 The Central *Thughūr*: The Steppe and the River

1. Ibn Buṭlān in G. Le Strange, *Palestine under the Moslems* (Beirut: Khayats, 1965), p. 370; on a journey from Ḥalab to Anṭākya in 1051 C.E. as quoted by *Mu'jam al-buldān* (1990), Yāqūt, *Mu'jam al-buldān* (1990), 2.266–70.
2. Ṭabarī, *Ta'rīkh*, III. 604 (Arabic) and vol. 30, p. 99 (English).
3. Which may have originally been named Nahr Ṭarṭar, Classical Dardas; see R. Dussaud, *Topographie Historique de la Syrie Antique et Medievale* (Paris: P. Geuthner, 1927), p. 476.
4. T. J. Wilkinson, *On the Margin of the Euphrates: Settlement and Land Use at Tell es-Sweyhat and in the Upper Lake Assad area, Syria* (Chicago, IL: Oriental Institute of the University of Chicago, 2004), pp. 20–2.
5. For a list of towns and products, written in the fourteenth century, see Mustawfī (1281–1349), *Nuzhat al-Qulūb*, trans. G. Le Strange (Leiden: Brill, 1919), pp. 102–6 (Persian-text volume), pp. 102–5 (English-text volume).
6. Their use in non-Islamic sources was not to define them clearly, but rather to define Christian Arabs generally. The *ṭu'āyē* might have been the tribes of Bakr, 'Ijl, Namir, and Taghlib. See C. Robinson, 'Tribes and Nomads in Early Islamic Northern Mesopotamia', in *Continuity and Change*, pp. 429–52.
7. M. N. van Loon, 'The Tabqa Reservoir Survey 1964', *Annales Archéologiques Arabes Syriennes* (Damascus: Direction Générale des Antiquités et des Musées, 1967), p. 4.

8. Ibid., p. 5.
9. Ibid., p. 6.
10. A. Bahnassi, 'Le Sauvetage des Vestiges de la Zone de Submersion du Barrage de Tabqa sur l'Euphrate', *Monumentum* 17 (1978), p. 60.
11. The surveyors did not consider the Islamic pottery published at the colloquium on the archaeology of the Middle Euphrates in Strasbourg in March 1977, which was later published: R. Harper, 'Athis-Neocaesareia-Qasrin-Dibsi Faraj', in J. Cl. Margueron (ed.), *Le Moyen Euphrate: zone de contacts et d'échanges* (Leiden: E. J. Brill, 1980), pp. 327–48. Unfortunately, details of the pottery, unlike the coins, are not published with findspots.
12. R. Maxwell Hyslop, J. du Plat Taylor, M. V. Seton-Williams, and J. D'Arcy Waechter, 'An Archaeological Survey of the Plain of Jabbul, 1939', *Palestine Exploration Quarterly* 74 (1942), pp. 8–40.
13. H. de Contenson, 'Le matériel archéologique des tells', in P. Sanlaville (ed.), *Holocene Settlement in North Syria*, BAR IS 238 (Oxford, 1985), pp. 99–161, 167–78.
14. Yāqūt, *Mu'jam al-buldān* (1990), p. 1.558.
15. A. Archi, P.E. Pecorella, and M. Salvini, *Gaziantep e la Sua Regione: Uno studio storico e topografico degli insediamenti preclassici* (Rome: Edizioni dell'ateno, 1971), pp. 109–10.
16. G. M. Schwartz, H. H. Curvers, F. A. Gerritsen, J. A. MacCormack, N. F. Miller, and J. A. Weber, 'Excavation and Survey in the Jabbul Plain, Western Syria: The Umm el-Marra Project 1996–1997', *American Journal of Archaeology*, 104/3 (2000), pp. 419–62.
17. T. J. Wilkinson, E. Peltenburg, A. McCarthy, E. B. Wilkinson, and M. Brown, 'Archaeology in the Land of Carchemish: Landscape Surveys in the Area of Jerablus Tahtani, 2006'. *Levant* 39 (2007), pp. 213–47.
18. G. Algaze, G. Breuninger, and J. Knudstad, 'The Tigris-Euphrates Archaeological Reconnaissance Project: Final Report of the Birecik and Carchemish Dam Survey Areas', *Anatolica* 20 (1994), pp. 1–96; G. Algaze, R. Breuninger, C. Lightfoot, and M. Rosenberg, 'The Tigris-Euphrates Archaeological Reconnaissance Project, A Preliminary Report of the 1989–1990 Seasons', *Anatolica* 17 (1991), pp. 175–240; G. Algaze, 'First Results of the Tigris-Euphrates Archaeological Reconnaissance Project', *Journal of Near Eastern Studies* 48 (1989), pp. 241–81.
19. Between 1998 and 2000, the Middle East Technical University (METU) and the Centre for Research and Assessment of the Historic Environment (TAÇDAM) conducted salvage excavations on several of the sites surveyed by Algaze. This was in preparation for the impending Carchemish Dam construction. In all, 250 sites were recorded, 16 of which were excavated. See N. Tuna et al., *Ilısu ve Karkamış Baraj Gölleri Altında Kalacak Arkeolojik ve Kültür Varlıklarını Projesi* (Salvage Project of the Archaeological Heritage of the Ilısu and Carchemish Dam Reservoirs Activities), four yearly volumes (Ankara: METU, 1999–2002).

20. J. Matthers (ed.), *The River Qoueiq, Northern Syria, and its Catchment: Studies Arising from the Tell Rifa'at survey 1977–79*, BAR International Series (Oxford: BAR, 1981).
21. Group II, the most prolific brittleware, is seen at 24 sites, and thus important to correctly date. In Northedge's ware description, he dates it either to the Late Roman or Umayyad (to the eighth century) period by parallels, although in his site chart, he gives it a Late Roman date. See A. Northedge, 'Selected Late Roman and Islamic Coarse Wares', in Ibid., pp. 459–71. In A. Vokaer, 'Some new results of archaeometric analysis of brittle wares', in M. Bonifay and J.-C. Tréglia (eds), *LRCW 2. Late Roman Coarse Wares, Cooking Wares and Amphorae in the Mediterranean: Archaeology and Archaeometry*, Volume II BAR Is 1662 (II) (Oxford: Archaeopress, 2007), the ware is dated to the fourth/fifth centuries (see Figure 4.7, p. 725); idem, 'Brittle Ware Trade in Syria Between the 5th and 8th Centuries'. In *Byzantine Trade*, Byzantine type, Figure 8.5, 129 a fifth-century date is more comfortable (A. Vokaer, personal communication with the author, 2012).
22. Wilkinson, *On the Margin of the Euphrates*, pp. 20–2; D. Whitcomb, 'The Ceramic Sequence from Surveyed Sites', in idem, p. 99.
23. C. Tonghini, Qal'at Jabar Pottery: Study of a Syrian Fortified Site of the late 11–14th centuries (New York, NY: Oxford University Press, 1998), p. 17–18.
24. R. P. Harper and T. J. Wilkinson, 'Excavations at Dibsi Faraj, Northern Syria, 1972–1974: A Preliminary Note on the Site and its Monuments with an Appendix', *Dumbarton Oaks Papers* 29 (1975), p. 324.
25. R. P. Harper, 'Athis-Neocaesareia-Qasrin-Dibsi Faraj', in J. Cl. Margueron (ed.), *Le Moyen Euphrate: zone de contacts et d'échanges* (Leiden: E. J. Brill, 1980), pp. 341–3. However, it is possible that the hoard was deposited for safekeeping after the floor of the building had been laid down, making the date, during the reign of the Caliph Hishām, a *terminus ante quem* for the floor. Harper describes it as being 'in the earth fill', which suggests that it was below and prior to the date of the building. Several coins, identified with mints, come from Dimashq (Damascus) and Ḥimṣ (Emesa).
26. Harper and Wilkinson, Appendix, in 'Excavations at Dibsi Faraj', p. 337; T. J. Wilkinson and L. Rayne, 'Hydraulic Landscapes and Imperial Power', *Water History* 2(2), pp. 126–7.
27. Balādhurī, *Futūḥ al-buldān* (1987), p. 205. In Pseudo-Dionysius of Tell Maḥrē, *Chronicle of Zuqnīn, parts III and IV: A.D. 488–775*, A. Harrak trans. (Toronto: Pontifical Institute of Mediaeval Studies, 1999), both Hishām and Maslama dug a canal known as the Bēth Balish in or around 717–18, pp. 160–1.
28. Wilkinson and Rayne, 'Hydraulic Landscapes', p. 128.
29. Harper, 'Athis-Neocaesareia-Qasrin-Dibsi Faraj', p. 339, nos 74–7.
30. Theophilus of Edessa, *Chronicle*, p. 147.
31. D. Whitcomb, 'The Ceramic Sequence from Surveyed Sites', in Wilkinson, *On the Margin of the Euphrates*, p. 99.
32. Wilkinson et al., 'Archaeology in the Land of Carchemish', pp. 239, 244; Wilkinson and Rayne, 'Hydraulic Landscapes', p. 128.

33. Algaze et al., 'Tigris-Euphrates Archaeological Reconnaissance Project: Final Report', p. 19.
34. Ibid., 22 and Fig. 32. Also, see G. Algaze, *Town and Country in Southeastern Anatolia*, Volume 2: *The Stratigraphic Sequence at Kurban Höyük* (Chicago, IL: Oriental Institute, 1990), pp. 390–1 and notes 1–5, for details of parallels.
35. P. Kenrick, 'On the Silk Route: imported and regional pottery at Zeugma', in *Byzantine Trade*, pp. 265–72.
36. Michael the Syrian, *Chronique*, vol. 3, p. 504.
37. D. Kennedy, *The Twin Towns of Zeugma on the Euphrates: Rescue Work and Historical Studies* (Portsmouth, RI: Journal of Roman Archaeology, 1998), pp. 160–1.
38. The Early Islamic diagnostic pottery consisted of an unglazed 'long amphorae handle with applied knob on top' (eighth to tenth century) and a 'bowl base with a central protuberance, serving as a lid' (the couvercle type, seventh/eighth century). Algaze et al., 'Tigris-Euphrates Archaeological Reconnaissance Project: Final Report', p. 44. Decker states that the drop in Early Islamic settlement in this area may be due to depopulation, presumably after the conquests and emigration/deportation of the population to Byzantine territory ('Frontier Settlement and Economy', p. 230). Another explanation might be unrecognized Early Islamic transitional ceramics. The pottery for this survey, stored in a museum depot, is now gone (Guillermo Algaze, personal communication with the author, 2011).
39. Yāqūt, *Mu'jam al-buldān* (1990), p. 2.381.
40. Although four sites (Tell Akhtereine/9, Qara Keupru/58, Tell Sourane–Azaz/72, and Tell Rahhal/86) had a gap between the fifth and eighth or ninth century, which can be interpreted either as continuity (assuming collections are only period-representative) or discontinuity. For the present, they are considered indefinite for the seventh century until the ceramics are republished, which will be forthcoming by T. Vorderstrasse and myself.
41. Matthers, *The River Qoueiq*, p. 78.
42. The name is Semitic: Hazazu.
43. Isḥāq b. Ibrāhīm al-Mawṣilī was one of the most celebrated court singers and poets in the early 'Abbāsid period, much loved by Mahdī and Hārūn among other caliphs. He was also known for various indiscretions, among them wine drinking, which he undoubtedly did at monasteries, reinterpreting the presence of nuns and ritual wine drinking in Christian services as tavern-style hospitality. At Dayr Tell 'Azāz, he says: 'And [there is] a tempting gazelle in Dayr Shaykh, a charming twinkle of my eye possessed of a pretty face and in it also. That my heart is in the tell of Tell 'Azaz with the gazelle of all possible gazelles with distinction, pretty and it is called this as well.' Yāqūt, *Mu'jam al-buldān* (1990), p. 4.132.
44. Matthers, *The River Qoueiq*, p. 13.
45. Schwartz et al., 'Excavation and Survey in the Jabbul Plain', p. 453.

46. Ṭabarī, *Ta'rīkh*, III. 52 (Arabic) and vol. 27, p. 176 (English). This may be the same as Nauar, used by Baldwin in 1121 as a base to attack Athārib. T. S. Asbridge, *The Creation of the Principality of Antioch, 1098–1130* (Rochester, NY: Boydell Press, 2000), p. 82. See Dussaud, *Topographie Historique*, p. 474; Ibn al-Shiḥna, *Al-Durr al-muntakhab fī ta'rīkh mamlakat Ḥalab* (Beirut: al-Maṭba'at al-Kāthūlīkīya, 1909), p. 4.
47. F. Rosenthal, 'Arabic Books and Manuscripts IV: New Fragments of as-Saraḫsī', *Journal of the American Oriental Society* 71/2 (1951), pp. 138–9.
48. Ṭabarī. *Ta'rīkh*, III. 52 (Arabic) and vol. 27, p. 176 (English).
49. Rosenthal, 'Arabic Books', p. 139.
50. Yāqūt, *Mu'jam al-buldān* (1990), 2.422–3.
51. Ṭabarī, *Ta'rīkh*, III. 2200 (Arabic) and vol. 38, p. 91 (English).
52. Y. Nishiaki, 'Tell Kosak Shamli: Preliminary Report of the Excavations (1994–1997)', in *Upper Syrian Euphrates*, p. 73; E. Peltenburg, 'Tell Jerablus Tahtani 1992–1996: A Summary', in ibid., p. 103; G. M. Séiquer, 'Tell Khamīs', in ibid., p. 207 and fn. 2; G. del Olmo Lete and E. Olavarri Goicoechea, 'Tell Qara Qūzāq: Enclave Comercial en el reino de Karkemish', *Revista de Arqueología* 135 (1992), pp. 12–15.
53. M.-O. Rousset-Issa, 'Les Ceramiques Recentes de la Prospection du Site de Tilbeshar (1994–1996)', *Anatolia Antiqua* VI (1998), pp. 177–9.
54. M.-O. Rousset, 'Projet de Travaux Archéologiques à Tilbeshar (Ancient Tell Bashir), Turquie'. Available at http://halshs.archives-ouvertes.fr/docs/00/35/97/66/PDF/projetTilbeshar.pdf (accessed 13 May 2013). A. Northedge believes this to be a mud-brick building, possibly a fortification, of the tenth century.
55. A. Gonzáliz Blanc, 'Christianism on the Eastern Frontier', *Upper Syrian Euphrates*, pp. 652–5.
56. Theodota of Amida, *Life*, forthcoming edition and translation by Jack Tannous, section p. 77.
57. Jack Tannous, 'Syria Between Byzantium and Islam: Making Incommensurables Speak', PhD dissertation, Princeton University, 2010, p. 345 and fn. p. 835.
58. Yāqūt, *Mu'jam al-buldān* (1990) 2.239.
59. I am grateful to Sarah Yukich and Glenn Schwartz for sharing some of the unpublished Jabbul Plain Survey material with me.
60. Yāqūt, *Mu'jam al-buldān* (1990) 2.446.
61. P.-L. Gatier, '"Grande" ou "Petite Syrie Seconde"? Pour une géographie historique de la Syrie intérieure Protobyzantine', in B. Geyer (ed.), *Conquête de la Steppe et appropriation des terres sur les marges arides du Croissant fertile* (Lyon: Maison de l'Orient Méditerranéen-Jean Pouilloux, 2001), p. 105.
62. Tonghini, *Qal'at Jabar Pottery*, pp. 70–1.
63. We see an evolution in the first settlements that: (1) continued until the end of the Late Roman period (G. Tchalenko, *Villages antiques de la Syrie du Nord*); (2) continued until the tenth century, but in a state of decline (J.-P. Sodini, G. Tate, B. Bavant, S. Bavant, D. Orssaud, and J.-L. Biscop, 'Déhès (Syrie du Nord), Campagnes I–III (1976–1978), Recherches sur l'habitat rural', *Syria* 57

[1980], pp. 1–303; G. Tate, *Les Campagnes de la Syrie du nord du Iie au VIIe siècle: Un exemple d'expansion démographique et économique dans les campagnes à la fin de l'antiquité* [Paris: Libr. orientaliste P. Geuthner, 1992]); (3) had already reached decline by the mid-sixth century due to natural disaster and plague (H. Kennedy, 'The Last Century of Byzantine Syria: A Reinterpretation', *Byzantinische Fosrschungen* 10 [1985], pp. 141–83); (4) instead of decline, stagnated until the tenth century (C. Foss, 'Syria in Transition, A.D. 550–750: An Archaeological Approach', *Dumbarton Oaks Papers* 51 [1997], pp. 189–269; or (5) continued from the Late Roman to the Early Islamic period until the tenth century (Magness, *The Archaeology of Early Islamic Settlement in Palestine*).

64. C. Wickham, *Framing the Early Middle Ages: Europe and the Mediterranean 400–800* (New York, NY: Oxford University Press, 2005), pp. 443–9.
65. F. Braemer, B. Geyer, C. Castel, and M. Abdulkarim, 'Conquest of New Lands and Water Systems in the Western Fertile Crescent (Central and Southern Syria)', *Water History* 2 (2010), pp. 101–2, and Figures 9 and p. 10.
66. Sodini et al., 'Déhès (Syrie du Nord)'; Tate, *Les Campagnes de la Syrie du nord.*
67. F. L. Kidner, 'Christianizing the Syrian countryside: an archaeological and architectural approach', in T. S. Burns and J. W. Eadie (eds), *Urban Centers and Rural Contexts in Late Antiquity* (East Lansing, MI: Michigan State University Press, 2001), pp. 349–79. Kidner's dating may have to be revised.
68. D. Hull, 'A Spatial and Morphological Analysis of Monastic Sites in the Northern Limestone Massif, Syria', *Levant* 40/1 (2008), pp. 89–113.
69. Magness, *The Archaeology of Early Islamic Settlement in Palestine*. Although pre-sixth century material was present, indicating that the site had been occupied previously.
70. I. Straughn, 'Sacrality and the afterlife of the Byzantine-Islamic frontier: A view of the border from the "Dead Cities" of Northern Syria', Paper given at the American Anthropological Association annual meeting, San Francisco, 13–18 November p. 2012.
71. I am grateful to Tony Wilkinson and the Durham–Edinburgh Land of Carchemish Project for sharing more, as yet unpublished details about the site with me.
72. Algaze et al., 'The Tigris-Euphrates Archaeological Reconnaissance Project: Final Report', pp. 28, 94.
73. Although a crossing point is not indicated, the way to Sumaysāṭ via a south–north land route that followed the river is also suggested in the map in D. Comfort, C. Abadie-Reynal, and R. Ergeç, 'Crossing the Euphrates in Antiquity: Zeugma seen from Space', *Anatolian Studies* 50 (2000), Figure 2, p. 101.
74. Ibn Khurradādhbih, *al-Masālik wa-al-Mamālik* (Leiden: Brill, 1889), pp. 75, 253.
75. Ibid., p. 75.
76. Balādhurī, *Futūḥ al-buldān* (1987), p. 180.
77. Yāqūt, *Mu'jam al-buldān* (1990) 1.390–1.

78. L. Golvin, 'À la recherche de la cité médiévale de Balis (Moyen-Euphrate)', in J. Cl. Margueron (ed.), *Le Moyen Euphrate:* Zone de contacts et d'échanges (Leiden: Brill, 1980), pp. 389–396.
79. T. Leisten, 'For Prince and country(side)-the Marwanid Mansion at Balis on the Euphrates', in *Residences, Castles, Settlements*, p. 382. In Figure 21, Leisten plots some of these small, apparently Umayyad villages: Tall Makhrum, Khirbat al-Fār, Madināt al-Far (not the one in the Balikh), and Maskana, but these were not surveyed.
80. Yāqūt *Mu'jam al-buldān* (1990), p. 3.59.
81. Ṭabarī, *Ta'rīkh*, III. 3261 (Arabic) and vol 17, p. 6 (English).
82. C. Konrad, personal communication with the author, p. 2012.
83. Ṭabarī, *Ta'rīkh*, III. 568 (Arabic) and vol. 30, p. 39 (English).
84. The Adıyaman Survey in the eastern *thughūr* included the uplands region in the Gölbaşı Valley in the central *thughūr*. Also, the Çakırhoyuk-Kizilin Plain around Kaysūm was surveyed, revealing many mounds, and the Besni area revealed very few mounds but many Classical and Islamic sites. See S. R. Blaylock, D. H. French, and G. D. Summers, 'The Adıyaman Survey: An Interim Report', *Anatolian Studies* 40 (1980), pp. 81–135.
85. Yāqūt hardly gives any information about it, other than that it is a *madina*: *Mu'jam al-buldān* (1990), p. 2.219.

Chapter 3 The Eastern *Thughūr*

1. Theodota of Amida, *Life*.
2. T. J. Wilkinson, 'Settlement and land use in the zone of uncertainty in Upper Mesopotamia', in R. M. Jas (ed.), *Rainfall and Agriculture in Northern Mesopotamia* (Istanbul: Nederlands Historisch Archaeologisch Instituut te Istanbul, 2000), p. 10.
3. Ibn Serapion, 'Description of Mesopotamia and Baghdād, written about the year 900 A.D. by Ibn Serapion'. Translation and notes by G. Le Strange, *Journal of the Royal Asiatic Society of Great Britain and Ireland* (January 1895), p. 58 (notes).
4. Theodota of Amida, *Life*, sections 115–16.
5. G. H. Willcox, 'A History of Deforestation as Indicated by Charcoal Analysis of Four Sites in Eastern Anatolia', *Anatolian Studies* 24 (1974), pp. 117–33, esp. 118. Of the four sites, one was primarily 'Medieval' (Taşkun Kale). Unfortunately, periodization is not explained (Late Medieval, Early Medieval, Roman and Hellenistic phases are employed).
6. R. Whallon, *An Archaeological Survey of the Keban Reservoir Area of East Central Turkey*, Memoirs of the Museum of Anthropology, University of Michigan 11 (Ann Arbor, MI: Regents of the University of Michigan, 1979), p. 9; M. B. Rowton, 'The Woodlands of Ancient Western Asia', *Journal of Near Eastern Studies* 26/4 (1967), p. 274.

7. V. W. Yorke, 'A Journey in the Valley of the Upper Euphrates', *The Geographical Journal* 8/5 (1896), pp. 463–4. He describes a fourth mountain route via another tributary of the Tokhma Su past Abdul Kharab. The third route, via the Kahta, may have joined either this one or the second via the Gerger Çay to the Euphrates before arriving at Malaṭya. Yorke is skeptical about the first route via the Qarāqis tributary.
8. Ü. Serdaroğlu, *Surveys in the Lower Euphrates Basin, 1975 (Aşaği Firat Havzasında Arastırmalar 1975)*, Lower Euphrates Project Publications Series 1, no. 1 (Ankara: Türk Tarih Kurumu Basimevi, 1977).
9. S. Blaylock, 'Adıyaman Survey 1985–1991', in R. Matthews (ed.), *Ancient Anatolia: Fifty Year's Work by the British Institute of Archaeology at Ankara* (London: British Institute of Archaeology at Ankara, 1998), p. 105.
10. Blaylock et al., 'The Adıyaman Survey: An Interim Report', p. 125.
11. G. M. di Nocera, '2003 Archaeological Survey in the Malatya Territory', *AST* 22/2 (2004), pp. 325–36. The Roman and post-Roman materials are awaiting publication by Francesca Dell'Era.
12. T. J. Wilkinson, *Town and Country in Southeastern Anatolia*, Volume 1: *Settlement and Land Use at Kurban Höyük and Other Sites in the Lower Karababa Basin* (Chicago, IL: Oriental Institute Publications, 1990), p. 126.
13. G. Stein, 'Medieval Regional Settlement Organization', in S. Redford, *The Archaeology of the Frontier in the Medieval Near East: Excavations at Gritille, Turkey.* (Philadelphia, PA: University Museum Publications, University of Pennsylvania, 1998), pp. 253–67.
14. Ch. Gerber, 'Die Umgebung des Lidar Höyük', in *Continuity and Change*, p. 306.
15. Blaylock et al., 'The Adıyaman Survey: An Interim Report', p. 125.
16. Stein, 'Medieval Regional Settlement Organization', p. 265, Figure 7.3.H.
17. Ibid., p. 266.
18. Ibid., p. 263.
19. Redford, *The Archaeology of the Frontier*, p. 277.
20. G. Algaze, A. Misir, and T. J. Wilkinson, 'Şanlıurfa Museum/University of California Excavations and Surveys at Titriş Höyük, 1991: A Preliminary Report', *Anatolica* 18 (1992), p. 44.
21. Ch. Gerber, 'Die Umgebung des Lidar Höyük', p. 309.
22. Ibid., p. 310.
23. The ceramics begin in the eighth century with some of the brittleware and lid types. Some flask neck and rims also appear to be eleventh/twelfth-century moulded buffware pilgrim-flask types and one base, also of later date – J. Moore, *Tille Höyük 1: The Medieval Period* (Ankara: British Institute of Archaeology, 1993), Figure 105.14. However, the lack of any of the decorative moulding of this later type of buffware is important. Given the format of the publication, it is unclear how these pits relate to the phasing and stratigraphy discussion. Ibid., pp. 193–6.
24. T. Goell and K. Otto-Dorn, 'Keramikfunde aus dem Mittelalter und der frühosmanischen Zeit', *Arsameia am Nymphaios: Die Ausgrabungen im Hierothesion*

des Mithradates Kallinikos von 1953–1956, Istanbuler Forschungen Band 23 (Berlin: Verlag Gebr. Mann, 1963), pp. 246–76.
25. These may date earlier. M. Thierry, 'Monuments chrétiens inédits de Haute-Mésopotamie', *Syria* 70/1–2 (1993) pp. 186–94.
26. Theodota of Amida, *Life*, section p. 106.
27. Whallon, *An Archaeological Survey of the Keban Reservoir*, p. 276.
28. G. Algaze, *Town and Country in Southeastern Anatolia*, p. 395, Fig. 124, photo Figure p. 132.
29. Ibid., pp. 128–9.
30. Redford, The Archaeology of the Frontier, 17, fn. p. 74.
31. Ibn Shaddād, p. 2.192.
32. Decker, 'Frontier Settlement and Economy', p. 232.
33. Michael the Syrian, *Chronique*, vol. 3, p. 10; vol. 4, p. 493; M. Morony, 'Michael the Syrian as a Source for Economic History', *Hugoye: Journal of Syriac Studies* 3, no. 2 (July 2000).
34. Ibn Serapion, 'Description of Mesopotamia and Baghdād', section IV, p. 13 (Arabic text) and p. 63 (English translation).
35. Ibn Serapion, 'Description of Mesopotamia and Baghdād', section III, p. 11 (Arabic text) and p. 54 (English translation).
36. Mustafa Poyraz (Kültür Varlıkları ve Müzeler Genel Müdürlüğünde – Office of the Director General of Culture and Museums), personal communication with the author, p. 2012.
37. Theodota of Amida, *Life*, section p. 115.
38. Bonner, *Aristocratic Violence and Holy War*, 143; Balādhurī, *Futūḥ al-buldān* (1987), p. 265 (Malaṭiya), p. 280 (Qālīqalā).
39. Wheatley, *The Places Where Men Pray Together*, p. 109.

Chapter 4 The Jazīra (Balikh and Khābūr River Valleys)

1. Arabic text from Jarīr, *Dīwān Jarīr* (Cairo: Dār al-Ma'āraf, 1969), vol. I, p. 345, lines 24–5. I am grateful to Tahera Qutbuddin for help with the translation. See R. Nadler, 'Die Umayyadenkalifen im Spiegel ihrer zeitgenössichen Dichter', inaugural dissertation, Friedrich-Alexander Universität, Erlangen-Nürnberg (1990), p. 261.
2. Ṭabarī, *Ta'rīkh*, I. 2497 (Arabic) and vol. 13, pp. 77–8 (English).
3. J. B. Segal, *Edessa: The Blessed City* (Oxford: Clarendon Press, 1970), pp. 155–6, 187–9; Wheatley-Irving, 'Samosata and its Environs in the 7th–9th Centuries CE', paper presented at the annual meeting of ASOR, Cambridge, MA, p. 1999.
4. Michael the Syrian, *Chronique*, vol. 3, p. 109; vol. 4, p. 542. Morony, 'Michael the Syrian as a Source', p. 144.

5. T. J. Wilkinson, 'Regional Approaches to Mesopotamian Archaeology: The Contribution of Archaeological Surveys', *Journal of Archaeological Research* 8/3 (2000), pp. 219–67.
6. Robinson, 'Tribes and Nomads', n. 26. F. Donner says that by *c*.600 CE, they were full-time shepherds or semi-nomads occupying riverside villages; see *The Early Islamic Conquests* (Princeton, NJ: Princeton University Press, 1981), p. 19.
7. Abu Ezzah, 'The Syrian Thughūr', p. 202.
8. C. Robinson, *Empire and Elites after the Muslim Conquest: The Transformation of Northern Mesopotamia* (New York, NY: Cambridge University Press, 2000), p. 61.
9. N. Yardımcı, *Harran Ovası yüzey araştırması* (Istanbul: Nurettin Yardımcı, 2004) p. 14.
10. Decker, 'Settlement and Agriculture in the Levant', pp. 1–2.
11. For more detail on this reinterpretation, albeit impressionistic at best, see Eger, 'The Spaces Between the Teeth: Environment, Settlement, and Interaction on the Islamic-Byzantine Frontier', PhD dissertation, University of Chicago, 2008, pp. 276–83.
12. Excavations at Aşağı Yarımca revealed a ninth-century Early Islamic farmhouse; S. Lloyd, 'Aşağı Yarımca', *Anatolian Studies* 2 (1952), pp. 11–13.
13. St. J. Simpson, 'From Tekrit to the Jaghjagh: Sasanian Sites, Settlement Patterns and Material Culture in Northern Mesopotamia', in *Continuity and Change*, n. 6, p. 89.
14. W. Van Liere and J. Lauffray, 'Nouvelle prospection archéologique dans la haute Jezireh syrienne', *Les Annales Archéologiques de Syrie* 4–5 (1954–5), p. 144.
15. V. Vezzoli, 'Islamic Period Settlement in the Tell Leilan Region (North Jazira): The Material Evidence from the 1995 Survey', *Levant* 40/2: (2008), pp. 185–202. This article is based on her MA thesis.
16. This count includes sites with three to five sherds, following the Amuq and Kahramanmaraş Survey methodologies. However, they do not count sites with one to two sherds as settlements, but as nomadic trace occupation; Wilkinson and Tucker, *Settlement Development in the North Jazira*, p. 71. See also W. Ball, D. Tucker, and T. J. Wilkinson, 'The Tell al-Hawa Project: Archeological Investigations in the North Jazira 1986–87', *Iraq* 51 (1989), pp. 1–66.
17. J. Eidem and D. Warburton's 1978 survey of a 170 km^2 area around Tell Brak – 'In the Land of Nagar: A Survey around Tell Brak', *Iraq* 58 (1996), pp. 51–64 – resurveyed Meijer's sites and found a total of 56. Their final periodization is coarse, dating 22 sites to the first millennium CE, but, unlike van Liere and Lauffray, offering little interpretation, rendering the data useless for our purposes.
18. T. J. Wilkinson, 'Archaeological survey of the Tell Beydar region, Syria, 1997: a preliminary report', in K. Van Lerberghe and G. Voet (eds), *Tell Beydar: Environmental and Technical Studies*, *Subartu* VI (2001), pp. 1–37; J. A. Ur and T. J. Wilkinson, 'Settlement and economic landscapes of Tell Beydar and its hinterland', in M. Lebeau and A. Suleiman (eds), *Beydar Studies I* (Turnhout, Belgium: Brepols, 2008), pp. 305–27.

19. J. A. Ur, *Tell Hamoukar* (Chicago, IL: Oriental Institute, 2010), pp. 120–2.
20. Fuller publication of the ceramics would have been useful to support Vezzoli's arguments, particularly as she provides very specific dates for the diagnostics, such as sgraffiato wares and cooking wares, often coming close to equating ceramic changes with political shifts. Vezzoli did consider assemblage size; however, this too was not systematically presented. Her divisions of 20 or more sherds, five to ten sherds, two to four sherds, and one sherd can roughly equate to our heavy, medium, and light categories; however, the table only indicates sites with five or more, or less than five sherds.
21. T. J. Wilkinson, 'Water and Human Settlement in the Balikh Valley, Syria: Investigations from 1992–1995', *Journal of Field Archaeology* 25/1 (1998), pp. 63–87.
22. L. De Jong, 'Resettling the steppe: the archaeology of the Balikh Valley in the Early Islamic period', in R. Matthews and J. Curtis (eds), *Proceedings of the 7th International Congress on the Archaeology of the Ancient Near East* (Wiesbaden: Harrassowitz Verlag, 2012), p. 519.
23. Theophilus of Edessa, *Chronicle*, p. 224.
24. Although this interpretation is possible, one should be cautious as there are hardly any parallels for such a structure. K. Toueir, 'Heraqlah, a unique victory monument of Harun-ar-Rashid', *World Archaeology* 14 (3), pp. 297 (plate 10) and p. 298.
25. Wilkinson, 'Water and Human Settlement'; Wilkinson and Rayne, 'Hydraulic Landscapes', pp. 132–5.
26. K. Bartl, 'The Balih Valley, Northern Syria, during the Islamic Period: Remarks Concerning the Historical Topography', *Berytus* 41 (1993/4), p. 36.
27. De Jong, 'Resettling the Steppe', p. 520.
28. Ibn Khurradādhbih, *Masālik wa-al-Mamālik*, p. 96.
29. Yāqūt, *Mu'jam al-buldān* (1955–7), 1.382.
30. C.-P. Haase, 'The excavations at Madīnat al-Fār/Ḥiṣn Maslama on the Balikh road', in H. Kennedy (ed.), *Muslim Military Architecture in Greater Syria: From the Coming of Islam to the Ottoman Period* (Leiden: Brill, 2006), pp. 56–9; idem, 'Is Madīnat al-Fār, in the Balikh Region of Northern Syria, an Umayyad Foundation?', *Aram* 6 (1994), 245–53; Idem, 'Une ville des débuts de l'Islam d'après les fouilles effectuées à Madinat al-Far (Syria du Nord). Les premières fondations urbaines umayyades', *Archéologie Islamique* 11 (2001), pp. 7–20.
31. A. A. Eger, '*Ḥiṣn, Ribaṭ, Thaghr, or Qaṣr?* The semantics of frontier forts in the Early Islamic period', in P. Cobb (ed.), *The Lineaments of Islam: Studies in Honor of Fred McGraw Donner* (Leiden: Brill, 2012), p. 433, fn. p. 23.
32. S. Heidemann, 'Settlement Patterns, Economic Development and Archaeological Coin Finds in Bilad al-Sham: The Case of Diyar Mudar', in *Residences, Castles, Settlements*.
33. For Ḥiṣn Maslama as way station and, at times, a garrison: Bartl, 'The Balih Valley', p. 37; Haase, 'Une ville des débuts de l'Islam', pp. 7–20.
34. Ur, Tell Hamoukar, p. 165.

35. Wilkinson and Tucker, *Settlement Development in the North Jazira*, pp. 70–1, 121, 153 Figure 7, Figure 78 for ceramics, Figure 20 for proximity to Tell al-Hawa.
36. Ball, Tucker, and Wilkinson, 'The Tell al-Hawa Project', 37–8.
37. J. A. Ur, 'Surface Collection and Offsite Studies at Tell Hamoukar, 1999', *Iraq* 64 (2002), p. 24.
38. See also W. Ball, 'The Upper Tigris Area: New Evidence form the Eski Mosul and North Jazira Projects', in *Continuity and Change*, p. 419.
39. A. Poidebard, *La Trace de Rome dans le desert de Syria: Le Limes de Trajan à la conquète Arabe, recherché aériennes (1925–1932)* [Paris: Librairie Orientaliste Paul Geuthner, 1934], p. 144 argued for a sixth-century date with an internal structure in the north-east corner that was a 'military chapel'. Oates argues for a fourth-century date. Gregory notes that the arrow-shaped corner towers, small size, closely spaced semicircular towers, and ditch are un-Roman elements, and posits a Sasanian or Early Islamic period date. S. Gregory, *Roman Military Architecture on the Eastern Frontier* (Amsterdam: Adolf M. Hakkert, 1997), vol. 2. pp. 94ff.
40. J. A. Ur, P. Karsgaard, and J. Oates, 'The Spatial Dimensions of Early Mesopotamian Urbanism: The Tell Brak Suburban Survey, 2003–2006'. *Iraq* 73 (2011), p. 16.
41. P. J. Ergenzinger, W. Frey, H. Kuhne, and H. Kurschner, 'The reconstruction of environment, irrigation, and development of settlement on the Ḥābūr in North-East Syria', in J. Bintliff et al. (eds), *Conceptual Issues in Environmental Archaeology* (Edinburgh: Edinburgh University Press, 1988), p. 122 and Figure p. 9.
42. M. Decker, *Tilling the Hateful Earth: Agricultural Production and Trade in the Late Antique East* (New York, NY: Oxford University Press, 2009), p. 184; see the larger discussion on canals, pp. 177–84.
43. Yāqūt, *Mu 'jam al-buldān* (1990), p. 3.15; H. Kennedy, 'Feeding of the Five Hundred Thousand: Cities and Agriculture in Early Islamic Mesopotamia', *Iraq* 73 (2011), p. 180; see also Wilkinson and Rayne, 'Hydraulic Landscapes', pp. 136–7.
44. De Jong, 'Resettling the Steppe', 520; for the latest on Kharab Sayyar, see J.-W. Meyer, 'Die deutsch-syrischen Ausgrabungen in Kharab Sayyar/Nordostsyrien', in *Residences, Castles, Settlements*, pp. 419–32.
45. M. Fuller, 'Archaeological Discoveries at Tell Tuneinir', *Journal of the Assyrian Academic Society* 12.2 (1998), pp. 68–82; idem, 'Continuity and Change in the Syriac Population at Tell Tuneinir, Syria', *ARAM* 6 (1994), pp. 259–77.
46. Ṭabarī, *Ta'rīkh*, II. 1735 (Arabic) and vol. 26, p. 778 (English).
47. D. Samuel, 'Archaeobotanical evidence and analysis', in S. Berthier (ed.), *Peuplement rural et aménagements hydroagricoles dans la moyenne vallée de l'Euphrate, fin VIIe-XIXe siècle* (Damascus: Institut français d'études arabes de Damas [IFEAD], 2001), pp. 381, p. 387.
48. L. Chaix and J. Studer, 'La Faune de Quelques sites Islamiques de la Moyenne Vallée de l'Euphrate', in ibid., pp. 303–40. Identification of the water buffalo remains is based, somewhat precariously, on the size of the second phalanges.

49. H. Kennedy, 'How to found an Islamic city', in C. Goodson, A. Lester, and C. Symes (eds), *Cities, Texts and Social Networks, 400–1500: Experiences and Perceptions of Medieval Urban Space* (Burlington, VT: Ashgate, 2010), pp. 60–1.
50. Balādhurī, *Futūḥ al-buldan* (1987), p. 247. See also Northedge, 'Archaeology and New Urban Settlement in Early Islamic Syria and Iraq', p. 248.
51. De Jong, 'Resettling the Steppe', p. 521; S. Heidemann, 'The History of the Industrial and Commercial Area of 'Abbasid al-Raqqa, called al-Raqqa al-Muḥtariqa', *Bulletin of the School of Oriental and African Studies* 69/1 (2006), pp. 32–52; J. Henderson et al., 'Experiment and Innovation: Early Islamic Industry at al-Raqqa, Syria', *Antiquity* 79 (2005), pp. 135–6; K. Toueir, 'Le Nahr el-Nil entre Raqqa et Heraqleh', in B. Geyer (ed.), *Techniques et pratiques hydro-agricoles traditionelles en domaine irrigué* (Paris, 1990), pp. 217–27.
52. H. Kennedy, 'Introduction', *Proche Orient*, pp. xiv–xv; S. Heidemann, 'The agricultural hinterland of Baghdād, al-Raqqa and Sāmarrā': settlement patterns in the Diyar Muḍar', in A. Borrut, M. Debié, A. Papaconstantinou, D. Pieri, and J.-P. Sodini (eds), *Le Proche-Orient de Justinien aux Abbasides: Peuplement et Dynamiques Spatiales* (Turnhout, Belgium: Brepols, 2011), p. 49.
53. Challis et al., 'Corona Remotely-Sensed Imagery in Dryland Archaeology: The Islamic City of al-Raqqa, Syria', *Journal of Field Archaeology* 29.1-2 (2002–2004), p. 141.
54. Yāqūt, *Mu'jam al-buldān* (1990) 2.173.
55. In Haase, 'Is Madīnat al-Fār', p. 247; Ibn Serapion, 'Description of Mesopotamia and Baghdād', section III, p. 12 (Arabic text) and p. 55 (English translation), and notes by Le Strange, pp. 58–9.
56. Robinson, *Empire and Elites*, pp. viii–ix.
57. As Robinson also notes, ibid., p. 71.
58. Heidemann, 'Settlement Patterns', p. 503. Raqqa may have been a mint for the local imitation of copper coins from Kūfa, as was Anṭākiya, see G. C. Miles, 'Islamic coins', in F. O. Waagé (ed.), *Antioch-on-the-Orontes, Vol IV, Part One* (Princeton, NJ: Princeton University Press, 1948), pp. 110, 116–17.

Chapter 5 The Western *Thughūr*: Crossroads of Cilicia

1. Sarakhsī in Yāqūt, *Mu'jam al-buldān* (1990), 1.161–2, translation in Rosenthal, 'Arabic Books', pp. 77–8.
2. Yāqūt, *Mu'jam al-buldān* (1990), p. 2.400.
3. Genesis ii, 11 and p. 13.
4. E. Özbayoğlu, 'Notes on Natural Resources of Cilicia: A Contribution to Local History', *Olba* 8 (2003), pp. 164–5.
5. Ananias of Sirak, *The Geography of Ananias of Širak: The Long and the Short Recensions*. Introduction, translation, and Commentary by Robert H. Hewsen (Dr. Ludwig Reichert Verlag: Wiesbaden, 1992), p. 54, long recension. See

Durak, 'Commerce and Networks of Exchange Between the Byzantine Empire and the Islamic Near East from the Early Ninth Century to the Arrival of the Crusaders'. PhD dissertation, Harvard University, 2008, pp. 177–84.

6. Although Strabo comments that 'the Pyramus of the silver-eddies shall silt up its sacred sea beach and come to Cyprus'. (*The Geography of Strabo*, p. 12.2.4).
7. T. Beach and S. Luzzadder-Beach, 'Aggradation around Kinet Höyük, an Archaeological Mound in the Eastern Mediterranean, Turkey', *Geomorphology* 17/1 (2008), pp. 416–28.
8. Eger, 'The Swamps of Home', pp. 55–79.
9. Examination of the three Turkish journals covering the region, *Olba*, *ANMED*, and *Adalya*, reveals no articles or reports from archaeological projects for this period whatsoever, save one or two passing references. Mustafa Sayar's Cilicia surveys have been mainly epigraphic in nature. A copious list of surveys is given in A. Ünal and K. Serdar Girginer, *Kilikya-Çukurova: İlk Çağlardan Osmanlılar Dönemi'ne Kadar Kilikya'da Tarihi Coğrafya, Tarih ve Arkeoloji* (Istanbul: Homer Kitabevi ve Yayıncılık, 2007), pp. 305–12. However, almost all of these are too specialized and insufficient to provide an assessment of settlement patterns on the plain.
10. M. V. Seton-Williams, 'Cilician Survey', *Anatolian Studies* 4 (1954), pp. 139–41.
11. For preliminary reports with site gazetteers, see G. Lehmann, A. E. Killebrew, and M.-H. Gates, 'Summary of the 2006 Cilicia Survey (İskenderun Bay Region)', *AST* 25.3 (2007), pp. 171–88; A. Killebrew, G. Lehmann, and M-H. Gates, 'Summary of the 2007 Cilicia Survey (İskenderun Bay Region)', *AST* 26/3 (2008), pp. 227–38; A. Killebrew, 'Summary of the 2008 Cilicia Survey (İskenderun Bay Region)', AST 27/3 (2009), pp. 319–58; idem, 'Summary of the 2009 Cilicia Survey (İskenderun Bay Region)', *AST* 28/1 (2010), pp. 39–46.
12. İ. Özgen and M.-H. Gates, 'Report on the Bilkent University Archaeological Survey in Cilicia and the Northern Hatay: August 1991', *AST* 10 (1992), pp. 387–94.
13. A. Eger, 'Ḥiṣn al-Tīnāt on the Islamic-Byzantine Frontier: Synthesis and the 2005–2008 Survey and Excavation on the Cilician Plain (Turkey)', *Bulletin of the American School of Oriental Research* 357 (February 2010), pp. 55–8.
14. F. Tülek, 'Osmaniye ili ve ilçelerinde Arkeolojik Yüzey Araştırması 2005 Yılı Çalışması', *AST* 25/1 (2007), pp. 305–26, see plan (çizim) 7). Yapılıpınar Höyuk, Taşlı H 4; idem, 'Osmaniye İli Yüzey Araştırması 2007 Çalışması', *AST* 26/1 (2008), pp. 135–40; idem, 'Osmaniye Arkeolojik Yüzey Araştırması 2008 Yılı Çalışması', *AST* 27/3 (2009), pp. 69–82; idem, '2010 Yılı Osmaniye İli Arkeolojik Araştırmaları, *AST* 29/1 (2011), pp. 491–504.
15. J. J. Rossiter and J. Freed, 'Canadian-Turkish Excavations at Domuztepe, Cilicia (1989)', *Echo du Monde Classique* 10 (1991), pp. 145–74. See also Decker, 'Frontier Settlement and Economy', pp. 164–5 and fn. 43 for other examples.
16. Seton-Williams ('Cilician Survey', 141) mentions two Islamic sites of unknown date in this area that may be possibilities, although they are mounds: Pekmezli II and Cebra.

17. T. Beach and S. L. Luzzadder-Beach, 'Geoarchaeology and aggradation', *Geomorphology* 17/1 (2008), p. 426. Higher exploration of the Amanus slopes was not permitted due to military activity.
18. Michael the Syrian, *Chronique*, vol. 3, p. 462.
19. I. Caneva and G. Koroğlu, *Yumuktepe* (Istanbul: Ege Yayinları, 2010).
20. The order and distance of these towns are for the most part accurate if one considers the towns to be Ṭarsūs, Kalanthia, Korykos, and Korasion. After this, it seems that he doubles back to Iskandariyya, which can be identified with Akkale, and then Sebasteia, heading west again. Nabik may be Nagidos, closer to Anemorium, according to F. Hild and H. Hellenkemper, *Kilikien und Isaurien* (Vienna: Verlag der Österreichischen Akademie der Wissenschaften, 1990); Ibn Khurradādhbih, *Masālik wa-al-Mamālik* (1889), p. 117.
21. R. Blanton, *Hellenistic, Roman and Byzantine Settlement Patterns of the Coast Lands of Western Rough Cilicia*, BAR International Series 879 (Oxford: Archaeoporess, 2000), pp. 29, 66.
22. M. Jackson, 'The Kilise Tepe Area in the Byzantine Area,' in *Excavations at Kilise Tepe, 1994–98: From Bronze Age to Byzantine in Western* Cilicia, Nicholas Postgate and David Thomas, eds. (Cambridge, UK: McDonald Institute for Archaeological Research, 2007), p. 27.
23. See Eger, 'Ḥiṣn al-Tīnāt on the Islamic-Byzantine Frontier', pp. 49–76
24. See entries in Eger, *The Spaces Between the Teeth: A Gazetteer*: Adhana had an encampment in 743 under Walīd II, and was not built up until 758/9 or 761/2 under Manṣūr. 'Ayn Zarba was settled and garrisoned in 827. Kanīsat al-Sawdā' was fortified and repaired in 799 and 806 by Hārūn al-Rashīd. Sīs was repaired in 851/2–862/3 during al-Mutawakkil's reign. See also Abu Ezzah, 'The Syrian Thughūr', pp. 15 and 82.
25. I am very thankful to A. Özyar for allowing me to make a preliminary and brief examination of the collections from Ṭarsūs. For recent reports, see, for Ṭarsūs: A. Özyar, 'Tarsus-Gözlükule 2007 Yılı Kazısı', *KST* 30/2 (2008), pp. 47–60. The Islamic ceramics from the Goldmann excavations are currently being worked on by O. Pancaroğlu (Boğaziçi) and Y. Bağcı, a PhD student at Leiden.
26. G. Salmeri and A. L. d'Agata, 'Cilicia Survey 2006', *AST* 25/2 (2007), pp. 1–6; idem, 'Cilicia Survey 2007', *AST* 26/2 (2008), pp. 119–24; idem, 'Cilicia Survey 2009', *AST* 28/2 (2010), pp. 21–4; idem, 'Cilicia Survey 2010', *AST* 29/3 (2011), pp. 165–70.
27. It is unpublished in English: 'Antik muayenehane bulundu', *Sabah*, 1 September 2011. Available at www.sabah.com.tr/Turizm/2011/09/01/antik-muayenehane-bulundu (accessed 20 May 2013).
28. For a recent overview, see R. Posamentir, 'Anazarbos in Late Antiquity', in O. Dally and C. Ratté, *Archaeology and the Cities of Asia Minor in Late Antiquity* (Ann Arbor, MI: Kelsey Museum of Archaeology, 2011), pp. 205–24.
29. An intensive site collection and mapping at 'Ayn Zarba was conducted in 2006 and 2007 under the direction of R. Posamentir, and I am currently preparing the Islamic ceramics for publication.

30. Posamentir, 'Anazarbos in Late Antiquity', pp. 217–24, esp. 222.
31. F. Tülek, 'Footsteps of the Arab-Byzantine Armies in Osmaniye Province, Cilicia', proceedings of the 7th ICAANE, London (2012) pp. 1, 149–61; idem, 'Osmaniye Arkeolojik Yüzey Araştırması 2008 Yılı Çalışması', pp. 69–81.
32. I am very grateful to F. Tülek for allowing me to prelimarily view the pottery from Örenşehir in p. 2009.
33. Özgen and Gates, 'Report on the Bilkent University Archaeological Survey', p. 390; J. Tobin, *Black Cilicia: A Study of the Plain of Issus during the Roman and Late Roman Periods*, BAR International Series (Oxford: John and Erica Hedges, 2004), pp. 16–17.

Part 2 Hydraulic Villages and Fortified Castles: A Narrative of Settlement

1. V. Minorsky, trans., *Ḥudūd al-'Ālam: 'The Regions of the World'* (Oxford, Printed at the University press for the Trustees of the E. J. Gibb Memorial, London: Luzac & Co., 1937), pp. 156–7.
2. *Incastellamento* was first introduced by P. Toubert and subsequently developed by Guichard and others. P. Toubert, *Les structures du Latium medieval: le Latium méridional et la Sabine du IXe siècle a la fin du XIIe siècle* (Rome: École française de Rome, 1973); P. Guichard, *Al-Andalus: Estructura antropológica de una sociedad islámica en occidente* (Barcelona: Barral, 1976). Guichard focused on the nature of rural social organization, particularly with the advent of Berber tribes. For Italy, see R. Francovich and R. Hodges, *Villa to Village: The Transformation of the Roman Countryside in Italy, c. 400–1000* (London: Gerald Duckworth & Co. Ltd., 2003). For an excellent synthetical and theoretical overview of the scholarship, see T. F. Glick, 'Tribal landscapes of Islamic Spain: history and archaeology', in J. Howe and M. Wolfe (eds), *Inventing Medieval Landscapes: Sense of Place in Western Europe* (Gainesville, FL: University Press of Florida, 2002), pp. 113–35, and idem, *From Muslim Fortress to Christian Castle*.
3. Wilkinson, 'Regional Approaches', p. 253.

Chapter 6 Prologue: Upland Settlements in the Late Roman Period (Fourth to Seventh Centuries)

1. Libanius, *Or.* 11.22. Libanius, *Antioch as a Centre of Hellenic Culture as Observed by Libanius*, translated by A. F. Norman. Translated Texts for Historians 34 (Liverpool: Liverpool University Press, 2000).
2. T. J. Wilkinson, 'Archaeological Landscapes of the Near East', particularly pp. 128–50.

3. R. Duncan Jones, 'Economic change in the transition to Late Antiquity', in S. Swaine and M. Edwards (eds), *Approaching Late Antiquity: The Transformations from Early to Late Empire* (New York, NY: Oxford University Press, 2004), pp. 20–52.
4. For a recent brief overview, see Decker, *Tilling the Hateful Earth*, p. 21.
5. Libanius, *Or.* 11.260–2.
6. D. R. Lightfoot, 'Syrian Qanat Romani: history, ecology, abandonment', *Journal of Arid Environments* 33 (1996), pp. 321–6; T. J. Wilkinson, 'Empire and environment in the northern Fertile Crescent', in I. P. Martini and W. Chesworth (eds), *Landscapes and Societies – Selected Cases*. (Dordrecht: Springer, 2010), pp. 144–5.
7. J. Casana and A. Gansell, 'Surface collection, off-site survey, and floodplain development at Tell Atchana', in K. A. Yener (ed.), *The Amuq Plain Regional Projects*, Volume 1: *Surveys in the Plain of Antioch and Orontes Delta, Turkey, 1995–2002* (Chicago, IL: Oriental Institute Press, 2005), p. 157; Casana, 'From Alalakh to Antioch', p. 262. Furthermore, a high-density field scatter north of the mound may suggest either off-site scatter or off-site settlement at the base of the tell in the form of a lower town.
8. These excavations of the 1930s were reanalysed by Vorderstrasse in 'The Romanization and Christianization', pp. 91–4; however, for the original publications, see R. C. Haines, *Excavations in the Plain of Antioch*, Vol. 2: *The Structural Remains of the Later Phases* (Chicago, IL: University of Chicago, 1971), pp. 10–13, 31–4, and plates 49C, 62, 63B.
9. S. Pollock and R. Bernbeck, 'Excavations at Fıstıklı Höyük', in *TAÇDAM* 1999, pp. 59–60; M. Frangipane and E. Bucak, 'Excavations and Research at Zeytinlibahçe Höyük, 1999', in *TAÇDAM* 1999, p. 122.
10. T. Vorderstrasse, 'A Countermarked Byzantine Coin of Heraclius (610–41) from Tell Kurdu', *The Numismatic Chronicle* 166 (2006), pp. 433–8.
11. These discrepancies reveal themselves when assemblage size is weighed against site size or height. Examples of this include AS 101, which was 17.5 ha in size but only had one or two Late Roman period sherds; and AS 86, which was almost 12 ha in area and 13 m high, but had a similarly small assemblage. AS 111, in contrast, was perhaps the largest non-urban Late Roman period site (18 ha) with a matching assemblage. From scanty evidence at Tell Atchana and Tell Kurdu, J. Casana argues that if one were to look hard enough, one would probably find some evidence of Late Roman (or Roman and Early Islamic) period occupation (personal communication with the author, 2008). See also L. Marfoe, 'Between Qadesh and Kumidi: A History of Frontier Settlement and Land Use in the Biqa, Lebanon', PhD dissertation, University of Chicago, 1978 for fewer but larger Byzantine sites than in the Roman period in the Biqāʿ Valley in Lebanon.
12. Although surveyors refer to it as a building of 'obscure purpose'. Blaylock, et al, 'The Adıyaman Survey: An Interim Report', pp. 122–4; Blaylock, 'Adıyaman Survey 1985–1991', p. 106.

13. Andrea di Giorgi, 'The Formation of a Roman Landscape', and idem, 'Socio-economic studies in the Territory of Antioch in the High Roman Empire', PhD dissertation, Bryn Mawr College, p. 2006.
14. For a thorough discussion of this problem, see M. Decker, 'Food for an empire: wine and oil production in North Syria', in S. Kingsley and M. Decker (eds), *Economy and Exchange in the East Mediterranean during Late Antiquity* (New York, NY: Oxford University Press, 2001), pp. 69–86; Foss, 'Syria in Transition'; P.-L., 'Villages du Proche-Orient protobyzantin (4ème -7ème s.), Étude régionale', in G. R. D. King and A. Cameron (eds), *The Byzantine and Early Islamic Near East*, Vol. 2: *Land Use and Settlement Patterns* (Princeton, NJ: The Darwin Press, Inc., 1994), p. 45.
15. Theodoret, *Histoire des Moines de Syrie 'Histoire Philothée'*, introduction, critical text, translation, and notes by P. Canivet and A. Leroy-Molinghen, Vol. 1 (Paris: Les Éditions du Cerf, 1977), p. 292 (Greek text); idem, *A History of the Monks of Syria*, p. 49.
16. G. Dagron, 'Entre Village et Cité: La Bourgade Rurale des IVe-VIIe Siècles en Orient', *Koinonia* 3 (1979), p. 32.
17. H. Pamir, 'The Orontes Delta Survey', in *The Amuq Valley Regional Reports*, pp. 67–98.
18. C. Foss, 'Lycia in History', in *Cities, Fortresses, and Villages of Byzantine Asia Minor* (Brookfield, VT: Variorum, 1996), pp. 19, 23.
19. See, most recently, L. Vanput, V. Köse, and M. Jackson, 'Results of the 2010 Pisidia Survey Project: Fieldwork in the Territory of Pednelissos', *AST* 29/3 (2011), pp. 269–92; and also previous preliminary reports.
20. Gatier, 'Villages du Proche-Orient protobyzantin', p. 45; Magness, *The Archaeology of Early Islamic Settlement in Palestine*, 198; F. R. Trombley, 'Demographic and Cultural Transition in the Territorium of Antioch, 6th–10th century', Topoi Supplement 5: *Antioche: Histoires, images et traces de la ville antique* (Lyons, 2004), pp. 341–62.
21. John of Ephesus, *Lives of the Eastern Saints*, edited and translated by E. W. Brooks in *Patrologia Orientalis* 17 (1923), pp. 233–4; Tannous, 'Syria Between Byzantium and Islam', pp. 384–8.
22. Glick, *From Muslim Fortress to Christian Castle*, p. 14.
23. Ibid., pp. 62–3.
24. Libanius, *Or.* 11.260–2.
25. Ibid., p. 11.230.
26. A. U. de Giorgi, 'Socio-economic Studies in the Territory of Antioch in the High Roman Empire', PhD dissertation, Bryn Mawr College, p. 2006.
27. See Gatier, 'Villages du Proche-Orient protobyzantin', p. 35 n. 69.
28. Dagron, 'Entre Village et Cité', pp. 32, 41–2, 52.
29. De Giorgi argues that this process also showed an endemic vulnerability, whereby a minority owned most of the land and controlled the markets, resulting in an inevitable collapse (de Giorgi, personal communication with the author, 2008).

30. J. H. W. G. Liebeschuetz, *Antioch: The City and the Imperial Administration in the Later Roman Empire* (New York, NY: Oxford University Press 1972), p. 60; see also Gerritsen et al, 'Settlement and Landscape Transformations', p. 266. For a discussion of similar patterns of late Sāsānian self-sufficient villages (more estates), see M. G. Morony, 'Landholding in seventh-century Iraq: Late Sasanian and Early Islamic patterns', in A. L. Udovitch (ed.), *The Islamic Middle East, 700–1900* (Princeton, NJ: Darwin Press, 1981), pp. 135–76.
31. E. Carlson, 'A Constantinian Coin Deposit from the Syro-Anatolian Frontier', poster presentation at ASOR Annual Meeting, Atlanta, GA, November 2010. The coins are available on open context: http://opencontext.org/sets/Turkey?proj=Domuztepe+Excavations&cat=Coin (accessed 20 May 2013).
32. Decker, 'Frontier Settlement and Economy', p. 264.
33. Eger, 'The Swamps of Home'.
34. Glick, *From Muslim Fortress to Christian Castle*, p. 12.
35. Wickham, *Framing the Early Middle Ages*.

Chapter 7 Hydraulic Villages in the Early Islamic Period (Seventh to Tenth Centuries)

1. Jarīr, *Dīwān Jarīr*, vol. I, p. 291, lines 39–45. I am grateful to Tahera Qutbuddin for assistance with the translation. For 'bite their fingertips' (line 6), see Qur'an 3:119; for 'pairs of fruit trees and date palms' (line 7), cf. Qur'an 50:10 and 55:52. See Nadler, 'Die Umayyadenkalifen im Spiegel ihrer zeitgenössichen Dichter', p. 262.
2. Wilkinson, 'Regional Approaches', p. 237.
3. Similar patterns of contraction and, in some cases, reduction around a fortified core (such as Ephesus, Ankara, and Amorium) have been noted throughout Anatolia as well from the seventh century onwards. For general discussion and examples, see Haldon, *Byzantium in the Seventh Century*, pp. 108–9.
4. Wilkinson, 'Regional Approaches', p. 242, Table III; 243, Figure 4; pp. 246, and 247, where he calls attention to these instances of 'differential growth'.
5. Anonymous, 'AG1022, Chronicle of AD 819', in Palmer, *The Seventh Century in the West-Syrian Chronicles*, p. 79; Hoyland, *Theophilus of Edessa's Chronicle*, p. 206, Appendix 2, p. 317.
6. Decker, 'Frontier Settlement and Economy', p. 252.
7. J. Bradbury, '"Presencing the Past": A case study of Islamic rural burial practices from the Homs region, Syria', in S. McPhillips and P. Wordsworth (eds), *Materiality of the Islamic Rural Economy: Archaeological Perspectives on Extra-Urban Life*, proceedings of the conference held 24–25 August 2013 at the University of Copenhagen (forthcoming).
8. See Chapter 2, fn. p. 43.

9. See Chapter 2, fn. p. 66.
10. See A. Palmer, *Monk and Mason on the Tigris Frontier* (Cambridge: University of Cambridge, 1990), pp. 111–12.
11. P. Brown, 'The Rise and Function of the Holy Man in Late Antiquity', *The Journal of Roman Studies* 61 (1971), pp. 85–90; Durak, 'Commerce and Networks of Exchange', pp. 368–70 and 394–5 for Jacobite (*Suryānī*) merchants.
12. Their isolation and contraction may also be due to the decline in the trans-Mediterranean trade and markets, which were important for their surplus production of olive oil. Kennedy suggests that economic and population pressures may have caused a shift in population whereby many left the rocky hills to settle in the Balikh and Khābūr and Euphrates valleys, thus contributing to the growth of settlement there. See Kennedy, 'Introduction', *Proche Orient?* p. xv; F. R. Trombley, 'Demographic and Cultural Transition in the Territorium of Antioch, 6th–10th century', pp. 341–62. This differs from the southern portion of Bilād al-Shām, particularly at church centers in Umm ar-Rasas and Madaba. H. Saradi, *The Byzantine City in the Sixth Century: Literary Images and Historical Reality* (Athens: Perpinia Publications, 2006), pp. 35–6. See also C. Foss, 'Byzantine Saints in Early Islamic Syria', *Analecta Bollandiana* 125 (2007), pp. 97–9; 'The Life of Timothy of Khākhustā', J. Lamoreaux and C. Cairala, eds and trans., *Patrologia Orientalis* 48/4 (2000), pp. 9–33.
13. De Giorgi, 'Socio-economic Studies'; see also Tannous, 'Syria Between Byzantium and Islam', pp. 361–2.
14. Yāqūt, *Mu'jam al-buldān* (1990), p. 3.283.
15. Theodota of Amida, *Life*, section p. 175.
16. Ur, Karsgaard, and Oates, 'The Spatial Dimensions of Early Mesopotamian Urbanism', p. 16.
17. The *thughūr* of al-Andalus includes not only the Pyrenees mountain area of Aragon, Castile, and Asturias, but also the eastern coastal area of Valencia, Murcia, and Almería, and the Balearic Islands. This area was also known as *sharq al-Andalus*.
18. Balearic Islands: M. Barceló, 'Immigration Berbère et établissements Paysans à Ibiza (902–1235)', in *Castrum* 7; H. Kirchner, 'Original design, tribal management and modifications in medieval hydraulic systems in the Balearic Islands (Spain)', *World Archaeology* 41/1, (2009) pp. 161. Granada and Almería: P. Cressier, 'Archéologie des structures hydrauliques en al-Andalus', in *El agua en zonas áridas: Arqueología e historia*, I Coloquio de Histora y Medio Físico, Vol. I (Almería: Instituto de Estudios Almerienses, 1989), pp. li–xcii; A. Malpica Cuello, 'Repoblaciones y nueva organización del espacio en zonas costeras granadinas', in M. A. Ladero Quesada (ed.), *La incorporación de Granada a la Corona de Castilla* (Granada: Diputación Provincial, 1993), pp. 513–58.
19. 'c'est la structure caractéristique du peuplement d'époque musulmane, éclatée en noyaux d'habitats peu distants les uns des autres et lies étroitement aux canaux d'irrigations, qui apparaît.' A. Bazzana, 'Villages et terroirs andalous:

Quelques aspects du peoplement medieval et de l'exploitation agraire dans al-Andalus', *Ruralia II* (Pamarky Archeologicke) Supplementum 11 (1998), p. 142.

20. Wilkinson and Rayne, 'Hydraulic Landscapes', p. 117.
21. For a recent example, see F. Braemer, D. Genequand, C. Dumond Maridat, P.-M. Blanc, J.-M. Dentzer, D. Gazagne, and P. Welch, 'Long-term management of water in the Central Levant: the Hawran case (Syria)', *World Archaeology* 41.1, (2009) pp. 36–57, especially 46–50 for local development; and Braemer et al., 'Conquest of New Lands and Water Systems', p. 110, for both local and centralized irrigation development. For al-Andalus, see Glick, *From Muslim Fortress to Christian Castle.*
22. Theodota of Amida, *Life*, section 85; in section 127, we learn of a monastery that becomes exempt from the *jizya*. Abu Yusuf (d. 798), in his *Kitab al-Kharaj*, states that *jizya* was only taken from monks living in monasteries if they were wealthy. If they were poor, it was to be paid on their behalf by wealthy monks. *Jizya* was also paid by ascetics who lived in towers (*ahl al-ṣawāmi'*, or stylites) only if they were wealthy; otherwise, monasteries paid for them. Abū Yūsuf Ya'qūb b. Ibrāhīm, *Kitāb al-kharāj* (Cairo: Matba'a al-Salafiya wa-Maqtabatuhā, 1962 or 1963), p. 146, via Tannous, 'Syria Between Byzantium and Islam', p. 364.
23. Balādhurī, *Futūḥ al-buldan* (1987), p. 237.
24. R. Stephen Humphreys, 'Christian communities in Early Islamic Syria and Northern Jazira: the dynamics of adaptation', in J. Haldon (ed.), *Money, Power, and Politics in Early Islamic Syria* (Burlington, VT: Ashgate, 2010), pp. 52–3.
25. For the most recent work, see the exhaustive study by G. K. Katbi, *Islamic Land Tax – *al-Kharāj*: From the Islamic Conquests to the 'Abbāsid Period*, Razia Ali, trans. (London: I.B. Tauris, 2010), who demonstrates the shifts and complexities of this tax from region to region and over time.
26. The definitions vary slightly in sources; see ibid., pp. 231–2.
27. Ibid., p. 247.
28. See Qudāma b. Ja'far, *Taxation in Islām, Vol. II. Qudāma b. Ja'far's Kitab al-Kharāj*, A. Ben Shemesh, trans. (Leiden: Brill, 1965), Chapter 6, p. 32; H. Kennedy, 'Feeding of the Five Hundred Thousand', pp. 181–2; Bonner, *Aristocratic Violence and Holy War*, pp. 140–5.
29. Michael the Syrian, *Chronique*, vol. 3, p. 470; vol. 4, p. 446; Morony, 'Michael the Syrian as a Source', p. 143.
30. For examples in 'Iraq and Iran, see I. M. Lapidus, 'Arab Settlement and Economic Development of Iraq and Iran in the Age of the Umayyad and Early Abbasid Caliphs', in A. L. Udovitch, *The Islamic Middle East, 700–1900* (Princeton, NJ: The Darwin Press, 1981), pp. 177–208; H. Kennedy, 'The impact of Muslim rule on the pattern of rural settlement in Syria', in P. Canivet and J.-P. Rey Coquais (eds), *La Syrie de Byzance à l'Islam VII-VIII siécles* (Damascus: Institut Français de Damas, 1992), p. 291.
31. Yāqūt, *Mu'jam al-buldān* (1990), p. 2.306; Ibn Serapion, 'Description of Mesopotamia and Baghdād', notes by G. Le Strange, p. 59. Maslama also built

canals in southern 'Iraq on *qaṭī'a* lands that he received, thereby gaining prestige among farmers. Balādhurī, *Futūḥ al-buldān* (1987), p. 413; H. Kennedy, 'Feeding of the Five Hundred Thousand', p. 179.

32. Haase, 'Is Madīnat al-Fār', p. 247; idem, 'Madinat al-Far, the Regional Late Antique Tradition of an Early Islamic Town', in *Continuity and Change*, p. 167; S. Heidemann, 'Finds in Bilad al-Sham: the Case of the Diyar Mudar', in *Residences, Castles, Settlements*, p. 501.
33. Wilkinson, 'Water and Human Settlement', p. 75.
34. H. Kennedy, 'Elite incomes in the Early Islamic state', in F. Donner (ed.), *The Articulation of Early Islamic State Structures* (Burlington, VT: Ashgate, 2012), p. 143; Katbi, 'Islamic Land Tax', pp. 239–40, 249.
35. Heidemann, 'The History of the Industrial and Commercial Area', pp. 32–52; Toueir, 'Le Nahr el-Nil', p. 218.
36. Challis et al., 'Corona Remotely-Sensed Imagery in Dryland Archaeology', pp. 148–9.
37. Agapius and Chronicle of 1234, in Theophilus of Edessa, *Chronicle*, pp. 258–9.
38. Ibn Shaddād, *al-'Alāq al-Khaṭīra*, p. 14. Other travellers noted canals around Ḥarrān; see Le Strange, *Palestine under the Moslems*, p. 103.
39. For Ra's 'Ayn see Sarakhsī via Yāqūt, *Mu'jam al-buldān* (1990), 3.15–16; F. Rosenthal, *Aḥmad b. aṭ-Tayyib as-Saraḫsī* (New Haven, CT: American Oriental Society, 1943), p. 71 (English translation). For Bājaddā, see Sarakhsī via Yāqūt, *Mu'jam al-buldān* (1955–7), 1.372, Rosenthal, *Aḥmad b. aṭ-Tayyib as-Saraḫsī*, p. 73.
40. Originally put forth by J. Sauvaget, 'Chateaux umayyades de Syrie', *Revue des Études Islamiques* 35 (1967), pp. 1–49; then H. Kennedy, 'The Impact of Muslim Rule', pp. 291–7. D. Genequand, "Lés etablissements dés elites Omèyyades en Palmyrene et au Proche-Orient (Beirut: Institut français du Proche-Orient, 2012)
41. The location of the Zaytūna Canal, mentioned in the *Chronicle of Zuqnīn* as having been built by Hishām along 'towns and forts and many villages' in 717–18, is not completely known but thought to be in the same region, around Raqqa. Pseudo-Dionysius, *The Chronicle of Zuqnin* (Toronto: Pontifical Institute of Mediaeval Studies, 1999), pp. 160–1; Michael the Syrian, *Chronique*, vol. 3, p. 490; vol. 4, p. 457; Sarre and Herzfeld, *Archäologische Reise im Euphrat und Tigris-Gebiet* (Berlin: D. Reimer, 1911); see M.-O. Rousset, 'La Moyenne Vallée de l'Euphrate d'Après les Sources Arabes', in S. Berthier, *Peuplement rural*, p. 565, n. 79. See Robinson, *Empire and Elites*, p. 87, fn. 189. Morony, 'Michael the Syrian as a Source', p. 143.
42. Hoyland, Theophilus of Edessa's Chronicle, pp. 223–4.
43. H. Kennedy, 'The Impact of Muslim Rule', p. 292.
44. Lapidus, 'Arab Settlement and Economic Development of Iraq and Iran', pp. 187–8. Lapidus argues that the focus then shifted to building up Baghdād and Samārrā'.

45. St. Simeon of the Olives, *Life*; Tannous, 'Syria Between Byzantium and Islam', p. 371.
46. Qudāma b. Ja'far, *Taxation in Islam*, pp. 60–2.
47. Ibid., pp. 61–2.
48. Balādhurī, *Futūḥ al-buldān* (1987), pp. 205–6.
49. H. Kennedy, 'Elite Incomes', pp. 142–3.
50. Wilkinson and Rayne, 'Hydraulic Landscapes', p. 138.
51. A. Wilson, 'Water-Mills at Amida: Ammianus Marcellinus 18.8.11', *The Classical Quarterly*, New Series, Vol. 51.1 (2001): pp. 231–6.
52. Robinson, *Empires and elites*, 85; Braemer et al, 'Long-term management', p. 50.
53. Al-Azdī, Ta'rīkh 26, 28, 33, p. 43.
54. See Wilkinson and Rayne, 'Hydraulic Landscapes', 138, and also for a chart and discussion showing that post-Iron Age irrigation works occurred in areas where there was more rainfall, and therefore supplemented a variety of functions including water supply to baths, latrines, nymphaea, and ablution areas in mosques.
55. See Wilkinson and Rayne, 'Hydraulic Landscapes', 138, and also for a chart and discussion showing that post-Iron Age irrigation works occurred in areas where there was more rainfall, and therefore supplemented a variety of functions including water supply to baths, latrines, nymphaea, and ablution areas in mosques. P. Bardhan, *'Symposium on Management of Local Commons,' Journal of Economic Perspectives* 7 (1993), pp. 87–92, esp. 90; Glick, *From Muslim Fortress to Christian Castle*, p. 69. See also M. Barceló, *The Design of Irrigation Systems in al-Andalus* (Bellaterra: Universitat Autònoma de Barcelona, Servei de Publications, 1998); L. P. Martínez Sanmartín, 'El studio social de los espacios hidráulicos', *Taller d'Història* (Valencia) 1 (1993), pp. 90–3; Kirchner, 'Original design', pp. 151–168.
56. M. Barceló, 'La arqueología extensiva y el studio de la creación del espacio rural', in M. Barceló (ed.), *Arqueología medieval: En las afueras del 'medievalismo'* (Barcelona: Crítica, 1988), p. 213; T. F. Glick, ibid., p. 69, Kirchner, 'Original design', p. 156; T.F. Glick, 'Irrigation in medieval Spain: a personal narrative across a generation', in J. Marcus and C. Stanish (eds), *Agricultural Strategies* (Los Angeles: Cotsen Institute of Archaeology, UCLA, 2006), p. 175. However, Stephen McPhillips, disagrees that mills have to be placed at the end of an irrigation system or reduce the flow of water to downstream sites or other mills (S. McPhillips, personal communication with the author, 14 March 2013).
57. Barceló, 'Immigration Berbère', pp. 291–321; Glick, *From Muslim Fortress to Christian Castle*, p. 32.
58. See Chapter 2, fn. p. 65.
59. S. Rost and A. Hamdani, 'Traditional Dam Construction in Modern Iraq', *Iraq* 53 (2011), pp. 213–14.
60. T. V. Pérez Medina, 'Regadiu i poblament als afores de l'Horta de València', *Afers* 33/34 (1999), pp. 603–17. See the foundational work by A. Bazzana, P. Cressier, and P. Guichard, *Les châteaux ruraux d'Al-Andalus* (Madrid: Casa de

Velázquez, 1988). See, also, an example of recent work by S. Gilotte: 'L'Estrémadure centre-orientale (VIIIe-XIIIe s.), peuplement et formes d'habitat aux marges d'al-Andalus', PhD dissertation, Université de Paris IV-Sorbonne, p. 2004.

61. Casana, 'From Alalakh to Antioch', p. 65.
62. For Sicily, see H. Bresc, 'Les eaux siciliennes: une domestication inachevée du XIIe au XVe siècle', in E. Crouzet-Pavan and J.-C. Maire-Vigueuer (eds), *Water Control in Western Europe, Twelfth-Sixteen Centuries*, proceedings of the Eleventh International Economic History Congress, vol. B2 (Milan: Università Bocconi, 1994), pp. 73–85; for Andalus, see fn. 63 above.
63. See, for example, S. Gutiérrez Lloret, 'La formación de Tudmir desde la periferia del estado islámico', *Cuadernos de Madīnat al Zahrā,* III (1991), pp. 9–21.
64. Glick, *From Muslim Fortress to Christian Castle*, p. 44.
65. R. Azuar Ruiz, 'La rábita califal de Guadamar y el paleoambiente del Bajo Segura (Alicante) en el siglo X', *Boletín de Arqueología Medieval* 5 (1991), pp. 135–50, esp. 145.
66. Glick, *From Muslim Fortress to Christian Castle*, p. 44.
67. Glick, 'Tribal Landscapes of Islamic Spain', p. 122.
68. Glick, *From Muslim Fortress to Christian Castle.*
69. Malaria is one reason, but it was likely not a deterrant for marsh settlement before the seventeenth century. See Eger, 'The Swamps of Home', p. 70 for discussion and bibliography.
70. Naval Staff Intelligence Department (British Admiralty), *A Handbook for Asia Minor*, Volume 4, Part 2 *Cilicia, Anti-Taurus and North Syria* (London: Naval Staff Intelligence Department, 1919), p. 13; V. Cuinet, *La Turquie d'Asie. Géographie administrative, statistique, descriptive et raisonée de chaque province de l'Asie-Mineure*, Volume 2 (Paris: E. Leroux, 1890–5), p. 23.
71. British Admiralty, *Handbook for Asia Minor*, p. 19.
72. Cuinet, *La Turquie d'Asie*, p. 23. Saltés near Huelva, Spain was a long-lasting Classical and Islamic site located on an island in a wetland delta and mentioned by Islamic geographers. Its Islamic name, Shaltīsh, alludes to the production of salt, and excavations revealed two *salina* basins dated to the Roman period. A. Bazzana, J. B. García, and J. de Meulemeester, '*Shaltīsh* (Huelva-Espagne) une ville dans les marais', *Archéologie Islamique* 4 (1994), p. 92.
73. Le Strange, *Palestine under the Moslems*, p. 61.
74. Challis et al., 'Corona Remotely-Sensed Imagery in Dryland Archaeology', p. 144.
75. H. Kennedy, 'Feeding of the Five Hundred Thousand', p. 180.
76. J. Pournelle, 'Marshland of Cities: Deltaic Landscapes and the Evolution of Early Mesopotamian Civilizations', PhD dissertation, University of California San Diego, 2003; Eger, 'The Swamps of Home'.
77. A reed mat with an Arabic inscription from Tiberias is a rare surviving example of such handicrafts, Benaki Museum in Athens (ΓΕ 14735);

Muqaddasī, *Aḥsan al-tāqasīm fi m'arifāt al-iqlīm*, in M. J. de Goeje (ed.), Bibliotheca Geographorum Arabicorum ma'rifat 3 (Leiden: Brill, 1906), pp. 161–2, talks about Qadas, a small town in Palestine, whose inhabitants' livelihood comes from weaving reed mats (*al-ḥuṣur*).

78. Rost and Hamdani, 'Traditional Dam Construction in Modern Iraq', p. 201; A. Na'aman, 'Le pays de Homs: étude de régime agraire et d'economie rurale', PhD dissertation, Sorbonne, 1950, p. 23.
79. Kirchner, 'Original design', p. 154.
80. M. Rowton, 'Urban Autonomy in a Nomadic Environment', *Journal of Near Eastern Studies* 32 (1973), pp. 201–15 discusses this; see also Wilkinson, 'Water and Human Settlement', p. 80.
81. Berthier, *Peuplement rurale*, p. 163.
82. Samuel, 'Archaeobotanical Evidence', in ibid.; M. Decker, 'Plants and Progress: Rethinking the Islamic Agricultural Revolution', *Journal of World History* 22/2 (2009), pp. 187–206.
83. Rice was already growing in the wetlands of southern Iraq when the Arabs conquered the area in the mid-seventh century, according to the Babylonian Talmud. See Decker, 'Plants and Progress', p. 195.
84. Anazarbus inscription: G. Dagron and D. Feissel, *Inscriptions de Cilicie.* Travaux et Mémoires du Centre de Recherche d'Histoire et Civilisation de Byzance, Collège de France, Monographies 4 (Paris: de Boccard, 1987), pp. 182 and n. 92. This is speculated based on the fragmentary word ζιον, which may read Ὀρύριον. See A. B. Finkelstein, 'Julian Among Jews, Christians, and "Hellenenes" in Antioch: Jewish Practice as a Guide to "Hellenes" and a Goad to Christians'. PhD dissertation, Harvard University, 2011, p. 109, n. 71, n. 112. For Ṭarsūs, see M. Canard, 'Le Riz dans le Proche Orient aux premiers siècles de l'Islam', *Arabica* 6/2 (1959), p. 118.
85. M. L. Venzke, 'Rice Cultivation in the Plain of Antioch in the 16th Century: The Ottoman Fiscal Practice', *Archivum Ottomanicum* XII (1987–92), pp. 175–271; H. İnalcık, 'Rice Cultivation and the *Çeltükci-Re'âyâ* System in the Ottoman Empire', *Turcica* 14 (1982), pp. 81, 86–8, 94–5, 102, 109, 112–13. In the Ottoman period, canal maintenance and rice cultivation involved a small team – as at Adana in Cilicia, where a canal system was headed by one headman (*re'īs*), who was responsible for the irrigation canal; three irrigation workers (*saqqās*); and 15 workers (*rencber*).
86. A. M. Watson, *Agricultural Innovation in the Early Islamic World: The Diffusion of Crops and Farming Techniques, 700–1100* (New York, NY: Cambridge University Press, 1983), p. 16, map 2; for Mar'ash, see E. Carter, Introduction, in E. Carter (ed.), *Survey and Excavation on the Syro-Anatolian Frontier* (forthcoming); British Admiralty, *A Handbook of Asia Minor*, Vol. 4, part 2, p. 115. The handbook observes that rice was exported, as it was better than the Indian variety but not as good as Italian or Egyptian rice.
87. Wilkinson would classify these as nomadic pastoralist camps – 'Regional Approaches', p. 251 – but this is not reflected in the historical record.

88. For more, see Eger, *'Ḥiṣn, Ribāṭ, Thaghr, or Qaṣr?'*. Differences between *funduq* and *khān* are similarly indistinguishable, although either term may have been used in different parts of the Islamic world; see O. R. Constable, *'Funduq, Fondaco*, and *Khān* in the wake of Christian commerce and crusade', in A. E. Laiou and R. P. Mottahadeh (eds), *The Crusades from the Perspective of Byzantium and the Muslim World* (Washington, DC: Dumbarton Oaks Research Library and Collection, 2001), p. 145.
89. Redford, *The Archaeology of the Frontier*, p. 13.
90. The two enclosures at Lidar Höyük and Site 11 from the Gritille Survey, although only 6 km east of Sumaysāṭ, sat across the river from one another and may have functioned not only as way stations but as a crossing point.
91. H. Kennedy, 'Feeding of the Five Hundred Thousand', pp. 179–180.
92. However, this frontier has been deconstructed as being solely a militarized boundary by Squatriti, 'Moving Earth and Making Difference', in *Borders Barriers*, pp. 59–90 and Rashev, 'Remarks on the Archaeological Evidence of Forts', in *Borders Barriers*, pp. 51–8.
93. Wilkinson, 'Settlement and Land Use', pp. 14, 20.
94. Wheatley, *The Places Where Men Pray Together*, pp. 114–15.
95. O. Constable, *Housing the Stranger in the Mediterranean World: Lodging, Trade, and Travel in Late Antiquity and the Middle Ages* (Cambridge: Cambridge University Press, 2003), pp. 50–1.
96. See ibid., p. 51.
97. See Eger, 'Ḥiṣn, Ribāṭ, Thaghr, or Qaṣr?'.
98. D. Whitcomb, 'Archaeological Research at Hadir Qinnasrin, 1998', *Archèologie Islamique* 10 (2000), p. 27.
99. R. Jarno, 'Tente et maison, le jeu annuel de la sédentarisation à Qdeir (Syrie)', in O. Aurenche (ed.), *Nomades et sédentaires* (Paris: Centre Jean Palerne, 1984), pp. 191–229.
100. Whitcomb, 'Archaeological Research at Hadir Qinnasrin', p. 27. This *ḥāḍir* was posited as the settlement of the Ṭayyi' and of the Tanūkh.
101. Michael the Syrian, *Chronique*, III, p. 1, IV, pp. 478–9; Morony, 'Michael the Syrian as a Source', p. 158.
102. Northedge ('Archaeology and New Urban Settlement in Early Islamic Syria and Iraq', pp. 234 and 239) suggests that Ḥiṣn Maslama may further be associated with 'Anjar, based on chronology and patronage. Based on Syriac texts, 'Anjar may be credited to the work of 'Abbās b. al-Walīd, a general who frequently campaigned with Maslama b. 'Abd al-Malik.
103. See Heidemann, 'The Agricultural Hinterland', pp. 43–57.
104. Balādhurī, *Futūḥ al-buldān* (1957–8), p. 245. Translation following P. K. Hitti, trans., *Origins of the Islamic State*, p. 278.
105. H. Kennedy, 'Feeding of the Five Hundred Thousand', p. 180. T. Bianquis, 'Raḥba et les tribus arabes avant les croisades', *Bulletin d'études orientales* 41–42 (1993), pp. 23–52.

106. Malaṭiya soldiers received 100-dīnār pay raises, while those in Ḥadath received 40 dīnār per soldier as well as bonuses and houses. For discussion, see von Sivers, 'Taxes and Trade', fn. 15 and 24 for other frontier fort-settling incentives with housing and land.
107. Al-Balādhurī, *Futūḥ al-Buldān* (1957–8), pp. 120–1; Abu Ezzah, 'The Syrian Thughūr', p. 49; but see H. Kennedy, *The Armies of the Caliphs: Military and Society in the Early Islamic State* (New York, NY: Routledge, 2001), p. 12 and fn. 74, which briefly mentions that it is maybe unclear whether Persians were moved to or from the city but were settled in the region.
108. Abu Ezzah, 'The Syrian Thughūr', p. 124.
109. Both father and son also patronized building projects on the way stations of another route, the Darb Zubayda. Ibid., pp. 89–91.
110. The family had lands around Ḥalab, Manbij, and the Euphrates in the central *thughūr*. See, for example, H. Kennedy, *The Early Abbasid Caliphate* (Totowa, NJ: Barnes and Noble Books, 1981), pp. 74–5.
111. See individual entries in Eger, *The Spaces Between the Teeth: A Gazetteer.*
112. Abu Ezzah, 'The Syrian Thughūr', p. 90.
113. Bonner, *Aristocratic Violence and Holy War*, pp. 71–5.
114. See M. Cooperson, 'The Grave of al-Ma'mūn in Ṭarsūs', *'Abbasid Studies: Occasional Papers of the School of 'Abbasid Studies, Cambridge, 6–10 July 2002* (2004), pp. 47–60.
115. Donner, *Early Islamic Conquests*, pp. 263–4.
116. Robinson, 'Tribes and Nomads', p. 439. He sees this not as a state-sponsored policy against nomads but a reaction to the ongoing security threat. Donner does view this as an example of state-sponsored sedentarization: *Early Islamic Conquests*, pp. 253, 266.
117. T. J. Wilkinson, 'Empire and environment in the northern Fertile Crescent', in I. P. Martini and W. Chesworth (eds), *Landscapes and Societies – Selected Cases* (Dordrecht: Springer, 2010), p. 137.
118. Acta S. Theodori 54B, cited in Trombley, 'The decline of the seventh-century town: the exception of Euchaita', in Sp. Vryonis (ed.), *Byzantine Studies In Honor of Milton V. Anastos* (Malibu, CA: Undena Publications, 1985), n. 63, n. 33, p. 80.
119. Bonner, *Aristocratic Violence and Holy War*, pp. 65–8.
120. Von Sivers, 'Taxes and Trade'.
121. Robinson, *Empire and Elites*, pp. 31–2.
122. Durak, 'Commerce and Networks of Exchange', pp. 356 and 367.
123. See the argument by Abu Ezzah, 'The Syrian Thughūr', pp. 212–21.
124. H. Kennedy, 'Introduction', in *Le Proche-Orient*, p. xv; Abu Ezzah, ibid., p. 222.
125. Shaban, *Islamic History*, Volume 2, pp. 28–32.
126. Durak, 'Commerce and Networks of Exchange', p. 28; for chronological developments, see pp. 413–21.

127. M. McCormick, *Origins of the European Economy: Communications and Commerce AD 300–900* (New York, NY: Cambridge University Press, 2002), see Chapter p. 19.
128. Tannous, 'Syria Between Byzantium and Islam', p. 373.
129. Straughn, 'Materializing Islam', p. 202.
130. Ceramic evidence does not point to ninth- or tenth-century decline; however, Heidemann, 'The Agricultural Hinterland', pp. 55–6, argues for decline between 880 and 900 on the basis of a decrease in coins. The difference between these two data sets needs to be investigated further.
131. R. Bulliet, *Conversion to Islam in the Medieval Period: An Essay in Quantitative History* (Cambridge: Harvard University Press, 1979), pp. 54–6; see also pp. 81, 104–13.
132. Humphreys, 'Christian Communities', p. 55.
133. Ṭabarī, *Ta'rīkh*, II.2374–75 (Arabic) and vol. 12, p. 159 (English). See also Tannous, 'Syria Between Byzantium and Islam', pp. 524–41.
134. Straughn, 'Sacrality and the afterlife of the Byzantine-Islamic frontier'.
135. Kennedy, 'Syrian Elites from Byzantium to Islam: Survival or Extinction?', pp. 185–7.
136. Katbi, *Islamic Land Tax*, pp. 239–240, 249.
137. Donner, *Early Islamic Conquests*, p. 247; Abu Ezzah, 'The Syrian Thughūr', pp. 212–21.
138. In the regions of Valencia on the eastern coast and Serrania de Ronda on the southern coast; see Glick, *From Muslim Fortress to Christian Castle*, p. 35 note 76; M. Acién Almansa, 'Cerámica a torno lento en Bezmiliana. Cronología tipos y diffusión', *I Congreso de Arqueología Medieval Española*, Vol. 4 (Zaragoza), p. 248.
139. Glick, ibid., p. 44; S. Gutiérrez Lloret, 'El origen de la huerta de Orihuela entre los siglos VII y XI: Una propuesta arqueológica sobre la explotación de las zonas húmedas del Bajo Segura', *Arbor* 151 (1995), p. 83.

Chapter 8 The Byzantine Frontier (Seventh to Tenth Centuries)

1. Ṭabarī, *Ta'rīkh*, III.1146 (Arabic) and vol. 32, p. 238 (English).
2. See, for example, Haldon and Kennedy, 'The Arab-Byzantine Frontier', p. 105; J. F. Haldon and L. Brubaker, *Byzantium in the Iconoclast Era* (New York, NY: Cambridge University Press, 2011); P. Niewöhner, 'Archäologie und die "Dunklen Jahrhunderte" im byzantinischen Anatolien' in J. Henning (ed.), *Post-Roman Towns, Trade and Settlement in Europe and Byzantium*, vol. 2, *Byzantium, Pliska, and the Balkans*, Millennium-Studien zu Kultur und Geschichte des ersten Jahrtausends n. Chr. 5.2 (Berlin, 2007), pp. 119–57.

3. Although this is not matched clearly by vegetation shifts. W. J. Eastwood et al., 'Integrating paleoecological and archaeo-historical records: land use and landscape change in Cappadocia (central Turkey) since Late Antiquity', in T. Vorderstrasse and J. Roodenberg (eds), *Archaeology of the Countryside in Medieval Anatolia* (Leiden: Nederlands Instituut voor het Nabije Oosten, 2009), pp. 50, 53; A. England et al., 'Historical landscape change in Cappadocia (central Turkey): a paleoecological investigation of annually laminated sediments from Nar lake', *The Holocene* 18 (2008), pp. 1,229–45.
4. See Wickham, *Framing the Early Middle Ages*, pp. 596–600.
5. Wickham's assertion may be complicated somewhat by the existence of some *curiales* who did not flee and remained elite, but gave up their titles; see W. Brandes and J. F. Haldon, 'Towns, tax and transformation: state, cities, and their hinterlands in the East Roman world, ca. 500–800', in N. Gauthier (ed.), *Towns and their Hinterlands Between Late Antiquity and the Early Middle Ages* (Leiden: Brill, 2000), pp. 144–5, 156–7.
6. Settlement in the Taurus can be suggested, but there is no specifici textual evidence – although there are some isolated cases of Syrians settling down in other parts of Anatolia. See J. Haldon, '"Citizens of ancient lineage…"? The role and significance of Syrians in the Byzantine élite in the 7th and 8th centuries', in W. J. Van Bekkum, J. W. Drijvers, and A. C. Klugkist (eds), *Syriac Polemics. Studies in Honour of Gerrit Jan Reinink* (Leuven 2007), pp. 91–102, esp. 93–4, fn. 10–11; Haldon and Kennedy, 'The Arab-Byzantine Frontier', pp. 92–3; idem, 'Some Considerations on Byzantine Society and Economy in the Seventh Century', in *State, Army, and Society in Byzantium: Approaches to Military, Social and Administrative History, 6th – 12th Centuries* (Brookfield, VT: Variorum, 1995), III. 89–94; although Wickham, *Framing the Early Middle Ages*, p. 241, argues against an aristocratic emigration specifically for Anṭakiya and Edessa.
7. Ṭabarī, *Ta'rīkh*, I. 2102 (Arabic) and vol. 11, p. 102 (English).
8. This occurred in either 711–12/712–13 (according to Ibn Shaddād, *al-'Alāq al-Khaṭīra*, 127, and others) or 808–9/809–10 (Balādhurī {after al-Wāqidī], *Futūḥ al-buldān* (1987), p. 233).
9. Haldon has argued that the *theme* system was a gradual development, rather than a creation of Heraklios, and should date from the mid-seventh century into the early ninth; see J. F. Haldon, 'Military service, military lands and the status of soldiers: current problems and interpretations', *Dumbarton Oaks Papers* 47 (1993), pp. 1–67, esp. 4–11, for an overview of the debate. The system included a largely fiscal administrative arrangement under Nikephoros I, *c.*809 and following, and was introduced in these various commands, which quickly came to be known as 'themata'. See the comment above for details; Haldon, *Byzantium in the Seventh Century*, p. 215; and Haldon and Brubaker, *Byzantium in the Iconoclast Era*, pp. 723–71.
10. As argued by Leonora Neville, *Authority in Byzantine Provincial Society: 950–1100* (New York, NY: Cambridge University Press, 2004).
11. See, for example, Haldon, *Byzantium in the Seventh Century*, pp. 153–60.

12. Whether this aspect of the local economy was negotiated by *kommerkiaroi* is not clear, given the absence of concrete evidence, although it is possible in the light of the other activities attributed to them: see W. Brandes, *Finanzverwaltung in Krisenzeiten. Untersuchungen zur byzantinischen Administration im 6.-9. Jahrhundert* (Frankfurt am Main, 2002) for detailed discussion and earlier literature.
13. See J. Haldon, 'Social élites, wealth, and power', in J. Haldon (ed.), *The Social History of Byzantium* (West Sussex: Wiley Blackwell, 2009), pp. 182ff.,
14. P. Charanis, *The Armenians in the Byzantine Empire* (Lisbon: Fundação Calouste Gulbenkian, 1963), pp. 33–4; see also M. Whittow, *The Making of Byzantium, 600–1025* (Berkeley, CA: University of California Press, 1996), pp. 337ff.
15. See, for a succinct account, H. Kennedy, *The Prophet and the Age of the Caliphates*, pp. 248–306, which has many various examples.
16. J. L. Ball, *Byzantine Dress: Representations of Secular Dress in Eighth-to Twelfth-Century Painting* (New York, NY: Palgrave Macmillan, 2005), pp. 57–77, disagrees, arguing that borderland populations did not distinguish between clothing from other cultures or their own (p. 60); J. Eric Cooper and M. Decker, *Life and Society in Byzantine Cappadocia* (New York, NY: Palgrave Macmillan, 2012), pp. 205–8.
17. Decker, 'Frontier Settlement and Economy', p. 266.
18. Theophanes, pp. 376–7, in Hoyland, *Theophilus of Edessa's Chronicle*, p. 201. See also Lilie, *Die Byzantinische Reaktion*, pp. 116–17.
19. On booty, see E. McGeer, 'Booty', *Oxford Dictionary of Byzantium* (New York, NY: Oxford University Press, 2005). All the military treatises – from Hellenistic and Roman texts on into the Byzantine period – note that plundering was acceptable. Selling or exchanging of prisoners was another type of booty (discussed in G. Dagron, 'Guérilla, places fortes et villages ouverts à la frontier orientale de Byzance vers 950', *Castrum 3*, p. 46). Pedro Chalmeta speaks about a Spanish system of booty between Christians and Muslims (published in the discussion following Dagron's article). See also G. T. Dennis (ed. and trans.), 'Three Byzantine Military Treatises', *Dumbarton Oaks Texts* 9, Corpus Fontium Historiae Byzantinae 25. (Washington, DC, 1985).
20. Dagron, 'Guérilla, places fortes et villages ouverts', pp. 45–6.
21. Ya'qūbī, *Kitāb al-Buldān* (Leiden: Brill, 1892), p. 362. *Jibāl al-rūm* could also refer to the mountains as a proper name, 'Byzantine Mountains', but this still implies a differentiation between upland and lowland settlement.
22. Ibn Ḥawqal, *Kitāb ṣūrat al-ārd*, p. 181. One textual mention shows a type of interaction that caused Christian settlers to leave their lands. The gradual sedentarization of tribes (and loss of military subsidies) caused some to work the lands themselves, displacing the former Christian tenants. Bonner, *Aristocratic Violence and Holy War*, p. 75.
23. Ibn Khurradādhbih, *Masālik wa-al-Mamālik*, pp. 105–8.
24. See Haldon, *Byzantium in the Seventh Century*, Revised Edition, p. 112. But, as I have argued elsewhere, one cannot extract too much specificity from the various

Arabic terms utilized for fortifications; see Eger, 'Ḥiṣn, Ribāṭ, Thaghr, or Qaṣr?'.

25. The italic emphasis is mine. Leo the Deacon, *History*, Book III, trans. A.-M. Talbot and D. F. Sullivan (Washington, DC: Dumbarton Oaks, 2005), p. 87; idem, *Brasídas Karalēs* (Athens: Ekdoseis Kanake, 2000), p. 154. Talbot (personal communication with the author, 2012) would reread the verb as a present inifinitive, thus: 'whose people were formerly called troglodytes, because they *dwell* in caves.'
26. J. Nollé, 'X. Tyana im Mittelalter', in D. Berges and J. Nollé, *Tyana: Archäologisch-historische Untersuchungen zum südwestlichen Kappadokien* (Bonn: Dr. Rudolf Habelt GMBH, 2000), vol. 2, p. 517.
27. G. H. Brown, 'Prehistoric Pottery in the Antitaurus', pp. 123–64.
28. V. Kalas, 'Rock-Cut Architecture of the Peristrema Valley: Society and Settlement in Byzantine Cappadocia', PhD dissertation, New York University, 2000: pp. 81, 98–100, 156–8; idem, 'The 2004 Survey of the Byzantine Settlement at Selime-Yaprakhısar in the Peristrema Valley, Cappadocia', *Dumbarto Oaks Papers* 60 (2006), pp. 274, 281.
29. Ibn Khurradādhbih, *Masālik wa-al-Mamālik*, pp. 106–7. Kharamah suggests a pierced mountain, i.e. cave dwellings. For commentary, see Zadeh, *Mapping Frontiers Across Medieval Islam*, pp. 35–7, where the rest of the anecdote is translated into English; E. Van Donzel and A. Schmidt, *Gog and Magog in Early Christian and Islamic Sources: Sallam's Quest for Alexander's Wall* (Leiden: Brill, 2009), pp. 208–9.
30. F. Tütüncü, 'Land of Beautiful Horses: Stables in Middle Byzantine Settlements of Cappadocia', MA thesis, Bilkent University, Ankara, 2008. See Kalas, 'Rock-Cut Architecture', pp. 94–6, 136–8.
31. R. Ousterhout, *A Byzantine Settlement in Cappadocia* (Washington, DC: Dumbarton Oaks Research Library and Collection, 2005), pp. 79–114; see Tütüncü, 'Land of Beautiful Horses', pp. 92 and 94, and Table 1 on p. 87 for comparative heights of stables – a key diagnostic in determining what animal was stalled there. Stables that went out of use acquired benches in some cases, and may have become extra spaces for refuge.
32. Philaretos, *Life*, p. 2, lines 5–15, in Lennart Rydén, *The Life of St. Philaretos the Merciful written by his Grandson Niketas* (Uppsala, 2002). See J. W. Nesbitt, 'The Life of Philaretos (702–792) and its Significance for Byzantine Agriculture', *The Greek Orthodox Theological Review* 14 (1969), pp. 150–8. These numbers cannot be taken at face value. In spite of the fact that it is not clear to what extent the account is actually a fiction. As Philaretos is cast as Job (see C. Ludwig, *Sonderformen byzantinischer Hagiographie und ihr literarisches Vorbild. Untersuchungen zu den Viten des Äsop, des Philaretos, des Symeon Salos und des Andreas Salos*, Berliner Byzantinistische Studien 3 (Frankfurt am Main: P. Lang, 1997)), the text clearly was intended to represent a recognizable reality to its ninth-century readers or audience. See also Haldon, *Byzantium in the Seventh Century*, p. 131.
33. Philaretos, ibid., p. 62 lines 45–6 (p. 63, English).

34. Ousterhout, *A Byzantine Settlement.* This system included Ḥiṣn Sinan (modern Akhısar), Aksaray to the north, Sivrihısar to the east, and al-Agrab (Late Roman Argalos) to the south. Based on dedicatory inscriptions, Akhısar is known to have also had a church and *strategos* that continued into the eleventh century. The presence of the *strategos*, a centrally-appointed military officer, denotes a connection with Constantinople. See also P. Magdalino, 'The Byzantine aristocratic *oikos*', in M. Angold (ed.), *The Byzantine aristocracy, IX to XIII Centuries* (Oxford: B.A.R., 1984) pp. 92–111; and idem, 'Honour among Romaioi: the framework of social values in the world of Digenes Akrites and Kekaumenos', *Byzantine and Modern Greek Studies* 13 (1989), pp. 183–218; Kalas, 'Rock-Cut Architecture', p. 158.
35. M. Rautman, *Daily Life in the Byzantine Empire* (Westport, CT: Greenwood Press, 2006), p. 217, P. Pattenden, 'The Byzantine Early Warning System', *Byzantion* 53 (1983), pp. 258–99, W. M. Ramsay, *The Historical Geography of Asia Minor*, Royal Geographic Society, Supplementary Papers, Vol. 4 (London: John Murray, 1890), pp. 187, 351–3.
36. See Haldon and Brubaker, *Byzantium in the Iconoclast Era*, pp. 555–6; and M. Restle, *Kappadokien (Kappadokia, Charsianon, Sebasteia und Lykandos)*, Tabula Imperii Byzantini 2 (Vienna, 1981) for sites. Some excavation has been done at Tyana/Kemerhisar, and an eighth- to tenth-century 'Christian' building was uncovered, but little else is known from the post-Byzantine occupation (G. Rosada and M. T. Lachin, 'Excavations 2007 at Tyana', *KST* 30/3 (2008), pp. 1–6; idem, 'Tyana/Kemerhisar Excavations 2008', *KST* 31/3 (2009), pp. 269–88; idem, 'Excavations at Tyana/Kemerhisar 2009', *KST* 32/3 (2010), pp. 196–215. Work at Zeyva/Porsuk has not revealed any post-seventh-century occupation of note. See also S. Métivier, 'L'organisation de la frontière arabo-byzantine en Cappadoce (VIIIe-IXe siècle),' in E. Couzzo, V. Déroche, A. Peters-Custot and V. Prigent, eds. *Puer Apuliae. Mélanges offerts à Jean-Marie Martin* (Paris, 2008), pp. 433–454.
37. R. Matthews, 'Landscapes of Terror and Control: Imperial Impacts in Paphlagonia', *Near Eastern Archaeology* 67 (2004), pp. 200–11.
38. In Euchaita, in the Pontus, textual reference to the population coming down from strongholds when the invaders had left implies this shift. C. Foss and D. Winfield, *Byzantine Fortifications: An Introduction* (Pretoria: University of South Africa, 1986), p. 142, p. 186, fn. p. 52.
39. See A. K. Vionis, J. Poblome, and M. Waelkens, 'Ceramic Continuity and Daily Life in Medieval Sagalassos, SW Anatolia (ca. 650–1250 AD)', in *Countryside*, pp. 191–213, esp. 201–2; H. Vanhaverbeke, A. K. Vionis, J. Poblome, and M. Waelkens, 'What Happened after the 7th century AD? A different Perspective on Post-Roman Rural Anatolia', in ibid., pp. 177–90; M. Waelkens, 'Sagalassos und sein Territorium. Eine interdisziplinäre Methodologie zur historischen Geographie einer kleinasiatischen Metropole', in K. Belke, F. Hild, J. Koder, and P. Soustal (eds), *Byzans als Raum: zu Methoden und inhalten der historischen Geographie des östlichen Mittelmeerraumes* (Vienna: Österreichische Akademie der Wissenschaften, 2000), pp. 261–88.

40. Foss, 'Lycia in History', p. 30.
41. Trombley, 'The Decline of the Seventh Century Town', pp. 65–90, see fn. 14 and 39. See also Haldon and Brubaker, *Byzantium in the Iconoclast Era*, pp. 536–72; Haldon, 'Some Considerations on Byzantine Society', III. 90–1. For discussion on the timber trade, see Durak, 'Commerce and Networks of Exchange', pp. 94–5.
42. Palynological data from Lake Nar cores suggest an increase in woodland growth, especially oak, during the seventh to ninth centuries. See Cooper and Decker, *Life and Society in Byzantine Cappadocia*, p. 66; Eastwood et al., 'Integrating Paleoecological and Archaeo-Historical Records', pp. 45–69; England et al., 'Historical Landscape Change in Cappadocia', p. 1,229–45; Wilcox, 'A History of Deforestation', pp. 117–33.
43. A. Dunn, 'The Exploitation and Control of Woodland and Scrubland in the Byzantine World', *Byzantine and Modern Greek Studies* 16 (1992), p. 235, fn. 104; J. Lefort, 'The rural economy, seventh-twelfth centuries', in A. Laiou (ed.), *The Economic History of Byzantium* (Washington, DC: Dumbarton Oaks Research Library and Collection, 2002), pp. 248ff., esp. 262.
44. Ü. Akkemik, H. Caner, G. A. Conyers, M. J. Dillon, N. Karlioğlu, N. Rauh, and L. O. Theller, 'The archaeology of deforestation in south coastal Turkey', *International Journal of Sustainable Development and World Ecology* (2012), pp. 4–5.
45. Al-Bīrūnī, *al-Biruni's Book on Pharmacy and Materia Medica*, ed. and trans., H. M. Said (Karachi: Hamdard Academy, 1973), p. 216 (Arabic text).
46. Brubaker and Haldon, *Byzantium in the Iconoclast Era*, pp. 682–705. But a high degree of economic localization and non-monetary exchange already existed. See, for instance, M. Hendy, *Studies in the Byzantine Monetary Economy c. 300–1450* (New York, NY: Cambridge University Press, 1985), pp. 640–44; and A. Laiou, 'Exchange and trade, seventh-twelfth centuries', in A. Laiou (ed.), *The Economic History of Byzantium*, vol. 3 (Washington, DC: Dumbarton Oaks, 2002), pp. 696–770; and papers in the recent volume, C. Morrisson (ed.), *Trade and markets in Byzantium* (Washington DC, Dumbarto Oaks, 2012).
47. A. Yener and A. Toydemir, 'Byzantine silver mines: an archaeometallurgy project in Turkey', in S. A. Boyd and M. M. Mango (eds), *Ecclesiastical Silver Plate in Sixth-Century Byzantium*. Papers of the Symposium held 16–18 May 1986 at The Walters Art Gallery, Baltimore, MD and Dumbarton Oaks, Washington, DC, (Washington, DC: Dumbarton Oaks, 1986), p. 162. But elsewhere on Table 1 the dates for early Byzantine are listed as 400–800. Nevertheless, many transitional period sites are mentioned, but no parallels are used with Islamic period ceramics. For more on mining, see K.-P. Matshke, 'Mining', in Laiou (ed.), *The Economic History of Byzantium*, p. 117; B. Pitarakis, 'Mines anatoliennes exploitées par les Byzantin: recherché récentes', *Revue Numismatique* 153 (1998), pp. 141–85, esp. 168–74.
48. Cooper and Decker, *Life and Society in Byzantine Cappadocia*, pp. 71–3.
49. See the itinerary into Bilād al-Rūm, or Byzantine lands, in Ibn Khurradādhbih, *Masālik wa-al-Mamālik*, p. 100.

50. S. Wolf, S. Stos, R. Mason, and M. S. Tite, 'Lead Isotope Analyses of Islamic Pottery Glazes from Fustat, Egypt', *Archaeometry* 45/3 (2003), pp. 405–20. Lead (*asrab* or *usrub*) was also imported from the eastern Islamic lands to Byzantium in the eleventh century, providing another example for same-commodity two-way trade of both raw and manufactured goods between regions in Byzantine and Islamic lands (see Durak, 'Commerce and Networks of Exchange', p. 128, for lead; pp. 152–4 for discussion on two-way trade; and p. 230). Durak attributes this phenomenon to differentiation in products and regions.
51. C. Foss, 'Late Antique and Byzantine Ankara', *Dumbarton Oaks Papers* 31 (1977), pp. 27–87, esp. 78; Ṭabarī, *Ta'rīkh*, III. p. 1,242 (Arabic text) and vol. 33, p. 105 (English text).
52. For detailed discussion and lists, see Durak, 'Commerce and Networks of Exchange', pp. 96–7; as gifts, pp. 246–8, 256, 259, 271; from raids and as tribute, pp. 280, 283, 334.
53. Saint Michael Maleinos, 'Vie de Saint Michael Maleinos', in L. Petit, (ed.), *Revue de l'Orient Chretien*, 7 (1902), pp. 557–8.
54. England, et al., 'Historical Landscape Change in Cappadocia', p. 1,243; Akkemik et al., 'The archaeology of deforestation', p. 16; Eastwood et al., 'Integrating Paleoecological and Archaeo-Historical Records', pp. 57, 62.
55. Dagron, 'Guérilla, places fortes et villages ouverts', discussion following article; Kalas, 'Rock-Cut Architecture', pp. 166–7.
56. J. de Meulemeester, 'Même problème, même solution: quelques réflexions autour d'un grenier fortifié', in L. Feller, P. Mana, and F. Piponnier (eds), *Le Village Medieval et son environnement: etudes offertes á Jean-Marie Pesez* (Paris: Publications de la Sorbonne, 1998), p. 104. See also M. Hassen, 'Les Ribāt du Sahel d'Ifrīqiya: Peuplement et évolution du territoire au Moyen Age', in *Castrum* 7, pp. 147–62.
57. G. Varınlıoğlu, 'Living in a Marginal Environment: Rural Habitat and Landscape in Southeastern Isauria', *Dumbarton Oaks Papers* 61 (2007), p. 316.
58. See the review by J. F. Haldon, 'Framing Transformation, Transforming the Network', *Millenium* 5 (2008), pp. 335–6.
59. For concepts of 'defensive agriculture' and pigeon raising, see Decker, *Tilling the Hateful Earth*, 166; idem, 'Frontier Settlement and Economy', pp. 257, 260, 265. See Lefort, 'The Rural Economy', pp. 264–6, for pastoralism and transhumance, although he argues that this occurs only from the eleventh century onwards, a contemporary practice with the arrival of the Saljūqs.
60. Nikephoros Ouranos, *Taktika*, 63.1–12, 63.84–97, 65.8, trans., McGeer, *Sowing the Dragon's Teeth* 143.1, 147.9–10. For the author, see p. 80; see Durak, 'Commerce and Networks of Exchange', Table 278, esp. p. 280 on animals taken in raids. Nicephoras Phocas, *Le Traité Sur la Geurilla (De Velitatione) de l'Empereur Nicéphore Phocas (963–969)*, text and trans., G. Dagron and H. Mihăescu (Paris: Éditions du Centre National de la Recherche Scientifique, 1986), for example p. 72 (English) and p. 73 (Greek).

61. A. Dain, 'Le Partage du Butin du guerre d'après les traits juridiques et militaries', in *Actes du Vie Congrès international d'études Byzantines, Paris, 27 Juillet-2 aout 1948* (Paris: École des Hautes Études, 1950), pp. 347–52; and see fn. 19, this chapter. For the Islamic system, see, e.g., Qudāma b. Ja'far, *Taxation in Islām*, Chapter 10, and pp. 51–3.
62. J. and P. Zepos, *Jus Graecoromanum* (Athens, 1931, repr. Aaelen, 1962), i.257–57, trans. by E. McGeer, *Sowing the Dragon's Teeth*, pp. 367–368.
63. Nicephorus Ouranus, *Tactica*, in ibid., 65.37–43 (Greek text), 156–157.7 (English translation).
64. Pseudo-Jāḥiẓ, *Kitāb al-tabaṣṣur bi-al-tijārah*, ed., H. Abd al-Wahhāb (Beirut: Dār al-Kitāb al-Jadīd, 1966), p. 34; Ibn al-Faqīh, *Mukhtasar kitāb al-buldān*, ed., M. J. de Goeje, Bibliotheca Geographorum Arabicorum (Leiden: Brill, 1967), p. 148; Ibn al-'Adim, *Zubdat al-Ḥalab min tar'īkh Ḥalab*, ed., S. Zakkār, vol. 1 (Damascus: Dār al-Kitāb al-'Arabī, 1997), p. 156. For further discussion, see Durak, 'Local, Regional, and International Trade in Medieval Cilicia', and 'Commerce and Networks of Exchange', pp. 96–7, 167.
65. Acien Almansa from Glick, *From Muslim Fortress to Christian Castle*, p. 28; as mentioned by A. Bazzana and P. Guichard, 'La Conquête de Région Valencienne d'Après la Chronique de Jacques 1er et les Données Archéologiques', in *Castrum 3*, pp. 21–31.
66. See also A. Harvey, *Economic Expansion in the Byzantine Empire* (Cambridge: Cambridge University Press, 1989), pp. 151–7; Cooper and Decker, *Life and Society in Byzantine Cappadocia*, pp. 102–3.
67. P. Cobb, *White Banners: Contention in 'Abbāsid Syria, 750–877* (Albany: SUNY Press, 2001), p. 111; Haldon and Kennedy, 'The Arab-Byzantine Frontier', p. 105; see also H. Kennedy, 'Introduction', in *Le Proche-Orient de Justinien aux Abbassides*, p. xv; and H. Kennedy, 'Arab Settlement on the Byzantine Frontier in the Eighth and Ninth Centuries', *Yayla*: Report of the Northern Society for Anatolian Archaeology 2 (1979), pp. 22–4.

Chapter 9 Epilogue: Fortified Castles of the Middle Islamic/Middle Byzantine Period (Tenth to Fourteenth Centuries)

1. K. Bartl, 'Balīh Valley Survey: Settlements of the Late Roman/Early Byzantine Period and Islamic Period', in *Continuity and Change*, p. 337; Berthier, *Peuplement rural*, pp. 148, 166–7.
2. Heidemann, 'Settlement Patterns, Economic Development', p. 505.
3. Ibn Buṭlān quoted in Yāqūt, *Mu'jam al-buldān* (1955–7), 1.267, translated in Le Strange, *Palestine Under the Moslems*, p. 370.

4. Adams, R. McC., *Heartland of Cities* (Chicago, IL: University of Chicago Press, 1981); Wilkinson, 'Regional Approaches', p. 250.
5. H. Kennedy, 'Feeding of the Five Hundred Thousand', p. 198; Wilkinson and Rayne, 'Hydraulic Landscapes', p. 122.
6. Heidemann, 'Settlement Patterns, Economic Development', p. 505.
7. Mas'ūdī, *Kitāb al-Tanbīh wa al-ishrāf*, pp. 131–2, cited in A. J. Cappel, 'The Byzantine Response to the 'Arab (10th-11th centuries)', *Byzantinische Forschungen* 20 (1994), p. 115. In the early eleventh century, the 20,000 tribesmen of the Ṭayyi' and Kalb settled in this area near Anṭākiya, between Qasṭūn and Inab, south-east of Anṭākiya, near Ma'arrat al-Nu'mān. See E. Honigman, *Die Ostgrenze des byzantinisches Reiches von 363 bis 1071*, Vol. 3 of A. A. Vasiliev, *Byzance et les Arabes* (Brussels: Éditions de l'Institut de Philologie et d'Histoire Orientales, 1935), pp. 117 and n. 6 for location.
8. Robinson, 'Tribes and Nomads'; R. Cribb, *Nomads in Archaeology* (New York, NY: Cambridge University Press, 1991), p. 25; J. S. Trimingham, *Christianity among the Arabs in Pre-Islamic Times*, p. 147ff.
9. H. Kennedy, *The Prophet and the Age of the Caliphates*, pp. 221–2, 225, 238–9. It should be noted that the Ḥamdānids often employed Kurds, Turks, and other Bedouin Arabs in their professional armies.
10. Ibid., p. 262.
11. The Ḥamdānids, based in Mosul and Aleppo, however, were the most strongly linked to urban centers. Cappel, 'The Byzantine Response to the 'Arab', p. 115.
12. Although the Early Islamic period Nahr al-Abbara, which replaced the Hellenistic to Late Roman period Saḥlan-Hammām, created more irrigation land, its more gradual gradient contributed to greater sedimentation and ultimately the collapse of the system. Wilkinson, 'Water and Human Settlement', p. 82.
13. Waagé, 'The Glazed Pottery', in *Antioch-on-the-Orontes*, Vol. IV, Part 1, *Ceramics and Islamic Coins*, pp. 101–2.
14. Eger, '(Re)Mapping Medieval Antioch'.
15. Gerritsen et al., 'Settlement and Landscape Transformations', p. 276; T. Vorderstrasse, 'Coin circulation in some Syrian villages (5th – 11th centuries)', in J. Lefort, C. Morrison, and J.-P. Sodini (eds), *Les Villages dans l'Empire Byzantin*, (Paris: Réalités Byzantines 11, 2005) pp. 495–510.
16. Muqaddasī, *Aḥsan al-taqāsīm fī ma'rifat al-āqālīm*, 155. 1–5.
17. Ibn Shaddād, *al-'Alāq al-Khaṭīra*, p. 423. The villages are al-Ḥaṭṭānīya, al-Barghārīya, al-Mash'ūfīya, and al-Jadīda (Tell al-Judaidah); Jacquot, *Antioche, centre de tourisme*, p. 442.
18. C. Barrionuevo and R. López, 'Territorios campesinos: una lectura del paisaje agrícola andalusí de Níjar y Huebro, en el distrito de Arsal-Yaman (Almería)', in *Agricultura y regadío en Al-Andalus, síntesis y problemas: actas del coloquio, Almería, 9 y 10 de junio de 1995* (Almeria: Instituto de Estudios Almerienses de la Diputación de Almería: Grupo de investigación 'Toponimia historia y

arquelogía del reino de Granada, 1995), pp. 233–4; Glick, 'Tribal Landscapes of Islamic Spain', p. 126.

19. Mezraa Höyük had Hellenistic, very little Late Roman and Middle Islamic, and no Roman or Early Islamic period finds (A. T. Ökse et al., 'Research at Mezraa Höyük, 1999', in *TAÇDAM* 1999, 213–29); Akarçay Höyük had Middle Islamic period (Y. Mergen and A Deveci, 'Akarçay Höyük Excavations: 2000', in *TAÇDAM* 2000, pp. 340–6); Şaraga Höyük had Middle Islamic period over Iron Age (K. Sertok and F. Kulakoğlu, 'Results of the 1999 Season Excavations at Şaraga Höyük', in *TAÇDAM* 2000, pp. 475–86); At Gre Virike, occupation went from fourth to first half of third millennia to Middle Islamic period (A. T. Ökse, 'Excavations at Gre Virike, 1999', in *TAÇDAM* 2000, pp. 292–307).
20. C. Alvaro and F. Balossi, 'Byzantine Occupation', in G. M. Di Nocera, 'The 2000 Campaign Zeytinlibahçe Höyük', in *TAÇDAM* 2000, pp. 89–96.
21. Blaylock et al., 'The Adıyaman Survey: An Interim Report', pp. 128–9.
22. Abū al-Fidā', *Kitāb taqwīm al-buldān*, p. 267.
23. M. Cassis, 'Çadır Höyük: A Rural Settlement in Byzantine Anatolia', in T. Vorderstrasse and J. Roodenberg, *Archaeology of the Countryside in Medieval Anatolia* (Leiden: Nederlands Instituut voor het Nabije Oosten, 2009), pp. 3–8.
24. Bernat Desclot, cited by J. Torró, 'El problema del hábitat forticado en el sur del reino de Valencia después de la segunda revuelta mudéjar (1276–1304)', *Anales de la Universidad de Alicante. Historia Medieval* 7 (1988–1989), p. 55. See also Glick, *From Muslim Fortress to Christian Castle*, pp. 17–18, and note 9.
25. J. de Meulemeester and A. Matthys, 'The Conservation of Grain and the Fortified Granaries from the Maghreb to Central Europe', *Ruralia II* (Pamarky Archeologicke) Supplementum 11 (1997), pp. 165–7; idem, 'Même problème, même solution', in L. Feller, P. Mana, and F. Piponnier (eds) *Le Village Medieval et son environnement: etudes offertes á Jean-Marie Pesez*, (Paris: Publications de la Sorbonne, 1998), p. 104.
26. Michael the Syrian, *Chronique*, III, pp. 207–8, 598; M. Morony, 'Michael the Syrian as a Source'.
27. O. Constable, *Housing the Stranger*, p. 223; Ibn Jubayr, *Riḥla* (Leiden: Brill, 1907), p. 287; *Travels of Ibn Jubayr*, trans., R. J. C. Broadhurst (London: Jonathan Cape, 1952), pp. 300–1.
28. Glick, *From Muslim Fortress to Christian Castle*, p. 23.

Chapter 10 Frontier or Frontiers? Interaction and Exchange in Frontier Societies

1. D. P. Cole, *Nomads of the Nomads: The Āl Murrah Bedouin of the Empty Quarter* (Arlington Heights, IL: AHM Publishing Corporation, 1975).

2. From the Ḥimṣ scholar Artā b. al-Mundhir al-Alhānī (d. 779/80), translated by W. Madelung, 'Apocalyptic Prophecies in Hims in the Umayyad Age', *Journal of Semitic Studies* 31/2 (1986). The battle of the 'Amāq is preserved only in the *Kitāb al-fitan wa-l-malāhim* of Nu'aym b. Hammād (d. 842), folio 122a–b, 135 (a-b), 139 (b), 144 (a). See also O. Livne-Kafri, 'A Muslim Apocalyptic Tradition', *al-'Usur al-Wusta* 71/2 (2005), p. 7; S. Bashear, 'Apocalyptic and Other Materials on Early Muslim-Byzantine Wars: A Review of Arabic Sources', *Journal of the Royal Asiatic Society* (third series) 1 (1991), pp. 183–9; D. Cook, 'Muslim Apocalyptic and Jihad', *Jerusalem Studies in Arabic and Islam* 20 (1996), p. 83.
3. From Madelung, 'Apocalyptic Prophecies', folio 63b, folio 28a.
4. Robinson also calls into this model the discussion of the Roman *limes* and fortification policies of policing nomads, see 'Tribes and Nomads', n. p. 63.
5. M. B. Rowton, 'Enclosed Nomadism', *Journal of the Economic and Social History of the Orient* 71/1 (1974), pp. 1–30.
6. Qudāma b. Ja'far, *Kitāb al-Kharāj*, Bibliotheca Geographorum Arabicorum 6 (Leiden: Brill, 1889), p. 259. I am grateful to Vanessa de Gifis for help with the translation.
7. P. Brown, 'The Rise and Function of the Holy Man', pp. 83–5.
8. Haldon and Kennedy, 'The Arab-Byzantine Frontier', p. 101. See also Hendy, *Studies in the Byzantine Monetary Economy*, pp. 114–17; and Durak's table on animals acquired in raids, Chapter 8, fn. 60.
9. Robinson, 'Tribes and Nomads', p. 434.
10. McGeer, *Sowing the Dragon's Teeth*, pp. 238–42.
11. Trans. M. Bonner, 'The Kitāb al-kasb attributed to al-Shaybānī: Poverty, Surplus, and the Circulation of Wealth', *Journal of the American Oriental Society* 121/3 (2001), p. 415. See the Qur'ān, 73.20.
12. See A. Bostom, *The Legacy of Jihad* (Amherst, NY: Prometheus Books, 2005).
13. Similarly, Byzantine *akritai* in the thirteenth century were frontier soldiers who were also tax-exempt and free to take booty from their raids on the upland tribes. Their allegiance was opportunistic, and they switched sides often. See R. P. Lindner, *Nomads and Ottomans in Medieval Anatolia* (Bloomington, IN: Research Institute for Inner Asian Studies, Indiana University, Bloomington, 1983), p. 11.
14. Balādhurī, *Futuḥ al-buldān* (1957–8), pp. 264–5, translation following Hitti, *Origins of the Islamic State*, pp. 292–3: see also Ibn Ḥawqal, *Kitāb ṣūrat al-arḍ*, p. 154.
15. J. E. Woods, *The Aqquyunlu: Clan, Confederation, Empire* (Salt Lake City: University of Utah Press, 1999), pp. 29–31, fn. 26, p. 239.
16. J. Shoup, 'Middle Eastern sheep pastoralism and the Hima system', in J. G. Galaty and D. L. Johnson (eds), *The World of Pastoralism: Herding Systems in Comparative Perspective* (New York, NY: Guilford Press, 1990), pp. 195–8; L. Gari, 'A History of the Hima Conservation System', *Environment and History* 12/2 (2006), pp. 213–28; Shahîd, *Byzantium and the Arabs in the Sixth Century*, Vol. 2, Part 1: *Toponymy, Monuments, Historical Geography, and Frontier Studies*

(Washington, DC: Dumbarton Oaks Research Library and Collection, 2002), pp. 57–60.

17. S. al-Rāshid, *al-Rabadhah: a Portrait of Early Islamic Civilization in Saudi Arabia* (Essex: Longman, 1986); Shahîd, *Byzantium and the Arabs in the Sixth Century*, pp. 66–7; J. Chelhod, 'Himā', EI2.
18. M. Hassen, 'Les Ribāt du Sahel d'Ifrīqiya'; Shoup, 'Middle Eastern Sheep Pastoralism', p. 197.
19. Straughn, 'Materializing Islam', p. 206.
20. Wickham discusses the comparisons between the Anatolian plateau and Spanish meseta, which can be seen as early as 400 CE: *Framing the Early Middle Ages*, p. 79. See J. Klein, *The Mesta, A Study of Spanish Economic History, 1293–1836* (Cambridge, MA: Harvard University Press 1920), pp. 5, 8.
21. See F. Donner, 'Sources of Islamic conceptions of war', in J. Kelsay and J. T. Johnson (eds), *Just War and Jihad: Historical and Theoretical Perspectives on War and Peace in Western and Islamic Traditions* (Westport, CT: Greenwood Press, 1991), p. 34, for pre-Islamic practices; Lindner, *Nomads and Ottomans*, p. 11 for Ottoman practices.
22. Abu Ezzah, 'The Syrian Thughūr', p. 202.
23. von Sivers, 'Taxes and Trade' and Abu Ezzah, 'The Syrian Thughūr', pp. 191–238. See C. Pellat, 'Ǧāhiẓiana, I: Le Kitāb al-Tabaṣṣur bi-l-tiǧara attribute à Ǧāḥiẓ', *Arabica* 1/2 (1954), p. 159. See also Durak, 'Commerce and Networks of Exchange', p. 288; for tribute, pp. 289–91.
24. A. Özyar, 'Tarsus-Gözlükule 2007–2009: The Early Islamic Remains', *7th International Congress on the Archaeology of the Ancient Near East ICAANE*, The British Museum and University College of London; see also Özbayoğlu, 'Notes on Natural Resources of Cilicia', p. 162.
25. G. Köroĝlu, 'Yumuktepe in the Middle Ages,' in I. Caneva and G. Köroĝlu (eds), Yumuktepe: A Journey Through Nine Thousand Years (Istanbul, 2010), pp. 81, fig. 126. This was a Viking sword found in an early 11th century house during the Byzantine re-occupation.
26. N. Thierry, 'De la Datation des Eglises de Cappadoce', *Byzantinische Zeitschrift* 88/2 (1995), pp. 437–9.
27. A. A. Vasiliev, *Byzance et les Arabes, extraits des sources Arabes*, vol. 2, p. 241. For an extensive discussion on incidence of trade, merchants, markets, and goods in both Byzantine and Islamic sources, see Durak, 'Local, Regional, and International Trade in Medieval Cilicia', who argues for the existence of vibrant trade across and within the frontier despite its militarization.
28. Lewond, *History of Lewond, The Eminent Vardapet of the Armenians*, trans. Z. Arzoumanian (Wynnewood, PA: St. Sahag and St. Mesrob Armenian Church, 1982), n. p. 37.
29. Balādhurī, *Futuḥ al-buldān* (1957–8), p. 228. See Haldon and Kennedy, 'The Arab-byzantine Frontier', p. 107; Eger, *The Spaces Between the Teeth: A Gazetteer*, p. 122.
30. Wheatley, *The Places Where Men Pray Together*, p. 106; Ibn Ḥawqal, *Kitāb ṣūrat al-arḍ*, p. 217.

31. For an excellent discussion, see A. Binggeli, 'Annual Fairs, Regional Networks, and Trade Routes in Syria, Sixth-Tenth Centuries', in C. Morrison, *Trade and Markets in Byzantium* (Washington, DC: Dumbarton Oaks, 2012), pp. 281–96, esp. 285–8 and 291 for a list of specific fairs and their feast-day attributions.
32. Binggeli, 'Annual Fairs', p. 292; and Ibn Hawqal, *Kitāb ṣūrat al-arḍ*, p. 177.
33. Wickham, *Framing the Early Middle Ages*, p. 630; Haldon and Brubaker, *Byzantium in the Iconoclast Era*, pp. 521–2.
34. Ibid.. See also Trombley, 'The Decline of the Seventh Century Town', p. 85, fn. p. 51.
35. For prisoners being incorporated into tribes, see the example from the winter raid on Euchaita (Chapter 7, footnote 120, above).
36. See Durak, 'Commerce and Networks of Exchange', pp. 292–303. Prisoners were in some instances acquired then sold right back to their people.
37. E. L. Daniel, 'The "Ahl Al-Taqadum" and the Problem of the Constituency of the Abbasid Revolution in the Merv Oasis', *Journal of Islamic Studies* 7/2 (1996), p. 174.
38. Ṭabarī, *Ta'rīkh*, III.1,451–2 (Arabic) and vol. 34, pp. 168–70 (English).
39. G. Le Strange, 'Al-Abrīk, Tephrikē, the Capital of the Paulicians: A Correction Corrected', *Journal of the Royal Asiatic Society of Great Britain and Ireland* (October 1896), p. 734.
40. Dagron, 'Minorités ethniques', p. 185, n. 43.
41. See, for example, Balādhurī, *Futuḥ al-buldān* (1987), p. 204. Faliḥ Ḥusayn, 'The participation of non-Arab elements in the Umayyad army and administration', in F. Donner (ed.), *The Articulation of Early Islamic State Structures* (Burlington, VT: Ashgate, 2012), pp. 279–80.
42. Ḥusayn, 'The Participation of Non-Arab Elements', p. 281.
43. Ṭabarī, *Ta'rīkh*, I.2,507 (Arabic) and vol. 13, pp. 88–90 (English). For *musta'riba*, see ibid., II.1,185, 1194 (Arabic) and vol. 23, pp. 134, 143 (English).
44. Ibid., III.1,235 (Arabic) and vol. 33, p. 95 (English).
45. Whittow, *The Making of Byzantium*, pp. 169–70.
46. Ibn Ḥawqal, *Kitāb ṣūrat al-arḍ*, pp. 211–13; M. Canard, *Histoire de la Dynastie des H'amdanides de Jazira et de Syrie* (Paris: Presses Universitaires de France, 1953), pp. 139–40, 303, 737–9.
47. Constantius VII Porphyrogenitus, *De Ceremoniis*, p. 694.22–695.14, trans. by McGeer, pp. 365–6.
48. Lindner, *Nomads and Ottomans*, p. 40. This is echoed by Blankinship for the Umayyads: 'The *jihād* policy had worked rather well for the Umayyads by concentrating attention at the distant frontiers, keeping the troops employed, dispersing discontented elements, and above all, by legitimating Umayyad rule.' *The End of the Jihād State: The Reign of Hishām ibn 'Abd al-Malik and the Collapse of the Umayyads* (New York, NY: State University of New York, 1994), pp. 78–9.
49. H. Eid, *Lettre du calife Hārūn al-Rashīd à l'empereur Constantin VI* (Paris: Cariscript, 1992), pp. 181–3 (French translation, pp. 79–80), English via N. Maria el-Cheikh, *Byzantium Viewed by the Arabs* (Camridge, MA: Harvard University Press, 2004), p. 92.

50. See Ṭabarī for various instances: (695/6) Ṣaliḥ b. Musarriḥ in Amīd, *Ta'rīkh*, II.881–892 (Arabic) and vol. 22, pp. 32–44; (754/5) Muqātil al-'Akkī in Ḥarrān, *Ta'rīkh*, III.93 (Arabic) and vol. 28, pp. 9–12 (English); (803) 'Abd al-Salām al-Khārijī in Amīd, *Ta'rīkh*, III.689 (Arabic) and vol. 30, p. 230 (English); (824–5) Naṣr b. Shabath al-'Uqaylī in Kaysūm, *Ta'rīkh*, III.1,068–72 (Arabic) and vol. 32, pp. 138–44 (English). See Robinson, *Empire and Elites after the Muslim Conquest*, pp. 111–26 for discussion.
51. Muqaddasī, *Aḥsan al-taqāsīm fī ma'rifat al-āqālīm* (Leiden: Brill, 1906), p. 252; M. Zakeri, *Sāsānid Soldiers in Early Muslim Society: the origins of the 'Ayārān and Futuwwa* (Wiesbaden: Harassowitz, 1995), p. 238; Cobb, *White Banners*, p. 118ff.
52. Blankinship, *The End of the Jihād State*, p. 23.
53. Donner, *Early Islamic Conquests*, p. 153ff.; M. Canard, 'al-'Awāṣim', EI2, pp. 761–2; Abu Ezzah, 'The Syrian Thughūr', p. 65.
54. Balādhurī, *Futuḥ al-buldān* (1957–8), pp. 217–18, 221.
55. Zakeri, *Sāsānid Soldiers in Early Muslim Society*, p. 188.
56. Ibid., 128, 170ff; E. L. Daniel, 'Arabs, Persians, and the Advent of the Abbasids Reconsidered', *Journal of the American Oriental Society* 117/2 (1997), pp. 542–8.
57. W. E. Kaegi, 'Observations on warfare between Byzantium and Umayyad Syria', in M.A. Bakhit and R. Schick (eds), *The Fourth International Conference on the History of Bilad al-Sham in the Umayyad Period* (Amman: University of Jordan Press, Bilad al-Sham History Committee, 1989), p. 62, n. 41; Keiko speculates if the name is associated with Gurgum, the Neo-Hittite kingdom of Mar'ash: O. Keiko, 'The Expansion of the Muslims and Mountain Folk of Northern Syria – The Jarājima in the Umayyad Period', *Orient* 27 (1991), pp. 74–94, esp. 75.
58. Alkım, 'The Road from Sam'al to Asitawandawa', p. 26.
59. Keiko, 'The Expansion of the Muslims', p. 78, n. 15.
60. Mango and Scott, *The Chronicle of Theophanes Confessor*, p. 496.
61. W. E. Kaegi, 'Reconceptualizing Byzantium's Eastern Frontiers in the Seventh Century', in *Shifting Frontiers*, pp. 83–92.
62. Theophilus of Edessa, *Chronicle*, pp. 180–2. Quote from *Chronicle* of 1234, p. 182; Mango and Scott, *The Chronicle of Theophanes Confessor*, p. 506.
63. Ṭabarī, *Ta'rīkh*, II.1,185 (Arabic) and vol. 23, p. 134 (English).
64. Cobb, *White Banners*, pp. 111–15. Theodore hailed from the village of Munayṭira.
65. Hild and Hellenkemper, *Kilikien und Isaurien*.
66. S. Dadoyan, 'The Armenian intermezzo in *Bilād al-Shām* between the fourth/tenth and sixth/twelfth centuries', in D. Thomas (ed.), *Syrian Christians under Islam: The First Thousand Years* (Leiden: Brill, 2001), pp. 164–5.
67. See Chapter 8, fn. 42; M. Moosa, *Extremist Shiites: The Ghulat Sects* (Syracuse, NY: Syracuse University Press, 1988), p. 112 and fn. p. 23.
68. Ṭabarī, *Ta'rīkh*, I.2,921 (Arabic) and vol. 15, p. 125 (English), in the year 653/4.
69. Bonner, *Aristocratic Violence and Holy War*, pp. 48–50.
70. Cappel, 'The Byzantine Response to the 'Arab', p. 116.
71. Ibid., pp. 116–17, fn. 7.

72. See Eger, 'The Swamps of Home', for a more extensive discussion.
73. From Zakeri, *Sāsānid Soldiers in Early Muslim Society*, p. 170ff. This is referring perhaps to them also settling in the 'Amq Tīzīn.
74. Muqqadasī, *Aḥsan*, p. 119, translated in Wheatley, *The Places Where Men Pray Together*, p. 89.
75. Wheatley, Ibid.
76. R. Levy states that the source for this information is the tenth-century Ḥamza of Iṣfahān and also Firdawsī's *Shahnameh*: 'A Note on the Marsh Arabs of Lower Iraq', *Journal of the American Oriental Society* 44 (1924), p. 133; M. J. de Goeje, *Memoire sur les Migrations des Tsiganes a travers l'Asie* (Leiden: E. J. Brill, 1903); Zakeri, *Sāsānid Soldiers in Early Islamic Society*, p. 158ff.
77. See Zakeri, *Sāsānid Soldiers in Early Muslim Society*, p. 158ff; Levy, 'A Note on the Marsh Arabs', pp. 130–3.
78. Zakeri, *Sāsānid Soldiers in Early Muslim Society*, p. 160. One canal in the Euphrates marshes near Babylon was called the Nahr al-Zuṭṭ.
79. Balādhurī, *Futuḥ al-buldān* (1957–8), p. 230.
80. Ṭabarī mentions that they were beset by Byzantines; *Ta'rīkh*, III.1,168–9 (Arabic) and vol. 33, p. 11 (English).
81. In Baṣra, there was a Nahr al-Sayābija. Zakeri, *Sāsānid Soldiers in Early Muslim Society*, p. 162. Wheatley, *The Places Where Men Pray Together*, p. 44.
82. Levy, 'A Note on the Marsh Arabs', pp. 130–3.
83. Zakeri, *Sāsānid Soldiers in Early Muslim Society*, p. 162. One other possibility is that they came from the Armenian district of Sīsajān; see M. J. de Goeje, *Memoire sur les Migration des Tsiganes a travers l'Asie.*
84. Ṭabarī, *Ta'rīkh*, III.1,167 (Arabic) and vol. 33, p. 8 (English) in the year 834; Zakeri, *Sāsānid Soldiers in Early Muslim Society*, p. 221. The Bāhila were another Arab tribe who lived in the swamps and were resistant to the central state. See Wheatley, *The Places Where Men Pray Together*, p. 44; and A. Popović, *The Revolt of African Slaves in the 3rd/9th century* (Princetonn, NJ: Markus Wiener Publishers, 1999), p. 86, n. p. 70.
85. Ṭabarī, *Ta'rīkh*, III.1,167 (Arabic) and vol. 33, p. 8 (English); idem, III.1069 (Arabic) and vol. 32, p. 140 (English).
86. See Popović, *The Revolt of African Slaves*, p. 11.
87. Balādhurī, *Futuḥ al-Buldān* (1957–8), p. 230. The animals were brought to counter a lion menace.
88. Ṭabarī, *Ta'rīkh*, III.1,426 (Arabic) and vol. 34, p. 137 (English).
89. Abū al-Fidā', *Kitāb taqwīm al-buldān*, p. 41.
90. B. D. Shaw, 'Bandit highlands and lowland peace: The mountains of Isauria-Cilicia', *Journal of the Economic and Social History of the Orient* 33 (1990), p. 210. Alexander, also, could not take this region – see idem, p. 217.
91. Ibid., p. 213. Shaw mentions a fascinating literary anecdote: Datames had to form an alliance with one such mountain tribal chief, named Thuys, who was depicted as a barbarian with a black face, huge body, and beard. Datames takes him down into the plains and washes him, i.e. attempts to civilize him.

92. Ibid., p. 264.
93. Ibid., p. 221ff. for Cicero (Cic. *ad. Att.* 5.20.5). See also Plutarch (*Cic.* XXXVI.4) and Lucan (III.244) for Cilicians.
94. Ibid., p. 244 for Cicero, (Cic. *de Div.* 1.42; Cic. *Verr.* 2.1.38.95).
95. Ibid., pp. 246–7.
96. Ibid., p. 200.
97. See work by J. Anderson, *The Rebel Den of Nùng Trí Cao* (Seattle, WA: University of Washington Press, 2007); J. C. Scott, *The Art of Not Being Governed: an Anarchist History of Upland Southeast Asia* (New Haven, CT: Yale University Press, 2010); W. van Schendel, *The Bengal Borderland: Beyond State and Nation in South Asia* (London: Anthem, 2005).

Conclusions Dismantling and Rebuilding the Frontier

1. A. Smith, *The Political Landscape: Constellations of Authority in Early Complex Polities* (Berkeley, CA: University of California Press, 2003), p. 154.
2. This literature served to create a sense of urgency and terror on the *thughūr*, showing how Islamic frontier towns were ravaged, creating an atmosphere of fear and a need for reinforcements. See W. Madelung, 'Apocalyptic Prophecies in Ḥimṣ in the Umayyad Age', *Journal of Semitic Studies* 31/2 (1986), pp. 141–85; and S. al-Zaid, 'The Apocalyptic Frontier: Tarsus and the End of the World', paper presented at the Middle Eastern History and Theory (MEHAT) conference, University of Chicago, p. 2004.
3. Kitāb al-Siyar (Book of Military Campaigns) was a genre of literature appearing in the ninth century, by Muḥammad b. al-Ḥasan al-Shaybānī (805) and others; see Shaybānī, *The Islamic law of nations: Shaybānī's Siyar*, Majid Khadduri, trans. (Baltimore, MD: Johns Hopkins Press, 1966).
4. The most famous of these is the late-thirteenth-/early-fourteenth-century poem of Digenes Akritas, similar to the Chanson de Rolande of Andalusia. There are two versions, the late-thirteenth-/early-fourteenth-century G version, and the late-fifteenth-century manuscript E version. H. Gregoire, *Ho Digenēs Akritas, hē vyzantinē epopoiia sten historia kais ten poiēsē, hypo Henri Gregoire. Me tēen synergasia tou K. Panou Morphopoulou. Prologoi tōn kathygētōn K. K. Richard Dawkins kai Gustave Cohen. Prōtotypa geōgraphika schediasmata tou K. Ernest Honigmann* (New York, NY: The National Herald, 1942); E. Jeffreys, ed. and trans., *Digenes Akritis: the Grottaferrata and Escorial versions* (New York, NY: Cambridge University Press, 1998). For more on literary frontiers and frontier literature, see Bonner, *Aristocratic Violence and Holy War.*
5. Speeches between caliphs and emperors travelled between Heraklios and the Prophet Muḥammad, Leo III and 'Umar II, and Nikephorus and al-Muti'. The tenth-century *qaṣīda* by Mutanabbī on the Battle of Ḥadath provoked a response by the Emperor Nikephoros Phokas in exactly the same style as the tradition of dueling poetry.

6. The search for the mythical and fantastic at the edges of civilization, like the lands of Gog and Magog (Yājūj and Mājūj) or the Cave of the Seven Sleepers, illustrates a desire to place an Islamic imperial and religious claim on even the most metaphysical frontiers. Zadeh, *Mapping Frontiers Across Medieval Islam*, p. 37.
7. Some studies have shown the prevalence of Andalusian-style facades that adorned the outside of these domestic structures in Cappadocia. The cross-adoption of styles of dress and adornment also has been studied, and it parallels the rise in trans-Mediterranean aesthetic-based consumerism of the exotic in material culture, such as the export of certain glazed wares from the frontier, with Arabic and pseudo-Arabic calligraphy, to the Aegean.
8. Such as the movement of architects, marble masons, and water engineers (*muhandis al-ma'*) from Byzantium to Islamic lands to work on monuments like Cordoba or the Great Mosque of Damascus, and *vice versa*. See J. Bloom, *The Revival of Early Islamic Architecture by the Umayyads of Spain*, in M. J. Chiat and K. L. Reyerson, *The Medieval Mediterranean: Cross-Cultural Contacts* (St. Cloud, MN: North Star Press of St. Cloud, 1988), p. 38. We also have textual references such as those of Theophanes, who mentions that the plan for the Bryas Palace on the Bosphorus came from Baghdād via an emissary. Cordoban masons in the eighth to tenth centuries also built churches in the northern Christian kingdoms, fitting them with unmistakable crenellations and other Islamic motifs; see María de los Ángeles Utrero Agudo, 'Building Churches in the 8th–10th Centuries in the Iberian Peninsula. Technology and Context', paper presented at the *Masons at Work* conference, University of Pennsylvania, Philadelphia, October 2012 (R. Ousterhout, R. Holod, and L. Haselberger, eds). Particular building supplies were also shipped, such as lapis from Aghanistan to Cappadocia and marble and mosaic to Ḥalab and Baghdād.
9. Abū 'Alī b. Zur'a (d. 1008) was a Christian scholar and translator who travelled to Byzantium as a merchant. Ibn Buṭlān, who we have already encountered, was a Christian physician travelling through the frontier. See ed. 'Ibn Zur'a', *EI2*: Ibn Buṭlan; see L. I. Conrad, 'Ibn Buṭlān in Bildad al–Shām: the career of a travelling Christian physician', in D. Thomas (ed.), *Syrian Christians under Islam: The First Thousand Years* (Leiden: Brill, 2001), pp. 131–58. The Archbishop Theodore (d. 690) journeyed from Ṭarsus to Constantinple, to Rome and then to Canterbury, stopping at Antioch and Edessa. Ananias of Shirak (d. *c.*650) was a traveller and geographer from Armenia. Merchants, like the Jewish *rādhāniyya* and Rūs merchants (Slavs or *saqāliba*) crossed the frontier. Emissaries on diplomatic missions also traversed the frontier, negotiating treaties and prisoner exchanges and exchanging gifts. Muslim b. Abī Muslim al-Jarmī, held prisoner in Byzantine lands, was released in 845 and returned to Islamic lands with geographical and other knowledge; see Zadeh, *Mapping Frontiers Across Medieval Islam*, pp. 88–9. See also A. Beihammer, 'Muslim Rulers Visiting the Imperial City: Building Alliances and Personal Networks between Constantinople and the Eastern Borderlands (Fourth/Tenth-Fifth/ Eleventh Century)', *al-Masaq: Islam and the Medieval Mediterranean* 24/2

(2012), pp. 157–77. See Durak, 'Commerce and Networks of Exchange', p. 39 and Table 1, who classifies all of these as forms of exchange.

10. See Durak, 'Commerce and Networks of Exchange', pp. 235–76 for gift exchange; pp. 304–15, esp. Table 12 for relics, many of which were taken on campaigns; and pp. 315–31 for books, many of which were not religious but military and scientific. From one raid to Amorium and Ankyra (Ankara), Hārūn al-Rashīd brought back old texts which he had translated by Yūḥannā b. Māsawayh, a prominent Christian physician from Jundīsābūr. [Tannous, 'Syria Between Byzantium and Islam', pp. 47, 564–5; Ibn Abī Uṣaybi 'a, *'Uyūn al-anbā' fī tabaqāt al-attibbā*, August Müller, ed. (Egypt: al-Maṭba'a al-Wahibīyah, 1882), p. 246.]. Caliph Ma'mūn obtained books from Byzantine lands; see el Cheikh, *Byzantium Viewed by the Arabs*, p. 110.

11. J. Tannous, 'The Book of Monasteries: Selections from al-Shahbushtī's Kitāb al-Diyārāt', BA Thesis, University of Texas, Austin, 2002; E. Campbell, 'A Heaven of Wine: Muslim-Christian Encounters at Monasteries in the Early Islamic Middle East', PhD dissertation, University of Washington, 2009; H. Kilpatrick, 'Monasteries through Muslim eyes: the *Diyārāt* books', in D. Thomas (ed.), *Christians at the Heart of Islamic Rule: Church Life and Scholarship in 'Abbasid Iraq* (Leiden: Brill, 2003), pp. 19–38.

BIBLIOGRAPHY

Abū al-Fidā', '*Kitāb taqwīm al-buldān*', in M. Reinaud and M. le Baron MacGuckin de Slane, *Géographie d'Aboulféda. Texte Arabe publié d'après les manuscrits de Paris et de Leyde aux frais de la Société Asiatique* (Paris: Imprimerie Royale, 1840).

Abu Ezzah, A.M., 'The Syrian Thughūr'. PhD dissertation, University of Exeter, 1980.

Abū Yūsuf Ya'qūb b. Ibrāhīm, *Kitāb al-Kharāj* (Cairo: Maṭba'a al-Salafiya wa Maqtabātuhā, 1962 or 63).

Acién Almansa, M., 'Cerámica a torno lento en Bezmiliana. Cronología tipos y Diffusion', vol. 4 of *I Congreso de Arqueología Medieval Española*, (Zaragoza, 1986), pp. 243–6.

Adams, R. McC., *Heartland of Cities* (Chicago, IL: University of Chicago Press, 1981).

Akkemik, Ü., H. Caner, G.A. Conyers, M.J. Dillon, N. Karlioğlu, N. Rauh, and L.O. Theller, 'The archaeology of deforestation in south coastal Turkey', *International Journal of Sustainable Development and World Ecology* (2012), pp. 1–11.

Algaze, G., 'First Results of the Tigris-Euphrates Archaeological Reconnaissance Project', *Journal of Near Eastern Studies* 48 (1989), pp. 241–81.

——— *The Stratigraphic Sequence at Kurban Höyük*, vol. 2 of *Town and Country in Southeastern Anatolia* (Chicago, IL: Oriental Institute, 1990).

——— R. Breuninger, and J. Knudstad, 'The Tigris-Euphrates Archaeological Reconnaissance Project: Final Report of the Birecik and Carchemish Dam Survey Areas', *Anatolica* 20 (1994), pp. 1–96.

——— R. Breuninger, C. Lightfoot, and M. Rosenberg, 'The Tigris-Euphrates Archaeological Reconnaissance Project, A Preliminary Report of the 1989-1990 Seasons'. *Anatolica* 17 (1991), pp. 175–240.

——— A. Misir, and T.J. Wilkinson, 'Şanlıurfa Museum/University of California Excavations and Surveys at Titriş Höyük, 1991: A Preliminary Report', *Anatolica* 18 (1992), pp. 33–60.

Alizadeh, K. and J.A. Ur, 'Formation and Destruction of Pastoral and Irrigation Landscapes on the Mughan Steppe, North-Western Iran'. *Antiquity* 81/311 (2007), pp. 148–60.

Alkım, U.B., 'The Road from Samal to Asitawandawa'. *Anadolu Araştırmaları* 2 (1965), pp. 1–45.

——— 'The Amanus Region in Turkey: New Light on the Historical Geography and Archaeology', *Archaeology* 22 (1969), pp. 280–9.

Alvaro, C. and F. Balossi Restelli, 'Byzantine Occupation', in 'The 2000 Campaign Zeytinlibahçe Höyük', *TAÇDAM* 2000, G.M. Di Nocera, pp. 89–96.

Amitai-Press, R., 'Northern Syria Between the Mongols and Mamluks: Political Boundary, Military Frontier, and Ethnic Affinities', *Frontiers in Question*, pp. 128–52.

Ananias of Sirak, *The Geography of Ananias of Širak: The Long and the Short Recensions*. Introduction, Translation and Commentary by Robert H. Hewsen (Wiesbaden: Dr. Ludwig Reichert Verlag, 1992).

Anderson, J., *The Rebel Den of Nùng Trí Cao* (Seattle, WA: University of Washington Press, 2007).

'Antik muayenehane bulundu'. *Sabah*, 1 September 2011. Available at www.sabah.com.tr/Turizm/2011/09/01/antik-muayenehane-bulundu (accessed 20 May 2013).

Antrim, Z., *Routes and Realms: The Power of Place in the Early Islamic World* (New York, NY: Oxford University Press, 2012).

Archi, A., P.E. Pecorella, and M. Salvini, *Gaziantep e la Sua Regione: Uno studio storico e topografico degli insediamenti preclassici* (Rome: Edizioni dell'ateno, 1971).

Asbridge, T.S., *The Creation of the Principality of Antioch, 1098-1130* (Rochester, NY: Boydell Press, 2000).

Avni, G., *Nomads, Farmers, and Town-Dwellers: Pastoralist-Sedentist Interaction in the Negev Highlands, Sixth-Eighth Centuries CE* (Jerusalem: Israel Antiquities Authority, 1996).

Al-Azdī, *Ta'rīkh futūḥ al-Shām*.

Azuar Ruiz, R., 'La rábita califal de Guadamar y el paleoambiente del Bajo Segura (Alicante) en el siglo X', *Boletín de Arqueología Medieval* 5 (1991), pp. 135–50.

Bahnassi, A., 'Le Sauvetage des Vestiges de la Zone de Submersion du Barrage de Tabqa sur l'Euphrate'. *Monumentum* 17 (1978), pp. 57–71.

Balādhurī, A., *Futūḥ al-buldān* (Beirut: Dār al-Nashr lil-Jāmi'īyīn, 1957–8).

——— *Futūḥ al-buldān* (Beirut: Mu'assasa al-Ma'arif, 1987).

——— *Origins of the Islamic State*. Translated by P. Hitti (Piscataway, NJ: Gorgias Press, 2002).

Ball, J.L., *Byzantine Dress: Representations of Secular Dress in Eighth to Twelfth Century Painting* (New York, NY: Palgrave Macmillan, 2005).

Ball, W., 'The Upper Tigris Area: New Evidence from the Eski Mosul and North Jazira Projects'. In *Continuity and Change*, pp. 415–28.

——— D. Tucker, and T.J. Wilkinson, 'The Tell al-Hawa Project: Archaeological Investigations in the North Jazira 1986-87', *Iraq* 51 (1989), pp. 1–66.

Barceló, M., 'La arqueología extensiva y el studio de la creación del espacio rural', in M. Barceló (ed.), *Arqueología medieval: En las afueras del 'medievalismo'* (Barcelona: Crítica, 1988), pp. 195–274.

——— *The Design of Irrigation Systems in al-Andalus* (Bellaterra: Universitat Autònoma de Barcelona, Servei de Publications, 1998).

——— 'Immigration Berbère et établissements Paysans à Ibiza (902-1235)', *Castrum* 7, pp. 291–321.

Bardhan, P., 'Symposium on Management of Local Commons'. *Journal of Economic Perspectives* 7 (1993), pp. 87–92.

Barrionuevo, C. and R. López, 'Territorios campesinos: una lectura del paisaje Agrícola andalusí de Níjar y Huebro, en el distrito de Arsal-Yaman (Almería)', in *Agricultura y regadío en Al-Andalus, síntesis y problemas: actas del coloquio, Almería, 9 y 10 de junio de 1995* (Almeria: Instituto de Estudios Almerienses de la Diputación de Almería: Grupo de investigación 'Toponimia historia y arquelogía del reino de Granada, 1995), pp. 229–59.

Bartl, K., 'The Balih Valley, Northern Syria, during the Islamic Period: remarks concerning the Historical Topography', *Berytus* 41 (1993/4), pp. 29–38.

——— 'Balīh Valley Survey: Settlements of the Late Roman/Early Byzantine Period and Islamic Period', in *Continuity and Change*, pp. 333–48.

Bashear, S., 'Apocalyptic and Other Materials on Early Muslim-Byzantine Wars: A Review of Arabic Sources'. *Journal of the Royal Asiatic Society* (third series) 1 (1991), pp. 173–207.

Bazzana, A., 'Villages et terroirs andalous: Quelques aspects du peoplement medieval et de l'exploitation agraire dans al-Andalus', *Ruralia II* (Pamarky Archeologicke) Supplementum 11 (1998), pp. 140–51.

——— P. Cressier, and P. Guichard, *Les châteaux ruraux d'Al-Andalus* (Madrid: Casa de Velázquez, 1988).

——— J.B. García, and J. de Meulemeester, '*Shaltīsh* (Huelva-Espagne) une ville dans les marais', *Archéologie Islamique* 4 (1994), pp. 87–116.

——— and P. Guichard, 'La Conquête de Région Valencienne d'Après la Chronique de Jacques 1er et les Données Archéologiques', *Castrum 3*, pp. 21–31.

Beach, T. and S. Luzzadder Beach, 'Aggradation around Kinet Höyük, an Archaeological Mound in the Eastern Mediterranean, Turkey', *Geomorphology* 71/1 (2008), pp. 416–28.

Behā ed-Dīn, *Life of Saladin*, translated by L.-C. Condor, Palestine Pilgrims' Text Society 13 (New York, NY: AMS Press, 1971).

Beihammer, A., 'Muslim Rulers Visiting the Imperial City: Building Alliances and Personal Networks between Constantinople and the Eastern Borderlands (Fourth/Tenth-Fifth/Eleventh Century)', *Al-Masaq: Islam and the Medieval Mediterranean* 24/4 (2012), pp. 157–77.

Berthier, S., *Peuplement rural et aménagements hydroagricoles dans la moyenne vallée de l'Euphrate, fin VIIe-XIXe siècle* (Damascus: Institut français d'études arabes de Damas [IFEAD], 2001).

Bianquis, T., 'Raḥba et les tribus arabes avant les croisades', *Bulletin d'études orientales* 41–42 (1993), pp. 23–52.

Binggeli, A., 'Annual fairs, regional networks, and trade routes in Syria, sixth-tenth centuries', in C. Morrison (ed.), *Trade and Markets in Byzantium* (Washington, DC: Dumbarton Oaks, 2012), pp. 281–96.

Al-Bīrūnī, *Al-Biruni's Book on Pharmacy and Materia Medica*, edited and translated by H.M. Said (Karachi: Hamdard Academy, 1973).

Blankinship, K.Y., *The End of the Jihād State: The Reign of Hishām ibn 'Abd al-Malik and the Collapse of the Umayyads* (New York, NY: State University of New York, 1994).

Blanton, R., *Hellenistic, Roman and Byzantine Settlement Patterns of the Coast Lands of Western Rough Cilicia*, BAR International Series 879 (Oxford: Archaeopress, 2000).

Blaylock, S., 'Adıyaman Survey 1985–1991', in R. Matthews (ed.), *Ancient Anatolia: Fifty Year's Work by The British Institute of Archaeology at Ankara* (London: British Institute of Archaeology at Ankara, 1998), pp. 101–10.

Blaylock, S.R., D.H. French, and G.D. Summers, 'The Adıyaman Survey: An Interim Report', *Anatolian Studies* 40 (1990), pp. 81–135.

Bloom, J., 'The revival of Early Islamic architecture by the Umayyads of Spain', in M.J. Chiat and K.L. Reyerson (eds), *The Medieval Mediterranean: Cross-Cultural Contacts* (St. Cloud, MN: North Star Press of St. Cloud, 1988), pp. 35–41.

Bonner, M., 'The Naming of the Frontier: 'Awāṣim, Thughūr, and the Arab Geographers', *Bulletin of the School of Oriental and African Studies* 57 (1994), pp. 17–24.

——— *Aristocratic Violence and Holy War: Studies in the Jihād and the Arab-Byzantine Frontier* (New Haven, CT: American Oriental Society, 1996).

——— 'The Kitāb al-kasb attributed to al-Shaybānī: Porverty, Surplus, and the Circulation of Wealth', *Journal of the American Oriental Society* (2001), pp. 410–27.

——— (ed.), *Arab-Byzantine Relations in Early Islamic Times* (Burlington, VT: Ashgate, 2004).

Bostom, A., *The Legacy of Jihad* (Amherst, NY: Prometheus Books, 2005).

Bradbury, J., 'Presencing the past: a case study of Islamic rural burial practices from the Homs region, Syria', in S. McPhillips and P. Wordsworth (eds), *Materiality of the Islamic Rural Economy: Archaeological Perspectives on Extra-Urban Life.* Proceedings of the conference held 24–25 August 2013, University of Copenhagen, forthcoming.

Braemer, F., D. Genequand, C. Dumond Maridat, P.-M. Blanc, J.-M Dentzer, D. Gazagne, and P. Welch, 'Long-term management of water in the Central Levant: the Hawran case (Syria)', *World Archaeology* 41/1 (2009), pp. 36–57.

——— B. Geyer, C. Castel, and M. Abdulkarim, 'Conquest of New Lands and Water Systems in the Western Fertile Crescent (Central and Southern Syria)', *Water History* (2010), pp. 91–114.

Braidwood, R., *Mounds in the Plain of Antioch* (Chicago, IL: University of Chicago, 1937).

Brandes, W., *Finanzverwaltung in Krisenzeiten. Untersuchungen zur byzantinischen Administration im 6.-9. Jahrhundert* (Frankfurt am Main: Löwenklau, 2002).

——— and J. Haldon, 'Towns, tax and transformation: state, cities, and their hinterlands in the East Roman world, ca 500-800', in N. Gauthier (ed.), *Towns and their Hinterlands Between Late Antiquity and the Early Middle Ages* (Leiden: Brill, 2000).

Brands, G. and C. Meyer, 'Antioch-on-the-Orontes and Seleucia Pieria 2004: Preliminary Results of the Geophysical Survey', *Arkeometri Sonuçları Toplantısı* (2006), pp. 149–54.

Brauer, R.W., *Boundaries and Frontiers in Medieval Muslim Geography* (Philadelphia, PA: American Philosophical Society, 1995).

Bresc, H., 'Les eaux siciliennes: une domestication inachevée du XIIe au XVe siècle', in E. Crouzet-Pavan and J.-C. Maire-Vigueuer (eds), *Water Control in Western Europe, Twelfth-Sixteen Centuries.* Proceedings of the Eleventh International Economic History Congress, vol. B2 (Milan: Università Bocconi, 1994), pp. 73–85.

Brown, G.H., 'Prehistoric Pottery from the Antitaurus', *Anatolian Studies* 17 (1967), p. 162.

Brown, P., 'The Rise and Function of the Holy Man in Late Antiquity', *The Journal of Roman Studies* 61 (1971), pp. 80–101.

Bulliet, R., *Conversion to Islam in the Medieval Period: an Essay in Quantitative History* (Cambridge: Harvard University Press, 1979).

Butzer, K., J.F. Mateu, E.K. Butzer, and P. Kraus, 'Irrigation Agrosystems in Eastern Spain: Roman or Islamic Origins?', *Annals of the American Association of Geographers* 75.4 (1985), pp. 479–509.

Campbell, E., 'A Heaven of Wine: Muslim-Christian Encounters at Monasteries in the Early Islamic Middle East', PhD dissertation, University of Washington, 2009.

——— *Histoire de la dynastie des H'amdanides de Jazira et de Syrie* (Paris: Presses Universitaires de France, 1953).

——— 'Le Riz dans le Proche Orient aux premiers siècles de l'Islam', *Arabica* 6/2 (1959), pp. 113–31.

Campbell, S., 'Domuztepe 2003'. *Anatolian Archaeology* 9 (2003), pp. 4–6.

——— 'Domuztepe 2004 Excavation Season', *Anatolian Archaeology* 10 (2004), pp. 4–6.

——— 'Domuztepe 2005', *Anatolian Archaeology* 11 (2005), pp. 13–15.

Canard, M., 'al-'Awāṣim', *EI2*, pp. 761–2.

Caneva, I. and G. Koroğlu, *Yumuktepe* (Istanbul: Ege Yayınları, 2010).

Cappel, A.J., 'The Byzantine Response to the 'Arab (10th-11th centuries)', *Byzantinische Forschungen* 20 (1994), pp. 113–32.

Carlson, E., 'A Constantinian Coin Deposit from the Syro-Anatolian Frontier', Poster presented at the American Schools of Oriental Research (ASOR) Annual Meeting, Atlanta, GA, November 2010.

Carter, E., Introduction, in E. Carter (ed.), *Survey and Excavation on the Syro-Anatolian Frontier*. Forthcoming.

——— and S. Campbell, 'Report on the 2004 Excavation Season at Domuztepe', *KST* 27/1 (2005), pp. 313–24.

Casana, J., 'The archaeological landscape of Late Roman Antioch', in I. Sandwell and J. Huskinson (eds), *Culture and Society in Late Roman Antioch: Papers from a Colloquium, London, 15*th December 2001 (Oakville, CT: David Brown Book Company, 2002), pp. 102–25.

——— 'From Alalakh to Antioch: Settlement, Land Use, and Environmental Change in the Amuq Valley of Southern Turkey', PhD dissertation, University of Chicago, 2003.

——— 'Structural Transformations in Settlement Systems of the Northern Levant', *AJA* 111/2 (2007), pp. 195–222.

——— 'Mediterranean Valleys Revisited: Linking Soil Erosion, Land Use, and Climate Variability in the Northern Levant', *Geomorphology* 101/3 (2008), pp. 429–42.

——— J. Cothren, and T. Kalaycı, 'Swords into Ploughshares: Archaeological Applications of CORONA Satellite Imagery in the Near East', *Internet Archaeology* 32 (2012). Available at http://dx.doi.org/10.11141/ia.32.2 (accessed 29 May 2013).

——— and A. Gansell, 'Surface collection, off-site survey, and floodplain development at Tell Atchana', in K.A. Yener (ed.), *The Amuq Valley Regional*

Projects, Volume 1, Surveys in the Plain of Antioch and Orontes Delta, Turkey, 1995-2002 (Chicago, IL: Oriental Institute Press, 2005), pp. 153–70.

——— and T.J. Wilkinson, 'Settlement and landscapes in the Amuq region', in K. Aslıhan Yener (ed.), *The Amuq Valley Regional Reports, Vol. 1. Surveys in the Plain of Antioch and Orontes Delta Survey, 1995-2002* (Chicago, IL: Oriental Institute Publications, 2005), pp. 25–66.

Cassis, M., 'Çadır Höyük: A Rural Settlement in Byzantine Anatolia', *Countryside*, pp. 1–24.

Chaix, L. and J. Studer, 'La faune de quelques sites Islamiques de la moyenne vallée de l'Euphrate', in S. Berthier (ed.), *Peuplement rural et aménagements hydroagricoles dans la moyenne vallée de l'Euphrate, fin VIIe-XIXe siècle* (Damascus: Institut français d'études arabes de Damas [IFEAD], 2001), pp. 303–40.

Challis et al., 'Corona Remotely-Sensed Imagery in Dryland Archaeology: The Islamic City of al-Raqqa, Syria', *Journal of Field Archaeology* 29/1-2 (2002–2004), pp. 139–53.

Chapot, V., *La frontière de l'Euphrate de Pompée à la conquiste Arabe* (Paris: A. Fontemoing, 1907).

Charanis, P., *The Armenians in the Byzantine Empire* (Lisbon: Fundaçäo Calouste Gulbenkian, 1963).

el-Cheikh, Nadia Maria, *Byzantium Viewed by the Arabs* (Cambridge, MA: Harvard University Press, 2004).

Cheïra, M.A., *La Lutte Entre Arabes et Byzantines: La conquête et l'organisation des frontières aus XIIe et VIIIe siécles* (Alexandria: Société de publications Égyptiennes, 1947).

Chelhod, J., 'Ḥimâ', *EI2*.

Cobb, P., *White Banners: Contention in 'Abbasid Syria, 750–877* (Albany, NY: SUNY Press, 2001).

de Coca Castañer, J.E.L., 'Institutions on the Castilian-Granadan Frontier, 1369-1482', in *Medieval Frontier Societies*, pp. 127–50.

Cole, D.P., *Nomads of the Nomads: The Āl Murrah Bedouin of the Empty Quarter* (Arlington Heights, IL: AHM Publishing Corporation, 1975).

Comfort, D., C. Abadie-Reynal, and R. Ergeç, 'Crossing the Euphrates in Antiquity: Zeugma seen from Space', *Anatolian Studies* 50 (2000), pp. 99–126.

Conrad, L.I., 'Ibn Buṭlān in Bildad al-Shām: the career of a travelling Christian physician', in D. Thomas (ed.), *Syrian Christians under Islam: The First Thousand Years* (Leiden: Brill, 2001), pp. 131–58.

——— 'Heraclius in Early Islamic Kerygma', in G.J. Renink and B.H. Stolte (eds), *The Reign of Heraclius (610–641): Crisis and Confrontation* (Dudley, MA: Peeters, 2002), pp. 113–56.

Constable, O.R., '*Funduq, Fondaco,* and *Khān* in the wake of Christian commerce and crusade', in A.E. Laiou and R.P. Mottahadeh (eds), *The Crusades from the Perspectives of Byzanium and the Muslim World* (Washington, DC: Dumbarton Oaks Research Library and Collection, 2001), pp. 145–56.

——— *Housing the Stranger in the Mediterranean World: Lodging, Trade and Travel in Late Antiquity and the Middle Ages* (Cambridge: Cambridge University Press, 2003).

Constantius VII Porphyrogenitus, *De Ceremoniis aulae Byzantinae*, edited by J.J. Reisk (Bonn: Weber, 1829).

de Contenson, H., 'Le matériel archéologique des tells', in P. Sanlaville (ed.), *Holocene Settlement in North Syria*. British Archaeological Reports (BAR) International Series 238, Oxford, 1985, pp. 99–178.
Cook, D., 'Muslim Apocalyptic and Jihad', *Jerusalem Studies in Arabic and Islam* 20 (1996), pp. 66–104.
Cooper, J. Eric and M. Decker. *Life and Society in Byzantine Cappadocia* (New York, NY: Palgrave Macmillan, 2012).
Cooperson, M., 'The Grave of al-Ma'mūn in Ṭarsūs', *'Abbasid Studies: Occasional Papers of the School of 'Abbasid Studies, 6-10 July, 2002* (2004), pp. 47–60.
Cressier, P., 'Archéologie des structures hydrauliques en al-Andalus', in *El agua en zona áridas: Arqueología e historia*, I Coloquio de Histora y Medio Físico, vol. I (Almería: Instituto de Estudios Almerienses, 1989), pp. li-xcii.
Cribb, R., *Nomads in Archaeology* (New York, NY: Cambridge University Press, 1991).
Cuinet, V., *La Turquie d'Asie. Géographie administrative, statistique, descriptive et raisonée de chaque province de l'Asie-Mineure*, vol. 2 (Paris: E. Leroux, 1890–5).
Curta, F., 'Frontier Ethnogenesis in Late Antiquity: The Danube, the Tervingi, and the Slavs', *Borders Barriers*, pp. 173–204.
——— Introduction to *Borders Barriers*, pp. 1–9.
Dadoyan, S., 'The Armenian intermezzo in *Bilād al-Shām* between the fourth/tenth and sixth/twelfth centuries', in D. Thomas (ed.), *Syrian Christians under Islam: The First Thousand Years* (Leiden: Brill, 2001).
Dagron, G., 'Minorités ethniques et religieuses dans l'Orient Byzantin à la fin du Xe et au Xie siècles: L'immigration Syrienne', *Travaux et Memoires* 6 (1976), pp. 177–216.
——— 'Entre Village et Cité: La bourgade rurale des IVe-VIIe siècles en Orient', *Koinonia* 3 (1979), pp. 29–52.
——— 'Guérilla, places fortes et villages ouverts à la frontière orientale de Byzance vers 950', *Castrum 3*, pp. 43–8.
——— and D. Feissel, *Inscriptions de Cilicie.* Travaux et Mémoires du Centre de Recherche d'Histoire et Civilisation de Byzance, Collège de France, Monographies 4 (Paris: de Boccard, 1987).
Dain, A., 'Le partage du butin du guerre d'après les traits juridiques et militaries', in *Actes du VIe Congrès international d'études Byzantines, Paris, 27 juillet-2 aout 1948* (Paris: École des Hautes Études, 1950), pp. 347–52.
Dalché, P.G., 'De la liste a la carte: limite et frontière dans la géographie et la cartographie de l'occident medieval', *Castrum 4*, pp. 19–31.
Daniel, E.L., 'The "Ahl Al-Taqadum" and the Problem of the Constituency of the 'Abbasid Revolution in the Merv Oasis', *Journal of Islamic Studies* 7/2 (1996), pp. 150–79.
——— 'Arabs, Persians, and the Advent of the 'Abbasids Reconsidered', *Journal of the American Oriental Society* 117/3 (1997), pp. 542–8.
Davies, G., 'The Roman Fort at Yotvata in its Regional Context', paper presented at the annual meeting of ASOR, San Diego, CA, 2007.
Decker, M., 'Food for an empire: wine and oil production in North Syria', in S. Kingsley and M. Decker (eds), *Economy and Exchange in the East Mediterranean during Late Antiquity* (New York, NY: Oxford University Press, 2001), pp. 69–86.

——— 'Frontier Settlement and Economy in the Byzantine East', *Dumbarton Oaks Papers* 61 (2007), pp. 217–67.

——— *Tilling the Hateful Earth: Agricultural Production and Trade in the Late Antique East* (New York, NY: Oxford University Press, 2009).

——— 'Plants and Progress: Rethinking the Islamic Agricultural Revolution', *Journal of World History* 20/2 (2009), pp. 187–206.

——— 'Settlement and agriculture in the Levant, 6th – 8th centuries', in A. Borrut, M. Debié, A. Papaconstantinou, D. Pieri, and J.-P. Sodini (eds), *Le Proche-Orient de Justinien aux Abbasides: Peuplement et Dynamiques Spatiales* (Turnhout, Belgium: Brepols, 2011). pp. 1–6.

Dennis, G.T. (ed. and trans.), *Three Byzantine Military Treatises*. Dumbarton Oaks Texts 9. Corpus Fontium Historiae Byzantinae 25 (Washington, DC: Dumbarton Oaks, 1985).

Devonshire, R.L., 'Relation d'un voyage du sultain Qâitbây en Palestine et en Syrie', *Bulletin de l'Institut Français d'Archéologie Orientale* 20 (1922), pp. 1–43.

al-Dimashqī, *Manuel de la Cosmographie du Moyen Age*, translated by A.F. Mehren (Copenhagen: C.A. Reitzel, 1874).

Dodd, L., A. Green, N. Highcock, L. Cadwell, and A. Yener, 'The 2010 Amuq Valley Regional Projects Survey', *AST* 29/2 (2011), pp. 205–24.

——— A. Green, A. Yener, 'The Amuq Valley Regional Survey Project 2009', *AST* 28/1 (2010), pp. 435–52.

Donner, F., *The Early Islamic Conquests* (Princeton: Princeton University Press, 1981).

——— 'The Sources of Islamic Conceptions of War', in J. Kelsay and J.T. Johnson, *Just War and Jihad: Historical and Theoretical Perspectives on War and Peace in Western and Islamic Traditions* (Westport, CT: Greenwood Press, 1991), pp. 31–69.

Van Donzel, E. and A. Schmidt, *Gog and Magog in Early Christian and Islamic Sources: Sallam's Quest for Alexander's Wall* (Leiden: Brill, 2009).

Drinkwater, J.F., ' "The Germanic Threat on the Rhine Frontier": A Romano-Gallic Artefact?', in *Shifting Frontiers*, pp. 20–30.

Duncan Jones, R., 'Economic change in the transition to Late Antiquity', in S. Swaine and M. Edwards (eds), *Approaching Late Antiquity: The Transformations from Early to Late Empire* (New York, NY: Oxford University Press, 2004), pp. 20–53.

Dunn, A., 'The Exploitation and Control of Woodland and Scrubland in the Byzantine World', *Byzantine and Modern Greek Studies* 16 (1992), pp. 235–98.

Durak, K., 'Commerce and Networks of Exchange Between the Byzantine Empire and the Islamic Near East from the Early Ninth Century to the Arrival of the Crusaders', PhD dissertation, Harvard University, 2008.

——— 'Local, Regional, and International Trade in Medieval Cilicia: A Case Study of Byzantine-Islamic Trade in the 10th Century', in *The Center and Periphery in the Age of Constantine VII Porphyrogennetos* (12–14 November 2009), Oxford Studies in Byzantium, 2013 (in press).

——— 'Traffic across the Cilician Frontier: Movement of People Between Byzantium and the Islamic Near East in the Early Middle Ages', in *Byzantium and the Arab World, Encounter of Civilizations* (16–18 December 2011), Thessalonica, 2013 (in press).

Dussaud, R., *Topographie Historique de la Syrie Antique et Medievale* (Paris: P. Geuthner, 1927).

Eadie, J., 'Transformation of the Eastern Frontier', *Shifting Frontiers*, pp. 72–82.

Eastwood, W.J., O. Gümüşçü, H. Yiğitbaşioğlu, John F. Haldon, and A. England, 'Integrating paleoecological and archaeo-historical records: land use and landscape change in Cappadocia (central Turkey) since Late Antiquity', in T. Vorderstrasse and J. Roodenberg (eds), *Archaeology of the Countryside in Medieval Anatolia*, (Leiden: Nederlands Instituut voor het Nabije Oosten, 2009), pp. 45–70.

Edwards, R.W., *The Fortifications of Armenian Cilicia* (Washington, DC: Dumbarton Oaks Research Library and Collection, 1987).

Eger, A., 'The Spaces Between the Teeth: Environment, Settlement, and Interaction on the Islamic-Byzantine Frontier', PhD dissertation, University of Chicago, 2008.

——— 'The Early Islamic Period (mid 7th to mid 10th centuries)', in Gerritsen, F., A.U. de Giorgi, A. Eger, R. Özbal, and T. Vorderstrasse, 'Settlement and Landscape Transformations in the Amuq Valley, Hatay: A Long-Term Perspective', *Anatolica* 34 (2008), pp. 241–314.

——— 'Ḥiṣn al-Tīnāt on the Islamic-Byzantine Frontier: Synthesis and the 2005-2008 Survey and Excavation on the Cilician Plain (Turkey)', *Bulletin of the American School of Oriental Research* 357 (February 2010), pp. 49–76.

——— 'The Swamps of Home: Marsh Formation and Settlement in the Early Medieval Near East', *Journal of Near Eastern Studies* 70/1 (April 2011), pp. 55–79.

——— '*Ḥiṣn, Ribaṭ, Thaghr, or Qaṣr?* The semantics of frontier forts in the Early Islamic period', in P. Cobb (ed.), *The Lineaments of Islam: Studies in Honor of Fred McGraw Donner* (Leiden: Brill, 2012, Second Edition, 2014 forthcoming).

——— *The Spaces Between the Teeth: A Gazetteer of Towns on the Islamic-Byzantine Frontier* (Istanbul: Ege Yayınları, 2012).

——— '(Re)Mapping Medieval Antioch: Urban Transformations from the Early Islamic to Crusader Periods', *Dumbarton Oaks Papers* 67 (2013), pp. 95–134.

——— 'Patronage and Commerce at the Twilight of Mamluk Rule: Two New Fifteenth Century Inscriptions from the Amuq Plain, Turkey.' *Journal of Islamic Archaeology* 1.1 (2014), pp. 53–72.

Eid, H., *Lettre du calife Hārūn al-Rashīd à l'empereur Constantin VI* (Paris: Cariscript, 1992).

Eidem, J. and D. Warburton. "In the Land of Nagar: A Survey around Tell Brak." *Iraq* 58 (1996), pp. 51–64.

Ellenblum, R. "Were there Borders and Borderlines in the Middle Ages? The Example of the Latin Kingdom of Jerusalem." In *Frontiers in Question*, pp. 105–19.

Elton, D. "The 'Ahl al-Taqadum' and the Problem of the Constituency of the Abbasid Revolution in the Merv Oasis," *Journal of Islamic Studies* 7/2 (1996), pp. 150–179.

——— "Arabs, Persians, and the Advent of the Abbasids Reconsidered." *Journal of the American Oriental Society* 117/3 (1997), pp. 542–548.

Elton, H. "Defining Romans, Barbarians, and the Roman Frontier." In *Shifting Frontiers*, pp. 126–35.

England, A., W.J. Eastwood, C. Neil Roberts, R. Turner, and J. Haldon. "Historical Landscape change in Cappadocia (central Turkey): a paleoecological investigation of annually laminated sediments from Nar lake." *The Holocene* 18 (2008), pp. 1229–1245.

Ergenzinger, P.J., W. Frey, H. Kuhne, and H. Kurschner. "The Reconstruction of Environment, Irrigation, and Development of Settlement on the Ḥābūr in North-East Syria." In *Conceptual Issues in Environmental Archaeology* (Edinburgh: Edinburgh University Press, 1988), pp. 108–28.

Evliya Çelebi, *Seyahatnâmesi*. Transliterated by S.A. Kahraman and Y. Dağlı (Istanbul: Yapı Kredi Kültür Sanat Yayıncılık, 1999).

Farag, W.A., 'Byzantium and its Muslim Neighbours During the Reign of Basil II (976-1025)', PhD dissertation, University of Birmingham, 1979.

Fiey, J.-M., 'The Syriac population of the Thughūr al-Shāmiya and the 'Awāṣim, and its relation with the Byzantines and Muslims', in M.A. al-Bakhit and R. Schick (eds), *Bilād al-Shām during the 'Abbāsid Period (132 A.H./750 A.D.–451 A.H./1059 A.D.)*, proceedings of the Vth International Conference on Bilad al-Sham, (Amman: Lajnat Tārīkh Bilād al-Shām, 1991), pp. 45–53.

Finkelstein, A.B., 'Julian Among Jews, Christians, and "Hellenenes" in Antioch: Jewish Practice as a Guide to "Hellenes" and a Goad to Christians', PhD dissertation, Harvard University, 2011.

Foss, C., 'Late Antique and Byzantine Ankara', *Dumbarton Oaks Papers* 31 (1977), pp. 27–87.

——— 'Lycia in History', in *Cities, Fortresses, and Villages of Byzantine Asia Minor* (Brookfield, VT: Variorum, 1996).

——— 'Syria in Transition, A.D. 550–750: An Archaeological Approach', *Dumbarton Oaks Papers* 51 (1997), pp. 189–269.

——— 'Byzantine Saints in Early Islamic Syria', *Analecta Bollandiana* 125 (2007), pp. 93–119.

——— and D. Winfield, *Byzantine Fortifications: An Introduction* (Pretoria: University of South Africa, 1986).

Francovich, R. and R. Hodges, *Villa to Village: the transformation of the Roman countryside in Italy, c. 400-1000* (London: Gerald Duckworth & Co. Ltd, 2003).

Frangipane, M. and E. Bucak, 'Excavations and Research at Zeytinlibahçe Höyük, 1999', *TAÇDAM* 1999, pp. 109–31.

Fuller, M., 'Continuity and Change in the Syriac Population at Tell Tuneinir, Syria', *ARAM* 6 (1994), pp. 259–77.

——— 'Archaeological Discoveries at Tell Tuneinir', *Journal of the Assyrian Academic Society* 12/2 (1998), pp. 68–82.

Gabbay, A., *Islamic Tolerance: Amīr Khusraw and Pluralism* (New York, NY: Routledge, 2010).

Galiatsatos, N., T.J. Wilkinson, D.N.M. Donoghue, and G. Philip, 'The Fragile Crescent Project (FCP): analysis of settlement landscapes using satellite imagery', *CAA 2009: Making history interactive*, Williamsburg, VA, 22–26 March 2009.

Gari, L., 'A History of the Hima Conservation System', *Environment and History* 12/2 (2006), pp. 213–28.

Gatier, P. -L., 'Villages du Proche-Orient protobyzantin (4ème -7ème s.), étude régionale', in G.R.D. King and A. Cameron (eds), *The Byzantine and Early Islamic Near East*, Volume 2: *Land Use and Settlement Patterns* (Princeton: The Darwin Press, Inc., 1994), pp. 17–48.

——— ' "Grande" ou "Petite Syrie Seconde"? Pour une géographie historique de la Syrie intérieure Protobyzantine', in B. Geyer (ed.), *Conquête de la Steppe et appropriation des terres sur les marges arides du Croissant fertile* (Lyons: Maison de l'Orient Méditerranéen-Jean Pouilloux, 2001.

Genequand, D., 'Les établissements des élites Omeyyades en Palmyrene et au Proche-Orient (Beirut: Institut Français du Proche-Orient, 2012).

Gerber, Ch., 'Die Umgebung des Lidar Hoyuk von hellenistischer bis frühislamischer Zeit: Interpretation der Ergebnisse einer Gelandebeguhung'. *Continuity and Change*, pp. 324–32.

Gerritsen, F., A.U. de Giorgi, A. Eger, R. Özbal, and T. Vorderstrasse, 'Settlement and Landscape Transformations in the Amuq Valley, Hatay: A Long-Term Perspective'. *Anatolica* 34 (2008), pp. 241–314.

Gilotte, S., 'L'Estrémadure centre-orientale (VIIIe-XIIIe s.): peuplement et forms d'habitat aux marges d'al-Andalus'. PhD dissertation, Université de Paris IV-Sorbonne, 2004.

de Giorgi, A.U., 'Socio-economic Studies in the Territory of Antioch in the High Roman Empire', PhD dissertation, Bryn Mawr College, 2006.

——— 'The Formation of a Roman Landscape: The Case of Antioch', *Journal of Roman Archaeology* 20 (2007), pp. 283–98.

Glick, T.F., *From Muslim Fortress to Christian Castle: Social and Cultural Change in Medieval Spain* (Manchester: Manchester University Press, 1995).

——— 'Tribal landscapes of Islamic Spain: history and archaeology', in J. Howe and M. Wolfe (eds), *Inventing Medieval Landscapes: Sense of Place in Western Europe* (Gainesville, FL: University Press of Florida, 2002), pp. 113-35.

——— 'Irrigation in medieval Spain: a personal narrative across a generation', in J. Marcus and C. Stanish (eds), *Agricultural Strategies* (Los Angeles: Cotsen Institute of Archaeology, UCLA, 2006), pp. 162–87.

de Goeje, M.J., *Memoire sur les Migrations des Tsiganes a travers l'Asie* (Leiden: E.J. Brill, 1903).

Goell, T. and K. Otto-Dorn, 'Keramikfunde aus dem Mittelalter und der frühosmanischen Zeit'. *Arsameia am Nymphaios: Die Ausgrabungen im Hierothesion des Mithradates Kallinikos von 1953-1956*, Istanbuler Forschungen Band 23 (Berlin: Verlag Gebr. Mann, 1963), pp. 246–76.

Golvin, L., 'À la recherche de la cité médievale de Balis (Moyen-Euphrate)', in J. Cl. Margueron (ed.), *Le Moyen Euphrate. Zone de contacts et d'échanges* (Leiden: Brill, 1980), pp. 389–96.

Gonzáliz Blanc, A., 'Christianism on the Eastern Frontier', *Upper Syrian Euphrates*, pp. 652–5.

Gregoire, H., *Ho Digenēs Akritas, hē vyzantinē epopoiia sten historia kais ten poiēsē, hypo Henri Gregoire. Me tēen synergasia tou K. Panou Morphopoulou. Prologoi tōn kathygētōn K.K. Richard Dawkins kai Gustave Cohen. Prōtotypa geōgraphika schediasmata tou K. Ernest Honigmann* (New York, NY: The National Herald, 1942).

Gregory, S., *Roman Military Architecture on the Eastern Frontier* (Amsterdam: Adolf M. Hakkert, 1997).

Guichard, P., *Al-Andalus: Estructura antropológica de una sociedad islámica en occidente* (Barcelona: Barral, 1976).

Gutiérrez Lloret, S., 'La formación de Tudmir desde la periferia del estado islámico', *Cuadernos de Madīnat al Zahrā*, III (1991), pp. 9–21.

——— 'El origen de la huerta de Orihuela entre los siglos VII y XI: Una propuesta arqueológica sobre la explotación de las zonas húmedas del Bajo Segura', *Arbor* 151 (1995), pp. 65–93.

Haase, C. -P., 'Is Madinat al-Far, in the Balikh Region of Northern Syria, an Umayyad Foundation?', *Aram* 6 (1994), pp. 245–57.

——— 'Madinat al-Far, the Regional Late Antique Tradition of an Early Islamic Town', *Continuity and Change*, pp. 165–72.

——— 'Une ville des débuts de l'Islam d'après les fouilles effectuées à Madinat al-Far (Syrie du Nord)', *Archéologie islamique*, 11 (2001), pp. 7–20.

——— 'The excavations at Madīnāt al-Fār/Ḥiṣn Maslama on the Balikh road', in H. Kennedy (ed.), *Muslim Military Architecture in Greater Syria: From the Coming of Islam to the Ottoman Period* (Leiden: Brill, 2006), pp. 54–60.

Haines, R.C., *Excavations in the Plain of Antioch*, vol. 2: *The Structural Remains of the Later Phases*, Oriental Institute Publications 95 (Chicago, IL: University of Chicago, 1971).

Haldon, J.F., and H. Kennedy, 'The Arab-Byzantine Frontier in the Eighth and Ninth Centuries: Military Organization and Society in the Borderlands', *Zbornik Radova Vizantoloski Institut* (*Recueil des Travaux de l'Institut d'Etudes Byzantines*) (Belgrade) 19 (1980), pp. 79–116.

——— 'Military service, military lands and the status of soldiers: current problems and interpretations', *Dumbarton Oaks Papers* 47 (1993), pp. 1–67.

——— 'Some Considerations on Byzantine Society and Economy in the Seventh Century', in *State, Army, and Society in Byzantium: Approaches to Military, Social and Administrative History, 6th-12th Centuries* (Brookfield, VT: Variorum, 1995).

——— *Byzantium in the Seventh Century: The Transformation of a Culture*, revised edition (New York, NY: Cambridge University Press, 1997).

——— ' "Citizens of ancient lineage.?" The role and significance of Syrians in the Byzantine elite in the 7th and 8th centuries', in W.J. Van Bekkum, J.W. Drijvers, and A.C. Klugkist (eds), *Syriac Polemics, Studies in Honour of Gerrit Jan Reinink*. (Leuven: Peeters, 2007), pp. 91–102.

——— 'Framing Transformation, Transforming the Network', review of C. Wickham, *Framing the Early Middle Ages*, *Millenium* 5 (2008), pp. 327–51.

——— 'Social élites, wealth, and power', in J. Haldon *The Social History of Byzantium* (West Sussex: Wiley Blackwell, 2009), pp. 168–211.

——— and L. Brubaker, *Byzantium in the Iconoclast Era, c. 680-850* (New York, NY: Cambridge University Press, 2011).

Harper, R., 'Athis-Neocaesareia-Qasrin-Dibsi Faraj', in J. Cl. Margueron (ed.), *Le Moyen Euphrate: zone de contacts et d'échanges* (Leiden: E.J. Brill, 1980), pp. 327–348.

——— and T.J. Wilkinson, 'Excavations at Dibsi Faraj, Northern Syria, 1972-1974: A Preliminary Note on the Site and Its Monuments with an Appendix', *Dumbarton Oaks Papers* 29 (1975), pp. 319–38.

Harvey, A., *Economic Expansion in the Byzantine Empire* (Cambridge: Cambridge University Press, 1989).

Hassen, M., 'Les Ribāt du Sahel d'Ifrīqiya: Peuplement et Évolution du Territoire au Moyen Age', *Castrum* 7, pp. 147–62.

Haug, R., 'The Gate of Iron: The Making of the Eastern Frontier', PhD dissertation, University of Michigan, 2010.

Hava, J.G., *al-Faraid Arabic-English Dictionary*, fifth edition (Beirut: Dar el-Mashreq, 1982).

Heidemann, S. 'The History of the industrial and commercial area of 'Abbāsid al-Raqqa, called al-Raqqa al-Muḥtariqa', *Bulletin of the School of Oriental and African Studies* 61/1 (2006), pp. 32–52.

——— 'Settlement Patterns, Economic Development and Archaeological Coin Finds in Bilad al-Sham: The Case of Diyar Mudar', *Residences, Castles, Settlement*, pp. 493–516.

——— 'The agricultural hinterland of Baghdād, al-Raqqa and Sāmarrā': settlement patterns in the Diyar Mudar', in A. Borrut, M. Debié, A. Papaconstantinou, D. Pieri, and J.-P. Sodini (eds), *Le Proche-Orient de Justinien aux Abbasides: peuplement et dynamiques spatiales* (Turnhout, Belgium: Brepols, 2011), pp. 43–58.

Henderson, J. et al., 'Experiment and Innovation: Early Islamic Industry at al-Raqqa, Syria', *Antiquity* 79 (2005), pp. 130–45.

Hendy, M., *Studies in the Byzantine Monetary Economy c. 300-1450* (New York, NY: Cambridge University Press, 1985).

Heywood, C., 'The Frontier in Ottoman History: Old Ideas and New Myths', *Frontiers in Question*, pp. 228–50.

Hild, F. and H. Hellenkemper, *Kilikien und Isaurien* (Vienna: Verlag der Österreichischen Akademie der Wissenschaften, 1990).

Honigmann, E., *Die Ostgrenze des byzantinisches Reiches von 363 bis 1071*, vol. 3 of A.A. Vasiliev (ed.), *Byzance et les Arabes* (Brussels: Institut de philology et d'histoire orientales, 1935).

——— *Le Couvent de Barsaumā et le Patriarcat Jacobite d'Antioch et de Syrie* (Louvain: L. Durbecq, 1954).

Hoyland, R. (trans.), *Theophilus of Edessa's Chronicle and the Circulation of Historical Knowledge in Late Antiquity and Early Islam* (Liverpool: Liverpool University Press, 2011).

Hull, D., 'A Spatial and Morphological Analysis of Monastic Sites in the Northern Limestone Massif, Syria', *Levant* 40/1 (2008), pp. 89–113.

Humphreys, R. Stephen, 'Christian communities in Early Islamic Syria and Northern Jazira: the dynamics of adaptation', in J. Haldon (ed.), *Money, Power, and Politics in Early Islamic Syria* (Burlington, VT: Ashgate, 2010), pp. 45–56.

Huntington, S.P., 'The Clash of Civilizations?' *Foreign Affairs* 72/3 (Summer 1993), pp. 22–49.

Ḥusayn, F., 'The participation of non-Arab elements in the Umayyad army and administration', in F. Donner (ed.), *The Articulation of Early Islamic State Structures* (Burlington, VT: Ashgate, 2012), pp. 265–89.

Hyslop, R. Maxwell, J. du Play Taylor, M.V. Seton-Williams, and J. D'Arcy Waechter, 'An Archaeological Survey of the Plain of Jabbul, 1939', *Palestine Exploration Quarterly* 74 (1942), pp. 8–40.

Ibn Abī Uṣaybi'a, *'Uyūn al-anbā' fī tabaqāt al-attibbā*, edited by August Müller (Egypt: al-Maṭba'a al-Wahibīyah, 1882).

Ibn al-'Adīm, *Zubdat al-Ḥalab min tar'īkh Ḥalab*, edited by S. Zakkār, Volume 1 (Damascus: Dār al-Kitāb al-'Arabī, 1997).

Ibn al-Faqīh, *Mukhtasar kitāb al-buldān*, edited by M.J. de Goeje, Bibliotheca Geographorum Arabicorum 5 (Leiden: Brill, 1967).

Ibn Ḥawqal, *Kitāb ṣūrat al-ārḍ* (Beirut: Manshūrāt Dār Maktabat Al-Ḥayā, 1964).

Ibn Jubayr, *Riḥla*, edited by William Wright, second edition revised by M.J. de Goeje, E.J.W. Gibb Memorial Series, vol. 5 (Leiden: Brill, 1907).

——— *Ibn Jubayr being the chronicle of a mediaeval Spanish Moor concerning his journey to the Egypt of Saladin, the holy cities of Arabia, Baghdad the city of the caliphs, the Latin kingdom of Jerusalem, and the Norman kingdom of Sicily*, translated by R.J.C. Broadhurst (London: Jonathan Cape, 1952).

Ibn Khurradādhbih, *Kitāb al-masālik al-mamālik* (Leiden: Brill, 1889, 1967).

Ibn Manẓūr, *Lisān al-'Arab* (Egypt: Dar el-Hadith, 2003).

Ibn Serapion, 'Description of Mesopotamia and Baghdād, Written about the year 900 A.D. by Ibn Serapion', translation and notes by G. Le Strange, *Journal of the Royal Asiatic Society of Great Britain and Ireland* (January 1895), pp. 1–76 and 254–315.

Ibn Shaddād, *al-'Alāq al-Khaṭīra fī Dhikr Umarā' al-Shām wa'l-Jazīra*, vol. 2 (Damascus: Manshūrāt Wizārat al-Thaqāfah, 1956–1991).

Ibn al-Shiḥna, *al-Durr al-Muntakhab fī Ta'rīkh Mamlakāt Ḥalab* (Beirut: al-Maṭba'at al-Kāthūlīkīya, 1909).

'Ibn Zur'a', (written by editor), *EI2*.

İnalcık, H., 'Rice Cultivation and the Çeltükci-Re'âyâ System in the Ottoman Empire', *Turcica* 14 (1982), pp. 69–141.

Isaac, B., *The Limits of Empire: The Roman Army in the East* (New York, NY: Oxford University Press, 1992).

Jackson, M., 'The Kilise Tepe area in the Byzantine area', in N. Postgate and D. Thomas (eds), *Excavations at Kilise Tepe, 1994-98: From Bronze Age to Byzantine in Western Cilicia* (Cambridge: McDonald Institute for Archaeological Research, 2007).

Jacquot, P., *Antioch centre de tourisme* (Paris: Comité de tourisme d'Antioche, 1931).

Jalabert, L. and R. Mouterde, 'Gabal al-'Ala', in *Inscriptions Grecques et Latines de la Syrie*, vol. 2, 338 (#624) (Paris: Libraire Orientaliste Paul Geuthner, 1939).

Jarīr, *Dīwān Jarīr*, volume 1, (Cairo: Dār al-Ma'ārif, 1969).

Jarno, R., 'Tente et maison, le jeu annuel de la sédentarisation à Qdeir (Syrie)', in O. Aurenche (ed.), *Nomades et sédentaires* (Paris: Centre Jean Palerne, 1984) pp. 191–229.

Jeffreys, E. (ed. and trans.), *Digenes Akritis: the Grottaferrata and Escorial Versions* (New York, NY: Cambridge University Press, 1998).

John of Ephesus, *Lives of the Eastern Saints*, edited and translated by E.W. Brooks, *Patrologia Orientalis* 17 (1923), pp. 1–306.

de Jong, L., 'Resettling the steppe: The archaeology of the Balikh Valley in the Early Islamic period', in R. Matthews and J. Curtis (eds), *Proceedings of the 7th International Congress on the Archaeology of the Ancient Near East* (Wiesbaden: Harrassowitz Verlag, 2012), pp. 517–531.

Kaegi, W.E., 'The Frontier: Barrier or Bridge?', the 17th International Byzantine Congress: Major Papers (New Rochelle, NY: A.D. Caratzas, 1986), pp. 279–303.

——— 'Observations on warfare between Byzantium and Umayyad Syria', in M.A. Bakhit and R. Schick (eds)., *The Fourth International Conference on the History of Bilad al-Sham in the Umayyad Period* (Amman: University of Jordan Press, Bilad al-Sham History Committee, 1989), pp. 49–70.

——— *Byzantium and the Early Islamic Conquests* (New York, NY: Cambridge University Press, 1992).

——— 'Reconceptualizing Byzantium's Eastern Frontiers in the Seventh Century', *Shifting Frontiers*, pp. 83–92.

Kalas, V., 'Rock-Cut Architecture of the Peristrema Valley: Society and Settlement in Byzantine Cappadocia', PhD dissertation, New York University, 2000.

——— 'The 2004 Survey of the Byzantine Settlement at Selime-Yaprakhısar in the Peristrema Valley, Cappadocia', *Dumbarton Oaks Papers* 60 (2006), pp. 271–93.

Kazhdan, A. and G. Constable, *People and Power in Byzantium: An Introduction to Modern Byzantine Studies* (Washington, DC: Dumbarton Oaks Center for Byzantine Studies, 1982).

Keiko, O., 'The Expansion of the Muslims and Mountain Folk of Northern Syria – The Jarājima in the Umayyad Period', *Orient* 27 (1991), pp. 74–94.

Kennedy, D., *The Twin Towns of Zeugma on the Euphrates: Rescue Work and Historical Studies* (Portsmouth, RI: Journal of Roman Archaeology, 1998).

Kennedy, H., 'Arab Settlement on the Byzantine Frontier in the Eighth and Ninth Centuries', *Yayla: Report of the Northern Society for Anatolian Archaeology* 2 (1979), pp. 22–4.

——— *The Early Abbasid Caliphate* (Totowa, NJ: Barnes and Noble Books, 1981).

——— 'The Last Century of Byzantine Syria: A Reinterpretation', *Byzantinische Forschungen* 10 (1985), pp. 141–83.

——— *The Prophet and the Age of the Caliphates* (Essex: Longman, 1986).

———'The impact of Muslim rule on the pattern of rural settlement in Syria', in P. Canivet and J.-P. Rey Coquais (eds), *La Syrie de Byzance à l'Islam VII-VIII siécles. Actes du Colloque International*, Lyons: Maison de l'Orient Méditerranéen; Paris: Institut du Monde Arabe, 11–15 September 1990 (Damascus: Institut Français de Damas, 1992), pp. 291–7.

——— *The Armies of the Caliphs: Military and Society in the Early Islamic State* (New York, NY: Routledge, 2001).

——— 'Syrian elites from Byzantium to Islam: survival or extinction?', in J. Haldon (ed.), *Money, Power, and Politics in Early Islamic Syria: A Review of Current Debates* (Burlington, VT: Ashgate, 2010), pp. 181–200.

——— 'How to found an Islamic city', in C. Goodson, A. Lester, and C. Symes (eds), *Cities, Texts and Social Networks, 400-1500: Experiences and Perceptions of Medieval Urban Space* (Burlington, VT: Ashgate, 2010), pp. 45–64.

——— Introduction, in A. Borrut, M. Debié, A. Papaconstantinou, D. Pieri, and J.-P. Sodini (eds), *Le Proche-Orient de Justinien aux Abbasides: peuplement et dynamiques spatiales* (Turnhout, Belgium: Brepols, 2011), pp. xi–xv.

——— 'Feeding of the Five Hundred Thousand: Cities and Agriculture in Early Islamic Mesopotamia', *Iraq* 73 (2011), pp. 155–69.

——— 'Elite incomes in the Early Islamic state', in F. Donner (ed.), *The Articulation of Early Islamic State Structures* (Burlington, VT: Ashgate, 2012), pp. 135–50.

Kenrick, P., 'On the Silk Route: imported and regional pottery at Zeugma', *Byzantine Trade*, pp. 265–72.

Kidner, F.L., 'Christianizing the Syrian countryside: an archaeological and architectural approach', in T.S. Burns and J.W. Eadie (eds), *Urban Centers and Rural Contexts in Late Antiquity* (East Lansing, MI: Michigan State University Press, 2001), pp. 349–79.

Killebrew, A., 'Summary of the 2008 Cilicia Survey (Iskenderun Bay Region)', *AST* 27/3 (2009), p. 319.

——— 'Summary of the 2009 Cilicia Survey', *AST* 28.1 (2010), 39ff.

——— G. Lehmann, and M.-H. Gates. 'Summary of the 2007 Cilicia Survey (İskenderun Bay Region)', *AST* 26/3 (2008), pp. 227–38.

Kilpatrick, H., 'Monasteries through Muslim eyes: the Diyārāt books', in D. Thomas (ed.), *Christians At the Heart of Islamic Rule: Church Life and Scholarship in 'Abbāsid Iraq* (Leiden: Brill, 2003), pp. 19–38.

Kirchner, H., 'Original Design, Tribal Management and Modifications in Medieval Hydraulic Systems in the Balearic Islands (Spain)', *World Archaeology* 41.1 (2009), pp. 151–68.

Klein, J., *The Mesta, A Study of Spanish Economic History* (Cambridge: Harvard University Press, 1920), pp. 1,293–836.

Konyar, E., 'Kahramanmaraş Yüzey Araştırması 2007', *AST* 26/2 (2008), pp. 175–186.

——— 'Kahramanmaraş 2009 Yılı Yüzey Araştırması', *AST* 28/2 (2010), pp. 263–71.

——— 'Surveys in Kahramanmaraş in 2010', *ANMED* 9 (2011), pp. 174–9.

——— M. Doğan-Alparslan, and M. Alparslan, 'Kahramanmaraş Yüzey Araştırması 2010', *AST* 29/1 (2011), pp. 35–50.

Kopytoff, I., 'The internal African frontier: the making of African political culture'. in I. Kopytoff (ed.), *The African Frontier: The Reproduction of Traditional African Societies* (Bloomington: Indiana University Press, 1987), pp. 3–84.

Köroĝlu, G., 'Yumuktepe in the Middle Ages,' in I. Caneva and G. Köroĝlu (eds), Yumuktepe: *A Journey through Nine Thousand Years* (Istanbul, 2010), pp. 79–104.

Kulikowski, M., 'Ethnicity, Rulership, and Early Medieval Frontiers', *Borders Barriers*, pp. 247–54.

Laiou, A., 'Exchange and trade, seventh-twelfth centuries', in A. Laiou (ed.), *The Economic History of Byzantium*, vol. 2 (Washington, DC: Dumbarton Oaks, 2002), pp. 697–770.

Lamoreaux, J. and C. Cairala (eds and trans.), 'The Life of Timothy of Khākhustā', *Patrologia Orientalis* 48/4 (2000), pp. 9–33.

Lapidus, I.M., 'Arab settlement and economic development of Iraq and Iran in the age of the Umayyad and Early Abbasid caliphs', in A.L. Udovitch (ed.), *The Islamic Middle East, 700-1900* (Princeton, NJ: The Darwin Press, 1981), pp. 177–208.

Lefort, J., 'The rural economy, seventh-twelfth centuries', in A. Laiou (ed.), *The Economic History of Byzantium*, vol. 1 (Washington, DC: Dumbarton Oaks Research Library and Collection, 2002), pp. 231–310.

Lehmann, G., A.E. Killebrew, and M.-H. Gates, 'Summary of the 2006 Cilicia Survey (İskenderun Bay Region)', *AST* 25/3 (2007), pp. 171–88.

Leisten, T., 'For Prince and Country(side) – the Marwanid Mansion at Balis on the Euphrates', in *Residences, Castles, and Settlements.*

Leo the Deacon, *Brasídas Karalçs* (Athens: Ekdoseis Kanake, 2000).

——— *History*, translated by A. -M. Talbot and D.F. Sullivan (Washington, DC: Dumbarton Oaks, 2005).

Levy, R., 'A Note on the Marsh Arabs of Lower Iraq', *Journal of the American Oriental Society* 44 (1924), pp. 130–3.

Lewond, History of Lewond, *The Eminent Vardapet of the Armenian*, translated by Z. Arzoumanian (Wynnewood, PA: St. Sahag and St. Mesrob Armenian Church, 1982).

Libanius, *Antioch as a Centre of Hellenic Culture as Observed by Libanius*, translated by A.F. Norman, Translated Texts for Historians 34 (Liverpool: Liverpool University Press, 2000).

Liebeschuetz, J.H.W.G., *Antioch: the City and the Imperial Administration in the Later Roman Empire* (New York, NY: Oxford University Press 1972).

Van Liere, W. and J. Lauffray, 'Nouvelle prospection archéologique dans la haute Jezireh syrienne', *Les Annales Archéologiques de Syrie* 4–5 (1954–5), pp. 129–48.

Lightfoot, D.R., 'Syrian qanat Romani: history, ecology, abandonment', *Journal of Arid Environments* 33 (1996), pp. 321–36.

Lilie, R. -J., *Die Byzantinische Reaktion auf die Ausbreitung der Araber: Studien zur Strukturwandlung des byzantinischen Staates im 7. und 8. Jhd* (Munich: Institut für Byzantinistik und Neugriechische Philologie der Universität, 1976).

——— 'The Byzantino-Arab Borderland from the Seventh to the Ninth Century', *Borders Barriers*, pp. 13–21.

Lindner, R.P., *Nomads and Ottomans in Medieval Anatolia* (Bloomington, IN: Research Institute for Inner Asian Studies, Indiana University, Bloomington, 1983).

Livne-Kafri, O., 'A Muslim Apocalyptic Tradition Attributed to Daniel (in Light of a Jewish Tradition)', *al-'Usur al-Wusta* 17/1 (April 2005), pp. 7–8.

Lloyd, S., 'Aşağı Yarımca', *Anatolian Studies* 2 (1952), pp. 11–13.

Van Loon, M.N., 'The Tabqa Reservoir Survey 1964', *Annales Archéologiques Arabes Syriennes* (1967), pp. 1–36.

Luce, M., 'Frontier as Process: Umayyad Khurasan', PhD dissertation, University of Chicago, 2009.

Ludwig, C., *Sonderformen byzantinischer Kagiographie und ihr literarisches Vorbild. Untersuchungen zu den Viten des Asop, des Philaretos, des Symeon Salos und des Andreas Salos*, Berliner Byzantinistische Studien 3 (Frankfurt am Main: P. Lang, 1997).

Madelung, W., 'Apocalyptic Prophecies in Ḥimṣ in the Umayyad Age', *Journal of Semitic Studies* 31/2 (1986), pp. 141–85.

Magdalino, P., 'The Byzantine aristocratic *oikos*', in M. Angold (ed.), *The Byzantine Aristocracy, IX to XIII Centuries* (Oxford, B.A.R. [British Archaeological Reports], 1984), pp. 92–111.

——— 'Honour among Romaioi: the framework of social values in the world of Digenes Akrites and Kekaumenos', *Byzantine and Modern Greek Studies* 13 (1989), pp. 183–218.

Magness, J., *The Archaeology of the Early Islamic Settlement in Palestine* (Winona Lake, IN: Eisenbrauns, 2003).

Malalas, John, *The Chronicle of John Malalas*, translated by E. Jeffreys, M. Jeffreys, and R. Scott, Byzantina Australiensia 4 (Melbourne: Australian Association for Byzantine Studies, 1986).

Malpica Cuello, A., 'Repoblaciones y nueva organización del espacio en zonas costeras Granadinas', in M.A. Ladero Quesada (ed.), *La incorporación de Granada a la Corona de Castilla* (Granada: Diputación Provincial, 1993), pp. 513–58.

Manzano Moreno, E., 'The Creation of a Medieval Frontier: Islam and Christianity in the Iberian Peninsula, Eighth to Eleventh Centuries', *Frontiers in Question*, pp. 32–54.

Marfoe, L., 'Between Qadesh and Kumidi: A History of Frontier Settlement and Land Use in the Biqa, Lebanon', PhD dissertation, University of Chicago, 1978.

Martínez Sanmartín, L.P., 'El Estudio social de los espacios hidráulicos', *Taller d'Història* (Valencia) 1 (1993), pp. 90–3.

Mas'ūdī. *Kitāb al-Tanbīh wa al-ishrāf* (Maktabāt al-Muthannā: Baghdād, 1938).
Mathisen, R.W. and H.S. Sivan, Introduction to *Shifting Frontiers*, pp. 1–10.
Matshke, K.-P., 'Mining', in A. Laiou (ed.), *Economic History of Byzantium*, vol. 1 (Washington, DC: Dumbarton Oaks, 2002), pp. 115–120.
Matthers, J. (ed.), *The River Queiq, Northern Syria, and its catchment: studies arising from the Tell Rifa'at survey 1977-79*, BAR International Series (Oxford: BAR, 1981).
Matthews, R., 'Landscapes of Terror and Control: Imperial Impacts in Paphlagonia', *Near Eastern Archaeology* 67 (2004), pp. 200–11.
Mayerson, P., 'Towards a Comparative Study of a Frontier', *Israel Exploration Journal* 40/4 (1990), p. 267.
McCormick, M., *Origins of the European Economy: Communications and Commerce AD 300-900* (New York, NY: Cambridge University Press, 2002).
McGeer, E., 'Booty', in *Oxford Dictionary of Byzantium* (New York, NY: Cambridge University Press, 2005).
——— *Sowing the Dragon's Teeth: Warfare in the Tenth Century* (Washington, DC: Dumbarton Oaks, 2008).
——— Métivier, S. 'L'organisation de la frontière arabo-byzantine en Cappadoce (VIIIe-IXe siècle),' in E. Couzzo, V. Déroche, A. Peters-Custot and V. Prigent, eds. *Puer Apuliae. Mélanges offerts à Jean-Marie Martin* (Paris, 2008), pp. 433–454.
Mergen, Y. and A. Deveci, 'Akarçay Höyük Excavations: 2000', *TAÇDAM* 2000, pp. 340–6.
Métivier, S. 'L'organisation de la frontière arabo-byzantine en Cappadoce (VIIIe-IXe siècle),' in E. Couzzo, V. Déroche, A. Peters-Custot and V. Prigent, eds. *Puer Apuliae. Mélanges offerts à Jean-Marie Martin* (Paris, 2008), pp. 433–454.
de Meulemeester, J., 'Même problème, même solution: quelques réflexions autour d'un grenier fortifié', in L. Feller, P. Mana, and F. Piponnier (eds), *Le Village Medieval et son environnement: études offertes á Jean-Marie Pesez* (Paris: Publications de la Sorbonne, 1998), pp. 97–112.
——— and A. Matthys, 'The Conservation of Grain and the Fortified Granaries from the Maghreb to Central Europe', *Ruralia II* (Pamarky Archeologicke) Supplementum 11 (1997), pp. 161–171.
Meyer, J.-W., 'Die deutsch-syrischen Ausgrabungen in Kharab Sayyar/Nordostsyrien', *Residences, Castles, Settlements*, pp. 419–32.
Michael the Syrian, *Chronique de Michel le Syrien*, edited and translated by J.-B. Chabot (Paris: Ernest Leroux, 1901).
St. Michael Maleinos, 'Vie de Saint Michael Maleinos', edited by L. Petit, *Revue de l'Orient Chretien* 7 (1902), pp. 543–94.
Miles, G.C., 'Islamic coins', in F.O. Waagé (ed.), *Antioch-on-the-Orontes, Vol. IV, Part One* (Princeton: Princeton University Press, 1948).
Miller, D.H., 'Frontier Societies and the Transition Between Late Antiquity and the Early Middle Ages', *Shifting Frontiers*, pp. 158–71.
Minorsky, V. (trans.), *Hudud al-'Alam: 'The Regions of the World'* (London: Luzac & Co., 1937).
Moore, J., *Tille Höyük 1: The Medieval Period* (Ankara: British Institute of Archaeology, 1993).
Moosa, M., *The Extremist Shiites: The Ghulat Sects* (Syracuse, NY: Syracuse University Press, 1988).

Morony, M., 'Landholding in seventh-century Iraq: Late Sasanian and Early Islamic patterns', in A.L. Udovitch, *The Islamic Middle East, 700-1900: Studies in Economic and Social History* (Princeton, NJ: Darwin Press, 1981), pp. 135–76.

——— 'Michael the Syrian as a Source for Economic History', *Hugoye: Journal of Syriac Studies* 3/2 (2000), pp. 141–72.

Morrison, C. (ed.), *Trade and Markets in Byzantium* (Washington, DC: Dumbarton Oaks, 2002).

Mullane, E., 'Patterns in the Past: Model Building and the Identification of Settlement Change in the Kahramanmarash Archaeological Survey Project, Turkey', MA thesis, UCLA, 2005.

Muqaddasī, *Aḥsan al-taqāsīm fī ma'rifat al-āqālīm* (Leiden: Brill, 1906).

Mustawfī, *Nuzhat al-qulūb*, translated by G. Le Strange (Leiden: Brill, 1919).

Na'aman, A., 'Le Pays de Homs: étude de régime agraire et d'économie rurale', PhD dissertation, Sorbonne, 1950.

Nadler, R., 'Die Umayyadenkalifen im Spiegel ihrer zeitgenössichen Dichter', inaugural dissertation, Friedrich-Alexander Universität Erlangen-Nürnberg, 1990.

Naval Staff Intelligence Department (British Admiralty), *A Handbook for Asia Minor*, volume 4, part 2, *Cilicia, Anti-Taurus and North Syria* (London: Naval Staff Intelligence Department, 1919).

Nesbitt, J.W., 'The Life of Philaretos (702-792) and its Significance for Byzantine Agriculture', *The Greek Orthodox Theological Review* 14 (1969), pp. 150–8.

Neville, L., *Authority in Byzantine Provincial Society, pp. 95–1100* (New York, NY: Cambridge University Press, 2004).

Niewöher, P., 'Archäologie und die "Dunklin Jahrhunderte" im byzantinischen Anatolien', in J. Henning (ed.), *Post-Roman Towns, Trade and Settlement in Europe and Byzantium.* Vol. 2. *Byzantium, Pliska, and the Balkans*, Millennium-Studien zu Kultur und Geschichte des ersten Jahrausends n. Chr. 5.2, Berlin, 2007.

Nishiaki, Y., 'Tell Kosak Shamali: Preliminary Report of the Excavations (1994-1997)', *Upper Syrian Euphrates*, pp. 71–82.

di Nocera, G.M., '2003 Archaeological Survey in the Malatya Territory', *AST* 22/2 (2004), pp. 325–36.

Nollé, J., 'X. Tyana im Mittelalter', in *Tyana: Archäologisch-historisch Untersuchungen zum südwestlichen Kappadokien* (Bonn: Dr. Rudolf Habelt GmbH, 2000).

Northedge, A., 'Selected Late Roman and Islamic coarse wares', in J. Matthers (ed.), *The River Qoueiq, Northern Syria, and its Catchment: studies arising from the Tell Rifa'at Survey 1977-79* (Oxford: ?Publisher, 1981), pp. 459–71.

——— 'Archaeology and new urban settlement in Early Islamic Syria and Iraq', in G.R.D. King and A. Cameron (eds), *The Byzantine and Early Islamic Near East*, volume II, *Land Use and Settlement Patterns* (Princeton, NJ: The Darwin Press, Inc., 1989), pp. 231–65.

Ökse, A.T., 'Excavations at Gre Virike, 1999', *TAÇDAM* 2000, pp. 292–307.

——— et al., 'Research at Mezraa Höyük, 1999', *TAÇDAM* 1999, pp. 213–29.

del Olmo Lete, G. and E. Olavarri Goicoechea, 'Tell Qara Qūzāq: Enclave Comercial en el reino de Karkemish', *Revista de Arqueología* 135 (1992), pp. 12–15.

Olster, D., 'From Periphery to Center: The Transformation of Late Roman Self-Definition in the Seventh Century', *Shifting Frontiers*, pp. 93–104.

Ouranos, Nikephoros, *Taktika*, translated by E. McGeer in *Sowing the Dragon's Teeth: Byzantine Warfare in the Tenth Century* (Washington, DC: Dumbarton Oaks, 2008).

Ousterhout, R., *A Byzantine Settlement in Cappadocia* (Washington, DC: Dumbarton Oaks Research Library and Collection, 2005).

Özbayoğlu, E., 'Notes on Natural Resources of Cilicia: A Contribution to Local History', *Olba* 8 (2003), pp. 164–5.

Özgen, I. and M. -H. Gates, 'Report on the Bilkent University Archaeological Survey in Cilicia and the Northern Hatay: August 1991', *AST* 10 (1992), pp. 387–94.

Özyar, A., 'Tarsus-Gözlükule 2007 Yılı Kazısı', *KST* 30/2 (2008), pp. 47–60.

——— 'Tarsus-Gözlukule 2007-2009: The Early Islamic Remains', 7th International Congress on the Archaeology of the Ancient Near East (ICAANE), The British Museum and University College London, 12–16 April 2010.

Palmer, A., *Monk and Mason on the Tigris Frontier* (Cambridge: University of Cambridge, 1990).

——— *The Seventh Century in the West-Syrian Chronicles* (Liverpool: Liverpool University Press, 1993).

Pamir, H., 'The Orontes Delta Survey', in K.A. Yener (ed.), *The Amuq Valley Regional Reports*, vol. 1: *Surveys in the Plain of Antioch and Orontes Delta Survey, 1995-2002* (Chicago, IL: Oriental Institute, 2005), pp. 67–98.

——— 'Hatay İli Antakya, Samandağı, Altınözü ve Yayladağı Yüzey Araştırmaları 2009', *AST* 28.3 (2010), pp. 371–98.

——— and G. Brands, 'The Asi Delta and Valley Archaeological Project in 2004: Samandağ and Antakya Surveys', *Anadolu Akdenizi Arkeoloji Haberleri* 3 (2005), pp. 103–9.

——— and G. Brands, 'Asi Deltası ve Asi Vadisi Arkeoloji Projesi Antiocheia, Seleuceia Pieria ve Sabuniye Yüzey Araştırmaları 2004 Yılı Çalışmaları', *AST* 23/2 (2006), pp. 89–102.

——— and G. Brands, 'Asi Deltası ve Asi Vadisi Arkeolojisi Projesi Antakya ve Samandağ Yüzey Araştırmaları 2005', *AST* 24/2 (2007), pp. 397–418.

——— G. Brands, and F. Çevirici, 'Hatay İli, Antakya, Samandağ ve Yayladağı Yüzey Araştırması 2006', *AST* 25/3 (2008), pp. 393–412.

——— G. Brands, and S. Nishiyama, 'Hatay İli, Antakya, Samandağ ve Yayladağı Yüzey Araştırması 2007', *AST* 26/3 (2009), pp. 1–12.

——— and İ. Yamaç, 'Hatay Yüzey Araştırmaları 2010 Antakya, Samandağ, Yayladağı ve Altınözü', *AST* 29/2 (2011), pp. 361–78.

Parker, S.T., *Romans and Saracens: A History of the Arabian Frontier* (Winona Lake, IN: Eisenbrauns, 1986).

Pattenden, P., 'The Byzantine Early Warning System', *Byzantion* 53 (1983), pp. 258–99.

Pellat, C., 'Ǧāhiẓiana, I: Le Kitāb al-Tabaṣṣur bi-l-tiğara attribute à Ǧāḥiẓ', *Arabica* 1/2 (1954), pp. 153–65.

Peltenburg, E., 'Tell Jerablus Tahtani 1992-1996: A Summary', *Upper Syrian Euphrates*, pp. 97–105.

Pérez Medina, T.V., 'Regadiu i poblament als afores de l'Horta de València', *Afers* 33-4 (1999), pp. 603–17.

Phocas, Nicephoras, *Le Traité Sur la Geurilla (De Velitatione) de l'Empereur Nicéphore Phocas (963-969)*, text and translation by G. Dagron and H. Mihăescu (Paris: Éditions du Centre National de la Recherche Scientifique, 1986).

Pitarakis, B., 'Mines anatoliennes exploitées par les Byzantin: recherché récentes', *Revue Numismatique* 153 (1998), pp. 141–85.

du Plat Taylor, J., M.V. Seton-Williams, and J. Waechter, 'Excavations at Sakçe Gözü', *Iraq* 12 (1950), pp. 53–138.

Pohl, W., 'Frontiers and Ethnic Identities: Some Final Considerations', *Borders Barriers*, pp. 255–65.

Poidebard, A., *La Trace de Rome dans le desert de Syria: Le Limes de Trajan à la conquète Arabe, recherché aériennes (1925-1932)* (Paris: Librairie Orientaliste Paul Geuthner, 1934), p. 144.

Pollock, S. and R. Bernbeck, 'Excavations at Fıstıklı Höyük', *TAÇDAM* 1999, pp. 59–60.

Popović, A., *The Revolt of African Slaves in Iraq in the 3rd/9th Century* (Princeton: Markus Wiener Publishers, 1999).

Posamentir, R., 'Anazarbos in Late Antiquity', in O. Dally and C. Ratté (eds), *Archaeology and the Cities of Asia Minor in Late Antiquity* (Ann Arbor: Kelsey Museum of Archaeology, 2011), pp. 205–24.

Pournelle, J., 'Marshland of Cities: Deltaic Landscapes and the Evolution of Early Mesopotamian Civilizations', PhD dissertation, University of California San Diego, 2003.

Procopius, *Of the Buildings of Justinian*, translated by A. Stewart, Palestine Pilgrims' Text Society 2 (New York, NY: AMS Press, 1971).

Pseudo-Dionysius of Tell Maḥrē, *The Chronicle of Zuqnīn*, parts III and IV: AD 488–775, translated by A. Harrak (Toronto: Pontifical Institute of Mediaeval Studies, 1999).

Pseudo-Jāḥiẓ, *Kitāb al-tabassur bi-al-tijārah*, edited by H. 'Abd al-Wahhāb (Beirut: Dār al-Kitāb al-Jadīd, 1966).

Qudāma b. Ja'far, *Kitāb al-Kharāj*, Bibliotheca Geographorum Arabicorum 6 (Leiden: Brill, 1889).

——— *Taxation in Islam*, vol. II, *Qudāma b. Ja'far's Kitāb al-Kharāj*, Part 7, translated by A. Ben Shemesh (Leiden: Brill, 1965).

Rambaud, A., *L'Empire Grec au Dixième Siècle: Constantin Porphyrogénète* (New York, NY: Burt Franklin, 1963).

Ramsay, W.M., *The Historical Geography of Asia Minor*, Royal Geographic Society Supplementary Papers, Vol. 4 (London: John Murray, 1890).

Rashev, R., 'Remarks on the Archaeological Evidence of Forts and Fortified Settlements', *Borders Barriers*, pp. 51–8.

al-Rāshid, S., *al-Rabadhah: a Portrait of Early Islamic Civilization in Saudi Arabia* (Essex: Longman, 1986).

Rautman, M., *Daily Life in the Byzantine Empire* (Westport, CT: Greenwood Press, 2006).

Redford, S., *The Archaeology of the Frontier in the Medieval Near East: Excavations at Gritille.* (Philadelphia: University Museum Publications, University of Pennsylvania, 1998).

Restle, M., *Kappadokien (Kappadokia, Charsianon, Sebasteia, und Lykandos)*, Tabula Imperii Byzantini 2, (Vienna, 1981).

Riley-Smith, J., 'Government and the Indigenous in the Latin Kingdom of Jerusalem, *Medieval Frontiers*, pp. 121–31.

Robinson, C., 'Tribes and Nomads in Early Islamic Northern Mesopotamia', *Continuity and Change*, pp. 429–52.

——— *Empire and elites after the Muslim conquest: the transformation of northern Mesopotamia* (New York, NY: Cambridge University Press, 2000).

Rooke, T., 'Writing the boundary: Khitat al-Shām by Muhammad Kurd 'Ali', in Y. Hiroyuki (ed.), *The Concept of Territory in Islamic Law and Thought* (London: Kegan Paul International, 2000), pp. 165–86.

Rosada, G. and M.T. Lachin, 'Excavations 2007 at Tyana', *KST* 30/3 (2008), pp. 1–6.

——— and M.T. Lachin, 'Tyana/Kemerhisar Excavations 2008', *KST* 31/3 (2009), pp. 269–88.

——— and M.T. Lachin, 'Excavations Tyana/Kemerhisar 2009', *KST* 32/3 (2010), pp. 196–215.

Rosenthal, F., *Aḥmad b. aṭ-Tayyib as-Saraḫsī* (New Haven, CT: American Oriental Society, 1943)

——— 'Arabic Books and Manuscripts IV: New Fragments of as-Saraḫsī', *Journal of the American Oriental Society* 71/2 (1951), pp. 135–42.

Rossiter, J.J. and J. Freed, 'Canadian-Turkish Excavations at Domuztepe, Cilicia (1989)', *Echo du Monde Classique* 10 (1991), pp. 145–74.

Rost, S. and A. Hamdani, 'Traditional Dam Construction in Modern Iraq', *Iraq* 53 (2011), pp. 201–20.

Rousset, M. -O., 'Projet de Travaux Archéologiques à Tilbeshar (Ancien Tell Bashir), Turquie'. Available at: http://halshs.archives-ouvertes.fr/halshs-00359766/ (accessed 12 August 2013).

——— 'La moyenne vallée de l'Euphrate d'après les sources arabes', in S. Berthier (ed.), *Peuplement rural et aménagements hydroagricoles dans la moyenne vallée de l'Euphrate, fin VIIe-XIXe siècle* (Damascus: Institut français d'études arabes de Damas [IFEAD], 2001).

Rousset-Issa, M.-O., 'Les Ceramiques Recentes de la Prospection du Site de Tilbeshar (1994-1996)', *Anatolia Antiqua* VI (1998), pp. 177–9.

Rowton, M.B., 'The Woodlands of Ancient Western Asia', *Journal of Near Eastern Studies* 26/4 (1967), pp. 261–77.

——— 'Urban Autonomy in a Nomadic Environment', *Journal of Near Eastern Studies* 32 (1973), pp. 201–15.

——— 'Enclosed Nomadism', *Journal of the Economic and Social History of the Orient* 17/1 (1974), pp. 1–30.

Ryden, L., *The Life of St. Philaretos the Merciful written by his Grandson Niketas* (Uppsala: Uppsala University, 2002).

Salmeri, G. and A.L. D'Agata, 'Cilicia Survey 2006', *AST* 25/2 (2007), pp. 1–6.

——— and A.L. D'Agata, 'Cilicia Survey 2007', *AST* 26/2 (2008), pp. 119–24.

——— and A.L. D'Agata, 'Cilicia Survey 2009', *AST* 28/2 (2010), pp. 21–4.

——— and A.L. D'Agata, 'Cilicia Survey 2010', *AST* 29/3 (2011), pp. 165–70.

Samuel, D., 'Archaeobotanical evidence and analysis', in S. Berthier (ed.), *Peuplement rural et aménagements hydroagricoles dans la moyenne vallée de l'Euphrate, fin VIIe-XIXe siècle* (Damascus: Institut français d'études arabes de Damas [IFEAD], 2001), pp. 347–481.

Sanlaville, P. (ed.), *Holocene Settlement in North Syria*, British Archaeological Reports (BAR) International Series 238 (Oxford, 1985).

Sanuto, M., *Secrets for True Crusaders to Help Them Recover the Holy Land*, part 14 of book 3, translated by Aubrey Stewart, Palestine Pilgrims' Text Society 12 (New York, NY: AMS Press, 1971).

Saradi, H., *The Byzantine City in the Sixth Century: Literary Images and Historical Reality* (Athens: Perpinia Publications, 2006).

Sarre, F. and E. Herzfeld, *Archaologische Reise im Euphrat- und Tigrisgebiet* (Berlin: D. Reimer, 1911).

Sauvaget, J., 'Chateaux umayyades de Syrie', *Revue des Études Islamiques* 35 (1967), pp. 1–49.

Van Schendel, W., *The Bengal Borderland: Beyond State and Nation in South Asia* (London: Anthem, 2005).

Schwartz, G., H.H. Curvers, F.A. Gerritsen, J.A. MacCormack, N.F. Miller, and J.A. Weber, 'Excavation and Survey in the Jabbul Plain, Western Syria: The Umm el-Marra Project, 1996-1997', *American Journal of Archaeology* 104/3 (2000), pp. 419–62.

Scott, J.C., *The Art of Not Being Governed: an Anarchist History of Upland Southeast Asia* (New Haven, CT: Yale University Press, 2010).

Segal, J.B., *Edessa: The Blessed City* (Oxford: Clarendon Press, 1970).

Séiquer, G.M., 'Tell Khamīs', *Upper Syrian Euphrates*, pp. 205–25.

Serdaroğlu, Ü., *Surveys in the Lower Euphrates Basin, 1975 (Aşağı Firat Havzasında Arastırmalar 1975)*, Lower Euphrates Project Publications, series I, no. 1 (Ankara: Türk Tarih Kurumu Basımevi, 1977).

Sertok, K. and F. Kulakoğlu, 'Results of the 1999 Season Excavations at Şaraga Höyük', *TAÇDAM* 2000, pp. 475–86.

Seton-Williams, M.V., 'Cilician Survey', *Anatolian Studies* 4 (1954), pp. 121–74.

Shaban, M.A., *Islamic History: A New Interpretation*, vols 1 and 2 (Cambridge: Cambridge University Press, 1976).

Shahîd, I., *Byzantium and the Arabs in the Sixth Century*, vol. II, part I: *Toponymy, Monuments, Historical Geography, and Frontier Studies* (Washington, DC: Dumbarton Oaks Research Library and Collection, 2002).

Shaw, B.D., 'Bandit highlands and lowland peace: The mountains of Isauria-Cilicia', *Journal of the Economic and Social History of the Orient* 33 (1990), pp. 199–233, 237–70.

Shaybānī, *The Islamic Law of Nations: Shaybānī's Siyar*, translated by Majid Khadduri (Baltimore, MA: Johns Hopkins Press, 1966).

Shoup, J., 'Middle Eastern sheep pastoralism and the Hima system', in J.G. Galaty and D.L. Johnson (eds), *The World of Pastoralism: herding systems in comparative perspective* (New York, NY: Guilford Press, 1990), pp. 195–215.

Simpson, St. J., 'From Tekrit to the Jaghjagh: Sasanian Sites, Settlement Patterns and Material Culture in Northern Mesopotamia', *Continuity and Change*, pp. 87–123.

von Sivers, P., 'Taxes and Trade in the 'Abbāsid Thughūr, 750–962/133–351', *Journal of the Economic and Social History of the Orient* 25 (1982), pp. 71–99.

Smith, A., *The Political Landscape: Constellations of Authority in Early Complex Polities* (Berkeley: University of California Press, 2003).

Smith II, A.M., 'Reconsidering the Territorium of Roman Aila', paper presented at the annual meeting of the American Schools of Oriental Research (ASOR), San Diego, 2007.

Smith, J.Z., 'Map is not Territory', *Map Is Not Territory: Studies in the History of Religions* (Chicago, IL: University of Chicago Press, 1993), pp. 289–310.

Snead, J., 'The Local Survey around Domuztepe', UCLA Archaeological Projects in Turkey. Available at: http://www.humnet.ucla.edu/humnet/nelc/stelasite/james.html (accessed 3 June 2013).

Sodini, J. -P., G.Tate, B. Bavant, S. Bavant, D. Orssaud, and J. -L. Biscop, 'Déhès (Syrie du Nord), Campagnes I–III (1976-1978), Recherches sur l'habitat rural', *Syria* 57 (1980), pp. 1–303.

Squatriti, P., 'Moving Earth and Making Difference: Dikes and Frontiers in Early Medieval Bulgaria', *Borders Barriers*, pp. 59–90.

Stein, G., 'Medieval Regional Settlement Organization in the Gritille Hinterlands', in *The Archaeology of the Frontier in the Medieval Near East: Excavations at Gritille, Turkey* (Philadelphia: University Museum Publications, University of Pennsylvania, 1998).

Strabo, *The Geography of Strabo*, translated by H.L. Jones, vol. 7 (New York, NY: G.P. Putnam's Sons, 1917–1932).

Le Strange, G., 'Al-Abrīk, Tephrikē, the Capital of the Paulicians: A Correction Corrected', *Journal of the Royal Asiatic Society of Great Britain and Irleland* (October 1896), pp. 733–41.

Le Strange, G., *Palestine under the Moslems* (Beirut: Khayats, 1965).

Straughn, I., 'Materializing Islam: An Archaeology of Landscape in Early Islamic Period Syria (c. 600-1000 CE)', PhD dissertation, University of Chicago, 2006.

——— 'Sacrality and the Afterlife of the Byzantine-Islamic Frontier: A View of the Border from the "Dead Cities" of Northern Syria', paper presented at the American Anthropological Association Annual Meeting, 2012.

St. Symeon of the Olives, *Life*, text and translation by Jack Tannous, unpublished.

Tannous, J., 'The Book of Monasteries: Selections from al-Shahbushtī's Kitāb al-Diyārāt', BA thesis, University of Texas, Austin, 2002.

——— 'Syria Between Byzantium and Islam: Making Incommensurables Speak', PhD dissertation, Princeton University, 2010.

Tate, G., *Les Campagnes de la Syrie du nord du IIe au VIIe siècle: Un exemple d'expansion démographique et économique dans les campagnes à la fin de l'antiquité* (Paris: Libraire Orientaliste P. Geuthner, 1992).

Tchalenko, G., *Villages antiques de la Syrie du Nord: Le massif du Bélus a l'époque romaine, I–III* (Paris: Paul Geuthner, 1953–8).

Theodoret of Cyrrhus, *Histoire des Moines de Syrie 'Histoire Philothée'*, introduction, critical text, translation, and notes by P. Canivet and A. Leroy-Molinghen, vol. 1 (Paris: Les Éditions du Cerf, 1977).

——— *A History of the Monks of Syria*, translated by R.M. Price, Cistercian Study Series 88 (Kalamazoo, MI: Cistercian Publications, 1985).

Theodota of Amida, *Life*, translated by Jack Tannous, forthcoming.

Theophanes Confessor, *The Chronicle of Theophanes Confessor. Byzantine and Near Eastern History, AD 284-813*, translated by C. Mango and R. Scott (New York, NY: Oxford University Press, 1997).

Theophilus of Edessa, *Theophilus of Edessa's Chronicle and the Circulation of Historical Knowledge in Late Antiquity and Early Islam*, translated by R. Hoyland (Liverpool: Liverpool University Press, 2011).

Thierry, M., 'Monuments chrétiens inédits de Haute-Mésopotamie', *Syria* 71/1-2 (1993), pp. 179–204.

——— 'De la Datation des Èglises de Cappadoce', *Byzantinische Zeitschrift* 88/2 (1995), pp. 419–53.

Tobin, J., *Black Cilicia: A Study of the Plain of Issus during the Roman and Late Roman Periods*, BAR International Series (Oxford: John and Erica Hedges, 2004).

Tonghini, C., *Qal'at Ja'bar Pottery: A Study of a Syrian Fortified Site of the late 11th-14th centuries* (New York, NY: Oxford University Press, 1998).

Torró, J., 'El problema del hábitat forticado en el sur del reino de Valencia después de la segunda revuelta mudéjar (1276-1304)', *Anales de la Universidad de Alicante. Historia Medieval* 7 (1988–9), pp. 53–81.

Toubert, P., *Les structures du Latium medieval: le Latium méridional et la Sabine du IXe siècle a la fin du XIIe siècle* (Rome: École française de Rome, 1973).

Toueir, K., 'Heraqlah, a unique victory monument of Harun-ar-Rashid', *World Archaeology* 14/3 (February 1983).

——— 'Le Nahr el-Nil entre Raqqa et Heraqleh', in B. Geyer (ed.), *Techniques et pratiques hydro-agricoles traditionelles en domaine irrigué* I (Paris, Librarie Orientaliste P. Geuthner, 1990), pp. 217–27.

Trimingham, J.S., *Christianity among the Arabs in Pre-Islamic Times* (New York, NY: Longman, 1979).

Trombley, F., 'The decline of the seventh century town: the exception of Euchaita', in Sp. Vryonis (ed.), *Byzantine Studies In Honor of Milton V. Anastos* (Malibu, CA: Undena Publications, 1985), pp. 65–90.

——— 'Demographic and Cultural Transition in the Territorium of Antioch, 6th-10th century', *Topoi Supplement 5: Antioche: Histoires, images et traces de la ville antique* (Lyons: Topoi, 2004), pp. 341-62.

Tülek, F., 'Osmaniye ili ve ilçelerinde Arkeolojik Yüzey Araştırması 2005 Yılı Çalışması', *AST* 25/1 (2007), pp. 305–26.

——— 'Osmaniye ili Yüzey Araştırması 2007 Çalışması', *AST* 26/1 (2008), pp. 135–40.

——— 'Osmaniye Arkeolojik Yüzey Araştırması 2008 Yılı Çalışması', *AST* 27/3 (2009), pp. 69–81.

——— '2010 Yılı Osmaniye İli Arkeolojik Araştırmaları', *AST* 29/1 (2011), pp. 491–504.

——— 'Footsteps of the Arab-Byzantine Armies in Osmaniye Province, Cilicia', *Proceedings of the 7th International Congress on the Archaeology of the Ancient Near East (ICAANE), London*, Vol. 1, (2012), pp. 149–61.

Tuna, N. et al., *Ilısu ve Karkamış Baraj Gölleri Altında Kalacak Arkeolojik ve Kültür Varlıklarını Projesi* [Salvage Project of the Archaeological Heritage of the Ilısu and Carchemish Dam Reservoirs Activities], four yearly volumes (Ankara: METU, 1999–2002).

Tütüncü, F., 'Land of Beautiful Horses: Stables in Middle Byzantine Settlements of Cappadocia', MA thesis, Bilkent University, Ankara, 2008.

Unal, A. and K. Serdar Girginer, *Kilikya-Çukurova: İlk Çağlardan Osmanlılar Dönemi'ne Kadar Kilikya'da Tarihi Coğrafya, Tarih ve Arkeoloji* (Istanbul: Homer Kitabevi ve Yayıncılık, 2007).

Ur, J.A., 'Surface Collection and Offsite Studies at Tell Hamoukar, 1999', *Iraq* 64 (2002), p. 24.

——— *Tell Hamoukar* (Chicago, IL: Oriental Institute, 2010).

——— and E. Hammer, 'Pastoral Nomads of the Second and Third Millenia AD on the Upper Tigris River, Turkey: Archaeological Evidence from the Hirbemerdon Tepe Survey', *Journal of Field Archaeology* 34 (2009), pp. 37–56.

——— P. Karsgaard, and J. Oates, 'The Spatial Dimensions of Early Mesopotamian Urbanism: The Tell Brak Suburban Survey, 2003-2006', *Iraq* 73 (2011), pp. 1–19.

——— and T.J. Wilkinson, 'Settlement and economic landscapes of Tell Beydar and its hinterland', in M. Lebeau and A. Suleiman (eds), *Beydar Studies I* (Turnhout: Brepols, 2008), pp. 305–27.

Utrero Agudo, María de los Ángeles, 'Building Churches in the 8th – 10th Centuries in the Iberian Peninsula', paper presented at the Masons at Work Conference, University of Pennsylvania, Philadelphia, October 2012, edited by Robert Ousterhout, Renata Holod, and Lothar Haselberger.

Vanhaverbeke, H., A.K. Vionis, J. Poblome, and M. Waelkens, 'What Happened after the 7th Century AD? A different perspective on Post-Roman Anatolia', *Countryside*, pp. 177–90.

Vanput, L., V. Köse, and M. Jackson, 'Results of the 2010 Pisidia Survey Project: Fieldwork in the Territory of Pednelissos', *AST* 29/3 (2011), pp. 269–92.

Varınlıoğlu, G., 'Living in a Marginal Environment: Rural Habitat and Landscape in Southeastern Isauria', *Dumbarton Oaks Papers* 61 (2007), pp. 287–317.

Vasiliev, A.A., *Byzance et les Arabes* Brussels: Institut de Philologie d'histoire orientales, 1935).

Venzke, M.L., 'Rice Cultivation in the Plain of Antioch in the 16th Century: The Ottoman Fiscal Practice', *Archivum Ottomanicum* XII (1987–92), pp. 175–271.

Vezzoli, V., 'Islamic Period Settlement in the Tell Leilan Region (North Jazira): The Material Evidence from the 1995 Survey', *Levant* 40/2 (2008), pp. 185–202.

Vionis, A.K., J. Poblome, and M. Waelkens, 'Ceramic Continuity and Daily Life in Medieval Sagalassos, SW Anatolia (ca 650-1250 AD)', *Countryside*, pp. 191–214.

Vokaer, A., 'Brittle Ware Trade in Syria Between the 5th and 8th Centuries', *Byzantine Trade*, pp. 121–36.

——— 'Some New Results of Archaeometric Analysis of Brittle Wares', in M. Bonifay and J.-C. Tréglia (eds), *LRCW 2. Late Roman Coarse Wares, Cooking Wares and Amphorae in the Mediterranean: Archaeology and Archaeometry*, volume II, BAR Is 1662 (II) (Oxford: Archaeopress, 2007).

Vorderstrasse, T., 'The Romanization and Christianization of the Antiochene region: the material evidence from three sites', in I. Sandwell and J. Huskinson (eds), *Culture and Society in Later Roman Antioch* (Oakville, CT: David Brown Book Company, 2002), pp. 91–4.

——— 'Coin circulation in some Syrian villages (5th – 11th centuries)', in J. Lefort, C. Morrison, and J.-P. Sodini, *Les Villages dans l'Empire Byzantin* (Paris: Réalités Byzantines 11, 2005).

——— *Al-Mina: A Port of Antioch from Late Antiquity to the End of the Ottomans* (Leiden: Nederlands Instituut Voor Het Nabije Oosten, 2005).

——— 'A Countermarked Byzantine coin of Heraclius (610-41) from Tell Kurdu', *The Numismatic Chronicle* 166 (2006), pp. 433–8.

Waagé, F., 'The Glazed Pottery', *Antioch-on-the-Orontes*, vol. IV, part 1, *Ceramics and Islamic Coins* (Princeton, NJ: Princeton University Press, 1948).

Waelkens, M., 'Sagalassos und sein Territorium. Eine interdisziplinäre Methodologie zur historischen Geographie einer kleinasiatischen Metropole', in K. Belke, F. Hild, J. Koder, and P. Soustals (eds), *Byzans als Raum: zu Methoden und inhalten der historischen Geographie des östlichen Mittelmeeraumes* (Vienna: Österreichische Akademie der Wissenschaften, 2000), pp. 261–88.

Walmsley, A., *Early Islamic Syria* (London: Gerald Duckworth & Co. Ltd, 2007).

Ward-Perkins, B., 'Land, Labour, and Settlement', *Cambridge Ancient History* 14 (2001), pp. 315–45.

Watson, A.M., *Agricultural Innovation in the Early Islamic World: The diffusion of crops and farming techniques, 700-1100* (Cambridge: Cambridge University Press, 1983).

Whallon, R., *An Archaeological Survey of the Keban Reservoir Area of East Central Turkey*, Memoirs of the Museum of Anthropology, University of Michigan 11 (Ann Arbor, MI: Regents of the University of Michigan, 1979).

Wheatley, P., *The Places Where Men Pray Together: Cities in Islamic Lands, Seventh through the Tenth Centuries* (Chicago, IL: University of Chicago Press, 2001).

Wheatley-Irving, L., 'Samosata and its Environs in the 7th–9th Centuries CE', paper presented at the annual meeting of American Schools of Oriental Research (ASOR), Cambridge, MA, 1999.

Whitcomb, D., 'Archaeological Research at Hadir Qinnasrin, 1998', *Archèologie Islamique* 10 (2000), pp. 7–28.

——— 'Letters from the Field: In Search of Lost Mar'ash', *The Oriental Institute News and Notes* 171 (Fall 2001), pp. 8–10.

——— 'The ceramic sequence from surveyed sites', in T.J. Wilkinson (ed.), *On the Margin of the Euphrates: Settlement and Land Use at Tell es-Sweyhat and in the Upper Lake Assad Area, Syria* (Chicago, IL: Oriental Institute of the University of Chicago, 2004).

Whittaker, C.R., *Frontiers of the Roman Empire: A Social and Economic Study* (Baltimore, IL: Johns Hopkins University Press, 1994).

Whittow, M., *The Making of Byzantium* (Berkeley, CA: University of California Press, 1996).

Wickham, C., *Framing the Early Middle Ages: Europe and the Mediterranean 400-800* (New York, NY: Oxford University Press, 2005).

Willcox, G.H., 'A History of Deforestation as Indicated by Charcoal Analysis of Four Sites in Eastern Anatolia', *Anatolian Studies* 24 (1974), pp. 117–33.

Wilkinson, T.J., Appendix, in R.P. Harper and T.J. Wilkinson, 'Excavations at Dibsi Faraj, Northern Syria, 1972-1974: A Preliminary Note on the Site and Its Monuments with an Appendix', *Dumbarton Oaks Papers* 29 (1975), pp. 319–38.

——— *Settlement and Land Use at Kurban Höyük and other Sites in the Lower Karababa Basin,* vol. 1 of *Town and Country in Southeastern Anatolia* (Chicago, IL: Oriental Institute Publications, 1990).

——— 'Water and Human Settlement in the Balikh Valley, Syria: Investigations from 1992-1995', *Journal of Field Archaeology* 25/1 (1998), pp. 63–87.

——— 'Regional Approaches to Mesopotamian Archaeology: The Contribution of Archaeological Surveys', *Journal of Archaeological Research* 8/3 (2000), pp. 219–67.

——— 'Settlement and land use in the zone of uncertainty in Upper Mesopotamia', in R.M. Jas (ed.), *Rainfall and Agriculture in Northern Mesopotamia* (Istanbul: Nederlands Historisch Archaeologisch Instituut te Istanbul, 2000), pp. 3–36.

——— 'Archaeological Survey of the Tell Beydar region, Syria, 1997: A Preliminary Report', in K. Van Lerberghe and G. Voet (eds), 'Tell Beydar: Environmental and Technical Studies', *Subartu* VI (2001), pp. 1–37.

——— 'Archaeological Survey in the Amuq Valley', *The Oriental Institute 2001–2002 Annual Report* (2002), pp. 20–3.

——— *Archaeological Landscapes in the Near East* (Tucson, AZ: University of Arizona Press, 2003).

——— *On the Margin of the Euphrates: Settlement and Land Use at Tell es-Sweyhat and in the Upper Lake Assad area, Syria* (Chicago, IL: Oriental Institute of the University of Chicago, 2004).

——— 'Empire and Environment in the northern Fertile Crescent', in I.P. Martini and W. Chesworth (eds), *Landscapes and Societies – Selected Cases* (Dordrecht: Springer, 2010), pp. 135–51.

——— and D.J. Tucker, *Settlement Development in the North Jazira, Iraq: A Study of the Archaeological Landscape* (Baghdād: British School of Archaeology in Iraq, Department of Antiquities & Heritage, 1995).

——— E. Peltenburg, A. McCarthy, E.B. Wilkinson, and M. Brown, 'Archaeology in the Land of Carchemish: Landscape Surveys in the Area of Jerablus Tahtani, 2006', *Levant* 39 (2007), pp. 213–47.

——— and Rayne, L., 'Hydraulic Landscapes and Imperial Power', *Water History* 2 (2), pp. 115–44.

Williams, A., 'Crusaders as Frontiersmen: The Case of the Order of St. John in the Mediterranean', *Frontiers in Question*, pp. 209–27.

Wilson, A., 'Water-Mills at Amida: Ammianus Marcellinus 18.8.11', *The Classical Quarterly*, new series 51/1 (2001), pp. 231–26.

Wittek, P., 'Deux Chapitres de l'histoire des Turcs de Roum', *Byzantion* 11 (1936), pp. 285–319.

Wolf, S., S. Stos, R. Mason, and M.S. Tite, 'Lead Isotope Analyses of Islamic Pottery Glazes from Fustat, Egypt', *Archeometry* 45/3 (2003), pp. 405–20.

Woods, J.E., *The Aqquyunlu: Clan, Confederation, Empire* (Salt Lake City, UT: University of Utah Press, 1999).

Ya'qūbī, *Kitāb al-buldān*, Bibliotheca Geographorum Arabicorum 7 (Leiden: Brill, 1892).

Yāqūt, *Marāṣid al-ittilā' 'alā asmā' al-amkina wa al-biqā'* (Beirut: Dār al-Jīl, 1992).

Yardımcı, N., *Harran Ovası yüzey araştırması* (Istanbul: [Nurettin Yardımcı], 2004).

Yener, K.A., 'Amik Vadisi Bölgesel Projesi 2006 Yılı Yüzey Araştırmaları', *AST* 25/1 (2007), pp. 341–8.

——— and A. Toydemir, 'Byzantine silver mines: an archaeometallurgy project in Turkey', in S.A. Boyd and M.M. Mango (eds), *Ecclesiastical Silver Plate in Sixth – Century Byzantium*, papers of the symposium held 16–18 May 1986 at The Walters Art Gallery, Baltimore and Dumbarton Oaks, Washington, DC (Washington, DC: Dumbarton Oaks, 1986).

Yorke, V.W., 'A Journey in the Valley of the Upper Euphrates', *The Geographical Journal* 8/5 (1896), pp. 453–72.

Zadeh, T., *Mapping Frontiers Across Medieval Islam: Geography, Translation, and the ʿAbbasid Empire* (London: I.B.Tauris, 2011).

al-Zaid, S., 'The Apocalyptic Frontier: Tarsus and the End of the World', paper presented at Middle Eastern History and Theory Conference, University of Chicago, 2004.

Zakeri, M., *Sāsānid Soldiers in Early Muslim Society: the origins of ʿAyyārān and Futuwwa* (Wiesbaden: Harassowitz, 1995).

Zepos, J. and P., *Jus Graecoromanum*, translated by E. McGeer, in *Sowing the Dragon's Teeth: Warfare in the Tenth Century* (Washington, DC: Dumbarton Oaks, 2008).

INDEX

al-ʿAbbās b. al-Walīd I, 67, 351 n102
ʿAbbāsid, 9, 43, 97, 138, 140–143, 152, 156, 231–232, 250
  administration, 19, 211–213, 238–239
  coinage, 81
  Dynasty, *see* individual caliphs
  military, 4–5, 154, 234–236, 266, 268–269, 280–281, 301–304
  policy, 89–91, 239–241, 283
ʿAbd al-Malik (caliph), 173, 176, 210, 291, 296
Abnāʾ 235
Abū al-Fidāʾ, 51, 61, 63, 304–305
Abū Hurayra (Hararis), 81, 82
Abū al-Ward, 89
ʿAḍud al-Dawla, 269
Agapius of Manbij, 141, 212, 213, 296
Ahl al-Aswāq, 238, 288
Ajya (Aigai), 160
Ak Su, 35–36, 39, 49–50, 54, 57, 63, 66–68, 72, 149, 220
Alexander the Sleepless, 282
Alfonso II, 3–4, 193–194
Amanus Mountains, 6, 23, 34–35, 38, 58–63, 159–162, 167, 170, 172, 177, 181, 191–192, 274, 295–296, 306
  Gates 39, 158
  Survey, 169, 188, 205, 225, 297
ʿAmmān, 92,
ʿAmmurīyya (Amorion), 289
Amū Daryā (Jayḥūn), 160
Amuq
  agriculture, 38
  canals and irrigation, 36, 38, 47–48, 100, 200, 208, 217, 218, 224–225
  ecology and marshes, 34–38, 71, 161, 219–220, 222–224, 300
  Plain, 6, 20, 23, 33–68, 128, 153, 156, 170, 223, 225, 264, 277, 296
  settlement patterns, 38, 42–48, 58–60, 65, 69, 93, 112, 126, 152, 157, 183, 188, 190–196, 201, 202, 205, 251, 265, 270–274, 279
  Survey, xii–xiii, 25, 27–34, 38, 39–42, 50, 62–63, 65, 76, 79, 87, 115, 138, 148, 165, 189, 200–201, 204, 207, 335n16
Ananias of Širak, 160, 369 n. 9
al-Andalus (Spain), 197, 216, 260, 262, 275, 286, 368n7
  ecology and marshes, 220
  irrigation and canals, 208, 215–219
  settlement patterns, 184, 220–211, 244, 256

thughūr, 3–4, 21, 272, 274, 345n17
Visigothic, 193, 217, 251, 298, 308
Andarīn (Androna), 82, 189, 228
Ankara 163, 259, 316n14, 344n3, 369n10
Anṭākiya (Antioch), 20, 38, 40, 41, 53, 64–67, 96, 99, 108, 115, 143, 174, 176, 194–197, 200, 226, 235, 238, 267, 270, 291, 295–299, 304, 338n58, 354n6, 360n7
Lake, 38, 48, 220
Plain (*see also* Amuq)
road, 39, 49, 52, 56, 61–62, 71, 72, 91, 162, 195
Anti-Taurus Mountains, 4, 6, 105, 106, 107, 119, 193, 252, 269, 298
Aplekton, 255
Armenia, 4, 24, 105, 248, 283–284, 288, 302, 320n47
Armenian, 61, 62, 66, 273, 288, 291, 295, 297
Christian, 66, 106, 249
Artāḥ, 38, 53, 67, 91, 97, 271
Artūqid, 122–123
'Aṣabiya, 292
Asāwira, 302–303
al-Ashrāf Īnāl (sultan), 51
'Askar, 221
'Awāṣim
administrative province, 19, 81, 96, 127, 200, 250, 320n47
region, 20, 69, 129, 156–157, 202, 206, 222, 240, 320n48
towns, 64, 67, 72, 98–101, 154
'Aylān, 269
'Ayn Zarba (Anazarbos), 19, 99, 162, 168, 174, 177–179, 232, 235, 236, 273, 302, 304, 340n.24, n29
Ayyūbid, 82, 97, 138, 155, 266, 272, 273
'Azaz
Nahr, 104, 106–107
Tell, 88
Ba'alabakk (Heliopolis), 235, 297
Baghrās, 56, 58, 60, 62–63, 97, 99, 170, 200, 238, 273–274
road 39, 91
Bāghaddā/Bājaddā, 141, 211
Bāhila, 106
Bakhtiyār ('Izz al-Dawla), 269
Bakr (tribe), 106, 130–131, 326n6
Balādhurī, 2–3, 82, 96, 211, 234, 284, 295, 296, 302
Balearic Islands, 208, 217, 223, 345n17, n18
Balikh (river), 128, 142, 154, 155, 188, 200, 213, 217, 222, 234
Plain, 24, 130
Survey, 129, 138–139, 149, 189, 207, 266
Valley, 20, 79, 104, 106, 128, 131–132, 140–143, 148, 156–157, 201, 211, 264, 269
Bālis (Barbalissus), 64, 70, 72–73, 81, 82, 89, 91, 95, 97, 99, 211, 212, 214, 217–218, 229, 243
Ballāḍ, 92
Banū Bazrik, 298
Banū Boghousag, 298
Baradān (Cydnus), 160, 174, 222
Basil II (emperor), 249–250
Baṣra, 235, 304
Bayās, 171, 174, 179–180, 295
Bilād al-Kufr, 5
Bilād al-Rūm
see Byzantium
Bilād al-Shām, 8, 23, 289, 345n12
Bughā al-Saghrīr, 173
Buḥayrah al-Matkh, 70, 87
Būqā, 38, 61, 63, 96, 170, 226, 295, 304
road 39
Buṣayra, 148, 153
Būyid (Daylamī), 267, 269

Byzantium, 11–12, 17, 28, 39, 60, 66, 75, 99, 124, 148, 158, 160, 170, 183, 192, 223, 230, 239–240, 244–263, 270, 279, 282, 284, 286, 289, 291, 296, 306, 329n38
administration, 248–252, 257–258, 292
elite, 65, 210, 248–249, 268
military/raids, 1, 3–4, 21, 43, 100, 122, 126, 154, 158, 181, 222, 225, 227, 248, 250–253, 261–262, 267–269, 277, 287, 291, 296, 299, 304, 319n42, 355n19
policy, 12, 55, 117

Cappadocia, 39, 107, 124, 179, 248–251, 254, 260, 268, 275, 287, 316n14, 321n3, 368n7
ecology, 246–247
settlement patterns, 251–253, 255–256
Castellum, 146, 274
Chonai, 289
Christianity
see Miaphysite
Cilicia, 6, 158–181, 189, 214, 222, 232–233, 239, 306
ecology and marshes, 159–162, 307
Gates, 1, 158, 159, 162, 169, 258, 306
Plain, 3, 6, 23, 153, 158, 159, 163, 168, 174, 174, 180, 221, 224, 236, 287, 297, 306
rough, 23, 162, 170–172, 180, 181, 193, 256, 257, 260, 306, 307
Survey, 163–167, 170, 257
Constantine V (emperor), 5, 125, 250
Constantine VI (emperor), 259, 293
Constantine VII Porphyrygenitos (emperor), 292
Crusader, 61, 88, 92, 180, 273, 297, 320n49
Curiales, 248, 354n5

Dābiq (Dabekon), 98, 236
Dār ḍiyāfa, 63
Dār al-Ḥarb, 1, 5, 246, 312
Dār al-Islām, 1, 5, 312
Darbassāk (Trapezon), 60–61, 62, 97, 273–274
Darb al-'Ayn, 39, 178–179
Darb Zubayda, 228, 352n109
Dayr Seta, 243
Dayr Sim'ān, 95, 243
Déhès, 94, 95, 192
Derebeys, 307
Dhuhl, 130
Dibsi Faraj (Athis/Neokaisarea/Kaiserion), 81, 82–83, 97, 212, 217, 265
Dimashq (Damascus), 81, 99, 297
Dionysius of Tell Maḥrē, 100, 157, 333n3
Dioskorides, 287
Ḍiyā', 143, 211
Diyār Bakr, 106, 122, 131, 193
Diyār Muḍar, 128, 131, 154, 156, 234, 292
Diyār Rabī'a, 128, 131, 135, 288
Druze, 299
Dulūk (Doliche), 72, 96, 97, 98

Ephesos, 289, 316n14, 344n3
Euphrates (river), 6, 23, 100–101, 129, 141, 147, 192, 212, 214, 230, 273, 298
lower, 55
middle, 128, 130, 131, 138–140, 155–157, 189, 201, 223–224, 266, 327n11
settlement patterns, 70–73, 81–86, 91–100, 148, 153, 188, 190, 211–212, 215, 217, 229, 271
steppe, 6, 207
Survey, 25, 73–79
upper, 6, 23, 102, 189, 193, 273
Euchaita, 237, 289, 357n38, 364n35
Expelatores, 251

Farghāna, 235, 291
Fāṭimid, 241–242, 269, 350n88
Funduq (pl. *fanādiq*), 173, 231, 287–288
Funduq Bughā, 173
Funduq al-Ḥusayn, 91, 173
Funduq al-Jadīd, 173

Galatia, 255
Ghab, 161, 223, 304
Ghassānid, 99
Ghazī, 292–293
Gritille, 114–116, 188, 271
  Survey, 109–110, 121, 189, 200, 205, 229

Ḥabīb ibn Maslama al-Fihrī, 295
Ḥadath (Adata), 50, 71, 72, 95, 96, 99, 100, 106, 107, 122, 238, 288, 351n106, 368n5
Ḥāḍir, 233, 351n100
Hadhbaniya, 288
Ḥalab (Aleppo), 6, 34, 38, 64, 69, 87, 92, 98, 200, 212, 236, 266, 288–289
  road, 39, 56, 72, 81, 91, 201
  surrounding hinterland, 71–72, 86, 92–93, 100–101, 126, 127, 202, 240, 269, 272, 352n110
Ḥamdānid, 241, 266, 268–270, 282–283, 291, 361n9,n11
Ḥarrān (Karrhai), 106, 109, 131, 132, 134, 139, 140, 142, 143, 154, 155, 156, 157, 204, 212, 269, 294, 313, 347n38
  Plain, 128–131
  Survey, 132–134, 200
Hārūn al-Rashīd, 9, 67, 69, 124, 154, 156–157, 177, 178, 180, 211, 212, 222, 234–236, 250, 259, 293, 316n14, 320n47, 340n24
Hārūnīyya, 19, 39, 99, 162, 169, 174, 178, 179, 232–233, 236, 297
Hashyān, 92
Heraklios (emperor), 1–3, 9, 131, 159, 248, 287, 295, 314, 315n1,n3, 354n9, 368n5
Ḥesnā Ḥamūṣā, 168
Hetaireia, 291
Ḥimā, 286
Ḥimṣ (Emesa), 99, 235, 277, 297, 305
  administrative province, 19, 328n25
Hishām (caliph), 61, 63, 99, 124, 141, 152, 156, 169–170, 176, 180, 212–213, 215, 217, 328n25,27, 347n41
Ḥiṣn Āwlās, 180
Ḥiṣn Baghrās
  see Baghrās
Ḥiṣn Būqā
  see Būqā
Ḥiṣn Hiraqla, 141, 258
Ḥiṣn Kamkh, 106, 107, 125, 238, 288
Ḥiṣn Lu'lu'a, 258, 297
Ḥiṣn Manṣūr, 105, 106–107, 119, 122, 125, 144–145, 292
Ḥiṣn Maslama, 131, 139, 140, 142–143, 211, 226, 233
Ḥiṣn al-Minshār, 125
Ḥiṣn Mūra, 63, 169,
Ḥiṣn Qalawdhiya, 106, 107, 119, 125, 193, 209, 298
Ḥiṣn Qatraghāsh, 169–170
Ḥiṣn Ṣafṣaf, 258
Ḥiṣn al-Tīnāt, 19, 39, 115, 161, 165, 168, 171–174, 222, 226, 228, 231, 270
Ḥiṣn Ziyād, 106, 107, 124–125, 292
Ḥudūd al-'Alām, 252

Ibn al-'Adīm, 262, 288
Ibn Buṭlān, 52, 71, 99, 267, 369n9
Ibn al-Faqīh, 96, 262
Ibn Ḥawqal, 23, 62, 96–97, 160, 175, 252, 288, 289
Ibn Jubayr, 275–276
Ibn Khurradādhbih, 96, 142, 170, 252, 253, 256

Ibn Serapion, 105, 123–125, 129, 155, 332n3
Ibn Shaddād, 97, 124, 271
Idrīsī, 10, 180
'Ijl, 130, 326n6
'Imm (Imma), 38, 39, 41, 50–53, 56, 59, 67, 72, 200, 217, 218, 225, 243, 245, 265, 274, 279, 288
Incastellamento, 183–184, 197, 256, 273–274, 276, 341n2
'Iraq, 38, 71, 97, 127, 135, 153, 175, 228, 230, 236, 289, 319n36
  southern, 130, 156, 161, 201, 208, 210, 218, 222–224, 234, 245, 266–268, 291, 300–305
Irene (empress), 289
Isauria, 160, 162, 167, 256, 257, 260–261, 306
Isḥāq al-Mawṣilī 88
Iskandarūna (Alexandretta) 3, 39, 62, 91, 143, 161, 162, 169, 173, 174, 179–180, 228, 340n20
Ismā'īl b. Ṣubayḥ, 155
Issus, 171
  ecology, 160–162, 222, 224–225
  Plain, 159, 169, 177, 179, 183, 188, 191
  settlement patterns, 165, 179–181
  Survey, 164–165, 189, 264
Istakhrī, 23
Iqṭā', 184, 210, 234, 237, 269
Iwān, 81
Iyad, 71

Jabal al-'Alā, 70
Jabal al-'Aqra, 38, 59, 117, 192, 203, 205, 225, 265
Jabal Barisha, 70
Jabal Duwaylī, 70
Jabal Halaqa, 70
Jabal al-Lukkām, 299
Jabal Rīḥa, 70
Jabal Sim'ān, 70
Jabal al-Summāq, 70, 299
Jabal Waṣṭanī, 70
Jabal Zawiya, 70
Jabbūl, Lake, 23, 70–71, 78, 89, 91–92, 203, 212, 220, 222
  Survey, 75, 77, 98, 207–208
Jacob of Serugh, 123
Jacobite
  see Miaphysite
Jamūs, 153, 304
Jarājima, 162, 170, 192–193, 227, 295–300, 303, 307, 308
Jarīr b. 'Aṭiya, 213
Jayḥān (Pyramus), 60, 73, 160, 168, 173, 174, 177–179, 221, 252, 288
Jazīra, 20, 23, 24, 121, 128–157, 193, 210, 221, 235, 243, 249, 268–269, 291
  administrative province, 143, 156–157, 202, 206, 238–241, 242, 266
  ecology and marshes, 129–130, 153
  irrigation and canals, 156, 157, 213, 215
  monastic communities, 130–131, 154, 157, 281–282
  settlement patterns, 128, 131, 155–156, 201, 234
  Survey, 25, 136, 138, 141, 145, 189, 200, 229, 264, 321n5 *see also* individual river valleys
Jibāl, Syrian (Dead Cities), 15, 35, 38, 69, 73, 117, 187, 191, 195, 206, 218, 245, 265, 297
  monastic communities, 93, 95, 192, 203–204, 205
Jihād, 1, 5, 21, 228, 278, 283–284, 292, 293, 307, 312, 365n48
Jisr al-Ḥadīd, 39, 41, 48, 56, 60
Jisr Manbij, 72–73, 85, 95–96, 98, 131, 229
Jizya, 209, 243, 283, 346n22
John the Arab, 259, 282
John Tzimiskes (emperor), 249–250

al-Jurjuma, 295, 297
Justinian (emperor), 64, 140
Justinian II (emperor), 291, 296
Kahramanmaraş
ecology and marshes, 38, 222
irrigation and canals, 48–49, 208, 220, 265
Plain, 6, 23, 34–35, 39, 60, 76, 112, 126
settlement patterns, 33–34, 45–47, 54, 57, 59, 63, 67–68, 134, 157, 183–184, 195, 202, 279
Survey, 25, 27–28, 39–41, 44, 60, 79, 87, 200–201, 204, 207, 322n9
Kalb, 72, 130, 277–278, 360n7
Kara Su, 34, 39, 48, 61, 70, 97, 207, 225, 323n10, 335n16
Kastra, 92, 226, 255
Kataphygia, 253
Keban, 23, 102, 200
Dam, 105, 107
Survey, 108, 119–121
Khābūr (river), 128–129, 155, 156, 215, 217, 222, 234
Plain, 24, 130
Survey 132, 134–139, 189, 200
Valley, 20, 128, 131, 143–154, 153, 155, 201, 345n12
Khān (pl. *Khānāt*), 62, 147, 148, 232, 238, 272, 288, 350n88
Kharāj, 3, 145–146, 209–210, 214, 243, 346n22
Khunāṣira, 92
Khurāsānī, 9, 154, 235–236, 238, 242, 267–268, 276, 284
Khuzā'a, 106, 290
al-Khwārazmī, 302
Khwārzim, 235
Kilāb, 130, 268
Kinet Höyük, 165–168, 272
Kleisoura, 162
Koinobion (coenobium), 59–60
Konon of Bidana, 307
Konya, 162, 259
Kūfa, 127, 234, 235, 277, 300, 302
Kurban Höyük, 96, 109, 112, 114, 116, 119, 121–122, 123, 188, 189, 205, 225–226, 264, 271

Lamas (river), 6, 159–160, 162
Leo the Deacon, 252
Leo III (emperor), 67, 289, 316n14
Libanius, 64, 65, 189, 194
Lidar Höyük, 109–110, 116–117, 121, 188–189, 192
Limes, 11, 16, 134, 226, 230, 363n4
Lycia, 192, 256

Madaba, 228, 345n12
Madīna (pl. *Mudun*), 63, 88, 170, 271, 300, 301
Madīnat al-Fār
see Ḥiṣn Maslama
Magaritai, 291
al-Mahdī (caliph), 9, 99, 143, 156–157, 176, 178, 214, 235, 236, 288
Malalas, 60, 64
Malaṭiya (Melitene), 4, 23, 102, 118, 123–124, 193, 234, 251, 258, 269, 284, 291, 298, 313
ecology and marshes,
irrigation and canals, 224
Plain, 102, 105–107, 224
settlement patterns, 120–126
Survey, 108–109, 119
Mālik b. Ṭawq al-Taghlibī, 234
Mamlūk, 51, 67, 92, 138, 224, 266, 272, 273, 305
Manbij (Hierapolis), 64, 71–73, 75, 96, 97, 98, 99, 236, 287, 313, 352n110
Mar'ash (Germanikeia), 23, 38, 50, 57, 66–67, 99, 178, 269, 288, 295
canals and irrigation, 218–219, 224
Plain, 20, 55, 60, 217
road, 39, 48, 49, 61, 62, 72, 73, 106, 121, 162

Mardaites
see Jarājima
Marj (pl. *murūj*), 286
Marj al-Aḥmar, 70, 222
Marwān II (caliph), 67, 89, 124, 156, 176, 212, 234, 294
Marwānid
see Umayyad
Masjid al-Jāmi', 62, 87, 155
Maslaḥa, 102, 124
Maslama b. 'Abd al-Malik, 82, 89, 97, 142–143, 180, 201–202, 211–214, 243, 296–297, 328, n27, 346,n31, 351n102
Maṣṣīṣa (Mopsuestia), 9, 161, 162, 168, 169, 173–174, 176, 210, 232–233, 238, 288, 298, 304
Mas'ūdī, 268
Matmūra (pl. *matāmīr*), 253
Mawālī, 213, 242, 244, 245, 278, 290, 293, 302
Mawṣil (Mosul), 24, 81, 131, 145, 147, 212, 215, 236, 268, 269
Maymūn al-Jurjumānī, 296
Mayyafāriqīn, 298
Miaphysite
Christians, 8, 9, 60, 106, 124, 130, 209, 238, 242, 243, 281–282, 289, 315n3
communities/settlements, 27–28, 51, 53, 55, 60, 66, 71, 93, 98, 100, 116, 128, 148, 157, 174, 197, 199, 203, 206, 209–210, 218, 240, 244–245, 259, 272, 279, 305
displacement, 4, 55, 95, 355n22
monasticism, 9, 13, 53, 85, 88, 92, 95, 100, 118–119, 131, 143, 147, 154, 157, 168–169, 190–193, 203–206, 209, 213–214, 240, 243, 254, 273, 298, 313, 329n43, 346n22
Michael Maleinos of Charsanion, 259
Michael the Syrian, 60, 85, 123, 130, 169, 210–211, 213, 233, 296
al-Minā', 66, 270
Miṣr (pl. *amṣār*), 18
Miṣr (Egypt), 71, 228, 310, 350n87
Mokissos, 255
Mongol, 146, 266, 319n36
Mu'āwiya (caliph), 59, 67, 81, 83, 124, 125, 173, 176, 210, 234–235, 291, 304
Muhallabī, 38, 232, 304
Muḥammad b. al-'Abbās al-Kilābī, 89
Muḥammad b. al-Qāsim al-Thaqafī, 302
Mu'izz al-Dawla, 269
Munqidh, 299
Muqaddasī, 10, 24, 171, 271, 294, 300–301
Musta'riba, 291
al-Mu'taḍid (caliph), 91, 173
al-Muthaqqab, 162, 169, 171, 173, 174, 179, 180
Muṭī' (caliph), 267
Muwallad, 193
Myria, 289

Nahr 'Afrīn, 34, 39, 47–48, 56–57, 60, 70, 98, 100, 148, 192, 207, 211, 217–220, 225, 274
Nahr al-Amarna, 70, 76, 83–84
Nahr al-'Āṣī
see Orontes
Nahr al-Aswad
see Kara Su
Nahr Dawrīn, 151–152, 212, 215
Nahr Ḥūrīth
see Ak Su
Nahr Quwayq, 23, 27, 70, 72, 86–89, 99, 201, 208, 222, 264, 265, 270, 272
Nahr Sa'īd, 152, 212
Nahr Sajūr, 70, 188, 264
Survey, 75–76, 98
Namir, 130, 326n6
Naṣībīn, 129, 131, 147, 213–214, 215, 292

Na'ūra, (pl. *nawā'īr*) 221
Nazianzos, 260
Nikephoros Ouranos, 261–262
Nikephoros Phokas (emperor), 4, 62, 249–250, 252, 259, 368n5
Nikomedia, 289
Numayrid, 269–270

Ochyromata, 253, 259
Oppida, 193
Orontes, 39, 48, 56–57, 59, 65, 66, 161, 169, 174, 191–192, 204, 224, 268, 273, 299, 304–305
Ottoman, 62, 108, 118, 138, 169, 180, 190, 224, 292–293, 307, 319n36

Pamphylia, 256, 257
Pandocheion, 94, 213–214
Paphlagonia, 255, 256
Paulician, 106, 122, 124, 290–291
Peutinger Table, 52, 56, 60, 62, 107, 177
Phokades (family), 249–250
Phrouria, 255
Pınar Tarlası, 73, 96, 266
Pontus, 255, 256, 357n38
Prokourstores, 250
Pseudo-Jāhiẓ, 262
Pyrgoi, 94–95

Qadus Jar, 82, 212
Qaḥṭān, 72
Qalamya, 170, 180
Qal'at Sim'ān, 206, 273
Qanat, 82, 84, 141, 189, 207–209, 211, 224
Qantari, 147
Qarāmiṭa, 266, 268
Qarqīsiyā, 127, 131, 147, 153, 212
Qarya (pl. *qurā*), 53, 88, 99, 208, 271, 274
Qaṣabah, 122
Qaṣr (pl. *quṣūr*), 97, 99, 143, 156, 212, 226–228, 286
Qaṭi'a (pl. *qāṭ'ā'*), 142, 210, 211, 212, 218, 237, 346n31
Qays, 71, 97, 124, 268
Qaysarīya (Caesarea Mazaca), 107
Qenneshrē, 92, 203, 204, 207, 215, 229
Qinnasrīn (Chalcis), 52, 64, 70, 71, 89, 222, 233, 234
  administrative province, 19, 81
Quḍā'a, 72, 280–281
Qudāma b. Ja'far, 217
Qūrus (Cyrrhus), 52, 72, 96, 97, 98, 291
Qushayr, 269

Rabī'a (tribe), 92, 130, 131, 234
Rāfiqa, 154–157, 201, 222
Raḥba, 153, 212, 222, 234, 269, 289
Raqqa (Kallinikos), 71, 73, 97, 99, 108, 130, 131, 139, 141, 154–155, 156, 157, 201, 209, 211, 222, 226, 236, 266, 269, 288, 293, 313
  al-Funduq al-Qadīm, 154
  al-Raqqa al-Muḥtariqa, 154
  Raqqa al-Sawdā', 222
  road, 81, 91, 106–107, 112, 121, 122, 131, 142, 143, 157, 229
  Sūq al-Hishām, 154
  Tell Aswad, 154
Ra's al-'Ayn, 129, 131, 134, 143, 147, 212, 221
Rashidūn, 4, 64
  Dynasty, *see* individual caliphs
al-Rawādif, 295–296
Ribāṭ (pl. *ribāṭāt*), 98, 228, 286
al-Ruhā (Edessa), 96, 104, 106, 114, 128, 131, 140, 157, 269, 313
Ruṣāfa (Ruṣāfat Hishām), 98, 99, 156, 228

Sabuktakīn, 269
Sabuniye, 66
Sahārija, 288
Sa'id al-Khayr, 97, 152, 212

Ṣāliḥ b. al-ʿAlī, 124, 125–126, 235–236, 297
Sāliq, 301
Saljūq, 108, 268, 273, 359n59
Salūqiyya (Seleucia), 160, 162, 170–171, 180
Sāmarrā' 13, 145
Samarqand, 235
Sanjah, 72, 96, 100, 106
Saqiya, 82, 216
al-Sarakhsī, 89, 142
Sāsānid, 86, 117, 131, 134, 136, 139, 144–145, 189, 210, 215, 230, 302, 303
Sayābija, 290, 301–304
Sayḥān (Sarus), 160, 162, 168, 221
Sebastea, 275
Selime, 253, 255
Shaybān, 288
Shimshāṭ (Arsamosata), 106, 107, 124–125, 288
Sicily, 184, 208, 220
Ṣiffīn, 81, 82, 91, 98
Simeon the Elder, 273
Simeon the Mountaineer, 193, 259
Simeon the Younger, 273
Simeon of the Olives, 94–95, 204, 213
Sinope, 289
Sīr Daryā (Sayḥūn), 160
Sīs, Sīsiya (Sision), 3, 162, 179, 248, 340n24
Spain
  see al-Andalus
Strategides, 248
Strategos, 53, 248, 356n34
Sufyanid
  see Umayyad
Sulaym (tribe), 124, 142
Sulaymān (caliph), 4, 98
Sumaysāṭ (Samosata), 8, 96, 102, 105, 108, 112, 114, 116, 121, 122–123, 126, 193, 204, 209, 229, 238, 288, 291, 313
  road, 106, 107, 112, 114, 121, 157
Symeon Stylites
  see Simeon the Elder and Simeon the Younger

Ṭabarī, 3, 5, 9, 89, 98, 127, 152, 211, 212, 248, 290, 291, 301, 302, 304
Ṭabarīyya (Tiberias), 222
Tabqa
  Survey, 73–75, 79, 81, 82, 188, 200, 207, 264
Taghlib, 130, 153, 243, 268, 291, 326n6
Tamīm, 130, 234, 290
Tanūkh, 72, 234, 351n100
Ṭaranda (Taranta), 67, 106, 107, 124
al-Ṭarsūsī, 158–159
Ṭarsūs, 1, 3, 8, 9, 19, 108, 115, 123, 159, 162, 169, 170, 173–176, 178, 180, 224, 226, 228, 232, 235–236, 257, 287, 288, 290, 298, 306, 340n20,n25; 369n9
Taurus Mountains, 4, 6, 8, 10, 19, 34, 35, 39, 60, 61, 66, 68, 72, 99, 102, 104–106, 129–130, 157, 161–162, 178, 181, 192, 219, 223, 230, 236, 247–248, 252, 256, 258–259, 282, 285, 287, 297, 299, 354 n .6
Ṭayyi', 71, 72, 106, 351n100, 360n7
Tell Beydar, 130, 136
Tell Brak, 135, 136, 146, 208, 226–227
Tell Hamoukar, 136, 144, 145
Tell Jarablus, 77, 91
Tell al-Judaidah, 59–60, 190, 202, 203, 271, 361n17
Tell Khusāf, 231
Tell Leilan, 136, 138, 144–145, 147, 264
Tell Rifaʿat, 78–79, 86–87, 188, 189, 264
Tell Sweyhat, 79, 83
Tell Tuneinir, 203, 272
Thaghr, 4, 8, 174, 180, 243

Tha'laba, 130
Thekla, 307
Theme, 253, 257, 316n14, 354n9
Theodoret, 52, 192
Theodota of Amida, 92, 105, 106, 125, 207, 346n22
Theophanes, 82, 251, 296, 369n8
Thessaloniki, 289
Thomas the Apostle, 92
Thughūr, 16, 21, 23, 121, 156–159, 222, 224–225, 239, 253, 262, 277, 289, 294, 311–314
  administrative province, 6, 10, 19, 127, 215, 238, 243, 269, 284
  central, 34–68, 70–73, 98–101, 115, 170, 201, 234, 268
  definition, 4, 8, 313, 320n48
  eastern, 24, 96, 102–126, 188, 234
  monastic communities, *see* Miaphysite
  region, 14, 20, 69, 203, 210, 221, 236, 280, 305–306
  settlement patterns, 13, 50–53, 93, 105, 122, 185, 198–199, 202, 231–232, 268, 296, 304
  Survey, 25–32, 107, 310
    see also individual Surveys
  Syro-Anatolian4, 217
towns, 18, 19, 54–55, 64–67, 81, 96–99, 154, 203–204, 226, 288
    see also individual towns
  al-thughūr al-'alā', 275
  western, 91, 99, 115, 159–181, 226, 268, 270
Thughūr al-Bakriya, 106
Thughūr al-Jazarīya, 23, 66, 284
Thughūr al-Shāmīya, 23, 66, 284
Tigris (river) 23–24, 102, 130, 146, 155, 189, 212, 214, 215, 229, 288, 302
Ṭirāz, 250
Trebizond, 289
Ṭonrakians, 298
Tourmarchai, 255
Ṭūr 'Abdin, 129, 131, 193, 204, 213, 215
Ṭuwāna (Tyana), 251, 258

Ubaydalla b. 'Abd al-Malik, 125
'Umar I (caliph), 97, 122, 124, 283, 286, 291
'Umar II (caliph), 4, 176, 180, 242, 316n14, 368n5
Umayyad, 3, 6, 9, 43, 64, 67, 97, 138, 140, 141–143, 156, 209, 233, 234–236, 241, 302, 328n21, 332n79
  administration, 91, 99, 128, 152, 210–213, 232, 245, 320n47
  coinage, 81
  Dynasty, *see* individual caliphs
  Marwānid (general), 97, 215, 240–241
  military, 174, 316n14
  policy, 4, 209–210, 365n48
  Sufyanid (general), 240
Ummahāt al-Ḥuṣūn, 193, 268, 269
'Uqayl 72
'Uyūn 271

Waqf (pl. *awqāf*), 231, 240
Wasiṭ, 81
al-Wāthiq, (caliph) 253

Yaghrā
  River, 34, 38, 48, 142, 152, 265, 271
  settlement, 39, 50, 56, 207, 218–220, 245, 279, 324n18
Ya'qūbī, 124, 251
Yāqūt, 52, 76, 87, 88, 91, 96, 97, 98, 99, 142, 147 159, 168, 332n84
Yazīd I (caliph), 159, 210–211, 304
Yazīd II (caliph), 125

Zangid, 266, 272
Zanj, 291, 301–304
Zeugma, 71, 73, 85, 96, 229, 233
Zubayda, 63
Zuqnīn (chronicle), 82, 212, 347n41
Zuṭṭ, 66, 162, 224–225, 245, 276, 290, 301–304

www.ingramcontent.com/pod-product-compliance
Lightning Source LLC
Chambersburg PA
CBHW071223230426
43668CB00011B/1286
* 9 7 8 1 7 8 4 5 3 9 1 9 1 *